AN MMY MONOGRAPH

Publications of
THE INSTITUTE OF MENTAL MEASUREMENTS
Edited by Oscar Krisen Buros

FOREIGN LANGUAGE
TESTS AND REVIEWS

FOREIGN LANGUAGE
TESTS AND REVIEWS

A Monograph
Consisting of the Foreign Language Sections of the
SEVEN MENTAL MEASUREMENTS YEARBOOKS (1938–72)
and
TESTS IN PRINT II (1974)

Edited by
OSCAR KRISEN BUROS
Director, The Institute of Mental Measurements

THE GRYPHON PRESS
HIGHLAND PARK · NEW JERSEY
1975

MANUFACTURED BY QUINN & BODEN COMPANY, INC., RAHWAY, NEW JERSEY
PRINTED IN THE UNITED STATES OF AMERICA

To
Mabel and Art

TABLE OF CONTENTS

MMY TEST REVIEWERS

Frederick B. Agard	3:208, 3:211, 3:213
Lawrence Andrus	2:1371, 2:1373
Christian O. Arndt	2:1371, 2:1374
Samuel D. Atkins	1:1065
	2:1363, 2:1367
James C. Babcock	2:1372, 2:1375
Ralph C. Bedell	5:256, 5:258
Hubert E. Brogden	3:178, 3:179
Nelson Brooks	1:984, 1:985
	2:1343, 2:1354, 3:183, 3:185
	4:242, 4:243, 5:255, 5:266, 6:364, 6:376
Donald G. Burns	4:242, 4:243
W. L. Carr	2:1366, 2:1369
John B. Carroll	6:360, 7:260
Clinton I. Chase	7:266
Henry Chauncey	6:375, 6:410, 6:431
John L. D. Clark	7:279, 7:280
John A. Cox, Jr.	5:256, 5:257, 5:258
Paul B. Diederich	2:1370
George Domino	7:266
Harold B. Dunkel	2:1359, 2:1365
	3:190, 3:194, 4:250
	5:272, 5:276, 6:384, 6:393
Bateman Edwards	2:1344, 2:1351
C. E. Ficken	2:1342, 2:1349
Wayne D. Fisher	6:355, 6:357, 6:417
Konrad Gries	4:251, 4:253
	4:258, 5:277, 5:280
John Flagg Gummere	2:1365, 2:1368
Michio P. Hagiwara	7:277, 7:279
A. Ralph Hakstian	7:255, 7:256
C. H. Handschin	2:1357, 2:1360
Harry Heller	2:1345, 2:1349
Elton Hocking	3:199, 4:238, 4:239
Warren S. Holmes	2:1342, 2:1350
Charles Holzwarth	2:1345, 2:1346
Joseph F. Jackson	2:1348
	2:1349, 3:180, 3:184
Laura B. Johnson	2:1348, 2:1356
Walter V. Kaulfers	1:986
	1:1156, 1:1157, 2:1340
	2:1341, 2:1355, 3:211, 3:213
	4:237, 5:265, 5:270, 6:427, 7:253, 7:323
Gilbert C. Kettlekamp	6:382, 6:383
W. C. Kvaraceus	4:254
Robert Lado	7:320, 7:322
Charles R. Langmuir	5:256
Walter F. W. Lohnes	7:286, 7:292
Herschel T. Manuel	5:255, 5:261
Bertram B. Masia	6:355, 6:357
John H. Meyer	3:182, 3:186
William B. Michael	4:232
Joseph A. Murphy	7:276, 7:281
Theodor F. Naumann	6:382, 7:290
Charles W. Odell	3:205, 3:207
Josephine B. Pane	7:301, 7:302
Gino Parisi	7:319, 7:325
Kathleen N. Perret	5:265, 5:291
Paul Pimsleur	6:379
Norman T. Pratt, Jr.	1:1064
	2:1366, 2:1370
Glen W. Probst	7:321
James H. Ricks, Jr.	6:379
Harry J. Russell	2:1372
	2:1373, 3:209, 3:212
Jean-Guy Savard	7:276

PREFACE

I T IS my considered belief that most standardized tests are poorly constructed, of questionable or unknown validity, pretentious in their claims, and likely to be misused more often than not. This conviction began to form 48 to 50 years ago when I was taking courses in testing at the University of Minnesota. I vividly recall presenting a paper entitled "Common Fallacies in the Use of Standardized Tests" in an advanced educational psychology class taught by Professor W. S. Miller, a paper in which I criticized some of the views of my instructors. Shortly thereafter, I had the good fortune to read a book which was a landmark in the consumer movement—*Your Money's Worth* by Stuart Chase and F. J. Schlink. It was this book which led to the founding of Consumers' Research, Inc., an organization which tests and evaluates commonly used commercial products. This book and the establishment of Consumers' Research stimulated me to begin thinking about a test users' research organization to evaluate tests.

After failing to secure financial support for the initiation of a test users' research organization, I scaled down my objectives to the establishment of a cooperative test reviewing service which would report on and evaluate standardized tests used in education, industry, and psychology. One hundred thirty-three specialists in a wide variety of disciplines cooperated by contributing "frankly critical reviews" for *The 1938 Mental Measurements Yearbook* (also called *The First Yearbook*). Later yearbooks (each volume supplementing earlier volumes) were published in 1941, 1949, 1953, 1959, 1965, and 1972.

The objectives of the *Mental Measurements Yearbooks* (MMY's) have remained essentially the same since they were first presented in detail in *The 1940 Mental Measurements Yearbook* (also called *The Second Yearbook*): (*a*) to provide information about tests published as separates throughout the English-speaking world; (*b*) to present frankly critical test reviews written by testing and subject specialists representing various viewpoints; (*c*) to provide extensive bibliographies of verified references on the construction, use, and validity of specific tests; (*d*) to make readily available the critical portions of test reviews appearing in professional journals; and (*e*) to present fairly exhaustive listings of new and revised books on testing along with evaluative excerpts from representative reviews in professional journals.

As important as the above objectives are, I place even greater importance on these less tangible objectives: (*f*) to impel test authors and publishers to publish better tests and to provide test users with detailed information on the validity and limitations of these tests; (*g*) to inculcate in test users a keener awareness of the values and limitations of standardized tests; (*h*) to stimulate contributing reviewers to think through more carefully their own beliefs and values relevant to testing; (*i*) to suggest to test users better methods of appraising tests in light of their own particular needs; and (*j*) to impress upon test users the need to suspect all tests unaccompanied by detailed data on their construction, validity, uses, and limitations—

even when products of distinguished authors and reputable publishers.

As the number of published tests and, especially, the related literature increased tremendously over the years, the MMY's became increasingly more encyclopedic in scope. Many test users, however, are interested in only one or two areas of testing. To meet their needs, we announced in 1941 plans for publishing monographs in English, foreign languages, intelligence, mathematics, personality, reading, science, social studies, and vocations. Unfortunately, we were too optimistic; it was over a quarter of a century before we were able to finance the publication of the first monograph, *Reading Tests and Reviews* (RTR I), published in 1968.

The next monograph, *Personality Tests and Reviews* (PTR I), was published in 1970. The core of these two monographs, RTR I and PTR I, consists of a reprinting of the reading and personality sections, respectively, of the first six MMY's and a new section listing both in print and out of print tests in the area represented by the monograph.

Despite the use of a large amount of reprinted material, the preparation and publication of these two monographs turned out to be very costly. Since sales later proved insufficient to finance similar monographs in other areas, we temporarily abandoned our plans for additional monographs.

Following the publication of *The Seventh Yearbook* in early 1972, we began devoting all of our time to the completion of *Tests in Print II: An Index to Tests, Test Reviews, and the Literature on Specific Tests* (TIP II). In mid-1974, while TIP II was in press, it suddenly occurred to me that up-to-date monographs could be prepared at a manageable cost by reprinting a given section of TIP II along with the corresponding sections of the seven MMY's. As a consequence, we are now publishing monographs in nine areas: second monographs in personality and reading, and first monographs in English, foreign languages, intelligence, mathematics, science, social studies, and vocations. Hopefully, the publication of these

monographs will make our material available to many test users who might otherwise not consult the MMY's and TIP II. Broadening the readership of our test reviews will bring us closer to achieving our objectives.

This monograph, *Foreign Language Tests and Reviews*, faithfully reflects the state of the art in foreign language testing over the past 50 years. I cannot but wonder why more progress has not been made in the development of foreign language testing, both in quality and quantity. For each of the languages most commonly taught—French, German, and Spanish—there is only one published test for use in grades as low as 7, and no tests for use in lower grades. Although some better tests have been constructed in recent years, I would have expected more progress not only in quality but in a much wider grade and language coverage. Since tests in languages other than French, German, and Spanish (and possibly even tests in these languages for grades 1–6) are not likely to be profitable commercially, I hope that nonprofit testing organizations will make available tests covering more languages and tests for use in elementary schools.

It has been particularly hectic preparing nine MMY monographs simultaneously. Fortunately, I have been assisted by a dedicated staff. Although other people worked for shorter periods of time, there are seven whom I would like to name for special recognition: Mary Anne Miller Becker, Sandra Boxer Discenza, Doris Greene McCan, Barbara Ruis Martko, Mary T. Mooney, Joan Stein Paszamant, and Natalie J. Rosenthal Turton. I am greatly indebted to my staff colleagues for their assistance in producing these nine derivative monographs.

We plan to publish *The Eighth Mental Measurements Yearbook* in 1977, followed by *Tests in Print III* in 1978. The foreign language sections of these volumes will supplement and update the material in this monograph.

OSCAR KRISEN BUROS

Highland Park, New Jersey
February 24, 1975

INTRODUCTION

FOR THE past 40 years we have been providing test users in education, industry, and psychology with a series of publications designed to assist them in the selection and use of tests which best meet their needs. We maintained an annual production schedule for our first four volumes (1935–38); since then, however, the intervals between books have been quite irregular with publication dates 1941, 1949, 1953, 1959, 1961, 1965, 1968, 1970, 1972, and 1974. Our publications through 1974 include three test bibliographies, seven *Mental Measurements Yearbooks,* two monographs, and two *Tests in Print.*[1] Nine derivative monographs—this volume and eight others—are being published in 1975. A brief description of our first fourteen publications follows.

FIRST THREE PUBLICATIONS

Although the earliest three publications are noncritical bibliographies, the original intent had been to prepare an annual critical review of new tests for journal publication. It soon became apparent, however, that this was far beyond the capacity of a single individual. A more modest goal was substituted, the publication of an annual bibliography of tests, as described in the Introduction to the first one:

To locate the standard tests recently published in specific areas is a laborious task. The usual bibliographic aids for locating periodical, monograph, and book publications are of little value in locating standard tests. New tests are being published so rapidly that the test technicians themselves find it difficult to locate the test titles of the past year without an inordinate amount of searching. For these reasons, the writer has undertaken the task of preparing a bibliography of psychological, achievement, character, and personality tests published in 1933 and 1934. This bibliography will be the first of a series to be published annually by the School of Education, Rutgers University.[2]

This 44-page bibliography lists 257 tests that were new, revised, or supplemented in 1933 and 1934. Many of these tests, usually revised editions, are still in print today.

Similar test bibliographies [3] were published in 1936 and 1937. During this time, attempts were being made to obtain a grant to initiate a

---

1 The first fourteen publications (1935–1974), edited by Oscar K. Buros and now published by The Gryphon Press, are listed from the most recent to the oldest:

a) *Tests in Print II: An Index to Tests, Test Reviews, and the Literature on Specific Tests,* December 1974. Pp. xxxix, 1107. $70.

b) *The Seventh Mental Measurements Yearbook,* Vols. I and II, 1972. Pp. xl, 935; vi, 937–1986. $70 per set.

c) *Personality Tests and Reviews: Including an Index to The Mental Measurements Yearbooks,* 1970. Pp. xxxi, 1659. $45. For reviews, see 7:B120.

d) *Reading Tests and Reviews: Including a Classified Index to The Mental Measurements Yearbooks,* 1968. Pp. xxii, 520. $20. For reviews, see 7:B121.

e) *The Sixth Mental Measurements Yearbook,* 1965. Pp. xxxvii, 1714. $45. (Reprinted 1971) For reviews, see 7:B122.

f) *Tests in Print: A Comprehensive Bibliography of Tests for Use in Education, Psychology, and Industry,* 1961. Pp. xxix, 479. $15. (Reprinted 1974) For reviews, see 6:B105.

g) *The Fifth Mental Measurements Yearbook,* 1959. Pp. xxix, 1292. $35. (Reprinted 1961) For reviews, see 6:B104.

h) *The Fourth Mental Measurements Yearbook,* 1953. Pp. xxv, 1163. $30. (Reprinted 1974) For reviews, see 5:B84.

i) *The Third Mental Measurements Yearbook,* 1949. Pp. xv, 1047. $25. (Reprinted 1974) For reviews, see 4:B71.

j) *The Nineteen Forty Mental Measurements Yearbook,* 1941. Pp. xxv, 674. $20. (Reissued 1972) For reviews, see 3:788 and 4:B70.

k) *The Nineteen Thirty Eight Mental Measurements Yearbook,* 1938. Pp. xv, 415. $17.50. (Reissued 1972) For reviews, see 2:B858.

l) *Educational, Psychological, and Personality Tests of 1936: Including a Bibliography and Book Review Digest of Measurement Books and Monographs of 1933–36,* 1937. Pp. 141. Out of print. For reviews, see 1:B326.

m) *Educational, Psychological, and Personality Tests of 1933, 1934, and 1935,* 1936. Pp. 83. Out of print. For reviews, see 36:B46.

n) *Educational, Psychological, and Personality Tests of 1933 and 1934,* 1935. Pp. 44. Out of print. For a review, see 36:B45.

2 *Educational, Psychological, and Personality Tests of 1933 and 1934,* p. 5.

3 *Educational, Psychological, and Personality Tests of 1933, 1934, and 1935.*
Educational, Psychological, and Personality Tests of 1936.

research organization which would serve as a bureau of standards for the evaluation of educational and psychological tests. It was only after we despaired of raising such funds that we decided to set up a test reviewing service.

THE SEVEN MMY'S

Since tests, unlike books, were rarely reviewed in professional journals, it was a revolutionary step forward when we published *The 1938 Mental Measurements Yearbook* 37 years ago. In his Foreword, Clarence E. Partch's comments reflect our excitement and mood in those early days:

The publication of *The 1938 Mental Measurements Yearbook of the School of Education, Rutgers University* is likely to prove a landmark of considerable importance in the history of tests and measurements. Heretofore, despite the obvious need of test users for frank evaluations of tests by competent reviewers, few standardized tests have been critically appraised in the professional journals and textbooks for students of education and psychology. Now, for the first time, a large number of frankly evaluative reviews by able test technicians, subject-matter specialists, and psychologists are available to assist test users in making more discriminating selections from among the hundreds of tests on the market.[4]

Except for a few test authors and publishers who objected to unfavorable reviews, *The 1938 Yearbook* (also referred to as *The First Yearbook*) was enthusiastically acclaimed in this country and abroad. It took some time, however, before most of the protesting publishers were able to accept unfavorable test reviews with equanimity.

Before *The 1938 Yearbook* was off the press, we began sending out invitations to review tests for a 1939 yearbook. Unfortunately, because of financing and production problems, we were unable to maintain our annual production schedule. It took us over two years to publish the next volume, *The 1940 Mental Measurements Yearbook*.

Much enlarged and greatly improved over its predecessor, *The 1940 Yearbook* (also referred to as *The Second Yearbook*) has been the prototype for all later yearbooks. In addition to the increased number of tests, reviews, and references, there were many qualitative changes: (*a*) The objectives which have characterized all MMY's were presented in detail for the first time. (*b*) The format was standardized. (*c*) The classification of tests was

4 *The 1938 Mental Measurements Yearbook*, p. xi.

changed from 40 specific categories to 12 broad categories. (*d*) The practice of including very short reviews of 100 words or less was discontinued. (*e*) The review coverage was extended to old tests and to tests previously reviewed as well as new tests. (*f*) The instructions given to reviewers concerning the preparation of their test reviews were presented. (*g*) The reactions of test authors and publishers—most of them objecting strenuously to unfavorable reviews—were reprinted for the first and last time.

In the Preface of *The 1940 Yearbook* we announced that the yearbooks would be published every two years. Because of World War II, however, *The Third Mental Measurements Yearbook* was not published until 1949. Except for its larger size and more thorough preparation, *The Third Yearbook*—like all later yearbooks—is very similar in its coverage, format, indexing, and organization to *The 1940 Yearbook*. There were, however, several improvements: (*a*) The "Classified Index of Tests," an expanded table of contents, was introduced. (*b*) Stars and asterisks were used preceding test titles to indicate, respectively, tests listed in a yearbook for the first time and tests revised or supplemented since last listed. (*c*) Asterisks were used at the end of a reference to indicate that the reference had been examined personally for accuracy and relevance. (*d*) Whenever possible, the abstract in *Psychological Abstracts* was cited for each reference. (*e*) Two improvements were made in the name index. Previously authors of references for specific tests had been indexed merely by citing the test for which the reference appears. After locating the test, one then had to search through the references to find those by that author. The new index eliminated this searching by citing each reference both to the test number and the reference number. Secondly, the index was converted into an "analytic index" in which *"test," "rev," "exc," "bk,"* and *"ref"* were used to indicate whether a citation referred to authorship of a test, review, excerpted review, book, or reference. These five features have been included in all later yearbooks.

In *The Fourth Mental Measurements Yearbook*, published in 1953, our review coverage was extended for the first time to many tests restricted to testing programs administered by organizations such as the College Entrance Examination Board. Six years later, in 1959, *The Fifth Yearbook* was published. Upon the completion of that volume, we were concerned that some cutbacks would be necessary to stem the phenomenal growth of production costs, as well as the ever increasing length of each MMY. As a result, we decided to discontinue specific test bibliographies and almost all reviews of foreign tests. The appreciative reviews *The Fifth Yearbook* received, however, especially those mentioning the value of the specific bibliographies to students of testing, caused us to reconsider. Consequently, despite the expanding literature on specific tests, we decided to continue all features of the earlier volumes. As a result, it took us six years to publish in 1965 *The Sixth Mental Measurements Yearbook,* a 1,751-page volume, approximately one-third larger than the previous yearbook. In addition to its more extensive coverage, *The Sixth Yearbook* presents a comprehensive listing of all tests in print as of mid-1964. The latest yearbook to date, *The Seventh Yearbook,* was published in 1972. This massive two-volume work of 2,032 pages may well be considered the zenith of the MMY's.

Like all other volumes published since 1938, *The Seventh Yearbook* supplements rather than supplants earlier yearbooks. For complete coverage, therefore, a reader must have access to all seven MMY's. A person using only the latest, *The Seventh Yearbook,* will miss a tremendous amount of valuable information in the six earlier volumes. Although the more recent yearbooks—especially the last three—are of greatest value, the third and fourth yearbooks also contain much useful information on many in print tests. Even though the first two yearbooks are mainly of historical interest, they also include some critical information on currently used tests. Our faith in the value of the first four MMY's, published between 1938 and 1953, is attested to by our reissuing of the first and second yearbooks in 1972 and reprinting of the third and fourth in 1974. Consequently, all seven yearbooks are now in print.

EARLIER MMY MONOGRAPHS

It is with amusement and wonder that we look back at some of the dreams of our youth. *The 1940 Mental Measurements Yearbook* was the first yearbook published by my wife and myself. In those depression days, money was scarce but printing was cheap and penny postcards could be used for advertising. Borrowed capital of $3,500 was sufficient to launch us into book publishing. Even before our first book was off the press we were planning to publish not only a new MMY every two years, but also a series of derivative monographs. Our plans were confidently announced in the Preface of *The 1940 Yearbook* thus:

In order to make the material in the yearbooks more easily accessible to individuals who are interested in only a small part of each volume, a new series of monographs is being planned. If the first two or three monographs prove successful, others will eventually be prepared to cover tests in each of the following fields: business education, English and reading, fine arts, foreign languages, health and physical education, home economics, industrial arts, intelligence, mathematics, sciences, social studies, and vocational aptitudes. The first publication in each field will include: a comprehensive bibliography of all standard tests in print in that area; a reprinting, in part or in full, of all reviews of these tests which have appeared in previous yearbooks or in the journal literature; new reviews written especially for the monograph (to be, in turn, reprinted, in part or in full, in the following yearbook); and an extensive list of references on the construction, validation, use, and limitations of the tests. Separates in each field will be issued every four, six, or eight years depending upon the frequency of test publication. These monographs will range in size from fifty to two hundred pages. This new series will make it possible for an individual to purchase, at a nominal cost, every four, six, or eight years a monograph devoted solely to the tests and reviews of most interest to him.[5]

However, the publishing of the MMY's alone, even at intervals of 4 to 8 years, proved to be so time consuming and difficult that initiating the monograph series had to be continually postponed. But the dreams were never abandoned.

In 1968, 27 years after the monograph series was initially announced, the first monograph, *Reading Tests and Reviews* (RTR I), was published. This 542-page volume consists of a comprehensive bibliography of reading tests as of May 1968 and a reprinting of the reading sections of the first six MMY's. A second monograph, *Personality Tests and Reviews* (PTR I), was published two years later. This 1,695-page volume lists all personality tests as of June 1969 and provides a reprinting of the personality sections of the first six MMY's. The preparation of these two monographs turned out to be too costly and time consuming to justify working on monographs in other areas.

[5] *The 1940 Mental Measurements Yearbook,* p. xx.

TIP I AND TIP II

In 1961, we published the ninth volume in the MMY series: *Tests in Print: A Comprehensive Bibliography of Tests for Use in Education, Psychology, and Industry*. The objectives and nature of *Tests in Print* (hereafter called *Tests in Print I* or TIP I) are described in its Introduction as follows:

The objectives of *Tests in Print* are threefold: first, to present a comprehensive bibliography of tests—achievement, aptitude, intelligence, personality, and certain sensory-motor skills—published as separates and currently available in English-speaking countries; second, to serve as a classified index and supplement to the volumes of the *Mental Measurements Yearbook* series published to date; third, to give a wider distribution to the excellent recommendations for improving test manuals made by committees of the American Psychological Association, the American Educational Research Association, and the National Council on Measurements Used in Education.[6]

TIP I lists 2,967 tests—2,126 in print and 841 out of print as of early 1961, and also serves as a master index to the contents of the first five MMY's. Originally, we had planned to publish a new edition of TIP shortly after the publication of each new MMY, but poor sales of TIP I caused these plans to be abandoned. *The Sixth Yearbook*, in effect, served as a new edition of *Tests in Print* by referring to the tests in TIP I which were still in print as of mid-1964. Surprisingly, however, sales of the 1961 *Tests in Print* began to pick up after publication of *The Sixth Yearbook* in 1965. This unexpected upturn encouraged us to begin devoting all of our time to the preparation of a new edition of TIP immediately after approving the last proofs for *The Seventh Yearbook*.

Tests in Print II: An Index to Tests, Test Reviews, and the Literature on Specific Tests (TIP II) was published in December 1974. Like the 1961 volume, *Tests in Print II* presents: (*a*) a comprehensive bibliography of all known tests published as separates for use with English-speaking subjects; (*b*) a classified index to the contents of the test sections of the seven *Mental Measurements Yearbooks* published to date; and (*c*) a reprinting of the 1974 APA-AERA-NCME *Standards for Educational and Psychological Tests*.

In addition, TIP II introduces the following new features: (*d*) comprehensive bibliographies through 1971 on the construction, use,

[6] *Tests in Print*, p. xv.

and validity of specific tests; (*e*) a classified list of tests which have gone out of print since TIP I; (*f*) a cumulative name index for each test with references; (*g*) a title index covering in print and out of print tests, as well as inverted, series, and superseded titles in the MMY's and monographs; (*h*) an analytic name index covering all authors of tests, reviews, excerpts, and references in the MMY's and monographs; (*i*) a publishers directory with a complete listing of each publisher's test titles; (*j*) a classified scanning index which describes the population for which each test is intended; (*k*) identification of foreign tests and journals by presenting the country of origin in brackets immediately after a test entry or journal title; (*l*) inclusions of factual statements implying criticism such as "1971 tests identical with tests copyrighted 1961 except for format," and "no manual"; (*m*) listing of test titles at the foot of each page to permit immediate identification of pages consisting only of references or names; and (*n*) directions on how to use the book and an expanded table of contents printed on the endpages to greatly facilitate its use.

TIP II contains 2,467 in print test entries, 16.0 percent more than in TIP I. Table 1 presents a breakdown of the number of tests and new references in TIP II by classification. Personality—the area in which we know the least about testing—has, as it did in 1961, the greatest number of tests. Although the percentage of personality tests is 17.9, 44.9 percent of the TIP II references are for personality tests. Three categories—intelligence, personality, and

TABLE 1

TESTS AND NEW REFERENCES
IN TESTS IN PRINT II

Classification	Tests		References	
	Number	Percent	Number	Percent
Achievement Batteries	50	2.0	438	2.6
English	131	5.3	220	1.3
Fine Arts	35	1.4	229	1.4
Foreign Languages	105	4.3	81	.5
Intelligence	274	11.1	4,039	24.4
Mathematics	168	6.8	166	1.0
Miscellaneous	291	11.8	866	5.2
Multi-Aptitude	26	1.1	235	1.4
Personality	441	17.9	7,443	44.9
Reading	248	10.1	837	5.1
Science	97	3.9	72	.4
Sensory-Motor	62	2.5	382	2.3
Social Studies	85	3.4	49	.3
Speech and Hearing	79	3.2	216	1.3
Vocations	375	15.2	1,301	7.8
Total	2,467	100.0	16,574	99.9

vocations—make up 44.2 percent of tests and 77.1 percent of the references in TIP II.

FOREIGN LANGUAGE TESTS AND REVIEWS

This volume's subtitle, *A Monograph Consisting of the Foreign Language Sections of the Seven Mental Measurements Yearbooks (1938–72) and Tests in Print II (1974)*, succinctly describes its contents. In addition to the 15-page reprint from TIP II and the 249-page section of reprints from the seven MMY's, *Foreign Language Tests and Reviews* (FLTR) includes a publishers directory, title index, name index, and a foreign language scanning index. The TIP II scanning index is reprinted in full also.

TIP II TESTS REPRINT

The section of this volume reprinted from *Tests in Print II,* TIP II Tests, contains a bibliography of in print foreign language tests, references for specific tests, cumulative name indexes for specific tests with references, and lists of tests which have gone out of print since appearing in TIP I. (The out of print tests are listed alphabetically at the ends of the specific language subsections.) The first three of these categories will be described in more detail.

FOREIGN LANGUAGE TESTS

The TIP II reprint section lists 105 foreign language tests in print as of early 1974—14.1 percent more tests than were listed 14 years ago in TIP I (Table 2). Arabic and Chinese are represented for the first time with one test each. The number of tests in German, Hebrew, and Russian increased significantly. The number of tests in Latin dropped sharply from 20 to 7, a decrease of 65.0 percent. The three languages most widely taught in schools and colleges—French, German, and Spanish—continue to account for more than half of all foreign language tests. English, considered as a foreign language for non-native speakers of English, ranks fourth among the 11 languages in number of tests—tests commonly used to test the English proficiency of applicants from non-English-language countries for admission to American colleges.

Fifty-nine (56.2 percent) of the 105 in print tests are either new or revised since the publication of *The Seventh Mental Measurements Yearbook* in 1972.

Unlike the long test entries in the *Mental Measurements Yearbooks,* the TIP II entries in this volume are short entries supplying the following information:

a) TITLE. Test titles are printed in boldface type. Secondary or series titles by a colon. Titles are always presented exactly as reported in the test materials. Stars precede titles of tests listed for the first time in TIP II; asterisks precede titles of tests which have been revised or supplemented since last listed.

b) TEST POPULATION. The grade, chronological age, or semester range, or the employment category is usually given. Commas are used to indicate separate grade levels. "Grades 1.5–2.5, 2–3, 4–12, 13–17" means that there are four test booklets: a booklet for the middle of the first grade through the middle of the second grade, a booklet for the beginning of the second grade through the end of the third grade, a booklet for grades 4 through 12 inclusive, and a booklet for undergraduate and graduate students in colleges and universities. "First, second semester" means that there are two test booklets: one covering the work of the first semester, the other covering the work of the second semester. "1, 2 semesters" indicates that the second booklet covers the work of the two semesters. "Ages 10-2 to 11-11" means ages 10 years 2 months to 11 years 11 months and "Grades 4-6 to 5-9" means the sixth month in the fourth grade through the ninth month in the fifth grade. "High school and college" denotes a single test booklet for both levels; "High school, college" denotes two test booklets, one for high school and one for college.

c) COPYRIGHT DATE. The range of copyright dates (or publication dates if not copyrighted) includes the various forms, accessories, and editions of a test. When the publication date differs from the copyright date, both dates are given; e.g., "1971, c1965–68" means that the test materials were copyrighted between 1965 and 1968 but were not published until 1971. Publication or copyright dates enclosed in brackets do not appear on the test materials but were obtained from other sources.

d) ACRONYM. An acronym is given for many tests.

e) SPECIAL COMMENTS. Some entries contain special notations, such as: "for research use only"; "revision of the *ABC Test*"; "tests administered

TABLE 2

IN PRINT FOREIGN LANGUAGE TESTS
IN TIP II AND TIP I

Classification	TIP II		TIP I	
	Number	Percent	Number	Percent
General	6	5.7	5	5.4
Arabic	1	1.0		
Chinese	1	1.0		
English	14	13.3	11	12.0
French	22	21.0	21	22.8
German	15	14.3	8	8.7
Greek	1	1.0	1	1.1
Hebrew	5	4.8	2	2.2
Italian	5	4.8	3	3.3
Latin	7	6.7	20	21.7
Russian	7	6.7	2	2.2
Spanish	21	20.0	19	20.7
Total	105	100.3	92	100.1

monthly at centers throughout the United States"; "subtests available as separates"; and "verbal creativity." "For research use only" should be interpreted to mean that the *only* use of the test should be in research designed to assess its usefulness; contrary to what the implications seem to be, "for research use only" does not mean that a test has any use, whatsoever, as a research instrument. Tests used in research studies should have demonstrated validity before being selected as research tools. A statement such as "verbal creativity" is intended to further describe what the test claims to measure.

f) PART SCORES. The number and description of part scores is presented.

g) FACTUAL STATEMENTS IMPLYING CRITICISM. Some of the test entries include factual statements which imply criticism of the test, such as "1970 test identical with test copyrighted 1960" and "no manual."

h) AUTHOR. For most tests, all authors are reported. In the case of tests which appear in a new form each year, only authors of the most recent forms are listed. Names are reported exactly as printed on test materials. Names of editors are generally not reported.

i) PUBLISHER. The name of the publisher or distributor is reported for each test. Foreign publishers are identified by listing the country in brackets immediately following the name of the publisher. The Publishers Directory and Index must be consulted for a publisher's address.

j) FOREIGN ADAPTATIONS. Revisions and adaptations of tests for foreign use are listed in parentheses following the description of the original edition.

k) CLOSING ASTERISK. An asterisk following the publisher's name indicates that the entry was prepared from a first-hand examination of the test materials.

l) SUBLISTINGS. Levels, editions, subtests, or parts of a test which are available in separate booklets are sometimes presented as sublistings with titles set in small capitals. Sub-sublistings are indented with titles set in italic type.

m) CROSS REFERENCES. Except for tests being listed for the first time, a test entry includes a second paragraph with cross references to relevant material which may be found in the MMY reprint sections in this volume, or, in some instances (such as reviews of testing programs), to material in other sections of the MMY's. These cross references may be to "additional information" reported in longer entries, or to reviews, excerpts, and references for specific tests.

REFERENCES

The specific test bibliographies in this monograph contain 330 references on the construction, use, and validity of specific tests—266 of these references for tests currently in print. Forty-three percent of the references are for the last six years reported on, 1966–71. Relatively little research and writing is being done on standardized foreign language tests—currently about 20 such references per year. Only eight of the in print tests have generated bibliographies of 10 or more references: *Modern Language Aptitude Test,* 44 references; *Iowa Placement Examinations: Foreign Language Aptitude,* 16; *MLA Cooperative Foreign Language Proficiency Tests: French,* 14; *Test of*

English as a Foreign Language, 14; *College Board Achievement Test in French Reading,* 13; *MLA Cooperative Foreign Language Proficiency Tests: German,* 12; *MLA Cooperative Foreign Language Proficiency Tests: Spanish,* 10; and *Pimsleur Language Aptitude Battery,* 10.

These specific test bibliographies cover not only the literature of the English-speaking world, but also the literature in English published in non-English-speaking countries. Our goal has been to include all published material—articles, books, chapters, and research monographs—as well as unpublished theses. We do not list as references research reports prepared for internal organizational use, prepublication reports, ERIC material, or abstracts of documents which are reproduced only on receipt of a purchase order (e.g., JSAS manuscripts). Secondary sources (e.g., *Psychological Abstracts*) may provide leads, but if the original publication cannot be located and examined, the reference is not used. We do, however, rely on secondary sources (primarily *Dissertation Abstracts International*) for unpublished theses. Except for doctoral dissertations abstracted in DAI, in recent years all thesis entries have been checked for accuracy by the degree-granting institutions.

References for a given test immediately follow the test entry. They are numbered consecutively for each test as they appear in the first through the seventh MMY and TIP II. References which appeared in earlier volumes are referred to but not repeated; e.g., "1–10. See 6:357" means references 1–10 can be found following test 357 in the section "Sixth MMY Reviews" in this volume.

References are arranged in chronological order by year of publication and alphabetically by authors within years. No references later than 1971 have been included. Supplementary bibliographies will be provided in the forthcoming 8th MMY for those tests which are listed again in that volume; the bibliographies for other tests will be brought up to date in *Tests in Print III,* scheduled for publication after the 8th MMY.

CUMULATIVE NAME INDEXES

A cumulative name index has been provided for every in print test having references, to facilitate the search for an author's writings relevant to that test. To simplify indexing, forenames were reduced to initials. Authors not consistent in reporting their names may be listed under two or more citations. On the other hand, a given name may represent two or more persons. In all cases, however, the references present names exactly as they appear in the publication referenced.

MMY REVIEWS REPRINT

This chapter is a reprinting of the foreign language test sections of the seven *Mental Measurements Yearbooks* presented in their order of publication: 1st MMY (1938, 8 pages), 2nd MMY (1941, 41 pages), 3rd MMY (1949, 29 pages), 4th MMY (1953, 24 pages), 5th MMY (1959, 28 pages), 6th MMY (1965, 48 pages), and 7th MMY (1972, 71 pages). This chapter brings together in a single well-indexed volume a great deal of information on foreign language testing covering the past 50 years and more. The yearbooks must still be consulted, however, for information about books on foreign language testing. Monographs on foreign language testing are rarely reviewed. The seven yearbooks together contain only 12 excerpted reviews for 7 books.[7]

This chapter presents 184 original test reviews written by 66 specialists, 12 excerpted test reviews, and 330 references on the construction, use, and validity of specific tests (Table 3). Tests currently in print account for 51.7 percent of the tests, 56.6 percent of the reviews and excerpts, and 80.1 percent of the references in this volume.

The contributing reviewers represent a wide

TABLE 3

REVIEWS, EXCERPTS, AND REFERENCES FOR THE 203 FOREIGN LANGUAGE TESTS IN THIS VOLUME

Reprint	Tests	Rev's	Exc's	Ref's
TIP II	105			81
7th MMY	75	27	7	87
6th MMY	77	25	4	55
5th MMY	40	25		9
4th MMY	35	20		32
3rd MMY	36	33	1	19
2nd MMY	36	44		47
1st MMY	19	10		
Total	203 [1]	184	12	330

[1] The total number of different tests in all publications is 203—105 in print and 98 out of print.

range of interests and viewpoints. Every effort was made to select reviewers who would be considered highly competent by a sizable group of test users. Our practice of publishing multiple reviews of given tests makes it possible to give representation to differing viewpoints among reviewers. The test reviews in a given yearbook are not limited to new and revised tests; old tests, especially those generating considerable research and writing, are frequently reviewed in successive yearbooks.

In order to make sure that persons invited to review would know what was expected of them, a sheet entitled "Suggestions to MMY Reviewers" was enclosed with each letter of invitation. The suggestions follow:

1. Reviews should be written with the following major objectives in mind:
a) To provide test users with carefully prepared appraisals of tests for their guidance in selecting and using tests.
b) To stimulate progress toward higher professional standards in the construction of tests by commending good work, by censuring poor work, and by suggesting improvements.
c) To impel test authors and publishers to present more detailed information on the construction, validity, reliability, uses, and possible misuses of their tests.
2. Reviews should be concise, the average review running from 600 to 1,200 words in length. The average length of the reviews written by one person generally should not exceed 1,000 words. Except for reviews of achievement batteries, multi-factor batteries, and tests for which a literature review is made, longer reviews should be prepared only with the approval of the Editor.
3. Reviews should be frankly critical, with both strengths and weaknesses pointed out in a judicious manner. Descriptive comments should be kept to the minimum necessary to support the critical portions of the review. Criticism should be as specific as possible; implied criticisms meaningful only to testing specialists should be avoided. Reviews should be written primarily for the rank and file of test users. An indication of the relative importance and value of a test with respect to competing tests should be presented whenever possible. If a reviewer considers a competing test better than

[7] Cheydleur, Frederic D. *Placement Tests in Foreign Languages at the University of Wisconsin: A Forward Step in Education, 1930–1943.* Bulletin of the University of Wisconsin, Serial No. 2686, General Series No. 2470. Madison, Wis.: Bureau of Guidance and Records, the University, 1943. Pp. 39. * For a review by James B. Tharp, *see* 3:798.

Davies, Alan, Editor. *Language Testing Symposium: A Psycholinguistic Approach.* London: Oxford University Press, 1968. Pp. viii, 214. * For a review by W. A. Bennett, *see* 7:B164.

Frizzle, Arnold Luther. *A Study of Some of the Influences of Regents Requirements and Examinations in French.* Columbia University, Teachers College, Contributions to Education, No. 964. New York: Bureau of Publications, the College, 1950. Pp. xi, 154. * For a review by James B. Tharp, *see* 4:B158.

Lado, Robert. *Language Testing: The Construction and Use of Foreign Language Tests: A Teacher's Book.* London: Longmans, Green & Co. Ltd., 1961. Pp. xxiii, 389. * For reviews by Mary Margaret Heiser, Morgan E. Jones, Suzanne Stahl, H. H. Stern, and one other person, *see* 6:B300 and 7:B369.

Otter, H. S. *A Functional Language Examination: The Modern Language Association Examinations Project.* London: Oxford University Press, 1968. Pp. viii, 136. * For a review by John B. Carroll, *see* 7:B468.

Schenck, Ethel A. *Studies of Testing and Teaching in Modern Foreign Languages: Based on Materials Gathered at the University of Wisconsin by the Late Professor Frederic D. Cheydleur.* Madison, Wis.: Dembar Publications, Inc., 1952. For a review by Theodore Huebner, *see* 5:B373.

Valette, Rebecca M. *Modern Language Testing: A Handbook.* New York: Harcourt Brace Jovanovich, Inc., 1967. Pp. xvii, 200. * For reviews by John B. Dalbor and Michio Peter Hagiwara, *see* 7:B621.

the one being reviewed, the competing test should be specifically named.

4. If a test manual gives insufficient, contradictory, or ambiguous information regarding the construction, validity, and use of a test, reviewers are urged to write directly to authors and publishers for further information. Test authors and publishers should, however, be held responsible for presenting adequate data in test manuals—failure to do so should be pointed out. For comments made by reviewers based upon unpublished information received personally from test authors or publishers, the source of the unpublished information should be clearly indicated.

5. Reviewers will be furnished with the test entries which will precede their reviews. Information presented in the entry should not be repeated in reviews unless needed for evaluative purposes.

6. The use of sideheads is optional with reviewers.

7. Each review should conclude with a paragraph presenting a concise summary of the reviewer's overall evaluation of the test. The summary should be as explicit as possible. Is the test the best of its kind? Is it recommended for use? If other tests are better, which of the competing tests is best?

8. A separate review should be prepared for each test. Each review should begin on a new sheet. The test and forms reviewed should be clearly indicated. Your name, title, position, and address should precede each review, e.g.: John Doe, Professor of Education and Psychology, University of Maryland, College Park, Maryland. The review should begin a new paragraph immediately after the address.

9. All reviews should be typed double spaced and in triplicate. Two copies of each review should be submitted to the Editor; one copy should be retained by the reviewer.

10. If for any reason a reviewer thinks he is not in a position to write a frankly critical review in a scholarly and unbiased manner, he should request the Editor to substitute other tests for review.

11. Reviewers may not invite others to collaborate with them in writing reviews unless permission is secured from the Editor.

12. Most tests will be reviewed by two or more persons in order to secure better representation of various viewpoints. Noncritical content which excessively overlaps similar materials presented by another reviewer may be deleted. Reviews will be carefully edited, but no important changes will be made without the consent of the reviewer. Galley proofs (unaccompanied by copy) will be submitted to reviewers for checking.

13. The Editor reserves the right to reject any review which does not meet the minimum standards of the MMY series.

14. Each reviewer will receive a complimentary copy of *The Seventh Mental Measurements Yearbook.*

The long test entries in the MMY Reviews reprint sections give all the information in the short TIP II entries plus the following:

a) INDIVIDUAL OR GROUP TEST. All tests are group tests unless otherwise indicated.

b) FORMS, PARTS, AND LEVELS. All available forms, parts, and levels are listed with copyright dates.

c) PAGES. The number of pages on which print occurs is reported for test booklets, manuals, technical reports, profiles, and other nonapparatus accessories.

d) FACTUAL STATEMENTS IMPLYING CRITICISM. Much more so than short entries, the long entries include factual statements implying criticism of the following type: "no data on reliability," "no data on validity," "no norms," "norms for grade 5 only," "no description of the normative population," "no norms for difference scores," "test copyrighted in 1970 identical with test copyrighted in 1960," and "statistical data based on earlier forms."

e) MACHINE SCORABLE ANSWER SHEETS. All types of machine scorable answer sheets available for use with a specific test are reported: Digitek (OpScan Test Scoring and Document Scanning System), IBM 805 (IBM Test Scoring Machine), IBM 1230 (IBM Optical Mark Reader), MRC (MRC Scoring and Reporting Service), NCS (NCS Scoring and Reporting Service), and NCS Sentry/70, and a few other answer sheets less widely used.

f) COST. Price information is reported for test packages (usually 20 to 35 tests), answer sheets, all other accessories, and specimen sets. The statement "$5.20 per 35 tests" means that all accessories are included unless separate prices are given for accessories. The statement also means 35 tests of one level, one edition, or one part unless stated otherwise. Quantity discounts and special discounts are not reported. Specimen set prices include copies of each level and part—but not all forms—unless otherwise indicated. Since 1970 prices are reported, the latest catalog of a test publisher should be consulted for current prices.

g) SCORING AND REPORTING SERVICES. Scoring and reporting services provided by publishers are reported along with information on costs. Special computerized scoring and interpretation services are sometimes given in separate entries immediately following the test entry.

h) TIME. The number of minutes of actual working time allowed examinees and the approximate length of time needed for administering a test are provided whenever obtainable. The latter figure is always enclosed in parentheses. Thus, "50(60) minutes" indicates that the examinees are allowed 50 minutes of working time and that a total of 60 minutes is needed to administer the test. When the time necessary to administer a test has been obtained through correspondence with the test publisher or author, the time is enclosed in brackets.

RUNNING HEADS AND FEET

To use this volume most efficiently, it is important to take advantage of the information given at the top and bottom of each page in the test and review sections. Both test entry and page numbers are given in the running heads. However, since all citations in the indexes and cross references are to entry numbers, these numbers, found next to the outside margins on facing pages, can be used as guide numbers in locating a particular test. The entry number on the left-hand page corresponds to the test embodying the first line of type on that page; the entry number on the right-hand page refers to the test containing the last line of type on that page. The test titles corresponding to these guide numbers are given in the running feet at the bottom of the page. Thus, the reader can quickly identify the first and last test discussed on each pair of facing pages.

The first reprint section, from *Tests in Print II,* has guide numbers in the range 218 to 322; the second reprint section, from the seven MMY's, has the successive ranges: 1:984 to 1:1157, 2:1340 to 2:1375, 3:178 to 3:213,

4:232 to 4:266, 5:255 to 5:294, 6:355 to 6:431, and 7:253 to 7:327. The digit preceding the colon in the guide number corresponds to the number of the yearbook being reprinted. The numbers following the colon are the test entry numbers within that yearbook.

TIP II SCANNING INDEX

The complete TIP II Scanning Index, a classified listing of all tests in TIP II, has been reprinted to provide readers with an overview of tests available in areas other than foreign language. The 2,467 tests are divided into the categories delineated in Table 1 of this Introduction. Since the foreign language section of the TIP II Scanning Index will be of most interest to readers of this monograph, we have reprinted that section (entitled Foreign Language Scanning Index) at the end of this volume for convenient reference. These scanning indexes are especially useful for locating tests suitable for a given population, since descriptions of these populations are reported immediately following the test titles.

PUBLISHERS DIRECTORY AND INDEX

Instead of giving only the entry numbers of the tests of a given publisher, as in our earlier publications, this Publishers Directory and Index gives both test titles and entry numbers. Stars denote the 9 publishers with test catalogs listing 10 or more tests (not necessarily foreign language tests). All addresses have been checked by the publishers, and are accurate through 1973. However, with such a large number of publishers (including many author-publishers), some address changes must be expected.

Seven publishers have four or more foreign language tests: College Entrance Examination Board, 32 tests; Educational Testing Service, 17; Cooperative Tests and Services, 12; Bobbs-Merrill Co., Inc., 6; Bureau of Educational Measurements, 6; Follett's Michigan Book Store, Inc., 6; and Harcourt Brace Jovanovich, Inc., 4. Since CTS is a division of ETS and since ETS constructs all the CEEB tests, the first three publishers make up an interlocking conglomerate responsible for 58.1 percent of all in print foreign language tests.

INDEX OF TITLES

This cumulative title index includes foreign language tests in print as separates as of February 1, 1974, and out of print or status unknown foreign language tests.

Citations are to test entry numbers, not to pages. Numbers without colons refer to in print tests listed in the first reprint section (TIP II Tests) in this volume; numbers with colons refer to tests out of print or status unknown, and may be found in the next reprint sections (MMY Reviews) of this volume. Superseded titles are listed with cross references to the current title. Tests which are part of a series are listed under their individual titles and also their series titles.

INDEX OF NAMES

This cumulative index is an analytical index distinguishing between authorship of a test, test review, excerpted review, or reference dealing with a specific test. Furthermore, the index indicates whether the relevant test is in print or out of print. Numbers with colons refer to out of print or status unknown tests.

Forenames have been reduced to initials to lower the cost of indexing. Since authors are not always consistent in how they list their names, two or more listings may refer to the same person. On the other hand, the use of initials sometimes results in one name representing two or more persons. Reference to the cited material in the text will resolve these difficulties in almost all cases.

Except for test authors, the use of the Index of Names is a two-step process. For example, if the name index reports *"rev, 255"* for P. Pimsleur, the reader must look at the cross reference for test 255 in TIP II Tests to learn where Pimsleur's review may be found in the yearbooks. Similarly, if the name index reports *"ref, 221"* for J. B. Carroll, the reader must look at the Cumulative Name Index for test 221 to learn where, in this volume, Carroll's reference or references on that test may be found. The Cumulative Name Index for test 221 indicates that Carroll is the author of 6 references for this test, each cited by number, so the reader can quickly locate them in the list of references under the test entry.

FOREIGN LANGUAGES – TIP II

[218]
Foreign Language Prognosis Test. Grades 8–9; 1930–59; 2 tests labeled Forms A, B; 1958–59 tests identical with tests copyrighted 1930 except for cover page; Percival M. Symonds; Teachers College Press. *
a) FORM A. 5 scores: English inflection, word translation-English to Esperanto, sentence translation-Esperanto to English, related words, total.
b) FORM B. 5 scores: word translation-Esperanto to English, artificial language, sentence translation-English to Esperanto, formation of parts of speech in English, total.

For additional information and a review by Wayne D. Fisher (with Bertram B. Masia), see 6:355 (1 reference); for a review by William B. Michael, see 4:232; for a review by Walter V. Kaulfers, see 2:1340 (6 references).

REFERENCES THROUGH 1971
1–6. See 2:1340.
7. See 6:355.

CUMULATIVE NAME INDEX
Fisher, W. D.: *rev*, 6:355   Michael, W. B.: *rev*, 4:232
Kaulfers, W. V.: *rev*, 2:1340   Richardson, H. D.: 4
Lau, L. M.: 3   Symonds, P. M.: 1–2
Maronpot, R. P.: 6   Veon, D. H.: 7
Masia, B. B.: *rev*, 6:355   Virgil, *Sister:* 5

[219]
*The Graduate School Foreign Language Testing Program. Graduate level degree candidates required to demonstrate foreign language reading proficiency;

1963–73; GSFLT; French, German, and Spanish administered 4 times annually (January, April, June, October) at centers established by the publisher; Russian administered on a special basis; Educational Testing Service. *

For additional information, see 7:668 (3 references). For a review of the Spanish test, see 7:320; an earlier edition of the French test, see 6:377; and the German test, see 6:391.

REFERENCES THROUGH 1971

1–3. See 7:668.

CUMULATIVE NAME INDEX

Bartlett, A. A.: 1   Harvey, P. R.: 3
Clark, J. L. D.: 2

[220]

Iowa Placement Examinations: Foreign Language Aptitude. Grades 12–13; 1925–44; 2 editions; Bureau of Educational Research and Service. *
a) SERIES FAI, REVISED. 1925–26; test by G. D. Stoddard and G. E. Vander Beke (Form A).
b) NEW SERIES FA-2, REVISED. 1925–44; original test by G. D. Stoddard; revision by Grace Cochran, J. R. Nielson, and D. B. Stuit.

For additional information and a review by H. E. Brogden, see 3:178 (7 references).

REFERENCES THROUGH 1971

1–7. See 3:178.
8. HAMMOND, H. P., AND STODDARD, GEORGE DINSMORE. "A Study of Placement Examinations." *Univ Iowa Studies Ed* 4(7): 1–59 '28. * (*PA* 3:2069)
9. THARP, JAMES BURTON.. Chap. 10, "Sectioning in Romance Language Classes at the University of Illinois," pp. 365–432. In *Studies in Modern Language Teaching.* By E. W. Bagster-Collins and Others. New York: Macmillan Co., 1930. Pp. xxxi, 491. *
10. FEDER, DANIEL D. "An Evaluation of Some Problems in the Prediction of Achievement at the College Level." *J Ed Psychol* 26:597–603 N '35. * (*PA* 10:1681)
11. VEON, DOROTHY HELENE. *The Relationship of Learning Factors Found in Certain Modern Foreign-Language Aptitude Tests to the Prediction of Shorthand Achievement in College.* Foreword by M. Herbert Freeman. Stillwater, Okla.: Division of Commerce, Oklahoma Agricultural and Mechanical College, 1950. Pp. 74. *
12. MORGAN, WILLIAM J. "A Validity Study of the Iowa Language Aptitude Examination." Abstract. *Am Psychologist* 7:287 Jl '52. *
13. HASCALL, EDWARD ORSON, JR. *Predicting Success in High School Foreign Language Study.* Doctor's thesis, University of Michigan (Ann Arbor, Mich.), 1959. (*DA* 19:3245)
14. LANG, MARY JANE. *The Relationship Between Certain Psychological Tests and Shorthand Achievement at Three Instructional Levels.* Doctor's thesis, University of Missouri (Columbia, Mo.), 1960. (*DA* 21:2632)
15. HASCALL, EDWARD O. "Predicting Success in High School Foreign Language Study." *Personnel & Guid J* 40:361–7 D '61. * (*PA* 36:4KL61H)
16. LANG, MARY JANE. "Predicting Elementary Shorthand Achievement." *Balance Sheet* 45:300–2 Mr '64. *

CUMULATIVE NAME INDEX

Brogden, H. E.: *rev,* 3:178   Larsen, R. P.: 7
Feder, D. D.: 10   Miller, L. W.: 4
Gerberich, J. R.: 5   Morgan, W. J.: 12
Giesecke, G. E.: 7   Stoddard, G. D.: 1–2, 8
Hammond, H. P.: 8   Tharp, J. B.: 3, 9
Hascall, E. O.: 13, 15   Veon, D. H.: 11
Kamman, J. F.: 6   Wittenborn, J. R.: 7
Lang, M. J.: 14, 16

[221]

Modern Language Aptitude Test. Grades 9 and over; 1959, c1955–58; MLAT; earlier experimental form called *Psi-Lambda Foreign Language Aptitude Battery;* 6 scores: number learning, phonetic script, spelling clues, words in sentences, paired associates, total; John B. Carroll and Stanley M. Sapon; Psychological Corporation. *

For additional information, reviews by Wayne D. Fisher (with Bertram B. Masia) and Marion F. Shaycoft, and excerpted reviews by Edward S. Bordin, Harold B. Dunkel, Herschel T. Manuel, and Laurence Siegel, see 6:357 (10 references).

REFERENCES THROUGH 1971

1–10. See 6:357.
11. HARDING, FRANCIS D. "Tests as Selectors of Language Students." *Mod Lang J* 42:120–2 Mr '58. * (*PA* 34:2153)
12. CARROLL, JOHN B. Chap. 4, "The Prediction of Success in Intensive Foreign Language Training," pp. 87–136. In *Training Research and Education.* Edited by Robert Glaser. Pittsburgh, Pa.: University of Pittsburgh Press, 1962. Pp. xi, 596. * (*PA* 38:1380)
13. CARROLL, JOHN B. "Programed Instruction and Student Ability." *J Programed Instr* 2:7–11 w '63. * (*PA* 40:7018)
14. PIMSLEUR, PAUL. "A Study of Foreign Language Learning Ability: Parts 1 and 2," pp. 57–72. In *Report of the Twelfth Annual Round Table Meeting on Linguistics and Language Studies.* Edited by Michael Zarechnak. Monograph Series on Language and Linguistics, No. 14. Washington, D.C.: Georgetown University Press, 1963. Pp. 132. *
15. CLOOS, ROBERT IRA. *A Comparative Study of Fourteen Predictors of Success in the Audio-Lingual Approach to First-Year German at the High School Level.* Doctor's thesis, Rutgers University (New Brunswick, N.J.), 1964. (*DA* 25:7106)
16. COOPER, CARL J. "Some Relationships Between Paired-Associates Learning and Foreign-Language Aptitude." *J Ed Psychol* 55:132–8 Je '64. * (*PA* 39:5823)
17. GALLAGHER, JOSEPH W., AND SPENCER, RICHARD E. "Prediction of Success in Basic German at the College Level." *Ed & Psychol Meas* 24:955–60 w '64. * (*PA* 39:8701)
18. SCHERER, GEORGE A. C., AND WERTHEIMER, MICHAEL. *A Psycholinguistic Experiment in Foreign-Language Teaching.* New York: McGraw-Hill Book Co., 1964. Pp. xiii, 256. *
19. ACKERMAN, THOMAS J. *Language Laboratory Instruction and the Achievement of First-Year Students of Spanish in Florida.* Doctor's thesis, Florida State University (Tallahassee, Fla.), 1965. (*DA* 27:134A)
20. CLARK, MARGARET G. *The Modern Language Aptitude Test as a Predictor at the University of Rochester.* Master's thesis, University of Rochester (Rochester, N.Y.), 1965.
21. GARDNER, R. C. "A Language Aptitude Test for Blind Students." *J Appl Psychol* 49:135–41 Ap '65. * (*PA* 39:10107)
22. GARDNER, R. C., AND LAMBERT, W. E. "Language Aptitude, Intelligence, and Second-Language Achievement." *J Ed Psychol* 56:191–9 Ag '65. * (*PA* 39:15290)
23. KIZIOR, EUGENIA A. *A Study of Factors That Aid in the Prediction of Secondary School Foreign Language Achievement.* Master's thesis, Northwestern University (Evanston, Ill.), 1965.
24. CRAWSHAW, TED CATHCART. *Comparative Validities of Eleven Predictors of Student Success in Ninth Grade Spanish and French: Aurora-West Public Schools, 1961–63.* Master's thesis, Northern Illinois University (DeKalb, Ill.), 1966.
25. HORTON, DAVID L.; WILEY, RONALD E.; AND DIXON, THEODORE R. "Predicting Paired-Associate Learning Speed: An Alternate MLAT." *Psychol Rep* 18:93–4 F '66. * (*PA* 40:6249)
26. RENFER, MARY EMMA FEWELL. *Predicting Success in the Study of Descriptive Linguistics.* Doctor's thesis, University of Southern California (Los Angeles, Calif.), 1966. (*DA* 27:1268A)
27. ARENDT, JERMAINE DELOS. *Predicting Success in Foreign Language Study: A Study Made in Selected Minneapolis Schools From 1963 to 1964.* Doctor's thesis, University of Minnesota (Minneapolis, Minn.), 1967. (*DA* 28:4869A)
28. MASSAD, CAROLYN EMRICK. *A Comparative Study of Creativity, Language Aptitude, and Intelligence in Sixth-Grade Children From Low-Socioeconomic and Middle-Socioeconomic Levels.* Doctor's thesis, Kent State University (Kent, Ohio), 1967. (*DA* 29:4331A)
29. PAYNE, DAVID A., AND VAUGHN, HAROLD A. "Forecasting Italian Language Proficiency of Culturally Immersed Students." *Mod Lang J* 51:3–6 Ja '67. *
30. STURGIS, THEODORE GILBERT. *A Study of the Statistical Relationships Between Certain Variables and Success in Learning Certain African Languages.* Doctor's thesis, Syracuse University (Syracuse, N.Y.), 1967. (*DA* 28:4393A)
31. ZAHN, JANE C. "Some Characteristics of Successful and Less Successful Overseas Community Development Advisers." *Adult Ed* 18:15–23 f '67. *
32. MUELLER, THEODORE H. "Programmed Language Instruction—Help for the Linguistically 'Underprivileged.'" *Mod Lang J* 52:79–84 F '68. * (*PA* 44:20888)
33. BARTLEY, DIANA E. "A Pilot Study of Aptitude and Attitude Factors in Language Dropout." *Calif J Ed Res* 20(2):48–55 Mr '69. *
34. CARROLL, JOHN B. "What Does the Pennsylvania Foreign Language Project Tell Us?" *Foreign Lang Ann* 3(2):214–36 D '69. *
35. CHASTAIN, KENNETH. "Prediction of Success in Audio-Lingual and Cognitive Classes." *Lang Learning* 19(1–2):27–39 Je '69. *
36. DICKEN, CHARLES. "Predicting the Success of Peace Corps Community Development Workers." *J Consult & Clin Psychol* 33(5):597–606 O '69. * (*PA* 44:2919)

37. HALSALL, ELIZABETH. "Linguistic Aptitude." *Mod Lang* (England) 50(1):18–23 Mr '69. *

38. JAKOBOVITS, LEON A. "Research Findings and Foreign Language Requirements in Colleges and Universities." *Foreign Lang Ann* 2(4):436–56 My '69. *

39. NEUFELD, GERALD G. *How Personality, Foreign Language Aptitude, and Anomie Relate to Foreign Language Acquisition.* Doctor's thesis, University of California (Berkeley, Calif.), 1969. (*DAI* 31:1651A)

40. SMITH, PHILIP D., JR. "The Pennsylvania Foreign Language Research Project: Teacher Proficiency and Class Achievement in Two Modern Languages." *Foreign Lang Ann* 3(2):194–207 D '69. *

41. WEAVER, WENDELL W.; KINGSTON, ALBERT J.; BICKLEY, A. C.; AND WHITE, WILLIAM F. "Information-Flow Difficulty in Relation to Reading Comprehension." *J Read Behav* 1(3):41–9 su '69. * (*PA* 45:2355)

42. POLITZER, ROBERT L. "On the Use of Aptitude Variables in Research in Foreign Language Teaching." *IRAL* (West Germany) 8(4): 333–40 N '70. *

43. SMITH, PHILIP D., JR. *A Comparison of the Cognitive and Audiolingual Approaches to Foreign Language Instruction: The Pennsylvania Foreign Language Project.* Philadelphia, Pa.: Center for Curriculum Development, Inc., 1970. Pp. xxv, 380. *

44. CLOOS, ROBERT I. "A Four-Year Study of Foreign Language Aptitude at the High School Level." *Foreign Lang Ann* 4(4):411–9 My '71. *

CUMULATIVE NAME INDEX

[222]

Modern Language Aptitude Test—Elementary. Grades 3–6; 1960–67; EMLAT; downward extension of the *Modern Language Aptitude Test;* 5 scores: hidden words, matching words, finding rhymes, number learning, total; John B. Carroll and Stanley M. Sapon; Psychological Corporation. *

For additional information and a review by A. Ralph Hakstian, see 7:255.

REFERENCES THROUGH 1971

1. MILLER, BERNEICE BEADLES. *The Effects of Continuing or Changing Foreign Languages on Listening Comprehension and Selected Tests as Predictors of Success in Spanish or French at the Seventh-Grade Level.* Doctor's thesis, University of Oklahoma (Norman, Okla.), 1970. (*DAI* 31:2618A)

CUMULATIVE NAME INDEX

[223]

Pimsleur Language Aptitude Battery. Grades 6–12; 1966–67; 5 scores: grade-point average, interest, verbal, auditory, total; Paul Pimsleur; Harcourt Brace Jovanovich, Inc. *

For additional information, a review by A. Ralph Hakstian, and an excerpted review by Donald C. Ryberg, see 7:256 (5 references).

REFERENCES THROUGH 1971

1–5. See 7:256.

6. CLOOS, ROBERT I. "A Four-Year Study of Foreign Language Aptitude at the High School Level." *Foreign Lang Ann* 4(4):411–9 My '71. *

7. LAFAYETTE, ROBERT CLAUDE. *An Investigation of Causes Leading to Early Attrition in Foreign Language Study.* Doctor's thesis, Ohio State University (Columbus, Ohio), 1971. (*DAI* 32:1752A)

8. LEAL, AUREA M. *A Study of the Factors Involved in the Correlation Between Pimsleur's Aptitude Test Scores and Academic Achievement in Beginning Spanish.* Master's thesis, John Carroll University (Cleveland, Ohio), 1971.

9. LESTER, KENNETH ALLEN. *Factors Related to Dropouts Between Levels Two and Three of Modern Foreign Language Study in the Public Secondary Schools of Connecticut.* Doctor's thesis, Boston University (Boston, Mass.), 1971. (*DAI* 32:1839A)

10. VON WITTICH, BARBARA. *The Impact of Method of Evaluation Upon Achievement in Elementary Foreign Language Courses.* Doctor's thesis, Iowa State University (Ames, Iowa), 1971. (*DAI* 32:5576A)

CUMULATIVE NAME INDEX

[Out of Print Since TIP I]

Common Concepts Foreign Language Test, 7:253 (1 review)

Luria-Orleans Modern Language Prognosis Test, 2: 1341 (1 review, 3 references)

ARABIC

[224]

*First Year Arabic Final Examination, 1972 Edition. 1 year college; 1964–72; 1964 edition called *First-Year Arabic Qualifying Examination;* no manual; Sami A. Hanna; Middle East Center, University of Utah. *

For additional information concerning the 1964 edition, see 7:258.

CHINESE

[225]

Harvard-MLA Tests of Chinese Language Proficiency. College and adults; 1959–65; 2 tests; Modern Language Association of America and Educational Testing Service; program administered by Educational Testing Service (Atlanta Office). *

a) PICTORIAL AUDITORY COMPREHENSION TEST. 2 semesters; 1959–65; John B. Carroll and Wai-Ching Ho.

b) INTERMEDIATE READING COMPREHENSION TEST IN MODERN CHINESE. 4 semesters; 1964–65; 4 scores: vocabulary, structure, reading comprehension, total; K. P. Chou, John de Francis, Y. K. Kao, H. C. Mills, R. C. Pian, and J. Wrenn.

For additional information, see 7:259.

ENGLISH

[226]

A Comprehensive English Language Test for Speakers of English as a Second Language. Non-native speakers of English; 1970; CELT; 3 tests; David P. Harris and Leslie A. Palmer; McGraw-Hill Book Co., Inc. *

a) LISTENING.
b) STRUCTURE.
c) VOCABULARY.

For additional information and a review by John B. Carroll, see 7:260.

[227]

Diagnostic Test for Students of English as a Second Language. Applicants from non-English language countries for admission to American colleges; 1953; A. L. Davis; McGraw-Hill Book Co., Inc. *

For additional information and reviews by Nelson Brooks and Herschel T. Manuel, see 5:255.

REFERENCES THROUGH 1971
1. BLATCHFORD, CHARLES H. "A Theoretical Contribution to ESL Diagnostic Test Construction." *TESOL Q* 5(3):209–15 S '71. *

CUMULATIVE NAME INDEX
Blatchford, C. H.: 1   Manuel, H. T.: *rev*, 5:255
Brooks, N.: *rev*, 5:255

[228]

English Knowledge and Comprehension Test. High school; 1965; S. Chatterji and M. Mukerjee; S. Chatterji [India]. *

For additional information, see 7:261.

[229]

★**English Placement Test.** College entrants from non-English language countries; 1972; test by Mary Spaan and Laura Strowe; published by the English Language Institute, University of Michigan and distributed by Follett's Michigan Book Store, Inc. *

[230]

*English Usage Test for Non-Native Speakers of English.** Non-native speakers of English; 1955–72; distribution restricted to the Agency for International Development and the Bureau of Educational and Cultural Affairs of the U.S. Department of State; David P. Harris and Leslie A. Palmer assisted by B. Jean Longmire (Forms L and U-B); American Language Institute. *

For additional information, see 7:262.

[231]

Examination in Structure (English as a Foreign Language). College entrants from non-English language countries; 1947; published by the English Language Institute, University of Michigan and distributed by Follett's Michigan Book Store, Inc. *

For additional information, see 5:260.

REFERENCES THROUGH 1971
1. LADO, ROBERT. *Measurement in English as a Foreign Language With Special Reference to Spanish-Speaking Adults.* Doctor's thesis, University of Michigan (Ann Arbor, Mich.), 1950.

CUMULATIVE NAME INDEX
Lado, R.: 1

[232]

★**Michigan Test of Aural Comprehension.** College applicants from non-English language countries; 1969–72; MTAC; John Upshur, Mary Spaan, and Rudolph Thrasher; published by the English Language Institute, University of Michigan and distributed by Follett's Michigan Book Store, Inc. *

[233]

*Michigan Test of English Language Proficiency.** College applicants from non-English language countries; 1961–66; MTELP; test by John Upshur, Leslie

Comprehensive English Language Test

Palmer (Form A), John Harris (Forms A and E), Geraldine May (Forms A and B), Miho Tanaka (Form B), Rudolph Thrasher (Forms B and D), A. Palmer (Form D), M. Spaan (Forms D and E), and E. Loundon (Form E); manual by Division of Testing and Certification, English Language Institute, University of Michigan; distributed for the Institute by Follett's Michigan Book Store, Inc. *

For additional information, see 7:264 (2 references); for a review by John B. Carroll, see 6:360.

REFERENCES THROUGH 1971
1–2. See 7:264.
3. BEBEAU, DONALD E. "Administration of a TOEFL Test to Sioux Indian High School Students." *J Am Indian Ed* 9(1):7–16 O '69. *

CUMULATIVE NAME INDEX
Bebeau, D. E.: 3   Dizney, H.: 1
Carroll, J. B.: *rev*, 6:360   Ursua, A. R.: 2

[234]

Oral Rating Form for Rating Language Proficiency in Speaking and Understanding English. Non-native speakers of English; 1959–67; also called *AULC Interview Rating Form;* 6 ratings by interviewers: comprehension, pronunciation, grammar and word-order, vocabulary, general speed of speech and sentence length, total; 1962 form identical with form published 1959 except for title; [David P. Harris]; American Language Institute. *

For additional information, see 7:265.

[235]

★**Test A/65.** Matriculants and higher; [1956?]; also called *English Language Achievement Test;* 3 scores: spelling, comprehension, vocabulary; no manual; National Institute for Personnel Research [South Africa]. *

[236]

Test of Aural Perception in English for Japanese Students. Japanese students in American colleges; 1950; for research use only; Robert Lado and R. D. Andrade; published by the English Language Institute, University of Michigan and distributed by Follett's Michigan Book Store, Inc. *

For additional information, see 6:362.

REFERENCES THROUGH 1971
1. STRAIN, JERIS E. "Difficulties in Measuring Pronunciation Improvement." *Lang Learning* 13(3–4):217–24 '63. *

CUMULATIVE NAME INDEX
Strain, J. E.: 1

[237]

Test of Aural Perception in English for Latin-American Students. Latin-American students of English; 1947–57; Robert Lado; published by the English Language Institute, University of Michigan and distributed by Follett's Michigan Book Store, Inc. *

For additional information, see 5:262.

REFERENCES THROUGH 1971
1. LADO, ROBERT. *Measurement in English as a Foreign Language With Special Reference to Spanish-Speaking Adults.* Doctor's thesis, University of Michigan (Ann Arbor, Mich.), 1950.
2. SISSON, CYRUS R. "The Effect of Delayed Comparison in the Language Laboratory on Phoneme Discrimination and Pronunciation Accuracy." *Lang Learning* 20(1):69–88 Je '70. *

CUMULATIVE NAME INDEX
Lado, R.: 1   Sisson, C. R.: 2

[238]

*Test of English as a Foreign Language.** College applicants from non-English language countries; 1964–

73; TOEFL; test administered 4 times annually (January, March, June, October) in approximately 100 countries; 6 scores: listening comprehension, English structure, vocabulary, reading comprehension, writing ability, total; program sponsored jointly by the College Entrance Examination Board and Educational Testing Service; Educational Testing Service. *

For additional information and reviews by Clinton I. Chase and George Domino of earlier forms, see 7:266 (10 references).

REFERENCES THROUGH 1971

1–10. See 7:266.

11. ERICKSON, DOUGLAS EUGENE. *Differential Personality, Academic, and Biographical Characteristics of International Graduate Students at the University of North Dakota.* Doctor's thesis, University of North Dakota (Grand Forks, N.D.), 1970. (*DAI* 32:6756A)

12. ANGOFF, WILLIAM H., AND SHARON, AMIEL T. "A Comparison of Scores Earned on the Test of English as a Foreign Language by Native American College Students and Foreign Applicants to U.S. Colleges." *TESOL Q* 5(2):129–36 Je '71. *

13. MARTIN, GALE MACLANE. *A Model for the Cultural and Statistical Analysis of Academic Achievement of Foreign Graduate Students at the University of North Carolina at Chapel Hill.* Doctor's thesis, University of North Carolina (Chapel Hill, N.C.), 1971. (*DAI* 32:2311A)

14. REILLY, RICHARD R. "A Note on 'Clozentrophy: A Procedure' for Testing English Language Proficiency of Foreign Students.'" *Speech Monogr* 38(4):350–3 N '71. *

CUMULATIVE NAME INDEX

Angoff, W. H.: 12   Lado, R.: 2
Chase, C. I.: 5; *rev,* 7:266   Martin, G. M.: 13
Darnell, D. K.: 8   Maxwell, A.: 6
Dizney, H.: 3   Palmer, L. A.: 4
Dizney, H. F.: 9   Reilly, R. R.: 14
Domino, G.: *rev,* 7:266   Sharon, A. T.: 12
Erickson, D. E.: 11   Stallings, W. M.: 5
Harris, D.: 1   Vroman, C.: 10
Hwang, K. Y.: 7, 9   Wilcox, L.: 10

[239]

*A Vocabulary and Reading Test for Students of English as a Second Language. Non-native speakers of English; 1960–72; distribution restricted to the Agency for International Development and the Bureau of Educational and Cultural Affairs of the U.S. Department of State; David P. Harris and Leslie A. Palmer; American Language Institute. *

For additional information, see 7:267.

[Out of Print Since TIP I]

English Examinations for Foreign Students, 5:256 (3 reviews)
English Language Test for Foreign Students, 5:257 (2 reviews, 3 references)
English Reading Test for Students of English as a Foreign Language (status unknown), 5:258 (2 reviews)
Listening Test for Students of English as a Second Language, 7:263
Rating Language Proficiency in Speaking and Understanding English (status unknown), T:625
Test of Aural Comprehension, 5:261 (2 reviews)

FRENCH

[240]

*Advanced Placement Examination in French. High school students desiring credit for college level courses or admission to advanced courses; 1954–73; 2 tests (candidate elects one or both); available to secondary schools for annual administration on specified days in May; inactive forms are available to colleges for local administration in the *Testing Academic Achievement* program; program administered for the College Entrance Examination Board by Educational

Testing Service. * For the testing program entry, see 1045.
a) FRENCH LANGUAGE.
b) FRENCH LITERATURE.

For additional information concerning earlier forms, see 7:268 (1 reference); see also 6:368 (3 references). For reviews of the testing program, see 7:662 (2 reviews).

REFERENCES THROUGH 1971

1–3. See 6:368.
4. See 7:268.

CUMULATIVE NAME INDEX

Nelson, R. J.: 3   Valley, J. R.: 1
Niess, R. J.: 2

[241]

Baltimore County French Test. 1 year high school; 1962; 2 scores: parts A, B; Baltimore County French Language Committee; Bobbs-Merrill Co., Inc. *

For additional information and reviews by Nelson Brooks and Mary E. Turnbull, see 6:364 (1 reference).

REFERENCES THROUGH 1971

1. See 6:364.

CUMULATIVE NAME INDEX

Brooks, N.: *rev,* 6:364   Turnbull, M. E.: *rev,* 6:364
Jungeblut, A.: 1

[242]

*Canadian Achievement Test in French. Grade 10; 1961–68; CATF; a test in the *Canadian Test Battery, Grade 10;* Ontario Institute for Studies in Education; distributed by Guidance Centre [Canada]. * For the complete battery entry, see 1046.

For additional information and a review by Mary E. Turnbull, see 6:365 (2 references).

REFERENCES THROUGH 1971

1–2. See 6:365.

CUMULATIVE NAME INDEX

D'Oyley, V. R.: 1–2   Turnbull, M. E.: *rev,* 6:365

[243]

★College Board Achievement Test in French Listening-Reading. Candidates for college entrance with 2–4 years high school French; 1971–73; test administered each spring at centers established by the publisher; inactive forms, entitled *College Placement Test in French Listening-Reading,* are available to colleges for local administration; program administered for the College Entrance Examination Board by Educational Testing Service. * For the testing program entry, see 1048.

For reviews of the testing program, see 6:760 (2 reviews).

[244]

*College Board Achievement Test in French Reading. Candidates for college entrance with 2–4 years high school French; 1901–73; test administered on specified dates at centers established by the publisher; inactive forms, entitled *College Placement Test in French Reading,* are available to colleges for local administration; program administered for the College Entrance Examination Board by Educational Testing Service. * For the testing program entry, see 1048.

For additional information, see 7:269; see also 6:366 (4 references) and 5:263 (2 references); for a review by Walter V. Kaulfers of earlier forms, see 4:237 (7 references). For reviews of the testing program, see 6:760 (2 reviews).

REFERENCES THROUGH 1971

1–7. See 4:237.
8–9. See 5:263.
10–13. See 6:366.

[245]

*College Placement Test in French Listening Comprehension. Entering college freshmen; 1962–72, c1955–72; reprintings of inactive 1963 and 1967 forms of *College Board Achievement Test in French Listening Comprehension;* test available to colleges for local administration; program administered for the College Entrance Examination Board by Educational Testing Service. * For the testing program entry, see 1051.

For additional information, see 7:270 (1 reference). For a review of the testing program, see 7:665.

REFERENCES THROUGH 1971
1. See 7:270.

[246]

★College Placement Test in French Listening-Reading. Entering college freshmen; 1971–72; reprinting of inactive 1971 form of *College Board Achievement Test in French Listening-Reading;* test available to colleges for local administration; program administered for the College Entrance Examination Board by Educational Testing Service. * For the testing program entry, see 1051.

For a review of the testing program, see 7:665.

[247]

*College Placement Test in French Reading. Entering college freshmen; 1962–72, c1955–72; reprinting of inactive 1964 forms of *College Board Achievement Test in French Reading;* test available to colleges for local administration; program administered for the College Entrance Examination Board by Educational Testing Service. * For the testing program entry, see 1051.

For additional information, see 7:271 (1 reference). For a review of the testing program, see 7:665. For reference to a review of the *College Board Achievement Test in French Reading,* see 244.

REFERENCES THROUGH 1971
1. See 7:271.

[248]

Cooperative French Listening Comprehension Test. 2–5 semesters high school or college; 1955; Nelson Brooks; Cooperative Tests and Services. *

For additional information and reviews by Walter V. Kaulfers and Kathleen N. Perret, see 5:265 (1 reference).

REFERENCES THROUGH 1971
1. See 5:265.
2. VECCHIONE, NICHOLAS. "A Further Study of the Cooperative French Listening Comprehension Test." *Ed Rec B* 77:75–82 Jl '60. *
3. TRAXLER, ARTHUR E. "Some Further Information on the Cooperative French Listening Comprehension Test Among Independent School Pupils." *Ed Rec B* 82:61–2 Jl '62. *
4. SIMON-HERMANN, *Sister.* "A Report on an Applied Linguistics Method Used to Improve the Spoken French of French-Speaking Students at the Grade Seven Level." *Alberta J Ed Res* (Canada) 9:111–9 Je '63. *

5. GARDNER, R. C., AND LAMBERT, W. E. "Language Aptitude, Intelligence, and Second-Language Achievement." *J Ed Psychol* 56:191–9 Ag '65. * (*PA* 39:15290)

[249]

First Year French Test. High school and college; 1956–68; Jean Leblon and Minnie M. Miller; Bureau of Educational Measurements. *

For additional information, see 7:273; for reviews by Nelson Brooks and Mary E. Turnbull of an earlier edition, see 5:266.

[250]

Ford-Hicks French Grammar Completion Tests. High school; 1944; test booklet title is *Dents' Modern Language Tests: French Grammar;* H. E. Ford and R. K. Hicks; J. M. Dent & Sons (Canada) Ltd. [Canada]. *

For additional information, see 6:372.

[251]

French I and II: Achievement Examinations for Secondary Schools. 1–2 years high school; 1951–60; Form 4 ('55) is the only form in print; Midwest High School Achievement Examinations and Minnesota High School Achievement Examinations were also used as series titles; Lee Stark; Bobbs-Merrill Co., Inc. *

For additional information concerning later and earlier forms, see 6:373 and 5:268; for a review by Mary E. Turnbull of Form A [1955, same as A-E (1962)], see 5:267; for a review by Elton Hocking of Form 1 (1951), see 4:239.

[252]

*The Graduate Record Examinations Advanced French Test. Graduate school candidates; 1939–73; 3 scores: interpretive reading skills, literature and civilization, total; Educational Testing Service. * For the testing program entry, see 1053.

For additional information concerning earlier forms, see 7:274; for a review by Nelson Brooks, see 6:376; for a review by Walter V. Kaulfers, see 5:270. For reviews of the testing program, see 7:667 (1 review) and 5:601 (1 review).

[253]

*Graduate School Foreign Language Test: French. Graduate level degree candidates required to demonstrate reading proficiency in French; 1963–73; test administered 4 times annually (January, April, June, October) at centers established by the publisher; Educational Testing Service. * For the testing program entry, see 219.

For additional information, see 7:275 (3 references); for a review by Clarence E. Turner of an earlier edition, see 6:377.

REFERENCES THROUGH 1971
1–3. See 7:275.

[254]

Iowa Placement Examinations: French Training. Grades 12–13; 1925–26; test by G. E. Vander Beke, G. D. Stoddard, and C. E. Young (Form B); Bureau of Educational Research and Service. *

For additional information and a review by Geraldine Spaulding, see 3:189 (4 references).

REFERENCES THROUGH 1971

1-4. See 3:189.
5. HAMMOND, H. P., AND STODDARD, GEORGE DINSMORE. "A Study of Placement Examinations." *Univ Iowa Studies Ed* 4(7):1-59 '28. * (*PA* 3:2069)
6. RICE, GEORGE A. Chap. 11, "A Study of Achievement in French and Spanish in Junior and Senior High School, With Consideration of Some of the Factors That Condition Achievement," pp. 433-71. In *Studies in Modern Language Teaching.* By E. W. Bagster-Collins and Others. New York: Macmillan Co., 1930. Pp. xxxi, 491. *
7. THARP, JAMES BURTON. Chap. 10, "Sectioning in Romance Language Classes at the University of Illinois," pp. 365-432. In *Studies in Modern Language Teaching.* By E. W. Bagster-Collins and Others. New York: Macmillan Co., 1930. Pp. xxxi, 491. *

CUMULATIVE NAME INDEX

Hammond, H. P.: 5   Spaulding, G.: *rev*, 3:189
Miller, L. W.: 4   Stoddard, G. D.: 1-2, 5
Rice, G. A.: 6   Tharp, J. B.: 3, 7

[255]

MLA Cooperative Foreign Language Proficiency Tests: French. French majors and advanced students in college; 1960-68; formerly called *MLA Foreign Language Proficiency Tests for Teachers and Advanced Students: French;* 7 tests in 3 booklets; 1966 test identical with tests copyrighted 1961 except for format and directions; Modern Language Association of America and Educational Testing Service; Cooperative Tests and Services. *
a) BOOK 1: READING, LISTENING COMPREHENSION, SPEAKING.
b) BOOK 2: WRITING.
c) BOOK 3: APPLIED LINGUISTICS, CIVILIZATION AND CULTURE, PROFESSIONAL PREPARATION.

For additional information and reviews by Joseph A. Murphy and Jean-Guy Savard, see 7:276 (9 references); for reviews by Paul Pimsleur and James H. Ricks, Jr., see 6:379 (3 references).

REFERENCES THROUGH 1971

1-3. See 6:379.
4-12. See 7:276.
13. SMITH, PHILIP D., JR. "An Assessment of Three Foreign Language Teaching Strategies and Three Language Laboratory Systems." *French R* 43(2):289-304 D '69. *
14. VILLARREAL, JOSE A. *The MLA-Cooperative Foreign Language Proficiency Test as an Evaluating Instrument of the Competency of Prospective Student Teachers of Spanish, French, and German.* Master's thesis, University of Texas (Austin, Tex.), 1970.

CUMULATIVE NAME INDEX

Bashour, D. S.: 5   Perkins, J. A.: 9
Beaujour, M.: 5   Pimsleur, P.: *rev*, 6:379
Carroll, J. B.: 6, 10   Ricks, J. H.: *rev*, 6:379
Churchill, F. J.: 4   Savard, J. G.: *rev*, 7:276
Dizney, H. F.: 7   Sheppard, D. C.: 5
Ehrmann, J.: 5   Smith, P. D.: 12-3
Gromen, L.: 7   Spencer, R. E.: 4
Hull, A.: 5   Starr, W. H.: 1-3
Ladu, T. T.: 5   Tollinger, S.: 5
McKinney, J. C.: 5   Valette, R. M.: 5
Murphy, J. A.: *rev*, 7:276 Villarreal, J. A.: 14
Otto, F.: 11   Wallmark, M.: 4, 8
Paquette, F. A.: 4-5, 8

[256]

MLA-Cooperative Foreign Language Tests: French. 1-2 years high school or 2 semesters college, 3-4 years high school or 4 semesters college; 1963-65; 4 tests in a single booklet: listening, speaking, reading, writing; writing test available as separate; prepared in cooperation with the Modern Language Association of America; Cooperative Tests and Services. *

For additional information and a review by Michio Peter Hagiwara, see 7:277 (5 references). For an excerpted review by John L. D. Clark of the series, see 7:254.

REFERENCES THROUGH 1971

1-5. See 7:277.
6. SMITH, PHILIP D., JR. *A Comparison of the Cognitive and Audiolingual Approaches to Foreign Language Instruction: The Pennsylvania Foreign Language Project.* Philadelphia, Pa.: Center for Curriculum Development, Inc., 1970. Pp. xxv, 380. *

CUMULATIVE NAME INDEX

Aleamoni, L. M.: 5   Paquette, F. A.: 1
Churchill, F. J.: 1   Smith, P. D.: 6
Clark, J. L. D.: *exc*, 7:254 Spencer, R. E.: 1-2, 5
Hagiwara, M. P.: *rev*, 7:277 Vocolo, J. M.: 3
Mueller, T. H.: 4   Wallmark, M.: 1

[257]

*National Teacher Examinations: French. College seniors and teachers; 1970-73; derived from *MLA Foreign Language Proficiency Tests for Teachers and Advanced Students: French;* an inactive form (1967) entitled *Teacher Education Examination Program: French* is available to colleges for local administration; the same inactive form entitled *French* is available to school systems for local use as part of the program entitled *School Personnel Research and Evaluation Services;* Educational Testing Service. * For the testing program entry, see 869.

For additional information, see 7:278. For reviews of the testing program, see 7:582 (2 reviews), 6:700 (1 review), 5:538 (3 reviews), and 4:802 (1 review).

[258]

Pimsleur French Proficiency Tests. "First-level,... second-level" courses in grades 7-16; 1967; 4 tests; Paul Pimsleur; Harcourt Brace Jovanovich, Inc. *
a) TEST 1, LISTENING COMPREHENSION.
b) TEST 2, SPEAKING PROFICIENCY.
c) TEST 3, READING COMPREHENSION.
d) TEST 4, WRITING PROFICIENCY.

For additional information, reviews by John L. D. Clark and Michio Peter Hagiwara, and an excerpted review by C. Richards Pusey, see 7:279 (1 reference). For an excerpted review by A. Ralph Hakstian of this and other tests (German, Spanish) in the series, see 7:257.

REFERENCES THROUGH 1971

1. See 7:279.

CUMULATIVE NAME INDEX

Clark, J. L. D.: *rev*, 7:279   Pimsleur, P.: 1
Hagiwara, M. P.: *rev*, 7:279 Pusey, C. R.: *exc*, 7:279
Hakstian, A. R.: *exc*, 7:257

[259]

Second Year French Test. High school and college; 1956-68; Jean Leblon and Minnie M. Miller; Bureau of Educational Measurements. *

For additional information and a review by John L. D. Clark, see 7:280; for reviews by Geraldine Spaulding and Clarence E. Turner of an earlier edition, see 5:271.

[260]

*Teacher Education Examination Program: French. College seniors preparing to teach secondary school; 1957-72; reprinting of inactive 1967 form of *National Teacher Examinations: French;* test available to colleges for local administration; Educational Testing Service. * For the testing program entry, see 898.

For additional information concerning an earlier form, see 6:374. For a review of the testing program, see 5:543.

[261]

*The Undergraduate Program Field Tests: French Test. College; 1969-73; formerly called *The Undergraduate Record Examinations: French Test;*

test available to colleges for local administration; Educational Testing Service. * For the testing program entry, see 1062.

For additional information and a review by Joseph A. Murphy of an earlier form, see 7:281. For reviews of the testing program, see 7:671 (2 reviews).

[Out of Print Since TIP I]

American Council Beta French Test, 2:1344 (1 review, 2 references)
Cohen French Test, 4:236 (1 review)
College Entrance Examination Board Achievement Test: French Listening Comprehension, 6:367
Common Concepts Foreign Language Test: French, 7:272
Cooperative French Test: Elementary and Advanced Forms, 3:181 (7 reviews, 7 references)
French Recognition Vocabulary Test: State High School Tests for Indiana, 4:240 (1 review, 1 reference); for a revision, see *French, First Year—Second Semester: State High School Tests for Indiana,* T:639
French Test (Two-Year Course): Affiliation Testing Program for Catholic Secondary Schools, 6:375 (1 review)
Lundeberg-Tharp Audition Test in French, 2:1354 (1 review, 3 references)
Standard French Test: Vocabulary, Grammar, and Comprehension, 2:1356 (1 review, 2 references)
Standardised French Grammar Test, 6:380 (2 reviews, 1 reference)
Standardised French Vocabulary Test, 6:381 (2 reviews, 1 reference)

GERMAN

[262]

*Advanced Placement Examination in German. High school students desiring credit for college level courses or admission to advanced courses; 1954–73; available to secondary schools for annual administration on specified days in May; inactive forms are available to colleges for local administration in the *Testing Academic Achievement* program; program administered for the College Entrance Examination Board by Educational Testing Service. * For the testing program entry, see 1045.

For additional information concerning earlier forms, see 7:282 (4 references); see also 6:385 (5 references); for a review by Herbert Schueler, see 5:273. For reviews of the testing program, see 7:662 (2 reviews).

REFERENCES THROUGH 1971
1–5. See 6:385.
6–9. See 7:282.

CUMULATIVE NAME INDEX
Lederer, H.: 7   Scheider, R. M.: 9
Newmark, M.: 5   Scherer, P.: 5
Presel, R.: 1   Schueler, H.: *rev,* 5:273
Reichard, J. R.: 2, 4, 8 Valley, J. R.: 3

[263]

★College Board Achievement Test in German Listening-Reading. Candidates for college entrance with 2–4 years high school German; 1971–73; test administered each spring at centers established by the publisher; inactive forms, entitled *College Placement Test in German Listening-Reading,* are available to colleges for local administration; program administered for the College Entrance Examination Board by Educational

Testing Service. * For the testing program entry, see 1048.

For reviews of the testing program, see 6:760 (2 reviews).

[264]

*College Board Achievement Test in German Reading. Candidates for college entrance with 2–4 years high school German; 1901–73; test administered on specified dates at centers established by the publisher; inactive forms, entitled *College Placement Test in German Reading,* are available to colleges for local administration; program administered for the College Entrance Examination Board by Educational Testing Service. * For the testing program entry, see 1048.

For additional information, see 7:283; for a review by Gilbert C. Kettelkamp of earlier forms, see 6:383; for a review by Harold B. Dunkel, see 5:272 (3 references); for a review by Herbert Schueler, see 4:244 (3 references). For reviews of the testing program, see 6:760 (2 reviews).

REFERENCES THROUGH 1971
1–3. See 4:244.
4–6. See 5:272.

CUMULATIVE NAME INDEX
College Entrance Examination   Kettelkamp, G. C.: *rev,* 6:383
  Board: 4   King, R. G.: 5
Dunkel, H. B.: *rev,* 5:272   Schueler, H.: *rev,* 4:244
Dyer, H. S.: 1–2   Tucker, L. R.: 3
Hollmann, W.: 6

[265]

*College Placement Test in German Listening Comprehension. Entering college freshmen; 1962–72, c1955–72; reprintings of inactive 1966 and 1967 forms of *College Board Achievement Test in German Listening Comprehension;* test available to colleges for local administration; program administered for the College Entrance Examination Board by Educational Testing Service. * For the testing program entry, see 1051.

For additional information, see 7:284 (2 references). For a review of the testing program, see 7:665. For reviews of the *College Board Achievement Test in German Listening Comprehension,* see 6:384 (2 reviews).

REFERENCES THROUGH 1971
1–2. See 7:284.

CUMULATIVE NAME INDEX
Aleamoni, L. M.: 2   Seguin, E. L.: 1
Matsunaga, A.: 2   Spencer, R. E.: 1

[266]

★College Placement Test in German Listening-Reading. Entering college freshmen; 1971–72; reprinting of inactive 1971 form of *College Board Achievement Test in German Listening-Reading;* test available to colleges for local administration; program administered for the College Entrance Examination Board by Educational Testing Service. * For the testing program entry, see 1051.

For a review of the testing program, see 7:665.

[267]

*College Placement Test in German Reading. Entering college freshmen; 1962–72, c1957–72; reprintings of inactive 1965 and 1966 forms of *College Board Achievement Test in German Reading;* test available to colleges for local administration; program administered for the College Entrance Examination Board by Educational Testing Service. * For the testing program entry, see 1051.

For additional information, see 7:285 (2 references). For a review of the testing program, see 7:665. For reference to reviews of the *College Board Achievement Test in German Reading,* see 264.

REFERENCES THROUGH 1971

1–2. See 7:285.

CUMULATIVE NAME INDEX

Aleamoni, L. M.: 2   Seguin, E. L.: 1
Matsunaga, A.: 2   Spencer, R. E.: 1

[268]

German I and II: Achievement Examinations for Secondary Schools. 1–2 years high school; 1951–60; Form 4 ['54] is the only form in print; Midwest High School Achievement Examinations and Minnesota High School Achievement Examinations were also used as series titles; Emma Marie Birkmaier; Bobbs-Merrill Co., Inc. *

For additional information concerning earlier forms, see 6:390 and 5:275; for a review by Harold B. Dunkel of Form A (1955) and Form B (1953, same as Form 2), see 5:276.

[269]

***The Graduate Record Examinations Advanced German Test.** Graduate school candidates; 1939–73; Educational Testing Service. * For the testing program entry, see 1053.

For additional information concerning earlier forms, see 7:287. For reviews of the testing program, see 7:667 (1 review) and 5:601 (1 review).

REFERENCES THROUGH 1971

1. SCHULTZ, MARGARET K., AND ANGOFF, WILLIAM H. "The Development of New Scales for the Aptitude and Advanced Tests of the Graduate Record Examinations." *J Ed Psychol* 47: 285–94 My '56. * (PA 32:2127)

CUMULATIVE NAME INDEX

Angoff, W. H.: 1   Schultz, M. K.: 1

[270]

***Graduate School Foreign Language Test: German.** Graduate level degree candidates required to demonstrate reading proficiency in German; 1963–73; test administered 4 times annually (January, April, June, October) at centers established by the publisher; Educational Testing Service. * For the testing program entry, see 219.

For additional information, see 7:288 (3 references); for a review by Jack M. Stein of an earlier edition, see 6:391.

REFERENCES THROUGH 1971

1–3. See 7:288.

CUMULATIVE NAME INDEX

Bartlett, A. A.: 1   Harvey, P. R.: 3
Clark, J. L. D.: 2   Stein, J. M.: *rev,* 6:391

[271]

MLA Cooperative Foreign Language Proficiency Tests: German. German majors and advanced students in college; 1960–68; formerly called *MLA Foreign Language Proficiency Tests for Teachers and Advanced Students: German;* 7 tests in 3 booklets; 1966 test identical with tests copyrighted 1961 except for format and directions; Modern Language Association of America and Educational Testing Service; Cooperative Tests and Services. *

a) BOOK 1: READING, LISTENING COMPREHENSION, SPEAKING.
b) BOOK 2: WRITING.
c) BOOK 3: APPLIED LINGUISTICS, CIVILIZATION AND CULTURE, PROFESSIONAL PREPARATION.

For additional information, see 7:289 (8 references);

for reviews by Harold B. Dunkel and Herbert Schueler, see 6:393 (3 references).

REFERENCES THROUGH 1971

1–3. See 6:393.
4–11. See 7:289.
12. VILLARREAL, JOSE A. *The MLA-Cooperative Foreign Language Proficiency Test as an Evaluating Instrument of the Competency of Prospective Student Teachers of Spanish, French, and German.* Master's thesis, University of Texas (Austin, Tex.), 1970.

CUMULATIVE NAME INDEX

Carroll, J. B.: 6, 10   Rehder, H.: 5
Churchill, F. J.: 4–5   Ryder, F. G.: 5
Dizney, H. F.: 7   Schueler, H.: *rev,* 6:393
Dunkel, H. B.: *rev,* 6:393 Sheppard, D. C.: 5
Gromen, L.: 7   Smith, P. D.: 11
Ladu, T. T.: 5   Spencer, R. E.: 4
McKinney, J. C.: 5   Starr, W. H.: 1–3
Marchand, J. W.: 5   Tollinger, S.: 5
Mueller, K. A.: 5   Villarreal, J. A.: 12
Paquette, F. A.: 4–5, 8   Wallmark, M.: 4, 8
Perkins, J. A.: 9

[272]

MLA-Cooperative Foreign Language Tests: German. 1–2 years high school or 2 semesters college, 3–4 years high school or 4 semesters college; 1963–65; 4 tests in a single booklet: listening, speaking, reading, writing; writing test available as separate; prepared in cooperation with the Modern Language Association of America; Cooperative Tests and Services. *

For additional information and a review by T. F. Naumann, see 7:290 (2 references). For an excerpted review by John L. D. Clark of the series, see 7:254.

REFERENCES THROUGH 1971

1–2. See 7:290.
3. SMITH, PHILIP D., JR. *A Comparison of the Cognitive and Audiolingual Approaches to Foreign Language Instruction: The Pennsylvania Foreign Language Project.* Philadelphia, Pa.: Center for Curriculum Development, Inc., 1970. Pp. xxv, 380. *

CUMULATIVE NAME INDEX

Aleamoni, L. M.: 2   Paquette, F. A.: 1
Churchill, F. J.: 1   Smith, P. D.: 3
Clark, J. L. D.: *exc,* 7:254 Spencer, R. E.: 1–2
Naumann, T. F.: *rev,* 7:290 Wallmark, M.: 1

[273]

***National German Examination for High School Students.** 2, 3, or 4 years high school; 1960-73; formerly called *AATG German Test* and *National German Contest for High School Students;* tests administered annually in February/March under auspices of high school guidance departments or centers established by the publisher; American Association of Teachers of German with the technical assistance of Educational Testing Service; program administered by American Association of Teachers of German, Inc. *

For additional information and reviews by Gilbert C. Kettelkamp and Theodor F. Naumann of an earlier edition, see 6:382.

[274]

***National Teacher Examinations: German.** College seniors and teachers; 1970–73; derived from *MLA Foreign Language Proficiency Tests for Teachers and Advanced Students: German;* Educational Testing Service. * For the testing program entry, see 869.

For additional information, see 7:291. For reviews of the testing program, see 7:582 (2 reviews), 6:700 (1 review), 5:538 (3 reviews), and 4:802 (1 review).

[275]

Pimsleur German Proficiency Tests. "First-level, . . . second-level" courses in grades 7–16; 1967; 4 tests; Paul Pimsleur; Harcourt Brace Jovanovich, Inc. *

a) TEST I, LISTENING COMPREHENSION.
b) TEST 2, SPEAKING PROFICIENCY.
c) TEST 3, READING COMPREHENSION.
d) TEST 4, WRITING PROFICIENCY.

For additional information, reviews by Walter F. W. Lohnes and Jack M. Stein, and an excerpted review by Garold N. Davis, see 7 :292. For an excerpted review by A. Ralph Hakstian of this and other tests (French, Spanish) in the series, see 7 :257.

[276]

*The Undergraduate Program Field Tests: German Test.** College ; 1969–73 ; formerly called *The Undergraduate Record Examinations: German Test;* test available to colleges for local administration ; Educational Testing Service. * For the testing program entry, see 1062.

For additional information, see 7 :293. For reviews of the testing program, see 7 :671 (2 reviews).

[Out of Print Since TIP I]

College Entrance Examination Board Achievement Test: German Listening Comprehension, 6 :384 (2 reviews, I reference)
Common Concepts Foreign Language Test: German, 7 :286 (I review)
First Year German Test, 5 :274 (I review)
German: Every Pupil Test, 6 :389
Lundeberg-Tharp Audition Test in German, 3 :194 (I review)

GREEK

[277]

*College Placement Test in Greek Reading.** Entering college freshmen ; 1962–72, c1957–72 ; formerly called *College Placement Test in Greek;* reprinting of inactive 1957 form of *College Board Achievement Test in Greek;* test available to colleges for local administration ; program administered for the College Entrance Examination Board by Educational Testing Service. * For the testing program entry, see 1051.

For additional information, see 7 :295. For a review of the testing program, see 7 :665. For a review of the *College Board Achievement Test in Greek,* see 5 :277.

[Out of Print Since TIP I]

College Board Achievement Test in Greek, 7 :294 (I review)

HEBREW

[278]

★Achievement Test—Hebrew Language.** Grades 5–7 ; 1973 ; Testing Bureau of the National Curriculum Research Institute ; American Association for Jewish Education. *

[279]

*College Board Achievement Test in Hebrew.** Candidates for college entrance with 2–4 years high school Hebrew ; 1961–73 ; test administered on a specified date at centers established by the publisher ; inactive forms, entitled *College Placement Test in Hebrew Reading,* are available to colleges for local administration ; program administered for the College Entrance Examination Board by Educational Testing Service. * For the testing program entry, see 1048.

For additional information, see 7 :296. For reviews of the testing program, see 6 :760 (2 reviews).

[280]

*College Placement Test in Hebrew Reading.** Entering college freshmen ; 1962–72, c1961–72 ; reprinting of inactive 1964 form of *College Board Achievement Test in Hebrew;* test available to colleges for local administration ; program administered for the College Entrance Examination Board by Educational Testing Service. * For the testing program entry, see 1051.

For additional information, see 7 :297. For a review of the testing program, see 7 :665.

[281]

[NCRI Achievement Tests in Hebrew.]** Grades 5–7, 7–9 ; 1965–67 ; Simon Bugatch and Judah Pilch (test) ; National Curriculum Research Institute, American Association for Jewish Education. *

For additional information, see 7 :298.

REFERENCES THROUGH 1971

I. KAPEL, MARILYN B., AND KAPEL, DAVID E. "Hebrew English Reading Achievement in a Jewish Day School: A Comparison Among Reading Achievements and Attitudes Towards the Two Languages." *Jewish Ed* 40(3):23–32 w '70. *

CUMULATIVE NAME INDEX

Kapel, D. E.: 1   Kapel, M. B.: 1

[282]

Test on the Fundamentals of Hebrew.** Grades 2–5, 3–6, 4–7 ; 1955–59 ; 4 or 5 scores : sentences (grades 3–7 only), vocabulary, stories, grammar, total ; Committee on Tests of the American Association for Jewish Education ; the Association. *

For additional information, see 6 :397.

ITALIAN

[283]

*College Placement Test in Italian Listening Comprehension.** Entering college freshmen ; 1962–72 ; reprinting of inactive 1966 form of *College Board Achievement Test in Italian Listening Comprehension;* test available to colleges for local administration ; program administered for the College Entrance Examination Board by Educational Testing Service. * For the testing program entry, see 1051.

For additional information and a review by Paolo Valesio, see 7 :299. For a review of the testing program, see 7 :665.

[284]

★College Placement Test in Italian Listening-Reading.** Entering college freshmen ; 1971–72 ; reprinting of inactive 1971 form of *College Board Achievement Test in Italian Listening-Reading;* program administered for the College Entrance Examination Board by Educational Testing Service. * For the testing program entry, see 1051.

For a review of the testing program, see 7 :665.

[285]

*College Placement Test in Italian Reading.** Entering college freshmen ; 1962–72, c1957–72 ; reprinting of inactive 1966 form of *College Board Achievement Test in Italian Reading;* test available to colleges for local administration ; program administered for the College Entrance Examination Board by Educational Testing Service. * For the testing program entry, see 1051.

For additional information and a review by Paolo Valesio, see 7:300. For a review of the testing program, see 7:665.

[286]

MLA Cooperative Foreign Language Proficiency Tests: Italian. Italian majors and advanced students in colleges; 1961–68; formerly called *MLA Foreign Language Proficiency Tests for Teachers and Advanced Students: Italian;* 7 tests in 3 booklets; Modern Language Association of America and Educational Testing Service; Cooperative Tests and Services. *
a) BOOK 1: READING, LISTENING COMPREHENSION, SPEAKING.
b) BOOK 2: WRITING.
c) BOOK 3: APPLIED LINGUISTICS, CIVILIZATION AND CULTURE, PROFESSIONAL PREPARATION.

For additional information and a review by Josephine Bruno Pane, see 7:301 (2 references); see also 6:403 (3 references).

REFERENCES THROUGH 1971
1–3. See 6:403.
4–5. See 7:301.

CUMULATIVE NAME INDEX
Castiglione, P. B.: 4   Pane, J. B.: *rev*, 7:301
Di Pietro, R. J.: 4   Paquette, F. A.: 4–5
Ladu, T. T.: 4   Sheppard, D. C.: 4
Lazzarino, G.: 4   Starr, W. H.: 1–3
MacAllister, A. T.: 4   Tollinger, S.: 4
McKinney, J. C.: 4   Wallmark, M.: 5
Olson, P. R.: 4

[287]

MLA-Cooperative Foreign Language Tests: Italian. 1–2 years high school or 2 semesters college, 3–4 years high school or 4 semesters college; 1963–65; 4 tests in a single booklet: listening, speaking, reading, writing; writing test available as separate; prepared in cooperation with the Modern Language Association of America; Cooperative Tests and Services. *

For additional information and a review by Josephine Bruno Pane, see 7:302. For an excerpted review by John L. D. Clark of the series, see 7:254.

[Out of Print Since TIP I]

College Entrance Examination Board Achievement Test: Italian Listening Comprehension, 6:398
College Entrance Examination Board Achievement Test: Italian Reading and Essay, 6:399; formerly called *College Entrance Examination Board Achievement Test in Italian,* 5:279

LATIN

[288]

*Advanced Placement Examination in Classics. High school students desiring credit for college level courses or admission to advanced courses; 1954–73; formerly called *Advanced Placement Examination in Latin;* 3 tests (candidate elects 1 or 2): Vergil, Lyric, Prose; available to secondary schools for annual administration on specified days in May; inactive forms are available to colleges for local administration in the *Testing Academic Achievement* program; program administered for the College Entrance Examination Board by Educational Testing Service. * For the testing program entry, see 1045.

For additional information concerning earlier forms, see 7:303. For reviews of the testing program, see 7:662 (2 reviews).

[289]

*College Board Achievement Test in Latin. Candidates for college entrance with 2–4 years high school Latin; 1901–73; test administered on specified dates at centers established by the publisher; inactive forms, entitled *College Placement Test in Latin Reading,* are available to colleges for local administration; program administered for the College Entrance Examination Board by Educational Testing Service. * For the testing program entry, see 1048.

For additional information, see 7:304; for a review by Konrad Gries of an earlier form, see 5:280 (1 reference); for a review by Harold B. Dunkel, see 4:250 (2 references). For reviews of the testing program, see 6:760 (2 reviews).

REFERENCES THROUGH 1971
1–2. See 4:250.
3. See 5:280.

CUMULATIVE NAME INDEX
Colby, J. K.: 2   Harwood, F. C.: 2
College Entrance Examination   Murphy, C. T.: 2
  Board: 3   Shero, L. R.: 2
Dunkel, H. B.: *rev*, 4:250   Spaeth, J. W.: 2
Gries, K.: *rev*, 5:280   Tucker, L. R.: 1

[290]

*College Placement Test in Latin Reading. Entering college freshmen; 1962–72, c1955–72; reprintings of inactive 1963 and 1964 forms of *College Board Achievement Test in Latin;* test available to colleges for local administration; program administered for the College Entrance Examination Board by Educational Testing Service. * For the testing program entry, see 1051.

For additional information, see 7:305. For a review of the testing program, see 7:665. For reference to reviews of the *College Board Achievement Test in Latin,* see 289.

[291]

Cooperative Latin Test: Elementary and Advanced Levels. 1–4 semesters high school or 1–2 semesters college, more than 4 semesters high school or more than 2 semesters college; 1932–41; 4 scores: reading, vocabulary, grammar, total; George A. Land; Cooperative Tests and Services. *

For additional information, see 3:204 (1 reference); for reviews by Harold B. Dunkel and John Flagg Gummere of an earlier form of the elementary level, see 2:1365; for a review by S. D. Atkins, see 1:1065; for a review by Norman T. Pratt, Jr. of an earlier form of the advanced level, see 1:1064.

REFERENCES THROUGH 1971
1. See 3:204.
2. TRAXLER, ARTHUR E. "The Correlation Between Achievement Scores and School Marks in an Independent School for Boys." *J Appl Psychol* 24:58–63 F '40. * (*PA* 14:3766)
3. TRAXLER, ARTHUR E. "Reliability of Cooperative Achievement Tests for Independent Secondary School Pupils." *Ed Rec B* 68:64–8 Jl '56. * (*PA* 31:8853)

CUMULATIVE NAME INDEX
Atkins, S. D.: *rev*, 1:1065   Pratt, N. T.: *rev*, 1:1064
Dunkel, H. B.: *rev*, 2:1365   Traxler, A. E.: 1–3
Gummere, J. F.: *rev*, 2:1365

[292]

Emporia First Year Latin Test. 1 year high school; 1962–64; first published 1962–63 in the Every Pupil Scholarship Test series; Bernadine Sitts, Minnie M. Miller, Lillian A. Wall, and M. W. Sanders; Bureau of Educational Measurements. *

For additional information, see 7:306.

[293]

Emporia Second Year Latin Test. 2 years high school; 1962–64; first published 1962–63 in the Every Pupil Scholarship Test series; Bernadine Sitts, Minnie M. Miller, Lillian A. Wall, and M. W. Sanders; Bureau of Educational Measurements. *

For additional information, see 7:307.

[294]

Latin I and II: Achievement Examinations for Secondary Schools. 1–2 years high school; 1951–59; Form 4 ('55) is the only form in print; High School Achievement Examinations, Midwest High School Achievement Examinations, and Minnesota High School Achievement Examinations were also used as series titles; Margaret M. Forbes; Bobbs-Merrill Co., Inc. *

For additional information concerning later and earlier forms, see 6:409, 5:284, and 5:286.

[Out of Print Since TIP I]

Cicero Test, 2:1363 (1 review)
First- and Second-Year Latin: Every Pupil Test, 6:407
First Year Latin: Every Pupil Scholarship Test, 6:408
First Year Latin: Manchester Semester-End Achievement Tests, T:670, 36:765
First Year Latin Test: State High School Tests for Indiana, 4:252
Holtz Vergil Test, 2:1366 (2 reviews)
Kansas First Year Latin Test, 5:283 (2 reviews)
Kansas Second Year Latin Test, 4:254 (2 reviews)
Latin Test (Two-Year Course): Affiliation Testing Program for Catholic Secondary Schools, 6:410 (1 review)
Orleans-Solomon Latin Prognosis Test, 3:207 (1 review)
Powers Diagnostic Latin Test, 2:1370 (2 reviews)
Second Year Latin: Every Pupil Scholarship Test, 6:411
Second Year Latin: Manchester Semester-End Achievement Tests, T:683, 36:771
Second Year Latin Test: State High School Tests for Indiana, 4:257
Ullman-Kirby Latin Comprehension Test, T:684

RUSSIAN

[295]

★**College Board Achievement Test in Russian Listening-Reading.** Candidates for college entrance with 2–4 years high school Russian; 1971–73; test administered each spring at centers established by the publisher; inactive forms, entitled *College Placement Test in Russian Listening-Reading,* are available to colleges for local administration; program administered for the College Entrance Examination Board by Educational Testing Service. * For the testing program entry, see 1048.

For reviews of the testing program, see 6:760 (2 reviews).

[296]

*College Placement Test in Russian Listening Comprehension.** Entering college freshmen; 1962–72; reprinting of inactive 1968 form of *College Board Achievement Test in Russian Listening Comprehension;* test available to colleges for local administration; program administered for the College Entrance Examination Board by Educational Testing Service. * For the testing program entry, see 1051.

For additional information, see 7:308 (1 reference). For a review of the testing program, see 7:665.

REFERENCES THROUGH 1971
1. See 7:308.

CUMULATIVE NAME INDEX
Aleamoni, L. M.: 1   Matsunaga, A.: 1

[297]

★**College Placement Test in Russian Listening-Reading.** Entering college freshmen; 1971–72; reprinting of inactive 1971 form of *College Board Achievement Test in Russian Listening-Reading;* test available to colleges for local administration; program administered for the College Entrance Examination Board by Educational Testing Service. * For the testing program entry, see 1051.

For a review of the testing program, see 7:665.

[298]

*College Placement Test in Russian Reading.** Entering college freshmen; 1962–72; reprintings of inactive 1964 and 1965 forms of *College Board Achievement Test in Russian;* test available to colleges for local administration; program administered for the College Entrance Examination Board by Educational Testing Service. * For the testing program entry, see 1051.

For additional information, see 7:309. For a review of the testing program, see 7:665.

[299]

*Graduate School Foreign Language Test: Russian.** Graduate level degree candidates required to demonstrate reading proficiency in Russian; 1963–73; test administered on a special basis; Educational Testing Service. * For the testing program entry, see 219.

For additional information, see 7:310 (4 references).

REFERENCES THROUGH 1971
1–4. See 7:310.

CUMULATIVE NAME INDEX
Aleamoni, L. M.: 4   Harvey, P. R.: 3
Bartlett, A. A.: 1   Matsunaga, A.: 4
Clark, J. L. D.: 2

[300]

MLA Cooperative Foreign Language Proficiency Tests: Russian. Russian majors and advanced students in college; 1960–68; formerly called *MLA Foreign Language Proficiency Tests for Teachers and Advanced Students: Russian;* 7 tests in 3 booklets; 1966 test identical with tests copyrighted 1961 except for format and directions; Modern Language Association of America and Educational Testing Service; Cooperative Tests and Services. *

a) BOOK 1: READING, LISTENING COMPREHENSION, SPEAKING.
b) BOOK 2: WRITING.
c) BOOK 3: APPLIED LINGUISTICS, CIVILIZATION AND CULTURE, PROFESSIONAL PREPARATION.

For additional information, see 7:311 (3 references); for a review by Wayne D. Fisher, see 6:417 (3 references).

REFERENCES THROUGH 1971
1–3. See 6:417.
4–6. See 7:311.

CUMULATIVE NAME INDEX
Baker, R. L.: 4   Moser, C. A.: 4
Carroll, J. B.: 5   Paquette, F. A.: 4
Chandler, D.: 4   Perkins, J. A.: 6
Fisher, W. D.: *rev,* 6:417   Sheppard, D. C.: 4
Ignatieff, E.: 4   Starr, W. H.: 1–3
Ladu, T. T.: 4   Tollinger, S.: 4
McKinney, J. C.: 4   Twarog, L. I.: 4

[301]

MLA-Cooperative Foreign Language Tests: Russian. 1–2 years high school or 2 semesters college, 3–4 years high school or 4 semesters college; 1963–65; 4 tests in a single booklet: listening, speaking, reading, writing; writing test available as separate; prepared in cooperation with the Modern Language Association of America; Cooperative Tests and Services. *

For additional information and an excerpted review by Raymond L. Bair, see 7:312 (2 references). For an excerpted review by John L. D. Clark of the series, see 7:254.

REFERENCES THROUGH 1971

1–2. See 7:312.
3. SHANE, ALEX M. "An Evaluation of the Existing College Norms for the MLA-Cooperative Russian Test and Its Efficacy as a Placement Examination." *Mod Lang J* 55(2):93–9 F '71.*

CUMULATIVE NAME INDEX

Aleamoni, L. M.: 2   Shane, A. M.: 3
Bair, R. L.: 1; *exc,* 7:312   Spencer, R. E.: 2
Clark, J. L. D.: *exc,* 7:254

[Out of Print Since TIP I]

College Entrance Examination Board Achievement Test: Russian, 6:412
College Entrance Examination Board Achievement Test: Russian Listening Comprehension, 6:413

SPANISH

[302]

*Advanced Placement Examination in Spanish. High school students desiring credit for college level courses or admission to advanced courses; 1954–73; available to secondary schools for annual administration on specified days in May; inactive forms are available to colleges for local administration in the *Testing Academic Achievement* program; program administered for the College Entrance Examination Board by Educational Testing Service. * For the testing program entry, see 1045.

For additional information concerning earlier forms, see 7:313 (2 references); see also 6:421 (1 reference). For reviews of the testing program, see 7:662 (2 reviews).

REFERENCES THROUGH 1971

1. See 6:421.
2–3. See 7:313.

CUMULATIVE NAME INDEX

Englekirk, J. E.: 2   Valley, J. R.: 1
Turner, A. R.: 3

[303]

Baltimore County Spanish Test. 1 year high school; 1962; 2 scores: parts A, B; Baltimore County Spanish Language Committee; Bobbs-Merrill Co., Inc. *

For additional information and a review by Mariette Schwarz, see 6:418.

[304]

★College Board Achievement Test in Spanish Listening-Reading. Candidates for college entrance with 2–4 years high school Spanish; 1971–73; test administered each spring at centers established by the publisher; inactive forms, entitled *College Placement Test in Spanish Listening-Reading,* are available to colleges for local administration; program administered for the College Entrance Examination Board by Educational Testing Service. * For the testing program entry, see 1048.

For reviews of the testing program, see 6:760 (2 reviews).

[305]

*College Board Achievement Test in Spanish Reading. Candidates for college entrance with 2–4 years high school Spanish; 1902–73; test administered on specified dates at centers established by the publisher; inactive forms, entitled *College Placement Test in Spanish Reading,* are available to colleges for local administration; program administered for the College Entrance Examination Board by Educational Testing Service. * For the testing program entry, see 1048.

For additional information, see 7:314; see also 6:419 (1 reference), 5:287 (1 reference), and 4:259 (3 references). For reviews of the testing program, see 6:760 (2 reviews).

REFERENCES THROUGH 1971

1–3. See 4:259.
4. See 5:287.
5. See 6:419.

CUMULATIVE NAME INDEX

Cabat, L.: 5   Godin, J. D.: 5
College Entrance Examination   Tucker, L. R.: 2
   Board: 4   Walsh, D. D.: 3
Dyer, H. S.: 1

[306]

*College Placement Test in Spanish Listening Comprehension. Entering college freshmen; 1962–72, c1955–72; reprintings of inactive 1969 and 1970 forms of *College Board Achievement Test in Spanish Listening Comprehension;* test available to colleges for local administration; program administered for the College Entrance Examination Board by Educational Testing Service. * For the testing program entry, see 1051.

For additional information concerning earlier forms, see 7:315 (1 reference); see also 6:422 (1 reference). For a review of the testing program, see 7:665.

REFERENCES THROUGH 1971

1. See 6:422.
2. See 7:315.

CUMULATIVE NAME INDEX

Aleamoni, L. M.: 2   Scheider, R. M.: 1
Matsunaga, A.: 2

[307]

★College Placement Test in Spanish Listening-Reading. Entering college freshmen; 1971–72; reprinting of inactive 1971 form of *College Board Achievement Test in Spanish Listening-Reading;* test available to colleges for local administration; program administered for the College Entrance Examination Board by Educational Testing Service. * For the testing program entry, see 1051.

For a review of the testing program, see 7:665.

[308]

*College Placement Test in Spanish Reading. Entering college freshmen; 1962–72, c1955–72; reprintings of inactive 1963 forms of *College Board Achievement Test in Spanish Reading;* test available to colleges for local administration; program administered for the College Entrance Examination Board by Educational Testing Service. * For the testing program entry, see 1051.

For additional information, see 7:316 (1 reference). For a review of the testing program, see 7:665.

REFERENCES THROUGH 1971

1. See 7:316.

CUMULATIVE NAME INDEX

Aleamoni, L. M.: 1   Matsunaga, A.: 1

[309]

First Year Spanish Test. High school and college; 1947–68; revision of *Kansas First Year Spanish Test;* Oscar F. Hernández and Minnie M. Miller; Bureau of Educational Measurements. *

For additional information, see 7:318.

[310]

Furness Test of Aural Comprehension in Spanish. 1–3 years high school or 1–2 years college; 1945–51; 2 editions; Edna Lue Furness; National Textbook Co. *

a) ORIGINAL EDITION. 1945–46; 4 scores: vocabulary, completion, identification, total; 1946 tests identical with tests copyrighted 1945.

b) RECORDED EDITION. 1951; 5 scores: vocabulary, completion, identification, question-answer, total.

For additional information, see 4:262; for reviews by Frederick B. Agard and Walter V. Kaulfers of *a,* see 3:213.

REFERENCES THROUGH 1971
1. FURNESS, EDNA L. *An Experiment in Objective Measurement of Aural Comprehension of Spanish.* Doctor's thesis, University of Colorado (Boulder, Colo.), 1952.

CUMULATIVE NAME INDEX
Agard, F. B.: *rev, 3:213*   Kaulfers, W. V.: *rev, 3:213*
Furness, E. L.: 1

[311]

The Graduate Record Examinations Advanced Spanish Test. Graduate school candidates; 1946–72; 4 scores: language knowledge, peninsular topics, Hispano-American topics, total; Educational Testing Service. * For the testing program entry, see 1053.

For additional information and a review by Gino Parisi of an earlier form, see 7:319. For reviews of the testing program, see 7:667 (1 review) and 5:601 (1 review).

[312]

Graduate School Foreign Language Test: Spanish. Graduate level degree candidates required to demonstrate reading proficiency in Spanish; 1963–73; test administered 4 times annually (January, April, June, October) at centers established by the publisher; Educational Testing Service. * For the testing program entry, see 219.

For additional information and a review by Robert Lado, see 7:320 (3 references).

REFERENCES THROUGH 1971
1–3. See 7:320.

CUMULATIVE NAME INDEX
Bartlett, A. A.: 1   Harvey, P. R.: 3
Clark, J. L. D.: 2   Lado, R.: *rev, 7:320*

[313]

Iowa Placement Examinations: Spanish Training. Grades 12–13; 1925–26; test by G. E. Vander Beke and G. D. Stoddard; Bureau of Educational Research and Service. *

For additional information and a review by Harry J. Russell, see 3:212 (2 references).

REFERENCES THROUGH 1971
1–2. See 3:212.
3. HAMMOND, H. P., AND STODDARD, GEORGE DINSMORE. "A Study of Placement Examinations." *Univ Iowa Studies Ed* 4(7):1–59 '28. * (*PA* 3:2069)
4. RICE, GEORGE A. Chap. 11, "A Study of Achievement in French and Spanish in Junior and Senior High School, With Consideration of Some of the Factors That Condition Achievement," pp. 433–71. In *Studies in Modern Language Teaching.* By E. W. Bagster-Collins and Others. New York: Macmillan Co., 1930. Pp. xxxi, 491. *

5. THARP, JAMES BURTON. Chap. 10, "Sectioning in Romance Language Classes at the University of Illinois," pp. 365–432. In *Studies in Modern Language Teaching.* By E. W. Bagster-Collins and Others. New York: Macmillan Co., 1930. Pp. xxxi, 491. *

CUMULATIVE NAME INDEX
Hammond, H. P.: 3   Russell, H. J.: *rev, 3:212*
Miller, L. W.: 2   Stoddard, G. D.: 1, 3
Rice, G. A.: 4   Tharp, J. B.: 5

[314]

MLA Cooperative Foreign Language Proficiency Tests: Spanish. Spanish majors and advanced students in college; 1960–68; formerly called *MLA Foreign Language Proficiency Tests for Teachers and Advanced Students: Spanish;* 7 tests in 3 booklets; 1966 test identical with tests copyrighted 1961 except for format and directions; Modern Language Association of America and Educational Testing Service; Cooperative Tests and Services. *

a) BOOK 1: READING, LISTENING COMPREHENSION, SPEAKING.

b) BOOK 2: WRITING.

c) BOOK 3: APPLIED LINGUISTICS, CIVILIZATION AND CULTURE, PROFESSIONAL PREPARATION.

For additional information and a review by Glen W. Probst, see 7:321 (6 references); for a review by Walter V. Kaulfers, see 6:427 (3 references).

REFERENCES THROUGH 1971
1–3. See 6:427.
4–9. See 7:321.
10. VILLARREAL, JOSE A. *The MLA-Cooperative Foreign Language Proficiency Test as an Evaluating Instrument of the Competency of Prospective Student Teachers of Spanish, French, and German.* Master's thesis, University of Texas (Austin, Tex.), 1970.

CUMULATIVE NAME INDEX
Carroll, J. B.: 6   Perkins, J. A.: 9
Churchill, F. J.: 4   Probst, G. W.: *rev, 7:321*
Ciruti, J. E.: 5   Ruisanchez-Lopez, L.: 5
Dizney, H. F.: 7   Sheppard, D. C.: 5
Griffin, D.: 5   Spencer, R. E.: 4
Gromen, L.: 7   Starr, W. H.: 1–3
Kaulfers, W. V.: *rev, 6:427* Tollinger, S.: 5
Ladu, T. T.: 5   Villarreal, J. A.: 10
McKinney, J. C.: 5   Wallmark, M.: 4, 8
Meade, R. G.: 5   Wilkins, G. W.: 5
Paquette, F. A.: 4–5, 8

[315]

MLA-Cooperative Foreign Language Tests: Spanish. 1–2 years high school or 2 semesters college, 3–4 years high school or 4 semesters college; 1963–65; 4 tests in a single booklet: listening, speaking, reading, writing; writing test available as separate; prepared in cooperation with the Modern Language Association of America; Cooperative Tests and Services. *

For additional information and a review by Robert Lado, see 7:322 (2 references). For an excerpted review by John L. D. Clark of the series, see 7:254.

REFERENCES THROUGH 1971
1–2. See 7:322.

CUMULATIVE NAME INDEX
Aleamoni, L. M.: 2   Paquette, F. A.: 1
Churchill, F. J.: 1   Spencer, R. E.: 1–2
Clark, J. L. D.: *exc, 7:254* Wallmark, M.: 1
Lado, R.: *rev, 7:322*

[316]

National Spanish Examination. 1, 2, 3, 4, 5 years junior high school and high school; 1957–73; NSE; new form issued annually for administration in April at local secondary schools or centers established by local chapters of the AATSP; 4 scores: aural, usage, reading comprehension, total; [Test Development Committee, American Association of Teachers of Spanish and Portuguese]; the Association (distributed by local chapter treasurers and the national chairman). *

For additional information and a review by Walter V. Kaulfers of earlier forms, see 7:323 (1 reference); see also 6:428 (8 references).

REFERENCES THROUGH 1971

1–8. See 6:428.
9. See 7:323.

CUMULATIVE NAME INDEX

Boyer, M. V.: 8   Kaulfers, W. V.: *rev*, 7:323
Charly, H. T.: 1, 3–9   Powell, J. D.: 2–4
Hartsook, J. H.: 4–6   Saporta, S.: 1

[317]

*National Teacher Examinations: Spanish. College seniors and teachers; 1970–73; derived from *MLA Foreign Language Proficiency Tests for Teachers and Advanced Students: Spanish;* an inactive form (1967) entitled *Teacher Education Examination Program: Spanish* is available to colleges for local administration; the same inactive form entitled *Spanish* is available to school systems for local use as part of the program entitled *School Personnel Research and Evaluation Services;* Educational Testing Service. * For the testing program entry, see 869.

For additional information, see 7:324. For reviews of the testing program, see 7:582 (2 reviews), 6:700 (1 review), 5:538 (3 reviews), and 4:802 (1 review).

[318]

Pimsleur Spanish Proficiency Tests. "First-level, …second-level" courses in grades 7–16; 1967; 4 tests; Paul Pimsleur; Harcourt Brace Jovanovich, Inc. *
a) TEST I, LISTENING COMPREHENSION.
b) TEST 2, SPEAKING PROFICIENCY.
c) TEST 3, READING COMPREHENSION.
d) TEST 4, WRITING PROFICIENCY.

For additional information, a review by Gino Parisi, and an excerpted review by E. E. Bilyeu, see 7:325. For an excerpted review by A. Ralph Hakstian of this and other tests (French, German) in the series, see 7:257.

[319]

Second Year Spanish Test. High school and college; 1953–68; revision of *Kansas Second Year Spanish Test;* Oscar F. Hernández and Minnie M. Miller; Bureau of Educational Measurements. *

For additional information, see 7:326.

[320]

Spanish I and II: Achievement Examinations for Secondary Schools. 1–2 years high school; 1951–55;

Form 4 ('55) is the only form in print; Midwest High School Achievement Examinations and Minnesota High School Achievement Examinations were also used as series titles; Emma Marie Birkmaier and Walter Pederson; Bobbs-Merrill Co., Inc. *

For additional information concerning earlier forms, see 6:429 and 5:292–3.

[321]

*Teacher Education Examination Program: Spanish. College seniors preparing to teach secondary school; 1957–72; reprinting of inactive 1967 form of *National Teacher Examinations: Spanish;* test available to colleges for local administration; Educational Testing Service. * For the testing program entry, see 898.

For additional information concerning an earlier form, see 6:430. For a review of the testing program, see 5:543.

[322]

*The Undergraduate Program Field Tests: Spanish Test. College; 1969–73; formerly called *The Undergraduate Record Examinations: Spanish Test;* test available to colleges for local administration; Educational Testing Service. * For the testing program entry, see 1062.

For additional information concerning an earlier form, see 7:327. For reviews of the testing program, see 7:671 (2 reviews).

[Out of Print Since TIP I]

College Entrance Examination Board Achievement Test: Spanish Listening Comprehension, 6:420
Common Concepts Foreign Language Test: Spanish, 7:317
Cooperative Spanish Test: Elementary and Advanced Forms, 2:1373–4 (4 reviews, 1 reference)
First Year Spanish Test: State High School Tests for Indiana, 4:261
Lundeberg-Tharp Audition Test in Spanish, 3:211 (2 reviews, 1 excerpt)
Silent Reading Test in Spanish, T:704b
Spanish and Latin American Life and Culture, 5:291 (1 review)
Spanish Test (Two-Year Course): Affiliation Testing Program for Catholic Secondary Schools, 6:431 (1 review)
Test of Spanish Vocabulary, T:704a

FOREIGN LANGUAGES — FIRST MMY

REVIEWS BY *Samuel D. Atkins, Nelson Brooks, Walter V. Kaulfers, Norman T. Pratt, Jr., and Curtis C. Vail.*

FRENCH

[984]

American Council on Education French Reading Test. Two semesters or more of college French or its equivalent; c1937; 1 form; 10 to 99 copies, 5¢ per test; 100 or more, 4½¢ per test; 25¢ per specimen set; 50(55) minutes; prepared for the Committee on Modern Languages by F. D. Cheydleur, V. A. C. Henmon, and M. J. Walker; Cooperative Test Service.

Nelson Brooks, Westover School, Middlebury, Connecticut. In evaluating this test, objection must be made to the presence of many questions that are debatable or unfair, to the choice of passages ill suited to minute questioning, to the use of questions that can readily be answered without reference to the text and to the lack of plausibility in a great many of the wrong answers. The test will give no indication of ability to read and think in French, but will undoubtedly prove whether or not a student has an extensive French vocabulary, familiarity with the patterns of French syntax and proficiency in grasping the meaning of a sentence or paragraph.

[985]

Cooperative French Test [Advanced Form]. 4 semesters or more, high school; or 1 year or more, college; c1937; 40- and 90-minute editions; lithotyped; 25¢ per specimen set (Form 1934 or N); 10¢ per sample test (Form 1934 or N); G. Spaulding and P. Vaillant; Cooperative Test Service.
a) FORM 1937. 4 earlier forms; no further forms scheduled; 90(95) minutes; 6¢ per test, 10 to 99 copies.
b) REVISED SERIES, ADVANCED FORM N. A new form is scheduled for publication each May 1; 40(45) minutes; 5¢ per test, 10 to 99 copies; 4½¢ per test, 100 or more; test booklets may be used repeatedly if separate answer sheets are used; 1½¢ per answer sheet, adapted to hand or machine scoring.

Nelson Brooks, Westover School, Middlebury, Connecticut. [*Review of Revised Series, Advanced Form N.*] Three aspects of linguistic training are examined in this test: reading ability, knowledge of isolated words and familiarity with essential points of grammar. Reading is tested by asking the student to indicate which of several words or phrases correctly completes a given sentence in French, and to specify which of several statements in French that concern a given sentence or brief passage is true. The method employed is fundamentally sound, for all the questions can theoretically be answered without reference to English, but many of the passages and the statements based on them are far too childish to appear in a test prepared for advanced high school and college students. In the vocabulary section, the student selects one of five French words which is synonymous with a given French word. The method here is sound also, but is not too successfully worked out, as many of the synonyms are English cognates that can easily be matched by a student knowing no French whatever. The grammar test consists in indicating which of several forms of a word or phrase will render a given sentence grammatically acceptable. In each case, an English translation of the grammar sentence is provided, although the correct answer can often be deduced from the French. This part of the test is the least artificial, for many of the wrong answers are precisely what a student learning grammar is likely to write. Many teachers, however, will question the advisability of presenting students with printed examples of incorrect French.

A test of this sort, in attempting to give a cross-section picture of achievement in language, can at best afford only an oblique and partial view. The student writes nothing in French, but in each question merely indicates by a number which one of five possible answers is correct. As in all such tests, there is a constant likelihood that a student who knows the right answer may put down the wrong number, the test then becoming one of digits and not of French. There is no check on spelling, use of accents or agreements of verb and adjective. Many a student will find himself dealing with problems that are artificial in the extreme, as they are quite foreign to French and are not likely to occur to the student's mind. If it is the intention of such tests to approximate the struggles of the youthful mind to comprehend, and that is the assumption, there must be a fairly high degree of association of some sort between the questions asked and the possible answers—more than is found in many of the answers here suggested. In the restricted field it covers, this test can be relied upon to examine the student in a manner that in itself exemplifies sound methods of linguistic training and to give dependable evidence of the student's acquaintance with certain prime requisites of a knowledge of French. The authors are to be commended for including one or two touches of humor, even though elementary, for, amid the rattle and clatter of such highly mechanized testing apparatus, the effect upon the student of working with material that possesses literary attractiveness or evokes a smile can only be to put him at his ease and enable him to approach more closely his normal stride in the work-a-day world.

[986]

Cooperative French Test [Elementary Form]. 3 semesters or less, high school; or 1 semester, college; c1937; 40- and 90-minute editions; lithotyped; 25¢ per specimen set (Form 1934 or N); 10¢ per sample test (Form 1934 or N); J. Greenberg and G. Spaulding; Cooperative Test Service.
a) JUNIOR FORM 1937. 4 earlier forms; no further forms scheduled; 90(95) minutes; 6¢ per test, 10 to 99 copies; 5½¢ per test, 100 or more.
b) REVISED SERIES, ELEMENTARY FORM N. A new form is scheduled for publication each May 1; 40(45) minutes; 5¢ per test, 10 to 99 copies; 4½¢ per test, 100 or more; test booklets may be used repeatedly if separate answer sheets are used; 1½¢ per answer sheet, adapted to hand or machine scoring.

Walter V. Kaulfers, Stanford University. [*Review of Revised Series, Elementary Form N.*] In Part I—Reading—many of the exercises are so short as to raise the question whether or not they are "reading" exercises in any functional sense at all. Moreover, test items Nos. 1, 3, 4, 7, and 8, of Part I contain cognate resemblances which, acting as specific determiners, may in a few cases invalidate the items as measures of the reading comprehension of individual pupils. Part II is adequate as a vocabulary recognition test in which the English meanings of isolated French words are to be identified. Part III tests a recognition knowledge of grammatical forms. Since proofreading ability of the type measured in this section generally shows little relationship to ability to speak or write a language fluently or correctly in actual life situations, the significance and value of measuring this type of skill is debatable. Nevertheless, of the objective tests in French occupying less than an hour of testing time, this test is probably the best measure of reading ability, vocabulary, and language usage published to date for pupils who begin the study of French below the tenth grade.

[987]

First Year French: State High School Tests for Indiana, 1936–1937 Edition. First, second semesters; p1936–37; 2 levels; a new first-semester form is scheduled for publication each December; a new second-semester form is scheduled for publication each March; mimeographed; 2¢ per test; 15¢ per sample test; 40(45) minutes; H. V. Wann and M. O. Peters; edited by H. H. Remmers; Division of Educational Reference.

[988]

Second Year French: State High School Tests for Indiana, 1936–1937 Edition. First, second semesters; p1936–37; 2 levels; a new first-semester form is scheduled for publication each December; a new second-semester form is scheduled for publication each March; mimeographed; 2¢ per test; 15¢ per sample test; 40(45) minutes; H. V. Wann and M. O. Peters; edited by H. H. Remmers; Division of Educational Reference.

GERMAN

[999]

American Council on Education German Reading Test. Two semesters or more of college German or its equivalent; c1937; 1 form; 10 to 99 copies, 5¢ per test; 100 or more, 4½¢ per test; 25¢ per specimen set; 50(55) minutes; prepared for the Committee on Modern Languages by E. P. Appelt and V. A. C. Henmon; Cooperative Test Service.

Curtis C. D. Vail, University of Buffalo. This test was originally prepared and administered to a wide high school and college population in 1936. The above form contains exactly the same materials as the experimental edition, except that wholesale revisions were necessary in the order of the German key words in Part I, and one change proved advisable in the order of the reading selections in Part II. Also two minutes additional time have been allotted the student on Part II, making the total for both parts 50 minutes. The validity of this examination for measuring solely a reading knowledge of German seems high; the correlation between results obtained from it and from school grades is fairly high (.54 to

.77), since many other outcomes are reflected in the school grades.

No Scaled Scores are available for this examination, but the results are given as to distribution, percentile ranks, and median scores for the various high school and college levels. For the first year of college the median score for Part I, which contains 100 multiple-choice vocabulary entries, is 32; for Part II, which contains ten German passages (which seem too difficult to allow much grading in this respect) on which a total of 50 German questions are to be answered in English, it is 10.4. These scores appear to be very reliable, and show a good increment between year levels. The raw scores, however, are obtained merely by totaling the number of correct answers—no correction is made for guessing, which seems unfortunate.

Part II is undoubtedly much easier to construct than other types of comprehension tests, and it is hard to say how much has been lost in the way of objectivity. The present writer can recall no instance where a free response on the part of the students has called for a decision on his part while grading this test.

The answer given on the scoring sheet to Part II, 4d, is incorrect; Gesellen is singular, not plural, in the reading passage.

[1000]

Cooperative German Test [Advanced Form].
4 semesters or more, high school; or 1 year or more, college; c1937; 40- and 90-minute editions; lithotyped; 25¢ per specimen set (Form 1934 or N); 10¢ per sample test (Form 1934 or N); M. Van D. Hespelt, E. H. Hespelt, and G. Spaulding; Cooperative Test Service.
a) FORM 1937. 4 earlier forms; no further forms scheduled; 90(95) minutes; 6¢ per test, 10 to 99 copies; 5½¢ per test, 100 or more.
b) REVISED SERIES, ADVANCED FORM N. A new form is scheduled for publication each May 1; 40(45) minutes; 5¢ per test, 10 to 99 copies; 4½¢ per test, 100 or more; test booklets may be used repeatedly if separate answer sheets are used; 1½¢ per answer sheet, adapted to hand or machine scoring.

Curtis C. D. Vail, University of Buffalo. [Review of Revised Series, Advanced Form N.] [For a more general discussion, see review No. 1001 by the same reviewer.] Despite the fact that we have called the designations of these tests as "elementary" and "advanced" rather arbitrary, it is immediately evident that the present test is far more difficult than the *Elementary Form N.* Part I consists of 45 multiple-choice comprehension items (reading); Part II of 40 multiple-choice questions on

vocabulary; and Part III of 40 multiple-choice completions on functional grammar for which, in each instance, the proper English equivalent is given. The raw score for each of these sections is arrived at by subtracting ¼ the wrong answers from the number of correct choices. Quite in contrast to the *Elementary Form,* the 50-point on the Scaled Scores shows that the average student of two years training is able to obtain a raw score of only 11 out of the 45 items in Part I, 14 of the 40 items in Part II, and 9–10 of the 40 items in Part III. For the entire examination, therefore, the average student answers correctly not significantly more than 27.6% of all the entries. This is ample evidence that this test is geared well above the level of the *Elementary Form.* The accuracy of the various portions of the test is indicated by the fact that at no level of the Scaled Scores does the standard error of measurement exceed ±4. Thus, although this test contains only 125 items to be answered in 40 minutes, it must be accorded a high measure of reliability and should prove almost as satisfactory as the longer 90-minute form. It should prove to be a valuable measuring instrument for diagnosis, prognosis, and placement at levels well above two years of high school, or one year of college German.

Part II is much more far-reaching in its implications than other existing types of vocabulary tests, since the solution of the German key word does not result from the selection of an English equivalent, but of a corresponding German synonym, e.g., *Empfang: Stab, Empfehlung, Reise, Aufnahme, Name.* Although we cannot deny that such a type of test is very hard to construct, it does seem that too many of the items are either far too easy or far too difficult. However, the Cooperative Test Service has performed here a valuable piece of pioneering which should be further developed.

The misprint of *lebte* as *nebte* in Part III, item No. 31, is hard to forgive; we expect such examinations to be immaculate in this respect.

[1001]

Cooperative German Test: Revised Series, Elementary Form N. 1–6 semesters: grades 6–9; c1937; a shorter edition of the *Cooperative German Test: Junior Form* series last issued in 1935; a new form is scheduled for publication each May 1; 40(45) minutes; lithotyped; 5¢ per test, 10 to 99 copies; 4½¢ per test, 100 or more; 25¢ per specimen set (Form N); 10¢ per sample test (Form N); test booklets may be used repeatedly if separate answer sheets are used;

American Council on Education German Reading Test

1½¢ per answer sheet, adapted to hand or machine scoring; E. Popper, A. Miller, and L. M. Will; Cooperative Test Service.

Curtis C. D. Vail, University of Buffalo. The above is one of the German tests issued by the Cooperative Test Service of the American Council on Education, which are the result of the cooperative efforts of subject matter specialists and experts in test construction. These tests have, in their experimental stages, been tried out on large populations and only those items have been retained in the final forms which have given definite assurance of yielding valid and reliable indications of the achievements of students.

One outstanding feature of these tests is that they exist in five 90-minute and two 40-minute forms, all of which yield comparable scores. This makes it possible to test each student with one form at the end of each semester German is studied, and thus to secure information on the growth both of classes as wholes and of pupils as individuals. Among the latter, of course, great individual differences are being found and these growth indices form a source that may be studied in connection with other data available on these students. Such an equivalent is again made possible, even for the layman, by a table which makes the conversion of raw scores into Scaled Scores a quite simple matter. The 50-point on all these Scaled Scores is intended to represent the score which would be made by the average unselected pupil who had received typical instruction and training at the two-year level. Since results for individual sections as well as for the whole examination are expressed in these same Scaled Score units, it is possible to detect areas of special strength and weaknesses for individual students. Although these Scaled Scores patently incorporate the concept of the norm in each score, the Cooperative Test Service further provides differentiated norms as to grade and subject status in varying types of institutions. Perhaps the outstanding feature of these is their constant revision—in the present instance the data have been revised to September, 1937.

The validity of the 90-minute forms of these tests is quite high since the time is ample to allow a careful sampling of the really important elements. This form, moreover, possesses an unusually high coefficient of reliability

($r = .979$). Many institutions, however, for reasons of cost and convenience will naturally prefer to use the shorter, 40-minute forms, such as the above, but it must be remembered that these of necessity do not rate as highly in validity and reliability as the longer forms. On the other hand they do represent much more accurate measures than the ratio of 40 to 90 minutes would suggest. In the present instance the standard error of measurement around the 50-point in the part scores is ± 4 (0.4σ).

Although these German tests are differentiated as "elementary" and "advanced" forms, these are rather arbitrary terms which mark the dividing line between the first to third, and the fourth to eighth semesters of high school German. They are thus all of a fairly elementary level though, as will be observed, the elementary form is geared quite low, and the advanced form quite high, and norms are thus available for four years of college instruction.

Such tests may, however, succeed very adequately in measuring what they are designed to measure and still fail to take into any account such outcomes of a study of German as the following: ability to pronounce the language understandably; to translate it into intelligible English; to write or speak it with some degree of freedom; and to comprehend it orally. Objective testing programs have so far been unable to provide adequate measuring devices for these skills. Although this leaves a definite gap in our knowledge of the modern foreign language student's progress, it is probably not without benefit in that it focuses attention above all on what should be the immediate objective of all foreign language teaching, i.e., the ability to read the language.

One feature of the Cooperative Test Service tests should not be overlooked. All forms of the Revised Series tests are set up in such a way that they can be scored either by hand, or by the use of the new electric scoring machine which scores tests more inexpensively, more accurately, and much more rapidly than can be done by the usual hand methods.

Elementary Form N consists of: Part I, 40 multiple-choice completions for comprehension (reading); Part II, 50 multiple-choice items on vocabulary; and, Part III, 35 multiple-choice completions on functional grammar (*Sprachgefühl?*) The 50-point on the Scaled Scores, referred to above, corresponds to raw scores of 30, 25, 21–22 in the three parts respectively. Since these raw scores are obtained by "right minus ¼-wrong," it is apparent that the average student with two years of training is able to answer correctly well over sixty per cent of the items. The student with two semesters falls somewhat below this, and the cluster of average scores at this level is practically identical with the cluster for sixth-semester students on the advanced form. Even so, the number of items the student is able to answer on the elementary form at the end of the second year suggests that it is approaching an altitude at which its usefulness is becoming limited.

The use of *ss* for ß on these tests can only result in confusion for many students, and should not be condoned.

LATIN

[1063]

Cicero Test. High school and college; p1937; 1 form; 60¢ per 25 tests, postpaid; 10¢ per specimen set; 40(45) minutes; M. A. Seller and H. E. Schrammel; Bureau of Educational Measurements.

[1064]

Cooperative Latin Test [Advanced Form]. 2 years or more, grades 9–14; c1937; 40- and 90-minute editions; lithotyped; 25¢ per specimen set (Form 1934 or N); 10¢ per sample test (Form 1934 or N); J. C. Kirtland, R. B. McJimsey, and B. M. Allen; Cooperative Test Service.
a) FORM 1937. 4 earlier forms; no further forms scheduled; 90(95) minutes; 6¢ per test, 10 to 99 copies; 5½¢ per test, 100 or more.
b) REVISED SERIES, ADVANCED FORM N. A new form is scheduled for publication each May 1; 40(45) minutes; 5¢ per test, 10 to 99 copies; 4½¢ per test, 100 or more; test booklets may be used repeatedly if separate answer sheets are used; 1½¢ per answer sheet, adapted to hand or machine scoring.

Norman T. Pratt, Jr., Princeton University. [*Review of Revised Series, Advanced Form N.*] This forty-minute "objective" test is designed for students with at least two years of Latin as an aid in "problems of placement, sectioning, and certification."

Part I (fifteen minutes) consists of three passages at the Caesar, Cicero, and Vergil levels respectively; each passage is followed by ten sentences in English of which the student is to indicate those which do and those which do not "agree with something that is said or implied in the paragraph under which they appear." Here only in the whole examination does Latin of any adequate quality and

quantity appear, and the time allotted thereto is distinctly insufficient both in proportion to the test as a whole and in respect to the amount and difficulty of the material contained in this part. It is not expected, of course, that the examinee will answer all the questions within the time limit, and the relative number of correct answers constitutes a valuable criterion for measuring individual differences in rapidity of "comprehension." Of greater importance, however, is the testing of accuracy, which can be properly done only when sufficient time is allowed. It may be suggested that the valuable device of "comprehension" should be used in combination with translation, which is the only completely adequate means now known for testing the accuracy with which a student understands a particular passage.

The two remaining parts may be discussed together: Part II (ten minutes) contains sixty Latin words, each followed by five English words of which the student selects the one "which most nearly corresponds in meaning to the Latin word"; in Part III (fifteen minutes), for each of fifty English sentences an incomplete Latin version is given, to be completed by the selection of one of the five Latin words or phrases listed. The fundamental objection to both is the same: well over half of the whole examination is devoted to the testing of vocabulary and syntax, divorced from continuous context, as self-sufficient ends; this directly violates the praiseworthy avowed purpose of the Cooperative Tests to emphasize the use of information, not mere information itself.

In general, it is very desirable to attain objectivity in testing and to ensure uniform and intelligent use of test results, but it is advisable not to standardize any one type of examination until our knowledge concerning the complex problems involved in test designing is more complete. At least for the present, the newer methods should be used in conjunction with the best traditional techniques, such as translation and composition. A really serious effort should be made to secure accuracy in the formulation and correction of the unduly-maligned essay question which tests the use and organization of information as no other device yet known can do. Above all, in the designing of tests objectivity of correction must never take precedence over testing value.

Finally, certain deficiencies perhaps inevitably inhere in the purely objective Latin test. It allows no place for either translation or composition, perhaps the most searching tests of the student's linguistic understanding and grasp of Latin. Most important of all, the student cannot be asked directly to draw his own inferences or to express his own thoughts concerning the more intangible but more valuable matters of historical and literary import which constitute the core of all good Latin teaching and for which provision must be made in any adequate test. In a word, the objective examination, at least in its present form, is ill-adapted to a field of study of which the essential nature and value are not scientific but human.

[1065]

Cooperative Latin Test [Elementary Form]. 1-6 semesters, grades 6-9; c1937; 40- and 90-minute editions; lithotyped; 25¢ per specimen set (Form 1934 or N); 10¢ per sample test (Form 1934 or N); W. L. Carr and G. R. Humphries; Cooperative Test Service.
a) JUNIOR FORM 1937. 4 earlier forms; no further forms scheduled; 90(95) minutes; 6¢ per test, 10 to 99 copies; 5½¢ per test, 100 or more.
b) REVISED SERIES, ELEMENTARY FORM N. A new form is scheduled for publication each May 1; 40(45) minutes; 5¢ per test, 10 to 99 copies; 4½¢ per test, 100 or more; test booklets may be used repeatedly if separate answer sheets are used; 1½¢ per answer sheet, adapted to hand or machine scoring.

S. D. Atkins, Princeton University. [*Review of Revised Series, Elementary Form N.*] Part I (15 minutes) contains three reading passages together with appended true-false statements. Its apparent aim is to test the student's progressive development of ability to read and comprehend Latin as Latin. Such an attempt is commendable; in this test, however, it succeeds only to the extent that it examines the student's power to read Latin which has been composed by an American in the twentieth century and which derives its dubious inspiration from word-lists. Furthermore, the banality of the first and last of these passages is appalling. Even an examination-passage of "easy" Latin ought to make some sense. A few years ago the recommendation was made that "easy" Latin "should conform to the genius of the Latin language, . . . should from the first deal mainly with themes readily adaptable to the attainment of the historical-cultural objectives."[1] These requirements are poorly satisfied by the Latin passages under discussion.

[1] *The Classical Investigation: Part 1, General Report.* Princeton, N.J.: Princeton University Press, 1924, pp. 127-8.

The true-false statement might prove more effective if supplemented by the question-sentence which demands specific information. Of course the question-sentence permits a certain variety in answer which makes correction by machine impossible. But then a good examination concerns itself with a thorough evaluation of the student's ability and a stimulation of his intellect, not with the ease and comfort of the examiner.

Part II (10 minutes) is a vocabulary test of the multiple-choice type which ignores altogether the emphasis that in recent years has been given to the functional approach. It puts a premium upon the senseless equating of one English word with one Latin word, whereas it is obvious that no one English word always covers the same ground as any one Latin word, whereas, too, it is a linguistic truism that, as the speaker and the speaker's situation changes, the semantic value of a word changes and so the word employed to translate it usually changes. The sort of listing that we have in this test encourages the impoverishment of the student's Latin and English vocabularies alike. Furthermore, though it may not be too important, it is interesting to see that in this particular examination a clever student could limit possibilities by disregarding all English words that have the same initial letter as the Latin word under which they are listed. For example: "*angustus* (1) angry (2) august (3) questionable (4) narrow (5) angelic." Here 1, 2, and 5 could be struck out immediately. This holds for forty-two out of the fifty items in this section. This type of test should be abandoned. The continuous narrative in which underlined words are given for translation would be a good substitute.

Part III (15 minutes) examines a knowledge of the principles of syntax by means of a modified matching type, employing detached sentences. Again it is my opinion that the continuous narrative is the better medium. Grammatical principles are only a means to an end, the reading of Latin, and the emphasis should be upon their utility for the attainment of that end.

In conclusion the question should be raised as to whether this kind of test emphasizes enough the comprehension of Latin. It might be advisable to reduce Parts II and III and to enlarge Part I by adding passages of "adapted"

Cooperative Latin Test

Latin that would cover more adequately some of the many cultural and historical aims considered valid for the elementary course. Such an examination, let us hope, would establish a trend away from the rigidity and narrowness so characteristic of the usual objective test. We are approaching that point where facility of computation conditions the content of the examination and thus becomes the all-important determinant of subject-matter.

[1066]

First and Second Year Latin: Every Pupil Test, December 1937 and April 1938. High school; p1937–38; a new form is scheduled for publication each December and April; 2¢ per test; 1¢ per key; specimen set free; 40(45) minutes; E. S. Buck and M. Hahn; Ohio Scholarship Tests.

[1067]

First Year Latin Test: State High School Tests for Indiana, 1936–1937 Edition. First, second semesters; p1936–37; 2 levels; a new first-semester form is scheduled for publication each December; a new second-semester form is scheduled for publication each March; mimeographed; 2¢ per test; 15¢ per sample test; 40(45) minutes; R. L. Alexander; edited by H. H. Remmers; Division of Educational Reference.

[1068]

Holtz Vergil Test. High school and college; p1937; 1 form; 60¢ per 25 tests, postpaid; 10¢ per specimen set; 40(45) minutes; W. L. Holtz and H. E. Schrammel; Bureau of Educational Measurements.

[1069]

Iowa Every-Pupil Test in Latin Reading Comprehension: Ninth Annual Iowa Every-Pupil High School Testing Program. p1937; a new form is scheduled for publication each May; 4¢ per test; 5¢ per key; 10¢ per summary report of norms; 60(65) minutes; F. H. Potter and H. M. Eddy; edited by [E. F. Lindquist]; distributed by the Bureau of Educational Research and Service.

[1070]

Second Year Latin Test: State High School Tests for Indiana, 1936–1937 Edition. First, second semesters; p1936–37; 2 levels; a new first-semester form is scheduled for publication each December; a new second-semester form is scheduled for publication each March; mimeographed; 2¢ per test; 15¢ per sample test; 40(45) minutes; J. L. Lee; edited by H. H. Remmers; Division of Educational Reference.

SPANISH

[1155]

Cooperative Spanish Test [Advanced Form]. 4 semesters or more, high school; or 1 year or more, college; c1937; 40- and 90-minute editions; lithotyped; 25¢ per specimen set (Form 1934 or N); 10¢ per sample test (Form 1934 or N); E. H. Hespelt, R. H. Williams, and G. Spaulding; Cooperative Test Service.

a) FORM 1937. 4 earlier forms; no further forms scheduled; 90(95) minutes; 6¢ per test, 10 to 99 copies; 5½¢ per test, 100 or more.
b) REVISED SERIES, ADVANCED FORM N. A new form is scheduled for publication each May 1; 40(45) minutes; 5¢ per test, 10 to 99 copies; 4½¢ per test, 100 or more; test booklets may be used repeatedly if separate answer sheets are used; 1½¢ per answer sheet, adapted to hand or machine scoring.

[1156]

Cooperative Spanish Test: Revised Series, Elementary Form N. 1–6 semesters, grades 6–9; c1937; a shorter edition of the *Cooperative Spanish Test, Junior Form* series last issued in 1935; a new form is scheduled for publication each May 1; 40(45) minutes; lithotyped; 5¢ per test, 10 to 99 copies; 4½¢ per test, 100 or more; 25¢ per specimen set (Form N); 10¢ per sample test (Form N); test booklets may be used repeatedly if separate answer sheets are used; 1½¢ per answer sheet, adapted to hand or machine scoring; J. Greenberg, R. H. Williams, and G. Spaulding; Cooperative Test Service.

Walter V. Kaulfers, Stanford University. [*Review of Revised Series, Elementary Form N.*] Although the assurance is strong that the test is both a valid and reliable measuring instrument, the actual evidence on statistical reliability, etc., is seemingly confined to the standard errors of measurement and standard deviations of norms, and to such statements in the *Handbook,* as "all test material was given to large numbers of students in order to obtain data from which indices of difficulty and validity could be secured. All items which did not prove to be valid were discarded."

From the viewpoint of content, the test may be regarded as ranking high. The three parts of the test show due regard for frequency counts with respect to vocabulary and idioms. Keniston's *Spanish Syntax List* would have been a better guide in the selection of items for the section on Spanish usage (grammar) than the approach used by the authors, but the syntax study was obviously unavailable at the time of the construction of the test.

The norms for each part are adequate both from the standpoint of range and number of cases, and geographical distribution. The segregation of norms by geographical areas, and for public and private secondary schools, possesses some advantages, though the trend in education is obviously away from emphasis on normative comparisons.

As a measure of ability to get meaning from short elementary sentences (five to thirty words long), to recognize the English meanings of isolated Spanish words, and to proofread sentences for grammatical correctness, the test is seemingly adequate. The organization of the test, the directions for administration, and the keys for scoring leave little to be desired. Since the pupils' responses are entirely in terms of numbers, no knowledge of Spanish whatever is required on the part of the scorer.

With respect to format there is some question as to whether the constant repetition of the number of the test item along with each of the five alternative choices—for example: 30(1)—may not be confusing at the start to pupils unfamiliar with this technique, particularly since no fore-exercises are provided by way of example in Parts I or II.

Of the objective tests in Spanish occupying less than an hour of testing time, *Elementary Form N* is probably the best measure of reading ability, vocabulary, and language usage published to date for pupils who begin the study of Spanish below the tenth grade. Of the 125 items comprising the test only two (exercises 6 and 8 in Part I) permit of justifiable answers different from those contained in the key.

Since grammar exercises of the proofreading type show little relationship to ability to use a language fluently or correctly in actual speech, it is doubtful whether Part III is worth administering in first or second year high school classes. By omitting Part III the examiner can reduce the length of the test to 25 minutes.

[1157]

Spanish Life and Culture. 2 years: high school; or 1 year: college; p1937; 1 form; 60¢ per 25 tests, postpaid; 15¢ per specimen set; 40(45) minutes; M. M. Miller, Bureau of Educational Measurements.

Walter V. Kaulfers, Stanford University. The reliability of .73 of this test could undoubtedly be raised by using a more objective type of response item in Part I, and by arranging all test items in order of difficulty throughout. At present, two of the simplest items (for example, 99 and 100) occur at the very end of the test, and can probably be guessed correctly by most pupils. With respect to validity there is room for doubt concerning the significance of some of the items of information tested. The river on which Madrid is located, for example, is of no particular consequence beyond the fact that the Manzanares has been made the subject of ridicule for being "navigable either in a coach or on horseback." The table of percentile norms offered should be used with extreme caution since it is based upon only 343 cases. As one of the pioneers in the field of foreign culture testing, however, the author deserves credit for having made an able beginning.

FOREIGN LANGUAGES — SECOND MMY

Reviews by Lawrence Andrus, Christian O. Arndt, S. D. Atkins, James C. Babcock, Nelson Brooks, W. L. Carr, Paul B. Diederich, Harold B. Dunkel, Bateman Edwards, C. E. Ficken, John Flagg Gummere, C. H. Handschin, Harry Heller, Warren S. Holmes, Charles Holzwarth, Joseph F. Jackson, Laura B. Johnson, Walter V. Kaulfers, Norman T. Pratt, Jr., Harry J. Russell, James B. Tharp, and Clarence E. Turner.

[1340]

Foreign Language Prognosis Test. Grades 8-9; 1930; 2 forms; $7.35 per 100; 25¢ per specimen set; 44(60-65) minutes; Percival M. Symonds; New York: Bureau of Publications, Teachers College, Columbia University.

REFERENCES

1 SYMONDS, PERCIVAL M. Chapter 6, "A Modern Foreign Language Prognosis Test," pp. 91-126. In *Prognosis Tests in the Modern Foreign Languages*: Reports Prepared for the Modern Foreign Language Study and the Canadian Committee on Modern Languages. By V. A. C. Henmon and others. Publications of the American and Canadian Committees on Modern Languages, Vol. 14. New York: Macmillan Co., 1929. Pp. xviii, 182. Paper. Out of print.

2 SYMONDS, PERCIVAL M. "A Foreign Language Prognosis Test." *Teach Col Rec* 31:540-56 Mr '30.

3 LAU, LOUISE MARGARET. *The Use of the Symond's Foreign Language Tests in Beginning French.* Unpublished master's thesis, University of Chicago, 1933. Pp. 41.

4 RICHARDSON, H. D. "Discovering Aptitude for the Modern Languages." *Mod Lang J* 18:160-70 D '33.

5 VIRGIL, SISTER. "Prognosis in German." *Mod Lang J* 20:275-87 F '36.

6 MARONPOT, RAYMOND P. "Discovering and Salvaging Modern Language Risks." *Mod Lang J* 23:595-8 My '39.

Walter V. Kaulfers, Associate Professor of Education in Foreign Language, Stanford University. Prepared some ten years ago, this test is apparently designed to forecast achievement in foreign language classes taught by the formal grammar-translation method. An eighth or ninth grader who can pass this examination should be able to qualify in almost any subject, for the test is hardly more than a linguistically weighted intelligence test. At that, its correlation with foreign language achievement (when both forms are combined into one test) averages only .71. Since no probable errors are given, nor statements made concerning

the number of cases upon which the coefficient is based, it is difficult to judge the true significance of this measure. It is certain, however, that the correlations of .60 and .61 between prognosis test scores and achievement test scores when only one form of the test is used, are not sufficiently high to warrant the rejection of any particular student on the basis of his test score alone. For purposes of homogeneous grouping, in the relatively few schools having large enough enrollments in any one language to make such grouping possible, the IQ alone would be just about as satisfactory.

From the standpoint of testing time (44 minutes per form) and ease of administration and scoring, the test ranks high among such foreign language prognosis tests as are available to date.

The validity of almost any prognosis test in foreign languages, however, varies with the type of course offered. Almost every foreign language prognosis test published to date has for certain groups yielded correlations as high as the test under discussion. The correlation is often high when the types of abilities involved (grammar-translation, in this case) are identical in the test and course work. The correlation tends to be low when different abilities are utilized in the course from those measured in the test. The user of this test should, therefore, make certain that the course in which the success of any student is to be predicted follows more or less closely the traditional grammar-translation method. Otherwise, the test is not likely to be any more valid in predicting ability to learn a foreign language than an ordinary intelligence test. This fact is emphasized because most schools are now breaking away from the traditional approach to foreign languages.

Moreover, the relative difficulty of many of the items makes the use of the test below the eighth grade undesirable. Whether or not the test predicts achievements equally well in German, French, Spanish, or Latin, as claimed, is debatable in view of the absence of separate data for the several languages. Since no norms are available, the interpretation of pupils' scores is still to some extent a matter of personal discretion. On the basis of a tryout of the test with prospective pupils of Spanish, the author advises that "pupils scoring under 50 on Form B and under 25 on Form A should have considerable difficulty in learning a foreign language."

Foreign language prognosis tests of the Symonds and Luria-Orleans type are usually excellent means for reducing foreign language enrollments in nonfunctional courses taught by teachers incapable of adjusting either method or content to the needs, interests, and abilities of children.

[1341]

Luria-Orleans Modern Language Prognosis Test. Grades 7-13; 1928-30; 1 form; $1.30 per 25; 15¢ per specimen set; 76(85) minutes; Max A. Luria and Jacob S. Orleans; Yonkers, N. Y.: World Book Co.

REFERENCES

1 KAULFERS, WALTER VINCENT. *The Forecasting Efficiency of Current Bases for Prognosis in Junior High School Beginning Spanish.* Unpublished doctor's thesis, Stanford University, 1933. Pp. 381.
2 YOUNG, JOSEPHINE A. *Derived Practical Instruments for Predicting Success in High School French.* Unpublished master's thesis, University of Pittsburgh, 1933. Pp. 46.
3 SEAGOE, MAY V. "Prediction of Achievement in Foreign Languages." *J Appl Psychol* 22:632-40 D '38.

Walter V. Kaulfers, Associate Professor of Education in Foreign Languages, Stanford University. The theory underlying the construction and organization of this test is that "to determine how well one can do a job, it is best to let him try it." Consequently, the examination consists of vocabulary exercises (recognition of cognates, memorization, etc.) and some eight grammar-translation lessons in Spanish and French. The test, therefore, is seemingly designed to predict achievement in the traditional grammar-translation type of course of a

decade or more ago. The correlation between the prognosis test scores and achievement test scores was .68 before the test was revised. In its present form the validity is estimated at .75.

Since this type of test cannot be standardized, no norms or standards are available. This makes the interpretation of scores rather difficult. According to the authors, "the usual per cent failing in the school should be the main basis of determining how many and which pupils should be eliminated."

Although fairly easy to score, the test is by virtue of its length and numerous subtests, by no means economical in administration or scoring.

In 1930 the reviewer administered the prognosis test to 461 pupils beginning Spanish in the eighth grade, and to 209 pupils beginning Spanish in the ninth grade. The correlation between prognosis test scores and achievement test scores at the end of the first semester was .35 for the eighth grade group, and .51 for the ninth grade group. For teachers' marks in Spanish, the correlations with prognosis test scores were .43 and .52 respectively. In this study the test did not prove itself sufficiently superior to ordinary intelligence tests to warrant use. In general, the test seems to be too difficult to provide a fair measure of pupil ability below the ninth grade. Above the eighth grade, the test may have some validity for predicting achievement in traditional grammar-translation types of work—at least for purposes of homogeneous grouping, but for this purpose it has not demonstrated itself sufficiently superior to IQ's, English test scores, or even to a simple twelve-minute test of English vocabulary, to claim any significant practical advantage.

Reliability is difficult to compute for a test of this type. It can be assumed, however, to be at least as high as the validity coefficient for the test.

FRENCH

[1342]

American Council Alpha French Test. Grades 9-16; 1926-27; 2 parts, 2 forms; 35¢ per specimen set; 40(50) minutes per part; V. A. C. Henmon, Algernon Coleman, and Marion R. Trabue; Yonkers, N. Y.: World Book Co.
a) PART I, [VOCABULARY AND GRAMMAR]. $1.25 per 25.
b) PART II, [SILENT READING AND COMPOSITION]. $1.25 per 25.

REFERENCES

1 HENMON, V. A. C. *French Word Book: Based on a Count of 400,000 Running Words.* University of Wisconsin,

Bureau of Educational Research, Bulletin No. 3. Madison, Wis.: the University, 1924. Pp. 84. Paper. Out of print.

2 SYMONDS, PERCIVAL M. *Ability Standards for Standardized Achievement Tests in the High School.* New York: Bureau of Publications, Teachers College, Columbia University, 1927. Pp. x, 91. $1.05.

3 BEATLEY, BANCROFT. Appendix 2, "A Comparative Study of Two Tests of French Vocabulary: The American Council Test and the Twigg French Vocabulary Test," pp. 346-53. In *Achievement Tests in the Modern Foreign Languages:* Prepared for the Modern Foreign Language Study and the Committee on Modern Languages. By V. A. C. Henmon. Publications of the American and Canadian Committees on Modern Languages, Vol. 5. New York: Macmillan Co., 1929. Pp. xxvii, 363. Paper. (London: Macmillan & Co., Ltd. 4s. 6d.)

4 HENMON, V. A. C. *Achievement Tests in Modern Foreign Languages:* Prepared for the Modern Language Study and the Canadian Committee on Modern Languages, pp. 1-266. Publications of the American and Canadian Committees on Modern Languages, Vol. 5. New York: Macmillan Co., 1929. Pp. xxvii, 363. $1.00. Paper. (London: Macmillan & Co., Ltd. 4s. 6d.)

5 VANDER BEKE, GEORGE E. *French Word Book.* Publications of the American and Canadian Committees on Modern Languages, Vol. 15. New York: Macmillan Co., 1929. Pp. xiii, 188. $1.10. Paper. (London: Macmillan & Co., Ltd. 5s. 6d.)

6 BREED, FREDERICK S. Chapter 4, "The Reliability of the Trabue French Composition Scale," pp. 187-98. In *Studies in Modern Language Teaching:* Reports Prepared for the Modern Foreign Language Study and the Canadian Committee on Modern Languages. By E. W. Bagster-Collins and others. Publications of the American and Canadian Committees on Modern Languages, Vol. 17. New York: Macmillan Co., 1930. Pp. xxxi, 491. $1.75. Paper. (London: Macmillan & Co., Ltd. 9s.)

7 FORD, H. E. Chapter 5, "The Reliability of the Trabue French Composition Scale for Scoring Ten-Minute Compositions," pp. 201-10. In *Studies in Modern Language Teaching:* Reports Prepared for the Modern Foreign Language Study and the Canadian Committee on Modern Languages. By E. W. Bagster-Collins and others. Publications of the American and Canadian Committees on Modern Languages, Vol. 17. New York: Macmillan Co., 1930. Pp. xxxi, 491. $1.75. Paper. (London: Macmillan & Co., Ltd. 9s.)

8 SEIBERT, LOUISE C., AND GODDARD, EUNICE R. "The Use of Achievement Tests in Sectioning Students." *Mod Lang J* 18: 289-98 F '34.

9 STEVENSON, MARY LOU. "The Use of Modern Language Placement Tests at the University of Pittsburgh." *Mod Lang J* 18:433-50 Ap '34.

C. E. Ficken, Dean of the College and Professor of French, Macalester College. This test, first copyrighted in 1926, has the distinction of having pioneered in its field and yet remains one of the best tests on the market for the objective measurement of silent reading, recognition vocabulary, and English-French grammar. The publishers are to be commended for reporting that "reliability for different parts for single years is from .84 to .95," while "probable error of a score is about two points." Validity coefficients are not given but have undoubtedly become available since the first printing and should therefore be added.

Part I, i.e., booklet one, contains a fifteen minute vocabulary test of seventy-five words and a twenty-five minute English-French grammar test of fifty items. Part II devotes thirty-two minutes to a silent reading test of twenty-eight responses, and eight minutes to a free composition based upon a picture to be scored on the basis of a composition scale.

Words for the vocabulary test were "chosen at regular intervals from each successive fifty words in a word count of 400,000 running words" and therefore measure in accurate

American Council Alpha French Test

progression of difficulty the recognition power of students into fairly advanced levels. The five-responses answer-words are in English, thereby avoiding the ambiguities which the French synonym technique involves for the English speaking student.

The grammar test likewise contains items chosen according to frequency in textbooks and presented in the order of progressive decrease in difficulty from semester to semester. "The testing technique varies throughout the test in accordance with what seems best for each grammatical point," being of the recall type in twenty-seven cases. Sixteen items require mutation of forms and hence involve the disturbing factor of nomenclature. Only the remaining seven items use the now prevalent multiple-choice technique.

The silent reading test "consists of seven paragraphs of increasing difficulty, with questions on the text in French, the answers to be given in English." Again the gradation is admirable to test the power of the advanced student as well as the student of limited training.

To the authors and publishers this reviewer urges revised editions and ventures several suggestions. For convenience of scoring, the answer-words of the vocabulary test should be numbered for response in blanks on the margin. The grammar test as well as the reading test should use the multiple-choice technique throughout. This would not only facilitate scoring but permit either economizing of time or the lengthening of the content with a consequent improvement of reliability. Furthermore, the procrustean pairing of subtests into two booklets, each to fit a forty-minute period is too arbitrary. If, as seems probable, the composition part is rarely used anyway, a single booklet built on lines of maximum efficiency and greatly reduced cost should bring this test back to the wider use which it merits.

Warren S. Holmes, Department of French, The Gunnery School, Washington, Connecticut. Each of the two forty-minute tests consists of two sections: Part I, Vocabulary and Grammar; and Part II, Silent Reading and Written Composition. Together they form a good test, as would be expected from the distinguished names of their authors. However, there are a few points that should be brought out in examining this instrument.

First, it is a comparatively old test (1926). This fact necessarily affects the vocabulary section, as it is based on the Henmon[1] count rather than on the considerably more extensive and scientific work of Vander Beke,[5] which was not to appear until eight years later. Although the statement in the manual dealing with this section is not wholly clear, it would appear that the words were selected from the first 4,000 in the Henmon count. Yet, there are several words that do not appear at all in the Vander Beke list (over 6,000 words), and others that are in very low frequency ranges. Does this react on the value of the test as an implement of measurement? Probably not seriously.

In the grammar section, I do not like the use, in the directions, of such expressions as partitive, possessive adjective, demonstrative pronoun, etc., although in fairness it should be added that illustrations of these somewhat formidable labels make clear what is desired.

My principal objections to Part II are in the matter of time required for scoring. The comprehension section, while raising no great difficulties of scoring, would demand more time on the part of the reader than, for example, multiple-choice items, and the reader would have to be thoroughly familiar with the language. The written composition test offers undeniable problems, both in the amount of material to be read and in the scoring. The difficulty of scoring is somewhat alleviated, but certainly not removed, by the careful scale prepared by M. R. Trabue. As the reader must familiarize himself with seventeen sample compositions in order to use this scale, the question as to whether the result obtained justifies the effort expended arises of itself. My inclination would be to answer in the negative. The Cooperative tests of the American Council on Education, which may be machine-scored throughout, if desired, would surely provide nearly, if not quite, as accurate a measurement, and the time saved in dealing with a large number of papers would be very considerable. And the Cooperative tests, at least the recent ones, require only 40 minutes to administer as against 80 minutes for the test under consideration.

[1343]

American Council Alpha French Test: Aural Comprehension. 1 to 6 semesters, high school; 1933; 2 forms; $4.20 per 100; 25¢ per specimen set; (35)

minutes; Agnes L. Rogers and Frances M. Clarke; prepared for the Committee on Modern Language Teaching under the auspices of the American Council on Education; New York: Bureau of Publications, Teachers College, Columbia University.

REFERENCES

1 HENMON, V. A. C. *Achievement Tests in Modern Foreign Languages*: Prepared for the Modern Language Study and the Canadian Committee on Modern Languages, pp. 311-21. Publications of the American and Canadian Committees on Modern Languages, Vol. 5. New York: Macmillan Co., 1929. Pp. xxvii, 363. $1.00. Paper. (London: Macmillan & Co., Ltd. 4s. 6d.)
2 CLARKE, FRANCES MARGUERITE. "Results of the Bryn Mawr Test in French Administered in New York City High Schools." *B High Points* 13:4-13 F '31.
3 ROGERS, AGNES L., AND CLARKE, FRANCES M. "Report on the Bryn Mawr Test of Ability to Understand Spoken French." *Mod Lang J* 17:241-8 Ja '33.

Nelson Brooks, Instructor in French, Westover School, Middlebury, Connecticut. The authors of this test have made a serious effort to isolate and measure a single ability, the ability to comprehend spoken French. Such information, if it can be obtained, is valuable indeed, and there is much of value in this test. Yet many users will have occasion to question some points of the theory on which it is constructed and certain details of its printed form.

The test is composed of eighty questions in French, each with five possible answers in English. The questions are short and simple and, to quote the authors, of "such a selection of content that the maximum degree of intelligence and of information required is below that possessed by the poorest student to be examined." To test comprehension in a language by giving questions in that language and answers in another raises immediate and serious objection, for there is no assurance that the student does not merely translate a few isolated words from the foreign tongue into his own, in which he then comprehends them as a sentence and makes an answer. As every language teacher knows, this is a process to be avoided at all costs, and the form of this test seems not only to provide the student with a crutch but also to insist that he use it. All classroom methods of teaching a foreign language, while not necessarily actual verbal processes in that language, should at least be projected against the natural use of the language as a background. The thought process required in answering a question on this test is something which simply never happens in a French person's mind.

To reduce the intelligence level of the questions to a point far below that of most of the students to be tested is a dubious procedure also, for the student remains a human being even while he is being analyzed by devices such as this, and the test may turn into a measure of his resentment at being asked questions that seem to him stupid.

The questions are of different types, and differ considerably in their value for a test of this kind. In one type, the answer is implicit in the question itself, such as Item 76 of Form B: "Qui appelle-t-on en cas de maladie?" In another type, no answer can be given until further information is supplied, as, for example, Item 47 of Form A: "Quel est le plus fier de ces animaux?" A third type is a question so wide in scope that one is, to say the least, bewildered until some limits are given, as in Item 61 of Form B: "Qu'est-ce qui ne dure qu'un instant?" Only questions of the first type can fairly be included in a test of ability to understand spoken French; the others obviously test something quite different, that is, the ability to understand a language pattern composed of a sentence spoken in French and five words written in English.

The test would be more satisfactory to both student and teacher if the questions were arranged in order of difficulty, and the student's mind would be clearer for the main business of the test if the perplexing chart for indicating his previous experience in French were at the end rather than at the beginning.

The dullness of many of the questions and the generally stuffy atmosphere of this test suggest that perhaps the advice of Otto Jespersen to makers of language textbooks, "It seems never to have occurred to the authors of some (schoolbooks) that there might be a limit to the amount of rubbish that can be offered children under the pretext of teaching them grammar," should be taken to heart by the makers of language tests as well.

[1344]

American Council Beta French Test. Grades 7-11; 1926-27; 2 forms; $1.30 per 25; 20¢ per specimen set; 90(100) minutes; prepared for the Modern Language Study under the auspices of the American Council on Education and the Conference of Canadian Universities; Jacob Greenberg and Ben D. Wood; Yonkers, N. Y.: World Book Co.

REFERENCES

1 WOOD, BEN D. *New York Experiments with New-Type Modern Language Tests*: Including a Survey of Modern Language Achievement in the Junior High Schools of New York City, June, 1925; the Regents Experiment of June, 1925, with New-Type Tests in French, German, Spanish, and Physics; and a Second Survey of Modern Language Achievement in the Junior High Schools of New York City, June, 1926, pp. 3-103, 323-39. Publications of the American and Canadian Committees on Modern Languages, Vol. 1. New York: Macmillan Co., 1928. Pp. xxii, 339. Paper. Out of print.

2 GIDUZ, HUGO. "The 1935 French Placement Tests at The University." *H Sch J* 18:227-8 N '35.

Bateman Edwards, Head of the Department of Romance Languages, Washington University. This test is published in two forms which the makers claim to be equivalent. In the year which elapsed between the copyrighting of Form A and Form B certain improvements were introduced, such as the provision of a place for recording the score at the end of each part, and the instruction at the bottom of the odd-numbered pages for the student to go right on to the next page. With these exceptions, the material form of the two tests is identical. Since the key for Form A alone was included with the tests, all references, unless indicated, are to that form.

Part I, a vocabulary test of 100 items, presents four or five English words as possible translations of a given French word. It would be difficult to invent a method better designed to elicit misinformation from the student. Series of words, lacking their context, soon lose all power to provoke response, and the confusion is not reduced by the occasional inclusion, among the correct equivalents, of words possessing several meanings, such as: "grave," "to oblige," "nail," or by the inconsistent use of "to" as the sign of the infinitive. To avoid bewilderment, the student would be wise to translate in his mind each French word, before referring to the suggested possibilities. And even then his problem may be complicated by one of the following: (a) the required translation is not the best or the most usual (*ménager* "to manage," *vœu* "vow"); (b) the translation required by the key is not the only acceptable one among the given possibilities (*fin* "end" also "fine," *souris* "mouse" also "smile," and in Form B *que* "that" also "why"); (c) the key is in error (*border* is translated as "to bare").

Part II is a comprehension test, offering 60 French sentences to be completed, at the end, by the addition of one out of five suggested words or phrases. Here the objections to Part I do not apply, since the words are presented in their context. However, the extreme platitude of these synthetic sentences is not conducive to inspiring the student with any enthusiasm for the French language. Since only the ability to understand French is here in question, an English answer to a question based on a passage of real French prose, of the type adopted by the College Entrance Examination Board, presents a far more interesting and trustworthy means of evaluation. The only objection to such a test could be that it is not susceptible of mechanical marking. Part II presents one typographical error in the omission of the question mark in Item 14. In Item 41 the use of *sept jours,* even in quotation marks, as synonymous with *une semaine* is of dubious correctness.

Part III, a grammar test, requires the insertion of one to four French words to complete the meaning in 60 French sentences of which the English translation is given. In five cases the omitted words comprise the entire sentence. This is the only part of the examination in which the scoring can not "be done mechanically by clerks who know nothing of French." The intention of the makers of the key has been "to include all satisfactory forms of possible answers," but in a good number of cases this has not been done. The long form of the interrogation may be used in Items 15, 29, and 42; the feminine pronoun is as correct as the masculine in Items 32, 53, and 60; the second person singular may be used in Item 30; the past definite is correct for Item 40. It is possible to accept *quelques pommes* instead of *des pommes* for "some apples" (Item 5), *fort* instead of *très* for "very" (Item 47), and *il doit travailler* instead of *il lui faut travailler* for "he must work" (Item 58), not to mention the less obvious possibility of circumlocutions in several of the other sentences. In addition, the key is in error for Item 48 in omitting the definite article which is not translated in the test. No uses of the conditional or subjunctive are included.

In the Manual of Directions the authors point to the difficulties inherent in an objective test of this sort in order to explain the lack of measurement of any cultural or oral-aural elements. A still greater lack is, I fear, that of material capable of giving the student any confidence whatsoever that he can handle the French language as a living means of communication. A French sentence for complete translation, where the student will have to conquer problems not only of vocabulary but also of syntax, is far more valuable than the recognition of any number of isolated words. When reading for comprehension the student should feel that the information imparted is mature enough not to insult his intelligence. In translating into French, the value of expressing a complete thought with all its elements is far superior to that of spotting a series of unrelated grammatical points in sentences artificially designed for the purpose. Perhaps the fault lies in the very conception of the wholly objective examination. An examination which subordinates the encouragement of independent thought to speed and objectivity in marking, and which does not require, on the part of the marker, intelligence and a knowledge of the subject superior to that of the examinee, may very likely prove not worth administering.

[1345]

American Council French Grammar Test. Grades 9-16; 1927; 2 forms; $1.25 per 25; 20c per specimen set; 22(27) minutes; prepared for the Modern Foreign Language Study under the auspices of the American Council on Education and the Conference of Canadian Universities; Frederic D. Cheydleur; Yonkers, N. Y.: World Book Co.

REFERENCES

1 CHEYDLEUR, F. D. *The American Council French Grammar Test (Selection Type)*: A Preliminary Experiment at the University of Wisconsin. University of Wisconsin, Bureau of Educational Research, Bulletin No. 8. Madison, Wis.: the University, 1927. Pp. 35. Out of print.
2 CHEYDLEUR, F. D. "The Construction and Validation of a French Grammar Test of the Selection or Multiple-Choice Type." *J Ed Res* 17:184-96 Mr '28.
3 CHEYDLEUR, FREDERIC D. "Results and Significance of the New Type of Modern Language Tests." *Mod Lang J* 12:513-31 Ap '28.
4 HENMON, V. A. C. *Achievement Tests in Modern Foreign Languages*: Prepared for the Modern Language Study and the Canadian Committee on Modern Languages, pp. 1-8, 10-11, 18-19, 295-300. Publications of the American and Canadian Committees on Modern Languages, Vol. 5. New York: Macmillan Co., 1929. Pp. xxvii, 363. $1.00. Paper. (London: Macmillan & Co., Ltd. 4s. 6d.)
5 CHEYDLEUR, FREDERIC D. "The Relationship between Functional and Theoretical Grammar: An Experiment Carried on with the American Council French Grammar Test, Selection Type, in Seven State Institutions." *Mod Lang J* 16:310-33 Ja '32.

Harry Heller, Head of the French Department, Fieldston School, New York, New York. This is an old and well-known test, prepared originally for the Modern Foreign Language Study. Much that this reviewer has said elsewhere in these pages concerning the *Cooperative French Test* in general, and its grammar section in particular, applies here too. Further comparison reveals that the publishers of the Cheydleur test have been much less generous with research data on the test's construction, etc. The reliability coefficient for 9,664 cases, given in the accompanying manual, is .87, but for some single years and semesters is too low for accurate measurement of individual students, ranging from .72 to .92. Correlation coefficients with other tests appear for the most part adequate although based on relatively few cases. Tables of percentile norms are given but it is not indicated how recently they were compiled.

Both alternate forms of this test are composed of 50 items of the selection type. An English sentence is followed by four alternative French translations among which the student chooses the correct one. As stated elsewhere, the device of confronting the student with incorrect alternatives is suspect to this reviewer who holds it to be educationally unsound, especially in the language arts where no governing "logic" can be posed in the early stages of study but is acquired only with a long mastery that few students achieve. Experimental evidence on this point would be valuable. However, in most of the items the alternative French translations are arranged around a common correct portion, thus throwing into better relief the grammatical usage being tested—an improvement over the grammar section of the *Cooperative French Test*.

A record of student achievement in French based on this one objective test alone would be a barren thing. Unless a grammar test is needed for some special reason the teacher would do well at least to combine this measure with a comprehension test or use the three-part *Cooperative French Test*.

Charles Holzwarth, Principal of the West High School, Rochester, New York. Since this test is also of the recognition type, the objections which I voiced in my review of the *American Council on Education French Reading Test* are applicable here, although to a somewhat lesser degree since the responses offered for the choice of the pupil are not so tricky and there seems to be only one possible choice. Personally I much prefer to test pupils by the actual translation into French of sentences based on a known vocabulary and with a controlled grammatical range of difficulty, something which is impractical in a standard test.

If one has to use a standard test, I see considerable merit in this one, but I believe it should be revamped. Of course, the minute even minor changes are made, goodbye standards and comparisons!

As to the range of grammar topics, I find it touches on most of the points covered in our school grammars. There are, however, a few rough spots, e.g.,

1. *There is little testing of verb forms.* (*a*) In the classroom we spend a great deal of time on tense formation, conjugation of verbs, principal parts of irregular verbs, etc. Yet this test which purports to evaluate our work fails to take them into account. (*b*) Tense usage is tested in Items 38, 39, 42, of Form A and in Items 1, 3, 6, 27 and 32 of Form B. (*c*) Verbs conjugated with *être,* which we classroom teachers consider rather important, appear only in B17 (i.e., Item 17 in Form B) and in A43, which latter case tests not only this principle but also the use of the subjunctive. (*d*) The agreement of the past participle with *avoir* appears only in B24. Surely this is cavalier treatment for such an important topic—or do we classroom teachers merely think it important? (*e*) The agreement of the past participle in reflexive verbs appears in A2 and B5, B43, while we find the perplexing agreement with *entendre parler* in A29 and *voir se battre* in B31.

2. *Pronouns.* (*a*) Personal pronouns, which we teachers believe relatively important, are tested only in A7 and A37, B7, B22, and B46. The position of pronouns (word order) is stressed apparently only in A7. The emphatic forms occur in A22 and B20. (*b*) Relative and interrogative pronouns seem more adequately handled. (*c*) Possessive pronouns occur only in A19.

3. *Prepositions are neglected.* They occur only in A4, B11 (à + place name), A26, B48 (*dans* + country), and A25 (*avant de*).

4. *Idiomatic and tricky usages are tested* (whether adequately enough, who shall say?) e.g., (*a*) se fait faire, A36; faire couper, B43; (*b*) venir de, B14; (*c*) plus de, A46, B35; (*d*) first (last) two, A40, B45; (*e*) enseigner à Louise à chanter, A30; (*f*) penser à (de), B39; and (*g*) gender of gens, B40.

Naturally some of the examples are hard to classify or present double difficulties, e.g., B1 (verb form and position of adjective), B22 (use of conjunction or preposition and indicative or subjunctive), B28 (use of *dont* and confusing word order), A25 (pronouns and preposition), etc.

If one of the strong points of the recognitional type of test is to concentrate attention on a single point, this has been overlooked in a number of cases.

To sum up, the test gives me the impression of a cross section of grammar cut on somewhat of a bias—but I don't say I could do better, for I appreciate the difficulties which

American Council French Grammar Test

faced the author. I merely affirm that some review and reconstruction would seem to be in order.

[1346]

American Council on Education French Reading Test. 2 semesters or more of college French; 1937-39; Forms A, B, and C; 5¢ per test, 10 to 99 copies; 25¢ per specimen set; 50(55) minutes; prepared for the Committee on Modern Languages; F. D. Cheydleur, V. A. C. Henmon, and M. J. Walker; New York: Cooperative Test Service.

REFERENCES

1 VANDER BEKE, GEORGE E. *French Word Book.* Publications of the American and Canadian Committees on the Modern Languages, Vol. 15. New York: Macmillan Co., 1929. Pp. xiii, 188. $1.10. Paper. (London: Macmillan & Co., Ltd. 5s. 6d.)

Charles Holzwarth, Principal of the West High School, Rochester, New York. This test is what is known as an objective, standardized test. Is there, however, such a thing as a purely objective test? Possibly so far as scoring is concerned but certainly not so far as the subject matter of the test is concerned for this, despite the best efforts of the editor or editors, is bound to be subjective in choice of materials, manner of presentation, etc. Any competent classroom teacher can make up a test better suited to test the progress and the knowledge of his own particular classes but, of course, it will not be standardized. Score one, therefore, for the standardized test.

This test is of the recognition type. Whatever advantages may inhere in this type of test, there are certainly just as inherent disadvantages, one of the most important of which, to my mind, is the fact that only passive knowledge is tested. This observation will stamp me at once as being a conservative of the old school who actually believes that pupils should achieve a certain oral-aural mastery of the language which the "new type" or "standardized" tests do not attempt to measure or even more or less highhandedly consider a mere ancillary of the power to read for comprehension. I grant, of course, that oral-aural ability is very difficult to measure except aurally, but I do not grant the premise that because a pupil does well on a reading test, he will necessarily do well in oral-aural work.

My chief additional objection to the recognition type test is that its very form makes it a guessing game or sets up an additional hazard which tests not one's comprehension of the written word in the basic paragraph but rather one's ability to choose carefully among the solutions offered, making the test one of

logical ability and clear thinking. This is particularly true of the first test of this kind undertaken by a given pupil. He has to learn the technique before he can show his real ability, i.e., before the test becomes really a fair and accurate test of his comprehension of the paragraph set for comprehension. Let me illustrate.

Let us consider Item 111, Form B. The question is: "Que ferait-elle quand elle serait riche?" Response 1 states: "She would have a beautiful house and magnificent dresses" (cf. "J'aurais une belle maison et des robes magnifiques" of the text) but that is not the correct answer, for Response 3 says: "She would marry the richest farmer in the country" ("J'épouserais le plus riche fermier du pays"). Both answers agree with the text but, of course, the question asks: Que *ferait*-elle? Here it hinges on the ability of the pupil to comprehend the question, not on his ability to comprehend the reading selection. My point is merely this, is the test supposed to test the pupil's ability to comprehend the passage set or his ability to comprehend questions based on the passage?

Consider also Item 112, Responses 2 and 3—here is a logical distinction rather than a factual distinction. Consider also Item 126, Responses 2 and 3. Here the pupil has to have not casual comprehension but mastery of *raille.*

In Item 108 the test tempts the pupil with Response 1 to see if he will fall for village. But the question itself says to *a* nearby city rather than *the* nearby city as in the text. Why be more critical of the pupil than the test?

Sometimes the questions are harder than the text, e.g., "châteaux en Espagne" of Item 113 or cf. Item 129 or Item 143. Here again the test is rather of the pupil's ability to understand the question rather than to comprehend the text.

Do you now see why I prefer to ask a pupil to translate into English rather than read a French question and pick an English answer which may trip him?

Or consider Item 149 (where I assume that Response 1 is the correct answer). Yet the passage doesn't really say so, it leaves the pupil to make the connection between "remplissait son assiette à fleurs" and "Oh! la bonne odeur de soupe au fromage!" And the author tries to trip the pupil with Response 2.

Consider Item 147 (where I assume Response 3 is the acceptable answer) and yet the text says "il va trouver *sa chambre* encore chaude . . . et tout *son petit chez lui* bien rangé," i.e., the pupil must be logical. Heaven forfend that I should object to setting up training in logical thinking as one of the by-products of language well taught; I merely question the validity of such procedure in a test which aims to discover whether the pupil can read and comprehend. Do we arrive at the goal via a double aim?

I object also to Item 107. Here the author is testing the pupil's concept of morality rather than his understanding of the story.

Have I illustrated what I consider to be some of the inherent faults of recognitional testing? For the classroom I believe translation is the most reliable form of testing comprehension. For purposes of comparison I grant the value of the standard test, but, oh, how careful must the author be!

I now come to a different type of objection to this particular test (Form B), namely extent of vocabulary. The description of the reading test given by the publishers says that the passages of Form A contain no words of a frequency above 2,000 except "22 words, such as proper names, cognates, and a few others whose meanings can be inferred from the text or whose English meanings are given." I have before me only Form B, but since A and B are held to be interchangeable, I assume that the above should apply to the passages of Form B also.

Is *confiseur* one of the 22? It is a vital word in the first selection but it is not translated in the text nor would I classify it as one of the cognates whose meaning an average pupil could guess. On the other hand it is not in the Vander Beke word list [1] and hence cannot be a particularly common word. Hence the pupil is entirely out of luck on Item 101.

Laitière of the second selection is also foreign to the Vander Beke list and yet is important to the understanding of the text. Do we infer that this is one of the 22 easy-to-guess words? Try it on a high school pupil!

The verb *quereller* of the third selection does not appear in Vander Beke. Another to be guessed at? And yet Item 116 depends upon it. I believe also that the wording of Item 117 is likely to stump the average high school pupil, i.e., this use of *offrir* is not commonly met in high school reading.

Again *conseillères* of the fourth selection is

not in Vander Beke. Hence I object to Item 123 which might well tempt the pupil to guess at *consolation*. The verb *railler* seems to rank 5,115 in Vander Beke. Although, to be sure, I have Form B before me rather than Form A for which the claim is made not to go above 2,000 (i.e., only 3 words between 1,500-2,000 and none between 2,001 and 2,500).

In the fifth selection *blanchâtre* is not in Vander Beke. *S'assombrir* ranks 5,057 in Vander Beke, while *terne* is 4,399, *étain* is 5,459, *réseau* is 5,236, and *s'enlacer* and *déformer* are not in Vander Beke.

In the sixth selection *culbuter* is not in Vander Beke, *assaillir* ranks 4,556, *égorger* 5,172, *narine* 5,988, and *désordonné* and *marmite* are not in Vander Beke.

Part I, the vocabulary test, is open to the same general objection that I have offered against Part II, i.e., that it is a guessing game where technique must be mastered before it is fair to gauge the pupil by what he accomplishes. My objection here is, however, much less strong for there is not the ambiguity of question to lead the pupil astray.

Inasmuch as the words which make up the vocabulary test are carefully chosen from the Vander Beke list, I believe it has decided value once the pupil knows the technique.

For a review by Nelson Brooks, see 984.

[1347]
Columbia Research Bureau Aural French Test. Grades 9-16; 1930; 2 forms; $1.25 per 25, 20¢ per specimen set; (45-60) minutes; Louise C. Seibert and Ben D. Wood; Yonkers, N. Y.: World Book Co.

REFERENCES

1 VANDER BEKE, GEORGE E. *French Word Book*. Publications of the American and Canadian Committees on Modern Languages, Vol. 15. New York: Macmillan Co., 1929. Pp. xxvii, 363. $1.10. Paper. (London: Macmillan & Co., Ltd. 5s. 6d.)

Clarence E. Turner, Assistant Professor of the Romance Languages, Rutgers University. This test is designed to measure the extent to which students, when listening to spoken French, can (*a*) understand a question, (*b*) understand the relation of facts, (*c*) understand a continuous paragraph, and (*d*) understand dictated sentences and copy them. In Part I the examiner reads a series of statements concerning each of three pictures which are before the student, who then indicates whether each statement is true or false. In Part II the examiner reads a series of questions which the student answers by indicating "yes" or "no." In Part III the examiner reads a paragraph, then identifies it by a letter. The student turns to that letter in his booklet, where he finds in English three statements concerning the paragraph, each statement to be completed by indicating the best of four possible answers. Part IV consists of a dictation exercise of fifteen sentences. The material in the test booklet is well arranged, without crowding or ambiguity.

The accompanying manual discusses the construction and validity of the test. Validity is claimed because of the wide sampling of items, the selection of content, the number of distinct functions measured, and the extent of differentiation among students who have had the same number of years of the subject, and between the averages of students who have had different amounts of training. Statistical support is offered for the claim of differentiation. The authors explain how they have sought to control the extent to which the test becomes a measure of vocabulary: 827 of its words are found in the Vander Beke list,[1] 47 per cent in the first thousand, 67 per cent in the first two thousand, 85 per cent in the first four thousand, and 92 per cent in the first six thousand. They state further that the selection of content was made with a view to avoiding as far as possible the measurement of general intelligence, information, or memory. Nevertheless, particularly in Part III, general intelligence and recall seem clearly to be measured. The authors' assertion that, "In Part III, for instance, all the paragraphs were first tested in English as to length, grasp of general meaning, perception of details and so on," does not prove, or mean, anything as it stands. The authors have sought to meet the objection that Part IV measures factors other than comprehension (e.g., grammar, spelling) by a method of scoring which minimizes errors not primarily of comprehension.

The reviewer believes this to be on the whole a sound and well-constructed test, capable of furnishing a usable measure of aural comprehension. Its usefulness and validity are somewhat reduced, perhaps unavoidably, by certain factors relating to the examiner, and to the means used for securing discrimination among students of superior ability.

The examiner is intended to be the teacher of the students tested. He must be able to pronounce French, which the authors optimistically take for granted, and he must furthermore train himself to read at three different speeds and to time pauses accurately. The speeds are those at which a sentence like *L'ouragan déracine les arbres les plus vigoureux* would be read in 30 (normal), 50 (slow), and 80 (very slow) seconds respectively. While an intelligent person can with reasonable practice arrive at an accurate performance, one can not help wondering whether some verification of the examiner's skill should not be requisite to the inclusion of scores in the norm-tables. The latter would have their maximum utility if based on scores obtained when the test is administered by *any* person of proven ability to pronounce French and to follow the authors' directions. Comparable scores could then be obtained for large groups of students from different schools, like college freshmen whom it might be wished to place according to their aural comprehension.

An examination of the more difficult items reveals a paradox underlying the test's construction. Fundamentally, the test, like the Vander Beke list with which it has been checked, is based on written French. It measures the ability to understand written French read aloud. This is a useful measure, but it must not be mistaken for a measure of the ability to understand spoken French. The simpler items when read aloud are like sentences which may be heard spoken, but the more difficult ones owe their difficulty in considerable part to the introduction of processes characteristic of literary French—longer sentences, more difficult syntax, less familiar words. Now spoken French becomes harder to understand as the speakers change, as the speed increases, as the vocabulary is extended, and as the style grows colloquial. In this test the speaker does not change. The vocabulary is carefully controlled, and though it increases, does not increase colloquially. The speed increases only to that rate called "normal," and which is definitely slower than that of rapid colloquial French. The style never grows colloquial either. Hence, the only devices left to secure discrimination among the better students are essentially those of literary French.

[1348]

Columbia Research Bureau French Test. Grades 9-15; 1926; 2 forms; $1.30 per 25; 20¢ per specimen set; 90(100) minutes; A. A. Méras, Suzanne Roth, and Ben D. Wood; Yonkers, N. Y.: World Book Co.

REFERENCES

1 MÉRAS, A. A.; ROTH, SUZANNE; AND WOOD, BEN D. Chapter 25, "A Placement Test in French," pp. 247-63. In *Contri-*

butions to Education, Vol. 1. Edited by J. Carleton Bell. New York Society for the Experimental Study of Education. Yonkers, N. Y.: World Book Co., 1924. Pp. ix, 364. Out of print.

2 WOOD, BEN D. New York Experiments with New-Type Modern Language Tests: Including a Survey of Modern Language Achievement in the Junior High Schools of New York City, June, 1925; The Regents Experiment of June, 1925, with New-Type Tests in French, German, Spanish, and Physics; and A Second Survey of Modern Language Achievement in the Junior High Schools of New York City, June, 1926, pp. 105-319. Publications of the American and Canadian Committees on Modern Languages, Vol. 1. New York: Macmillan Co., 1927. Pp. xxii, 339. Paper. Out of print.

3 CHEYDLEUR, FREDERIC D. "The Relative Reliability of the Old and New Type Modern Language Examinations." French R 2:530-50 My '29.

Joseph F. Jackson, Professor of French, University of Illinois. Forms A and B are equivalent and are similarly constructed. Part I, Vocabulary, consists of 100 French words for each of which the student is to choose the nearest English equivalent from 4 or 5 alternates; Part II, Comprehension, 75 true-false statements in French; and Part III, Grammar, 100 English sentences, each followed by an incomplete translation to be completed by the student.

In Form A the items of Part I are well chosen, excepting two cognates (Items 29 and 90) and several alternates which could serve as well in certain contexts as the expression desired (Items 16, 48, 62, and 100). For an objective test the items of Part II are less generally satisfactory, as the answers in some cases depend at least as much on the student's judgment, opinion, or experience as on his knowledge of French (e.g., Items 40, 45, 55, 61, 67, 72, and 73). Granted that any test of intellectual ability involves the use of intelligence and memory, it is possible to devise a sounder gauge of a student's language skill than is provided by the type of sentences indicated. The grammar-completion elements of Part III are quite satisfactory, but the scoring of them is less objective than the manual of directions indicates. All the possible alternate answers are not given in the key. In the directions for using the key, it is stated that "the student's answer should receive credit even if it is not in the key, provided there is no doubt that it is correct." One naturally wonders whether a scorer's doubt necessarily invalidates a student's answer.

Form B is less acceptable than Form A. There are more debatable points in Part I (Items 4, 13, 37, 58, 68, and 100) and in Part II (Items 17, 18, 22, 23, 29, 30, 39, 41, 43, 45, 51, 53, 55, 61, 65, and 72). In connection with Part II of both forms, it is interesting and perhaps significant to note that the reliability

coefficient for Part II is .84, while those of Part I and Part III are respectively .93 and .94. Similarly the correlation of Part II with each of the other parts is .71, while the correlation between Parts I and III is .74.

The manual of directions treats in detail validity, derivation, construction, application, administration, establishment of norms, scoring and interpretation of scores. The vocabulary of the test was drawn from words common to at least four of sixteen recognized textbooks. Items were pretested for validity and practicability; those retained were then arranged according to order of difficulty. It is affirmed that this test "affords a measure two or three times as reliable as those of old-type examinations of three hours' duration," but the basis of this affirmation is not indicated. In a discussion of possible limitations of the test, there is no mention of lack of measurement of the student's ability to translate connected passages thoroughly and accurately from and into French, yet this is an ability which is considered of primary importance in instruction. There seems to be some confusion about the character of Part II (Comprehension) which, according to the manual, was intended to afford a wide sampling of French grammar. It is difficult to see what grammatical points are included in Part II. Norms were established from the results obtained in giving the test to high school students of New York State. These norms should be too high for some sections of the country. The key is somewhat awkward to operate. One of the alternate answers given for Item 77 of Part III, Form A, is incorrect.

In summary, the material and makeup of this test are interesting and significant within the indicated limits, but in execution it falls short of its potentialities.

Laura B. Johnson, Assistant Professor in the Teaching of French, The University of Wisconsin. These tests are among the most satisfactory standardized French tests for high-school students. Divided into three parts they test quite adequately recognition of vocabulary, reading ability, and grammar knowledge. The 75 items in the vocabulary test are well chosen. The multiple-choice technique is used, five English words being given as possible translations of each French word. Cognates are avoided and misleading similar words are suggested. One may question the validity of *instance* as a translation of *cas,* or *carry out* as a translation of *accomplir,* but, on the whole, it seems as good a way to measure recognition of isolated words as has yet been devised.

The comprehension part of the test is based on 75 disconnected statements to be identified as true or false. The statements are based on a reasonable vocabulary and increase gradually enough in difficulty to permit of clear differentiation in each year of language study. In at least two instances there is sufficient ambiguity to permit of two possible interpretations which make them invalid as testing instruments. One wonders, however, if accurate interpretation of isolated sentences is as good a test of reading power as comprehension of a connected passage with opportunity for cumulative inference, correlation of ideas, understanding of implication, emphasis, idiomatic phrasing, etc.

The 100 items which make up the grammar test are fairly representative of the grammatical points stressed in high-school classes. However, in some cases, there seems to be rather too much emphasis on unimportant idiomatic usage rather than on significant constructions as such. Because the French words to be inserted into the French context in translating a given English sentence are to be written in the margin apart from the sentence, students often omit a vital word and hence are penalized for an omission rather than a commission.

The chief advantage of this examination is that it includes a sufficient number of relatively easy items to measure adequately achievement in the first- and second-year work and has sufficient range to challenge the most advanced students in fourth-year work. Forms A and B are considered equivalent and duplicable forms.

[1349]

Cooperative French Test [Advanced Form]. 4 semesters or more: high school, or 2 semesters or more: college; 1933-40; 40- and 90-minute editions; 25¢ per specimen set of either edition; Advanced Form P: Geraldine Spaulding and Paule Vaillant; Advanced Form Q: Geraldine Spaulding and Paule Vaillant with the editorial assistance of Algernon Coleman, E. B. DeSauzé, Henry M. Fiske, Stephen L. Pitcher, and Lenore Thomas; New York: Cooperative Test Service.
a) FORMS 1934, 1936, AND 1937. Forms 1933 and 1935 are out of print; 6¢ per test, 10 to 99 copies; 90(95) minutes.
b) REVISED SERIES, ADVANCED FORMS N, O, P, AND Q. 1937-40; 5¢ per test, 10 to 99 copies; 40(45) minutes.

REFERENCES

1 VANDER BEKE, GEORGE E. *French Word Book.* Publications of the American and Canadian Committees on the Modern Languages, Vol. 15. New York: Macmillan Co., 1929. Pp. xiii, 188. $1.10. Paper. (London: Macmillan & Co., Ltd. 5s. 6d.)
2 FICKEN, CLARENCE ELWOOD. *Intercorrelations of Part Scores in Foreign Language Tests.* Unpublished doctor's thesis, University of Wisconsin, 1937. Pp. 120.
3 HANNA, JOSEPH V. "A Comparison of Cooperative Test Scores and High School Grades as Measures for Predicting Achievement in College." *J Appl Psychol* 23:289-97 Ap '39.
4 GIDUZ, HUGO. "The 1939 French Placement Tests at the University of North Carolina." *H Sch J* 23:28-31 Ja '40.

C. E. Ficken, Dean of the College and Professor of French, Macalester College. [Review of Advanced Form P.] This test "is recommended for those students who have had four or more semesters of study in high school French, or at least a year in college, and has the same scope and objectives as indicated . . . for the 90-minute edition." It, therefore, purports to measure throughout this range in forty minutes the nonliterary elements of linguistic achievement other than free composition, pronunciation, and aural skill. The pattern of the longer test is followed in designating the three parts as Reading, Vocabulary, and Grammar but the time proportions of 25, 25, and 40 minutes are revised to 15, 10, and 15 minutes respectively. Test item totals of 80, 100, and 100 are consequently reduced to 45, 40, and 40.

Without a test supply for obtaining empirical data the reviewer undertakes merely an armchair appraisal. The authors give but small consolation when they admit that the shorter tests "are slightly less reliable than the longer tests but are adequate for most purposes," while the manual of directions does not give a reliability coefficient for either. A nonprofit organization of first-rate prestige thereby misses a valuable opportunity to discipline the more mercenary test makers. Meanwhile the cautious examiner can scarcely be blamed for questioning the reliability of a ten or fifteen minute test.

It is encouraging to find that "all test material was given to large numbers of students in order to obtain data from which indices of difficulty and validity could be secured." But again there are no coefficients to demonstrate the statistical validity of the test or any of its three parts. We are merely assured that the successive forms are comparable and equivalent measures of whatever they measure. In short, evaluation of the test is reduced to an analysis of its probable curricular validity.

Part I, Reading, contains twenty-nine items involving word and sentence meaning, while the remaining sixteen items require a multiple-choice interpretation of four brief paragraphs. The proportion suggests that we are measuring vocabulary rather than reading. Ninety-five per cent of the vocabulary used is from Vander Beke's *French Word Book* [1] and hence within the six thousand commonest reading words. This evidence of scientific care is commendable but also points to the absence of sufficiently difficult passages to test the recognition power of a fourth-semester college student. In spite of these limitations, the test probably measures reading ability as well as it can be done in fifteen minutes.

Part II, Vocabulary, adds little of value and should either have been pooled with Part I or omitted. Out of forty words, no fewer than ten are English cognates, whose response word (in French) is likewise a cognate. "Gigantesque" for example, is rendered by "énorme," which would be evident without the slightest knowledge of French. Of the remaining thirty words four or five have answer-synonyms of lower frequency than the test word. In four other cases the answer word merely categorizes the test word and hence credits a most hazy response, as for example, "cigale" is rendered by "insecte." In short, the "direct" method may be good technique for *teaching* vocabulary but becomes a very "indirect," if not abortive, method of *measuring* vocabulary. Furthermore, this reviewer fails to detect any "decoy" elements among the incorrect answer-words. And finally, there is no perceptible progression from easy to difficult question-words.

Part III, Grammar, consists of forty English sentences, each with five French translations. It, therefore, directly measures composition grammar rather than a recognition knowledge of reading essentials. As such it appears to be entirely successful.

To examiners, this reviewer suggests the reduction of the test to thirty minutes by omitting Part II, thus measuring comprehension in a broad sense with Part I and composition grammar with Part III. The results should then be treated as approximations to be interpreted in the light of past or future performance or additional testing. With all its limitations we must recognize that this test is a far better measuring instrument than the traditional examination of yesterday.

Harry Heller, Head of the French Department, Fieldston School, New York, New York. [Review of Advanced Form P.] A survey of our achievements to date in the field of objective modern foreign language testing is, in general, discouraging. Test makers continue to address themselves, with varying degrees of moderate success, to those aspects of language learning that are most obviously measurable. Nowhere would our survey yield evidence of any concerted pioneering effort to measure the outcomes sought by the best practices of progressive language teaching. A lag between good teaching practice and the production of corresponding instruments of measurement may well be inevitable but, far from assuming any large responsibility for progress, test makers continue to produce instruments—in some cases, as in the one under review, ably constructed and validated on the basis of what it is proposed to measure—that sanction the outworn materials, if not methods, of the days before the Modern Foreign Language Study. These assertions are difficult to support fully within the scope of this review although general and specific considerations bearing upon them will be noted.

In the light of our poor achievements in this field and measured merely against its own claims, this latest form of the *Cooperative French Test* stands favorable comparison with other tests on the market. A teacher or supervisor content to understand the skills of reading, vocabulary, and grammar as presented by the authors, implicit in their test, will find that this instrument attains its stated goal with better than average success. Descriptive and explanatory material concerning the test's construction, validation, norms, etc., is available in rather extensive accompanying booklets, some at a small extra cost. This material appears to be the fruit of considerable research and is marked throughout by sincerity. Useful tables for the conversion of raw scores into special scaled scores for greater comparability are supplied. Tables of percentile norms of recent compilation and for different types of secondary schools and colleges represent another real advantage. The test is adapted to hand or machine scoring.

The three divisions of the test have already been indicated. Part I is made up of short passages of French. The student is invited to select from five choices the word, or small group of words, which completes the prefaced statement. These passages are for the most part too meager to be considered real reading situations. The power to comprehend the un-

Cooperative French Test [Advanced Form]

familiar when it is in context with the known is barely called into play. In many cases only one of the five choices has any relevance or plausibility. In fact, many items reduce themselves to questions of vocabulary, *acheter* suggesting *argent* and *livre* eliciting *bibliothèque*. The authors will claim that "easy" items must be inserted to provide measurement of individual differences in the lower percentiles. This may not be the place to point out that our tests so far do not reveal important individual *human* differences but only differences from an artificial norm, although it may fairly be asked whether the range of difficulty is wide enough on the upper level to measure individual differences in the higher percentiles. What is involved here, however, is not the difficulty of the reading items but the very definition of the reading skill.

Part II is a vocabulary test of the multiple-choice type. It is difficult to justify, or even discover, any unifying basis on which the words given may have been chosen. Some are common or useful only in specific forms or connections, like *agréer*. Here, too, as in the reading section, many items offer only one alternative, out of five, that is in any way related to the given word. Here even to a lesser extent than on the reading portion will "careful judgment" and "shrewd guessing based on intelligent inference," both invited by the authors' directions to the student, enter into performance. But, above all, this reviewer wishes to question whether vocabulary can usefully be tested by giving words *out of context*.

The grammar section, Part III, contains forty items. In Items 1 to 8 the student chooses the correct form among five to complete the French translation of an English sentence. In Items 9 to 40 he selects the correct French translation among five of an English sentence. It would be difficult to formulate a definition of functional grammar to which competent teachers could subscribe that is met by this test. The most inept French student with the greatest gift for whimsy should feel most at home among these wrong alternative translations! The multiple-choice question admittedly lends itself to objective measurement but is this use of it a good educational procedure? Is it psychologically sound? Many of the items on this part of the test cover fundamental forms, verb tenses, etc., that good teaching and testing alike must treat as simple habit

responses not to be dislocated by offering confusing choices that cannot be distinguished from one another by any process of reasoning or even useful rules. And as for the properly functional aspects of grammar, why not build a multiple-choice test where four out of five alternatives are *correct* or *approximately correct* and only one wrong for some *important reason*? The student could be asked to indicate the best answer as well as the wrong one. The choices he made among items placed in such a juxtaposition would reflect his acquisition of functional grammar concepts in an interesting way.

It should be repeated in all fairness that the *Cooperative French Test* is a relatively good contribution to the measurement of the reading, vocabulary, and grammar skills, although important *redefinitions* of these skills have been suggested. Yet the skills measured, while fundamental in any language teacher's hierarchy of values, received but a few scant lines, and with different emphasis, in the list of desirable outcomes promulgated recently by a "records" committee of language teachers on which this reviewer sat. A director of languages in a large school system has declared publicly that his teachers are not primarily teachers of French, German, or Spanish, but of the social studies! In the second place, said he, they were teachers of language in general. Only lastly, and almost incidentally, were they concerned with the French subjunctive or German word order. This reviewer has little sympathy for this viewpoint. It is like looking through the wrong end of a telescope! It is cited, however, as a symptom of real and growing concerns among language teachers. The test makers are challenged to redefine their old goals and to essay new roads—a difficult task, indeed. They must look to the best, as well as to the most usual, educational procedures for material that is socially significant and interesting to maturing minds and developing personalities. They are challenged to devise tests that are significant educational experiences, the standard by which the teaching art measures itself.

Joseph F. Jackson, Professor of French, The University of Illinois. [Review of Advanced Form P.] According to a descriptive pamphlet, this form is designed for students who have studied French for four or more semesters in high school or at least one year in college. It consists of three parts. Part I, Reading, 15 minutes, 29 sentences or brief passages, each to be completed by a choice of one of five words or phrases, and 4 longer passages with 16 questions based on them, each to be answered by a choice of one of five words or phrases. This part is entirely in French. Part II, Vocabulary, 10 minutes, 40 French words, each with a series of five French words from which the one most nearly corresponding in meaning to the original is to be selected. Part III, Grammar, 15 minutes, 8 English sentences, each with an incomplete translation to be completed by a choice of one of five expressions, and 32 English sentences, the correct translation of each to be indicated by a choice of one of five options.

The material, which is based almost entirely on the Vander Beke and Cheydleur lists, is well chosen and carefully prepared. The items were pretested for validity and for order of difficulty. The student indicates throughout by number his choice of answers. The test can thus be scored purely objectively, as there is no question of interpretation or of alternate answers.

From the standpoint of rigid measurement a test which lends itself completely to objective scoring is most satisfactory, but the teacher may well find this type of test highly mechanical and narrowly limited. The student is not called upon to write any French, he is asked only to identify correct answers. Nowhere is he required to dip into his own fund of knowledge. The authors of the test recognize as the most generally accepted objectives of modern foreign language study "the acquisition of skill in reading, writing, speaking, and understanding the language." Yet they admit that, since ability to compose in writing and speaking, as well as general oral and aural skill, do not readily lend themselves to objective techniques of testing, there is no attempt made to measure them. This raises a broad, fundamental question which is applicable to all tests of this type. If there are important aspects of language study which can not be scientifically tested and objectively measured, does the objective test furnish an adequate description of the student's general ability?

With reference to the test under consideration, the second section of Part III, which offers for each of 32 English sentences five

French versions, four-fifths of which are barbarisms, represents a device which is antagonistic to sound teaching. Students learn largely by example. Eighty per cent of bad examples in an important section of a formal test can not have a good effect, particularly in the case of a student who chooses and retains a number of improper constructions.

The explanatory and descriptive material dealing with derivation, validity, applicability, establishment of different norms, scoring and interpretation of the scores from various points of view is instructive and interesting. The key is ingeniously constructed and easy to use.

For a review by Nelson Brooks, see 985.

[1350]

Cooperative French Test [Elementary Form]. First 3 semesters: high school, or first semester: college; 1933-40; 40- and 90-minute editions; 25¢ per specimen set of either edition; Elementary Form P: Jacob Greenberg and Geraldine Spaulding; Elementary Form Q: Jacob Greenberg and Geraldine Spaulding with the editorial assistance of Algernon Coleman, E. B. De Sauzé, Henry M. Fiske, Stephen L. Pitcher, and Lenore Thomas; New York: Cooperative Test Service.

a) JUNIOR FORMS 1936 AND 1937. Forms 1933, 1934, and 1935 are out of print; 6¢ per test, 10 to 99 copies; 90(95) minutes.

b) REVISED SERIES, ELEMENTARY FORMS O, P, Q. 1937-40; Form N is out of print; 5¢ per test, 10 to 99 copies; 1½¢ per machine-scorable answer sheet; 40(45) minutes.

REFERENCES

1 VANDER BEKE, GEORGE E. *French Word Book*. Publications of the American and Canadian Committees on Modern Languages, Vol. 15. New York: Macmillan Co., 1929. Pp. xiii, 188. $1.10. Paper. (London: Macmillan & Co., Ltd. 5s. 6d.)

2 EMERY, M. A. *The Composition and Amount of a Minimum Vocabulary for Reading Ungraded French Texts*. Unpublished master's thesis, University of Chicago, 1931. Pp. 39.

3 PURIN, C. M. *A Standard German Vocabulary of 2000 Words and Idioms*. Chicago, Ill.: University of Chicago Press, 1931. Pp. xvi, 195. Out of print.

4 HAYGOOD, J. D. *A Minimum Essential French Reading Vocabulary*. Unpublished master's thesis, University of Chicago, 1932. Pp. 51.

5 THARP, JAMES B. *A Basic French Vocabulary*, Revised edition. New York: Henry Holt and Co., Inc., 1934. Pp. 222. $0.72.

6 GREENBERG, JACOB. *Le Français et la France*: Premier Cours. New York: Charles E. Merrill Co., 1939. Pp. xiii, 433. $1.48.

Warren S. Holmes, Department of French, The Gunnery School, Washington, Connecticut. [Review of Elementary Form P.] This is an excellent test. It is divided into three parts: reading, vocabulary, and grammar. The multiple-choice technique has been used throughout, making the following of directions extremely simple and allowing very rapid and accurate scoring. In fact the test may be machine scored if desired. The accompanying material is abundant, and includes all that could be desired in the matter of use, validation, administration, scoring, and tabulation.

Cooperative French Test [Advanced Form]

Prospective buyers of this test should realize, however, that it attempts to measure only those skills which "lend themselves readily to objective techniques of testing." It is not a test of the ability to translate a connected passage of French into English or to write connected French prose, either free or from an English model. Yet these are still important objectives, if one is to judge by the emphasis placed upon them in class and preparation time, as well as in examinations set for entrance to many of our universities. Would it not be possible to show a correlation between an objective test of this sort and ability to translate from English to French and vice versa? Such a correlation, if obtainable and made readily accessible in the manual, would be sure of a welcome from practical teachers.

James B. Tharp, Associate Professor of Education, The Ohio State University. [Review of Elementary Form P.] When one considers the careful research and attention to detail based on an expert knowledge of testing techniques and sensitivity to educational purposes that have characterized the construction, validation, and interpretation of the Cooperative tests, one must, generally speaking, accord them first place among educational measurements today. The tests have employed the most objective techniques and have been organized to avoid misunderstanding of directions and to facilitate rapid scoring. Besides a carefully annotated catalogue of test forms, there have been prepared booklets of directions, of norms, and of "purpose, content, and interpretation."

That the French tests have profited from these professional contributions goes without saying. From the thousands of administrations of the 90-minute regular and junior forms from 1933 ending with 1937 among all types of high schools and colleges there have accumulated enough cases to permit establishing norms for three categories of secondary schools and three types of colleges. In each of these six groups hundreds if not thousands of students were tested—sufficient to level off the variation in types of instruction, methods, and content. Reliability coefficients and intercorrelations with other types of measurements are so high that few other tests may rival them. The system of scaled scores and the elaborate tables of percentile ranks make possible many kinds of educational uses with reasonable confidence in the accuracy of interpretation.

With the highest possible statements of confidence and praise in the mechanical and statistical features, the same cannot be said for the range and selection of content. While some users may quarrel with the lack of variety in the technique of response, this reviewer recognizes the accuracy in objective scoring and accepts the principles of selection. With respect to measurement of grammar, the selection response comes the nearest to testing that type of grammar needed for comprehension, rather than that usually stressed in testing—the grammar needed for expression and creative composition. I say "nearest" because even yet the system of completion of partial translations of English sentences is mainly a measurement of powers of composition rather than of comprehension. When we shall invent nearly pure measurements of the latter, the writer just now cannot predict.

Of 35 items in the grammar portion, 27 are these completions and the remaining 8 are best-answer (5-item choice) exercises, testing the correct rendering in French of an idea expressed in English. It is only by having this second type that word position and order can be measured. This type is also the best device to measure comprehension as well as expression of idioms. The items are well chosen in range of coverage and reflect well the estimated frequency of grammatical phenomena in French discourse. (Only in Spanish has a frequency count in syntax been completed.) Other than to say that there seem to be too many items based on inflections in proportion to the total number of items, the reviewer has only praise for the grammar test.

Part I, Reading, and Part II, Vocabulary, cannot have the same bill of health from this reviewer. In the booklet on purposes, the test authors subscribe to current objectives of reading skill, and while making no promise to use only vocabulary items from the frequency lists for fear that "rigid exclusion . . . would seriously restrict the range of subject matter," state that at least the vocabulary portions "are based directly on the Modern Foreign Language word lists for the respective languages." These statements are made for all the languages, but on the junior forms there is a variation: "The vocabulary part of the Spanish test is derived from the first half of the word book, only. In the German test, the vocabulary items are taken from Purin's *Standard German Vocabulary*.[3] In the French test, it was decided not to limit the choice of words to those of higher frequency in the word book, partly because of the considerable number of 'environmental' words which are widely taught in the first years of French study, but which do not rank high in the frequency list."

It is apparent that these differences represent the different opinions of the authors working in the three languages, for it is especially in French and Spanish that surveys by Haygood,[4] Emery,[2] and others have shown that 80 per cent to 93 per cent of ordinary discourse stays within the first 2,000 words in the word lists. If there still remains a considerable number of low frequency words "widely taught" in French, the reviewer submits that the proportion of environmental words runs quite similar with respect to frequency in each of the languages measured. If the authors of this test accept the word counts as quoted above, it must be that teachers and school syllabi continue to use books written before the word counts or that they do not put first the reading objective. That it is the present trend for authors of new books to use the frequency lists and even restricted selection therefrom is generally accepted. Greenberg, in the preface of his beginners' text *Le Français et la France*[6] says: "The total basic vocabulary of the book is limited to a minimum number of useful words and phrases that are generally chosen on the basis of their range as rated by the Vander Beke *French Word Book*."[1]

Recent published vocabulary syllabi in French (The New York State List, the Secondary Education Board List, the *Basic French Vocabulary*,[5] etc.) all contain at least the first 2,000 words, and idioms proportionately, and add a scattering of words of lower frequency —less than a fifth of the total—somewhat as indicated by the Haygood, Emery, and similar studies.

Finally, there is another reason to question the quoted reasons for validity of a higher proportion of low-frequency words in French than in Spanish or German. While the 90-minute Junior Form may have been devised for and widely used "within the narrow range of junior high school work," this new 40-minute Elementary Form is "especially adapted to beginning classes" (according to the cata-

logue) both in junior and senior high schools and in colleges. The vocabulary problem of beginners at various levels varies only by quantity and speed of assimilation, not by range of selection.

Of the 50 items of the vocabulary test, 30 are from the first thousand, 9 more from the second thousand, the remaining 11 of still lower frequency, the whole having an Index of Frequency of 2.74. Form N (1937) of this series has an index of 2.80 in the Elementary Form as against an index of 6.01 in the Advanced Form. (In this Advanced Form, 27 out of 50 items are beyond the 2,000 range and 26 of these are not found in the *Basic French Vocabulary*. The 50 odd-numbered items in the vocabulary portion of the 1934 "regular" test have an index of 6.6; and 30 of the 50 do not appear in the *Basic French Vocabulary*.) Noting that the Miller-Davis second-year test has an index of 2.37, it is the opinion of the reviewer that on a frequency basis the vocabulary portion of the *Cooperative French Test* seems placed somewhat too high for an elementary test.

The same criticism is advanced on the reading portion. Many of the key words of the sentences set for comprehension, are not among the 3,340 words in *Basic French Vocabulary*; two, *ragoût* and *réveille-matin*, are not among Vander Beke's 6,136 words. A large proportion of words in the 5-item selection responses are not in the *Basic French Vocabulary*; words like *muguets, boucher, épicier*, are not in Vander Beke.

The reading portion of the regular 90-minute forms and of the advanced 40-minute forms begin with short sentences describing an idea or establishing a situation which only one of the selection choices will complete, but the items grow longer and become short paragraphs. The Elementary Form uses exclusively the incomplete sentence, a device that requires the authors to assemble "universally known facts" to which responses are not ambiguous. Of 40 of such sentences, the reviewer judges only 10 to be plain facts; the other 30 are intelligence-test type, of which several are arithmetic problems.

Some of the factual items are ambiguous: e.g., Item 3, Part I, "La fête nationale des États-Unis a lieu (1) très souvent (2) très rarement (3) au mois de juillet (4) en hiver (5) à Paris seulement." May a reader not

---

Cooperative French Test [*Elementary Form*]

reason that one day a year is "très rarement"? And suppose the test is measuring reading achievement in Canada and some luckless boy doesn't know the United States' national holiday (do we know that of Canada?)! Another example is Item 38, Part I: "On dit que les chiens qui aboient (1) sont très grands (2) mangent beaucoup de viande (3) aiment à jouer (4) courent dans les rues (5) ne mordent pas." If a reader perchance had never met this famous proverb, must his comprehension of French suffer? He reasons that dogs do two or three things and that the "barking" is merely a confusion item, so he does *not* mark the last choice. It must be admitted that this technique runs the risk of other factors affecting a pure measurement of comprehension of written French. Moreover, the series of disconnected sentences puts too strong a stress on mere vocabulary memory, a factor being measured in a separate part. There is lacking the successive build-up of connected ideas in longer passages and the operation of syntax and idiom as affecting comprehension.

Unfortunately, the tables of norms in terms of scaled scores merge the raw scores of all four types of test, so there is no evidence given of successive achievement levels on this test. It would be interesting to see intercorrelations of the reading and vocabulary measurements— of the relations of the reading and vocabulary measurements, of the regular with the revised series. The high coefficients of reliability (lowest in the vocabulary portion) do not give evidence of validity.

The reviewer would recommend a selection of vocabulary test items (some of them idioms which should not be tested as grammar) more in harmony with research on frequency burden in typical French prose rather than that in widely used beginners' textbooks, until the gap between these two bases becomes narrowed by more genuine adoption of the frequency criterion. For the reading test the reviewer would suggest a series of short paragraphs, each long enough to establish a central idea on which the language, which has been used to express the idea, may be tested on broader factors of comprehension. If a series of sentences is used, why cannot they be connected in thought, perhaps in groups of five or six, based on story pictures so that the hazard of "universally known fact" need not be present to inject a variable error? There are several other types

of reading that we must find ways of measuring before we can consider the field covered.

Although the reviewer sees the difficulty of change of style in maintaining norms on earlier forms, it is probable that the system of scaled scores would safeguard a revision of the reading and vocabulary portions of this test. There is no shadow of doubt that the Cooperative tests, as a general battery of measurements, offer the best instruments available at this date. They have taken testing many strong strides forward.

For a review by Walter V. Kaulfers, see 986.

[1351]

French Life and Culture. High School and College; 1935; 1 form; 50¢ per 25; 15¢ per specimen set; 40(45) minutes; Minnie M. Miller; Emporia, Kan.: Bureau of Educational Measurements, Kansas State Teachers College.

REFERENCES

MILLER, MINNIE. "A Test on French Life and Culture." *Mod Lang J* 20:158-62 D '35.

Bateman Edwards, Head of the Department of Romance Languages, Washington University. This test raises the problem of the possibility of imparting to students in elementary French courses a grasp of the essentials of French life and culture. The objective is admirable, but, if this knowledge were to be gained in the French course alone, it is difficult to see how teachers could maintain normal progress in the acquisition of the language and at the same time furnish the necessary "information on French geography, history, government, art, literature, science, and customs." Even if some one of the manuals of French civilization which are now on the market were to be included in the student's reading, their necessarily summary treatment of a large number of subjects would not be sufficient to impress detailed points on the student's mind. Consequently, the test becomes, in some measure, one of general information gleaned from a variety of sources, requiring no knowledge of French as a language.

Leaving aside the question of how cultural information is to be obtained, the value of such information is obvious. The test under discussion organizes its material of 100 questions into three parts, which represent differing techniques of examination. Part I is the most valuable, since it tests the student's own factual information by means of 40 questions with no prompting lists of answers. Part II consists of 30 questions grouped into two equal sections, the first covering geography, history, and government, the second covering art, literature, and science. Corresponding to each section is an alphabetical list of 20 possible answers. Part III contains 30 statements to be completed by one of three possibilities.

The need for inclusion of some of the items represented may be questioned. For example: questions based on the comparison of French and American systems of measure lack value if there has been no practical experience with both; a knowledge of the present-day population of France and of Paris is significant only when related to that of other countries and cities, or of other centuries; the ability to choose between the Place de la Concorde and the Place de la République as the largest public square in Paris does not necessarily imply any worth-while grasp of French life and culture.

A graver criticism results from the fact that a test of cultural values is, of all tests, the least suited to the present fashion for examinations which can be marked by clerks who need have no knowledge of the subject. Of what value is it to be able to state that the French Renaissance took place in the sixteenth century, unless one can also state what the qualities and influence of that Renaissance are? Is the student who, from a list of twenty names, can pick out that of André Maurois as "a well-known writer of present-day France" to be compared to one who could state some significant fact about the writings of Maurois or of any one of a number of authors of greater merit? The ultimate test of our knowledge of a civilization is not the ability to fit a word into its proper place, to recall or select the isolated fact, but to understand the meaning and importance of the fact, to put in order a number of facts so that their relations and the implications of those relations are apparent. Insistence on the single unrelated and undefined fact, such as demanding the word "gothic" to characterize the style of architecture used in the French medieval cathedrals, leads to partial and ill-digested knowledge. Certainly, a factual examination has its place in any study of a civilization, and the present examination is well-balanced and comprehensive in the facts it demands, but it would be ridiculous to claim that its results could point to more than a superficial knowledge of the subject.

In at least three cases in Part III (Items 86, 88, and 89), the words offered to complete the

sense suffer from a lack or a superfluity of definite articles. It is impossible to speak of "the Notre-Dame de Paris" or of "Jardin du Luxembourg," and to call the wood or park in the west part of Paris "Boulogne" is distressingly ambiguous. A more careful wording of the sentences might remove such faults.

Clarence E. Turner, Assistant Professor of the Romance Languages, Rutgers University. This test purports to measure "such information on French geography, history, government, art, literature, science, and customs as students may reasonably be expected to acquire in two years of high school, or one year of college French." All the questions are in English. Part I calls for one- to three-word answers in English to forty factual questions. Part II calls for the matching of fifteen questions on geography and history with twenty possible answers, and of fifteen questions on literature and the fine arts with twenty other answers. Part III offers a choice of best answer from among three to each of thirty questions representing all of the fields mentioned. The material is somewhat crowded on the page, especially in Parts II and III.

The accompanying manual gives no account of the test's construction and validity beyond the following assertion: "The items were selected from valid sources. The items themselves, as well as their proportional distribution among the various fields of subject matter, were carefully checked by teachers of French in high schools and colleges." The omission of some further demonstration of the test's validity is particularly regrettable for two reasons. First, because it purports to measure achievement in a field where there is no readily accepted valid criterion of achievement. Second, because many of the items appear to have little or no discriminatory power with reference to the achievement under test.

Actually, the test measures factual information. Much of this information is often, and some of it is almost always, acquired by students prior to the study of French: "Name one Frenchman who aided the thirteen colonies during the American Revolution." "Who was commander-in-chief of the allied armies at the close of the World War?" Other questions may be answered by a significant number of students on the basis of information acquired elsewhere in the curriculum: "Is the kilogram

French Life and Culture

more or less than the pound?" "What duke of Normandy conquered England?" Some are both extraneous and trivial: "What colors are used in the French flag?"

About seventy of the items call for information which would normally be encountered only in the French classroom, and then only if emphasis were there placed upon one or more of the manuals which convey that thin mixture of geography, history, sociology, and literature which is sometimes called Civilization. Information gained from one of these books is necessarily superficial and unrelated to that which gives it significance. Consequently, some items of the test under review remind one, by their stressing of the small fact for its own sake, of a well-known radio program: "What is the largest public square in Paris?" "The approximate population of Paris is: (1) 3,000,000 (2) 5,000,000 (3) 1,500,000."

There are a few inaccuracies. The key wrongly insists on "No" as the answer to Item 21, "Are the church and state separated in France?" Dumas *père* and not just Dumas ought perhaps to be exacted as the answer to Item 39. Item 46 may be missed by the student with the best information, who knows that the chateau of Versailles was begun under Louis XIII. Item 86 offers a choice of three impossible answers, since the wood or park in the west part of Paris is not called *Boulogne,* any more than it is called *Tuileries* or *Luxembourg.*

One's total judgment of the test is bound up with that of the curriculum which it reflects, since it has been noted that only for a certain type of curriculum could the test claim validity. It will seem to many teachers that there is no possibility on this earth of building a significant knowledge of any national life and culture without founding it upon a fluent command of the language of that culture. Imparting such command of the printed and spoken language is surely the legitimate business of the modern language teacher, and no other comparable contribution to the student's ultimate knowledge and understanding of a national culture lies within his power. The time spent in preparing students to produce odd bits of information about kilograms, bridges, and authors one-to-a-century, is time spent at the expense of the student in his progress toward meaningful knowledge.

[1352]
French Reading: Dominion Tests. Grade 10; 1940; 2 forms; 2¢ per test in quantity; 15¢ per preliminary manual; 5¢ per sample test; 30(40) minutes; Toronto, Canada: Department of Educational Research, University of Toronto.

[1353]
French Vocabulary Test: Dominion Tests. Grades 9-10; 1940; 2 forms; 2¢ per test in quantity; 15¢ per preliminary manual; 5¢ per sample test; 30(40) minutes; Toronto, Canada: Department of Educational Research, University of Toronto.

[1354]
Lundeberg-Tharp Audition Test in French. High school and college; 1934; 2 forms; $2 per 100; 75¢ per 25; percentile rank norms furnished on request; 10¢ per specimen set; James B. Tharp and Olav K. Lundeberg; Columbus, Ohio: James B. Tharp, Ohio State University.

REFERENCES

1 THARP, JAMES B. "Effect of Oral-Aural Ability on Scholastic Achievement in Modern Foreign Languages." *Mod Lang J* 15:10-26 O '30.
2 THARP, JAMES B. "Lundeberg-Tharp Audition-Pronunciation Test in French." *Mod Lang Forum* 16:4-7 Ja '31.
3 THARP, JAMES B. "A Modern Language Test." *J Higher Ed* 6:103-4 F '35.

Nelson Brooks, Instructor in French, Westover School, Middlebury, Connecticut. The first question that arises when one is confronted with a highly objective test is this: what is the relation between the score one makes on this test and one's actual success in applying in real life the ability being measured? The maker of a test in oral comprehension of a foreign language has an unusual opportunity, for he can make his test of problems that are almost identical with those of normal social contact. The makers of this test have profited well by this opportunity, and have devised problems that are as natural as that of understanding a name over the telephone.

The test contains three groups of questions. In the first, the student sees before him four words or word groups that are similar but not identical in sound, and upon hearing one of them pronounced, indicates which one he has heard. In the second, the student listens while the examiner reads aloud in French a sentence that is complete except for the final word. The student then writes, in either French or English, the word that rightly completes the thought of the sentence. In the third type, the examiner reads aloud a definition of an object or an idea and the student then writes in a single word what it is that has been described. In these last two groups, the answer is to be found in the question itself, and a well-trained student can do all parts of the test without any reference to English.

Part III, the definition series, is the least satisfactory section, for definitions are devious at best, and such a one as Item 20 (Form B, Part III) "action de se mettre la nourriture dans la bouche, la mâcher avec les dents, l'infiltrer de salive and ensuite de l'avaler" seems to go a very long way around. But such heaviness and artificiality occur only rarely, and a much more typical item is Item 24 of the same section: "plante dont on fume les feuilles desséchées."

The authors provide one or two reassuring bits of information that may forestall criticism on certain points. In the first part, the test of "phonetic accuracy," two methods of administration were employed, one in which the student heard four words or word groups and saw one, the other in which he saw four groups and heard one. As there was no appreciable difference in the results of these two methods, the second and obviously shorter method was retained. Also, the scores on this part of the test were compared with ratings based on phonograph recordings of individual pronunciation by several classes of high school and college students, with correlations as high as .84 on the two types of test. The writers feel, therefore, that they have devised what is a reasonably reliable index of a student's pronunciation.

The test contains many useful reminders such as "account for every test sheet; avoid pantomime; do not finish the incompleted sentence inadvertently" and to the students "avoid coughing and shuffling of feet." The presence of such practical details gives the user confidence that the authors have done a thorough job in perfecting this test in the only way such a test can be perfected, that is, in collaboration with the student.

[1355]

Miller-Davis French Test. First, second years; 1935; 1 form, 2 levels; 50¢ per 25; 15¢ per specimen set; 40(45) minutes; Minnie Miller and Vera Davis; Emporia, Kan.: Bureau of Educational Measurements, Kansas State Teachers College.
a) TEST I. First year.
b) TEST II. Second year.

REFERENCES

1 VANDER BEKE, GEORGE E. *French Work Book.* Publications of the American and Canadian Committees on Modern Languages, Vol. 15. New York: Macmillan Co., 1929. Pp. xiii, 188. $1.10. Paper. (London: Macmillan & Co., Ltd. 5s. 6d.)

Walter V. Kaulfers, Associate Professor of Education in Foreign Languages, Stanford University. Tests I and II are about as reliable and valid as any short 40-minute omnibus tests of general achievement in a foreign language can be. Whether or not the tests serve adequately to measure all the things claimed—vocabulary, pronunciation, grammar, translation, reading for thought content, and information on French life and culture, is questionable. No effort has seemingly been made to compute the reliability and validity of the individual parts devoted to vocabulary, grammar, pronunciation, etc. Consequently, the test cannot be considered diagnostic except in the sense of indicating general areas of weakness. Even for this purpose, however, the items on French culture are too few (only 8 in Test II, and only 5 in Test I) to be indicative of anything at all. In Test II these few items are included among purely vocabulary items with the result that the validity of the section is jeopardized.

Nevertheless, this innovation, feeble as it is, represents a significant beginning in achievement testing in the foreign languages. It represents the probable trend of the future. Indeed, many frontier workers in the foreign languages are ready even now to evaluate their offerings primarily in terms of functional reading ability and functional cultural acquirements in the way of useful information and desirable attitudes, interests, and appreciations acquired in and through the foreign language conceived as a means of communication. Apparently the cultural objective is taking root sufficiently to be given incidental consideration in testing programs. However, if the *Miller-Davis French Tests* truly represent answers to the prayers of high-school teachers for tests that will do justice to what they teach, then it is evident that most French teachers are still spending most of their time drilling students on nonfunctional grammar-translation or proofreading exercises. In reality, Parts III and IV in both tests might well be omitted as failing to measure anything worth measuring as an indication of the student's ability to use French correctly in his *own* original oral or written speech. The transfer value of proofreading or translation exercises in formal grammar to actual extemporaneous or impromptu speech has yet to be demonstrated in any language. The evidence to date tends overwhelmingly to indicate that there is little or no transfer value at all. Despite this fact Tests I and II devote more items to grammar than to any other phase of French. The number of items devoted

Lundeberg-Tharp Audition Test in French

to grammar even exceeds the number assigned to reading. The reading sections are, in fact, the least objective of the six parts of the tests. It is unfortunate that multiple-choice or true-false correction-type items could not have been used here.

By and large the tests are about as satisfactory and inexpensive as any brief omnibus measures of general achievement in conservative French courses. The tests have the advantage of brevity and simplicity in giving and scoring (except Part VI in both tests which involves handwriting). One disadvantage is the small type in which the tests are printed. Moreover, the norms must be used with some caution since they are based on only 469 cases for Test I and 500 cases for Test II. Fortunately these norms represent the achievement of students in several different schools and localities.

James B. Tharp, Associate Professor of Education, The Ohio State University. Of the 100 points to be scored, 5 points each are given to pronunciation and to cultural information in Test I, and similarly, 10 and 8 points respectively in Test II. While highly desirable from the point of view of coverage, the smallness of the sampling renders this use of the time consumed rather dubious. These areas merit measurement each by a separate test. Unless the samplings can be increased to a point more safely valid, these sections had better be omitted.

Part I of each test lists 30 vocabulary items (of which the last 5 are high-frequency idioms). The items have been well chosen and the selection responses thoughtfully arranged. There are 19, 8, and 3 items respectively from the first three 500-word groups of the *French Word Book*[1] in Test I; and 12, 4, 8, 3, and 3 items from respective groups in Test II. On a point-ratio basis, calling the first 500 groups worth 1, the second, 2, etc., the Index of Frequency of Test I is 1.13; of Test II, 2.37. Again the only danger is the small size of the sampling; the range is excellent. Of the various techniques employed to measure grammar, the most nearly valid is that of Part III of Test I, a completion exercise with 4-item selection responses. The partial-translation completions of Part IV, as usual, permit only the testing of forms and agreements. The translation to

French of English verb forms of Part III, Test II, is valid for composition aims, but the arrangement of the partial-translation completions of Part IV leaves much to be desired. It causes such a hybrid as *"nous of it avons besoin,"* a child that neither a French nor an English mother would recognize. Had the English phrase been placed in front of the incomplete French sentence with no blank indicated, both form and position could have been measured by requiring the complete sentence to be written with the missing item in its proper place. Preferably, with a preceding sentence to set the problem, a mutation exercise could have measured this phenomenon much more effectively.

In Part VI, paragraph comprehension is tested by two and three paragraphs of 100 to 200 running words, very well chosen as to advance of vocabulary burden between the two levels. Unfortunately, there are too many questions on each paragraph, and of the 25 in Test I, 12 are of yes-no type, good only for vocabulary testing through the requirement to respond only in English. Fewer items, factual and thought questions, weighted if it is desired to give more value to reading, would probably give a more valid measurement of comprehension.

One serious defect of all the multiple-choice sections of the test is the failure to provide for the correction formula [Score $= R - W/(N-1)$]. For example, when a four-choice response is used, one may score 25 per cent by a random guess. The writer tried this out in the 30-item vocabulary tests, marking the third response down the list. There were 7 and 9 items on Tests I and II, respectively, correct by this guess. The test author virtually spotted the candidate fourteen points on each test, as proved when the reviewer guessed at all the other selection type exercises in the same way. With correction formulas provided for, a stiffening of the questions on paragraph comprehension, a refinement of technique in measuring grammar, and omission of pronunciation and culture tests in favor of more extensive testing of these areas by other instruments (in particular the *Miller Test on French Life and Culture* and one of several aural tests), the excellent range and choice of content of these tests could be reworked into highly desirable measurements of general achievement in French.

Miller-Davis French Test

[1356]

Standard French Test: Vocabulary, Grammar, and Comprehension. Semesters 1-5: high school; 1929; 1 form; $1.50 per 25; 15¢ per specimen set; Peter Sammartino and Carl A. Krause; Bloomington, Ill.: Public School Publishing Co.
a) PART I. 28(35) minutes.
b) PART II. 32(40) minutes.

REFERENCES

1 SAMMARTINO, PETER. "An Experiment in Modern Languages." B High Points 10:15-21 N '28.
2 SAMMARTINO, PETER. "A Standardized Test in Modern Languages." J Ed Res 20:231-3 O '29.

Laura B. Johnson, Assistant Professor in the Teaching of French, The University of Wisconsin. This test covers vocabulary, grammar, and comprehension in each of its two parts. The reviewer's opinion that Part II is definitely more difficult than Part I is corroborated by the higher score made throughout Part I by first, second, third, and fourth semester students in all but two instances. It leads one to wonder why first or even second semester students should spend time taking the second part on which they can hope to recognize relatively few items. If one considers both parts as a whole, the test includes 100 words to be identified in five-response multiple-choice exercises, 50 grammatical items to be filled in with the correct French words, and five brief reading passages on each of which five English questions are to be answered. The words in the vocabulary test are wisely chosen, with few exceptions, and the grammatical items are based on constructions most frequently drilled in class. The test on comprehension seems quite inadequate because of the extreme brevity of the passages chosen and the nature of the questions which seem to reduce interpretation of the reading passage to almost verbatim translation. The test can be easily and quickly administered, graded, and scored.

GERMAN

[1357]

American Council Alpha German Test. Grades 9-16; 1926-27; 2 forms; 2 parts; 35¢ per specimen set; 40(45) minutes per part; V. A. C. Henmon, B. Q. Morgan, Stella M. Hinz, C. M. Purin, and Elizabeth Rossberg; prepared for the Modern Language Study under the auspices of the American Council on Education and the Conference of Canadian Universities; Yonkers, N. Y.: World Book Co.
a) PART I [VOCABULARY AND GRAMMAR]. $1.30 per 25.
b) PART II [SILENT READING AND COMPOSITION]. $1.25 per 25.

REFERENCES

1 MORGAN, B. Q., EDITOR. *German Frequency Word Book*: based on Kaeding's Häufigkeitswörterbuch der deutschen Sprache. Publications of the American and Canadian Committees on Modern Languages, Vol. 9. New York: Macmillan Co.,

1928. Pp. xv, 87. $0.75. Paper. (London: Macmillan & Co., Ltd. 2s. 6d.)
2 HENMON, V. A. C. *Achievement Tests in Modern Foreign Languages*: Prepared for the Modern Language Study and the Canadian Committee on Modern Languages, pp. 1-266. Publications of the American and Canadian Committees on Modern Languages, Vol. 5. New York: Macmillan Co., 1929. Pp. xxvii, 363. $1.00. Paper. (London: Macmillan & Co., Ltd. 4s. 6d.)
3 American Association of Teachers of German, Committee on the Word List. "Minimum Standard Vocabulary for German." German Q 7:87-119 My '34.

C. H. Handschin, Professor of German and Executive Officer of Graduate Work, Miami University. REVIEW OF PART I. This is an effective test, as far as the general technique goes. An adequate manual of directions and key are supplied. The first item is a multiple-choice vocabulary test, and consists of 100 German words, each followed by five English words, one of which is the equivalent of the German word. The task is to select this equivalent from among the five English words.

This multiple-response exercise is well known. However, it is not suited in this form to modern language testing because the one being tested must spend his time studying English words, instead of German words; i.e., he must compare the English words, one after another, with his idea of what the German word means. His attention is therefore predominantly on the English words.

It would be far better in these multiple-choice responses as used in foreign language tests, if there were one English word and five German words, one of which were the equivalent of the German word. It would be presumed that he knew the English word and his time would be spent on trying to recall the meaning of the five German words, all of which would redound to his knowledge of German.

Another weakness of this vocabulary test is the fact that the words were taken from Morgan's adaptation [1] of Kaeding's frequency list. It should instead be based on the "Minimum Standard Vocabulary for German," [3] the official list of the American Association of Teachers of German. This list was not available when this test was written.

This official list is far superior to Kaeding's list. (*See* Morgan's *German Frequency Word Book*, which is based on Kaeding's list.) In the first place, about 400 words were eliminated as belonging to realms not needed by our American students, and then quite a number of use-words eminently useful for our students were added. Future tests should be based only on this list.

The second item in the test is made up of multiple-choice exercises on grammatical forms in sentences. There are fifty English sentences. Each one is followed by four German sentences, one of which is correct. This is the proper technique, as the time and effort of the one being tested is spent in studying the four German sentences.

The grammatical knowledge necessary to do these exercises is what is known as recognitional (not functional) knowledge of grammar. Since the recognitional grammar is now in many schools the sole grammatical objective, this sort of test may be welcomed.

The test shows another weakness in that it is nowhere stated what stage of ability (how many semesters of work) the test proposes to test. It is assumed that it is meant to test two years of college, or four years of high school work.

REVIEW OF PART II. Item 1 of this test is writing a composition in eight minutes about the picture reproduced on the first inside cover page. This is a difficult task and should be demanded only of classes that have had considerable work in writing German. Writing is a perfectly legitimate objective, if time is ample. In most schools the first, sometimes the only objective, is a reading knowledge. In such classes as this the exercise might be omitted.

The scoring is not as simple as on the other parts of the test. It is done by the aid of the scale supplied and can be done only by the teacher, or other competent person.

Item 2 is a test of silent reading, and consists of seven paragraphs of increasing difficulty, chosen on the basis of preliminary testing. Whether the gradation of difficulty is absolutely correct or not makes no great difference.

The technique employed is to base a number of German questions on each paragraph. These are to be answered in English. This is a proper gauge of comprehension, as the precise thought must be reproduced.

The weakness of the test is that it does not state what portion of the frequency word list it tests, whether the first 1,000, 1,500 or 2,000 words, or what.

It is necessary that the test be based on a certain portion or on the entire frequency word list, and that this be then stated in the description of the test. For no teacher can guarantee that his pupils know any portion of the frequency word list—no matter how

many ordinary reading texts his class has read, unless he teaches the words of the word list somehow in addition. If, therefore, his class is to take a test successfully he should know what portion of the frequency word list it tests.

[1358]
American Council on Education German Reading Test. 2 semesters or more of college German; 1937-38; Forms A and B; 5¢ per test, 10 to 99 copies; 25¢ per specimen set; 50(55) minutes; prepared for the Committee on Modern Languages; E. P. Appelt and V. A. C. Henmon; New York: Cooperative Test Service.

For a review by Curtis C. D. Vail, see 999.

[1359]
Columbia Research Bureau German Test. Grades 9-15; 1926-27; 2 forms; $1.30 per 25; 20¢ per specimen set; 90(95) minutes; C. M. Purin and Ben D. Wood; Yonkers, N. Y.: World Book Co.

REFERENCES

1 WOOD, BEN D. *New York Experiments with New-Type Modern Language Tests*: Including a Survey of Modern Language Achievement in the Junior High Schools of New York City, June, 1925; The Regents Experiment of June, 1925, with New-Type Tests in French, German, Spanish, and Physics; and A Second Survey of Modern Language Achievement in the Junior High Schools of New York City, June, 1926, pp. 105-319. Publications of the American and Canadian Committees on Modern Languages, Vol. 1. New York: Macmillan Co., 1927. Pp. xxii, 339. Paper. Out of print.

Harold B. Dunkel, Examiner, Board of Examinations, The University of Chicago. These tests consist of three parts: I, Vocabulary, 25 minutes; II, Comprehension, 20 minutes; and III, Grammar, 45 minutes. The norms are derived from the New York Regents examination of 1925.

Part I presents 100 isolated German words with the answers in multiple-choice form. That the words are not given in context is certainly a serious objection. Whatever the instructional method followed, reading is always an important, and usually the primary, objective; and vocabulary is usually taught and learned with reading in view. Hence it seems logical that vocabulary should be tested in some manner which approximates the reading situation. But even granting the present technique, we find flaws in its execution. In a good many cases, the student selects his answer, not from all four or five possibilities offered (unfortunately only four possibilities are printed for some items), but from fewer. For example, although the capitalization plainly indicates which German words are nouns—English verbs, adverbs, and adjectives are offered as possible distractors for them. These possibilities the student immediately rules out. Or, frequently the correct answer and its opposite (e.g., wet, dry) are both included. The experienced test-taker guesses that the correct answer is one of these, and his chances become one out of two, not one out of five.

Part II contains 75 statements of the true-false type and shows all the faults of this form. The familiar determiners (manchmal, alle, nie, immer, oft selten, and the like) frequently betray the answer. Even worse are some statements of doubtful validity in a German examination. That "Ein Pfund Eisen wiegt mehr als ein Pfund Wolle" is obviously a false statement, but one can catch too many people on this item in English for it to be a valid item in a German test. Similarly, to decide the truth or falsity of "Damit der Luftballon in die Höhe steige, muss er mit einem Gase gefüllt werden, das schwerer ist als die atmosphärische Luft" demands some knowledge of physics as well as of German. Even worse are statements of the proverbial sort like: "Oft sprechen die Leute am meisten, welche nichts zu sagen haben," or "Jede Dummheit findet einen, der sie macht." Before I can pass judgment on "Nach einem heissen Tage folgt manchmal eine kühle Nacht," I must have some idea of what the author means by "manchmal" and some reports from the weather bureau. With items like these, it is nothing short of miraculous that this section ever attained its published reliability of .80. In any event, I doubt whether the ability here tested is ability to read with some comprehension continuous passages of German.

Part III, though called grammar, really tests, through sentence completion, active ability to use the language in writing and speaking rather than ability to read. Aside from such help as this power may give in reading, writing and speaking have a legitimate place in modern foreign language instruction. I wonder, however, whether this place is sufficiently great to merit one-half the testing time. If we dismiss this objection, this section of the test, as might be expected from the time devoted to it, does seem an adequate sampling of the actual knowledge required for writing and speaking on an elementary level, and appears to merit its reliability of .95.

The norms are based on examinations of 1925. Considering the changes in language instruction which have taken place since that date, I am extremely dubious of the value of these norms. The fact that they are based on pupils from New York state alone also makes them of questionable national value. Furthermore, they are entirely in terms of high school years; consequently, for high school no semester norms are available, and the college instructor must content himself with his best guess as to how his semesters or quarters correspond with high-school years in New York during the year 1925.

In the past thirteen years more progress has been made in testing than in automobile construction. To say that this test and a 1926 Ford appear odd to us is no reflection on the authors or Mr. Ford. Both the test and the car were good in their day; but that day has passed.

[1360]

Cooperative German Test [Advanced Form]. 4 semesters or more: high school; or 1 year or more: college; 1933-40; 40- and 90-minute editions; 25¢ per specimen set of either edition; Advanced Form P: Miriam Van Dyck Hespelt, E. Herman Hespelt, and Geraldine Spaulding; Advanced Form Q: Miriam Van Dyck Hespelt, E. Herman Hespelt, and Geraldine Spaulding with the editorial assistance of E. W. Bagster-Collins, E. E. Cochran, Warner F. Gookin, C. M. Purin, and E. H. Zeydel; New York: Cooperative Test Service.
a) FORMS 1935, 1936, AND 1937. Forms 1933 and 1934 are out of print; 6¢ per test, 10 to 99 copies; 90(95) minutes.
b) REVISED SERIES ADVANCED FORMS N, O, P, AND Q. 1937-40; 5¢ per test, 10 to 99 copies; 1½¢ per machine-scorable answer sheet; 40(45) minutes.

REFERENCES

1 MORGAN, B. Q. *A German Frequency Word Book*: Based on Kaeding's Häufigkeitswörterbuch der deutschen Sprache. Publications of the American and Canadian Committees on Modern Languages, Vol. 9. New York: Macmillan Co., 1928. Pp. xiii, 87. $0.75. Paper. (London: Macmillan & Co., Ltd. 2s. 6d.)
2 HAUCH, EDWARD F. *A German Idiom List*: Selected on the Basis of Frequency and Range of Occurrence. Publications of the American and Canadian Committees on Modern Languages, Vol. 8. New York: Macmillan Co., 1929. Pp. xi, 98. $0.80. Paper. (London: Macmillan & Co., Ltd. 2s. 6d.)
3 PATERSON, DONALD G.; SCHNEIDLER, GWENDOLEN G.; AND WILLIAMSON, EDMUND G. *Student Guidance Techniques*, pp. 143-5. New York: McGraw-Hill Book Co., Inc., 1938. Pp. xviii, 316. $3.00. (London: McGraw-Hill Publishing Co., Ltd. 18s.)
4 HANNA, JOSEPH V. "A Comparison of Cooperative Test Scores and High School Grades as Measures for Predicting Achievement in College." *J Appl Psychol* 23:289-97 Ap '39.

C. H. Handschin, Professor of German and Executive Officer of Graduate Work, Miami University. [Review of Advanced Form P.] This test is designed for groups having had four semesters or more of high school work, or at least one year of college work. The test is divided into three parts. Part I, Reading, consists of 45 sentence-completion exercises. An incomplete German sentence is given, followed by five German words or phrases, only one of which makes sense. Beginning with Item 32, several exercises are based on a single portion of text. There are 45 exercises all told in this part.

Part II is a multiple-choice vocabulary test. A German word is followed by five other German words, only one of which is an equivalent of the first word given. The task is to select the equivalent word.

This also is a proper technique; i.e., giving one German word or phrase, followed by a number of German words or phrases. This technique can be employed whether the test attempts to test single words, phrases, sentences, or syntactical expressions.

Part III contains 40 multiple-choice completion exercises, the part to be supplied consisting in this case of grammatical forms. An English sentence is given, followed by a correct German translation except that one word is omitted. There follow five forms, only one of which is correct in the sentence as given. The task is to choose and insert this correct form.

The knowledge called for includes articles, interrogative pronouns, verb forms, personal pronouns, adjectives, possessives, relative pronouns, case and inflections of nouns and pronouns, auxiliary verbs, and cases after (prepositions, word position, etc.).

The knowledge called for is of functional grammar, since the examinee must not only recognize the form in question but must choose a form to fit into the sentence.

This is an effective test. Here again, however, there is no proper account of the derivation of the test given. There is merely a footnote on page eighteen of the Handbook implying that the source of the material used is Morgan's *German Frequency Word Book*,[1] and Hauch's *German Idiom List*.[2] As in the case of the other texts discussed above, there is no statement as to what portions of the word or idiom list the test is based on. To be sure there is no frequency list of syntactical expressions for German yet.

For a review by Curtis C. D. Vail, see 1000.

[1361]

Cooperative German Test [Elementary Form]. 1-6 semesters: grades 6-9; 1937-39; 25¢ per specimen set of either edition; Elementary Form P: Emma Popper, Alice Miller, and Lucy M. Will; New York: Cooperative Test Service.
a) JUNIOR FORMS 1933 and 1934. Form 1935 is out of print; 6¢ per test, 10 to 99 copies; 90(95) minutes.
b) ELEMENTARY FORMS N, O, AND P. 1937-39; 5¢ per test, 10 to 99 copies; 1½¢ per machine-scorable answer sheet; 40(45) minutes.

For a review by Curtis C. D. Vail, see 1001.

ITALIAN

[1362]

Cooperative Italian Test. 2 semesters or more: high school or college; 1940; Experimental Form Q; 6¢ per test, 10 to 99 copies; 25¢ per specimen set; 70(75) minutes; Peter Riccio and Anthony Cuffari; New York: Cooperative Test Service.

LATIN

[1363]

Cicero Test. High school and college; 1937; 1 form; 50¢ per 25; 10¢ per specimen set; 40(45) minutes; Mary Alice Seller and H. E. Schrammel; Emporia, Kan.: Bureau of Educational Measurements, Kansas State Teachers College.

S. D. Atkins, Department of Classics, Princeton University. Part I contains a long passage taken from Cicero's second speech against Verres and twenty appended true-false statements. Its aim is to test the student's ability to read and comprehend Ciceronian Latin. That aim has been admirably achieved by a careful choice of the reading passage and a skillful construction of the true-false statements. This is the most important and valuable section of a test that has many good features, but is very badly proportioned. This first portion is almost a complete test of 40 minutes in itself and yet that is the time allowance for the whole test. The reading selection consists of 1½ Teubner pages or, more exactly, 54 lines. Even the most brilliant student at the Cicero level cannot read and really comprehend 54 lines of a Verrine oration which he has not previously seen, and adequately handle the appended statements in less than 20 or 25 minutes. That leaves 15 or 20 minutes to answer the 56 other items on the test. All items weigh equally in the determination of the final score. It is my opinion that the time limit for this test should be extended 20 minutes at least and Part I should count much more heavily than the other two parts or the whole test should be drastically pruned. In either case the time allotments *for each part* ought to be clearly indicated.

Part II (14 items) examines a knowledge of syntax through the medium of the continuous narrative. Certain words and phrases are printed in bold face in the narrative and then are printed again below followed by technical terms descriptive of various grammatical constructions. The student is required to make a correct choice from the several possibilities. For example: "( ) 22. *nullīs*. 1. dative, ind. obj. 2. dat. of possession. 3. dat. of person judging." The Latin passage consists of 36 Teubner lines taken from the third speech *In Catilinam*. The employment of the continuous narrative as an instrument for testing syntax is praiseworthy. The attachment thereto of questions that emphasize correct "pigeonholing" rather than correct perception of relations is deplorable, particularly when it necessitates a familiarity with such absurd artificial refinements as a "dative of person judging" which, according to the key, is the correct answer in the example cited above.

Part III, comprising 42 true-false statements, is divided into two sections. Section A continues the examination of an ability to remember technical labels and formal rules of grammar. The statements are of this kind: "( ) 41. There are at least seven ways of expressing purpose in Latin." For some reason not apparent to me there are two statements in this group totally unrelated to the rest, one concerning consuls and the other the praetorship. It is my belief that this section might be deleted with little loss. Section B tests a factual knowledge of social life, political events and figures, and governmental organization in the Ciceronian period. In general, the statements are well-formulated, of a sufficiently wide range, and as thought-provoking as any of a true-false type can be.

The following corrections are suggested: *causa* for *causā* in line 45, Part I; "Sicily" for "Italy" in Item 5 of Part I (or − for + on the answer key); *ac* for *as* in line 4, Part II, Section A; *restitisse* for *resistisse* in line 4, Part II, Section B; and "causal" for "casual" in Item 28 of Part II. It is also suggested that the words translated or explained in the footnotes to the comprehension selection in Part I receive some sort of identification mark in the text itself.

With some revision this could be made an acceptable test of the objective type.

[1364]

Cooperative Latin Test [Advanced Form]. 2 years or more of Latin; 1933-40; 40- and 90-minute editions; 25¢ per specimen set of either edition; Advanced Form P: John C. Kirtland assisted by Ruth B. McJimsey and Bernard M. Allen; Advanced Form Q: George A. Land; New York: Cooperative Test Service.
a) FORMS 1933, 1936, AND 1937. Forms 1934 and 1935 are out of print; 6¢ per test, 10 to 99 copies; 1½¢ per

machine-scorable answer sheet for Form 1937; 90(95) minutes.
b) REVISED SERIES, ADVANCED FORMS N, O, P, AND Q. 1937-40; 5¢ per test, 10 to 99 copies; 1½¢ per machine-scorable answer sheets; 40(45) minutes.

For a review by Norman T. Pratt, Jr., see 1064.

[1365]

Cooperative Latin Test [Elementary Form]. 1-3 semesters: high school; 1933-40; 40- and 90-minute editions; 25¢ per specimen set of either edition; Elementary Form P: John C. Kirtland assisted by Ruth B. McJimsey and Geraldine Spaulding; Elementary Form Q: George A. Land; New York: Cooperative Test Service.
a) JUNIOR FORMS 1934, 1936, AND 1937. Forms 1933 and 1935 are out of print; 6¢ per test, 10 to 99 copies; 1½¢ per machine-scorable answer sheet for Form 1937; 90(95) minutes.
b) REVISED SERIES, ELEMENTARY FORMS O, P, AND Q. 1937-40; Form N is out of print; 5¢ per test, 10 to 99 copies; 1½¢ per machine-scorable answer sheet.

Harold B. Dunkel, Examiner, Board of Examinations, The University of Chicago. [Review of Form P.] This test consists of the three sections common to the Cooperative foreign language tests: Part I, Reading, is tested by the paragraph-question method; Part II, Vocabulary, is represented by 100 isolated words; Part III, Grammar, is tested by the correct completion of Latin sentences. All sections are in multiple-choice form.

If we are sincere in our claims that the student's ability to read Latin understandingly is the primary aim in elementary instruction, Part I is the most important part of the test. Yet I doubt whether Part I is an instrument able to bear the responsibility of measuring the primary objective. The difficulties of producing adequate passages with words drawn from a frequency list, of framing searching yet unambiguous questions on them, and of cramming all this material into one testing period are familiar to anyone who has attempted the task himself. Yet even to a kindly judge, this section appears to have serious shortcomings. The passages themselves are not bad; but the thought moves very jerkily with little by way of transition. Hence, the stories rather fly along, and I was tempted to mark the first passage as "absurd" though the key indicates "sorrowful." The chief fault lies in the questions which are too few in number to test adequately the student's comprehension. Very few of the questions are searching. Some of them are slightly ambiguous; some of them even answer preceding questions. These shortcomings are surprising since many of the items are good. My main criticism is, however, that there are too few penetrating questions for even the necessarily elementary subject matter. In its present form this section gives unnecessary aid and comfort to those who believe that translation is the only valid test of reading ability.

Part II would be much more valuable if the words were presented in context. Depending upon the context, a rare word may be easily understandable or a common word puzzling. Vocabulary in itself is nothing; it is only an aid to reading, and we test it only because of its relation to reading. Hence, the student's vocabulary is important only in context and should be tested there.

The desirability of Part III is even more questionable. In the case of the modern foreign languages which the student may sometimes write or speak, the ability tested by this section (which might better be labeled composition rather than grammar) may be important. But in Latin, the student needs only enough grammatical knowledge to be able to read intelligently. Certainly that is not the ability tested here. The active knowledge demanded by this section may well contribute to reading ability, but I should consider it questionable whether its contribution entitles it to fifteen minutes of a forty-minute test.

In general, I feel that Part I should have better questions and more of them so that it is, in itself, a valid test of reading comprehension. This change would involve lengthening this section. Why not take time for an adequate measurement of our prime objective? Measurement of vocabulary is important only in diagnosis of reading progress. It should, then, probably be measured on the reading passages. Then we shall know that Johnny can't read because he doesn't know the words. If he doesn't know the words and yet can read, knowing the words is not important. The same statement is true of grammar. In short, if—and it is no easy task—Part I could be expanded to form the entire test with certain items included which would yield part-scores on functional vocabulary and grammar, we should have a much better instrument than the present one whose value in testing attainment of the reading objective seems very limited.

John Flagg Gummere, Chairman of the Latin Department, William Penn Charter School, *Philadelphia, Pennsylvania.* [Review of Form P.] Part I consists of reading for comprehension. There are four passages of made Latin of approximately the same length, but graded in difficulty. Each passage is followed by five incomplete statements. With each incomplete statement there are given five words or phrases, and the pupil is to select the word or phrase in each instance which "most correctly" (sic!) completes the statement. It is difficult to say much in a short Latin passage with the limited vocabulary permitted in an elementary test; as a result, little could be said for the literary quality or narrative attainment of the four selections. Yet this should not be considered as preventing pupils from revealing their ability to comprehend Latin. Moreover, the type of question is necessitated by the fact that the tests are to be marked objectively. Translation is a better guide to an evaluation of a pupil's knowledge of Latin, but this test does not pretend to furnish that kind of evaluation.

Part II is a multiple-choice vocabulary test. With each Latin word are given five words or phrases, and the pupil is to select the word or phrase "which most nearly corresponds in meaning." It is true that such a test tends to equate the meaning of a Latin word with a definite English word; such practice is a direct violation of the principles of real semantic study. On the other hand, we are dealing with a test that is supposed to reveal a pupil's knowledge, and this type of multiple-choice exercise will be done well by a pupil who has a good Latin vocabulary, and poorly by one who has not. It is my opinion that no real harm is done by equating Latin *socius* and English *ally,* for instance. If the classroom work emphasizes the fact that *sequor* and *socius* are from variant forms of the same root, the semantic development of the word *socius* will be clear; if not, the situation will be made no worse by the equation of meaning. It is evident that a better test could be made by asking the meaning of words in a context, but that procedure is prevented by practical considerations of testing. Some multiple-choice tests of this type include nonsense words among the possibilities offered to the pupil. In this test objection could be made to the giving of such words as *pulley* and *comport.* An intelligent student knows quite well that he has not met the word for *pulley*; a great many students, regardless of intelligence would, at this age, be entirely ignorant of the meaning of the verb *comport*.

Part III contains thirty-five incomplete sentences each to be completed by selecting one of a group of five words or phrases. I object to giving, among the possible answers, forms that do not actually exist in Latin (e.g., viren, hominos, mitteberis), since it is not good practice to permit pupils to see such pseudo forms at any time, least of all in print.

The time and percentage of questions are divided thus: Part I—15 minutes, 19 per cent; Part II—10 minutes, 48 per cent; Part III—15 minutes, 33 per cent. I think that the time and the value given to Part I is proportionately too small, and should prefer that it be given half the time and half the questions.

The examiner is furnished with every possible assistance: a scoring key, complete tables of norms, and a 16-page booklet giving directions for administering the tests and interpreting the results. Percentile scores have been compiled from a satisfactorily large number of student scores; the tables are divided according to the location and type of schools so that public-school records are separated from independent-school records.

The test has been so carefully proofread that nowhere is there an error; in fact, misprints are limited to exactly one piece of type, from a wrong font, in Part III, Item 17-2. This bespeaks the great care that has been exercised in its preparation.

For a review by S. D. Atkins, see 1065.

[1366]

Holtz Vergil Test. High school and college; 1937; 1 form; 60¢ per 25; 10¢ per specimen set; 40(45) minutes; W. L. Holtz and H. E. Schrammel; Emporia, Kan.: Bureau of Educational Measurements, Kansas State Teachers College.

W. L. Carr, Professor of Latin, Columbia University. This test, which is offered in only one form, is described as including "translation, thought content, syntax, scansion, and mythology based on selected passages from the Aeneid I-IV." This description is inaccurate in four particulars. No "translation" is called for; Part V, ostensibly on scansion and requiring a choice of one of five words which "correctly completes" each of five incomplete "hexameter verses," is really a test in recalling the verse as Vergil wrote it; the 18 items in Part III and the 22 items in Part V call for a knowledge of the content and back-

ground of Aeneid I-VI and not of Aeneid I-IV alone; and Parts I and II are based on a single passage, not on "passages."

Part I consists of 23 true-false statements based on a thirty-line passage taken from the beginning of the second book of the Aeneid and is obviously intended to test the "thought content" (i.e., the pupil's comprehension) of the passage. This passage is almost sure to have been read by the pupils taking the test, and one or more passages which the pupil had presumably *not* seen would provide a better test of his ability to comprehend Latin. The 18 items in Part III also test comprehension, for they consist of questions in Latin with multiple-choice answers in Latin, although these questions would seem to be intended primarily as a test of the pupil's ability to identify certain persons, places, and events mentioned in Aeneid I-VI. Part VI also calls for some comprehension, but it is obviously primarily intended to test the pupil's knowledge of the identity of the twelve persons and places listed.

The test consists of a total of 96 items arranged in six parts, but except for Part II (on forms and syntax) it would be hard to say just what each part really tests. Furthermore, the 96 items are lumped together in the scoring, a procedure which would be justifiable only if all the items were of equal weight and if a wrong response in the true-or-false portions of the test were no more serious than a wrong response in the multiple-choice portions. This lump score would have some value as a measure of general proficiency in Latin and of a general knowledge of the content of Aeneid I-VI, but its diagnostic value would seem to this reviewer to be very low.

Careless proofreading in the matter of macrons seriously lessens the value of the test, e.g., *Troia eversa* is used as an ablative absolute phrase in a Latin question in which all the other long vowels are indicated. Some of these Latin questions are pretty bad in other ways; e.g., "Qui cognatus Ascanio erat Hector"?

Norman T. Pratt, Jr., Department of Classics, Princeton University. This test, including "items concerned with translation, thought content, syntax, scansion, and mythology based on selected passages from the *Aeneid*, Books I-IV," "was constructed for use as an achievement test for classes pursuing work in this field in high school or college." It is crowded in format and appears to contain more material than can properly be tested in the forty minutes allotted. Of its six parts two are, laudably, based directly upon the first thirty lines of the fourth book of the *Aeneid*. Part I consists of twenty-three questions on thought content, some of which seemingly could easily be guessed by anyone familiar with the general context and none of which touch the pathos of the passage very deeply; indeed, it is doubtful that the significance of such a passage *can* really be penetrated by any such technique as the true and false questions here employed. Also appended to the passage are sixteen Latin words selected therefrom; beside each is a designation of form and construction to be marked true or false. Knowledge of forms and syntax is thus well tested in context. There are a few minor imperfections: the case of Item 27 might as well be dative as ablative; in Item 31 *vellum* is misprinted for *vellem*; and the grammatical terminology of Item 35, "substantive volitive clause," is unnecessarily obscure. Parts III and IV may be considered together. The former contains eighteen questions in Latin concerning the story and background of the *Aeneid*, each with five brief Latin answers of which the correct one is to be indicated; their function is to test knowledge of factual details. In the latter there are twenty-two incomplete statements in English concerning the story, meter, mythology, and literary matters, each to be completed by the selection of one of five possibilities also given in English. Most of these questions, too, are of a mechanical nature, and it is noteworthy that the attempt to introduce more weighty matters results in a question of the following type: "From the Roman standpoint the strongest element in the character of Aeneas was: 1. courage in battle; 2. consideration for his companions in distress; 3. obedience and submission to the will of Fate; 4. devotion to his father; 5. affection for his son." Number three is the correct answer, but it is at least very presumptuous to rule out numbers one, four, and five. Herein lies an indication of the most serious deficiency in the objective Latin test in general. Even if the faults of inanity, transparency, and over-subtlety are avoided in the construction of the questions, there still remains the unavoidable shortcoming that the examinee can not be asked to give a synthesis of his own knowledge. The fundamental capacities to apprehend meaning and to organize material are thus left unexamined and unstimulated. Implicit in any good test should be the examiner's conception of what is significant in his subject matter, and one may be so bold as to say that the objective Latin test never will succeed in representing satisfactorily what is valuable in the study of Latin.

In the fifth part are five incomplete hexameters which the student is to complete by selecting one of five Latin words. This is a good functional test of memory and of skill in meter; it should be made clear in the directions, however, that both the meter and the original reading of each line are to be restored. Finally, Part VI consists of twelve proper names to be identified from a list of seventeen possibilities given in Latin. Here again, whereas it is necessary and desirable that the student of Latin have a knowledge of ancient folklore and geographical terminology, the objection is not so much to this test as to any objective Latin test, namely, that there is much too much emphasis upon mechanical knowledge rather than real comprehension and the use of knowledge.

[1367]

Hutchinson Latin Grammar Scale. High school; 1928; 2 forms; 50¢ per 25; 10¢ per specimen set; 25(30) minutes; Mark E. Hutchinson; Bloomington, Ill.: Public School Publishing Co.

REFERENCES

1 HUTCHINSON, MARK E. "A Standard Latin Grammar Test." *Sch and Soc* 27:47-8 Ja 14 '28.
2 AMERICAN CLASSICAL LEAGUE, ADVISORY COMMITTEE. *The Classical Investigation*: Part One, General Report: A Summary of Results with Recommendations for the Organization of the Course in Secondary Latin and for Improvement in Methods of Teaching. Princeton, N. J.: Princeton University Press, 1924. Pp. vi, 305. Out of print. (An abridged edition, consisting of a reprint of pp. 29-235, may be obtained from the American Classical League, New York University, New York, N. Y. at fifty cents a copy. The abridged edition was published in 1928 and has paper covers.)

S. D. Atkins, Department of Classics, Princeton University. This test involves no knowledge of technical terms usually employed to describe features of syntax but only requires from the student an ability to select from four choices offered the Latin sentence which correctly renders the syntactical principle presented in a complete English sentence. Measured by the recommendations made in *The Classical Investigation*[2] with respect to the principles to be incorporated in the normal four-year course and the distribution of these by semesters, the test, both Scales A and B, covers the first six semesters. Approximately 34 per cent of the items of Scale A belong to the first-semester level, 14 per cent to the second, 23 per cent to the third, 12 per cent to the fourth, and 17 per cent to the fifth and sixth. The corresponding percentages of Scale B are 34 per cent, 17 per cent, 25 per cent, 12 per cent, and 12 per cent. (These figures are only roughly approximate.) As far as constructions tested are concerned Scales A and B are exactly identical in some 25 or 26 items out of 35. The testing sentences and their order, of course, are different. The difficulty value assigned to these sentences by the test author is, in the majority of cases, greater for Scale B. The prospective consumer might like to know how the author can arrive at an assessment of 90 for Item 13, let us say, in Scale A and 96 for Item 17 in Scale B, both of which test the use of the ablative of description in sentences that are quite similar. Such information regarding value-criteria might well be included in the direction folder or references, at least, to sources where that information may be obtained, should be made therein.

The coverage of both scales is satisfactorily comprehensive, save that the pronoun and the uses of the dative should, perhaps, have greater representation, and more time, certainly, should be devoted to the verb, even to the point of lengthening the test. None of the tasks on either scale appears to be excessively difficult. The average time of 42 seconds per item is a generous allowance. The ocular energy required of the student could be reduced considerably and much time, space, and expense saved by changing the format. For example, Item 1 (Scale A), instead of being set up in five separate sentences, could be presented as follows: 1. ( ) The consul, a friend of the soldiers, has set out. *Cōnsul* (a. *amīcus*, b. *amīcī*, c. *amīcō*, d. *amīcum*) *militum profectus est.* All items on both scales, without exception, are adaptable to such revision.

The reviewer must raise the question as to whether a test of this type has justification for existence. The primary immediate objective of an elementary Latin course is to develop an ability to read and understand Latin. For the attainment of that objective educators in recent years have insisted upon a very early introduction of connected reading into the initial stages of Latin study and have emphasized the use of this continuous narrative as a more effec-

Hutchinson Latin Grammar Scale

tive instrument for developing principles of syntax than detached, isolated sentences. It is my opinion that the continuous narrative and questions built thereupon make a far better testing agent than the collection of colorless insipid drill-sentences found in this test.

[1368]

Kansas First Year Latin. First, second semesters: high school; 1936; 2 forms, 2 levels; 50¢ per 25; 15¢ per specimen set; 40(45) minutes; Mary Alice Seller, H. E. Schrammel, and Lois Bellinger; Emporia, Kan.: Bureau of Educational Measurements, Kansas State Teachers College.
a) TEST I, FORMS A AND B. First semester.
b) TEST I, FORMS C AND D. Second semester.

REFERENCES

1 College Entrance Examination Board. *A Latin Word List:* Prepared in Accordance with the Recommendation of the Commission Which Revised the Definition of the Requirement in Latin. New York: the Board, 1927. Pp. 31. $0.25. Paper.

John Flagg Gummere, Chairman of the Latin Department, William Penn Charter School, Philadelphia, Pennsylvania. It is difficult to believe that these tests are actually in use. In spite of an evidently sincere effort to provide valid testing material, the authors have signally failed to provide the thoroughly accurate and well-edited material which the users of tests have a right to demand. The very title omits a hyphen that belongs in the compound modifier "first-year." The directions for securing the raw score state that from the "possible score" should be subtracted the "number wrong and omitted" instead of the number wrong *or* omitted. These are small points, but typical of the tests as a whole. It is quite proper to mark vowel length, but there are almost twenty errors in the markings in each form. There are downright blunders such as *"lex Romanus,"* "King Philippi" (both in Form C), "they are lead" (Form B). Further examples are:

FORM A. The word *cicada,* marked feminine in the vocabulary, is referred to seven times in the questions by a masculine pronoun. Misprints are *prevēnit* and *thonsand.* Two verbs in the Latin reading, supposedly referring to the same time, are in different tenses (*rogāvit* and *respondet*). *Comparābās* is wrongly divided into syllables. *Impecunious* is supposed to mean *lack of money; amiable* to mean *affectionate.* The use of *inquit* outside the quotation which it accompanies is questionable.

FORM C. *Dicione* is written three times with long *e,* suggesting that it is not a mere misprint. The word *imperātor,* used to refer to Flamininus we find translated as *emperor* though the event described took place in 195 B.C. The Latin reading deals with events in Greece after the war between the Romans under Flamininus and King Philip. The following statement appears in the true-false questions: " 'S. P. Q. R.' meant that it was the will of the emperor alone." Observe that the sentence is not English; it is precisely this kind of inexactness that a study of foreign language, particularly of Latin, should eliminate. The question is the more objectionable because S. P. Q. R. is given in its full form in a footnote. Misprints are *adivisse* and *fratem*.

FORM D. Certain rules of grammar, to be used in answering questions in Part III, are said to be "at the right"; as a matter of fact, they are on the next page (not good) and below the questions that run over onto the next page. *Amābant* is to be translated as *did love*. Misprints are *appelāvit* and *mītibus*.

The Latin text is set in small type and in Forms A, C, and D the lines are very close together. We are told that "the content of these tests is based on . . . recommendations of the national committee on Latin teaching." What national committee?

The proportion of questions in the two types of test is as follows: Forms A and B, about 43 per cent on comprehension of Latin and Latin grammar, 23 per cent on word study, and 33 per cent on "background" material; Forms C and D, 57, 17, and 26 per cent respectively. The ratio of questions on Latin itself to other questions is, therefore, in Forms A and B, about 2 to 3; in Forms C and D, about 3 to 2. The ratio should be higher in both types.

With the tests are furnished: a mimeographed sheet of directions (erroneously called a "manual"), a scoring key, and a class record sheet.

The direction sheet gives directions and tables of percentile scores with suggestions for translating such scores into school marks. The percentile scores have been based, for Forms A and B, on 4,035 student scores; for Forms C and D, on 4,354 scores. All these scores were sent in by "410 cooperating schools in four nation-wide testing programs."

If thoroughly edited and revised, the tests would be useful to some schools.

[1369]

Kansas Second Year Latin Test. First, second semesters: high school; 1935; 2 forms, 2 levels; 50¢ per 25; 15¢ per specimen set; 40(45) minutes; W. L.

Holtz and H. E. Schrammel; Emporia, Kan.: Bureau of Educational Measurements, Kansas State Teachers College.
a) TEST II, FORMS A AND B. First semester.
b) TEST II, FORMS C AND D. Second semester.

REFERENCES

1 College Entrance Examination Board. *A Latin Word List*: Prepared in Accordance with the Recommendation of the Commission Which Revised the Definition of the Requirement in Latin. New York: the Board, 1927. Pp. 31. $0.25. Paper.

W. L. Carr, Professor of Latin, Columbia University. This test appears in four forms. Forms A and B, outwardly comparable, are intended for use at the end of the first semester of second-year Latin and Forms C and D, also outwardly comparable, are intended for use at the end of the second semester. The manual of directions gives percentile norms computed from 4,217 student scores.

FORM A. Form A consists of four parts. Part I is intended to test comprehension. It consists of a single 184-word Latin passage taken from Ritchie's "Fabulae Faciles," followed by 25 true-or-false statements. This story about Hercules and the Amazons is found in several second-year textbooks and is, furthermore, fairly familiar to a good many pupils from sources other than Latin. The pupil's responses, therefore, might be based in part on something other than comprehension of the Latin passage. The use of several sight passages dealing with less familiar themes would provide a better test of comprehension. Furthermore, Item 5 calls for the identification of Mars as the Roman god of war, a response not to be secured from the passage alone. Two minor faults are noted in the true-or-false statements: first, the tricky linking of Items 2 and 3 by the word "however" and, second, the use of a negative in Item 8. Part II consists of a multiple-choice test of 20 points of syntax in the Latin passage set for comprehension in Part I. Devoting 20 out of 65 items to formal syntax and only 25 to comprehension does not seem to this reviewer justifiable, especially when Parts III and IV are also mainly concerned with forms and syntax, Part III consisting of 16 completion exercises and Part IV calling for the choice of the Latin sentence which best translates each of 5 English sentences.

The "final score," and the only score apparently used in the validation of the test, is found by subtracting the "wrong and omitted" items from the total number of items, a procedure which would be acceptable only if all the items were of equal weight, if a wrong response were no more serious than an omitted response, and if a wrong response in the true-or-false portions of the test were no more serious than a wrong response in the multiple-choice portions of the test. This criticism of the scoring technique applies also to Forms B, C, and D.

FORM B. Form B is constructed on the same pattern as Form A and the same general criticisms are applicable. The single Latin passage set for comprehension in Part I consists of 193 words and is a continuation of the Hercules-Amazon episode begun in Form A. A minor fault is the use of the tie-up words "nevertheless" and "however" to introduce three of the true-or-false statements. A much more serious fault, as this reviewer sees it, is the overemphasis given to syntax in Parts II, III, and IV, which have a total of 40 items while Part I on comprehension contains only 25 items.

FORM C. Form C follows in general the pattern of Forms A and B, but consists of a total of 70 items, only 20 of which are concerned primarily with testing the pupil's ability to comprehend Latin. This lack of emphasis upon comprehension seems even less justifiable in Forms C and D than in Forms A and B. Part I consists of a single Latin passage of 143 words, adapted from Caesar's *Gallic War,* Book I, Chapter 36, followed by 20 true-or-false statements. Pupils taking this test may or may not have previously read this particular passage. It is found in several second-year Latin text-books.

Part II consists of 18 true-or-false statements about syntax in the Latin passage set for comprehension in Part I. Part III calls for the completion of 14 Latin sentences to test the pupil's functional knowledge of forms and syntax. Part IV employs the multiple-choice technique for testing the pupil's recognition knowledge of 18 Latin words or phrases mostly of technical nature. Examples are: lorica, vexillum, vinea, aquilifer, sarcina, speculator, and testudo. Only ten of the 18 words in Part IV are included in the College Entrance Examination Board's *Latin Word List* [1] for the first two years. The "final score" is found by subtracting the number of "wrong and omitted" items from the "possible score" of 70 unweighted items.

FORM D. Form D follows the pattern of Form

C in its distribution of items by parts and in the testing techniques used. The single 123-word passage set for comprehension in Part I is taken without adaptation from Caesar's *Gallic War,* Book I, Chapter 52. Item 2 requires more than ability to comprehend the Latin, namely, the background knowledge that a Roman *quaestor* was a "quartermaster" and that probably there was only one such officer assigned to Caesar's army. Item 20 likewise demands the background knowledge that *tertiam aciem* here means the "reserve line." Minor criticisms are the use of the tricky tie-up word "nevertheless" in Item 9 and of a negative in Item 14. Part II employs a true-or-false technique for testing knowledge of formal syntax and Part III consists of completion exercises to test a functional knowledge of forms and syntax. Item 44 practically repeats Item 45 in Form C and Item 51 is ambiguous. Part IV tests the pupil's understanding of certain technical terms, proper names, and background material in connection with the Gallic War. Unfortunately, Items 54, 61, 63, 64, and 65 exactly repeat items in Form C.

In the opinion of this reviewer any of these four tests would serve as rough measure of the knowledge and abilities which the authors claim that the tests measure, with the single exception of "derivatives," for which there is no provision whatsoever. Furthermore, their diagnostic value would seem to be very low, because of the failure to distinguish clearly among the objectives the attainment of which each part is supposed to measure.

[1370]

Powers Diagnostic Latin Test. First year; 1930; 2 forms; $1.25 per 25; 15¢ per specimen set; non-timed (90) minutes; Francis F. Power; Bloomington, Ill.: Public School Publishing Co.

Paul B. Diederich, Assistant Professor of Education, The University of Chicago. The test consists of fifteen parts of English sentences to be translated into Latin, 21 noun forms to be diagnosed and then written in some other form, 21 verb forms ditto, 60 Latin words to match with English equivalents, 2 Latin stories of 44 words each about which 10 comprehension questions are asked, and from which ten words are selected to match with their construction, and 25 English derivatives for which the student finds Latin roots. It is appropriate for first year Latin, requires two 45-minute periods, and yields

Kansas Second Year Latin Test

part scores of high statistical reliability. Norms for each part are based upon 571 scores from 33 schools after 7 months of instruction in Latin. Two comparable forms of the test are available.

It is a perfectly conventional objective test of the usual elements of a first-year Latin course. The words and constructions used give evidence of a careful study of their frequency of occurrence in first-year Latin texts. The only grave objection a conservative teacher might have would be that the ability to read Latin receives scant attention. Eighty-eight words of very simple Latin prose, followed by comprehension questions which can be figured out one at a time are hardly an adequate sample of the ability to read Latin.

A more progressive teacher would be likely to complain that no one needs a standardized test to find out how well students have learned these simple mechanical elements of Latin grammar. The ultimate objectives of the study of Latin are represented only by the 25 very easy derivatives, with no attempt to determine what increment of meaning is added by knowing the Latin root. The effect of Latin on English, the study of classical civilization, a beginning acquaintance with the great stories of the classics, and the discipline of thinking which this study can give are all ignored. It is true that these outcomes are more difficult to test, but these are the points at which the Latin teacher really needs the help of the test technician.

Norman T. Pratt, Jr., Department of Classics, Princeton University. These tests are designed "to measure the extent to which pupils in first-year Latin have mastered the vocabulary, word forms, and translating skills necessary for a good foundation in the subject" and may be used also "in canvassing the basal preparation of a second, third, or fourth year class at the beginning of a term." The two forms are planned exactly alike, and their "high reliability (.80 to .90 by parts)" renders them valuable for determining the results of remedial instruction. The time required is estimated at "two forty-five-minute periods." Except for one misprint in the key for Form 2, English-Latin Translation, Item 4 (*magnam* for *magnum*), the accompanying literature is clear and useful.

There are seven parts. The first consists of twelve sentences in English followed by partial Latin versions thereof to be completed by the insertion of one Latin word in each of the total of fifteen blank spaces; this constitutes an adequate functional test of memory for the rules governing such constructions as object, complementary infinitive, ablative of cause, etc., as well as vocabulary.

Parts 2 and 3 are constructed alike. The former contains a column of 21 Latin nouns and adjectives, each followed by five spaces in which the student enters the number, gender, case, nominative singular, and another designated form from the declension of the word. The third section serves the same purpose for verb forms, calling for the identification of voice, tense, person, and number (all 21 forms are in the indicative) and for the construction of another form; the items herein are apparently of graded difficulty. Both parts seem well constructed, even to the nicety that for the purpose of initiation the first item is much like the model given at the beginning of each section. In Part 4 there are three columns of twenty Latin words each. Below each column is a list of twenty English words arranged alphabetically from which the student is to select the one which translates the meaning of each Latin word. In addition to the objection which may be made to all such techniques, namely, that the testing of the mental process involved in finding the correct answer amid a group of possibilities is less rigid and fundamental than the testing of independent and original knowledge, a more serious charge must be brought against the whole group of Parts 2-4: they test aspects of the knowledge of Latin through media completely detached from any context. This is especially serious in the province of vocabulary wherein context is so important, and could have been avoided by attaching the analysis of forms and meanings to real passages of Latin, perhaps in conjunction with the two following sections.

There follow two brief passages of inferior quality to each of which are attached ten English questions concerning the contents to be answered briefly in English. It is praiseworthy that the factor of ease of correction has not eliminated this section as it has in some marketed tests. The questions should, however, include some of a more inferential variety; all of them as now constituted can be answered by the bald translation of one, two,

Powers Diagnostic Latin Test

or at the most three words. Also appended to each passage are ten Latin words from the passage and ten constructions to be matched with the words by which they are illustrated. The test is concluded with a column of twenty-five English words; the student is to give the Latin word from which the English is derived.

These tests are in the reviewer's opinion essentially good and could easily be improved, chiefly by basing Parts 2-6 upon more, continuous Latin of better calibre and by so designing the comprehension-questions as to test and develop the students' imagination and insight which are not merely valuable translating skills but indispensable ends in themselves.

SPANISH

[1371]

American Council Alpha Spanish Test. Grades 9-16; 1926-28; 2 forms, 2 parts; $1.25 per 25; 35¢ per specimen set; 45(50) minutes; prepared for the Modern Language Study under the auspices of the American Council on Education and the Conference of Canadian Universities; Milton A. Buchanan, J. P. W. Crawford, Hayward Keniston, and V. A. C. Henmon; Yonkers, N. Y.: World Book Co.
a) PART I [VOCABULARY AND GRAMMAR].
b) PART II [SILENT READING AND COMPOSITION].

REFERENCES

1 HEMMERLING, WALTER. "A Study of Four Standardized Achievement Tests in Spanish." *Mod Lang Forum* 14:10-4 O '29.
2 HENMON, V. A. C. *Achievement Tests in Modern Foreign Languages*: Prepared for the Modern Language Study and the Canadian Committee on Modern Languages, pp. 1-266. Publications of the American and Canadian Committees on Modern Languages, Vol. 5. New York: Macmillan Co., 1929. Pp. xxvii, 363. $1.00. Paper. (London: Macmillan & Co., Ltd. 4s. 6d.)
3 BUCHANAN, MILTON A. *A Graded Spanish Word Book*, Fourth edition. Publications of the American and Canadian Committees on Modern Languages, Vol. 3. Toronto, Canada: University of Toronto Press, 1933. Pp. 195. $1.25. Paper.
4 KENISTON, HAYWARD. *Spanish Syntax List*: A Statistical Study of Grammatical Usage in Contemporary Spanish Prose on the Basis of Range and Frequency. Publications of the Committee on Modern Languages, American Council on Education. New York: Henry Holt and Co., 1937. Pp. xi, 278. $1.75. Paper.

Lawrence Andrus, Examiner, Board of Examinations, The University of Chicago. The vocabulary section contains 100 items, using the 5-response multiple-choice technique, with responses in English. A check of the Spanish words in the Buchanan *Graded Spanish Word Book*[3] shows the following percentages (for Forms A and B respectively) in the 500-word groups in Buchanan's word book (arranged in descending order of range and frequency)—first 500: 23, 23; second 500: 10, 10; third 500: 11, 11; fourth 500: 9, 9; fifth 500: 8, 9; sixth 500: 9, 8; seventh 500: 10, 10; eighth 500: 10, 10; ninth 500: 8, 8; tenth 500: 2, 2. The validity of vocabulary

selection and the equivalence of Forms A and B in vocabulary are obvious. For lower and intermediate levels of instruction, this section should still give excellent results.

In the grammar section there are 50 items, using multiple-choice and completion techniques. Eight items in each form demand merely the recall of verb forms, by no means the most significant type of item. One item in Form A and two in Form B involve very common idioms. The remaining items are syntactical in nature. Following are the percentages (for Forms A and B respectively) of these syntactical items found in the different ranges of the Keniston *Spanish Syntax List*,[4] the range figures representing the number of 10,000-word units (out of a total of 60 such units counted) in which a given construction occurs—range 60: 29.27 and 35; range 55-59: 7.32 and 5; range 50-54: 14.64 and 17.5; range 45-49: 2.44 and 0; range 40-44: 14.64 and 12.5; range 35-39: 0 and 2.5; range 30-34: 2.44 and 5; range 25-29: 0 and 0; range 20-24: 4.88 and 5; range 15-19: 9.76 and 7.5; range 10-14: 4.88 and 2.5; range 5-9: 7.32 and 7.5; and range 0-4: 2.44 and 0.

The foregoing data show remarkably good validity and fair equivalence of Forms A and B in a test published eleven years before the *Spanish Syntax List*. Unquestionably better could now be done in both respects. The adoption of a uniform technique throughout the grammar section would enable more items to be tested in the same allotted time.

The silent reading section has eight Spanish paragraphs accompanied by 50 questions in Spanish to be answered in English. The paragraphs are well graded in difficulty and varied in content. The questions are generally well phrased and well chosen, with the exception of two in Form A and one in Form B where the student has merely to choose between two possibilities.

The composition section is undoubtedly the weak point of the test. The student is confronted with an "action picture" of a rather emotional type and told to write in Spanish the best composition he can in eight minutes about the picture. Compositions are to be graded by means of a Spanish Composition Scale. While such a scale is admittedly an attempt to remedy the evils of purely subjective grading, the difficulties arising in its use are so great that it is probably better to omit altogether free composition as such from achievement tests.

Reliability coefficients based on apparently adequate samplings of high school pupils are reported as follows: Vocabulary, .92; Grammar, .84 to .91; Silent Reading, .86. We are not told by what procedure these coefficients were obtained. The probable error of measurement for each of these three parts is given as approximately two score points.

Distribution of scores, percentile ranks, and norms are given in the manual of directions for eight semesters of high school in all four sections and for six semesters of college in vocabulary and grammar, five in silent reading, and four in composition. Some of the norms for vocabulary, grammar, and silent reading in both high school and college are based on a rather small number of cases. Adequate directions for administration and scoring are furnished in the manual.

Christian O. Arndt, Assistant Professor of Education, Northwestern University. Although this test suffers from certain weaknesses it nevertheless possesses considerable value as a measuring device for evaluating the progress of students.

The test is divided into four sections which deal with vocabulary, grammar, silent reading, and composition. Two class periods are required for administration. In reference to the vocabulary section it should be said that words are generally well chosen, although the reviewer questions the functional value of the inclusion of such words as *ajo, aguantar, pereza, tez, bóreda,* and *desollar*. It is doubtful whether the vocabulary test measures ability other than general intelligence, and whether word tests without context should therefore be given if one would test vocabulary in a foreign language.

The section dealing with grammar gives the student a good opportunity to make direct application to his knowledge of Spanish. By way of criticism of this part in Form B, the examiner would point out the disproportionate emphasis of questions on the irregular verb at the expense of the regular verb (*see* Item 11). Again in Item 13, could the number of examples not be increased above one!

Some teachers may raise the criticism that the sections devoted to silent reading and composition involve a certain amount of subjective evaluation in scoring. Though this be true, however, these sections nevertheless afford a valuable instrument for determining the actual ability of the examinee to comprehend written Spanish.

The reliability of the separate parts of this test vary from .84 to .92. Scores are presented in terms of percentile ranks.

Unfortunately, no data are available in the manual of directions concerning the validity of this test. Until more information is at hand to show that such language tests are actually measuring what they purport to measure the results can only be accepted with considerable reservation.

Several other Spanish tests are available which offer advantages beyond those afforded by this test.

[1372]

Columbia Research Bureau Spanish Test. Grades 9-15; 1926-27; 2 forms; $1.30 per 25; 20¢ per specimen set; 90(100) minutes; Frank Callcott and Ben D. Wood; Yonkers, N. Y.: World Book Co.

REFERENCES

1 KENISTON, HAYWARD. "Common Words in Spanish." *Hispania* 3:85-96 My '20.
2 CARTWRIGHT, C. W. "A Study of the Vocabularies of Eleven Spanish Grammars and Fifteen Spanish Reading Tests." *Mod Lang J* 10:1-14 O '25.
3 WOOD, BEN D. *New York Experiments with New-Type Modern Language Tests*: Including a Survey of Modern Language Achievement in the Junior High Schools of New York City, June, 1925; The Regents Experiment of June, 1925, with New-Type Tests in French, German, Spanish, and Physics; and A Second Survey of Modern Language Achievement in the Junior High Schools of New York City, June, 1926, pp. 105-319. Publications of the American and Canadian Committees on Modern Languages, Vol. 1. New York: Macmillan Co., 1927. Pp. xxii, 339. Paper. Out of print.
4 HEMMERLING, WALTER. "A Study of Four Standardized Achievement Tests in Spanish." *Mod Lang Forum* 14:10-4 O '29.
5 KENISTON, HAYWARD. *A Spanish Idiom List*: Selected on Basis of Range and Frequency of Occurrence. Publications of the American and Canadian Committees on Modern Languages, Vol. 11. New York: Macmillan Co., 1929. Pp. xiii, 108. $0.60. Paper. (London: Macmillan & Co., Ltd. 2s. 6d.)
6 BUCHANAN, MILTON A. *A Graded Spanish Word Book*, Fourth edition. Publications of the American and Canadian Committees on Modern Languages, Vol. 3. Toronto, Canada: University of Toronto Press, 1933. Pp. 195. $1.25.
7 KENISTON, HAYWARD. *Spanish Syntax List*: A Statistical Study of Grammatical Usage in Contemporary Spanish Prose on the Basis of Range and Frequency. Publications of the Committee on Modern Languages, American Council on Education. New York: Henry Holt and Co., 1937. Pp. xi, 278. $1.75. Paper.

James C. Babcock, Assistant Professor of Romance Languages, The University of Chicago. It is not easy to find exact information on the derivation of the present test. In the manual of directions it is stated that "the derivation of the test is exactly like that of the *Columbia Research Bureau French Test* as described in the manual of directions for that test." If the user or potential user of the Spanish test happens to have the French manual at hand, which can by no means be assumed, he will find that the derivation of the French test "is described in detail in *Yearbook of the New York Society for the Experimental Study of Education*, Volume I." Without continuing his search beyond the French manual, however, he will learn that the criterion governing the construction of the French test was the degree of community shown in sixteen well-known French texts (twelve grammars and four composition books). From this he may deduce that the Spanish test is based on the common content of a number of Spanish texts, all published, necessarily, before the date of the test (1926). It seems scarcely necessary to point out at the present time the serious limitation of a criterion involving the assumption that the subject matter found in texts (especially those written at least fourteen years ago) is what should appear there. The test, then, is out of date. If it is to be of use, it must be revised in the light of the frequency counts of vocabulary, syntax, and idiom, and other information made available since its publication. In Part I (vocabulary), of Form A, for example, a check of the words tested with the Buchanan *Graded Spanish Word Book* [6] would seem to indicate the presence in the test of a number of unprofitable items. Approximately one-third of the items are either among the starred words or the first 500, while about 13 per cent are above 3,000. Regardless of the teaching method employed and the degree of advancement of the students, it is obvious that in classes taught with recently published texts, a number of these items would be either too easy or entirely beyond the range of the student's vocabulary experience. Similar criticisms could be made of the content of Part II (comprehension) and Part III (grammar).

The alternative-response recognition technique employed in Part I is satisfactory, the four or five English words which follow each Spanish word being, on the whole, well chosen. The Spanish words, however, are not arranged in order of difficulty. The comprehension section is much less satisfactory. It is composed entirely of true-false sentences, no attempt being made to test the comprehension of paragraphs. In Part III, grammar is tested by use of the completion type in which the student writes out the Spanish word or words necessary to complete correctly the Spanish translation of 100 rather short English sentences. The manual's claim that this section is "equally objective" is debatable, especially since the key is not entirely adequate. A few of the items in Part III test vocabulary rather than usage.

The manual states that the reliability coefficient for the test as a whole is .97; for Parts I, II, and III separately the figures are .92, .68, and .95 respectively.

Harry J. Russell, Associate Professor of Romanic Languages, Miami University. Two forms of this test are available, Forms A and B. They are supposed to be comparable, and the results, if administered simultaneously, should be the same.

The format is all that could be desired, the type is clear, and the items are arranged in a comprehensible manner.

The reliability coefficient, arrived at by finding the correlation between random halves of the same form of the test, is given as .97. The validity coefficient, found by correlating the test scores with college grades in Spanish courses, and the Regents examinations for 1925, is given at .70 in the college group, and for second-, third-, and fourth-year high school students as, .55, .65, and .71.

Each test consists of three parts, vocabulary, comprehension, and grammar, to be completed in 20, 25, and 45 minutes respectively. The 100 vocabulary items are tested by giving a Spanish word followed by 5 English words, one of which is right. Comprehension is tested with 75 Spanish sentences, some of which are true and others false. The division on grammar consists of 100 English sentences, each one followed by an incomplete Spanish translation, to be completed by supplying the untranslated word or words.

At the time these tests were formulated there were no scientific studies on vocabulary and syntax. The authors did have access, however, to the Keniston [1] and Cartwright [2] word lists.

A brief analysis of the vocabulary content of Part I reveals many low frequency words such as *almohada, legumbre, panadería, oveja, sugerir*, etc., however, there are a surprising number of words belonging to the first 1,500 in the *Graded Spanish Word Book*, [6] (75 per cent of the first 50 words falling in that category).

The items found in the grammar test are principles of common occurrence in Spanish

Columbia Research Bureau Spanish Test

texts of the time. Many of these syntax items have been proven relatively unimportant by the recent *Spanish Syntax List*,[7] but, of course, that was not available to the authors at the time the test was constructed.

The device of testing the foreign word by means of a native one has been improved upon by recent test technicians. True-false tests are not very reliable. Some of the statements made in Part II of this test might be either true or false; e.g., Items 1, 12, 17, 23, 35, etc. A more satisfactory measure of comprehension could be devised.

There should be some sort of reading test that would measure reading ability in a natural reading situation. This division of the test should carry the bulk of the weight, being given the major role in the test rather than the minor one that it occupies in this test. The test on grammar should be changed from the present active type to some sort of passive, recognition exercise. It should be given the least weight in the total test. As the tests now stand, fifty per cent of the time is devoted to Part III, Grammar.

The tests need re-editing in the light of the above criticisms, making full use of available scientific studies, and the more advanced techniques developed within the past few years.

[1373]

Cooperative Spanish Test [Advanced Form]. 4 semesters or more: high school; or 1 year or more: college; 1933-40; 25¢ per specimen set of either edition; 40- and 80-minute editions; Advanced Form P: E. Herman Hespelt, Robert H. Williams, and Geraldine Spaulding; Advanced Form Q: same authors with the editorial assistance of Helen B. Collins, Mary B. MacDonald, Nell Morris, Trudie Wilson, and G. W. Umphrey; New York: Cooperative Test Service.
a) FORMS 1934, 1936, AND 1937. Forms 1933 and 1935 are out of print; 6¢ per test, 10 to 99 copies; 90(95) minutes.
b) REVISED SERIES, ADVANCED FORMS N, O, P, AND Q. 1937-40; 5¢ per test, 10 to 99 copies; 1½¢ per machine-scorable answer sheet; 40(45) minutes.

REFERENCES

1 BUCHANAN, MILTON A. *A Graded Spanish Word Book*, Fourth Edition. Publications of the American and Canadian Committees on Modern Languages, Vol. 3. Toronto, Canada: University of Toronto Press, 1933. Pp. 195. $1.25. Paper.
2 KENISTON, HAYWARD. *Spanish Syntax List*: A Statistical Study of Grammatical Usage in Contemporary Spanish Prose on the Basis of Range and Frequency. Publications of the Committee on Modern Languages, American Council on Education. New York: Henry Holt and Co., 1937. Pp. xi, 278. $1.75. Paper.
3 HANNA, JOSEPH V. "A Comparison of Cooperative Test Scores and High School Grades as Measures for Predicting Achievement in College." *J Appl Psychol* 23:289-97 Ap '39.

Lawrence Andrus, Examiner, Board of Examinations, The University of Chicago. [Re-

view of Advanced Form P.] This **test** has three parts: I, Reading (45 items, 15 minutes); II, Vocabulary (40 items, 10 minutes); III, Grammar (40 items, 15 minutes). The multiple-choice technique, with five suggested responses for each item, is used. Timing for each part is reasonable.

The reading section is too easy throughout to provide sharp discrimination at the third and fourth year levels in high school or the second and third year levels in college. Possibly the time limit may help overcome this deficiency.

The vocabulary section contains no English, for which it is to be commended. Each of the forty lead words is followed by five words from which the student must select the one closest in meaning to the lead word. A check of the lead words and the responses in the Buchanan *Graded Spanish Word Book* [1] shows the following percentages of lead and response words respectively in the 500-word groups in Buchanan's word book (arranged in descending order of range and frequency)—first 500: 25, 16; second 500: 25, 19.5; third 500: 15, 14.5; fourth 500: 0, 7; fifth 500: 2.5, 9.5; sixth 500: 7.5, 7.5; seventh 500: 5, 5.5; eighth 500: 0, 4.5; ninth 500: 2.5, 2; tenth 500: 5, 3.5; eleventh 500: 7.5, 4; twelfth 500: 5, 2.5; thirteenth 500: 0, .5; fourteenth 500: 0, 0; not in the *Graded Spanish Word Book*: 0, 3.5.

While individual users may not approve the exact percentage chosen from each 500-word group, it is evident that an attempt has been made to use the most valid criterion available in choice of vocabulary, i.e., the word count. It may be noted that the words used are practically all content words. It would be advisable to include more form words among those chosen from the commonest two thousand. This test is inferior in distribution of vocabulary difficulty to the *American Council Alpha Spanish Test*, but does include more difficult words, which should make it more discriminating than the Alpha Spanish test at higher levels of instruction.

Of the forty items in the grammar section, three are idiomatic in nature. The remaining thirty-seven items are definitely syntactical. The following table shows the percentage of these syntactical items found in the different ranges of the Keniston *Spanish Syntax List*,[2] the range figures representing the number of 10,000-word units (out of a total of sixty such units counted) in which a given construction occurs—range 60: 43.24; range 55-59: 5.45; range 50-54: 8.11; range 45-49: 8.11; range 40-44: 10.81; range 35-39: 8.11; range 30-34: 8.11; range 25-29: 0; range 20-24: 0; range 15-19: 2.70; range 10-14: 2.70; range 5-9: 2.70; range 0-4: 0. This distribution of construction difficulty is satisfactory, although it could be made more even.

No reliability coefficients for Form P have yet been reported. Percentile norms for both secondary schools and colleges are differentiated, for secondary schools according to geographical location and type of institution, for colleges on the basis of the performance of entering college freshmen on the *American Council on Education Psychological Examination.* College norms are given for entering freshmen and for college students who have had no instruction in Spanish in secondary school. These types of differentiation show a wholly laudable effort to make the norms mean more for individual students than published norms often do mean. Although we are told in the booklet of norms that "these norms represent carefully smoothed and weighted values so that the numbers of cases do not provide a proper basis for judging their accuracy of sampling," this reviewer would feel safer in using norms based on at least one hundred cases—which is not true for certain norms given—particularly in the absence of details about the smoothing and weighting. Furthermore, all these norms are presented in terms of the scaled scores, the critical worth of which must be evaluated in the light of the information finally available in a bulletin devoted especially to them.

A complete and very satisfactory manual of instructions for administration and scoring accompanies the test.

Harry J. Russell, Associate Professor of Romanic Languages, Miami University. [Review of Advanced Form P.] The users of this test would undoubtedly like to know (*a*) exactly who could be tested by it, (*b*) precisely what they were being tested in, or for, (*c*) what the test means in terms of achievement and, (*d*) what learning possibilities it has. Questions one and three are answered adequately by the handbook, the booklet of norms, and other data supplied. to prospective users. The information contained in the handbook answering questions *b* and *d* are definitely in-

adequate. The rather vague statements made about the vocabulary range of the reading and vocabulary divisions, and the grammar content of the test leave much to be desired from the point of view of the teacher who wishes to administer it, or the examiner who would like to critically evaluate it.

Part I, the reading section of this test consists of 45 items, and is to be completed in fifteen minutes. Items 1 to 26 are, for the most part, single sentences of the completion type, five choices being given after each incomplete statement, one of which is correct. The remaining nineteen items are based upon five separate short paragraphs and one letter. There are from two to four incomplete sentences, similar to those found in the first twenty-six items, based on each paragraph or letter.

The vocabulary basis of this test is nowhere stated other than the rather vague statement made in the handbook. A brief analysis of various items reveals the fact that many words, such as *neumáticos, perforado, melocotones, tenis,* do not occur in the *Graded Spanish Word Book.*[1] Of course, some of these words are partially cognate, and might be understood in spite of their unusualness, but why include such problematical items when legitimate ones could just as easily be found?

Items 27 to 45 are more nearly true reading situations than the others. It is the author's opinion that reading ability can best be tested by items more nearly comparable to the normal reading activities engaged in by Spanish students than those found in Items 1 to 26 inclusive.

Part II, the vocabulary division of this test, is composed of forty words, each one followed by five choices, one of which is an exact, or near synonym of the item being tested. The test is to be completed in ten minutes.

The vocabulary chosen for the test consists of 19 words (47.5%) taken from the first 1,000 words in the *Graded Spanish Word Book;* 7 words (17.5%) from the second 1,000; 5 words (12.5%) from the third 1,000; 4 words (10%) from the fifth 1,000; and 5 words (12.5%) from the sixth 1,000.

The answer words, contrary to the statement made in the handbook, are not usually of a higher frequency than the words being tested. As proof of this statement see Items 1, 3, 4, 5, 6, 9, 10, 11, 12, 13, 14, etc. The answer word,

Cooperative Spanish Test [*Advanced Form*]

being more difficult than the test word, makes the test somewhat unfair.

The items that go into the test might have been selected more scientifically to give a more adequate cross section of the specific vocabulary being tested. If the test, for instance, is to examine the student on his knowledge of the 3,000 most common Spanish words the tester might pick every seventy-fifth word, thus eliminating the element of chance selection that seems to have been employed in choosing the words used in this test.

Part III, the grammar division, is made up of forty items. The first 21 items consist of English sentences partially translated into Spanish, the student to supply the one missing word or part of word from the five Spanish choices that are given after each item. The remainder of the test consists of 19 English sentences, each of which is followed by five possible Spanish translations one of which is correct.

We are not told whether the recent study [2] on Spanish syntax was used in selecting the grammatical items to be tested. A hurried comparison, however, of the most common grammatical phenomena as revealed in Keniston's *Spanish Syntax List* with those contained in this test proves that some of the items tested are relatively unimportant.

The validity of the techniques employed in this test, the translation of English to Spanish, might well be questioned.

[1374]

Cooperative Spanish Test [Elementary Form]. 1-6 semesters: grades 6-9; 1933-39; 40- and 90-minute editions; 25¢ per specimen set of either edition; Elementary Form P: Jacob Greenberg, Robert H. Williams, and Geraldine Spaulding; New York: Cooperative Test Service.
a) JUNIOR FORM 1934. Forms 1933 and 1935 are out of print; 6¢ per test, 10 to 99 copies; 90(95) minutes.
b) REVISED SERIES, ELEMENTARY FORMS N, O, AND P. 1937-39; 5¢ per test, 10 to 99 copies; 1½¢ per machine-scorable answer sheet; 40(45) minutes.

Christian O. Arndt, Assistant Professor of Education, Northwestern University. [Review of Elementary Form P.] This test should meet the practical needs of all teachers who desire an accurate measuring device for the evaluation of progress in Spanish in secondary schools. The test is divided into three parts covering reading, vocabulary, and grammar. The multiple-choice method whereby words are selected for completing sentences is used in the section devoted to reading. This method

has been widely used by psychologists for many years and is set up to good advantage in this test. There may be some legitimate questioning of the value of Part II devoted to vocabulary since the meaning of words is contingent upon their context. Results of vocabulary tests have long been known to correlate highly with the intelligence of those tested and do not necessarily indicate proficiency in language. The section dealing with grammar should test for grammar and not be concerned with idioms as well. Idioms might better be tested under the section on vocabulary.

Some of the examples employed in Part III are open to criticism because of the choice of alternative words; for instance, Item 8: "The maid will serve us right away." Instead of the pronouns *yo, me, mi*, it would appear better to use *nuestros, usos,* and *os*. In Item 3, two things are tested, the object pronoun and the idiom. This is obviously undesirable. Giving the first few letters of the verb rather than the infinitive in the case of Items 23, 26, 27, 28, and 33 is confusing to the examinee. In general more aspects of grammar should be treated in this section.

The short time (40 minutes) required for administering the test will be appreciated by all busy teachers. Scores are presented in terms of percentiles which makes for ready understanding.

Norms are based upon adequate sampling from widely separated geographical areas. This enables one to compare the relative standing of students in various parts of the country. Furthermore, interesting comparisons may be drawn between the work done in public and independent secondary schools.

The test has a reliability coefficient of .93 which indicates that it possesses value as a reliable diagnostic device. It is regretted by the examinee that no information is at hand concerning the validity of the test.

The three authors of this test are to be commended for the objective approach and meticulous care with which the test has been constructed and standardized. It should find wide acceptance by teachers of Spanish in secondary schools throughout the country.

For a review by Walter V. Kaulfers, see 1156.

[1375]

Spanish Life and Culture. Two years: high school, or 1 year: college; 1937; 1 form; 50¢ per 25; 15¢ per specimen set; Minnie M. Miller; Emporia, Kan.: Bureau of Educational Measurements, Kansas State Teachers College.

James C. Babcock, Assistant Professor of Romance Languages, The University of Chicago. The construction of useful tests of students' knowledge of foreign "life and culture" is perhaps one of the most difficult tasks confronting those who are trying to improve the standard tests for use in foreign language courses. The difficulty arises from the lack of uniformity in cultural background instruction in our elementary courses, both with regard to the relative importance of this part of the course and, in the case of Spanish, the question of emphasis on Spain or Spanish America. It arises also from the fact that the significant objective of an understanding and appreciation of the peculiar genius of a people and the role of that people's civilization in world culture is much less easily tested than the less meaningful aim of memorizing dates and names.

The author of the present test does not attempt to test understanding and appreciation. The test "covers such information on geography, history, government, art, literature, science, and customs of Spain and Spanish America as students may reasonably be expected to acquire in two years of high school, or one year of college Spanish." The word "information" should be taken to mean primarily a knowledge of the subjects listed sufficient to identify, recognize or (in Part I) produce the names of people and places. No explanation of the choice of materials is given in the manual of directions other than the assertion that "the items were selected from valid sources" and "the items themselves, as well as their proportional distribution among the various fields of subject matter, were carefully checked by teachers of Spanish in high schools and colleges." In the opinion of the reviewer, some six or eight at least out of the total of 100 items are of too little significance to merit inclusion in the test. It is likely that many teachers would have preferred more than five items dealing with art. This number could easily be increased without adding to the length of the test by omitting a few very easy and probably unprofitable items such as: "There are many Spanish names for towns in: I. Virginia, 2. California, 3. Wisconsin." Approximately forty per cent of the items have to do primarily with Spanish America or the activities of Spaniards in Spanish America.

Three types of responses are called for in the three parts of the test. In Part I, the student is to write out the answers to short questions. Since these questions call for nothing other than the names of people, cities, mountains and the like, a more objective type of response might be preferred. The matching type in Part II and the multiple-choice type in Part III are more satisfactory, although it would probably have been well to include more detractors in the answer columns of Part II and use four rather than three possible responses in Part III. The items are not arranged in order of difficulty.

It should be noted that the table of percentile norms was computed from the scores of only 343 students. The test showed a reliability coefficient of .73.

For a review by Walter V. Kaulfers, see 1157

FOREIGN LANGUAGES—THIRD MMY

REVIEWS BY *Frederick B. Agard, H. E. Brogden, Nelson Brooks, Harold B. Dunkel, Elton Hocking, Joseph F. Jackson, Walter V. Kaulfers, John H. Meyer, C. W. Odell, Harry J. Russell, Herbert Schueler, Geraldine Spaulding, Hazel M. Toliver, Clarence E. Turner, Roland Vinette.*

[178]

Iowa Placement Examinations: Foreign Language Aptitude. Grades 12-13; 1925-44; IBM; 2 editions; G. D. Stoddard and G. E. Vander Beke; Bureau of Educational Research and Service, State University of Iowa.
a) SERIES FAI, REVISED. 1925; Forms A, B; $4 per 100; 50¢ per specimen set including the other 10 tests in the series, postpaid; 45(50) minutes; prepared under the direction of C. E. Seashore and G. M. Ruch.
b) NEW SERIES FA-2, REVISED. 1925-44; also called Quick-Scoring Edition; IBM; Form M; separate answer sheets need not be used; $1.15 per 25; 30¢ per specimen set including the other 4 tests in the series, postpaid; $1.50 per 100 machine-scorable answer sheets; 15¢ per stencil for scoring answer sheets; 45(50) minutes; revised by Grace Cochran, J. R. Nielson, and D. B. Stuit.

REFERENCES

1. STODDARD, GEORGE DINSMORE. *Iowa Placement Examinations.* University of Iowa, Studies in Education, Vol. 3, No. 2. Iowa City, Iowa: the University, 1925. Pp. 103. Paper. $1.00. *
2. STODDARD, GEORGE D. "Iowa Placement Examinations." *Sch & Soc* 24:212-6 Ag 14 '26. *
3. THARP, JAMES B. "Sectioning Classes in Romance Languages." *Mod Lang J* 12:95-114 N '27. *
4. MILLER, LAWRENCE WILLIAM. *An Experimental Study of the Iowa Placement Examinations.* University of Iowa Studies in Education, Vol. 5, No. 6. Iowa City, Iowa: the University, 1930. Pp. 116. Paper. $1.00. * (*PA* 5:799)
5. GERBERICH, J. R. "Validation of a State-Wide Educational Guidance Program for High-School Seniors." *Sch & Soc* 34:606-10 '31. * (*PA* 6:1622)
6. KAMMAN, JAMES FOSTER. *A Statistical Analysis of the Foreign Language Aptitude Test, Form B, of the Iowa Placement Examinations.* Unpublished master's thesis, University of Iowa, 1939.
7. LARSEN, R. P.; WITTENBORN, J. R.; AND GIESECKE, E. G. "Factors Contributing to Achievement in the Study of First Semester College German." *J Exp Ed* 10:265-71 Je '42. * (*PA* 16:5024)

H. E. Brogden, Research Psychologist, Personnel Research Section, The Adjutant General's Office, Washington, D. C. The *Foreign Language Aptitude* test of the *Iowa Placement Examinations* appears to be a well-planned and competently constructed test. Earlier forms, Series FAI, include six subtests concerned with facility in translation from singular to plural forms, in changing the tense of verbs, and forming nouns from verbs—all in the English language—and three subtests concerned with facility in guessing the meaning of Esperanto words, applying Esperanto grammar rules, and matching a series of sentences in Esperanto with corresponding sentences in English having different ordering of the component words or phrases. In Form M, a recent, machine-scored

edition, the student is tested by his ability to deduce the meaning of italicized words in sentences written in Esperanto, to translate sentences in a new language, and to answer correctly or solve correctly questions and problems in English grammar.

Validity of the earlier forms in predicting first-semester foreign-language grades is reported as .50 and reliability as .97. Form M is reported to have validities of .67, .65, and .69 (N's not given) for predicting, respectively, first-semester grades in French, German, and Spanish. The reliability is given as .979. Percentile norms, based on something over 1,200 cases are given.

While it would be desirable to base the norms on more than 1,200 cases, Form M, at least, appears quite adequate for its intended use. More information than is usual is given on validity and reliability. The validities reported are satisfactorily, even surprisingly, high.

[179]

Language Aptitude Test: George Washington University Series. Grades 9-16; 1929; Form 1; $7.50 per 100; 10¢ per specimen set, postpaid; 36(45) minutes; T. Hunt, F. C. Wallace, S. Doran, K. C. Buynitzky, and R. E. Schwarz; Center for Psychological Service, George Washington University.

H. E. Brogden, Research Psychologist, Personnel Research Section, The Adjutant General's Office, Washington, D. C. The *Language Aptitude Test* consists of ten subtests. Four of these might be described as artificial language tests. These include Meaning of Prepositions, Memory for Foreign Language, Use of Prefixes and Suffixes, and Use of Language Rules. Two are verbal intelligence tests, namely, Comprehension and Vocabulary. Two tests which appear to be grammar achievement tests—English Grammar and Following Directions for Word Order—together with two tests entitled Recognition of Similarities in Sound and Knowledge of Accent complete the listing. There are 200 items in all.

Apparently no serious attempt has been made

to achieve ease in scoring. Scoring keys are not provided, and the format of the test appears to be such that keys cannot be simply constructed for rapid hand scoring. Actually there seems no reason why a test of this sort—if it is to be used extensively—should not be adapted for machine scoring.

A mimeographed sheet accompanying the test gives no information concerning the validity or reliability of the test. Although the test was published in 1929, only medians and quartile points are given as provisional norms. The number of cases employed in determining these is not given.

Judged from the content, the validity of the test should be high. Artificial language and verbal ability are known to be efficient predictors of achievement in foreign languages. The effect of use of several varieties of unorthodox structure in the artificial language subtests is difficult to judge, although the subjective reaction of the reviewer to these tests is favorable. The two grammar tests and the test entitled Recognition of Similarities in Sound also impress the reviewer favorably. A seemingly desirable characteristic of the memory and comprehension tests is the time interval between the study of the memory and comprehension material and the administration of the actual test. A sheet containing an English passage—for the reading comprehension test—and the vocabulary and the prefixes and suffixes for two of the artificial language tests is studied prior to the administration of the test proper.

Since the test contains 200 items, the reliability of the total score is very probably quite adequate. It is doubtful if many of the subtests are sufficiently reliable so that the subscores will be of use in profiles or for differential diagnosis.

It would be interesting to have available the standard deviations of the various subtest scores and the distribution of the difficulties of their component items. The reviewer would guess that many of the tests would be found to be very much easier than others. Because of this suspected variation in difficulty, suspected variation in reliability of the subtest content, and the evident variation in length of subtests, it is probable that the actual weighting of the subtests scores is far from equal and may be at variance with their intended and their optimal weighting.

While the test impresses the reviewer favorably and is judged by him to be valid for pre-

dicting achievement in foreign languages, it is still difficult to recommend it without adequate information as to its validity and reliability. One of the most unfortunate aspects of the testing movement is the tendency to write tests in large numbers—expending considerable ingenuity in the process very often—without adequate determination of validity, reliability, and proper norms. Since the latter steps are the more laborious and possibly the more important aspects of test construction, it would seem—especially in the case of a commercial test—that adequate information in these respects would be a primary requirement. Otherwise it can only be said that another test has been added to the tremendous number already available.

FRENCH

[180]
★[Cooperative French Comprehension Test.] 1-2 years high school or 1 year college, more than 2 years high school or more than 1 year college; 1942-47; this test is, as the booklet title indicates, Part I of the *Cooperative French Test: Lower and Higher Levels;* IBM; Forms S, X; 2 levels; separate answer sheets need not be used; $1.75 per 25; 25¢ per specimen set of either level, postpaid; 40¢ per 25 machine-scorable answer sheets; 15¢ per stencil for scoring answer sheets; 40(45) minutes; Geraldine Spaulding, Laura Towne, and Sarah Wolfson Lorge; Cooperative Test Service.
a) LOWER LEVEL. 1-2 years high school or 1 year college.
b) HIGHER LEVEL. More than 2 years high school or more than 1 year college.

Joseph F. Jackson, Professor of French, University of Illinois, Urbana, Illinois. [Review of Lower Level Form S.] This examination (40 minutes) is planned to test comprehension of isolated words, single sentences, and rather brief connected passages. It is divided into two sections: Section I (15 minutes), 50 words and 10 sentences, and Section II (25 minutes), 8 connected passages with a total of 45 statements to be completed correctly. All items are of the multiple-choice type, with five options for each. The possible equivalents for the single words are given in English. The rest is entirely in French, thus constituting a double comprehension test, both of the original and of the paraphrases or completions.

The test is comprehensive and well designed to explore a wide range and variety of vocabulary. The isolated words include some false cognates and near homonyms which should trap the unwary but which should give no real trouble to the careful and well-prepared student. The sentences of Section I involve so-called "idiomatic" expressions. The connected passages of Section II embrace a diversity of situations and of pertinent vocabulary.

On the whole, the test is carefully designed and executed. The proposed equivalents are good, with the possible exception of Items 51 and 94. There are a few misprints which should be corrected in Items 53 and 77 and in the second passage, page 6, line 6.

Regarding the large number of items and choices for the relatively short time indicated for the test, it should be pointed out that the examiners, seeking a wide spread in results for differentiation, do not expect the examination to be completed in the given period. Thus facility is measured and rewarded along with accuracy.

Aside from the few minor defects noted above, this examination is to be recommended for general purposes.

Joseph F. Jackson, Professor of French, University of Illinois, Urbana, Illinois. [Review of Higher Level Form S.] This test is constructed on the same pattern as Form S, Lower Level; it consists of isolated words for recognition of equivalents in English, idiomatic expressions in complete sentences with possible equivalents in French, and short passages, each having three to six statements to be completed or questions to be answered, all in French. For each of the 105 items involved there are five possible alternate choices.

There is a good spread and variety of isolated words tested in Section I. A possible criticism is that over 80 per cent are nouns and verbs, with the former far exceeding the latter. Granted that nouns and verbs constitute the principal working stock in language, it would seem advisable to give more attention to other parts of speech than we find here and to have such elements as conjunctions and adverbial phrases at least represented. The locutions included in the complete sentences are well chosen. For a matter of detail, normal tense sequence is violated in Item 59, choices 3 and 4. Although this does not affect the point specifically tested, such questionable models should be avoided.

The second section is consistently good, with two minor exceptions. Item 80 depends largely on the meaning of a single word, which is rather uncommon in itself and which is not used in the text. In general, it is better not to have evidence of comprehension of a passage hinge on the understanding of one word; this is particularly true in this case, as the item is designed to test comprehension of the general subject of the entire passage given. The second exception concerns the eighth passage (p. 8), which offers a *casse-tête* in the sequence of events rather than a clear test of comprehension of French. The reviewer cheerfully admits the validity of testing intelligence along with verbal knowledge, but undue complications or confusions are likely to obscure both types of ability. In any case, the unraveling of involved situations demands an amount of time disproportionate to the particular end in view.

Taken all in all, this is a good test in its planning, execution, and validity.

Clarence E. Turner, Associate Professor of the Romance Languages, Rutgers University, New Brunswick, New Jersey. [Review of Lower and Higher Levels, Form S.] Specimen sets of these tests do not include norm tables and related data. The scoring key gives parallel columns of raw scores and "tentative" scaled scores. The accompanying booklet does not discuss the construction and validation of particular tests.

The tests follow the same pattern at both levels. Section I calls for the choice of the best of five English translations for each of fifty French words. Roughly half of the items are nouns, and one-third are infinitives. Ten items follow which call for the best from among five French paraphrases of French sentences containing crucial locutions. Section II, of forty-five items, calls for the best of five French sentence-completions based on a series of short prose paragraphs in French.

The tests have many merits. The reading passages in Section II are interesting and varied in style and subject. Real ingenuity has been shown throughout in the choice of distractors, and in their combination so as to throw specific points into relief. In Section I, the five possible responses typically include one false cognate, one translation of a superficially similar French word, and vague echoes of other foreign languages. Not to any objectionable degree does exact comprehension of the French text fail to furnish all that is required for selection of the right answer. Wild guessing is penalized by the subtraction of a proportion of wrong answers from the total of correct ones. Subtle management of the difficulties promises discriminatory power for the tests at all levels of ability.

Cooperative French Comprehension Test

Two criticisms should be made. First, comprehension of the force of moods and tenses of the verb is not sufficiently tested. Here is, for many students, the principal obstacle to the understanding of written French. Second, fifty items, or just short of half the test, combine two assailable features: they involve English, and they test words out of context. This is mentioned because of the frequent and weighty objections which teachers have made to such practices. To the writer, they seem defensible. Even the best student, in building his French vocabulary, has got to do more than simply read and understand: he must use some form of memory drill, to the end that one day he may, like the cultivated native, understand any word in any context. Such drill can scarcely take any practical form other than the memorizing of words out of context in terms of their English equivalents. A practice which, with all its pitfalls, can scarcely be avoided by the learner would seem therefore to be admissible in a test, though the proportion of items involving it ought perhaps to be reduced.

A final reservation, applicable to all reading comprehension tests in foreign languages, must be made. Given present trends in the curriculum, any such test will need to be combined with other tests having oral-aural features.

For reviews by John H. Meyer and Roland Vinette of the Cooperative French Test: Lower and Higher Levels, *see 182.*

[181]

Cooperative French Test: Elementary and Advanced Forms. 1-3 semesters high school or 1 semester college, more than 2 years high school or at least 1 year college; 1939–41; IBM; Forms P, Q, R; 2 levels; separate answer sheets need not be used; $1.75 per 25 copies of Elementary Form; $2 per 25 copies of Advanced Form; 25¢ per specimen set of either level, postpaid; 40¢ per 25 machine-scorable answer sheets; 15¢ per stencil for scoring answer sheets; 40(45) minutes; Cooperative Test Service.
a) ELEMENTARY FORM. 1-3 semesters high school or 1 semester college; Jacob Greenberg and Geraldine Spaulding.
b) ADVANCED FORM. At least 2 years high school or 1 year college; Geraldine Spaulding and Paul Vaillant.

REFERENCES

1-4. *See* 40:1349.
5. SMITH, FRANCIS PRESCOTT. "The Use of Standardized Objective Tests for Sectioning French Courses According to Student Ability." *Mod Lang J* 26:123-32 F '42. *‡
6. SMITH, FRANCIS PRESCOTT, AND CAMPBELL, HELEN S. "Objective Achievement Testing in French: Recognition Versus Recall Tests." *Mod Lang J* 26:192-8 Mr '42. *
7. TRAXLER, ARTHUR E. "The Relation of Vocabulary and Grammar to Reading Achievement in Latin, French, and Spanish," pp. 61-5. In *1947 Achievement Testing Program in Independent Schools and Supplementary Studies.* Educational Records Bulletin, No. 48. New York: Educational Records Bureau, June 1947. Pp. xii, 66. Paper, lithotyped. $2.00. * (PA 22:449)

Cooperative French Comprehension Test

For reviews by Nelson Brooks, C. E. Ficken, Harry Heller, Warren S. Holmes, Joseph F. Jackson, Walter V. Kaulfers, and James B. Tharp, see 38:985, 38:986, 40:1349, and 40:1350.

[182]

★**Cooperative French Test: Lower and Higher Levels.** 1-2 years high school or 1 year college, more than 2 years high school or more than 1 year college; 1942–47; IBM; Forms S, X; 2 levels; separate answer sheets need not be used; $2 per 25; 25¢ per specimen set of either level, postpaid; 60¢ per 25 machine-scorable answer sheets; 30¢ per stencil for scoring answer sheets; 80(85) minutes; Geraldine Spaulding, Laura Towne, and Sarah Wolfson Lorge; Cooperative Test Service.
a) LOWER LEVEL. 1-2 years high school or 1 year college.
b) HIGHER LEVEL. More than 2 years high school or more than 1 year college.

REFERENCES

1. TRAXLER, ARTHUR E. "Some Data on the Results of the Cooperative Tests in French, Latin, and Secondary School Mathematics, Form S," pp. 55-9. In *1942 Achievement Testing Program in Independent Schools and Supplementary Studies.* Educational Records Bulletin, No. 36. New York: Educational Records Bureau, June 1942. Pp. xiii, 59. Paper, lithotyped. $1.50. *

John H. Meyer, Former Assistant Examiner, Board of Examinations, The University of Chicago, Chicago, Illinois. [Review of Form S.] The older forms of this test have been so long and widely used that the characteristic virtues and limitations of the series are by now a familiar story. The S forms (80 minutes) do, however, include a new feature: a 15-minute Part III labeled, somewhat ambitiously, Civilization. Grammar (Part II) takes 25 minutes; Part I, rather vaguely entitled Comprehension, is split into a 15-minute vocabulary section and a 25-minute reading comprehension section. Parts II and III are thus designed exactly to balance the two sections of Part I.

Vocabulary (Items 1 to 50) is tested not in context (i. e., specific words in complete sentences) but by the traditional and somewhat artificial device of a succession of isolated words. In the Lower Level test, the parts of speech are represented as follows: adverbs 5, adjectives 7, nouns 23, verbs 15; in the Upper Level: prepositions 1, adverbs 4, adjectives 3, nouns 27, and verbs 15. These proportions seem slightly faulty in view of the trouble which most students encounter in grappling with (*a*) verbs and (*b*) the "little words" (conjunctions, prepositions, etc.).

Items 51 to 60 sample (in context) the student's knowledge of common French idioms. But their position, at the end of the vocabulary section, means that many students either will not reach them at all or will be able to give them only very hurried attention.

The content of the passages in the reading section, on which Items 61 to 105 are built, seems a trifle thin, elementary, and even trivial. This is particularly true of the selections in the Lower Level form, which are, moreover, written in a rather wilted and limping French. The items suffer accordingly and betray, moreover, from time to time, a certain clumsiness of form (for an acute case of tense trouble see Item 67, Higher Level). One feels, therefore, that, at both levels: (a) the reading burden might have been lightened by the use of fewer passages (five or six, for example, instead of eight or nine); (b) choice of more significant and interesting material, and slightly longer passages, would have permitted the writing of better (and at least equally reliable) items; and (c) the prose style of certain of the passages might well have received first aid within the prescribed vocabulary limits.

The 50 grammar items, while necessarily easy, in view of the constantly diminishing emphasis on grammar in present-day teaching, offer a fair sampling of the indispensable minimum of grammatical knowledge. Items 1 (Lower Level) and 42 (Higher Level) might perhaps have been more happily placed in the idiom section; Items 19 and 18 in the Lower Level duplicate to some extent the work of Items 4 and 5 in the same test. About one-third of the points tested at the lower level are retested at the higher level, but this proportion does not seem too great in view of the fact that so large a portion of second-year grammatical teaching is necessarily devoted to a review of fundamentals. It is true that a larger sampling of verb forms (and especially those of the most common irregular verbs) might have been included, although, strictly speaking, the verbs might better be tested under the heading of vocabulary. Irregular verbs, at any rate, seem inadequately represented in the test.

The last 50 items (on Civilization), apparently chosen in accordance with no well-defined or logical plan, are not, generally speaking, impressively significant. The effect is one of scrappiness—of stray facts arbitrarily coordinated by an "Information, please!" technique. At best they offer a few vague tags and set formulas. The cultural content of elementary French courses in the United States varies widely and is largely dependent upon such factors as (a) the personal culture and taste of the individual teacher, and (b) the scope and approach of the individual textbook. In the absence of objective criteria governing the selection and arrangement of cultural material, the validity of "civilization" items remains dubious. Responses to such items are, therefore, determined largely and almost inevitably by chance.

To enlarge upon the advantages and merits of the *Cooperative French Tests* would be almost an impertinence. In the case of so popular and long-established a series they may be taken for granted. The foregoing criticisms, it was felt, might prove useful. It is with that intention that they are offered.

Roland Vinette, Professor of Measurement and Testing, Institute of Psychology, University of Montreal, Montreal, Canada. [Review of Form S.] Each of these tests consists of three parts: I, Comprehension, which has two sections; II, Grammar; and III, Civilization. Part I, Comprehension, Section 1, contains first 50 French words, each of which is followed by five English words or phrases. The subject must decide which one of the English words or phrases is the best translation for the French word. We have compared the 50 French words in each test with an unpublished list of the 6,000 words most used by French-Canadian pupils and found the following distribution: for the Lower Level Test, 50 per cent of the French words fall in the first thousand, 30 per cent in the second thousand, and the rest in the third and the fourth thousands; for the Higher Level Test, about 30 per cent in the first thousand, about 15 per cent in each of the second, third, fourth, and fifth thousands. That is a fairly good proof of validity.

Section 1 also includes 10 French sentences, each of which is followed by five other French sentences. The subject must decide which of these five choices best explains the meaning of the first sentence. To make his choice, the subject must have an exact understanding not only of the French vocabulary but also of the French sentence.

Section 2 consists of French passages followed by several questions. To answer these questions correctly, the subject must show an understanding of the paragraph as a whole.

Part II, Grammar, contains 50 questions. Each question consists of an English sentence followed by a translation in which there is a blank to be filled by one of the five words or phrases suggested. To fill in the blank correctly, the subject must know the appropriate rule in French grammar. Rules concerning pronouns and verbs are the most employed in the test; those concerning nouns and adjectives are rather neglected. However, those used are among the most important in the French language and among the most difficult for the English speaking person to apply correctly.

Part III, Civilization, consists of 50 questions about great French men (authors, politicians, etc.) ; and French monuments, geographical facts, history, and usages.

Norms are provided for each part separately, for Parts I and II together, and for the total score. Data about reliability and validity are omitted.

As a whole, each of these tests represents an interesting device for measuring the student's level in French.

For reviews by Joseph F. Jackson and Clarence E. Turner of Part I of this test, see 180.

[183]
★**Examination in French Grammar.** 1-2 years high school or 1 year college, 2½ years high school or 2 years college; 1944–45; IBM; 1 form (usually called Form B) ; 2 levels; separate answer sheets must be used; $1.75 per 25 of either level; 40¢ per 25 machine-scorable answer sheets for either level; 15¢ per scoring key for either level; 25¢ per specimen set of either level, postpaid; 40(45) minutes; prepared by the Examinations Staff of the United States Armed Forces Institute; published by the American Council on Education; distributed by Cooperative Test Service. (Also distributed by Science Research Associates: $2 per 25 of either level; 65¢ per 25 machine-scorable answer sheets for either level; 50¢ per key; 50¢ per specimen set.)
a) LOWER LEVEL. 1944; 1-2 years high school or 1 year college; Form LFG-1-B-4.
b) UPPER LEVEL. 1945; 2½ years high school or 2 years college; Form UFG-1-B-4.

Nelson Brooks, Instructor in French, Westover School, Middlebury, Connecticut. For some reason, the fixed-response type of test turns out to be less dependable in the field of grammar than in either vocabulary or comprehension. Unfortunately the authors of the present tests seem not to have understood even the basic problems involved; much less have they contributed anything of value to the tests of this kind already available. There are some satisfactory items, such as Items 6 and 8, Lower Level, and Items 34 and 56, Upper Level; the series is at its worst in Item 39, Lower Level or Item 48, Upper Level, where the incorrect French of the

distractors is lamentably bad. Of the 120 grammar items offered, at least one-third must be rejected as unsatisfactory for one reason or another. Sometimes there are not five choices in the answers (this is true in 12 cases; in Items 18 and 41, Lower Level, there are only two) ; sometimes the French in the question is dubious e.g., Item 58, Lower Level; often there is the sad business of putting incorrect French in the answers (there are 16 examples of this, in addition to the sample items). Again, the question is not one of grammar but vocabulary (e.g., Item 27, Lower Level), or the distractors are not likely enough (e.g., Item 60, Lower Level, where the most obvious wrong answer, *a demeuré,* is overlooked), or there are two possible right answers (e.g., Item 47, Lower Level), or the problem is simply too far-fetched, as in Item 13, Lower Level, in which the manipulation of " 'My husband does not understand me,' she sobbed. 'He always keeps me from doing as I please.' " in order to test for the use of the preposition *de* seems like serving a very small fruit in a very large bowl.

Of these deficiencies, the two major ones are the lack of likelihood in the distractors, or their absence, and the use of incorrect French in the answers. The first of these is very serious for the worth of the test. Unless there is an obvious degree of plausibility in the wrong answer, it might as well be an ampersand or a Rorschach blot, and chance becomes a dominant factor. Of course, the tests will give impressive statistics, but let us not forget that it is possible to distinguish between students by dealing them cards from a deck. The point here is, have they been distinguished in accordance with their knowledge of French grammar? The authors overlook the fact that the student has a method in his wrongness, and seem content to suggest for his logically right but grammatically wrong answer sheer nonsense or nothing at all.

Equally serious is the use of incorrect French in the wrong answers. It is painful indeed to see such monstrosities in print and it is little wonder that many people, teachers and students alike, receive a bad impression of this kind of test when they read them. To offer the student a puzzle with a part missing and ask him to choose which of several pieces fits the missing part seems natural and reasonable enough. To offer him some of these pieces forced violently and unnaturally together is to offend his intelligence and to violate the first principles of teaching. It is one thing for the student to make errors in his attempts to master syntax; it is quite another for the teacher or the testmaker to do violence to language in an attempt to imitate the struggles of the student. It is the equivalent of baby talk and is of profit to no one. Furthermore, it is quite unnecessary. If a given number of acceptable items of this kind can be devised, twice that number can be devised, provided the testmakers understand what they are about and will firmly and patiently reject all but suitable material. Let those who use this form in making tests be aware of its possibilities and of its absurdities, and not give the method a bad name for not having themselves measured up to its exacting standards.

[184]

★Examination in French Reading Comprehension. 1-2 years high school or 1 year college, 2½ years high school or 2 years college; 1944-45; IBM; 1 form (usually called Form B); 2 levels; separate answer sheets must be used; $1.75 per 25 of either level; 40¢ per 25 machine-scorable answer sheets for either level; 15¢ per scoring key for either level; 25¢ per specimen set of either level, postpaid; 50(55) minutes; prepared by the Examinations Staff of the United States Armed Forces Institute; published by the American Council on Education; distributed by Cooperative Test Service. (Also distributed bv Science Research Associates: $2 per 25 of either levels; 65¢ per 25 machine-scorable answer sheets for either level; 50¢ per key; 50¢ per specimen set.)
a) LOWER LEVEL. 1944; 1-2 years high school or 1 year college; Form LFR-1-B-4.
b) UPPER LEVEL. 1945; 2½ years high school or 2 years college; Form UFR-1-B-4.

Joseph F. Jackson, Professor of French, University of Illinois, Urbana, Illinois. [Review of Lower Level.] In attempting to evaluate this test, it is well to have in mind the general conditions and purposes determining its conception. According to the Manual, the original tests were intended "for use in reporting the educational achievements and status of service personnel to the educational institutions from which these men and women may wish to secure credit." Objectives were described by examiners, specialists, and teachers; materials were collected accordingly and they were pretested in schools or colleges, sometimes with adult groups; then revisions were made on the basis of results recorded. The ensuing revised examination forms were then submitted to one or more critics designated by professional organizations. According to these criticisms (for comprehensiveness, accuracy, and validity), the examination forms were subject to still further revision and to additional pretesting, if possible. In this process there was sufficient material for two forms, one for the Armed Forces Institute, the other for civilian use in schools and colleges. It is this second or alternate form that is reviewed here.

Specifically, the examination consists of seven French passages, 8 to 20 lines each, with a total of 47 completion-type statements in French to test comprehension. The completions are multiple choice. Choices are limited to three, reducing the number and diversity of alternatives found in other similar tests.

The examination is less carefully executed than would be suggested by the procedures indicated for it in the Manual. At least six of the seven passages, depending on irony, subtlety, or knowledge of politics, demand a maturity of judgment which cannot be assumed in younger students. Thus, the actual comprehension of French may not be adequately tested, and the real validity of the examination may well be questioned. For example, the first passage, a verse selection, depends for its effect on the attitude of the poet. This is nowhere stated, it is only implied, particularly for those who happen to know the poet. A student might comprehend the French perfectly (although part of the sense derives from a Spanish word, the meaning of which is not given) without grasping the unexpressed emotional tone. Similarly, Section II depends for full comprehension on knowledge of court gallantry and intrigues, religious attitudes, irony and personal relations incompletely explained in the selected context. A fuller acquaintance with the author and with his entire work would supplement understanding of the French text itself. Section IV depends on irony for its effect. Sections V and VI presuppose some knowledge of "useful relations" and of political science and political attitudes. Section VII, a Merovingian scene, is remote and obscure for the uninitiated; its effect is achieved by indirection rather than by the precise meaning of words.

The authors state that the educational objectives "are defined as clearly as possible in terms of behavior; that is, a student should be able to do definite things which are indicative of his attainment of each objective." We should suggest that the student's behavior is conditioned to a large extent by his experience. In comprehension passages material should be considered not only for its linguistic difficulty but for its content in relation to the student's probable experience—social, intellectual, and emotional. The fact that the original USAFI tests were intended for scattered age groups may have something to do with this problem. It is surprising, however, that the difficulties indicated were not revealed in pretesting, particularly with high school students.

Beside this general question of appropriateness or validity of the passages chosen for comprehension, there are matters of detail which could be improved. Items 4, 8, and 15 do not represent a clear choice. In Item 28C, an intensification has been added to the original; this might be misleading. Without attempting to proofread the examination, which is a second printing, the reviewer has picked up some unfortunate misprints: *la père* (p. 2); *le comtesse* (p. 3); *soit* for *soir*, *Théatre* (p. 4); *ce* for *ces* (p. 7); *médicins* and (*la reine*) *étant allé* (p. 8). Finally, the examiners offer (p. 1) an example for the students in which *l'insouciance* is gratuitously translated as "carelessness." Surely in the context it means rather "unconcern" or "lack of concern."

Considering the procedures and purposes of this test, the performance fails to live up to its promise.

Joseph F. Jackson, Professor of French, University of Illinois, Urbana, Illinois. [Review of Upper Level.] For the general make-up of this examination and for considerations regarding its purpose and procedure, see the above review of the Lower Level. Form UFR contains six passages, with 44 completion-type statements in French, with three choices for each.

While the Upper Level Form would ordinarily be addressed to older students, a difference of one or two years in age would scarcely compensate for the added difficulty in content of the Upper Level examination.

Section I, in verse, is a particularly complex dramatic scene, the partial resolving of a real imbroglio. The number of characters and the involved relations and implications make the scene very confusing. Without referring to the original context, the reviewer had difficulty with two of the five items for comprehension. Section II involves Roman military and political history. Section IV is a rather remote social situation, strained in its humor and effect. Sec-

tion V is heavily historical and political. It is extremely perplexing in the number of personages involved, in their relationships and interests, in the factions and intrigues represented. Section VI deals with the press and with the formation of public opinion. It is deliberately paradoxical and in part quite obscure. (I have reread this passage several times with diminishing returns in trying to find apparent sense in it.)

It is important to test intelligence as well as verbal ability but, unless the material itself is readily comprehensible to the student, the particular purpose of testing the accuracy and scope of his understanding of the foreign language is defeated. At the same time, the range of vocabulary tested is limited by insistence on particular types of subjects. In this case, history, politics, public opinion, and the press constitute half the content of the examination. Surely there could and should be more diversity of subject matter, related more closely to the student's field of experience. A conceivable desire to include in examinations for the armed forces material of a social, political, and historical nature has no valid relation to civilian tests. The mere reference here to armed forces and to civilians suggests the source of the difficulty in attempting to evaluate such tests for ordinary purposes.

Apart from the question of suitability and comprehensiveness of material for general use, the examination is quite well constructed. In addition to the two items mentioned earlier for Section I, only Item 41 is not clear-cut. All the others are well confined to one reasonable choice. The test seems to have been carefully prepared. Two questions of detail arise: page 3, *quelques* for "some"; page 4, "chilly" for *frileux*. This last appears to be a *contresens* in the context. Might it not rather be "sensitive to the cold"?

With the reservations noted, which should not affect older students unduly, the examination is good of its kind.

Clarence E. Turner, Associate Professor of the Romance Languages, Rutgers University, New Brunswick, New Jersey. The USAFI booklet accompanying these and the other academic-subject tests states, without attempting proof, that the present forms are "equivalent to" those prepared for the testing of service personnel. Their use is recommended in order

Examination in French Reading Comprehension

to evaluate justly the educational experiences of the veteran. The development of local norms by particular educational institutions is quite rightly urged. The separate norm tables accompanying these tests give parallel columns of raw scores and percentile ratings together with the number of cases (for Form A only, ranging from 103 to 810) on which the norms for each class level are based. The booklet discusses the construction of the tests in the most general terms, and one wishes one might know for these particular tests what the defined objectives were.

At both levels, the tests consist of forty-odd triple-choice completions in French based on six French passages which include some poetry. The distractors vary from the ingenious to the quite obvious and do not as a rule contain a core of elements in common with the best answer so as to throw a point into relief. A good deal is tested besides comprehension of French, notably intelligence, logic, and the ability to give close attention to something not very interesting. We are told that it is hard to decide whether cats, when tested for intelligence, are stupid or just bored, and there are moments when these tests threaten to create the same problem. At bottom, what is being tested here is the ability to recognize and match two different ways of saying the same thing, and the authors have devised one or two clever traps for those who match on an uncomprehending mechanical basis. If the directions called for the best answer rather than for "the correct" one, the student's perplexity would be diminished at some points.

While it is necessary to grant without question the usefulness of the tests for the purpose we have cited from the booklet, doubts arise as to their wider value. Their claims to superiority in the field would be that they avoid the use of English (save for rare bracketed explanations) and that they test no item out of context. But even the most perfect reading comprehension test would no longer reflect to a useful degree the prevailing curriculum, now that the teaching profession seems to be abandoning the notion (entertained for the quarter century between two global wars!) that Americans need to know no more of foreign languages than how to read them.

[185]

★**Examination in French Vocabulary.** 1-2 years high school or 1 year college, 2½ years high school or

2 years college; 1944–45; IBM; 1 form (usually called Form B); 2 levels; separate answer sheets must be used; $1.75 per 25 of either level; 40¢ per 25 machine-scorable answer sheets for either level; 15¢ per scoring key for either level; 25¢ per specimen set of either level, postpaid; 40(45) minutes; prepared by the Examinations Staff of the United States Armed Forces Institute; published by the American Council on Education; distributed by Cooperative Test Service. (Also distributed by Science Research Associates: $2 per 25 of either level; 65¢ per machine-scorable answer sheets for either level; 50¢ per key; 50¢ per specimen set.)
a) LOWER LEVEL. 1944; 1-2 years high school or 1 year college; Form LFV-1-B-4.
b) UPPER LEVEL. 1945; 2½ years high school or 2 years college; Form UFV-1-B-4.

Nelson Brooks, Instructor in French, Westover School, Middlebury, Connecticut. There is much of value in these two tests, yet one cannot examine them carefully without concluding that they have been based on a doubtful assumption and constructed in the wrong way. The authors seem to feel that all vocabulary should be tested for in context, although the test itself proves this to be wrong. They also seem to assume that a suitable context is any complete sentence that contains the expression to be tested, which is debatable indeed. The series is at its best in such items as 41 and 61, Upper Level, in which the vocabulary expression is well integrated with the entire sentence. However, in such an item as 46, Lower Level (Réfléchissez bien avant de choisir votre *métier*), the sentence adds exactly nothing and is merely a waste of time. In Item 7, Lower Level, dealing with the word *malgré*, the sentence, whose English equivalent is "She is old in spite of her blond horses," becomes a definite liability. The misprint here is bad enough, although the student can probably correct it if the testmakers could not (even in a second printing), but it is less serious than the use of a sentence so obviously carpentered for a test. To have anything like its proper validity, the context must be a sentence taken from something that a writer has written for some purpose other than to make a test. Not only is the student entitled to deal with sentences that have the tang of plausibility rather than the woodenness of makeshift, but the test will prove far more if he does.

A context has been supplied in all 160 items of the two tests, yet the results seem to substantiate the case for testing many of them by themselves. There should be, of course, no doubt about the value of testing isolated words. Of two lists of, say, 50 words selected within the same limits in the frequency list, the student will always make approximately the same score on the second as on the first, as any teacher can easily prove for himself. This would hardly be true if it were not the measurement of something very definite indeed and therefore worth measuring.

Testing for words in context, though by no means the only or the most efficient method of measuring vocabulary, can be very fruitful if the words and the context are rightly chosen. In not more than half of the items in these tests can it be said that the context limits or complements the test word in terms of the equivalents offered. In the other half, the word might as well, or might better, be set down opposite its five possible meanings, in which form it can be handled twice as fast. In the forty minutes allowed for one test, the student could then handle 120 items instead of 80 and would be measured that much more accurately. If the test for vocabulary in context is to be fully exploited, the equivalents should all be right translations of the single word, only one of which is right for the particular context. There is no example of this throughout the two tests.

It is, of course, much more difficult to devise distractors for single words than for words in context, and it is significant that in these tests the majority of wrong answers are suggested not by the word in question but by the rest of the sentence. Yet this can be done, and anyone in search of likely distractors has only to ask a group of students to write what they think the foreign word means in English, and he will get a crop that will be highly useful and often surprising. He will discover that in every case there is a logical, even though erroneous, connection in the student's mind, for logic can be very misleading when it comes to handling verbal symbols. It is in this region of false analogies that the author must look for his distractors if he is to duplicate the processes of the student's mind.

To be specific, take the sample item on the first page of the tests. As equivalents for *travail* in the sentence "Ce travail est difficile," the authors suggest *game, work, chair, book, bed.* Three of these are acceptable, *work* being right and *game* and *book,* though in no way resembling *travail,* at least being among things that are sometimes difficult. *Chair* and *bed* are worthless, for they are in no way connected

Examination in French Vocabulary

with *travail,* and, whatever else they are, they simply aren't difficult. A far more likely list of wrong answers would be *trial, journey, trail, crossing,* all of which may be difficult and all of which are enough like *travail* directly or through synonyms to distract the student who does not immediately respond to the combination *travail—work* and thus to separate him from those who do. If half the items in these tests were to be remade along these lines, the series might become a useful, even accurate, instrument.

[186]
★French Grammar Test: Dominion Tests. Grades 9-10; 1940–41; Forms A, B; 65¢ per 25; 30¢ per specimen set; specimen set must be purchased to obtain the manual; 27(35) minutes; prepared by the Department of Educational Research, Ontario College of Education, University of Toronto; Vocational Guidance Centre.

John H. Meyer, Former Assistant Examiner, Board of Examinations, The University of Chicago, Chicago, Illinois. On the basis of a detailed analysis of the major points covered by the two forms of this test, this reviewer questions the accuracy of the statement in the test manual that the difference between Forms A and B is "probably small." The differences between the two parts of the test in both A and B are purely formal. Both within and between forms, there is considerable overlapping. For flagrant instances of reduplication, see especially: Item 49 in both forms (identical item); Items 77 and 80, 79 and 82, in Form A; 70 and 74 in Form B. For examples of items which test more than one point, see especially: Form A, Items 69, 70, 76, 77, 78, 80, 81; Form B, Items 72, 75, 77, 78, 82.

The material presentation of the test (especially Part I) is clumsy, confusing for the student, and arduous for the scorer. The manual admits that "the pupils occasionally misunderstand the directions," which in themselves are explicit enough. The items in Part I are presented in groups of two to four with a common set of five possible completions, of which the student is to choose one. Actually, in many cases, he does nothing of the sort. In answering Item 1, Form A (a typical case), he (a) distinguishes between the conjunctive personal pronoun and the definite article, eliminating three possible responses, and (b) makes a true-false choice between the two remaining responses.

Any attempt at tightening up, correcting, and improving this test would mean practically rewriting it.

[187]
★French Reading: Dominion Tests. Grade 10; 1940–41; Forms A, B; 65¢ per 25; 30¢ per specimen set; specimen set must be purchased to obtain the manual; 30(35) minutes; prepared by the Department of Educational Research, Ontario College of Education, University of Toronto; Vocational Guidance Centre.

Geraldine Spaulding, Editor, National Teacher Examinations, New York, New York. This is a reading test designed for use in Canadian high schools, and recommended for grade 10 only. Each form contains eight very simple anecdotes, with three to five questions on each. The passages are well selected and furnish appropriate material for reading at a very elementary level. There is very little use of past tenses, and there are no subjunctives.

The questions are in French, and are to be answered in English. This arrangement has the advantage that French questions tend to "give away" the meaning of the passage much less than do English questions. Some of the questions leave room for a good deal of variation in the responses (thus complicating the scoring), but it is difficult to phrase questions that will avoid such variation and still test more than the comprehension of details. On the whole, the questions achieve a very satisfactory compromise between the need for minimizing variation in correct responses, and the need for testing comprehension of a sustained thought.

A booklet furnished with the tests contains very explicit instructions for administering and scoring, keys, percentile norms (Canadian), reliability data, and (addressed to the expert in statistics) measures of internal consistency.

[188]
★French Vocabulary Test: Dominion Tests. Grades 9–10; 1940–41; Forms A, B; 65¢ per 25; 30¢ per specimen set; specimen set must be purchased to obtain the manual; 30(35) minutes; prepared by the Department of Educational Research, Ontario College of Education, University of Toronto; Vocational Guidance Centre.

Roland Vinette, Professor of Measurement and Testing, Institute of Psychology, University of Montreal, Montreal, Canada. Each of these vocabulary tests contains 100 questions. Each question consists of a French word followed by five English words or phrases. The subject must decide which one of the English words or phrases is the best translation for the French word.

A careful comparison of these 200 French words (100 for each form) with an unpublished list of the 6,000 words most used by French-Canadian pupils reveals that about 50 per cent of the 200 words fall among the first thousand. The remaining 50 per cent are distributed from the second to the fifth thousand. This proves the validity of these tests as a measure of knowledge in the more common French vocabulary.

These tests are also reliable and easy to give. However, a more practical key, directly adjustable to the test, would be desirable; at present the examiner has to make the key from answers listed in the manual. This minor disadvantage should not reduce the value of the test.

[189]
Iowa Placement Examinations: French Training: Series FT1, Revised. Grades 12-13; 1924–26; Forms A, B; $4 per 100; 50¢ per specimen set including the other 10 tests in the series, postpaid; 45(50) minutes; prepared under the direction of C. E. Seashore and G. M. Ruch; C. E. Young, G. E. Vander Beke, and G. D. Stoddard; Bureau of Educational Research and Service, State University of Iowa.

REFERENCES

1. STODDARD, GEORGE DINSMORE. *Iowa Placement Examinations.* University of Iowa, Studies in Education, Vol. 3, No. 2. Iowa City, Iowa: the University, 1925. Pp. 103. Paper. $1.00. *
2. STODDARD, GEORGE D. "Iowa Placement Examinations." *Sch & Soc* 24:212-6 Ag 14 '26. *
3. THARP, JAMES B. "Sectioning Classes in Romance Languages." *Mod Lang J* 12:95-114 N '27. *
4. MILLER, LAWRENCE WILLIAM. *An Experimental Study of the Iowa Placement Examinations.* University of Iowa Studies in Education, Vol. 5, No. 6. Iowa City, Iowa: the University, 1930. Pp. 116. Paper. $1.00. * (PA 5:799)

Geraldine Spaulding, Editor, National Teacher Examinations, New York, New York. This test is quite old, Form A being dated 1925 and Form B, 1926. The norms which are furnished presumably date back to the same period and are of questionable value after twenty years. Since only one percentile table is supplied for each form (apparently based on students with one year of high school study), no basis is furnished for the interpretation of results for students with other amounts of study.

With respect to content, Form B is somewhat superior to Form A. In the vocabulary part of Form A, at least a fourth of the words are almost identical in English, while Form B contains no particularly obvious cognates. The frequency range of the words in this part is quite wide, covering the entire range of the *French Word Book.* Part 2, on grammar and idiom, offers stereotyped problems, primarily on very elementary grammar points. Part 3, on verb forms, is rather heavily weighted with uses of the subjunctive. The passages presented for reading in Part 4 appear pretty difficult for students with one year of high school study.

The techniques used include both multiple choice and completion. However, the advantages of each technique are not well utilized. Teachers often disapprove the presentation of unidiomatic constructions and incorrect or nonexistent forms, which is practically unavoidable in multiple-choice items on inflected forms and syntax. In this test, the only multiple-choice part is the one on verb forms, where this disadvantage is most obvious. And this same defect is introduced unnecessarily in Part 2, where incorrect sentences are to be corrected, in free-response items. Multiple-choice items might better have been used for the vocabulary and reading (where acceptable answers in free-response form are likely to include more variants), and completion items for the verb forms.

Since three of the four parts consist of completion items, the scoring of the test is more time-consuming and less objective than the scoring of a straight multiple-choice test, and some knowledge of French on the part of the scorer is advisable.　•

GERMAN

[190]

Cooperative German Test: Advanced Form. At least 4 semesters high school or 1 year college; 1938–40; Forms O, P, Q; separate answer sheets need not be used; $2 per 25; 25¢ per specimen set, postpaid; 40¢ per 25 machine-scorable answer sheets; 15¢ per stencil for scoring answer sheets; 40(45) minutes; Miriam Van Dyck Hespelt, E. Herman Hespelt, and Geraldine Spaulding; Cooperative Test Service.

REFERENCES

1-4. *See* 40:1360.

Harold B. Dunkel, Examiner, Board of Examinations, The University of Chicago, Chicago, Illinois. [Review of Advanced Forms O, P, and Q.] The existence of several comparable forms, the availability of norms, and the general care with which the materials for administration and for scoring have been prepared, all give these tests (like other products of the Cooperative Test Service) a considerable handicap over other competitors. Fortunately the merits of the tests themselves justify this additional apparatus.

The reliabilities of the parts and of the total tests are not reported, but the standard errors of measurement are plotted beside the scale of scores. It is unfortunate, however, that the directions do not give a simple explanation of what these lines mean, one that would be intelligible and serviceable to the average language teacher, who is unacquainted with statistics. What "error" means in the context of deciding whether to give Willie Johnson a D or an F is something that every teacher should know; and a better understanding of this concept would do much to correct the misapprehensions of those who believe either that test scores possess the infallibility of the Holy Writ or that they are the invention of the Devil. The present effort to report standard errors is undoubtedly a step in the right direction, but I doubt whether it goes far enough to accomplish its purpose.

The tests cover reading, vocabulary (with the words in isolation), and grammar. Though this last part demands only the recognition of the correct structure, it demands a more active manipulation of the language than does reading. As a result, the teacher will probably get most information not from the total score but from the scores on those parts most relevant to the objectives he stresses. This flexibility of the tests for varied teaching procedures is one of their strong points.

A feature of the tests which many teachers like is that the multiple-choice answers are all in German. Thus in the reading section, the student exhibits his comprehension by correctly completing the sentence which forms the item or, in the few longer items, by completing statements about a short passage. Similarly in the vocabulary section he selects that one, of the five German words offered, which is most closely connected with the German word tested. As usual, however, this procedure is attended by some difficulties. The answer must sometimes be apparently more difficult than the question (e.g., Item 3, Part II, Form Q, *erblicken* the answer for *sehen*) and cognates must be used freely (*Energie—Kraft*, 21, II, O). Sometimes the distractors are so farfetched in difficulty (*Lerche* as a possible answer for *Ding*, 6, II, P) or sense (Response 2, 35, I, O) that they can scarcely perform their function.

But these and others like them are relatively minor matters and involve a negligible fraction of the almost 400 items in the three forms reviewed. Of the standardized tests for the abilities covered, therefore, these tests remain the most useful and usable.

For reviews by C. H. Handschin and Curtis C. D. Vail, see 38:1000 and 40:1360.

[191]

★**Examination in German Grammar: Lower Level.** 1-2 years high school or 1 year college; 1945; IBM; Form LGG-1-B-4 (usually called Form B); separate answer sheets must be used; $1.75 per 25; 40¢ per 25 machine-scorable answer sheets; 15¢ per scoring key; 25¢ per specimen set, postpaid; 60(65) minutes; prepared by the Examinations Staff of the United States Armed Forces Institute; published by the American Council on Education; distributed by Cooperative Test Service. (Also distributed by Science Research Associates: $2 per 25; 65¢ per 25 machine-scorable answer sheets; 50¢ per key; 50¢ per specimen set.)

Herbert Schueler, Assistant Professor of Education, Queens College, Flushing, New York. This test of German grammar uses the familiar device of translation from English into German as the basis for the test items. Each English sentence is followed by a stem giving a partial translation (except in the case of very short items) followed by five alternative completions from which the student is to choose the correct one. It is a test of eighty-five items with a time allotment of sixty minutes, which makes it much longer than the grammar sections of both the *American Council Alpha German Test* and the *Cooperative German Tests.*

Since no lists of syntax frequency are available for comparison, any estimate of the adequacy of the sampling of grammar items tested will be largely subjective. About half of the items tested involve case inflections, about a third involve forms of verbs. Only five items involve a problem of word order. No subjunctive forms are tested directly. In the main, the sentences offered are quite short, their form colloquial, and their subject matter practical, with a minimum of the bookishness and old-fashioned style that so often afflict grammar textbooks and tests.

The norm tables are even less adequate than those supplied with the USAFI vocabulary and reading tests. Less than three hundred cases and only a dozen schools are involved, and only students with a background of one year of high school and two years of high school were tested. For this reason, and for the reason that standards for the amount of grammar to be taught at the various levels vary so greatly from school to school and school system to school system, it is imperative that every school expecting to use this test establish its own norms. It will be necessary, in addition, for every school expecting to use this test for grade placement of students seeking credit for work taken in the Armed Forces to compare its course of study in German with the range of items in structure tested here, to help determine its validity for use in each particular situation. A school using the reading method will obviously find less use for a test of this kind, especially in the early terms of the subject, than a school relying on the grammar-translation method. No one-year college norms are available for this test. Since the test is quite difficult for the one-year and two-year high school groups tested (one-year group, 76th percentile, 44 out of a possible 84; two-year group, 71st percentile, 56 out of a possible 84), some norms for more advanced levels, both high school and college, would have been helpful. The results obtained for this test should be used cautiously, pending the publication of more extensive norms. In any case, because of the variability in the amount and extent of the teaching of structure in various schools and school systems, its use as a basis for individual grade placement and the assigning of individual letter grades for work taken in the armed forces is less to be recommended than its use as a means of individual diagnosis and group comparisons.

[192]

★**Examination in German Reading Comprehension: Lower Level.** 1-2 years high school or 1 year college; 1945; IBM; Form LGR-1-B-4 (usually called Form B); separate answer sheets must be used; $1.75 per 25; 40¢ per 25 machine-scorable answer sheets; 15¢ per scoring key; 25¢ per specimen set, postpaid; 50(55) minutes; prepared by the Examinations Staff of the United States Armed Forces Institute; published by the American Council on Education; distributed by Cooperative Test Service. (Also distributed by Science Research Associates: $2 per 25; 65¢ per 25 machine-scorable answer sheets; 50¢ per key; 50¢ per specimen set.)

Herbert Schueler, Assistant Professor of Education, Queens College, Flushing, New York. This test of reading comprehension consists of six reading selections (from about 200 to 300 words in length), each followed by a set of four-alternative multiple-choice completion exercises in German. Of the six selections, one is an excerpt from a poem by Conrad Ferdinand Meyer, two are narrative, two are expository, and one is a short dialogue. All of

Examination in German Reading Comprehension

them are obviously literary in flavor and represent a rather one-sided choice of reading material designed to test reading comprehension. One is reminded too much of the foreign-language classroom in which the newspaper, the popular magazine, the science journal, and the cookbook never play a part in the development of reading skill. This restriction to the "literary" is a definite limitation on the validity of this test.

This reviewer does not feel that the best way to test reading comprehension in a test of this kind is to use the foreign language in the multiple-choice completions. There are at least three serious disadvantages to the use of the foreign language in the test items: (a) It is difficult to construct alternatives in which the correct answer cannot be taken directly from the test. For instance, if in the text you have the sentence, "Ich hatte den Eindruck . . . als fügte sie Worte hinzu" and then have as one of the choices in the test—"Der Held hatte den Eindruck, dass Mademoiselle im Lesen Worte hinzufügte," a student who has no idea of what the key word "hinzufügen" means can get the correct answer by a simple process of matching. (This example was taken from the test.) (b) If, however, the test constructor is careful to avoid such direct matching possibilities, he is in serious danger of yielding to the temptation of constructing items that involve something much more than the ability to comprehend exactly what a paragraph says. For instance, in a short dialogue between a man and a woman about life, love, and the relations between a woman who wishes to give herself freely to a man and a man who rejects her open devotion because he is concerned about his financial ability to found a family, the student is asked to consider whether this story is laid during a time when young people generally could look forward with confidence into the future, or when they felt like starting a revolution, or when they had little hope for the future, or when they didn't worry too much about any of those things. The reading selection may give clues, to be sure, as to what might conceivably have been the most probable era in which the story was played, but there is little direct evidence in the material given to justify confidence in any speculation as to the social atmosphere of the time when it occurred. For this selection in the test, there are two such questions out of the total of seven, each

of which requires either a knowledge of what went on before or pure speculation based on clues given in the selection, which make these items more a test of intelligence and imagination and less of reading comprehension. In another selection, the student is asked to judge whether the selection is written for the purpose of teaching, amusing, or angering the reader, which involves a skill of judging literary tone not necessarily associated with reading ability. (c) A third disadvantage is, that with the test item in the foreign language, you are posing the problem of comprehending the question as well as the paragraph on which it is based. If key words in the test item introduce additional difficulties for the student, for instance, then a student comprehending the paragraph may nevertheless get the wrong answer because he did not comprehend the question. In one item on this test the student sees the following alternative: "Diese Geschichte spielt in einer Zeit, in der junge Menschen mit Zuversicht in die Zukunft sehen." The comprehension of the sentence hinges on the word Zuversicht; if the student doesn't know the meaning, his judgment is based not on his comprehension of the original reading selection but on his knowledge of the meaning of one word in the test item. There are many such examples throughout the test, which seriously limit the test's usability, especially if discriminating measures of the lower levels of reading ability are sought. It would have been much better had the test constructors used English instead of German in the test items. In that way many of the pitfalls mentioned above could have been avoided rather easily, and the problem of reading comprehension could have been narrowed down much more effectively to the actual reading selection.

This test, and the tests of German vocabulary and grammar reviewed below, were designed to offer a basis for evaluating the work done in the subject by returned servicemen in the armed forces for the purpose of securing credit and grade placement in civilian schools. A table of percentile norms for one year of high school, two years of high school, and one year of college are furnished with the test. Unfortunately, these norm tables, especially for the high school levels, are based on too few cases to be used with any degree of confidence. The one-year high school norms were secured from testing only 128 students in seven schools, a sample

Examination in German Reading Comprehension

much too small to form the basis for any reliable comparisons. It is imperative, therefore, as the manual accompanying the test takes great pains to point out, that each school secure its own norms based on the administration of these tests to its own students, before any attempt is made to use the test as a basis for assigning credit to returned servicemen. However, because of the limitations of this test as a test of reading ability, as mentioned above, this reviewer would recommend use of such tried tests as the *Cooperative German Tests*, if not as a replacement for, then at least as a supplement to, this USAFI test.

[193]

★**Examination in German Vocabulary: Lower Level.** 1-2 years high school or 1 year college; 1945; IBM; Form LGV-1-B-4 (usually called Form B); separate answer sheets must be used; $1.75 per 25; 40¢ per 25 machine-scorable answer sheets; 15¢ per scoring key; 25¢ per specimen set, postpaid; 45(50) minutes; prepared by the Examinations Staff of the United States Armed Forces Institute; published by the American Council on Education; distributed by Cooperative Test Service. (Also distributed by Science Research Associates: $2 per 25; 65¢ per 25 machine-scorable answer sheets; 50¢ per key; 50¢ per specimen set.)

Herbert Schueler, Assistant Professor of Education, Queens College, Flushing, New York. This 45-minute vocabulary test contains 75 five-alternative multiple-choice items. Each item consists of a short German sentence containing the word or expression to be tested in boldface type. The five alternative responses are in English and include the correct translation of the expression to be tested. Incorporating the expression to be tested in a sentence is an improvement over the practice followed both in the *American Council Alpha German Test* and in the *Cooperative German Tests* of giving in the stem just the words to be tested. Even though other variables are introduced by this expansion of the stem, especially if the rest of the sentence contains other words of equal or greater difficulty to the candidate, these additional variables are more than compensated for by the advantages gained by placing the expression in natural semantic surroundings. The question of whether to use English or German in the alternatives is one of those oft-debated questions that probably will never be settled to the satisfaction of foreign-language teachers. By placing the alternatives in English, a wider sampling of vocabulary may be secured, especially among those expressions of greatest fre-

quency and therefore of greatest importance. Use of alternatives in the foreign language, however, involves testing by means of synonyms, which in the case of those words of greatest frequency, are almost invariably of lower frequency and therefore less adapted to test the candidates' knowledge of basic vocabulary. For this reason the form of item followed in this test seems to this reviewer to be the best of those so far used.

The choice of expressions to be tested is, in the main, quite good and is well distributed over the frequency ranges, as revealed by a check with the Eaton Semantic Frequency List (which in German is based on Kaeding). About one-third of the expressions tested are verbs or verb phrases, about one-fifth nouns or noun phrases, and another fifth adjectival and adverbial modifiers. One weakness of the test's coverage of verbs is that the seven strong (irregular) verbs tested all appear in the imperfect tense. The German sentences of the stems only occasionally have an armed forces flavor and are, with some exceptions, simple and colloquial in style.

Because of its length and the frequency range of the vocabulary tested, this test should offer a useful measure of vocabulary range of civilian students. If used as a measure for placing students seeking credit for study with the armed forces into grade levels in foreign-language classes, it must be used cautiously. The norm tables provided with the test represent, especially in the case of the norms for the one-year and the two-year high school levels, a sample that is much too small. Less than three hundred students and fourteen schools are involved, hardly a basis for accurate comparisons and placement. As the very helpful manual accompanying this test points out, it will be necessary for schools expecting to use these tests for placement purposes to determine their own local norms first, and if they are found to deviate significantly from the published norms, to use the former as a basis for comparison. This determining of local norms would be necessary even with adequate national norms, since the content of foreign-language courses is so highly variable from one institution to the next. In any case, the use of this test for diagnostic and guidance purposes, as suggested by the manual, may represent a clue to its best usefulness.

[194]

Lundeberg-Tharp Audition Test in German. High school and college; 1929; Forms A, B; $2 per 100; 10¢ per specimen set; Olav K. Lundeberg and James B. Tharp assisted by C. A. Williams; James B. Tharp, College of Education, Ohio State University, Columbus, Ohio.

Harold B. Dunkel, Examiner, Board of Examinations, The University of Chicago, Chicago, Illinois. These are the pioneering efforts to measure the aural comprehension of German and are probably the most widely used tests in this general area at present. The two forms are parallel and generally comparable. In the 50 items of Part I, Phonetic Accuracy, the student selects, from four German words printed on the answer sheet, the one read by the examiner. In Part II, Completion Series, the student writes, in English or German, the word which best completes each of 25 incomplete sentences which are read to him one by one. In Part III he writes the object or idea defined by a short German sentence. Instructions for reading and administering are given, as well as norms for high school semesters, though the size and nature of the groups used in standardizing are not reported. No data on reliability or on the intercorrelations between the parts are given, but the reviewer believes from personal experience with these and similar materials that the reliabilities are probably sufficiently high.

Reviewers of tests, like the reviewers of anthologies, are often critical merely because the authors did not select the same material the reviewers would have chosen. And certainly it is unfair to ask a test to measure everything in forty minutes. With this disclaimer, I mention two points. In exercises like Part I, "phonetic accuracy" is, for some languages, only part of the skill demanded; the student also must be able to translate the sounds he hears into the conventional spelling of that language. In these cases, the test is as much a measure of "orthographic" as of "phonetic" accuracy. The former is an important skill and, though it should not be confused with aural proficiency, is probably worth measuring in some aural tests. In a language having such relatively phonetic spelling as does German, however, the task is quite simple (as the norms for these tests show); and once the student is past the very elementary stages, the test may reflect primarily the artificial situation produced by

the words being isolated from context or the failure of the reader to make his phonetic distinctions perfectly clear. Some of us, consequently, would prefer to see Part I for German replaced by a measure of ability to comprehend longer continuous passages. This ability is not highly correlated with the ability measured by the completions and definitions; the beginner can often cope with single sentences but gets swamped by the longer units he is certain to meet in conversations, movies, and radio broadcasts. Teachers using the present form can easily supplement it in this regard.

The major problem of standardizing aural tests is, of course, that of standardizing their oral administration. In the directions the authors have done what they can to obtain comparable situations when the tests must be read by many different readers under different circumstances. But that variable remains and should be remembered by teachers in interpreting the norms.

Some minor infelicities (e.g., the misprint in Item 29, Part I, Form A and Item 15, Part I, Form B or the keying of Item 18, Part III, Form B) can be easily cleared up in revision and need not affect the present utility of the tests. With increased interest in the aural-oral skills, teachers will (or should) want to know how their classes stack up. This test, within its necessary limitations, can be recommended to them for this purpose.

HEBREW

[195]

★**Group Test in Siddur Reading.** 1943–47; 1 form; 5¢ per test; 15¢ per sample test; Noah Nardi; Jewish Education Committee of New York, Inc.

[196]

★**Hebrew Aptitude Test.** Ages 8-17 and adults; 1946; 1 form; 5¢ per test; 15¢ per sample test; 48(60) minutes; Noah Nardi; Jewish Education Committee of New York, Inc.

REFERENCES
1. NARDI, NOAH. "A Test to Measure Aptitude in the Hebrew Language." *J Ed Psychol* 38:167-76 Mr '47. * (PA 22:537)

[197]

★**Hebrew Intermediate Test.** 1946; Forms A, B; 5¢ per test; 15¢ per sample test; Noah Nardi; Jewish Education Committee of New York, Inc.

[198]

★**Hebrew Primary Test.** First 2 years of a Talmud Torah curriculum; 1943; Forms A, B; 5¢ per test; 15¢ per sample test; (60) minutes; Noah Nardi; Jewish Education Committee of New York, Inc.

ITALIAN

[199]

★Cooperative Italian Test. At least 2 semesters; 1947; revision of Experimental Forms Q and S; IBM; Form X (experimental Forms Q and S are available on order for large quantities); separate answer sheets need not be used; $1.75 per 25; 25¢ per specimen set, postpaid; 40¢ per 25 machine-scorable answer sheets; 15¢ per stencil for scoring answer sheets; Form X: 40(45) minutes; Forms Q and S: 70(75) minutes; Peter Riccio and Anthony Cuffari; Cooperative Test Service.

Elton Hocking, Professor of Modern Languages and Head of the Department, Purdue University, Lafayette, Indiana. These tests are in the familiar pattern of the Cooperative tests in foreign languages, scorable by key or machine. However, no information is supplied concerning construction, validation, norms, etc.

Of the seventy items in Part I of Form Q, 27 per cent are based on four anecdotes averaging ten lines each. The correct responses are frequently mere synonyms or paraphrases of expressions in the anecdote, and they are often located for the student by the key statement which quotes the anecdote almost verbatim. This is valid testing, but it is usually classified as vocabulary. The only essential difference between such items and those of Part II (Vocabulary) is that the latter lists the vocabulary equivalents in English. Eleven items in Part I are concerned with matters of geography, history, music, etc. Such questions would perhaps be justified in a test of "Italian culture," but they have no place in a test of reading comprehension. This tendency to stray from the purposes of the test is found also in connection with the anecdotes, where some of the "correct" responses (Items 57, 58, 61) are based not on the facts of the narration but on inferences which the authors have drawn from those facts. If the student draws another inference, his response is "wrong." This tendency reaches the point of absurdity in Item 56, which requires the student to pass judgment on the anecdote in question. If he judges it to be "silly," his response is "wrong"; the only "correct" response is "amusing." Of the remaining 40 items in Part I, the majority should be classified as vocabulary rather than reading, for the statements (averaging less than one line in length) are so brief that the student can only compare the key word with the five responses. These words, in turn, are too frequently concerned with food and drink and "daily life"

vocabulary in general; a student with a fair reading knowledge in the Italian classics might conceivably be embarrassed by these bread-and-butter details. His knowledge of constructions and idioms, his ability to deduce meanings from the context will not help him here.

Parts II and III of Form Q show a better balance of materials and a good spread in degree of difficulty. However, they seem not to have been checked against Part I for duplications, and the whole test shows lapses in technique, such as wrong responses which are obvious for external reasons and the use, in Part III, of only the blank-filling technique. Unfortunately, some constructions, such as the use or omission of the article, do not lend themselves to this device. Again, mere blank-filling is too cumbersome to handle the delicate questions of word order or correlative constructions. Such difficulties could have been overcome by a series of items using complete responses and, with the fill-ins, the "No additional word needed" response.

In general, the above comments apply also to Form S, except that in Part I the statements are even shorter, consisting frequently of only subject and verb; "cultural" items have risen to 28 per cent; the anecdotes and exercises on them are somewhat better. Part III gives verb forms complete, and the number of such items has risen to 40 per cent. Although the total number of items in Form S is 223, and in Form Q 245, the same working time (70 minutes) is specified for each.

These tests lack the expert workmanship which generally characterizes the Cooperative tests in foreign languages. This is unfortunate because these are the only tests of this type yet available for Italian. However, the 1947 catalog announces Form X, "made up of items selected and revised from the two experimental forms." No doubt this will be a more useful test.

[200]

★Examination in Italian Grammar: Lower Level. 1-2 years high school or 1 year college; 1945; IBM; Form LIG-1-B-4 (usually called Form B); no norms available; separate answer sheets must be used; $1.75 per 25; 40¢ per 25 machine-scorable answer sheets; 15¢ per scoring key; 25¢ per specimen set, postpaid; 50(55) minutes; prepared by the Examinations Staff of the United States Armed Forces Institute; published by the American Council on Education; distributed by Cooperative Test Service. (Also distributed by Science Research Associates: $2 per 25; 65¢ per 25 machine-scorable answer sheets; 50¢ per key; 50¢ per specimen set.)

[201]

★**Examination in Italian Reading Comprehension: Lower Level.** 1-2 years high school or 1 year college; 1945; IBM; Form LIR-1-B-4 (usually called Form B) ; no norms available; separate answer sheets must be used; $1.75 per 25; 40¢ per 25 machine-scorable answer sheets; 15¢ per scoring key; 25¢ per specimen set, postpaid; 50(55) minutes; prepared by the Examinations Staff of the United States Armed Forces Institute; published by the American Council on Education; distributed by Cooperative Test Service. (Also distributed by Science Research Associates: $2 per 25; 65¢ per 25 machine-scorable answer sheets; 50¢ per key; 50¢ per specimen set.)

[202]

★**Examination in Italian Vocabulary: Lower Level.** 1-2 years high school or 1 year college; 1945; IBM; Form LIV-1-B-4 (usually called Form B) ; no norms available; separate answer sheets must be used; $1.75 per 25; 40¢ per 25 machine-scorable answer sheets; 15¢ per scoring key; 25¢ per specimen set, postpaid; 50(55) minutes; prepared by the Examinations Staff of the United States Armed Forces Institute; published by the American Council on Education; distributed by Cooperative Test Service. (Also distributed by Science Research Associates: $2 per 25; 65¢ per 25 machine-scorable answer sheets; 50¢ per key; 50¢ per specimen set.)

LATIN

[203]

★**[Cooperative Latin Comprehension Test.]** 1-2 years high school or 1 year college, more than 2 years high school or more than 1 year college; 1942; this test is, as the booklet title indicates, Part 1 of the *Cooperative Latin Test:* Lower and Higher Levels; IBM; Form S; 2 levels; separate answer sheets need not be used; $1.75 per 25; 25¢ per specimen set of either level, postpaid; 40¢ per 25 machine-scorable answer sheets; 15¢ per stencil for scoring answer sheets; 40(45) minutes; Harold V. King and Geraldine Spaulding. Cooperative Test Service.
a) LOWER LEVEL. 1-2 years high school or 1 year college.
b) HIGHER LEVEL. More than 2 years high school or more than 1 year college.

Hazel M. Toliver, Instructor in Latin, Indiana University, Bloomington, Indiana. With these tests is furnished a pamphlet containing an abundance of material on administering and scoring the tests and on tabulating and interpreting the results. Tables of norms and percentile scores based on the scores of a large number of students are supplied.

Both tests are unusually accurate and well edited. The only error seems to be in the key for Item 14 in Section 2 of the Higher Level test.

Each test contains three divisions of multiple-choice questions: a vocabulary section of sixty words; ten Latin sentences to be completed; and Latin passages (five in the Lower Level test and seven in the Higher Level) upon which are based statements to be completed.

The vocabulary section is useful in checking

the student's knowledge of Latin words, although isolated words do not measure real understanding of words in context.

The Latin sentences to be completed offer a fair representation of typical Latin idioms and constructions and should, to some extent, measure general knowledge of grammar and syntax. Actually, however, the lists of words and phrases from which the student must complete the sentences are such that the choice depends much more upon the actual meanings involved than upon any grammatical or syntactical differences among the answers. Hence, this division tests vocabulary and comprehension more effectively than it does grammar and syntax. Perhaps the test would be better if this division were lengthened and the vocabulary section shortened or eliminated.

The Latin passages in the third division become progressively more difficult and are well calculated to test the comprehension ability of even the best students. The statements based upon the passages involve both factual and thought answers. In some cases, because the statements fail to cover the material sufficiently, a student whose understanding of the whole passage was rather hazy could answer most of the questions. Since such passages must be taken out of context and usually offer some difficulty because of this fact, this section might be improved by reducing the number of passages, lengthening those retained, and supplying more questions—preferably such as would require real insight on the student's part.

On the whole, these tests could be expected to measure with reasonable accuracy what they claim to measure—ability to comprehend the thought contained in the Latin.

[204]

Cooperative Latin Test: Elementary and Advanced Forms. 1-3 semesters high school or 1 semester college, at least 2 years high school or 1 year college; 1939-41; IBM; Forms P, Q, R; 2 levels; separate answer sheets need not be used; $1.75 per 25; 25¢ per specimen set of either level, postpaid; 40¢ per 25 machine-scorable answer sheets; 15¢ per stencil for scoring answer sheets; 40(45) minutes; Form P: John C. Kirtland; Forms Q and R: George A. Land; Cooperative Test Service.
a) ELEMENTARY FORM. 1-3 semesters high school or 1 semester college.
b) ADVANCED FORM. At least 2 years high school or 1 year college.

REFERENCES
1. TRAXLER, ARTHUR E. "The Relation of Vocabulary and Grammar to Reading Achievement in Latin, French, and Spanish," pp. 61-5. In *1947 Achievement Testing Program in Independent Schools and Supplementary Studies.* Educational Records Bulletin, No. 48. New York: Educational Records Bureau, June 1947. Pp. xii, 66. Paper, lithotyped. $2.00. * (PA 22:449)

For reviews by S. D. Adkins, Harold B. Dunkel, John Flagg Gummere, and Norman T. Pratt, Jr., see 38:1064, 38:1065, and 40:1365.

[205]

★Cooperative Latin Test: Lower and Higher Levels. 1-2 years high school or 1 year college, more than 2 years high school or more than 1 year college; 1942; IBM; Form S; 2 levels; separate answer sheets need not be used; $2 per 25; 25¢ per specimen set of either level, postpaid; 60¢ per 25 machine-scorable answer sheets; 30¢ per stencil for scoring answer sheets; 80(85) minutes; Harold V. King and Geraldine Spaulding; Cooperative Test Service.
a) LOWER LEVEL. 1-2 years high school or 1 year college.
b) HIGHER LEVEL. More than 2 years high school or more than 1 year college.

REFERENCES

1. TRAXLER, ARTHUR E. "Some Data on the Results of the Cooperative Tests in French, Latin, and Secondary School Mathematics, Form S," pp. 55-9. In 1942 *Achievement Testing Program in Independent Schools and Supplementary Studies.* Educational Records Bulletin, No. 36, New York; Educational Records Bureau, June 1942. Pp. xiii, 59. Paper, lithotyped. $1.50. *

C. W. Odell, Professor of Education, University of Illinois, Urbana, Illinois. Although these tests probably deserve rank as the best tests dealing with the phases of Latin which they cover, they are still subject to a number of adverse criticisms. Each consists of three parts, one of which is subdivided. Part I, Comprehension, calls for selecting the proper one of five English words for each of a number of Latin words, of five Latin words or phrases to complete each of a number of incomplete Latin statements, and of English words, phrases, or clauses to complete statements about Latin passages which have been read. Part II, Grammar, calls for a selection of proper endings and forms to complete Latin sentences for which the English translations are given. Part III, Civilization, is likewise in multiple-answer form and deals with varied aspects of Roman history, society, literature, private life, and so forth. The general form and setup of the tests is good. The fact that the answers are to be placed in parentheses instead of blanks makes scoring somewhat slower. The directions for giving and scoring, the norms, and other supplementary materials likewise appear to be satisfactory.

The content appears to be based almost entirely on the traditional sequence of Caesar, Cicero, and Virgil, so that the tests are not well adapted for use in schools following the modern trend in the selection of content. In Part I, Section 1, it would be desirable to have all of each group of five suggested answers the same part of speech. As they are, alert pupils may derive some clues as to which ones to eliminate

from consideration. In the Lower Level, Part I, Section 2, Item 15, ten days are referred to as "a little more than a week"; in Item 29, "to be" should be "to have been"; in Item 36, Choice 4 seems a correct answer as well as 5. In Part II, Item 28, "his" is in italics for no apparent reason. In Part III, Item 20, the correct answer is that clocks were unfamiliar to the Romans, a statement which is not true unless limited to modern types of clocks. In the Higher Level, Part II, Item 20, "these" is translated "illae" rather than "hae"; in Items 22 and 27 similar constructions are differently translated, that used in Item 27 being poor usage if not absolutely incorrect.

The third parts of the two levels contain five elements that are exactly the same and two others almost so. Moreover, there are several items in this part of both levels that call for knowledge that probably would have been acquired only by reading specific sections of Latin authors that might easily not be included in a high school course.

The form "Antonius" rather than "Anthony" is used, but inconsistently "Pompey" rather than "Pompeius" and "Octavian" rather than "Octavianus."

[206]

Kansas First Year Latin Test. First, second semesters high school; 1936; 2 forms; 2 levels; 90¢ per 25, postpaid; 15¢ per specimen set, postpaid; 40(45) minutes; Mary Alice Seller, Lois Bellinger, and H. E. Schrammel; Bureau of Educational Measurements, Kansas State Teachers College of Emporia.
a) TEST I, FORMS A AND B. First semester.
b) TEST V, FORMS C AND D. Second semester.

Hazel M. Toliver, Instructor in Latin, Indiana University, Bloomington, Indiana. The four forms of this test are similar in structure and also in the amazing number of errors which they contain. Misprints include *prevēnit* and *thonsand* in Form A, *dābēs* and *lead* in Form B, *adīvīsse* and *urnos* in Form C, and *appelāvit* and *mūitibus* in Form D. Mistakes and omissions in the markings of long vowels are inexcusably frequent. Other errors are the incorrect syllable division of *comparābās* in Form A and *King Philippi* in Form C, and the illogical tense of *respondet* in the reading passage of Form A and of *exclāmat* in Form B.

Part I of each form contains a Latin passage with true-false statements based upon it. The value of such questions depends upon careful selection of material and carefully worded questions requiring real insight on the student's part.

Kansas First Year Latin Test

Yet Form A offers a story commonly read in grade school. Most students could probably answer at least 6 of the 15 questions without having looked at the Latin. In Form C the selection is none too clear; the first true-false statement is not completely covered in the passage; the fifth is couched in extremely odd English; the ninth is puzzling and cannot be answered from the Latin; and the truth or falsity of the eleventh and sixteenth statements is not clearly ascertainable from the Latin passage. This part of the test is better handled on Forms B and D, although there might be some question about the material used on Form D, since many first-year Latin textbooks contain accounts of Aeneas's adventures.

Part II on Forms C and D, designed to test knowledge of forms and syntax, is poor because only one true-false explanation for the construction of each of several words and phrases from the reading passage is offered. Part II on Forms A and B, with multiple-choice questions with the same objective, is more effective. Item 22 on Form C explains *sub diciōne* as "ablative with preposition, *sub,* to indicate place where something is carried on." Since no actual place is involved, such a true-false statement could be confusing for the student. For Item 27 the key is wrong. A practice pedagogically objectionable is followed in Part II of Forms A and B and in Part III of Form C, where nonexistent forms of Latin words are presented as possible answers.

Part III on Forms C and D tests knowledge of certain elementary principles of grammar and syntax. On Form C some five of the rules listed are hardly appropriate because many first-year students never hear of them. On Form D this part is badly arranged, and the scoring is made awkward by the fact that the number arrangement on the key does not correspond to that on the test. In Item 33 the rule itself supplies the correct answer.

Part V on Forms C and D and Part III on Form B, word-study questions, merely list the English derivatives. Part III on Form A is better because the English words appear in sentences. There are two blunders in definition: *impecunious* is defined as "lack of money" and *amiable* as "affectionate."

All four forms of this test have too many yes-or-no questions, which invite guessing and reduce the effectiveness of the test. No penalty for guessing is provided in the scoring, and the questions are not weighted properly since the yes-or-no type has the same value as the multiple-choice. Furthermore, the proportion of questions testing language elements compared with those on background and derivatives is much too small.

Although there is some good testing material in these tests, this reviewer could not honestly recommend them, in their present form, to any teacher who desired effective and accurate measuring instruments.

For review by John Flagg Gummere, see 40:1368.

[207]

Orleans-Solomon Latin Prognosis Test. Grades 9-16; 1926; Form A; $1.70 per 25; 35¢ per specimen set, postpaid; 50(55) minutes; Jacob S. Orleans and Michael Solomon; World Book Co.

C. W. Odell, Professor of Education, University of Illinois, Urbana, Illinois. Although it has been more than 20 years since this test appeared, it still merits use for the prediction of probable success in Latin courses. The test consists mainly of a series of short lessons to be studied followed by tests over their content. It is therefore valid only for those who have never studied Latin previously. Its use indicates that a coefficient of correlation of .70 or higher can usually be secured between the scores on this test and success in beginning Latin courses.

The scoring provisions are one of the points of weakness. The form of answer called for in some cases is such as to allow some element of subjectivity in scoring, but it is doubtful whether this can be avoided without weakening the functioning of the test. In some of the tests only certain aspects of the answers are scored, and others, even if incorrect, do not count. It is at least doubtful whether this is better than scoring on all aspects of the answers. The scoring key for Tests 8 and 9 is not sufficiently specific. For example, for "puella" it is not clear whether to be considered correct, the answer must be "the girl," as given in the key, or whether "girl" or even "girls" should be accepted. The maximum score on the test is only 222, but the form for tabulation goes up to 242. Moreover, all the intervals provided therein are not the same, thus violating good statistical practice.

In several instances there appears to have been carelessness in wording. Thus, in Lesson 2, the practice as to whether or not an article is used before a Latin noun is not consistent. In Test 2,

(b) and (e) contain "if," which it would have been better to omit. Lessons 3 and 4 are so nearly repetitions that they might well have been combined. Lesson 4 and some others thereafter close with the statement, "Think what this lesson teaches you." It would seem better to have followed this with more specific statements or reminders.

Some of the suggested answers to Test 1 are probably not commonly known to ninth grade pupils. Examples are "equitant," "equitation," "militate," "matriarch." Latin words for which English derivatives would be more commonly known might well have been chosen. Test 4 contains the sentence, "The eagle destroys the land," which is utter nonsense insofar as its meaning is concerned.

Other points about which questions might well be raised are the desirability of having pupils tear off the list of study words rather than of merely placing it at the first and not allowing them to turn back; the reason why Lessons 3 and 4 and the following tests, and also Tests 8 and 9, are not united into one since they are very similar; and the practice of translating first person singular, present active indicative verbs by infinitives, for example, "narro—to tell."

SPANISH

[208]

★Examination in Spanish Grammar: Lower Level. 1-2 years high school or 1 year college; 1944; IBM; Form LSG-1-B-4 (usually called Form B); separate answer sheets must be used; $1.75 per 25; 40¢ per 25 machine-scorable answer sheets; 15¢ per scoring key; 25¢ per specimen set, postpaid; 40(45) minutes; prepared by the Examinations Staff of the United States Armed Forces Institute; published by the American Council on Education; distributed by Cooperative Test Service. (Also distributed by Science Research Associates: $2 per 25; 65¢ per 25 machine-scorable answer sheets; 50¢ per key; 50¢ per specimen set.)

Frederick B. Agard, Associate Professor of Modern Languages, Cornell University, Ithaca, New York. This forty-minute test of elementary Spanish grammar, now available in the civilian language-teaching field, employs the established multiple-choice technique for objective tests of the achievement type. The composition of its sixty items is the same as that used in the grammar sections of the Cooperative Test Service and the College Entrance Examination Board tests. In each item, a short English sentence is followed by its Spanish equivalent in which one word or phrase, embodying the grammatical point to be tested, is omitted. Below the pair of sentences appear two, three, four, or five (in most items five) words or phrases, one of which is the grammatically correct missing element of the Spanish version. The student indicates his answer on a separate sheet (which may be machine scored). The distractors are all composed of real Spanish forms; in most cases they are merely syntactically incorrect within the given sentence, and in a few items they offer meaningless sequences of forms (e.g., *soy yendo a abrir*).

Of the sixty points of syntax tested, fifty-two have a range of 35 or higher in Keniston's *Spanish Syntax List* and are thus to be regarded as having the same relative importance as the first 500 words in Buchanan's *Graded Spanish Word Book* or Keniston's *Standard List of Spanish Words and Idioms*. Nearly half of the fifty-two have a range of 55 or above, and eighteen of these are in the top range of 60 or in the assured high frequencies which were not counted. Within the high ranges a considerable weight is given to the handling of personal pronouns and possessive forms; some teachers may well feel that this occurs at the expense of verb-form treatment (tense, person, number). In the ranges below 35, we find the following eight items: *contigo* (Item 22), *ser* in impersonal expression of time (Item 23), relative *a quienes* object of verb (Item 23), possessive *su propio* (Item 33), subjunctive after *quienquiera que* (Item 12), imperfect subjunctive after *si* in conditional sentence (Item 22), interrogative *cuál* before a *de*-phrase (Item 6), and *acaba de* plus infinitive (Item 21). Since the range goes as low as 14 before passing the 2,000-mark in vocabulary, most teachers will find no objection to these eight items which, moreover, are dealt with in most elementary grammars. For example, the use of *cuál* before a *de*-phrase (range of 6) merges, at the pedagogical level, with the generalized use of that interrogative form. Actually, only the one item *quienquiera que* plus subjunctive seems to fall outside the reasonable limits of grammatical testing at the level set by this test.

There is one disadvantage connected with the scoring. Since the number of answer choices varies from two to five, there can be no practicable formula for subtracting a fraction of wrong answers from the rights and thus compensating for guesswork. Except for this drawback, which not all teachers will consider important, this test seems to be as good as, but no better than, competing tests of Spanish grammar at the basic level.

[209]

★**Examination in Spanish Reading Comprehension: Lower Level.** 1-2 years high school or 1 year college; 1944; IBM; Form LSR-1-B-4 (usually called Form B); separate answer sheets must be used; $1.75 per 25; 40¢ per 25 machine-scorable answer sheets; 15¢ per scoring key; 25¢ per specimen set, postpaid; 40(45) minutes; prepared by the Examinations Staff of the United States Armed Forces Institute; published by the American Council on Education; distributed by Cooperative Test Service. (Also distributed by Science Research Associates: $2 per 25; 65¢ per 25 machine-scorable answer sheets; 50¢ per key; 50¢ per specimen set.)

Harry J. Russell, Associate Professor of Romanic Languages, Miami University, Oxford, Ohio. The test technique employed in the construction of the examination is to present passages of varying length, both prose and verse, upon which from four to seven incomplete Spanish statements are based, with three Spanish completions furnished for each statement. The procedures used in constructing the test are not too clearly defined except in the rather general statements furnished in the manual.

The test items are, generally speaking, fairly normal reading situations. The examination, however, seems to have the following defects: (*a*) The level measured is not too clearly defined. (*b*) The vocabulary difficulty is not carefully controlled. (*c*) The cognates that were probably assumed by the test technicians to be "gift words" are frequently not known to the students for whom the test was designed. (*d*) The reading materials are not arranged in the order of progressive difficulty. (*e*) The reading passages are made up of prose as well as verse and are of a decidedly unequal length, and comprehension of them is tested by many or few test items, depending upon whims of the test technicians that seem to have no relationship to either their length or their difficulty. (*f*) The time allowed for the completion of the test is inadequate.

For some time it has been rather generally accepted that the maximum foreign-language vocabulary of a one-year high school student is 1,000 words; that of a two-year high school, or a one-year college student, is 2,500 words. If this assumption is correct, there are 53 words, or 6.6 per cent, in this test that are beyond the two-year high school level, and 70 words, or 7.4 per cent, that are beyond the one-year high

school level. The burden of unknown words as compared with known ones is entirely too high in both cases for the levels specified. It would seem, therefore, that the term "Lower Level" is erroneous as applied to this test.

The vocabulary difficulty of the reading passages varies considerably. Passage VI, for instance, contains only two words that would not be known to a two-year high school student, while II, containing only ten more running words than VI, has seven such words. The most difficult selection in terms of known to unknown words is III rather than the last passage in the test. It ought to be possible to assume that a reading test is arranged in progressive order of difficulty, that is, graduated from easiest to hardest in terms of test items.

Words that look like English, and that have the same meaning as their English counterpart, are only considered to be cognates when they are known to the person being tested. A series of tests designed by E. I. Dale of Ohio State University to test the English vocabulary knowledge of juniors and seniors in high school and freshmen in college proves that such words as "eminent," "opulence," "preponderance," "presumptious," etc., all used in this test, are not likely to be known by this age student. They must, therefore, be considered "burden words" rather than "recognizable cognates."

It is questionable whether the inclusion of poetry in a "lower level" test is either legitimate or wise, especially when that verse is as highly philosophical as Passage V is and when so much depends upon the student being able to comprehend it (17.5 per cent of the test items in this examination are based on this passage).

Passage I contains 205 running words; VII, 133, III, 188, and V, 127. The average test technician would go from simple to complex rather than reverse the process. The passage that contains 205 words is tested by 6 test items, while the one that contains 127 words has 7 test items. There seems to be no correlation between the length and difficulty of the passage to the number of test items based on it.

There are 1,057 running words in the seven passages of this examination. One is considered to be a slow reader, and therefore inefficient, who reads at a rate of less than 250 words per minute. At that rate the students should be able to read all of the test passages in less than five minutes. It seems strange to allow 45 minutes to decipher 40 test items based on passages that

Examination in Spanish Grammar

should take no longer than five minutes to read.

Only three completion items are furnished with each incomplete statement in this test. The penalty for guessing (a penalty that should be imposed for all multiple-choice type examinations) when only 3 completion items are furnished is very heavy. It would seem that the normal of five completion items should be furnished with each incomplete statement in order to diminish the penalty imposed.

The correct answer to a majority of the test items is almost a repetition of the exact language used in the passage being tested. A clever student need only match up these words to get the correct answer. There is no way of ascertaining whether he actually comprehended what he read or was merely astute in matching. This is a departure from the accepted technique which, it would seem, is inadvisable.

[210]

★**Examination in Spanish Vocabulary: Lower Level.** 1-2 years high school or 1 year college; 1944; IBM; Form LSV-1-B-4 (usually called Form B); separate answer sheets must be used; $1.75 per 25; 40¢ per 25 machine-scorable answer sheets; 15¢ per scoring key; 25¢ per specimen set, postpaid; 40(45) minutes; prepared by the Examinations Staff of the United States Armed Forces Institute; published by the American Council on Education; distributed by Cooperative Test Service. (Also distributed by Science Research Associates: $2 per 25; 65¢ per 25 machine-scorable answer sheets; 50¢ per key; 50¢ per specimen set.)

[211]

Lundeberg-Tharp Audition Test in Spanish. High school and college; 1929; Forms A, B; $2 per 100; 10¢ per specimen set; (30) minutes; Olav K. Lundeberg and James B. Tharp; James B. Tharp, College of Education, Ohio State University, Columbus, Ohio.

Frederick B. Agard, Associate Professor of Modern Languages, Cornell University, Ithaca, New York. This is a time-tested instrument for measuring Spanish auditory apprehension, constructed by qualified experts in the field of testing. Accompanying norm tables, compiled for each form separately, are furnished for two or four high school semesters; for two or four college semesters; or for one, two, or three college quarters. The test has three parts: I, Phonetic Accuracy; II, Completion Series; III, Definition Series.

The spoken material in Part I consists of fifty utterances, ranging progressively from two through seven syllables each. Corresponding to each spoken item (uttered twice in succession), there are printed on the test paper four partially homophonous words or expressions, one of which is identical to the spoken stimulus. The

student is to determine which one of the four was pronounced. The choices are all real Spanish but are mere segments of hypothetical speech with no importance attached to their meaning; the student does not need to know their meaning, but merely to apprehend accurately their phonetic pattern; in addition, he needs to use an exact knowledge of the written representation of Spanish sounds, in order to distinguish in writing the heard utterance from its partial homophones.

In Part II the examiner reads 25 incomplete sentences in Spanish. After listening to a sentence once only, the student is to write down in English (or in Spanish if he prefers) a word or phrase which will reasonably complete the unfinished spoken sentence. A key of acceptable answers is supplied with the test.

The vocabulary employed in the incomplete sentences is carefully controlled. Six words in Form A and seven in Form B are not listed in the Keniston *Standard List of Spanish Words and Idioms.* These few, most of which have English cognates (e.g., *invención, alfabeto, aritmético*), are all understandable within their context or are unessential to comprehension of the sentence as a whole; in one item the key word is *pizarra,* a class-room term which can be assumed to be known by most students.

In Part III, the examiner reads 25 statements in Spanish, each defining some object, person, or action. After listening to a definition once only, the student identifies what has been defined by writing down the English (or Spanish) word for it. A key of acceptable answers is supplied.

The vocabulary of the Definition Series, slightly more difficult than that of the completion items, is no less rigidly controlled. Sixteen words in Form A and 21 in Form B are not in the *Standard List;* most of these are cognates of English words; and all are either deducible from context or are nonessential elements of the sentence, with the sole exception of *muñeca,* a key word in one item. The sentence structure and style, while uncomplicated, has the inevitable dictionary flavor of definitions and thus confronts the student with turns of phrase not commonly met with in the spoken language under normal conditions of its use.

As a whole the Lundeberg–Tharp Test represents a valuable pioneer contribution to the field of aural testing. It succeeds in eliminating the variables of unknown vocabulary and of knowledge any more specialized than the common fund possessed by all people as social beings. It is true that Part I does not measure ability to apprehend meaningful speech; and it is doubtful that Parts II and III measure differing degrees of aural skill, since the utterances are of equal length in both parts. The test does not, for example, measure the ability to apprehend sustained discourse such as conversations or anecdotes of fifty or a hundred words. I have come to believe that for students completing one or two years of Spanish the ideal aural test, which to my limited knowledge has yet to be built, will measure the ability to apprehend utterances of varying length, graduated from *Buenos días* and *¿A dónde va Vd.?* to a five-minute conversation or talk. Rather than incomplete sentences and definitions (which are not normal forms of speech) the student ought to be tested with realistic "slices of speech" similar to utterances he would hear in real conversation and would be expected to react to by speech or action. In the test situation we would then provide for a "substitute reaction" in the form of choosing among different possibilities a reply, or an act, or a restatement of content.

Walter V. Kaulfers, Associate Professor of Education, Stanford University, Stanford, California. The reliability coefficients of .92 and .92 for Forms A and B, respectively, of this relatively short and easy-to-administer aural-comprehension test indicate that it deserves publication in a more attractive form than the present "tentative edition" affords. In case the publication of a more finished edition is contemplated, the utility of the test could be improved by substituting a strictly objective multiple-choice form of response in Parts II (completion of sentences dictated in Spanish) and III (identifying descriptive definitions) for the handwritten (Spanish or English) response that is now required of students. As Parts II and III now stand, only a corrector with a knowledge of both Spanish and English (and his own notions of fairness in accepting or rejecting answers) can undertake to score the test —and at a considerable expenditure of time in the case of large groups. It is unfortunate that the multiple-choice form of response used in Part I (identifying the printed form of a word, in a group of four words, from hearing the key

word pronounced twice) could not have been adapted for use in Parts II and III.

In revising the tentative edition for final publication, the authors may also wish to consider the possibility of making the test far more objective and valid by providing for its (optional) administration entirely via records on tone-control talking machines, capitalizing on different native speakers. As the test now stands, it is likely to guarantee only a rough measure of how well the students can understand their own teacher. The norms do not indicate whose voice(s) the experimental groups heard during the tryouts. For this reason, intergroup comparisons based on the test would be difficult to interpret.

Needless to add, any test that requires ability to handle printed words (as in Part I) measures more than just aural comprehension. Any of the thousands of Spanish-speaking natives who understand Spanish without serious difficulty, but who have never learned to read or write, would fail every part of the present edition. If it is to have other than intramural scholastic interest, the final revision might well capitalize on some of the practical devices used in machine-scorable group performance scales. As the first venture in aural-comprehension testing to appear on the foreign language horizon, the *Lundeberg–Tharp Audition Test* deserves credit as a promising pioneering start toward a more finished product. It is doubtful, however, if an aural-comprehension test useful for purposes of vocational placement can be developed without the aid of a substantial grant from some educational or government foundation to finance the cost of deriving and validating norms defined in operational terms.

Mod Lang J 28:699 D '44. Winthrop H. Rice. This audition test in Spanish is made up of three parts; part I, "Phonetic Accuracy," 50 multiple choice items wherein the student indicates which of four words has been pronounced by the examiner; part II, "Completion Series" (25 items), wherein the examiner reads a statement lacking the final word which the student is to supply in either Spanish or English (as determined by the examiner); part III, "Definition Series" (25 items), wherein the examiner reads a definition and the student sets down, in Spanish or English, the name of the thing defined. * In general, the construction of the test is excellent. The selection of words for the multiple choice part has been done with great care and, one might add, ingenuity. The elements are sufficiently different so that a moderately well-trained ear can grasp the differences yet they are sufficiently similar to permit of mistakes through careless listening or poor training. The other two parts are constructed with similar care. There are, however, one or two questions which might be raised. First, one wonders why the single words of part I are read twice while the long, and some times involved, sentences of parts II and III are to be read only once. This seems to put the student at some disadvantage in the latter parts where not only sound but comprehension of vocabulary and sentence structure are involved. For example, it seems a bit strong to read only once, and *at normal speed,* such a definition as "Instrumento de hierro con anzuelo doble que está afirmado al extremo de un cable y que se arroja al mar para asegurar y detener las embarcaciones," while such words as "zozobras" and "jayán" (to pick two of the most difficult) are read twice. The same remark might apply to such a completion question as "Si se saca al pez de su ambiente natural, se muere dentro de pocos minutos porque no puede respirar fuera del. . . ." It would be the suggestion of this reviewer that the number of readings for the three parts be changed to one for the first and two for each of the others. Such a change would probably bring the level of the norms for the different parts more in line with one another. The norms for fourth semester high school are given as 45.7 (out of 50) for part I; 11.2 (out of 25) for part II; and 6.2 (out of 25) for part III. It will be noted also that the norms are considerably lower on the parts where more than pure audition is involved. Three remarks concerning form B: 1) in part I, number 5, the key word is *pazo;* the four possibilities are *paso, vaso, pazo* and *pazco.* In classes using the *seseo,* this would allow two correct answers, and a change seems indicated; 2) in number 47, the key *nos esperad* is grammatically incorrect; 3) in part II, statement 11 (La leche es blanca pero el vino es generalmente . . .) which expects the answer *red* or *rojo* is open to question on the basis of fact. In spite of these minor difficulties, the test remains one of the best of its kind available to teachers. Statistical data show good reliability and validity which were reflected in sample testings made at this reviewer's institution,

where several classes of different levels of experience and of ability definitely showed these differences in their scores on the test.

[212]

Iowa Placement Examinations: Spanish Training: Series ST1, Revised. Grades 12-13; 1924–26; Forms A, B; $4 per 100; 50¢ per specimen set, including the other 10 tests in the series, postpaid; 43(50) minutes; prepared under the direction of C. E. Seashore and G. M. Ruch; G. E. Vander Beke and G. D. Stoddard; Bureau of Educational Research and Service, State University of Iowa.

REFERENCES

1. STODDARD, GEORGE DINSMORE. *Iowa Placement Examinations.* University of Iowa, Studies in Education, Vol. 3, No. 2. Iowa City, Iowa: the University, 1925. Pp. 103. Paper. $1.00. *
2. MILLER, LAWRENCE WILLIAM. *An Experimental Study of the Iowa Placement Examinations.* University of Iowa Studies in Education, Vol. 5, No. 6. Iowa City, Iowa: the University, 1930. Pp. 116. Paper. $1.00. * (PA 5:799)

Harry J. Russell, Associate Professor of Romanic Languages, Miami University, Oxford, Ohio. The examinations consist of Part 1, a vocabulary test of 50 items; Part 2, a grammar test of 40 items; Part 3, a verb test of 40 items; and Part 4, a reading test containing three paragraphs on which are based 20 questions. The technique employed in testing the vocabulary is to give the Spanish word and then list five possible English translations, one of which is correct. The grammar technique is to give a Spanish sentence containing one grammatical error. The student is to underline this error and then write the correct word on a dotted line to the right. The verbs are tested by sentences in which the verbs occur in the infinitive form inclosed in parentheses. The student is to write each verb in the correct tense and person required by the remainder of the sentence. The reading paragraphs are tested by English questions to be answered briefly in English.

There is no way of determining what the basis of selection of the vocabulary items comprising the vocabulary test might have been because a statement clarifying this point is not contained in the manual, nor was it possible for the reviewer to find it in any of the literature on the subject which was consulted. The following analysis of this test, however, may be of some value to the reader. If we are justified in assuming that the first-year high school student, or the first-semester college student, has a vocabulary of approximately 1,000 most common Spanish words, this section of the examination is entirely too difficult to test this level of instruction. The vocabulary in Form B contains 27 words, or 54 per cent, that would not be known to first-year high school students. There are 10 words, or 20 per cent, that would not be known to second-year high school, or first-year college students, provided that it is safe to assume that at this level of instruction they would have a vocabulary consisting of the 2,500 most common Spanish words. Form A is much better on this score since only 14, or 28 per cent, of the words tested would be beyond the 1,000-word level; and 4, or 8 per cent, beyond the 2,500-word level. The technique employed in testing these words is a well-established one and, therefore, entirely acceptable.

The grammar test was constructed without the benefit of *The Spanish Syntax List* and is, therefore, a random choice of the grammatical phenomena to be tested. Considerable stress is placed on phenomena that are now known to be obscure or of decidedly low frequency. The technique of writing grammatically incorrect sentences to test the student's acumen in recognizing the errors has been seriously questioned by psychologists. This test is, of course, not the least bit objective, since all of the information required is active and to be written in by the student. The same criticism is registered concerning Part 3 of the test since the student is supposed to write the correct form of the infinitive in the space provided for that purpose and also for Part 4 since he is to answer English questions based on the reading of passages briefly in English.

An analysis of the reading passages used in Part 4 reveals that there are 34 words that would not be known to a first-year high school student. The first paragraph, the most difficult of the three contained in the test, averages one new word to 6 known ones. The minimum of one unknown word to from 50 to 70 known ones is a commonly accepted technique. Any reading passage that is more heavily weighted with unknown words than that is considered unreadable. The research of numerous investigators establishes the veracity of this statement; consequently, it is doubtful whether the reading section of this examination is a valid test for the instruction level stated above.

These "placement tests" are a curious mixture of objective, passive and subjective, active techniques. The amount of time that one would have to spend in grading the subjective, active parts of the test could hardly be justified when one considers that there are several reputable standardized objective tests available that would be far more satisfactory and that would require only a fraction of the time for grading.

[213]

★**Furness Test of Aural Comprehension in Spanish.** Grades 9-16; 1945; Forms A, B; $2.00 per 25; 10¢ per sample copy; (45) minutes; Edna Lue Furness; Banks Upshaw & Co.

Frederick B. Agard, Associate Professor of Modern Languages, Cornell University, Ithaca, New York. This recently published test of aural skill in Spanish is, as far as one can judge, intended for first- or second-year students of the language. Available in two forms (A and B) seemingly intended to be equivalent in level of difficulty, the test consists of three parts: I, Vocabulary (10 minutes); II, Completion (15 minutes); III, Identification (15 minutes). The technique is that of multiple-choice response throughout the three parts, which may profitably be discussed separately.

PART I, VOCABULARY. The spoken material consists of 50 isolated words. The examiner is directed to utter the stimulus twice in succession. The student is to select his answer from five printed Spanish words (occasionally phrases), one of which is closely associated in meaning with the word pronounced.

The purpose of this section is to measure skill in aurally apprehending single lexical units presented in their conventional dictionary form (verbs, for instance, are uniformly given as infinitives). This objective seems open to question on the ground that such units do not constitute *speech;* in conversational situations language is not transmitted in this fragmentary form, as single words devoid of context. However, admitting for the moment the desirability of aural vocabulary testing, one may legitimately inquire about the basis for selecting the words. All 50 are "basic" in that they fall within the first four groups (words 1 to 2,000) of the Keniston *Standard List.* Distribution according to frequency varies in the respective forms, however. Form A contains 14 words from 1 to 500, 17 from 501 to 1,000, 10 from 1,001 to 1,500, and 9 from 1,501 to 2,000. Form B, considerably easier from the point of view of frequency, has 34 from 1 to 500, 15 from 501 to 1,000, 1 between 1,001 and 1,500, and none above 1,500. Within the battery of 250 answer choices (five per item), a good 80 per cent of the words are distributed evenly enough through the first four groups, with the addition of some 10 per cent of derivatives (words 2,001 to 3,060) and another 10 per cent (roughly) not found in the *Standard List* at all. Of these last, a majority are obvious cognates of English words; but it is difficult to justify from the student's point of view such ponderous items as *auxiliar, intercesor, antepasado,* or *astro luminoso* as correct answers (corresponding to the spoken items *ayudar, abogado, abuelo, sol*) or such comparative strangers as *encarnar, jarabe, consuelo, guisar, agarrar* even as distractor-items. The form *ayanzar* (Form A, Item 11, Choice 5) is seemingly a misprint for *avanzar,* as is *carcel* (Form B, Item 10, Choice 1) for *cárcel.*

Apart from the few questionable word-selections mentioned, this part has a serious flaw in construction. The make-up of a large number of the items is such that the correct answer can be spotted at a glance, simply because some or all of the *distractors* are partially homophonous with the *spoken stimulus* while the correct choice is entirely different in form and in some cases appears as an obvious paraphrase: e.g., spoken item *ojo,* answer-choices *olor, odio, oreja, ola, visión;* spoken item *prometer,* answer-choices *dar mutua (!) palabra, pronunciar, proponer, pronto, estar.* It seems vain to pretend that even an average student would not discover, after working through the first few items, that he could deduce the answers without even listening to the spoken stimuli. It may be that the author became aware of the structural weakness in this part of the test before building Form B, where in many items there is no giveaway phonetic similarity between distractors and stimulus and where correct answering depends, as it should, wholly on apprehension of the utterance.

PART II, COMPLETION. In this section the examiner reads 25 incomplete sentences in Spanish. After listening to a sentence twice, the student is to select one of five possible completions printed in the folder.

Correct answering of these completion items depends on two factors in addition to apprehension of the utterance: (*a*) possession of the vocabulary used in both utterance and answer choices; (*b*) in many instances, a rudimentary knowledge of geography and cultural history, especially of the Western Hemisphere. As for the lexical factor, the utterances themselves range rather freely outside the first four *Standard List* groups, particularly in the use of cognates such as *eclesiástico, unidad monetaria, alfabeto, independencia,* and numerous geographical proper names. Reading a cognate is rarely a problem, but the student who knows well enough what a monetary unit is, may find his ear quite unresponsive to the sounds that make up *unidad monetaria* when he hears them for the first time. Nevertheless, it is fair to say that in substantially all these items apprehension of the cognates is facilitated by their context; they are not "key words," as are *cueca* and *jarabe* in one item whose value depends wholly on the knowledge of at least one of these two unusual words. Also the derived word *azucarera,* essential to one item, seems of doubtful fairness; and among the answer choices, it is disconcerting to find such words as *vocales, cazuela, férreo, licenciado, prelado, dramaturgo, valses.* Furthermore, the factual knowledge required to answer some of the items, e.g., that Velázquez was a Spanish artist or that Brazilians alone in America speak Portuguese, invalidates the section as an exact measure of aural apprehension. For if a student fails to answer, is it because his ear did not register the speech utterance (which is what we would want to know) or simply because he didn't happen to know who Velázquez was?

PART III, IDENTIFICATION. In this part the examiner reads 25 statements in Spanish, each defining some object, person, or action. After listening to a definition twice, the student is to identify what has been defined by selecting one of five possibilities. Example: spoken definition *Producto útil que se encuentra en las minas;* answer choices *el máiz, la hierba, el guante, el carbón, la torre.* This section is presumably intended to be harder than Part II, but the utterances are not perceptibly longer; and therefore one cannot see that it measures any different skill, or degree of skill, than the preceding section. Furthermore, the composition being essentially the same as that of the completion section, the same requirements are present in addition to mere apprehension of the statements uttered: vocabulary knowledge and, in some items, factual knowledge. The style of these utterances is ponderous; it is a dictionary style, quite dissimilar to the normal arrangement of spoken idiom. Words outside the *Standard List* 1 to 2,000 set are more frequent here than in Part II; apart from numerous cognates we find *encuadernades* (misprint for *encuadernados*), *platicar, predicador, limosna, puntero, frondoso* (all however deducible from context or not essential to the item) and, as key words, *deporte, joya, uva, grosella, arbolado.* Among the answer choices are *salsa, mestizo, codo, olfato, casimir, lienzo, volcar, mensajero, vara, rienda, reja.* Certain of the items also depend, as in Part II, on knowledge of special facts.

Adequate "reception" or "comprehension," which constitutes one-half of the act of speech communication, is composed of at least three elements: (*a*) auditory apprehension of the spoken utterance and transmission of the acoustic image to the brain for the purpose of physical or linguistic response; (*b*) knowledge of the meaning to be attached to the acoustic image; (*c*) awareness of certain facts or assumptions bearing on the subject of discourse but not uttered in the actual speech situation. Success on Parts II and III of the Furness Test depends in varying degree on all three of these factors. Teachers who expect their students' recognition vocabulary, both auditory and visual, to extend somewhat beyond the 2,000 words of the *Standard List* and who likewise expect them to control certain semispecialized facts as part of their Spanish-language training will find Form B of the Furness test usable. Many teachers, on the other hand, in order to evaluate precisely their students' skill in using Spanish and to ascertain their individual weaknesses, will feel it desirable to isolate the factor of auditory apprehension. A test devised for this purpose must eliminate other variables (*a*) by using only words which the student can with fair certainty be assumed to know and (*b*) by setting no further obstacles to correct response, such as answer choices which draw on reading skill or vocabulary control in the language or which require knowledge of particular facts. Carefully planned tests of this type already exist, such as the University of Chicago Language Investigation Tests of Aural Comprehension (available on two levels in French, German, and Russian as well as Spanish); the *Spanish Aural Comprehension Test* prepared by the Spanish staff of Stephens College, Columbia, Missouri; or the *Lundeberg–Tharp Audition Tests.* An advantage of the Chicago and Stephens tests is that the spoken material is recorded on phonograph records, thus assuring provision of native speech at standardized speed.

Walter V. Kaulfers, Associate Professor of Education, Stanford University, Stanford, California. This attractively printed, easily scorable, 40-minute, multiple-choice dictation test should appeal to teachers who want a measure of aural comprehension that is easy to administer and readily scorable from a key. Since only right answers are counted, the danger of clerical error is reduced without injury to the value of the test in providing a percentile ranking of students. Users of the test, however, should realize that its scores are destined to be more than a measure of aural comprehension. Since the examinees are required to choose right Spanish answers (words or phrases) from among a group of five printed responses, the examination tests a considerable amount of what might more properly be termed audio-visual-association and phrase-reading ability in Spanish. Part I, Vocabulary, for example, requires the examinee to find among the words *apoyer, atacar, auxiliar, ayer, ayanzar* (?) the one that "most nearly corresponds in meaning to" the key word *ayudar* (to be pronounced twice by the examiner). In Part II, Completion, the examinee is asked to complete statements like "Cervantes es famoso por ser ..." by choosing the right answer from among (1) un cura italiano (2) un abogado francés (3) un autor español (4) un maestro chileno (5) un doctor argentino. Exactly the same technique is used in Part III, Identification.

Since this test, like the *Lundeberg–Tharp Audition Test in Spanish,* is a pioneer in the foreign-language field, the suggestions for improvements in subsequent forms of that test apply with equal relevance to the present edition. Inasmuch as the English directions in the test show that it is primarily designed for English-speaking students of Spanish, it would seem that all the printed multiple-choice responses could well be English words of high frequency, rather than a mixture of Spanish words of both common and, too often, exceedingly rare frequency.

If a teacher does a great deal of vocabulary work with synonyms in Spanish in elementary and intermediate as well as advanced classes, his first-year students should probably have no difficulty in associating the dictated key word *ayudar* with its nearest given equivalent *auxiliar* (Item 11, Part I, Form A). If, however, such work is reserved for second or third year courses, this item would merely disqualify students without giving them any opportunity to demonstrate their ability to understand words of much higher frequency than *auxiliar* that have formed the basis of most of their work in elementary and intermediate courses. In its present form,

Furness Test of Aural Comprehension in Spanish

Part II would seem to be much fairer to college students taught by the synonym method than to freshmen or sophomores in most of our high schools.

Whether any aural comprehension test should include cultural information, no matter how simple, or how well "anybody of average intelligence ought to know it"—to quote a common remark—is still questionable; for, while it is unlikely that a student will attend a Spanish class for any length of time without hearing of Cervantes, it is not at all certain that he will necessarily remember the author of *Don Quixote* clearly at the time of the examination, no matter how well he might be able to comprehend Spanish. If the use of English, instead of Spanish, for the printed multiple choices does not seem desirable, the use of techniques similar to those suggested for the *Lundeberg–Tharp Audition Test* would, perhaps, be even more satisfactory. In its present form, few high school teachers of Spanish will want to administer the test without first making a careful study of the individual items in a specimen set to see whether the students have been exposed to the vocabulary included among the acceptable choices.

No information is supplied in the manual about the reliability of the test and the extent to which an effort was made to scale the individual items on the basis of their actual difficulty as shown by the number of examinees missing them during experimental tryouts. A tentative table of norms is given for students who have completed two or more semesters of Spanish in high school or college. Since no mention is made of the number of cases on which the norms are based, however, teachers will hardly be justified in drawing serious conclusions from a comparison of the performance of their own students with the averages reported in the Examiner's Manual. If the test, in its present form, is administered by a teacher to his own students, it can hardly afford more than a rough measure of how well they can understand him when he dictates items to be identified among a printed list consisting of both oft-used and rather-seldom-used words.

How well an examinee can understand the oral Spanish most likely to be encountered in routine travel situations abroad, in telephone conversations dealing with the routine business of daily life, in radio news commentaries, or in formal lectures, would not be evident from the scores of either the present test, or of the *Lundberg–Tharp Audition Test in Spanish,* except by very indirect inferential guessing. In their present forms, both are primarily intramural scholastic examinations—for "marking purposes only."

FOREIGN LANGUAGES — FOURTH MMY

REVIEWS BY *Nelson Brooks, Donald G. Burns, Harold B. Dunkel, Konrad Gries, Elton Hocking, Walter V. Kaulfers, W. C. Kvaraceus, William B. Michael, Herbert Schueler, James B. Tharp, Mary E. Turnbull, and Clarence E. Turner.*

[232]

Foreign Language Prognosis Test. Grades 8–9; 1930; 2 forms (listed below); author recommends use of both forms; norms ['30]; $9.90 per 100; 35¢ per specimen set; postpaid; 44(60) minutes; Percival M. Symonds; Bureau of Publications, Teachers College, Columbia University. *

a) FORM A. 5 scores: English inflection, word translation (English to Esperanto), sentence translation (Esperanto to English), related words, total.

b) FORM B. 5 scores: word translation (Esperanto to English), artificial language, sentence translation (English to Esperanto), formation of parts of speech in English, total.

REFERENCES

1–6. See 40:1340.

WILLIAM B. MICHAEL, *Director, The Testing Bureau, University of Southern California, Los Angeles, California.*

Designed to predict the degree of success that pupils in the eighth or ninth grade will realize in the study of a foreign language, this test consists of two forms of somewhat different content. The manual states that either form may be used successfully but recommends that both forms be employed whenever feasible.

Although the test appears to possess considerable face validity, the rather confident statements expressed in the manual regarding its guidance value in the selection of students who should pursue foreign language courses and in the formation of groups of homogeneous ability do not seem to be entirely justified with respect to the evidence presented concerning its reliability and validity. Estimates of the coefficient of reliability ranging between .73 and .78 are expressed in terms of the correlation between total scores on Form A and Form B (which do not begin to approximate equivalent forms) for four schools concerning which no explanation is given regarding size, location, or scope of curriculum. No reliability coefficients are reported for part scores, although it may be expected that they would be rather low in view of the relatively small numbers of items in several of the parts.

As to validity, average coefficients of .60 and .61 are reported between total scores on one or the other of the two forms and achievement test scores of classes studying French, Spanish, or Latin. For four schools the coefficient was .71 when both forms were used. Since descriptive information regarding size of samples, type or name of achievement test, and grade placement of pupils is lacking, it is difficult to evaluate the genuine worth of these coefficients. No inter-correlations among part scores are presented. No mention is made as to whether an item analysis was undertaken. In fairness, it should be mentioned that two references are listed in a foot-note that yield further information regarding previous work in validating the test. Nevertheless, more data should be available in the manual than has been presented.

Although the manual states that no norms are available, a supplementary sheet is included on which the decile equivalents for part scores and for total scores are furnished for 261 and 120 pupils who took Form A and Form B, respectively. The groups are not identified except that they were tested in September and that they intended to take Latin. It is interesting to note that, as would be expected, the range of scores is exceedingly narrow on the subtests. Similar normative data are presented for 45 pupils intending to take Spanish; again there is no further identification of the group.

In addition, one other potential point of weakness should be cited. In view of the extremely short time limits of many parts, there is a substantial risk that sources of extraneous variance in test scores may be introduced. Since the completion of a large number of items in a short time would be likely if one had a good rote memory, many examinees high in other abilities related to success in language might be unfairly penalized. For example, the individual who possesses the superior reasoning and verbal comprehension abilities required in mastering the complex interrelationships of language structure and meaning may not have sufficient time to put his ability into practice and to demonstrate his potential superiority over the less capable individual whose highly developed memory places him at an advantage in answering many of the relatively low difficulty level items.

Although this test might prove to be a worthwhile prognostic instrument, it is difficult for one to recommend its widespread use in light of the meager data presented in the manual concerning reliability, validity, and norms. It would appear that one could make at least as dependable a prediction of success in foreign language study from several of the well known standardized tests that yield measures of verbal intelligence as one could from this test.

For a review by Walter V. Kaulfers, see 40: 1340.

ENGLISH

[233]

★**English Examination for Foreign Students: Including a Test of Non-Verbal Reasoning.** Applicants from non-English language countries for admission to American colleges; 1947; 7 scores (listed below); 3 parts; $3.50 per set, 10–19 sets of test and answer sheets; $3 per set, 20–99; $2.50 per set, 100–299; $2 per set, 300 or more; one set of phonograph records (78 rpm) provided with orders of 10–50 tests; two sets with orders of 51–100; two sets, plus one set for each multiple of 50 beyond 100, with orders of more than 100 tests; booklet of sample questions free; replacement answer sheets not supplied; postpaid; 270 (305) minutes in two sessions; Educational Testing Service. *

a) BOOK 1. 4 scores: reading comprehension, aural comprehension, pronunciation, total; separate answer sheets must be used; 140(155) minutes.

b) BOOK 2, ENGLISH COMPOSITION. Forms A, B; no norms; 40(45) minutes.

c) BOOK 3. 2 scores: scientific vocabulary, nonverbal reasoning; separate answer sheets must be used; 90 (105) minutes.

[234]

★**English Language Test for Foreign Students.** Applicants from non-English language countries for admission into American colleges; 1951; Form A; 25¢ per test; separate answer sheets must be used; 5¢ per answer sheet; $1 per set of scoring stencils; $1.30 per specimen set; postage extra; nontimed (60–90) minutes; Robert Lado; George Wahr Publishing Co. *

REFERENCES

1. LADO, ROBERT. "Phonemics and Pronunciation Tests.' *Mod Lang J* 35:531–42 N '51. *
2. LADO, ROBERT. "A Practical English Language Test for Foreign Students." *News B Inst Int Ed* 26:16–7 Ap 1 '51. *

CLARENCE E. TURNER, *Professor of Romance Languages, Rutgers University, New Brunswick, New Jersey.*

Much careful linguistic analysis and testing ingenuity have gone into the development of this test. It promises real usefulness in the advance evaluation of a foreign student's linguistic fitness to pursue college or university study in the United States. Its practical advantages are numerous and important, for it can be administered and scored by personnel without special training, if need be in a testing center abroad; it is simple, clear, and objective; and it requires no special equipment.

The mastery of an acquired language is seldom easy. English, for all its comparatively simple inflections, is a peculiarly difficult tongue for the foreigner. For that matter, what native speaker of it never mispronounces a word or flies to the dictionary to fill a gap in his vocabulary? The specific difficulties of English for most foreigners lie in the vast extent of its ever growing vocabulary, in the problems relative to the production and aural comprehension of its sounds, and in its oddly capricious relationship of pronunciation to spelling. ("What, are there no rules!" was the perceptive remark of a highly literate Italian gentleman on hearing English read aloud for the first time.)

The test at hand meets head on these very difficulties. All its 134 items test vocabulary to some extent, although careful control keeps this from becoming the major factor in Parts I and II. Pronunciation is quite rightly awarded the largest number of items (54). This part of the test is the most novel and has been discussed elsewhere (*1*) by the author. The student's oral-aural control of English is tested through his ability to distinguish and match (however spelled) English phonemes in situations like those where they are typically distinctive in English. (For example, *sink* becomes a different word, or no word at all, if we remove the [*s*]-phoneme or replace it with various others, so [*s*] is distinctive in this situation.) Each item has only three parts, yet offers five possible answers, since all three may contain matching phonemes, or none, or any combination of two. A random example, Item 34, will illustrate the principle. Many languages lack the [1]-phoneme, as in the English word *bit,* yet this sound is distinctive in this situation, since *bet, bat, bait,* and so on have meanings different from *bit.* The student is asked to match identical sounds in: (1) We had to b--ld a fence. (2) It keeps the r--ndeer out. (3) Last year they k–cked and broke many little trees. To give the correct answer, 1 and 3, the student must pronounce correctly to himself the three key words, avoid the distractor offered by the queer spelling *ui* in *build,* and distinguish the [1] of *kicked* and *build* from the [e] of *reindeer,* which is the sound most likely to be confused with [1] by most foreigners. Specific traps are laid for natives of various languages: the unwary Oriental may match *–ibrary* with *–ead books;* the Spanish speaker may match *Ri–er* and *La–or;* the Italian will tend to fail to match *La–or* with *ra– –its,* and so on. The reduction of unstressed vowels to [1] and [ə], a process so characteristic of English, receives due attention. To deal correctly with the groups *p– –ple, t– –m won, to s– – the game* and *–imple problem, –ure, ea–y* the student must have grasped the point that in English the same sound may be spelled in many ways, and the same spelling pronounced in many ways.

It is not necessary to discuss Part I (Structure) in detail. Here as in the more novel Part II, the items have been chosen by sound criteria. Can the student sense interrogation from word order? Can he trace pronouns to their antecedents and subjects to their verbs? Can he tell to what action *did so* refers? Here, as consistently throughout the test, the emphasis is upon those features of English which typically have the function of determining meaning.

Part III is more debatable. The sampling problem in measuring the English vocabulary is a staggering one. One clear and commendable trend in the present test may be mentioned. The author has included no fewer than 10 items (out of 40) which involve "two-word verbs," those tricky combinations so puzzling even to the foreigner who knows their elements, as in *ran out of wood, got over his headaches.* In other words, idiom is recognized as an aspect of vocabulary, a point that teachers of language often fail to discern.

In so carefully constructed a test, one feels that there must be a reason even for practices that appear illogical. There is a puzzling one in Part III. The majority of the items involve detecting one or more words which may be directly substituted for an underscored word, as *started* in "My classes *began* yesterday." One is therefore ill-prepared to match "My watch has a *luminous* dial" with *shines in the dark,* where the relationship, though real, is entirely different. Surely, too, some logical Frenchman will fail to equate *dog* with *an animal.* The ex-

English Language Test for Foreign Students

amples preceding the test items have, of course, prepared the student for some peculiar matchings, for in Example S we are told that *with wings, usually flies* and *with feathers* "are correct about *bird*" in the sentence, "That is a beautiful *bird*." This would be difficult to formulate either in English or in logic. If anything is gained by this sort of mental gear shifting, let us tolerate it, for the test as a whole is an unusually sound and practical one.

[235]

★**Test of Aural Comprehension in English as a Foreign Language.** Applicants from non-English language countries for admission into American colleges; 1946; Forms A, B, C; 10¢ per test; separate answer sheets must be used; 25¢ for examiner's materials; 50¢ per scoring stencil; $1 per specimen set; postpaid; nontimed (30–45) minutes; Robert Lado; English Language Institute, University of Michigan. *

FRENCH

[236]

★**Cohen French Test.** 1–3 years secondary school; 1945–49; 4 parts; Forms A ['45], B ['45]; manual ['49]; 7s. 9d. per 10; 2s. per 10 of any one part; 6d. per scoring key; 2s. 6d. per manual; 3s. 10d. per specimen set; cash orders postpaid within Australia; S. W. Cohen; Australian Council for Educational Research. *
a) PART 1, VOCABULARY. 20(30) minutes.
b) PART 2, SILENT READING. 25(35) minutes.
c) PART 3, GRAMMAR. 25(35) minutes.
d) PART 4, AURAL COMPREHENSION. (25) minutes.

MARY E. TURNBULL, *Formerly Head of Test Production, Educational Testing Service, Princeton, New Jersey.*

Part 1, Vocabulary, gives 75 short French sentences, a portion of each of which appears in boldface; five suggested English translations for the boldface expressions follow each sentence. A good sampling of easy vocabulary includes several parts of speech, although nouns and verbs are most numerous. The part would be more effective if it were well edited to remove the careless errors, repetitions, and extraneous clues to answers with which it is replete. For example, in Form A, Item 46 asks for the English equivalent of "craindre" and Item 54 for the translation of "crainte." "Early" appears as a choice in Items 6 and 8 of Form A and there are several further instances of this same fault. In other items (e.g., Items 20 and 40 of Form A) the fact that the key word is a noun is clearly indicated by the context (it follows "un"); yet some of the choices given are not nouns and so can be eliminated on the basis of this extraneous clue. The same carelessness has

crept into the proofreading: some boldface words are not translated and some choices are misnumbered.

Part 2, Silent Reading, consists of eight short paragraphs with four questions on each. The paragraphs, in general, appear in order of difficulty (except G and H of Form A) and they present rather interesting and complete situations. More questions and more searching ones could have been provided for some of the meatier paragraphs, and the difficulty of the questions and the passages could have been better matched. This part also shows a distressing lack of proofreading (e.g., Item 5 of Form B mentions "women" when "woman" was intended).

Part 3, Grammar, covers many of the basic points in French grammar by suggesting five French expressions or endings to complete each of the given French translations of 65 English phrases or sentences. This part occasionally becomes a vocabulary test (cf. Item 51 of Form A and Item 35 of Form B) and it concentrates too much on the same words, such as "finir," "venir," "nager," and "lire." On the other hand, some items, like Item 23 of Form A, test several points at once. There is great diversity in the difficulty of consecutive items. Misprints again occur throughout and unfortunately there is an error (duplication of choices) even in sample question 5.

Part 4, Aural Comprehension, consists of 50 items, each of which has five English words from which the correct answer can be selected. Here again a lack of variety lessens the potential usefulness of the test (Items 4 and 20, 7 and 29 of Form A, and Items 11 and 24 of Form B). This part is also weakened by poor choices: for example, Items 5, 15, and 16 of Form A each have one clue word which, if understood by the examinee, makes only one given choice possible; several items require the comprehension of only one word of the question (usually near the beginning of the question) to limit the possible choices to one or two (cf. Form B, Items 19 and 32). Again misspellings occur in the French questions (Item 33 of Form A and Item 5 of Form B).

Space for the answers is provided along the right margin of each test page; for each form there are neatly printed and easy to use answer keys. The directions for all parts seem clear and include useful examples. Adequate time limits are allowed for each part.

The manual gives short descriptions of the

Cohen French Test

parts, suggests possible uses, and provides tables of norms and a concise statistical appendix. Separate scale scores are provided for pupils in each year and in each of the six Australian states. The scale scores are obtained by reading from a norms table (the reverse of usual practice in this country) which is identical for Forms A and B. This identity implies the direct equivalence of raw scores on the two forms, but no evidence of such equivalence (which seems too good to be true) is presented. There are no data concerning validity. Reliability coefficients for the several parts, determined for samples of more than 100 cases, range in the .70's and .80's.

The *Cohen French Test* is an interesting attempt to test four of the basic elements of achievement in elementary French. It could be useful to both teachers and pupils in classroom situations where an easy, unspeeded measure is desired. It would be much improved by careful editing which would eliminate repetitions and the numerous proofreading errors.

[237]

★College Entrance Examination Board Achievement Test in French Reading. Candidates for college entrance; 1901–51; available only in College Entrance Examination Board Admissions Testing Program (see 526); 60(70) minutes; prepared by College Entrance Examination Board Committee of Examiners in French Reading in cooperation with the Staff of Educational Testing Service: 1951–52 membership: H. Linn Edsall (Chairman), Anne Marie de Commaille, Henry Dupont, Donald M. Frame, and Eleanor L. Michel; program administered by Educational Testing Service for the College Entrance Examination Board. *

REFERENCES

1. THARP, JAMES B. "College Entrance Examination Board Looks at Its French Examination. *French R* 13:380–4 Mr '40. *
2. WEBER, CHRISTIAN O. "Old and New College Board Scores and Grades of College Freshmen." *J Am Assn Col Reg* 20:70–5 O '44. * (*PA* 19:570)
3. DYER, HENRY S. "Validity of C.E.E.B. Placement Test in French: Studies at Harvard and Radcliffe." *Col Bd R* 1:1+ sp '47. * (*PA* 22:857)
4. DYER, HENRY S. "Some Observations on the College Board Language Tests." *Ed & Psychol Meas* 8:593–602 w '48. * (*PA* 24:1458)
5. TUCKER, LEDYARD R. "Interpreting Scores on the Foreign-Language Tests." *Col Bd R* 1:47–9 sp '48. *
6. DYER, HENRY S. "The Effect of Recency of Training on the College Board French Scores." *Sch & Soc* 70:105–6 Ag 13 '49. * (*PA* 26:2384)
7. BROOKS, NELSON. "The College Board Achievement Test in French." *French R* 24:141–8 D '50. *

WALTER V. KAULFERS, *Professor of Education, University of Illinois, Urbana, Illinois.* [Review of Forms VAC2, WAC2, XAC2, and YAC.]

With a consistent reliability of .97 and content graded on the basis of frequency counts of French vocabulary, idioms, and syntax, these strictly objective, machine scorable, one-hour multiple choice tests are probably as scientifically

efficient per unit of testing time as any standardized tests in any field of subject matter. A careful examination of the methods used in validating and scaling the individual test items shows strict conformity to the best in current statistical theory and practice. Similarly, in typography and use of standard idiomatic French, the tests are technically about all that can be desired.

The several types of five-item multiple choice statements employed in the different parts of the examination are generally well suited to the purpose, with the possible exception of the stress that the subtests place on the recognition of grammatical forms in context. A strategic phrasing of items here should eliminate the necessity of supplying English translations in a test of reading ability. Moreover, command of word order, which is often as important as grammatical form per se, is not measured by this syntax test, even though simple devices for measuring it objectively have been in use for several years. Fortunately, all these matters are of relatively minor importance.

Despite their generally excellent qualities, however, the examinations are somewhat confused as to their ultimate purpose. First, none of the "French Reading" examinations is strictly a *reading* test. All contain substantial sections devoted exclusively to vocabulary and also a separate section on the ability to select the most appropriate grammatical form from five tempting choices. Since vocabulary is inseparably related to reading comprehension as well as to usage, its separate measurement in a test to which reading comprehension scores are added to vocabulary scores means measuring the same ability at least twice—once directly and again indirectly—with a consequent confusion of the true meaning of the total score. It is doubtful if a separate section on vocabulary or recognition of grammatical forms as such is ever justified on an *achievement* test. The function of vocabulary tests and special form recognition tests is primarily *diagnostic;* for example, they aid teachers in locating specific reasons for a particular student's inability to use a language *in synthesis* as a means of communication in reading, writing, or speaking. Any process of adding scores obtained from subtests of closely interrelated or overlapping abilities leads to a total score whose significance can be established only by arbitrary academic fiat, with a gradual widening rather than narrowing of the schism between the real world and a strictly intramural school world. If pressures from college French departments do not permit the dropping of the separate vocabulary and grammar sections, the name of the examination should at least be changed to suit its present content. The term "Reading Test" is definitely a misnomer.

Secondly, the French reading tests are too narrow in scope to be considered *achievement* tests for high school students of French. A candidate who, through special effort on the part of himself and of a skillful teacher, has attained a commendable ability to understand spoken French and some ability to speak it would not receive even one point of credit on the entire examination. Like most language examinations, it does not distinguish between normal people and literate deaf-mutes. Moreover, a student who has attained some knowledge of French life and culture in keeping with the widely accepted social-cultural objectives of high school teaching would have no opportunity at all to display his achievement.

The undeniable fact that courses of study vary too much from one high school to another to permit the construction of an achievement examination that will be equally fair to all makes the term "achievement" test a misnomer. Both the specialized nature of the examination and the use to which it is put indicate that it is primarily a *college placement* examination to assist institutions of higher learning in placing people in courses for which the examination shows them to be best fitted in terms of such local offerings as are available. Even here, the examination would, by virtue of its content, limit its present placement value to reading courses stressing belles lettres and conducted primarily in English. With minor exceptions, the items test only French of the narrative or descriptive type, or conversational passages of the kind found in novels. Examples of expository writing, editorial writing, news reporting, etc., are tested indirectly, if at all. Moreover, since the examination does not include a measure of ability to understand spoken French, it does not guarantee satisfactory placement in courses featuring lectures or discussions in the foreign language. At best, it provides only a convenient indication of a student's ability to read the materials assigned for silent reading in literature courses where these are graded in difficulty.

Within the limitations noted above, however, the tests are as objective, reliable, and scien-

tifically valid as modern statistical theory and practice allow. By converting raw scores into College Entrance Examination Board standard ratings, student performance is equated to rule out the possible "halo" effect of having taken the test with a group of relatively mediocre candidates or, conversely, the penalty of having had to compete against relatively superior candidates. The new standard ratings also enable college admissions officers to compare scores directly, language to language. The average test score of a normal, representative group who have studied a language for two years, for example, is now 460 in German, Spanish, French, and Latin. For three years, it is 520, and for four years, 580. Each year of training beyond two thus yields, on the average, a 60-point rise in total score. The convenience of this arrangement cannot be overestimated in evaluating student performance for placement purposes, even though the ultimate validity of the examinations, either as measures of achievement or as placement tests, is limited by the considerations cited in preceding paragraphs.

In summary, the College Board French reading tests are superior to most standardized foreign language tests in scientific excellence as regards test construction and authoritative linguistic content. Their limitations arise from confusion of achievement testing and placement testing, both of which cannot be served effectively at the same time in present circumstances of variations in high school and in college courses of study. For this reason, the College Board should concentrate its time, efforts, and resources on what it can hope to do with some promise of success and give up what it can only pretend to do with respect to the evaluation of work in high school. Specifically, this means abandoning the achievement testing objective (as well as the use of the term *achievement* in connection with its tests) and concentrating exclusively on the improvement of the college placement and guidance function of the examinations. Such a revision might well include an objective test of ability to understand spoken French as an aid in guiding students with respect to enrollment in intermediate and advanced courses where lectures and discussions are likely to be in the foreign language. Recent improvements in the way of recording machines, nonbreakable long playing records, and portable record players with tone as well as volume controls (and multiple loud speakers to compensate for defective acoustics) remove nearly all the hazards that once beset the administration of a brief but thoroughly standardized, objective examination of aural comprehension.

A report to the college or university in the form of a profile chart showing a particular student's relative standing (e.g., percentile rank) on tests of ability to distinguish between correct and incorrect French usage, to understand spoken French, and to comprehend the printed page would be a more valid and discriminating indication of a student's fitness for work in a particular course than the present omnibus total score. Although a separate test of vocabulary may be included as a concession to institutions desiring a separate score for diagnostic or special guidance purposes, it should be evident that a good test of reading comprehension and aural comprehension will inevitably co-measure vocabulary in about the only context, apart from ability to speak the language, where its existence has any practical importance.

Inasmuch as implementation of the foregoing recommendations implies a change in the policy of the College Entrance Examination Board beyond the control of its able staff of testing experts, it is to be hoped that its officers will reconsider the functions of its language examinations. If a change in policy is not feasible in the immediate future, the present examination should be renamed *College Entrance Examination in French,* since it obviously leaves out too many worthwhile "achievements" to be an achievement test and is far too much interested in pure vocabulary and grammatical form to be just a "French Reading Test." With appropriate changes, as indicated, to conform to fundamental changes in College Board policy, the examinations might appropriately be called *College Placement Examination in French* with less invitation to criticism and considerable benefit to institutions of higher learning as a solution to the transfer problem in college foreign language.

[238]

*Cooperative French Test: Lower and Higher Levels. 3–6 semesters high school or 1–2 semesters college, more than 2 years high school or more than 1 year college; 1942–51; 4 scores: comprehension, grammar, civilization, total; IBM; 2 levels; Forms S (Lower Level, '49—same as test copyrighted in 1942; Higher Level, '42), X ('49 or '50—same as test copyrighted in 1947); no data on validity; no specific manual; no college norms; general Cooperative manual ('51); high school norms ['50]; $2.50 per 25 of any one level; 50¢ per specimen set of any one level, postpaid; separate answer sheets may be used; 90¢ per 25 IBM answer sheets; 30¢ per set of stencils for scoring

answer sheets; cash orders postpaid; 80(85) minutes; Geraldine Spaulding, Laura Towne, and Sarah Wolfson Lorge; Cooperative Test Division, Educational Testing Service. *

REFERENCES

1. TRAXLER, ARTHUR E. "Some Data on the Results of the Cooperative Tests in French, Latin, and Secondary School Mathematics, Form S," pp. 55–9. In *1942 Achievement Testing Program in Independent Schools and Supplementary Studies.* Educational Records Bulletin, No. 36. New York: Educational Records Bureau, June 1942. Pp. xiii, 59. Paper, lithotyped. *
2. BOVEE, ARTHUR G. AND FROEHLICH, GUSTAV J. "Some Observations on the Relationship Between Mental Ability and Achievement in French." *Sch R* 53:534–7 N '45. * (*PA* 20:2063)
3. JACOBS, ROBERT. "An Evaluation of the 80-Minute Forms of the Cooperative Tests in French, Latin, and Spanish," pp. 79–86. (*PA* 23:309) In *1948 Achievement Testing Program in Independent Schools and Supplementary Studies.* Educational Records Bulletin, No. 50. New York: Educational Records Bureau, July 1948. Pp. xiii, 86. Paper, lithotyped. *

ELTON HOCKING, *Professor of Modern Languages and Head of the Department, Purdue University, Lafayette, Indiana.*

Unlike the earlier Elementary and Advanced Forms of this test, which required only 40 minutes of working time, the Lower and Higher Levels require 80 minutes of working time distributed among three parts as follows: I, Comprehension: Section 1 (50 vocabulary items with choices in English, and 10 all-French sentence items), 15 minutes, Section 2 (eight to ten passages of French prose, usually narrative, on which are based 45 all-French items), 25 minutes; II, Grammar (50 items combining English and French), 25 minutes; and III, Civilization (50 questions of fact, entirely in English), 15 minutes. The Comprehension sections for Form S are available separately as the 40-minute *Cooperative French Comprehension Test,* Lower and Higher Levels, but the cost is excessive: $2.25 for 25 booklets and $.80 for 25 answer sheets, as compared with $2.50 and $.90 for the 80-minute test.

The advantage of the newer test, in both forms and at both levels, is clearly in the expanded treatment of Comprehension (Part I): the number of separate vocabulary items is increased somewhat; the ten sentence items are new; and the eight to ten prose passages offer considerably more reading material than is found in the older forms. The vocabulary words are well chosen in terms of both range and level of difficulty, and the reading passages are carefully graduated in difficulty. The content of the reading passages in the Lower Level tends to be over-sentimental, but to criticize them for this would be captious. The items throughout this part of the test reflect considerable professional skill in their selection and construction.

The items in Part II, Grammar, suffer from a fault that has long been chronic with the grammar items of the *Cooperative French Test* (Form R excepted). A large proportion of these items require only the selection of words to fill in blanks in French translations of English sentences, and some require only the selection of word endings, as, for example, in this item (Form X, Lower Level, Item 30) :

There were two blue hats in the shop window.
Il y avait deux chapeaux bleu- (_____)
   dans la vitrine.
30–1   -s
30–2   -x
30–3   -es
30–4   -se
30–5   *No ending needed*

Such butchery seems unjustified. No space is saved on the page; there is always space available for complete words, and usually for complete sentences. For the grammar items a much larger percentage of complete sentence choices should be used if the test is to be fair to students who learn by auditory and visual imagery rather than by matching French words with English words.

In this part of the test also, there are duplications of constructions, and sometimes even of the same word in the same construction (Form X, Lower Level, Items 3 and 8, 9 and 34, 10 and 31). However, since the constructions which are duplicated are those generally stressed in conventional grammar books, the student's score here should be a good index of his ability to translate textbook "sentences" into French.

Part III, Civilization, is an innovation in the Lower and Higher Levels. In 15 minutes the student is to answer 50 items covering several different aspects of French culture. This attempt to test the student's knowledge of French culture is highly questionable. There is no quarrel with the concept of culture as an important aim of the course, and there is no doubt that a mature and cultivated person would know the answers, incidentally, as a by-product of his general cultural background and reading. However, uncultivated young students do not know the answers incidentally or any other way. When once the nature of this part of the test becomes known locally (one administration is enough, for the pattern is painfully obvious), students will feel impelled to cram the answers by conning guidebooks and outline manuals. They can easily do so, for the repertory of conventional landmarks in history, geography, and the arts is limited. The situation here is very different from that of vocabulary, for instance, where there are thousands of valid items to be sampled, and where

recognition of each item is an end in itself. But civilization is not quantitative, nor is it assessed by identifying Hugo as a writer rather than a painter or a musician, or Debussy as a composer rather than a painter. No, this part of the test is not valid; and, much worse, the inclusion of it may encourage students to mistake the guidebook for the tour, the menu for the meal, the cliché for the experience. Civilization is traduced in the name of civilization.

Part III of this test is thus self-defeating. As for Part II, it has long been known that the scores on grammar tests like this one do not correlate highly with functional skills in a foreign language; hence, this part is not likely to prove particularly useful. On the other hand, Part I seems to be the most thorough and reliable test of reading ability in French yet to be published. This part is highly recommended. Teachers who are primarily interested in measuring skill in reading may prefer to use the Comprehension test alone rather than the complete test.

For reviews by John H. Meyer and Roland Vinette of Form S, see 3:182; for reviews by Joseph F. Jackson and Clarence E. Turner of Part 1, Form S, see 3:180.

[239]

★**French I and II: Achievement Examinations for Secondary Schools.** 1 or 2 years high school; 1951; orally administered in part; 1 form; no data on reliability and validity; no manual; Minnesota norms (median and quartile deviation) available; similar norms for other regions by special arrangement with publisher; 7¢ per test, postage extra; 60(65) minutes; edited by Walter W. Cook; prepared by a curriculum committee of high school teachers for use in the Minnesota State Board Achievement Examinations Program; Educational Test Bureau, Educational Publishers, Inc. *

ELTON HOCKING, *Professor of Modern Languages and Head of the Department, Purdue University, Lafayette, Indiana.*

This test is not recommended for use in any circumstances. It is faulty in construction, in French, in English, and even in layout, typography and spelling.

The heading calls for the names of both parents to be written in a space of two inches; asks the pupil to fill in a blank cryptically headed "time used"; admonishes him to "read directions carefully" (there are almost none); says nothing about guessing or the formula for scoring. There is a plethora of headings and subheadings. Thus, each individual French passage of the Reading Examination has a subheading, as for example, Article No. I, Section I of Section One. Each section is numbered; it is also called "examination" and "test." The nervous child who sees on page one "You have fifteen (15) minutes for this test" may well be reduced to panic.

The Reading Comprehension part (15 minutes) of the test involves four French passages (averaging ten lines) on which are based 15 items. Each item is an incomplete French statement followed by three completions in English. This dubious practice is complicated by the faulty French of the passages, the awkward or incorrect wording of the responses, the patent absurdity of some responses, and the "old chestnuts" used, doubtless familiar to some students but not to all.

The Vocabulary part (10 minutes) has 40 items, each a French sentence with a word or phrase underlined. Each is followed by five choices in English. The technique is faulty: distractors are too close (Items 42, 44, 52); some responses are disqualified because they are absurd (Item 54), or use the wrong tense (Item 36). Also, the key is wrong for Item 53, and there are mistakes of French in Items 17, 23, 42, 46, and 51.

Section III, Aural Examination (20 minutes), involves ten definitions (choice of three each) and three "anecdotes" totalling 34 lines of French. These are to be read aloud, once only, by the teacher. A very slow oral reading of the entire section consumes only five minutes, leaving 15 minutes for the student to choose his 22 responses, each from a choice of three. This is an absurdly long time.

There are no instructions about the speed of reading or the length of pauses during which the student responds. With these left to the whim of each teacher, the scores will vary accordingly. This aural examination should have been recorded on a disc, like the University of Chicago examination upon which it is obviously patterned although there is no acknowledgment. The latter, however, used five times as many items and a skill in construction that is not even approximated here. Twenty-two items are inadequate. Of the ten definitions, five are taken verbatim from the University of Chicago tests; two of the remainder are incoherent, even in print.

Two of the three "anecdotes" are old favorites ("Why don't they eat cake?" and the work of the Curies), and the third is exposition. All involve elementary blunders in French. The suggested responses are sometimes irrelevant or absurd, and frequently couched in tortuous English. The author has a weakness for redundant phrases and adverbs.

A technical blunder which can be of capital importance is the fact that the examiner reads the Aural Examination from a separate sheet on the back of which is printed the scoring key for the whole test. Presumably he will stand for 20 minutes holding the key up before the eyes of the students. If he stands close, as he should for an aural examination, the students near him should make perfect scores.

In Section Four (Grammar, 25 items, 10 minutes), each item is an English sentence with an incomplete French translation followed by five suggested completions. Twenty-five items are too few; there is no settled policy on distractors (they are sometimes in good French, and sometimes not); Items 81 and 94 require the identical word; Items 95 and 101 both supply two correct responses, although the key accepts only one; Item 85 supplies no correct response; there are misprints in Items 88, 95, and 100; the page is crowded, although the following page is blank.

In sum, this test is the product of persons who have little competence in test construction, in French, or even in English. It will not bear comparison with the work of experts, such as the Cooperative tests.

[240]

★**French Recognition Vocabulary Test: State High School Tests for Indiana.** High school; 1948; Forms K, L; mimeographed; no data on reliability and validity; no manual; no norms; 4½¢ per test; 15¢ per specimen set; postpaid; nontimed (30–40) minutes; E. R. Ryden; State High School Testing Service for Indiana, Purdue University. *

REFERENCES

1. RYDEN, EINAR RUDOLPH. *Vocabulary as an Index to Learning in a Second Language.* Doctor's thesis, Northwestern University (Evanston, Ill.), 1947. (*Summaries of Doctoral Dissertations....June–September 1947,* 1948, pp. 147–51.)

CLARENCE E. TURNER, *Professor of Romance Languages, Rutgers University, New Brunswick, New Jersey.*

It is obviously unfair to neglect the question of how well the authors have accomplished what they undertook in order to examine the value of the undertaking. In the case of any passive recognition test, it is really the latter question that haunts one. In the tragic confusion that exists among modern language teachers as to what they ought to be trying to achieve, it seems safe to the reviewer to assert that passive recognition of the correct English equivalents of foreign words constitutes one of the least significant of desirable objectives. This is the skill most likely to be concentrated on by poor teachers and poor students. It is one of the few skills which may to some extent be taken for granted. It is the thing which the entering college freshman who is going to fail French can do nothing else but.

Granted that language skills are intercorrelated. If we had no other way of measuring directly the skills we consider most important, a test of this sort would throw some light on a student's showing relative to that of his fellows. So would a good test of English grammar, or one of English vocabulary. Indeed, tests of the present type are to a considerable extent really tests of English vocabulary. To realize this, one has only to imagine the test being given to a Frenchman. What are we to say of a type of test which a literate Frenchman could not pass unless he knew English? But, it will be protested, our school children are not French! True, but they are being sadly cheated if they are not being led toward the possibility of doing the same things with their French that the French do. If such teaching is being done, tests like the one under review will no longer reflect the curriculum.

When we examine the fairer question of how good the test is of its type, we find merits and defects which are common in the field. The proportion of items too easy to have discriminatory power seems fairly high—*animal, nation, observer* (the really interesting question about the last word is whether the student knows how to pronounce it). Too often the distractors are obviously absurd words thrown in at random. Has anyone ever really thought that *nation* means "ragamuffin"? While the correct answer is not too often an evident English cognate, it is very frequently the synonym of one (*spécial,* "particular"). The authors have wisely included items of more than one word, e.g., *il fait beau,* the translation of which as "it is beautiful" is not unequivocally the best.

[241]
★Graduate Record Examinations Advanced French Test. Senior year college through graduate school and candidates for graduate school; 1939–51; available only in Graduate Record Examinations programs (see 527); 105(125) minutes; Educational Testing Service. *

[242]
★A Standardized French Grammar Test. Ages 11–17 with 1–5 years of French; 1951; Forms A ['51], B ['51]; manual ['51]; 1s. 9d. per 12; 2d. per single copy; 1s. 6d. per manual; 1s. 10d. per specimen set; postage extra; 35(40) minutes; T. S. Percival; University of London Press Ltd. *

REFERENCES
1. PERCIVAL, T. S. *Achievements Tests in French Grammar and Vocabulary.* Master's thesis, University of Durham (Durham, England), [1950?]. Abstract: *Brit J Ed Psychol* 21: 156–8 Je '51. * (*PA* 26:1085, title only)

NELSON BROOKS, *Westover School, Middlebury, Connecticut.*

A few points of difference between the English and the American languages catch the eye on the first page of this test prepared under the auspices of Durham University in England. In the U.S., the student does not "turn over," but turns the page; he does not "work" a test, but takes it; he is in a "form" only in certain independent schools; he is much more likely to be classified by grade or year. The student will find himself very much at home, however, in the problems presented in the test items, for the English attack upon the structural patterns of French seems to be very similar to our own. The test is, on the whole, very good and has clearly been prepared with the greatest care; such negative features as it has are connected with debatable points of procedure, a few details of fact, and a degree of inexperience.

This reviewer is concerned about the effect of interrupting the flow of a sentence by the interpolation of a word in the foreign language as: "An old (vieux) friend. Un (   ) ami." What is convenient and economical from the point of view of printing may well be psychologically harmful from the point of view of equating the two languages. Is not the true linguistic relationship more naturally expressed by a form like, "An old friend. (vieux) Un——— ami."? Printed thus, the coaching can be done from the sidelines without getting in the runner's way. This detail might be considered minor if it were not for the fact that this deliberate and unnatural mixing of the two languages is standard practice in grammars and exercise books on both sides of the Atlantic. The instructions on page 1 of the test are not quite accurate. The "phrases" are sometimes dependent clauses printed as sentences, a practice that should not be countenanced by any teacher of grammar. The "incomplete French translation" in a number of cases is reduced to a pair of parentheses. Such matters might seem trivial in another instance, but in a concentrated sampling exercise of this kind, there is no detail that does not influence the final result in some way.

The author has given careful thought to the principle of testing one thing at a time, and the test is very satisfactory on that score. Necessary vocabulary help is provided, verbs are given in the infinitive and are even conjugated when the emphasis is on word order rather than on the verb form. In some cases, the author seems to have gone almost too far in this direction. In the items, "A yellow (jaune) chair" and "Une chaise (   )," whatever problem there was seems to have been reduced to the vanishing point.

While it is well to have at the beginning of any test a few extremely easy items in order to complete the gamut of difficulty, by the time 15 per cent of the test has been done, the student should be meeting problems with a definite challenge. In Form A, Item 15, the student is asked to write "nous sommes" for "we are"; in Form B, Item 14, he is to write "nous avons" for "we have." The ability to do this is not an indication that one has traveled very far along the road to the Eiffel Tower. Furthermore, in Item 35 of Form A, the student is asked to deal with, "I am preparing myself. Je (   ) prépare." If such a problem has proved so difficult that it merits this position in the test, then there is something grossly wrong in the instruction the students are given. The proper relationship between teaching and testing needs far more analysis than it has so far received, but it seems clear that fixed response tests, rightly used, can be very helpful in indicating what can be taught and what should be emphasized. It seems to this reviewer that there are too many items in the two forms of this test that are scarcely entitled to a place in the measurement of students between the ages of 11 and 17, with up to five years of study of French.

One may take issue with the answers provided in at least two instances. In Form A, Item 50, not only "de" but also "ces" must be accepted; in Item 98, "soit venu" may be used for "fût venu." We must not forget that the French themselves are the loudest champions of the "tolérances."

Finally, to use these tests "repeatedly at intervals of a few months" would seem to be a dubious procedure. Surely some students, and particularly the bright ones, are going to remember certain exasperating little items, look them up, and jolly well get them right the next time. The true significance of such items as samples of the areas they represent will thus be lost.

In spite of these comments, the test is a good one; it demands that the student write his answers in the form of French words and that he write them correctly to receive credit. It will measure what is a major concern of all teachers of French a great part of the time.

DONALD G. BURNS, *Lecturer in Education, University of Leeds, Leeds, England.*

The principal purpose of this test is to facilitate a rapid grading of the pupils on the basis of their achievement in French grammar. The reliability of the test has been shown to be satisfactorily high at all levels within the grammar school. The procedure which has been followed in selecting and validating test items as well as the data obtained by comparing these tests with other criteria is a sufficient indication of the validity with which they will achieve this. Their chief merit is perhaps that they enable the teacher to assess pupils over a particularly wide range of achievement; and they will therefore be of special service in helping to allocate not only pupils transferred from one school to another but also those who have done three or four years' work in the language and for whom some independent but reliable measure of achievement is desirable.

[243]

★A Standardized French Vocabulary Test. Ages 11–17 with 1–5 years of French; 1951; Forms A ['51], B ['51]; manual ['51]; 1s. 9d. per 12; 2d. per single copy; 1s. 6d. per manual; 1s. 10d. per specimen set; postage extra; 35(40) minutes; T. S. Percival; University of London Press Ltd. *

REFERENCES

1. PERCIVAL, T. S. *Achievements Tests in French Grammar and Vocabulary.* Master's thesis, University of Durham (Durham, England), [1950?]. Abstract: *Brit J Ed Psychol* 21: 156–8 Je '51. * (PA 26:1085, title only)

NELSON BROOKS, *Westover School, Middlebury, Connecticut.*

There are many things to be kept in mind in the preparation of a vocabulary measuring device in which a French word is followed by five English words; some of these things have escaped the author of this test. In general, it will be easier for the student to write his answer and for the instructor to read it if the answer parentheses are placed in the right hand margin of the page; in this test the answer parentheses (referred to erroneously in the instructions as "brackets") are printed at the left of the page, just after the item numbers. All the distractors (the wrong answers) should be words that are in the working vocabulary of the student, but such words as "osier, aloes, portmanteau, aluminium, tyre, ewer, prequisite, reconnoitre, assises" are certainly not sufficiently available to the American student to play their proper role here. Every distractor should have some plausible connection with the test word if it is to do its work, and many of these wrong answers do not seem likely to lead very far astray. No student with a measurable knowledge of French is very likely to think that "là" is the equivalent of "towards," or that "mur" is translated "ready," or that "bouche" is "ankle." The greater the degree of likelihood in every distractor, provided it is clearly wrong, the more exact will the measurement be.

For best results, the right answer should fall in all five positions an approximately equal number of times. In Form A, the right answer occurs 10 times in the first position, but 29 times in the fifth position. There should be, obviously, only one right word in each item, but in a number of cases here there are two correct answers. Taking the *Concise Oxford French Dictionary* as arbiter, Item 32 of Form A, "champ," may be answered either "country" or "field"; in Item 94, Form A, "avis" may be answered either "advice" or "opinion"; in Form B, Item 8, "terre" may be answered either "earth" or "world." Furthermore, in Form A, Item 41, the translations of "vivre," "live" and "survive," are too nearly alike for one to be right and the other wrong. Item 9, Form A, "maintenant: maintain, now" is hardly acceptable either, for after all, the test word is also a form of the verb "maintenir," which might in certain contexts be rendered "maintain." In Form B, Item 30, the test word "chapeau" is an English word (given in *Webster's Collegiate Dictionary*) and as such hardly merits a place in this test. In Form A, Item 25, the words Negro and Negress are printed without the capital letter; the word Jewish occurs in the item immediately following.

The test contains too many repetitions of words in the possible answers (ideally, there should be none at all): "yesterday" occurs five times and "tomorrow" four times. The word "whilst" occurs four times, once as a right answer and three times as a wrong answer. It should be noted that "whilst," though commonly accepted on equal terms with "while" in Eng-land, is no longer usual in the United States.

This reviewer is concerned about the statement in the directions that "the meaning of 'plume' is pen." The meaning of "plume" is not "pen" but an instrument one writes with. "Pen" is the English equivalent of "plume"; both are verbal symbols referring to the same object. All language teachers are aware of this distinction, but it will be of great assistance to their pupils if such relationships are kept clear from the start. The *Concise Oxford French Dictionary* observes this distinction most carefully in its introduction, using "equivalent," "translation," and "rendering" but never "meaning" unless the symbol-thing relationship is intended.

A further device that does not seem to be quite cricket is the use of three or even four parts of speech in the same item. When dealing with isolated words, as in this test, one must remember that in real life there are no isolated words. To obtain best results, the test maker should contemplate his test words in context and choose distractors among the possible translations that suggest themselves when there is relationship with other words in a phrase or sentence. All class room procedure is far enough removed from life as it is; in these highly selective tests, it is of first importance that the greatest possible degree of naturalness be maintained.

This long list of criticisms should not obscure the fact that the test, in both its forms, contains a large majority of items of first quality. As it stands, it is a fairly good test, and with the severe editing that is obligatory in all measures of this kind, it can become an excellent one.

DONALD G. BURNS, *Lecturer in Education, University of Leeds, Leeds, England.*

The chief merit of these tests is that they offer a continuous scale against which to measure pupils' achievement in vocabulary at any stage during the first five years of study. The norms given in the manual are admittedly based on experience in grammar schools in Newcastle and Northumberland, but the tests should provide valuable information to teachers working under similar conditions in any part of the country.

Coefficents of reliability (between two forms of the test) range from .77 (for a first year group of 339 cases) to .90 (307 cases in the fourth year) and .89 (142 cases in the fifth year). Many investigators would find that these are not large enough to indicate a high degree of reliability, and it might be an advantage therefore if the manual included some indication of the internal consistency of the tests such as might be obtained by using a split half reliability coefficient.

Considerable care has been taken in the construction of these tests to select material which should make them suitable for application in English schools, and from this point of view their validity must be considered high. A correlation of .90 was obtained between this test and the vocabulary section of the *Cohen French Test*.

These are the first French vocabulary tests to be published with norms based on performance in English Schools for many years. The range of achievement covered by each form of the test is wide enough to provide the teacher with a ready and reliable means of comparing groups of pupils at different levels within the school, and the tests should be particularly useful in assessing the knowledge of pupils who are transferred or admitted to a school after the normal time of entry. They represent a valuable addition to the material available for the measurement of achievement in the schools.

GERMAN

[244]

★College Entrance Examination Board Achievement Test in German Reading. Candidates for college entrance; 1901–51; available only in College Entrance Examination Board Admissions Testing Program (see 526); 60(70) minutes; prepared by College Entrance Examination Board Committee of Examiners in German Reading in cooperation with the Staff of Educational Testing Service: 1951 membership: Robert W. Kesler (Chairman), Paul G. Graham, W. G. Hollman, Maxim Newmark, and Arthur J. Watzinger; program administered by Educational Testing Service for the College Entrance Examination Board. *

REFERENCES

1. DYER, HENRY S. "Validity of the German Placement Test: Relation Between Test Scores and College Grades." *Col Bd R* 1:24–6 f '47. * (PA 22:1877)
2. DYER, HENRY S. "Some Observations on the College Board Language Tests." *Ed & Psychol Meas* 8:593–602 w '48. * (PA 24:1458)
3. TUCKER, LEDYARD R. "Interpreting Scores on the Foreign-Language Tests." *Col Bd R* 1:47–9 sp '48. *

HERBERT SCHUELER, *Associate Professor of Education, and Director of the School of General Studies, Queens College, Flushing, New York.* [Review of Forms ZAC, YAC, XAC, WAC2, and VAC2.]

These examinations of the College Entrance Examination Board are not available for use outside of the official testing program of the Board. Their use is, therefore, largely confined to the area of admissions. The forms under review make use of multiple choice techniques of testing and are essentially measures of recognitional levels of language skill. The various parts of these examinations follow familiar language testing patterns. Each form contains the now inevitable vocabulary section which makes use of the four-alternative English translations of a single German word. In addition, there is a section in which the student is asked to determine which two of four German words or expressions are synonyms. Elements of language structure are tested in a third section in which the student is asked to choose one of four alternative translations of English words or phrases given within a German sentence. Another section in the forms beginning with WAC–2 (1948) is a short situational group in which the student is asked to choose one among four remarks which a person would be most likely to make in a number of situations. The device seems quite promising, although the test constructors seemed to have found it difficult to construct items that are sufficiently challenging to yield a wide spread of scores. It is, however, the one section in these tests which departs from conventional test patterns and should be developed further in future tests. Finally, each of the forms has a reading comprehension section consisting of four passages of approximately equal length followed by several multiple choice comprehension items in German.

In general, these tests are carefully constructed. The Board's process of conscientious evaluation, involving repeated review and pretesting before a final form is set, assures high reliability. The demonstrated reliability of these tests was from .96 to .97, surely an eminently praiseworthy record of internal consistency. Considering the population served by these tests (they are most commonly taken by students with a background of two years of secondary school German), they are quite difficult. As a result, they fail to discriminate as much as could be wished among those falling at and below the median scores. On the other hand, the scores among the higher levels are spread out quite well. From an inspection of the items by this reviewer, it would seem that more items of low and middle difficulty should be introduced, especially in the final section of the tests—the passages for reading comprehension. All four passages in each test are of approximately equal length. The comprehension of each is tested by five multiple choice questions. The student not familiar with the meaning area of any one of these passages is, therefore, at a considerable disadvantage, since so many questions depend on each. The introduction of more passages of shorter length with fewer questions depending on them would help in widening the range of difficulty and in giving more students of average and low average ability the opportunity to complete some items of this reading comprehension section.

The technique of recording scores of these examinations has been so refined that the interpretation is made extremely simple for admissions officers. The raw scores are converted into scaled scores in such a manner that the average test score of the normal representative group who have studied German for two years is 460, for three years 520, and for four years 580. (These figures apply to French, Spanish, and Latin as well, making it possible to compare students in different languages directly.) While this form of score reporting is an invaluable aid to the admissions officer, it means much less to the language department once the student has been admitted. The need for diagnosis of relative strengths and weaknesses in structure or vocabulary range and paragraph comprehension, etc. is clear to the language chairman interested in homogeneous sections of language classes and to the instructor interested in making plans for the class he is to teach. It is unfortunate that scores on the separate parts cannot be made available. The scores on the translation section and on the paragraph comprehension section are measures of sufficiently discrete elements of language competence to be extremely useful to the professionally enlightened instructor. Under the circumstances, however, an institution desiring this type of analytical score must administer another examination to those students already admitted. For this purpose, the later forms of the Cooperative German tests (reviewed in this volume) are among the most useful.

[245]

*Cooperative German Test: Advanced Form. More than 2 years high school or 1 year college; 1937–51; 4 scores: reading, vocabulary, grammar, total; IBM; Forms O ('50—same as test copyrighted in 1938), P ('51—same as test copyrighted in 1939), Q ('50—same as test copyrighted in 1940); Form N out of print; no data on validity; no specific manual; norms ('38); general Cooperative manual ('51); $2.50 per 25; 25¢ per specimen set; postpaid; separate answer sheets may be used; 80¢ per 25 IBM answer sheets; 15¢ per stencil for hand or machine scoring of answer sheets; cash orders postpaid; 40(50) minutes;

E. Herman Hespelt, Miriam Van Dyck Hespelt, and Geraldine Spaulding; Cooperative Test Division, Educational Testing Service. *

REFERENCES

1–4. See 40:1360.
5. GAEDE, WILLIAM R. [Editorial Note on the Cooperative German Test.] *German Q* 14:238–9 N '41; 15:37 Ja '42. *
6. HESPELT, MIRIAM VAN DYCK. "Cooperative German Tests." *German Q* 15:169–71 My '42.
7. SCHAEFFER, RUDOLF F. "What Kind of Tests for Oral-Aural Courses?" *German Q* 21:94–101 Mr '48. *

HERBERT SCHUELER, *Associate Professor of Education, and Director of the School of General Studies, Queens College, Flushing, New York.*

Each form of this test consists of three parts and can be administered within a single academic hour. Part I is basically a test of reading comprehension utilizing the five-alternative completion type item. Both stem and alternatives are in German. So cleverly are these items conceived that the usual objection to the all foreign language comprehension test—that it is too often possible to match correct alternative to stem without necessarily comprehending the meaning—has been successfully overcome. The authors are wise in avoiding long paragraphs with several questions based on each. By concentrating on relatively short items—many consist of one sentence—they have made it possible to test a much wider range of vocabulary without unduly penalizing the student who just happens not to know the vocabulary relating to a particular subject.

Part II consists of single word vocabulary matching items. The stem words and the alternatives are, in the main, well chosen, both as to frequency range and as to distribution among parts of speech. However, in view of the growing recognition among language teachers and linguists that the primary unit of language is not necessarily the single word but the contextual phrase, clause, or sentence, as the case may be, the single word vocabulary test stem seems somewhat archaic. A more satisfactory type of vocabulary item is that used in the foreign language tests developed for the United States Armed Forces Institute, where the word or phrase to be tested is presented in a sentence followed by English translation alternatives.

Part III consists of two subparts. The first of these presents English sentences followed by translations with an inserted blank which the student completes from five given alternatives. Such items of structure as adjective endings, verb endings, verb auxiliaries, and idiomatic expressions are tested in this section. The second subpart consists again of English sentences, followed, however, by complete alternative translations. This section tests such items as word order, tense sequence, and idioms. This reviewer has strong reservations as to the need and propriety of the English translations in this section of the test. In the overwhelming majority of items, they fulfill no legitimate function; the alternatives are in no way dependent on the translation. For example, consider the following item from Form O:

> 18. It was very cold in the cottage, so they built a fire.
> Es war sehr kalt im Häuschen,
> 18–1 darum sie haben gemacht Feuer.
> 18–2 darum sie Feuer haben gemacht.
> 18–3 darum sie Feuer gemacht haben.
> 18–4 darum sie haben Feuer gemacht.
> 18–5 darum haben sie Feuer gemacht.

The correct answer is the only possible one regardless of meaning, because it is the only one with the correct word order. The translation, therefore, fulfills no legitimate function. In Form O, 30 of the 40 items in this section are in no way dependent upon the English translation; for most of the rest of the items, if one or two alternatives were changed, the translation could be omitted without disturbing the item validity. Those few items in which the English translation is an integral part of the item—as, for example, in the case of idiomatic translations involving model auxiliaries—might well be dispensed with in this section and different ways found to test them in other sections of the test. These translations add to the reading time of each item and introduce English as an unnecessary distractor. It is unfortunate that the authors could not have seen fit at last to produce an all foreign language test, especially since it would have involved no fundamental change in the test.

These shortcomings do not, however, significantly impair the usefulness of this test. It is carefully constructed, has been proved in the field, and shows the evidence of steady improvement from form to successive form.

For a review by Harold B. Dunkel of Advanced Forms O, P, and Q, see 3:190; for a review by C. H. Handschin of Advanced Form P, see 40:1360; for a review by Curtis C. D. Vail of Revised Series, Advanced Form N, see 38:1000.

[246]

★**German I and II: Achievement Examinations for Secondary Schools.** 1 or 2 years high school; 1951; 1 form; no data on reliability and validity; no manual; Minnesota norms (median and quartile deviation) available; similar norms for other regions by special arrangement with publisher; 7¢ per test, postage extra; 60(65) minutes; edited by Walter W. Cook; prepared by a curriculum committee of high school teachers for use in the Minnesota State Board Achievement Examinations Program; Educational Test Bureau, Educational Publishers, Inc. *

[247]

★**Graduate Record Examinations Advanced German Test.** Senior year college through graduate school and candidates for graduate school; 1939–51; available only in Graduate Record Examinations programs (see 527); 105(125) minutes; Educational Testing Service. *

GREEK

[248]

★**College Entrance Examination Board Achievement Test in Greek Reading.** Candidates for college entrance; 1901–51; available only in the March series of College Entrance Examination Board Admissions Testing Program (see 526); 60(70) minutes; prepared by College Entrance Examination Board Committee of Examiners in Greek Reading in cooperation with the Staff of Educational Testing Service: 1951 membership: Henry Phillips (Chairman), Malcolm MacLaren, William H. Marnell, and James A. Notopoulos; program administered by Educational Testing Service for the College Entrance Examination Board. *

ITALIAN

[249]

★**College Entrance Examination Board Achievement Test in Italian Reading.** Candidates for college entrance; 1924–51; available only in the March series of College Entrance Examination Board Admissions Testing Program (see 526); 60(70) minutes; prepared by College Entrance Examination Board Committee of Examiners in Italian Reading in cooperation with the Staff of Educational Testing Service: 1951 membership: Maria Piccirilli (Chairman), Francis Baccari, Joseph De Simone, Camillo P. Merlino, and Louis Sorieri; program administered by Educational Testing Service for the College Entrance Examination Board. *

LATIN

[250]

★**College Entrance Examination Board Achievement Test in Latin Reading.** Candidates for college entrance; 1901–51; available only in College Entrance Examination Board Admissions Testing Program (see 526); 60(70) minutes; prepared by College Entrance Examination Board Committee of Examiners in Latin Reading in cooperation with the Staff of Educational Testing Service: 1951 membership: Charles T. Murphy (Chairman), George Land, Dorothy M. Robathan, John W. Spaeth, Jr., and J. A. Thayer; program administered by Educational Testing Service for the College Entrance Examination Board. *

REFERENCES
1. TUCKER, LEDYARD R. "Interpreting Scores on the Foreign-Language Tests." *Ccl Bd R* 1:47–9 sp '48. *

2. COLBY, JOHN K.; HARWOOD, FLOYD C.; MURPHY, C. T.; SHERO, L. R.; AND SPAETH, JOHN W., JR. "The College Board's Objective Tests in Latin: A Statement by the Committee of Examiners in Latin." *Classical J* 44:319–22 F '49. *

HAROLD B. DUNKEL, *Examiner in the University Examiner's Office, and Associate Professor of Education, The University of Chicago, Chicago, Illinois.* [Review of Forms VAC2, WAC2, XAC, YAC, and ZAC.]

Since all five forms reviewed follow the same general plan of organization and are similar in detail, they can be reviewed simultaneously. Each form contains three parts. In Part I the student selects from among four Latin words offered those two which are synonymous or related in some fashion. Part II is a set of multiple choice items requiring translation from English to Latin. In the earlier forms, often only a single English word is to be translated; later forms make more use of short phrases. Part III contains four short Latin passages (two of prose and two of poetry) on each of which three different exercises are based: (*a*) multiple choice items requiring the translation into English of selected words or phrases in the passage, (*b*) multiple choice completion-items in simple Latin, rephrasing parts of the passage or making comments about it, and (*c*) true-false statements in English about the passage in general or important elements in it. Each of these subparts for each passage contains 3 to 8 items. Only the total score is reported in the form of the usual CEEB standard scores, so corrected, however, in these and the other language tests that the standard scores are comparable from language to language and are interpretable in relation to the number of years' experience (two, three, or four) the student has had with the language.

The tests are meticulously prepared and the results analyzed with equal care. For those forms old enough for data to be available, the reliabilities reported are in the low .90's. Though these coefficients are slightly lower than those of the CEEB tests in other foreign languages, they are certainly adequate. And recent forms of the Latin test closely approximate CEEB's more than adequate standards for level of difficulty, length, and the like. Within the framework set, these tests are well executed, and it would be difficult even to quibble. The objective forms are probably as valid measures as the older essay forms they replaced a few years ago, and certainly more reliable ones.

It seems to me proper, however, to question this general framework even though it is easy to see how the Latin test committee and the Board are led to it. One debatable issue is the practice of using a single total score, with the items originally selected from the tryout forms on the basis of high correlation between the individual items and the total. Admissions officers in the colleges involved undoubtedly prefer to have to work with a single score; and the present total is a reliable measure of whatever it is it measures. Another value of the present procedure for public relations is that teachers whose students take the test will have little ground for complaint that any of their language drill goes unheeded. Translation (English-Latin and Latin-English), comprehension (expressed in Latin and expressed in English), and vocabulary command measured within Latin all get added into the total score. Others of us, however, would prefer to see more than one score or else a total which was somewhat less of a fruit salad; we would like to have part scores with low mutual intercorrelations and hence some diagnosis of the different skills involved (if they are different), or else a total score which would be less of a hash of these different tasks which are distinctions without a difference anyway since only those items are kept which show high correlation with the total score.

Another question might be raised concerning the objectives covered. One of the test committees has pointed out quite properly that some of the presumed outcomes of Latin instruction are measured elsewhere in the CEEB battery (e.g., the increased command of English should be reflected in higher scores on the *Scholastic Aptitude Test*) and need not be treated in the Latin test also. But the reviewer doubts whether this is true of some of the other objectives: understanding of a foreign culture, historical perspective, increased sympathy with a foreign people, and the like. As the battle continues over the place of Latin in the curriculum, one hears much about these outcomes as constituting a major justification for the study of the Latin language; yet these important and carefully prepared tests pay no attention to these objectives. Students, as well as parents, school administrators, and this reviewer, are inclined to suspect that outcomes which are not measured on such tests are not really considered by teachers to be worth bothering with or at least do not get much attention paid them. These comments may, of course, be more properly considered criticisms of the talk about Latin rather than of these

Latin tests. The schools concerned with CEEB tests might well ponder the issue and then change either the usual talk about Latin or the tests of Latin.

In summary, for those who accept the general principles on which these tests are based, they are admirable examinations and among the best, if not the best, in print today. This is not to say that the reviewer would not like to tinker with the principles.

[251]

*Cooperative Latin Test: Lower and Higher Levels. 3–6 semesters high school or 1–2 semesters college, more than 2 years high school or more than 1 year college; 1942–51; 4 scores: comprehension, grammar, civilization, total; IBM; 2 levels; Forms S (Lower Level, '51—same as test copyrighted in 1942; Higher Level, '42), Y (Lower Level, '50 or '51—same as test copyrighted in 1947; Higher Level, '47); no data on validity; no specific manual; no college norms; general Cooperative manual ('51); high school norms ['50]; $2.50 per 25 of any one level; 50¢ per specimen set of any one level, postpaid; separate answer sheets may be used; 90¢ per 25 IBM answer sheets; 30¢ per set of stencils for scoring answer sheets; cash orders postpaid; 80(85) minutes; Harold V. King and Geraldine Spaulding (S); Cooperative Test Division, Educational Testing Service. *

REFERENCES

1. TRAXLER, ARTHUR E. "Some Data on the Results of the Cooperative Tests in French, Latin, and Secondary School Mathematics, Form S," pp. 55–9. In *1942 Achievement Testing Program in Independent Schools and Supplementary Studies.* Educational Records Bulletin, No. 36. New York: Educational Records Bureau, June 1942. Pp. xiii, 59. Paper, lithotyped. *
2. TRAXLER, ARTHUR E. "The Relation of Vocabulary and Grammar to Reading Achievement in Latin, French, and Spanish," pp. 61–5. In *1947 Achievement Testing Program in Independent Schools and Supplementary Studies.* Educational Records Bulletin, No. 48. New York: Educational Records Bureau, June 1947. Pp. xii, 66. Paper, lithotyped. * (PA 22:449)
3. JACOBS, ROBERT. "An Evaluation of the 80-Minute Forms of the Cooperative Tests in French, Latin, and Spanish," pp. 79–86. (PA 23:309) In *1948 Achievement Testing Program in Independent Schools and Supplementary Studies.* Educational Records Bulletin, No. 50. New York: Educational Records Bureau, July 1948. Pp. xiii, 86. Paper, lithotyped. *

KONRAD GRIES, *Assistant Professor of Classical Languages and Chairman of the Department, Queens College, Flushing, New York.* [Review of Forms S and Y.]

One may safely agree with the previous reviewer that these tests "probably deserve rank as the best tests dealing with the phases of Latin which they cover."

Forms S and Y are the latest in a long series of tests based upon much experimentation, careful evaluation, and the most approved testing procedure. All items are of the multiple choice type, requiring either the writing of a number or, if the test is to be machine scored, the blacking of a vertical space. A sheet of "Percentile Ranks for Secondary School Students" gives percentile tables for part and total scores based on the results of varying numbers of students,

ranging from over two thousand third semester students in 50 different schools to 399 sixth semester students in eleven different schools. Provided with detailed directions, attractively and effectively printed, easily and scientifically scored, these tests are the professional product one would expect from the Cooperative Test Service. That there are defects and deficiencies lies in the nature of the world: *errare humanum est.*

The forms under consideration are all 80-minute tests. The disadvantage of so long a test is outweighed by the range and depth of the items, and by the fairness effected through the large number of items in each area tested. All four forms have three parts: comprehension (combining the vocabulary and reading of the older forms), grammar, and civilization (an innovation not appearing in previous forms).

In Part I there are 60 well chosen vocabulary items, as foolproof as such isolated matchings can be, and 40 comprehension items, based largely on Latin passages of some length and requiring in their answering both linguistic knowledge and considerable thought. The first 10 comprehension items are incomplete Latin sentences, the correct Latin completion of which is to be chosen from five possibilities listed. The remaining 30 items are based on five to seven excellent passages that are well graded, interesting, real units of thought adapted from a variety of sources and topics: anecdotes, mythology, Nepos, Caesar (Lower Level Y is unfortunately almost entirely taken from this author) for the Lower Level and Nepos, Cicero, Livy, Vergil, and even Lucretius for the Higher Level. The only general objection to this section is that the 30 minutes allotted to it would seem to be inadequate; 45 minutes would seem a minimum for the often thought-provoking questions, which require a real understanding of the Latin they refer to. Specifically, in Lower Level S the answer to Item 6 could be 3 or 4, and that to Item 18 could be 2 or 5; in Higher Level Y the answer to Item 28 could be 2 or 5; and in the Livian passage in Higher Level S, page 7, column 2, *praestarent* is an unfortunate replacement for Livy's *praesto essent.*

Part II consists of 40 (Lower Level) or 45 (Higher Level) items designed to show knowledge of forms and syntax. In each item a sensible English sentence is followed by an incomplete Latin version, the test being to choose the correct complement from a list of five suggestions.

College Entrance Examination Board Achievement Test in Latin Reading

Form S on both levels varies this procedure by reserving the first 10 items for a word completion test, in which correct endings are to be supplied from a long list of endings. As well suited for their purpose as these sentences are, they show too little differentiation in difficulty as between the two levels; also, 15 rather than 20 minutes seem an ample time allotment. It is too bad that the authors have seen fit to include some impossible forms as suggested answers: *geruit, militorum, eiam,* and *saxe.* Lastly, note that in Item 19 of Higher Level Y the word suggested as equivalent to "another" is not *alius* but *alter.*

Part III is made up of 60 items on civilization, in its broadest sense: it covers Latin abbreviations, derivation of English words, "antiquities," history, mythology, government, religion, later influence, etc., as well as specific questions on the triumvirate of the American high school curriculum—Caesar, Cicero, and Vergil. The general effect is one of patchiness and lack of direction (perhaps unavoidable in view of the broad field to be covered); most of the questions, however, appear to be valid in themselves, although here and there a question is overly obvious (e.g. about Dido's fate) or of no great significance (e.g. on the locale of the Second Catilinarian). Again, there could be more differentiation between the two levels, and the time allotment seems too generous for pure recall work.

In conclusion, some corrections should be cited. For all of Lower Level S and for all but the last two comprehension passages of Lower Level Y the length of the Latin vowels is indicated. Note these misprints: S I, 1, Item 48, *dedō* for *dēdō;* Y I, 1, Item 52, *cedō* for *cēdō;* page 6, column 2, line 9 of the passage *propōsitīs* for *prōpositīs.* Other misprints in the Latin are these: Lower Level S, page 6, column 2, line 9 of the passage, *classī* for the normal *classe;* Higher Level Y, page 6, column 1, line 5 of the passage, *eum in Bithynia regis hospitio esse,* where read *Bithyniae.*

For a review by C. W. Odell of Form S, see 3:205; for a review by Hazel M. Toliver of Part 1, Form S, see 3:203.

[252]

*First Year Latin Test: State High School Tests for Indiana. 1, 2 semesters high school; 1934–49; 2 levels; mimeographed; no data on reliability and validity; no manual; norms ['49]; 4½¢ per test; 15¢ per specimen set; postpaid; 40(45) minutes; Inez Painter; State High School Testing Service for Indiana, Purdue University. *

a) FIRST SEMESTER. Form A ['48].
b) SECOND SEMESTER. Form N ['48].

[253]

Godsey Latin Composition Test. High school; 1926; 2 scores: sentences, rules; Forms A, B; no data on reliability; $1.30 per 25, postage extra; specimen set not available; 30(35) minutes; Edith R. Godsey; World Book Co. *

REFERENCES

1. AMERICAN CLASSICAL LEAGUE, ADVISORY COMMITTEE. *The Classical Investigation: Part One, General Report: A Summary of Results With Recommendations for the Organization of the Course in Secondary Latin and for Improvement in Methods of Teaching.* Princeton, N.J.: Princeton University Press, 1924. Pp. vi, 305.
2. BRUECKNER, LEO J. "The Status of Certain Basic Latin Skills." *J Ed Res* 9:390–402 My '24. *

KONRAD GRIES, *Assistant Professor of Classical Languages and Chairman of the Department, Queens College, Flushing, New York.*

Potential users of this test should not be deceived. This is not a Latin composition test, nor does it fulfill its stated aim of measuring "the accuracy of Latin composition work, at the same time showing the correlation of sentence-writing skill to knowledge of Latin grammar"; for the student is nowhere required either to recreate Latin forms nor to assemble such forms independently into a Latin sentence, be it as translation or as original thought. Instead, he is confronted in each form with three sets of eleven English sentences, each followed by a Latin translation, one element of which is given in four different forms, of which only one is correct. This he is to encircle. Next to each sentence are four numbers referring to four of some 16 succinctly stated rules printed at the bottom of the page. His second job is to encircle the number of that rule which applies to the encircled Latin form. The abilities tested, therefore, are (*a*) the student's ability to eliminate impossible forms (e.g., *pācam* and *proficīscerēs*), the occasional presence of which is perhaps the most unfortunate aspect of the test; (*b*) his ability to recognize forms (e.g., in "These are the books which you lost. *Hī sunt librī (quī, quae, quem, quōs) āmīsistī,*" he must recall that *librī* is masculine and *quōs* accusative plural masculine); (*c*) his understanding of grammatical concepts (e.g., that of the indirect object if he is to choose *tibi* as the translation for "you" in "I granted you this favor"); and (*d*) his ability to select that rule which supports his choice of the correct Latin.

This is a good test of the areas covered. The sentences, based mainly on Caesar, but graded in difficulty from simple agreement to the passive periphrastic, make good sense. Except for the impossible forms mentioned above, the items of choice are well calculated to reveal the student's mastery of morphology and syntax; both sentences and rules (there are about 35 of the latter, when repetitions among the three sets are subtracted) are abundant enough to give fair coverage; and the rules are, for the most part, both well chosen, being all of functional importance, and well phrased. The accuracy of Rule 5, Part II, Form B, is questionable: "A *cum*-temporal clause has its verb in the....subjunctive," time as such being indicated by the indicative; as is also the advisability of including the rather technical "clause of volition."

Other virtues of this test are its brevity, its broad applicability (second semester through fourth year), its ease of administration and scoring (both the key and the manual are excellent), and the large number of cases upon which its norms were based. As the test was devised and administered in connection with the Classical Investigation of 1921–1923, over 20,000 papers were available for the determination of norms.

[254]

Kansas Second Year Latin Test. 1, 2 semesters high school; 1935–36; 2 levels; manual ('36); 90¢ per 25 of any one level; 20¢ per specimen set; postpaid; 40(45) minutes; W. L. Holtz and H. E. Schrammel; Bureau of Educational Measurements, Kansas State Teachers College of Emporia. *
a) TEST II. First semester; Forms A ('35), B ('36).
b) TEST II. Second semester; Forms C ('35), D ('36).

W. C. KVARACEUS, *Professor of Educational Measurement, Boston University, Boston, Massachusetts.*

These tests were constructed for use with second year Latin students in high schools. Forms A and B are available for use at the end of the first term; Forms C and D are to be used at the end of the second term. Forms A and B contain 65 items each and Forms C and D are made of 70 items each. Each of these forms contains four parts measuring proficiencies in the following areas: ability to determine the thought content from a Latin paragraph, knowledge of Latin forms and syntax, and vocabulary control. If the teaching of Latin still avows any objectives other than the knowledge of Latin grammar and the ability to translate a Latin passage, they are not visible in this test.

These tests have been poorly constructed and have been carelessly edited. Some of the items are lacking in objectivity and a number of seri-

ous errors are noted. To name a few examples: in Form A, *Amezonum* should read *Amazonum,* the acknowledgment should read *Fabulae* for *Faulae,* and the answer for Item 36 calls for a *cum* descriptive clause when temporal is more nearly correct; in Form B, Item 15 is ambiguous and unrelated to the specific passage, in Item 28 *genere* is better described as an ablative of means, in Item 32 there are two defensible answers, in Item 51 the answer calls for *isset* but could more probably be *erit,* in Item 53 the answer could also be *erint* (pl.), in Item 59 the answer could also be *at* or *ant,* the answer sheet has a misprint for Item 60 and should appear as *isset;* in Form C the translation text has been rewritten from indirect discourse to direct discourse and utilizes punctuation that is very misleading. In line 9 of the Latin paragraph *mihi* should be separated from *deteriora;* Items 21 and 24 could be keyed otherwise than false, in Item 61 *siege* not *seige;* in Form D, Items 22 and 23 could be scored plus, and the answer space under Item 46 is misleading. These errors and ambiguities are inexcusable.

Two pages of mimeographed statements constitute the manual. Percentile norms are available based on 805 cases for Form A, 1,001 cases for Form B, and 2,411 cases for Forms C and D. The inference is made that the norm sample was obtained on a nation-wide basis, but no information is given to substantiate the claim. In view of the age of the norms and the question of the determination of the norm sample, present-day use of these distributions for comparative purposes is seriously questioned, especially when one considers the marked falling off in Latin elections within the past years and the many selectivity factors operating in the election of this subject today. Any norms that are offered should be accompanied by specific descriptions of the grade and ability of the norm group.

These tests do not do a very discriminating job in showing up differences in achievement. The reported Q values range from 4.5 to 6 points of raw score with probable errors of measurement ranging from 2.46 to 3.27. At the same time there is a very heavy dependence on true-false items throughout the forms, but no provisions are made for corrections for guessing.

These one-sheet, poorly printed tests, vintage 1935–36, should either be completely revised and new norms established or they should be withdrawn from the market. A Latin teacher who has had a basic course in educational measurement should be able to serve his own evaluation needs more adequately by constructing his own objective tests for local use. If the teacher wants to obtain comparative test data, he will find a better tool in the *Cooperative Latin Test.*

For a review by W. L. Carr, see 40:1369.

[255]

★**Latin I and II: Achievement Examinations for Secondary Schools.** 1 or 2 years high school; 1951; 1 form; no data on reliability and validity; no manual; Minnesota norms (median and quartile deviation) available; similar norms for other regions by special arrangement with publisher; 7¢ per test, postage extra; 60(65) minutes; edited by Walter W. Cook; prepared by a curriculum committee of high school teachers for use in the Minnesota State Board Achievement Examinations Program; Educational Test Bureau, Educational Publishers, Inc. *

[256]

*****Latin I and II: Every Pupil Test.** 1 or 2 years high school; 1929–51; new form usually published each April and December; form April 1951; no data on reliability and validity; no manual; norms ('51); 2½¢ per test; 1¢ per answer key; postpaid; 40(45) minutes; Ohio Scholarship Tests, Ohio State Department of Education. *

[257]

*****Second Year Latin Test: State High School Tests for Indiana.** 1, 2 semesters high school; 1934–49; 2 levels; mimeographed; no data on reliability and validity; no manual; norms ['49]; 4¢ per test; 15¢ per specimen set; postpaid; 40(45) minutes; Josephine Lilian Lee; State High School Testing Service for Indiana, Purdue University. *
a) FIRST SEMESTER. Form A ['45].
b) SECOND SEMESTER. Form N ['45].

[258]

White Latin Test. High school; 1924; 3 scores: vocabulary, sentences, total; Form B; Form A out of print; no data on reliability; revised manual; $1.80 per 25, postage extra; 35¢ per specimen set, postpaid; 35(40) minutes; Dorrance Stinchfield White; World Book Co. *

REFERENCES

1. SYMONDS, PERCIVAL M. *Ability Standards for Standardized Achievement Tests in the High School.* New York: Bureau of Publications, Teachers College, Columbia University, 1927. Pp. x, 91. *

KONRAD GRIES, *Assistant Professor of Classical Languages and Chairman of the Department, Queens College, Flushing, New York.*

The manual indicates that this is "a comprehensive and standard Latin test suitable to measure growth in knowledge of Latin on the part of high school and college students through four years of Latin." In reality, the knowledge of Latin tested is strictly recognitional and is confined to vocabulary, sentence structure, and translation; one would hope that the term "knowledge of Latin" covers a somewhat broader field.

Within its limitations, however, the test is a well constructed instrument which will clearly show whether a student has mastered a basic vocabulary, and whether his study of grammar and his readings in Latin have given him the ability to see which of several suggested translations of a given Latin sentence is the correct one. The 100 vocabulary items (for each four equivalents are proposed) and the 20 sentences (for each, three or four translations are offered) which each of the forms contains are, in the one case, abundant enough to provide a fair selection, and, in the other, inclusive enough really to check the student's mastery of important principles. Both parts are graded in difficulty and based upon frequency of occurrence "in the works of authors that are read for college entrance." This seems to mean mainly Caesar and Cicero; Vergil (and verse) is omitted save for an occasional vocabulary item. The time allotments—15 and 20 minutes respectively—are adequate, and the scoring can be done "rapidly and accurately." The manual is helpful in its instructions on administration, scoring, and interpretation; it also contains tables of percentile norms, based on 3,500 cases for the one form and 1,650 cases for the other.

Administratively, then, this is a good test; and it undoubtedly measures a certain amount and kind of knowledge, Pedagogically, however, its value is not so definite. The advisability of presenting isolated words and sentences has been questioned before by *Mental Measurements Yearbook* reviewers (Atkins, 38: 1065; Dunkel, 40:1365; Toliver, 3: 203); it may be wise to question it again. Thus, in vocabulary, "word-matching" is possible, and even laudable, up to a certain point: *lacrima* does equal "tear," *surgo* "rise," and *sic* "thus." But the words that are univalent, or whose semantic range is equivalent in Latin and English, are strictly limited in number. To equate *pario* with "win," *largior* with "bribe," and *fides* with "protection" is of doubtful validity; and when *eripio* becomes "rescue," entirely too much emphasis is laid on the single context in which the student is expected to have met the word.

In the case of isolated sentences, there is, of course, the advantage of being able to increase the difficulty of structure gradually, almost scientifically, and to cover a large number of grammatical forms and principles efficiently. But how much is lost for the student who meets such inanities as *"Ille locus quem vos castris petebatis mihi deligendus est," "Pauci Athenis multos menses habitare poterant,"* or *"Pascere, crudelis, nostro dolore corque ferum satia; miserae mihi plura supersunt quam tibi felici."* (Incidentally, the first comma of this last sentence is missing, the only misprint noticed, although more commas in the longer sentences would be a legitimate aid to the student.) Even the best of the sentences, those taken or adapted from Latin authors, have no real life when deprived of their rightful context. No one has ever spoken or written in isolated sentences, nor does one learn Latin to be able to read Latin quotations. The self-sufficient paragraph is the normal unit of speech, and the most proper unit for testing comprehension in a foreign language, Latin or any other.

SPANISH

[259]

★**College Entrance Examination Board Achievement Test in Spanish Reading.** Candidates for college entrance; 1902-51; available only in College Entrance Examination Board Admissions Testing Program (see 526); 60(70) minutes; prepared by College Entrance Examination Board Committee of Examiners in Spanish Reading in cooperation with the Staff of Educational Testing Service: 1951 membership: Donald D. Walsh (Chairman), Linton L. Barrett, Amelia del Río, Rose E. Martin, and Naomi W. Zieber; program administered by Educational Testing Service for the College Entrance Examination Board. *

REFERENCES

1. DYER, HENRY S. "Some Observations on the College Board Language Tests." *Ed & Psychol Meas* 8:593-602 w '48. * (*PA* 24:1458)
2. TUCKER, LEDYARD R. "Interpreting Scores on the Foreign-Language Tests." *Col Bd R* 1:47-9 sp '48. *
3. WALSH, DONALD DEVENISH. "The College Board Spanish Test." *Hispania* 34:343-8 N '51. *

[260]

*Cooperative Spanish Test: Lower and Higher Levels. 3-6 semesters high school or 1-2 semesters college, more than 2 years high school or more than 1 year college; 1948-51; 4 scores: comprehension, grammar, civilization, total; IBM; 2 levels; Form Y (Lower Level, '50—same as test copyrighted in 1948; Higher Level, '48); no data on validity; no specific manual; no college norms; general Cooperative manual ('51); high school norms ['50]; $2.50 per 25 of any one level; 50¢ per specimen set of any one level, postpaid; separate answer sheets may be used; 90¢ per 25 IBM answer sheets; 30¢ per set of stencils for scoring answer sheets; cash orders postpaid; 80(85) minutes; William H. Shoemaker and Geraldine Spaulding; Cooperative Test Division, Educational Testing Service. *

REFERENCES

1. JACOBS, ROBERT. "An Evaluation of the 80-Minute Forms of the Cooperative Tests in French, Latin, and Spanish," pp. 79-86. (*PA* 23:309) In *1948 Achievement Testing Program in Independent Schools and Supplementary Studies.* Educational Records Bulletin, No. 50. New York: Educational Records Bureau, July 1948. Pp. xiii, 86. Paper, lithotyped. *
2. CLAPP, HAROLD L. "Meditations on a Placement Program or When Should a Foreign Language be Studied." *Mod Lang J* 31:203-7 Ap '47. *
3. TRAXLER, ARTHUR E. "The Relation of Vocabulary and Grammar to Reading Achievement in Latin, French, and Span-

ish," pp. 61-5. (*PA* 22:449) In *1947 Achievement Testing Program in Independent Schools and Supplementary Studies.* Educational Records Bulletin No. 48. New York: Educational Records Bureau, June 1947. Pp. xii, 66. Paper, lithotyped.

JAMES B. THARP, *Professor of Foreign Language Education, The Ohio State University, Columbus, Ohio.*

The Lower and Higher Levels of this test have the same pattern of items and the timing for all parts is the same. Throughout both levels the five-option multiple choice item is used, with provision for marking the appropriate answers in the test booklet or on a separate answer sheet. Answers in the booklet must be scored by hand with a fan key; the separate answer sheets can be scored either by machine or by hand with a scoring stencil.

Part I, Comprehension, is organized in two sections. Section 1 (15 minutes) contains 50 Spanish words, each accompanied by five numbered English meanings. About half of the words are nouns. According to ratings suggested by Spaulding,[1] the first 30 words in the Lower Level have an average frequency index of 2.3, that is, an average within the second 500-word group; and the next 20 words show an average index of 3.3, or an average within the third 500-word group. In the Higher Level this section is more difficult, the average frequency indices being 3.8, 4.1, 6.3, 5.9, and 8.4 for the 50 words taken in groups of ten.

The last 10 items of Section 1 represent a welcome innovation in vocabulary measurement. For these items an idiom is used in a Spanish sentence which is followed by five Spanish sentences, only one of which paraphrases the meaning of the test sentence. Rating the idioms by a self-made system similar to that of Spaulding, this reviewer found an average frequency index of 3.3 for the ten idioms in the Lower Level and an average frequency index of 6.0 for those in the Higher Level. Neither level contains a word that is not in the Buchanan Word-list or an idiom that is not in the Keniston Idiom List.

Section 2 (25 minutes) consists of several Spanish paragraphs, each followed by three to five paraphrasing sentences with five possible endings, only one of which conforms to the story in the paragraph. The reviewer applied Spaulding's Formula I to the ten paragraphs in the Lower Level and obtained difficulty ratings of 54, 69, 79, 45, 92, 50, 60, 82, 53, and 70. Based on word frequency and sentence length alone,

1 Spaulding, Seth. "Two Formulas for Estimating the Reading Difficulty of Spanish." *Ed Res B* 30:117-24 My 16 '51.

White Latin Test

these ratings indicate relatively easy prose. The reviewer analyzed only the first three and last three of the nine paragraphs in Section 2 of the Higher Level, obtaining for the six paragraphs difficulty ratings of 90, 70, and 80 (first three), and 118, 85, and 130 (last three). These data indicate the generally higher difficulty of the paragraphs of this level.

It must be remembered that the Spaulding formulas of necessity ignore idiomatic and syntactical complexities and the nature of the story content. With this in mind, the reviewer is of the opinion that, in spite of the apparently unsteady pattern of difficulty shown by the paragraph ratings for both the Lower and Higher Levels, there is probably little doubt that the paragraphs are arranged in order of ascending difficulty, as judged by actual performance of students who took the trial administration of the test.

Part II, Grammar (25 minutes), consists of a series of English sentences which set the grammatical problem, each followed by a partial Spanish translation and five numbered expressions, only one of which correctly completes the Spanish translation. The Lower Level has 40 of these completions, and the Higher Level 39. The second part of this section employs a selection-type response by which knowledge of correct word order and position in a sentence may be measured. An English sentence is followed by five translations in Spanish, only one of which is correct. There are 10 of these in the Lower Level and 11 in the Higher Level.

It is test items of this sort that some teachers object to on the complaint that the pupil must look at incorrect language and may, as a consequence, suffer harm to his language skill. Every classroom has similar errors cropping up in daily recitations, and the errors are successfully used for teaching purposes. It should be recognized that "proof-reading" is a valid testing technique, especially when the pupil is well aware that he is taking a test and not encountering model language that he should imitate.

Part III, Civilization (15 minutes), is another welcome innovation in a foreign language test. This part is made up of 50 items about geography, history, art, literature, and other aspects of Hispanic civilization. The statements and the five-choice completions are in English, except where Spanish places and titles make up the responses. The reviewer counted eight or ten items in each level that could be called

of general application to Hispanic life; the remainder are about equally divided between Spain and Latin America. In each level three pictures are included for identification.

Some teachers may raise the question as to whether some of the facts tested here are representative of a knowledge of Hispanic civilization. Let him who objects try to compose a better test, and at that, to compose two forms of the test, one easier than the other. Of course, there are some items in the Higher Level that are easier than some in the Lower Level, but the table of scores shows an overall difference. A Scaled Score of 50 is equivalent to a raw score of 24 on the Lower Level, but only 13 on the Higher Level.

No attempt will be made here to explain the system of Scaled Scores, which is described in some detail in the manual. Suffice it to say that the tables of percentile ranks given in terms of Scaled Scores for both levels together furnish data for six semesters of secondary-school study. No college norms are thus far available.

Form Y of the *Cooperative Spanish Test* shows evidence of the careful selection of materials and skillful execution of test exercises that have long characterized the Cooperative foreign language tests. The authors of this test are to be complimented for presenting the usual type of material well and for offering some new testing techniques much needed by the Spanish-teaching profession.

[261]

★First Year Spanish Test: State High School Tests for Indiana. 1, 2 semesters high school; 1945; 2 levels; mimeographed; no data on reliability and validity; no manual; norms ['45]; 4½¢ per test; 15¢ per specimen set; postpaid; 40(45) minutes; O. H. Patterson; State High School Testing Service for Indiana, Purdue University. *
a) FIRST SEMESTER. Form A ['45].
b) SECOND SEMESTER. Form N ['45].

[262]

*Furness Test of Aural Comprehension in Spanish. 1–3 years high school or 1–2 years college; 1945–51; 2 editions; no data on reliability and validity; $1.50 per 25; 10¢ per specimen set; postage extra; Edna Lue Furness; Banks Upshaw & Co. *
a) [ORIGINAL EDITION.] 1945–46; 4 scores: vocabulary, completion, identification, total; Forms A ('46—same as test copyrighted in 1945), B ('46—same as test copyrighted in 1945); manual ['46]; tentative norms; 40(45) minutes.
b) [RECORDED EDITION.] 1951; 5 scores: vocabulary, completion, identification, question-answer, total; Form C; no norms; manual ['51]; 3 types of recordings: "LP" 33⅓ rpm (28-inch records), wire (5-inch spool), dual-track tape (5-inch spool); $6 per "LP" record set; $7.50 per wire recording; $7.50 per dual-track tape recording; 32(37) minutes.

For reviews by Frederick B. Agard and Walter V. Kaulfers, see 3:213.

[263]

★**Graduate Record Examinations Advanced Spanish Test.** Senior year college through graduate school and candidates for graduate school; 1946–51; available only in Graduate Record Examinations programs (see 527); 105(125) minutes; Educational Testing Service. *

[264]

★**Kansas First Year Spanish Test.** First year high school or college; 1947; Form A; $1.05 per 25; 20¢ per specimen set; postpaid; 40(45) minutes; Minnie M. Miller; Bureau of Educational Measurements, Kansas State Teachers College of Emporia. *

[265]

★**Spanish I and II: Achievement Examinations for Secondary Schools.** 1 or 2 years high school; 1951; 1 form; no data on reliability and validity; no manual; Minnesota norms (median and quartile deviation) available; similar norms for other regions by special arrangement with publisher; 7¢ per test, postage extra; 60(65) minutes; edited by Walter W. Cook; prepared by a curriculum committee of high school teachers for use in the Minnesota State Board Achievement Examinations Program; Educational Test Bureau, Educational Publishers, Inc. *

[266]

The Stanford Spanish Tests. 1–4 years high school or 1–2 years college; 1927; 3 parts; Forms A, B; 80¢ per 25 of any one part; 25¢ per specimen set; cash orders postpaid; Aurelio M. Espinosa and Truman L. Kelley; Stanford University Press. *
a) PART I, GRAMMAR. 20(25) minutes.
b) PART II, VOCABULARY. 15(20) minutes.
c) PART III, PARAGRAPH MEANING. 20(25) minutes.

JAMES B. THARP, *Professor of Foreign Language Education, The Ohio State University, Columbus, Ohio.*

Five parts were originally planned for this test; the last two projected parts, Sentence Meaning and Pronunciation, were never published.

Separate norms are presented for high school and university classes by years. Within each year of study there are norms for a variety of groups, according to the amount of study given to other languages. This factor, usually neglected in other tests, seems to have considerable importance if one or more other languages have been studied for more than one year. For example, the total of all three norms for first year high school in group A (no other language or 1 year Latin or French) is 65.2. In group C (3 years Latin or French) each norm is 11 or 12 points higher, and the total is 103.4. The university group A (no other language) total is 90.6; group E (8 to 10 years of other languages in 4 different combinations of French and Latin) has a total of 130.2.

The arrangement of parts, beginning with the more difficult grammar and ending with the easier reading, may have a psychological value that other tests could copy.

The vocabulary test uses a matching technique: groups of 6 test words (7 in the last two groups) printed in a column, each word followed by a blank; to the right of each group appears a column of 12 English words containing the correct meanings plus confusion items.

It must be remembered that these tests came out the same year of the publication of Buchanan's *A Graded Spanish Word Book* [1] and probably without the advantage of its data. Consequently it is gratifying to see how each form of Part II, Vocabulary, checks against the Buchanan list. Of the 68 test words, there are 7 words in each form not found in the 6,702 items given by Buchanan. There are 39 words in Form A and 41 words in Form B which occur within the first 1,500 of the Buchanan list. When the remaining, less frequent words are given the Frequency Index suggested by Spaulding,[2] the average index for the 22 words in Form A and the 20 words in Form B is 8.17 and 8.44, respectively. These figures show a progression from easy to difficult, so far as the factor of frequency is concerned, and a close equivalence of difficulty between forms.

When the 10 paragraphs of Part III are analyzed by the Spaulding formula, the results are not so satisfactory. Although the paragraphs grow longer toward the last of the 10 selections, and the sentences are shorter at the beginning, simpler in content, and less idiomatic, the statistics of difficulty do not show progression to greater difficulty at the end or near equivalence of difficulty between the forms. According to Spaulding's Formula I, paragraphs VI to X are rated 77, 62, 58, 155, and 120 in Form A, and 45, 78, 55, 72, and 61 respectively in Form B. It would be interesting to learn whether Form A proves more difficult in the pupil responses to these paragraphs, a fact not revealed in the norms, which give one figure for both forms.

It is in the grammar test, Part I, however, that this reviewer finds the most to criticize for lack of validity. The 50 items of each form are presented in three types of test procedures: (*a*) Mutations, Form A, 27; Form B, 29. (*b*) Com-

---

1 Buchanan, Milton A. *A Graded Spanish Word Book.* Publications of the American and Canadian Committees on Modern Languages, Vol. 3. Toronto, Canada: University of Toronto Press, 1927. Pp. 195. Paper. *
2 Spaulding, Seth. "Two Formulas for Estimating the Reading Difficulty of Spanish." *Ed Rcs B* 30:117–24 My 16 '51. *

Furness Test of Aural Comprehension in Spanish

pletion, recall response, Form A, 6; Form B, 5. (c) Selection, 2-item choice, Form A, 17; Form B, 16. In each form nearly one fourth of the changes of form of completions in a blank depend on the knowledge of a grammatical term, such as "past absolute," "possessive adjective," "reflective pronoun," etc.: 13 cases in Form A; 15 in Form B. Does a failure to respond indicate lack of knowledge of the language form or of the grammatical nomenclature? Scoring directions say "The omission of accent marks.... should not be counted against the student," but should there not be added "unless vital to the meaning"? For example, the answer to Item 11 in Form A is *sé,* not *se;* and the answer to Item 35 in Form B is *Les hablé,* not *Les hable.* In both forms, Item 12 appears tricky. When asked to "Write the correct forms to complete the meaning," *Los peces viven en (el) agua* in Form B, the answer *el* remains the same, unless some culprit thinks he *must* change it, as nothing has been said about some items being correct as they stand. But in Form A, for *Necesito (un)zapatos,* the answer on the key sheet is *unos.* Suppose a pupil writes *dos* or says "nothing"; is this response wrong or does the scorer accept it in defiance of the key?

Since the *Stanford Spanish Tests* have continued in demand for many years, even as newer tests came on the market, there is ample evidence that teachers regard the tests highly and find themselves well served. The minor faults indicated above have not marred the solid results delivered in a quarter-century of popular usage.

Stanford Spanish Tests

REPRINTED FROM *The Fifth Mental Measurements Yearbook*

FOREIGN LANGUAGES—FIFTH MMY

REVIEWS BY *Ralph Bedell, Nelson Brooks, John A. Cox, Jr., Harold B. Dunkel, Konrad Gries, Walter V. Kaulfers, Charles R. Langmuir, Herschel T. Manuel, Kathleen N. Perret, Herbert Schueler, Geraldine Spaulding, Mary E. Turnbull, and Clarence E. Turner.*

ENGLISH

[255]

★**Diagnostic Test for Students of English as a Second Language.** Applicants from non-English countries for admission into American colleges; 1953; 1 form; manual ['53]; no data on reliability; no norms; separate answer sheets must be used; $3.50 per 10 tests; $1 per 10 answer sheets; 45¢ per specimen set; postpaid; 60(65) minutes; A. L. Davis; Educational Services. *

NELSON BROOKS, *Associate Professor of French, Yale University, New Haven, Connecticut.*

This is a pencil and paper test on a number of frequently used patterns of form and order in which vocabulary plays a minor role and sound no role at all. Each item offers a choice of three ways of writing a short utterance in English, two of which are unacceptable. All the items use English only. Some of the choices are wrong because the suggested forms are impossible: "severals," "gooder," "tooths," "mights," "absenced." Other choices are wrong because the words as given do not fit accepted patterns of English syntax: "in his coffee sugar he uses," "resemble to," "wants on time breakfast," "pair of shoe," "can to write," "had the tailor a coat make," "doesn't he can't." A third type of wrong answer results when the suggested forms—correct in themselves—are fitted into the entire utterance: "It is (hardly) (very) (much) difficult to write on a grain of rice"; "She buys (her own clothes) (his own clothes) (its own clothes)"; "If he had seen you, he (would have spoken) (would speak) (will have spoken) to you." In the opinion of this reviewer, only the last named type of distractor is allowable, although this renders invalid nearly a third of the test.

The issue is an old one, but can never be dismissed from the testmaker's mind: are the parts which the testee is asked to fit together all to be genuine, though sometimes incompatible, or must he distinguish between genuine and spurious parts as well? Beyond the questions of intellectual integrity and fair play there is the matter of wrong learning by the testee. There is no need to learn a thing wrong in order eventually to learn it right, and it is gratuitous on the part of the testmaker to assume wrong learning by the testee as a matter of course. To ask that such a standard of high-mindedness be applied to this test is merely to ask that all of it be as good as the larger part of it is.

There are some misprints, two of them serious. In Item 132 of the student's booklet the first choice is not accompanied by its code letter A, and for Item 127 the key indicates A as the correct answer; it should be C. In Item 14 there are two possible correct answers, "I hope he will go" and "I hope he would go," both being perfectly acceptable English.

In scoring, one-half of the number of wrong answers is to be deducted from the number right in arriving at a final evaluation. Missing answers are not counted at all. Neither of these facts is mentioned in the instructions to the student, though both are very likely to influence his performance on this or any other test and hence affect the accuracy of measurement.

No table of norms is provided, but the test is said to have been given to hundreds of students from foreign countries. Experience at the American Language Center of the American University has shown that students with scores of 125 or better are ready for college work, those between 100 and 125 need considerable extra training, and those between 40 and 80 need full time instruction in English.

While this test will doubtless serve to separate in a general way those who know English well from those who do not, the impression persists that this could be done with far greater accuracy if the test were based upon a more systematic analysis of the patterns of English, and if it included some work with English sounds—surely a matter of prime importance to those who intend to study in American classrooms.

HERSCHEL T. MANUEL, *Professor of Educational Psychology, The University of Texas, Austin, Texas.*

This test illustrates the type of measuring instrument which is developed to meet a need in a particular situation and then made available to other users without sufficient descriptive material on which the new user can base an independent judgment of its value. The test "has been given to hundreds of students from foreign countries," apparently with satisfactory results.

The test consists of 150 multiple choice items which are for the most part short sentences in which the student is to choose the best of three words or phrases—for example, "They meet (at) (to) (on) eight o'clock." The ability tested is primarily acquaintance with English idioms rather than extent of vocabulary, comprehension of reading material, or understanding of spoken language. Although ability to do college work depends upon much more than ability with the English language, and although ability with the English language is much more than acquaintance with idioms, the mastery of idiomatic usage, in the opinion of the reviewer, is undoubtedly an important variable in itself and an important index of progress toward general mastery of the language.

The method of selecting items (letter from author) was one of "checking all available texts for materials, having our teachers submit possible questions and criticising what we had done." Validity (same source) was based upon a comparison of test results with class scores. No item analyses or validity coefficients are given.

There is no indication in the available material that a method of comparative linguistic analysis such as that used by Lado was used in selecting items. There is, however, a classification of items on the answer sheet under 10 heads—pronouns, nouns, adjectives and adverbs, ellipses, prepositions, word order, verbs, tenses and voice, verbals, and idiomatic vocabulary. Thus, to a certain degree, the test does, as the title suggests, provide an opportunity to discover types of errors. Because of the small number of items in each division no attempt should be made to find part scores, or at least to regard them as reliable. Indeed, the author

makes no suggestion that part scores should be found; he does express an interest in using the results for lesson planning.

The format of the test is good except that perhaps something more should be done to facilitate keeping the right place on the answer sheet. (The reviewer once found himself shifting to a new column on the answer sheet when going to a new page in the test booklet!) The answer sheet is double, having a carbon paper insert which records the student's responses on the second sheet. The second sheet is preprinted to show the correct answers.

The Spearman-Brown split-half reliability (author's letter) is amazingly high (.96, *n* not reported), the range of scores is wide (31–145), and the mean score (103.5) is well below the total possible score. The author gives certain scores which have been found, by "experience at the American Language Center of the American University," to indicate corresponding degrees of preparation for college work.

In summary, the reviewer regards the test as useful in the practical situation for which it was empirically developed, but lacking in published information which would enable other testers to evaluate it for their own situations and use it most profitably. In addition, the reviewer would like to see more attention given to what the test measures as distinguished from the use which may be made of the scores. We need to know more about the relation of idiom mastery to other phases of language ability.

[256]

English Examinations for Foreign Students. Applicants from non-English language countries for admission to American colleges; 1947–56; 3 booklets; manual ['56]; practice booklet ['47]; norms ['51]; separate answer sheets must be used except with *b;* 10–19 tests, $3.50 each; one set of 12-inch records (78 rpm) provided with orders of 10–50 tests; postpaid; 270(305) minutes in 2 sessions; published for the College Entrance Examination Board; Educational Testing Service. *

a) BOOK 1. 4 scores: reading comprehension, aural comprehension, pronunciation, total; Form VFS; 140(155) minutes.
b) BOOK 2, [ENGLISH COMPOSITION]. Forms A, B ['47, also labeled Form VFS]; no norms; 40(45) minutes.
c) BOOK 3. Title on test is *English Examination for Foreign Students (Including a Test of Non-Verbal Reasoning)*; 2 scores: scientific vocabulary, nonverbal reasoning; Form VFS; 90(105) minutes.

RALPH BEDELL, *Specialist for Higher Education Programs, United States Office of Education, Washington, D.C.*

The large number of foreign students on our campuses and the still larger numbers to come are challenging some of our best educators to examine English with a new perspective —a view through the eyes of intelligent people whose first language is a language other than English.

The teaching of English as a foreign language presents many pedagogical and practical problems. To watch an intelligent adult struggling for the first time to learn English with its many nuances, its incessant flow of idioms, its casual disregard for grammar, is enough to bring out the best in any teacher. Is it any wonder that the student often turns to us who use English and asks, "Are there no rules?" And perhaps we whose first language is English might ask, "Who among us can say that he has learned English well?"

The trends of the times, nevertheless, bring constant pressure on our friends overseas to learn English. Since World War II, English has become the language of most of the scholars, business men, and officials throughout the free world. To many millions overseas success in learning English is the avenue to becoming well informed. The ability to use and understand English is especially important to keep abreast of modern technology. American colleges and universities are being pressed as never before to meet the English problems of foreign students, and one of the major chapters in any book of American higher education might be the success with which this is being done.

The *English Examination for Foreign Students* is designed to help select those whose English is sufficiently well advanced to permit profitable pursuit of college level courses in which the language of instruction is English. Further, the examination may be of considerable use to teachers of English as a foreign language in adjusting instruction to the needs of students.

The examination measures silent reading and auditory comprehension. The former is tested through sections on English vocabulary, recognition of correct and incorrect grammatical forms, and comprehension of sentences and short passages in English. Most of the vocabulary, sentence, and paragraph items sample words and ideas from everyday experience. There is a separate section, however, on scientific vocabulary, which includes words from elementary mathematics, physics, and chemistry. The large number of foreign students wishing to study the sciences in English speaking colleges and universities makes this section especially significant. The items testing paragraph comprehension place emphasis upon reading for detail and understanding of ideas. The paragraphs are short samples of those found in the first year of college history, social studies, and literature.

Auditory comprehension is tested through written questions based upon spoken passages played on phonograph records. The 16 spoken passages vary in length from about one quarter of a minute to about two minutes. Eleven paragraphs are spoken in a male voice and five in a female voice. At the conclusion of each paragraph the student is given time to mark multiple choice items which test recall of detail, understanding of ideas, or general significance of the paragraph. The number of such test items for each paragraph varies from one to six depending upon the length and content of the paragraph. The student is permitted to listen to the spoken paragraph only once and the test is so arranged that he cannot see the questions on a paragraph until after he has heard the paragraph spoken. After listening to a paragraph, the student answers the questions on it before proceeding to the next paragraph in the test.

Subordinate to the reading and auditory sections is a test purporting to measure the student's pronunciation of English words through his recognition of rhymes and correct accentuation. The student is asked to indicate whether or not the same sound is found in such pairs of words as *won—sun, did—ride,* and *air—bear.* Accentuation is tested by numbering the syllables of words and asking the student to indicate the number of the syllable most heavily accented. While these are strikingly clever devices for obtaining paper and pencil measures of pronunciation, tests of this type may at best be expected only to identify those whose pronunciation is very poor or who cannot relate their pronunciation to the printed word; that is, those who pass this test may still be in need of improvement in pronunciation.

The Test of Non-Verbal Reasoning, is obviously not intended as a measure of English attainment, but is designed to be helpful in determining the student's aptitude for school or college work independent of his proficiency in English. This test measures the ability of a student to determine the relationship that exists among a group of four line diagrams and select from a second group of diagrams the one that fits in with the relationship found in the first group.

The examination may be administered by anyone trained in the use of group tests of educational achievement. The publisher provides instructions for administration which are unusually complete and are clearly and precisely written. As some foreign students may have difficulty in following directions in English, and may not be generally familiar with testing procedures, it is desirable to have one or more proctors to assist the supervisor of the examination. The publisher recommends one proctor for each 20 students.

All persons who administer this examination will need to give it careful study in advance. The publisher recommends that each student who is to take the examination receive the practice book at least one week before the examination date with the direction to study it carefully. The practice book contains an answer sheet and questions like the ones in the examination. Correct answers are given to permit the student to check his work. The practice book does not contain any reference to the essay or auditory portions of the examination. This is not considered a serious fault, however, as the student will almost certainly have greater need for the very useful practice on other sections of the examination.

For administration of the aural comprehension section, it is necessary to have an electric phonograph that will play records at 78 revolutions per minute. The publishers provide a special phonograph needle with the records, and the use of this needle is recommended. The recordings are of good quality and can be understood when played on an ordinary phonograph. It is necessary, however, to have an advance tryout of the phonograph in the room where the examination is to be given to make sure the acoustics of the room are such that all students can hear the records distinctly.

The examination is published in one form only, except for the essay portion which is in two forms. Those who administer the examination will therefore need to exercise special care to see that no copy of it gets into unauthorized hands.

The scoring of the examination is objective except for the essay portion. The student marks an answer sheet which may be a copy of that supplied by the publisher, or an IBM or other similar answer sheet. With the exception of the essay portion, each copy of the examination may be reused by providing replacement answer sheets.

The publisher furnishes norms for each section of the examination (except for the essay portion) and for a composite score on reading comprehension, aural comprehension, and punctuation. The norms are based upon 507 foreign students tested at universities in the United States and abroad. There is no further description of these students. No data on the reliability and validity of the examination are available. Users of the examination are advised to conduct their own standardization and validation research.

The examination, especially those portions that deal with English, may have considerable use for groups of foreign students who are currently enrolled in colleges or universities in addition to those who are applicants for college entrance. A skilled teacher of English for foreign students may be able to make a number of inferences from responses to the questions of the examination that will be helpful in teaching. Pending further research, the examination should not, however, be considered suitable for individual counseling. The absence of sufficient validating data on the Test of Non-Verbal Reasoning makes this portion, especially, of little value unless an institution can obtain research on the predictive value of this test for its own students. Institutions lacking such research will be well advised to use one of the well standardizing nonverbal tests otherwise available for which validation data are available.

The examination originally was sponsored by the College Entrance Examination Board and the United States Department of State. It was first administered in 1947, and has found limited use since that time in colleges and universities, some divisions of the Armed Forces, and foreign affiliates of industrial corporations. It is a great pity that a test which is so well constructed and for which there is so much need should not be sufficiently well standardized and validated to warrant much wider use.

JOHN A. COX, JR., *Research Psychologist, Personnel Laboratory, Wright Air Development Center, Lackland AFB, Texas.*

This battery of tests gives every appearance of being a well planned and carefully prepared set of measures. It is rather complete, giving information about the examinee's ability to read English, compose in English, and comprehend spoken English, and about his intellectual level. The printed materials are well organized and editorially clean. The material presented orally is equally well prepared. There is no doubt that these tests were prepared by experts in the field of test construction.

Apart from the conversion tables, there is no indication of statistical analysis. No reliability estimates are presented. No validity information is given. In fact, the user is told that no validity studies are planned. Rather he is advised to validate the instrument for his own use. At least the publishers do not make unsubstantiated claims of validity for the instrument. There is no mention of the interrelationships among the several part scores, leaving the user to guess (or determine for himself) the utility of two or more part scores combined. This seems a waste of the data collected on the normative sample.

Strictly on the basis of subjective judgment, this examination bears the marks of a fine instrument. The user must be prepared to undertake validation studies and intercorrelation analysis along with the computation of reliability estimates before he will have the commonly accepted objective criteria to evaluate the instrument.

CHARLES R. LANGMUIR, *Director of Special Projects, The Psychological Corporation, New York, New York.*

Neither a foreign student adviser nor a foreign student is ever likely to forget the experience of this examination. A week prior to the scheduled testing the student works through nine pages of instructions and sample test questions. On the day of the test he appears for two sessions, totaling 4 hours and 50 minutes of working time plus incidental administration time.

In the first 60 minutes he is presented with Section A (Reading Comprehension), consisting of 35 vocabulary opposites, 10 vocabulary completion, and 20 two-choice usage items, followed by 25 paragraph reading questions based on seven passages. Section B (Aural Comprehension) uses the next 80 minutes. The student listens to 16 recorded passages and answers 50 four-choice questions. The paragraphs are spoken by several voices at rates varying from 130 to 160 words per minute. The simplest statement consists of two sentences, totaling 33 words, spoken in 15 seconds. The longest passage, between 300 and 400 words in length, is spoken in 2 minutes. The material has a descriptive-literary-philosophical character. After listening to a passage, the student turns the page to find the questions, which may vary in number from one to six. The first session ends with Section C, a 20-minute test of "pronunciation comprehension," consisting of 30 true-false rhymes and 30 words to mark for syllabic accent.

The second session opens with Section D, an essay part. The student has 15 minutes in which to write one or two sentences responsive to each of four statements and a related question. In the next 25 minutes he writes an essay of about 125 words on an assigned topic. The testing is concluded with a 30-minute test of 60 scientific vocabulary items (Section E) and a 60-minute nonverbal reasoning test (Section F) composed of two timed parts, 30 minutes for 30 three-by-three Penrose-Raven-type matrices, and 30 minutes for 60 two-choice figure classification items.

This is an impressive amount of business to find out whether a foreign student can read English and understand spoken English at a level sufficient to meet the demands of American colleges. Unfortunately, the examiner has a lot more work to accomplish before he discovers that he is not going to find out. First, he has to score four sides of two special hand scoring answer sheets, writing the scores in widely separated, unlabeled spaces on opposite sides of the answer sheets. The scores for Sections A, B, and C are then added, and the composite score is recorded on the front side of the first answer sheet. The five part scores and the composite score for the first three parts can then be looked up on six pages of conversion tables to get the six converted scores. These are presumably written down somewhere not identified. There are no scoring boxes of any kind on the answer sheets. These converted scores are now looked up in another table to get the percentile ranks, which are based on "foreign students tested at universities in this country and abroad" (n = 507). There is no other relevant information, except possibly that the converted scores are derived by a linear equating to an arbitrary scale of the raw scores of 119 foreign students tested somewhere. The publisher says the converted scores are "considerably more meaningful and much easier for interpretive work."

The examiner will reach this point much sooner if he is thoughtful enough to invent some way to register the key on the answer sheet. The keys supplied the purchaser are made by an unsteady hand—or by a steady hand with unsteady scissors—out of pieces of manila folders. Lines are ruled in pencil. The labeling is pen-and-ink, holograph. Scoring directions are omitted. If the examiner is planning a repeat performance with the reusable test booklets, he should design his own answer sheets and keys from scratch. The publisher says that replacement answer sheets are not available. The publisher recommends standard IBM answer sheets "or any other appropriate type devised or secured by the institution." It had better be devised by the institution since no standard IBM answer sheet will be in any way appropriate.

The second session involves the examiner in other difficulties. The essay section is not scorable. The publisher supplies no information, not even examples for normative or scale comparison, but does make one suggestion: "that the consensus of opinion of a group of readers be used in determining this score, but ETS leaves the method of scoring and the use of this score entirely to the discretion of the test user."

A scientific vocabulary test might have some utility in advising foreign students, especially if the choice of items were based on their specific differential content validity. The publisher offers no information about the ideas which generated this collection of science vocabulary. No rational basis is evident from an inspection of the items.

The final hour of the second session is given over to the nonverbal reasoning test. It is clearly not a part of the English examination, but is given with it "because most colleges would like an indication of the applicant's general reasoning ability." The normative and validity information required for such use by most colleges turns out to be some percentiles computed from 497 "foreign students tested at universities in this country and abroad." Who, where, level of education, age, sex, etc., are not mentioned.

About 200 words on the interpretation of scores accompanies the percentile table. The statements imply a powerful validity, e.g.,

"Scores of less than 40 on Reading Comprehension, Aural Comprehension, or Pronunciation suggest the need for special work in these areas," and "Candidates with (composite) scores above 50 will probably not be handicapped in their college work because of an English deficiency." No data in support of any validity statement are supplied, not even the intercorrelation of the parts, the reliabilities of the scores, or group differences of any kind. No follow-up studies are cited. In fact, it is not even known what kind of performance would be demonstrated by typical students whose native language is English. This situation is not likely to improve. The publisher states, "No additional normative studies are contemplated."

The test was put together immediately after the war with financial support of the State Department, and was published in its present form in 1947 by the College Entrance Examination Board for restricted rental. In 1951 it was made available by sale of materials to institutions and with the tacit understanding that the strict security conventional with College Board materials would be preserved. The materials supplied to current purchasers are apparently remainders from the original stock. The three test booklets are printed by offset on poor quality paper from a mediocre typescript much reduced. The reading paragraphs, for example, are printed in lines 7 inches long and packed 8 lines to the inch. The recorded material is presented on eight sides of four 12-inch discs, to be played at 78 rpm. The records are not packaged for storage. The pressings received for review were substandard in every respect.

[257]
English Language Test for Foreign Students. Applicants from non-English language countries for admission into American colleges; 1951; Form A; tentative norms; separate answer sheets must be used; 25¢ per test; 5¢ per answer sheet; $1 per set of scoring stencils; $1.30 per specimen set; postage extra; 120-(125) minutes; Robert Lado; George Wahr Publishing Co. *

REFERENCES
1–2. See 4:234.
3. LADO, ROBERT. "Improvements in Foreign Language Tests." *Univ Mich Sch Ed B* 24:3–5 O '52. *

JOHN A. COX, JR., *Research Psychologist, Personnel Laboratory, Wright Air Development Center, Lackland AFB, Texas.*

According to the author, this test measures "control of the English language by foreign students." The test contains 134 items of four types and requires no more than two hours' time to administer. The first part (40 items) is labeled "Structure"; the second (54 items), "Pronunciation." In both these parts the questions are in the form of multiple completion type items. In this form three alternatives are given, any combination of which, including "none," may be correct. The second part also contains 14 items with four and five choices consisting of syllabicated words whose accented syllables must be identified. The third part (40 items) is labeled "Vocabulary," and the items are, once again, in the multiple completion form. The format of the test is good and the booklet is editorially clean. Excellent sample items are presented separately for each part.

Special answer sheets are used and must be hand scored. Scoring stencils are provided which should make obtaining the raw scores (number correct) quite easy. A table for converting the raw scores to "per cent correct" is printed on the back page of the answer sheet.

The manual contains simple and satisfactory directions for administering the test and for scoring. There is a bare mention of using the time taken to finish as a separate score. The validity and reliability of this score are not discussed. A chance-half reliability coefficient is reported as .95 for the per cent correct score (based on 41 cases). Validity is implied by a table giving behavior descriptions of candidates scoring at various per cent levels. Thus, a testee earning a score falling between 90 to 100 per cent is described as follows: "This student is carrying a full time load and doing very good work in freshman English." This table is also based on 41 cases. The author implies that his test possesses "content" validity, but he gives no direct evidence of this. As evidence of validity, he presents the fact that this test correlates .89 with the average of scores from three other tests, two of which are "aural." This seems to be a type of construct validity. No information is given as to the size or character of the sample on which the relationship was found. This critic feels that more useful information would have been obtained by correlating scores from this test with those from each of the other three tests separately. The author's position that performance on the test is highly related to aural English proficiency possibly would be better supported by such data. Certainly, the author's position that this "silent test" measures "aural control" is still open to question.

In general, this test appears to be a satisfactory instrument for measuring proficiency in the comprehension of written English, but the evidence presented by the author that it is such an instrument is very weak. In truth, there are no norms given. There is a minimum of "validity" information, none of which is of the predictive variety. What little information is given is based on an undefined sample of 41 cases. The author's statement that the test has been thoroughly pretested should be verified in the manual by presenting results of the "pretesting." On the basis of the information given, the *English Language Test for Foreign Students* can be recommended for use only in an experimental way, not for any practical purposes such as selection of students for a training program.

For a review by Clarence E. Turner, see 4:234.

[258]

★An English Reading Test for Students of English as a Foreign Language. College entrants; 1956; 1 form; no data on reliability; 10 or more tests, 10¢ each; 18¢ per specimen set; postpaid; 30(35) minutes; Harold V. King and Russell N. Campbell; Washington Publications. *

RALPH BEDELL, *Specialist for Higher Education Programs, United States Office of Education, Washington, D.C.*

The test, developed in connection with the authors' work in the Costa Rican-American Cultural Center, measures certain aspects of silent reading comprehension in English. It is intended for use with students whose first language is other than English. Until further research is available this test, at best, is likely to be no more than a minor aid to a good teacher.

The test consists of 50 multiple choice items, of which 32 measure primarily paragraph comprehension. The remainder appear to measure ability to comprehend very short sentences, but they probably measure vocabulary also. The paragraph comprehension items measure principally reading for detailed information. Throughout the test, a student may refer from questions to paragraphs; consequently, scores may be more indicative of ability to search out details in a paragraph than of ability to recall what has been read. All items are concerned with common everyday words, expressions, and ideas; there is no attempt to measure any aspect of specialized subject matter fields.

The test may be administered by any teacher. The printed directions are so abbreviated that the student may not fully understand how he is to answer the questions unless the teacher enlarges upon them. The 30-minute time limit is designed to cut off extremely slow students rather than to enforce speed as an element of the test.

Scoring is done by multiplying the number of correct answers by 2 to obtain a percentage of the total items answered correctly. A key is provided. An interpretive table is given which describes scores for various percentages. For example, those who score in the range 70–80 per cent are said to "have no trouble in reading newspapers and magazines. May need a dictionary to read literary material."

The authors state that the interpretations are "based on the scores obtained by students on all levels of ability in the experimental try-outs." This quotation is the total published information available on the tryout group. There is not available in any published source the number or level of students included. No distribution of scores is available. Therefore, this test is without norms in the generally accepted sense. Although the authors state that the test includes "only items of the highest validity and reliability," no published evidence on either of these points is available.

The test is likely to be useful to teachers in institutions that have a sufficient number of students to establish their own normative data and research on validity. The extent to which the test would be useful would be revealed by these data and research studies. The absence of an alternative form greatly increases the chance that the test will be invalidated by copies getting into unauthorized hands or by knowledge of the items becoming too generally known.

JOHN A. COX, JR., *Research Psychologist, Personnel Laboratory, Wright Air Development Center, Lackland AFB, Texas.*

The 50-item test is proposed as a measure of reading skill among foreign students. The first 18 questions are multiple choice items testing knowledge of vocabulary and ability to select words and phrases which are logical in terms of the context given. Each is in the form of an incomplete sentence as a stem with four alternatives to complete the stem correctly. The other 32 questions are reading comprehension type items based on five paragraphs. The test is not intended as a speed test, but a time limit of 30 minutes is recommended "to insure comparable results." The answers are to be marked in the test booklets. A folding key is provided which should make hand scoring simple and fast. The score is per cent correct.

While taking the test, this reviewer found several faulty items. One item depends on the word "defray" and another on the word "rift." These words seem rather esoteric for most English usage, but they may fit into the scheme of difficulty the authors used in item selection. Another question seems to have two perfectly good answers. Answers to some of the reading comprehension items do not require ever having seen the paragraph. Other items require reasoning from information given in the paragraph, a factor which is not primarily a matter of comprehension. At least one item (Item 22) is ambiguous.

No manual is furnished. Information about the test is printed on the back of the front and back covers of the test booklet. No instructions are given for administration. No statistical analysis is presented. No reliability estimates are reported. Validity is implied in the form of descriptions of language and reading behavior to be expected from persons earning various "per cent right" scores. However, no information as to how these descriptions were arrived at is given. Norms are in the same condition. There is simply a statement that "over five hundred" students were used as the basis for the behavioral descriptions. There is also an implication that some sort of item analysis was performed. The authors say that "only items of the highest validity and reliability" were included, but no description of the techniques used in determining item validities and reliabilities is given. It is recommended that 70 (per cent right) be used as a cutoff score for entry into college. Nothing is said of the relationship between the two parts or item types.

In conclusion, this test seems too short for use as a screening device for college entrance. An instrument for diagnosis in areas of English proficiency would need to be longer and more reliable than one for selection, so this test should not be used for diagnosis. In an experimental situation (such as in a thesis where scores would be used for information but not as a basis for making practical decisions that would affect individuals) the need for accuracy is not so important. This test might be used in such an experimental program. Any other use would require that it be lengthened and the items made cleaner with respect to the points made above. A manual providing administrative directions and properly reported normative information, reliability data, and validity data would be most useful.

[259]

★**English Usage Test for Non-Native Speakers of English.** Non-native speakers of English; 1955–57; Forms A ['55], B ['57]; directions sheet for Form A ['55], directions sheet for Form B ['57]; no data on reliability; no norms; distribution is restricted to the International Cooperation Administration or the International Educational Exchange Service of the U.S. Department of State; separate answer sheets must be used; Form A: 60(65) minutes, Form B: 75(80) minutes; A. L. Davis and Kenneth Croft; Washington Publications. *

[260]

★**Examination in Structure (English as a Foreign Language).** Entering foreign college freshmen; 1947; Forms A, B, C; mimeographed directions sheet ['47]; no data on reliability; no norms; separate answer sheets must be used; 15¢ per test; 3¢ per answer sheet; 50¢ per scoring stencil; $1 per specimen set; postage extra; 60(65) minutes; English Language Institute, University of Michigan; distributed by Wahr's Book Store. *

[261]

*****Test of Aural Comprehension.** Applicants from non-English language countries for admission into American colleges; 1946–57; Forms A, B, C ('46); separate answer sheets must be used; 10¢ per test; 2¢ per answer sheet; 50¢ per set of scoring stencils; $1.50 per manual ('57); $1 per specimen set; postage extra; (40) minutes; Robert Lado; distributed by George Wahr Publishing Co. *

HERSCHEL T. MANUEL, *Professor of Educational Psychology, The University of Texas, Austin, Texas.*

This test consists of 60 three-choice items. The examiner reads a sentence (sometimes two or more sentences) and the student marks a picture, a phrase, or a sentence to indicate his understanding of what is read. For example, in one of the more difficult items the examiner reads the sentence "Had John been sincere he would have told me the truth," and the student marks one of the three sentences: "(a) John was sincere; (b) John told the truth; (c) John did not tell the truth."

The test is said to measure "understanding of spoken English by persons whose native language is not English." Apparently this understanding of spoken English is regarded as an index of a student's "control of English" in general. This is in contrast to the Davis *Diagnostic Test for Students of English as a Second Language,* in which the knowledge of written English idioms is the basis of measurement. The point is not that Lado and Davis think they are measuring the same aspects of language

ability but that they use different approaches to accomplish the same purpose—the measurement of the adequacy of the English of foreign students. Idioms are not lacking in Lado's test, but the student is required only to indicate his understanding of the language used and not to judge (as in the Davis test) which of different expressions is best.

Instead of taking samples of English at random, Lado has constructed items which present special comprehension difficulties to foreign students. Thus a foreign student might have difficulty distinguishing the sounds "sixty" and "sixteen," interpreting a phrase such as "tear up a paper," or interpreting a preposition like "on," which may have meanings somewhat different from those of the corresponding word in the native language. It would be interesting to know how the results of such a test correlate with the results of the usual test of reading. Although this information is not given, the reviewer believes that the approach to testing through a comparative analysis of different languages is a promising one. Lado's *Linguistics Across Cultures* [1] is a key to understanding this point of view.

The format of the test is good and the test is easy to score. "Proficiency" norms and "progress" norms, stated in simple terms, reflect experience with the test in the English Language Institute.

Data on reliability and validity are rather meager. The coefficient of reliability based upon administration of Forms A and C to the same students (.87) and the split-half reliability of Form A (.88) are satisfactory for a test of 60 items, but low enough to suggest the possibility of considerable error in measuring an individual student if only one form is used. The validity coefficient of .85 (*n* not given) resulting from the correlation of test scores and composite teacher judgments is good. It should be pointed out, however, that the statistics appear to be based solely upon results achieved in the English Language Institute where the test was developed. The test consumer would like to know how the test would perform in another setting.

It is clear that more information is needed for an independent evaluation of the test and for optimum use of the results. From the standpoint of test construction one may question why

1 LADO, ROBERT. *Linguistics Across Cultures: Applied Linguistics for Language Teachers.* Ann Arbor, Mich.: University of Michigan Press, 1957. Pp. 141.

English Reading Test for Students of English as a Foreign Language

the last 10 items in Form B are much longer than corresponding items in the other forms, whether the items chosen for the test reflect equally the learning difficulties of students of different mother tongues, and why the raw scores are converted to percentages of items correct rather than to standard scores or percentiles. However, in spite of the questions which may be raised, the reviewer believes that the test will be useful in judging the ability of foreign students to work in English speaking colleges and that it represents a significant approach to the evaluation of this ability. He hopes that the author will develop additional tests on the basis of comparative linguistic analysis, and that the relation of these tests to other tests and to general English proficiency will be shown.

CLARENCE E. TURNER, *Professor of Romance Languages, Rutgers University, New Brunswick, New Jersey.*

This test is devised to measure understanding of spoken English by persons not natives of that language, and has been developed largely in working with and for foreign born students in American academic institutions. Unlike the same author's *English Language Test for Foreign Students,* it does not seek either to measure pronunciation or to sample range of vocabulary. The present test may be thought of very roughly as an elaboration for the ear of the excellent structure portion of the other test, with the inclusion of a few items testing sound discrimination, and of a larger number of items testing not range of vocabulary but comprehension of vocabulary signals embodied in two-word verbs, prefixes, and the like.

There can be little doubt that the student's status will have been pretty clearly determined by the time he has finished following Mrs. Smith, Mary, John, and Charles through their deceptively basic activities. He will have met many of the characteristic problems which offer little difficulty to the native speaker of familiar English but which torment the learner of that idiom. He will have dealt with progressive tenses, contractions, *do* and *going* as auxiliaries, concealed negation, concealed subordination, contrary-to-fact conditions with negative result, nouns used as adjectives, *not any* with elements interposed, two-word verbs, adjectives and adverbs, auxiliary *had* with participle understood, and so on through a long list of

genuine problems ingeniously pinpointed. He will have shown whether he can catch the operative *when?* or *who?* in a question containing a few natural but distracting irrelevancies. He will have had to sense interrogation from structure in a question read with falling inflection. He will have sorted out *sinking* from *singing* and *thinking,* and *milk chocolate* from *chocolate milk.* The last two items alone would make a fair little pocket test.

The author has again shown that he is a keen analyst of language and a shrewd maker of tests. One can quarrel only with a few details. The Charles of the examiner's manual, evidently a sneaky fellow, turns up as Carlos in the test booklet in several items of Forms B and C. Even decent Mr. Smith passes as Dr. Smith in the test booklet, Form B, Part 2, Item 17. If we are told, "The man's horse is crossing the river," does it necessarily follow that the owner is not on the horse's back? If not, Form B, Part 1, Item 15, has two possible answers. "The boy is giving the rat a cat" pinpoints English by isolating it utterly from experience, but it is scarcely a fair item in a test where no other sentence does comparable violence to common sense. Finally, there is inconsistency concerning the flashback presentation of past action. In Form A, Part 1, Item 17, "The girl used the telephone" is not to be matched with the picture of a girl using a telephone, but rather with that of one walking away from the phone. "The girl has used the telephone" would seem a better verbalization of this. Again, in Form B, Part 1, Item 5, "Where did he put his hat? He put it on the table" is to be matched with the picture of a man walking away from hat and table, rather than with a flashback of the action being performed. But in Form C, Part 1, Item 16, "He opened the door of his room" is supposed to match a picture of a man actually engaged in opening a door. Here there is admittedly no other possible matching, but the items are inconsistent with each other, and the whole matter is confusing. How does one visualize the pastness of a past action? Is there a valid general visual difference between "She used the phone" and "She is using the phone"? Perhaps tense cannot be shown pictorially with any accuracy in cases like these.

There is fascination and instruction in this test for users or lovers of language, and anyone requiring an instrument to determine

Test of Aural Comprehension

whether a handicap exists in the aural comprehension of English need look no further.

[262]

★**Test of Aural Perception in English for Latin-American Students.** Latin-American students of English; 1947–57; 1 form ('57); separate answer sheets must be used; 4¢ per answer sheet ('47); $1.50 per manual ('57); postage extra; (60) minutes; Robert Lado; distributed by George Wahr Publishing Co. *

FRENCH

[263]

*College Entrance Examination Board Achievement Test in French.** Candidates for college entrance with 2–4 years high school; 1901–58; for more complete information, see 599; IBM; 60(80) minutes; program administered by Educational Testing Service for the College Entrance Examination Board. *

REFERENCES

1–7. See 4:237.
8. COLLEGE ENTRANCE EXAMINATION BOARD. *Foreign Languages: A Description of the College Board Tests in French, German, Latin, and Spanish.* Princeton, N.J.: the Board, April 1954. Pp. 31. * (*PA* 29:1444)
9. EVENSON, A. B., AND SMITH, D. E. "A Study of Matriculation in Alberta." *Alberta J Ed Res* 4:67–83 Je '58. *

For a review by Walter V. Kaulfers of earlier forms, see 4:237.

[264]

★**College Entrance Examination Board Advanced Placement Examination: French.** High school seniors desiring credit for college level courses; 1954–58; for more complete information, see 600; 2 scores: language, literary; IBM in part; 3 parts in 2 booklets; 180(200) minutes; program administered by Educational Testing Service for the College Entrance Examination Board. *

[265]

★**Cooperative French Listening Comprehension Test.** 2–5 semesters high school or college; 1955; Forms A, B; $12.50 per tape recording (3¾ or 7½ ips); $3.25 per 25 answer booklets; 25¢ per scoring stencil; $1 per manual; postage extra; 30(40) minutes; Nelson Brooks; Cooperative Test Division, Educational Testing Service. *

REFERENCE

1. SPAULDING, GERALDINE. "A Brief Study of the Cooperative French Listening Comprehension Test." *Ed Rec B* 68:61–3 Jl '56. * (*PA* 31:8847)

WALTER V. KAULFERS, *Professor of Education, University of Illinois, Urbana, Illinois.*

This relatively advanced standardized test of ability to understand spoken French can be administered either orally or by means of tape recordings. It claims to serve four purposes: to help determine a student's general ability in aural comprehension, to help locate weaknesses requiring attention, to provide a basis for ability grouping in French, and to afford examinees an objective measure of their relative achievement in comparison with that of other students.

To serve these purposes, the test is divided into four parts totaling 42 items of the 5-answer multiple choice type. The 10 items in Part 1 involve phonetic discrimination. In his answer booklet the examinee indicates which of five statements he hears spoken either by the examiner reading from the manual or by the voice recorded on tape. The second part requires the listener to check the best response, out of five in his answer booklet, to each of 10 questions posed in French.

Part 3 is essentially a 10-item completion test. The examinee indicates which of five answers best completes a statement or sentence spoken in the foreign language. The last part consists of 12 questions involving the comprehension of passages of 100–175 words in length. Here the examinee is required to select the best of five answers to each question.

The entire test, including the oral directions to students, is in French. The directions for each part are also printed in French in the answer booklet, so that the examinee can follow them as they are delivered orally. However, since the recorded version sometimes varies from the printed version of the directions (e.g., *je lirai* on tape versus *on lira* in print), some students may find these discrepancies momentarily distracting. Only if the script is to be read from the manual instead of broadcast is a knowledge of French absolutely essential on the part of the examiner.

The reliability coefficient of .87 indicates that the test is more accurate for the purposes which it claims to serve than "homemade" tests are likely to be. Correlations between teacher ratings of their pupils' ability to understand spoken French and scores made by the pupils on the test range from .42 to .79. There is reason to believe that the tape recorded version is much more valid for examinees who have frequently heard French spoken by different individuals than it is for students who have rarely heard anyone but their teacher speak the language.

The recordings, which use standard Parisian French, are generally satisfactory. Except in Part 4, where a woman speaker is introduced in the dialogue passages, the same male voice continues throughout. The delivery is clear and at a moderate pace. In a few cases elisions occur where a native speaking at this deliberate rate might not be likely to make them. Occasionally, the attempt to speak clearly does not necessarily facilitate comprehension. The French *sonner,* for example, comes out sounding very much like *son nez.* These limitations, as well as the discrepancies between the printed and oral directions, however, are minor. It should be easy for the publishers to correct them on the master tape. Examiners can avoid them by reading the script from the manual instead of using the recordings. In this case, however, comparison of results with the norms will not be fair, since norms are based on administration of the test via recordings exclusively.

Scoring is done by means of a stencil. The test is not scorable by machine. Because raw scores must be totaled and then translated into converted scores, a double checking of tests by two people is recommended.

Norms are available for public secondary schools, independent secondary schools, and colleges. High school students who have had less than three years of French, however, are likely to find the test discouragingly difficult unless they have been enrolled in intensive courses giving special attention to the spoken language. Because over 80 per cent of secondary school students take only two years of French, the examination will probably be useful primarily for purposes of advanced guidance-placement in college.

A less advanced test is needed to appraise the increasing amount of oral work being done in the first and second years of high school French. At this level the directions and choice of answers should probably be in English rather than in the foreign language. Otherwise the examination would be almost as much a test of comprehension in silent reading as of ability to understand the spoken language. To a certain extent this criticism applies even to the present relatively advanced form of the test.

If the scope of the present examination were extended somewhat it could be used as an aid in vocational placement. To this end a greater variety of voices and at least the commoner dialectal variations should be included. To this end also, comparison norms obtained from native speakers in France (e.g., by administering the recorded test to 100 students of the *premi-ère classe* in three or four widely separated *lycées* or *collèges*) would be desirable. The comparison norms could serve as a life criterion in answering the question "How far have the ex-

aminees progressed toward understanding spoken French as well as educated natives?"

It is an unfortunate limitation of foreign language tests published to date that their norms allow for little but an intramural interpretation. They do not tell us how well the examinee is qualified to get along in an exclusively foreign language environment. At best they usually tell us only whether the student has "covered" enough, or been exposed enough, in previous courses to make him eligible to sit in a more advanced classroom. Although the *Cooperative French Listening Comprehension Test* comes much closer to being a real-life performance test than most achievement examinations produced to date, the limitations noted in the preceding paragraphs still prevent it from fulfilling this qualification completely.

Kathleen N. Perret, *Interpreter, Department of Conference Services, Interpretation Division, United Nations, New York, New York*.

The testing of aural comprehension has been a vexed question ever since the inception of the standardized testing movement, and while the difficulties have been attributable in part to technical problems, the general attitude of the public toward foreign languages has also accounted in no small measure for the dearth of aural comprehension tests. Fortunately, the development of disc and tape recordings has opened up vast horizons in the testing field at a time when it is more important than ever before to verify actual achievement and to ensure that the schools are doing their job properly.

The *Cooperative French Listening Comprehension Test,* on tape, came like a breath of fresh air as the reviewer read the scripts through. It has so many virtues that it seems carping to pick up the relatively minor shortcomings, and the criticisms that follow should be read with this comment in mind.

The test includes four types of listening situation: phonetic discrimination, comprehension of isolated questions, sentence completion, and comprehension of conversation and conversational narrative as contained in four passages running from 50 to 75 seconds in length. After the instructions are read out, the tape is started and the test begins. From this moment on, the entire material, questions and answers, is in French. Before starting on the questions, the speaker first reads an introductory passage that is largely a restatement of the directions on the cover page so that the student has about 2 minutes to accustom his ear to the voice. Throughout the test the answers are all of the multiple choice type.

The Examiner's Manual, a 28-page booklet, gives ample statistical and historical background, as well as copious directions for administration and scoring. Presented in a smart kit with scoring key and explanatory leaflets, it also contains the complete script for the two forms, so that the test may be given "live" if necessary.

The phonetics of French probably offer more difficulty to the English speaking student than any other European language. Obviously, the student must be trained to distinguish between *il veut* and *ils veulent,* or between *allais* and *allez,* or between *je, j'ai* and *j'y,* to name some typical cases, and the 10 questions in Part 1 should give definite indication of the weaknesses or strengths of the student's grasp of fundamental French sounds. This is a particularly difficult type of question to construct, for not only must the decoy responses be plausible but they must offer a sequence of sounds reasonably similar to that of the correct response. At the same time, they should not degenerate into a pure vocabulary test, the common flaw in earlier tests. Item 7 in Form B, where some valid distractors might have been built on *entendre,* is thus too limited in its decoys. On the other hand, Item 2 in Form A, "Elle a quitté la cuisine," with decoys based on *quitte, quitta,* and *quittait* in various combinations with *la cuisine* and *la cousine,* is a good example of the best items in Part 1.

The first part of the test consists largely of phrases or very short sentences. Parts 2 and 3, which consist of sentences of varying length, provide a useful transition to the lengthy material in Part 4. The difference in approach in Parts 2 and 3, apart from purely functional considerations, serves to enliven the material and exploit the element of spontaneous recall. There are some items in these two parts, however, which are open to technical criticism. In Form A, Items 27 and 29 may depend largely on vocabulary. In particular, Item 29, which reads, "J'entends sonner. Je décroche le récepteur et je dis...." uses one key word which is at the very top of the Vander Beke list (*décrocher*) and one (*récepteur*) which does not appear in the list at all. The key word *dérapa*

in Item 30 does not appear in the Vander Beke list either. The same comment applies to Item 24 in Form B, where the key word is *contrôleur.* Otherwise the items are varied in tone and style and reflect an awareness of the commonest types of student error.

Part 4, consisting of four passages, clearly bears the stamp of contemporary conversational style. Interestingly enough, much of the material has been selected from Voice of America broadcasts, although two passages in Form A and one in Form B are taken from contemporary books and publications. Each form contains one historical-cultural narrative, one purely conversational passage, one personal anecdote or personal experience passage, and one travelogue narrative. Both forms use a male voice for two passages, a male and female voice for the conversational passage, and a female voice for the travelogue or cultural-type narrative. The voices are extremely clear and typical in their pronunciation and intonation.

Part 4 offers a considerable range of difficulty. Technically, the construction of the responses and the distractors in this part seems weaker than in any other part of the test. For example, in Form A, four decoys for Item 40 will be automatically eliminated if the student knows the answer to Item 42, while three decoys for Item 41 can be eliminated in the light of the answer to Item 40. A certain amount of inference might enter into the responses to Items 31 and 32 and to Item 39, in view of the responses required for Items 37 and 38. In Form B, the only negative response among the decoys for Item 33 happens to be the correct one, and the response marked as correct for Item 35 is open to question. Lastly, Item 40 is not quite fair because the only clear indication of the correct answer comes in the introduction to the passage which is read but once, while everything else is read twice.

As a general comment on style, it must be said that some of the language, although grammatically correct, smacks of translation from English; but, apart from this and certain minor errors, the test as a whole is impressive, particularly when set against the previous work done in the field. The two forms are, according to the publisher, comparable in range of difficulty and content. It is the opinion of the reviewer that Form A, particularly in Part 4, is somewhat easier than Form B.

Few of the earlier aural comprehension tests

Cooperative French Listening Comprehension Test

in any language were divorced to any considerable degree, if at all, from the visual approach and, on rereading now, they have a slightly archaic air. A notable exception to this is Part I of the *Lundeberg-Tharp Audition Test in French,* Part I (on phonetic accuracy); although it consists largely of words rather than phrases, thus simplifying the problem, many of the decoys are nevertheless extremely well chosen. The remainder of the test, however, is not so advanced in content or technique. The *Columbia Research Bureau Aural French Test,* despite the highly literary nature of many of the items, is interesting in that it includes pictures, a device that has many obvious advantages and might be further explored in testing aural comprehension.

In preparing an aural comprehension test, many authorities feel it is better to use the literary vocabulary characteristic of classroom texts. Others argue that, even with the usual textbook, enough vocabulary commonly used in conversation can be extracted to make a useful test. This reviewer rather thinks that what is needed is not a new and different course of study but more imagination in devising stimulating tests that will present the material available in current textbooks in a lighter and more contemporary style. In that respect, the test under review is a shining example.

Today there is a growing realization of the importance of teaching the student to speak as well as to read and write a language. This will not be satisfactorily accomplished in this country, however, until American schools begin to achieve the type of results obtained in European and British institutions. This means that, on the very first day of the first semester of French, teachers must begin developing the ability to speak and must use English themselves only when it is absolutely unavoidable. With such discipline, after three years of high school or two years of college French, every student should be able to express himself with some degree of fluency and, as techniques for teaching pronunciation tricks to overcome special hurdles such as *eu* and *u* become more widely used, with some ease and elegance. In these circumstances, this test will prove of increasing value. If, at times, the pronunciation used in the tapes is almost too French, as in Item 23 of Form A, where it takes a fine ear to hear the *ce* in the "J'aime bien ce chapeau"— this may provide a healthy shock to the American student whose penchant for wresting a loud "uh" out of every mute *e* has been the bane of many a teacher's existence.

The test is sound and well constructed and, what is perhaps more appealing, fresh and new in feeling and remarkably free of the visual approach. It constitutes a major breakthrough in the field of testing aural comprehension and, in addition to providing a valid measure of achievement, it should serve to set new standards for teacher and pupil alike.

[266]

★**First Year French Test.** High school and college; 1956; Form A; no manual; no data on reliability; tentative norms (no date); $1.20 per 25 tests, postage extra; 25¢ per specimen set, postpaid; 40(45) minutes; Minnie M. Miller, Jean Leblon, and Marguerite Rice Crain; Bureau of Educational Measurements. *

NELSON BROOKS, *Associate Professor of French, Yale University, New Haven, Connecticut.*

This 90-item test contains eight sets of directions and nine different procedures. The student is asked to match isolated words in two languages (paix-peace), to identify similar sounds as represented in printed words (the *i* of "midi" and the *y* of "type"), to match equivalents in two languages as they appear in statements ("Il will come bientôt."), to complete sentences in French ("Comment _____-vous ce matin?"), and to read with comprehension two prose passages (edited) of 20-odd lines. In 65 items the student makes a choice of four suggested answers, in 5 he separates true from false, and in 20 he must write one or two words in French. Twenty four items are concerned principally with matters of structure and 5 items with information that is other than linguistic. Sound is dealt with in 10 items, though only in terms of printed symbols.

All tests should measure subject matter rather than technique; for this reason everything possible should be done to make directions clear and procedure simple. This test needs considerable revision in this regard. In the attempt to present the entire test on two sides of a sheet the size of typewriter paper, very small type has been used, in which the difference between ordinary and boldface type, an important matter in some items, is not easily distinguished. In Part 1 numbers are used for both items and choices; the use of letters for the latter would have made things less confusing for the testee. Part 2, by far the most diffi-

First Year French Test

cult from the point of view of technique, has no example and depends upon the selection of letters which boldface type does not make sufficiently clear. Directions and arrangement in Part 3 are especially puzzling. "In the parenthesis before each word place the number of the word which has the *same* vowel sound as the vowel in the first word." In no case do the parentheses immediately precede a word, and in some cases the choices have two syllables and hence two vowel sounds. The wording of the first sentence in Part 7 is most unfortunate: "Read this passage carefully and then do the statements below." Even in American English, one does not "do" a statement.

Some points are covered twice: the problem in Item 31 is the same as that in 28, and Item 62 is essentially the same as 53. In some parts the test puts a high value upon what is relatively unimportant, if not detrimental, to the beginner. Part 1 is a lexicography test involving the matching of isolated words in two languages, something to be minimized at all costs by the beginner. The items in Part 4 employ a procedure which has done as much to negate successful language learning in America as any other practice one can think of. This is the arbitrary mixing of two languages within the confines of the same utterance, a behavior pattern that is characteristic only of speakers whose language is in a serious state of disintegration. (This is reflected in items of the type: "Je him ai vu.") The textbooks, the tests, and the teaching procedures that encourage the learner to link two languages at a less-than-complete-utterance level are the result of a colossal misunderstanding of the nature of language behavior. Whatever may be the dictates of economy in printing and whatever may be the heritage of learning traditions that compound the mother tongue with the language being studied, it is by now perfectly clear that the learning of a second language that may—at least in part—replace the mother tongue must be done in terms of *separating* the two rather than binding them tightly and permanently together. Early levels of language learning in American schools and colleges cannot greatly improve until they are freed from the fetters of textbooks, tests, and teachings that employ this practice.

In Parts 7 and 8, the precise indication of the origin of the passages used (author, editor, publisher, and page) disqualifies these items

for use in a "standardized" test. A test is either based upon knowledge of certain chosen materials known to and studied by the testee, or upon certain general linguistic facts for which one candidate has presumably had no more special preparation than any other. Accurate measurement can hardly be expected to result from performance with materials on which some candidates have had long and careful drill and some none at all, especially when this fact is made so explicit.

Some items in this test are to be commended. Many of the completion and comprehension exercises that involve only French are good; so is the use of recall as well as recognition. But the matching of isolated words in the manner of a bilingual dictionary, the use of single utterances composed of two languages, and the study of "pablumized" prose are pedagogical misdeeds which early levels of language teaching and testing cannot too soon renounce.

MARY E. TURNBULL, *Formerly Head of Test Production, Educational Testing Service, Princeton, New Jersey.*

This is a good, neatly printed, and carefully edited test of various aspects of French that should be covered during a first year course.

Part 1, a vocabulary test, consists of 19 French words, for each of which the appropriate English translation must be chosen from four possibilities, and then 6 French words or expressions, each with four possible French definitions. A good group of basic nouns, verbs, adjectives, and adverbs is included and the distractors are intelligently selected to entice the uncertain student. The words seem carefully arranged in order of difficulty, the French definitions at the end of the part being much harder than the words tested at the beginning.

Parts 2 and 3 are very short but good tests of pronunciation. In Part 2 the student must select from a column of given words the word containing the same sound as the boldfaced letters in each of five given words. In each of the five items of Part 3 the correct answer must be a word having the same vowel sound as the first word given. Again, good distractors are supplied; these should really test the student's ability to discriminate between the correct and incorrect sound.

Part 4 tests knowledge of five French verbs, since the student must complete each given French sentence by choosing the French word or words which best translate the boldfaced English word or expression included in the sentence. Basic verbs are tested and the choices should all seem logical or attractive to some pupils.

Part 5 consists of 20 French sentences, each of which is to be completed by one of four given French choices. This part tests vocabulary (especially verbs), grammar (a good variety of elementary points), and some geographical knowledge of France. In this part there occurs the rare (for this test) case of a missing accent (Item 53).

Part 6 consists of a French paragraph that includes a number of English words or expressions. For each of these English portions the student is to write the corresponding French word or words on dotted lines provided below. In two cases (Items 62, 63) the grammar or vocabulary tested has already been tested in the preceding part (Items 53, 42). Correct spelling influences the points given for this part. Scoring this part will require more time than that necessary for scoring a straight objective test, but having the student do some writing in French is well worthwhile.

Part 7 is a French paragraph-reading test with five multiple choice and five true-false questions. The selection is a rather difficult one, but the questions based on it are quite simple. The reader who skims through the paragraph, getting the gist but not necessarily understanding each word, will probably get a better score on this part than the more conscientious reader who may spend too much time on the paragraph.

Part 8 consists of a fairly difficult passage from *Les Misérables* on which are based 10 French questions that require only very short answers to be written in French. Again, the questions are very simple as compared with the passage and only one or two words will answer each. A careful reading of this selection will give the answers to Items 53 and 55 in an earlier part.

The *First Year French Test* is an interesting test of the basic elements of achievement in elementary French. It should be useful to both teachers and pupils in classroom situations where an unspeeded measure is desired.

[267]

French I and II: Achievement Examinations for Secondary Schools. 1 or 2 years high school; 1951–53; Forms 1 ('51), 2 ('53); no specific manual; direc-

tions sheets [1, '51; 2, '53]; no data on reliability; Form 1 norms ['52]; no norms for Form 2; 10¢ per test, postage extra; (60–90) minutes; Lee Stark; Educational Test Bureau. *

For a review by Elton Hocking of Form 1, see 4:239.

[268]

★French I and II: Midwest High School Achievement Examinations. 2 years high school; 1953–55; Forms A ('55), B ('53, identical with Form 2 of *French I and II: Achievement Examinations for Secondary Schools*); no specific manual; directions sheet ['55]; series manual ('57); no data on reliability; no norms; 10¢ per test, postage extra; 45(65–95) minutes; Lee Stark (A); Educational Test Bureau. *

MARY E. TURNBULL, *Formerly Head of Test Production, Educational Testing Service, Princeton, New Jersey.* [Review of Form A.]

The test begins somewhat ruggedly for the student with a 15-minute Reading Examination, consisting of 12 items based on three historical articles. Both articles and items are in French. Unfortunately, the articles, especially the first one, present well known facts, with the result that many of the succeeding items can be answered without reference to the article. More variety in content, closer attention to accents (cf. Article 1, line 7, *Pétain;* Item 6, choice C, *maîtres;* Item 7, choice A, *très*), and more care in wording the questions (inclusion of *quoique* in Item 10 makes A the only possible answer) would have improved this section.

Section 2, Civilization and Culture Identification, tests knowledge of French geography, history, and the arts by means of 23 items to be answered in 10 minutes. These are interesting and varied, but they are marred by careless errors in spelling (Item 26, *gouvernement*) and omissions of accents (four are omitted from the sample item alone).

Section 3, Vocabulary Examination, consists of two parts for which 10 minutes in all are allowed. Part 1 gives 20 short French sentences in which the italicized words are to be translated; more than half of the words tested are nouns. Many of the items show a distressing lack of correlation between the italicized words and the given translations (e.g., Item 40, where *du* is italicized but ignored in all choices; Item 47, where *ma* receives similar treatment; and particularly Item 51, where "formidable" is the only word in italics but where "wonderful team" is supposed to be the correct answer). In some items the definite article is translated in the given choices whether it is italicized or not; in others the article is ignored even though it is italicized. The word *entrer* is misspelled in the sample item. Part 2 is much more difficult than Part 1 and tends to be a test of reasoning powers rather than vocabulary. There are 10 items, each consisting of five French words or phrases; in each item the one word or phrase "which least follows the pattern set by the other words" is to be selected. In Item 61, where the correct answer is E, the choices have been labeled A, B, C, D, and 1; and in Item 62 choice B is needlessly capitalized and only choice A is given without the definite article.

Section 4, Aural Examination, allows 15 minutes for two parts, a definition series and an anecdote series. In this section the teacher reads the definitions and the anecdotes "ONLY ONCE." The answer choices to the 15 definitions are in French (although the example gives English choices), whereas the questions based on the French anecdotes are in English. Part 1 gives some interesting definitions that test knowledge of Paris as well as geography, history, and straight vocabulary. Part 2 consists of three historical anecdotes. These appear in order of difficulty, but the student of history may find the correct answers easy to select without paying much attention to the French. Again in this section careless errors appear in the test copy. In Item 66 *gouvernement* is again misspelled; two choices are capitalized in Item 75 while the other three are not; and the first choice in Item 80 is not labeled. For Item 82 "by" is included in the premise of the item and repeated at the beginning of choice B; and in choice C of Item 90 "Gauls" is not capitalized.

Section 5, a 10-minute Grammar Examination, consists of 20 items, each with four or five possible French translations of a given English expression or sentence. This section occasionally becomes a vocabulary test (cf. Items 101, 103, 104, 106, and 111). The adjective *prêt(e)* accounts for two errors in this section, being given no accent in the sample item and the wrong accent in Item 103.

Section 6, Matching Famous Personalities of the Current and Historical Scene, allows 5 minutes for selecting from a list of 20 names the name of the individual who best fits each of 11 given descriptions. Emphasis here seems to be on the arts.

Space for the answer is provided beside each test question; there is a neatly printed scoring key. The directions are adequate, and examples are given for all but the last section of the test. Time limits seem appropriate for each section, except possibly for the Aural Examination, where 15 minutes, if this includes the time taken by the teacher to read the definitions and the anecdotes, may not give the student sufficient time to answer the questions.

No norms are currently available for the test. The manual gives a short review of the changing purposes of the American High School during the past 50 years (!) and also states the purpose of the Midwest High School Achievement Examination—to motivate efforts of accomplishment and to motivate thinking ability. There are no data concerning validity and no reliability coefficients.

French I and II is an interesting test in which a good variety of elements of achievement in French language, history, and culture are included; the inclusion of an aural test is especially praiseworthy. The test could be useful for student motivation as well as for checkup on teaching emphasis on the different phases of the subject. It could be improved by careful editing which would eliminate the numerous proofreading errors and by a rearrangement of the various sections in order of difficulty.

[269]

★**French: Teacher Education Examination Program.** College seniors preparing to teach secondary school; 1957; for more complete information, see 543; IBM; no data on reliability; no norms; 80(95) minutes; Educational Testing Service. *

For a review by Walter W. Cook of the entire series, see 543.

[270]

*****The Graduate Record Examinations Advanced Tests: French.** College seniors and graduate students; 1939–58; for more complete information, see 601; IBM; 180(200) minutes; Educational Testing Service. *

WALTER V. KAULFERS, *Professor of Education, University of Illinois, Urbana, Illinois.* [Review of Form GGR.]

This 3-hour objective, machine scorable examination is not to be confused with the *Graduate Record Examinations Advanced French Test,* which requires only 1¾ hours. The purpose of Form GGR is fourfold: (*a*) to aid in assessing the qualifications of college majors in French for graduate work, and in predicting their success in graduate study; (*b*) to serve as part of a comprehensive departmental examination or proficiency examination for college seniors; (c) to assist in guiding and placing advanced students transferring from other institutions; and (d) to help in evaluating curriculum and instruction in French at the college level by providing a common yardstick comparable for all examinees.

Except for the directions to students, the 200 5-response multiple choice items comprising the test are entirely in French. Approximately one eighth deal with the history, geography, and civilization of France (including a few items on architecture, music, painting, science, and products). Since this section is brief, considering the range of coverage, only the highlights of French history and civilization are included. Some of these should be familiar to examinees from other sources besides offerings in French.

About two-fifths of the examination stresses comprehension and interpretation of passages of prose and poetry varying in length from 90 to approximately 300 words. The remainder—nearly half the test—measures knowledge of literary history and terminology, and ability to identify important figures and characters in French literature, including some from the postwar period.

A conscious effort has been made to measure sensitivity to style and literary values, and to test ability to follow the development of an author's thoughts as well as to draw proper inferences. An idea of the nature of the examination can be obtained from the following excerpts from directions selected at random:

Line 13 means....
Verses 10 and 11 convey the idea of....
In line 12, the *il* refers to....
Of the dates assigned below which one is clearly false?
Which of the lettered words or phrases is nearest in meaning to the underlined word in the sentence?
The name of a character from literature is given and followed by five suggested descriptions of the character. Select the best characterization.

The content of the examination has apparently been based on expert judgment regarding items of French literature, history, and civilization commonly included in college French courses and the syllabi, readings, or departmental tests accompanying them. As a general measure of ability to read and interpret French literature, and of knowledge of the highlights of French history, literature, and civilization, Form GGR leaves little to be desired.

It is not, however, a diagnostic test. In its present form only a very time-consuming analysis of each examinee's answer sheet would indicate whether a relatively low score on the test were attributable to inability to read and interpret literary selections, to inadequate knowledge of French literary history, to ignorance of the vocabulary of literary criticism, or to a lack of acquaintance with French culture outside the field of literature. This is a significant limitation, since for the guidance and placement of students in graduate courses such knowledge is almost imperative.

Although the answer sheets could easily be redesigned to yield diagnostic subscores, there is no question but that this would seriously complicate machine scoring. Until a convenient method for recording diagnostic subscores as well as the overall achievement score is devised, however, the examination should be used only in connection with other measures, such as grades in previous courses, or ratings by the candidates' major professors.

Because ability to understand and use the spoken language is now a common objective of instruction in the modern languages, Form GGR must obviously be supplemented by tests of aural comprehension and rating scales of ability to speak French if an adequate evaluation of a candidate's ability to do graduate work in courses making extensive use of the spoken language is to be obtained. Form GGR does not distinguish between students who are well prepared to hold their own in courses conducted entirely in French, and those who by virtue of previous training are qualified only to enter courses conducted in English where use of the foreign language is limited almost exclusively to silent reading of assigned works outside of class. The latter type of offering is by no means extinct.

Now that communication with French *lycées, collèges,* and *universités* is readily possible, scores obtained from an administration of the test to 200–300 representative students in France would be of considerable value in helping to appraise both the validity and the real life significance of the examination.

To date Form GGR has not been used widely enough to yield representative norms or dependable measures of statistical reliability. Estimates of reliability furnished by the Educational Testing Service range between .93 to .96. These estimates, however, need confirmation from a wider tryout of the test than has so far been possible. For some of the uses suggested for the examination, such as retesting of students to measure growth, more than one 3-hour form of the test would be desirable.

Like nearly all standardized tests, this examination follows the ladder principle of progressing from easy to difficult as a means of determining how high an examinee can climb. All test results are translated into 3-digit scaled scores ending in zero. These range from approximately 200 to 950. Eventually, when enough data have been assembled from a wider administration of the test, the scaled scores should make it possible to tell whether a candidate's performance on the French examination was higher or lower than his performance on another test relative to the same group of examinees. The Educational Testing Service is also in process of developing norms for particular levels and types of institutions.

For a review by Harold Seashore of the entire series, see 601.

[271]

★**Second Year French Test.** High school and college; 1956; Form A; no manual; no data on reliability; tentative norms (no date); $1.20 per 25 tests, postage extra; 25¢ per specimen set, postpaid; 40(45) minutes; Minnie M. Miller, Jean Leblon, and Marguerite Rice Crain; Bureau of Educational Measurements. *

GERALDINE SPAULDING, *Consultant, Educational Records Bureau, New York, New York.*

From the point of view of subject matter, the content of this test is, for the most part, well chosen. Since the total of 95 items includes a little bit of everything, there is necessarily rather limited coverage of any one area. However, the test yields only a total score, and makes no attempt to provide differential measures in various phases of achievement.

Though the subject matter content is satisfactory, a number of criticisms can be made of the formal characteristics of the test. First of all, the chief consideration in the design of the test sheet seems to have been economy in the use of paper—an economy that is costly in terms of resulting difficulties for both examinee and scorer. The entire test is printed on the two sides of a single 8½ by 11 inch sheet, with very small type. Many of the spaces provided for students to write in their answers are barely large enough for a legible response by a student having small, neat handwriting. The response parentheses provided for the multiple choice items are small and very close together, and are at the left of the item, which is awkward. The cramming of so much material onto a single sheet results in unreasonable difficulties for both examinee and scorer.

There are several shortcomings in the directions. There is at present no manual, and perhaps none would be needed, at least for presentation of administering and scoring instructions, if the test directions and key were complete and clear. But the directions are involved, none too clear, and not always complete, so that procedure is not made plain to either examinee or scorer.

With respect to the techniques of item writing, the multiple choice items are well constructed. The decoys are suitable and the correct answers clear-cut, with one or two exceptions. Five of the 25 reading questions are true-false items. In the 10 items of Part 6, the student supplies the appropriate verb form, in context, writing out the form himself. In the remaining 30 items, the student also writes out the answers; but it is difficult to see what is gained by this, since most of the 30 items are so restricted, either in the directions or in the wording of the question, that relevant answers are limited to a small number of choices, usually only two. Such items have no clear advantages over items in which the choice of an answer is indicated by code, as in the ordinary fixed choice item. They have definite disadvantages when it comes to scoring. Even if questions are phrased so that answers *can* be single words, anyone with scoring experience knows that there is no limit to the number of variant answers that examinees can think of—including many borderline answers to the simplest question, requiring judgment in deciding whether or not to give credit. Coded choice items eliminate such scoring problems, and reduce those due to illegible writing.

Items requiring spontaneous answers have their place in tests not designed for machine scoring, and in many situations, especially in language tests, are probably more valid than coded choice items. But for the sake of reliability of scoring, items with answers written out by the student should be confined to situations where the examinee really must "think up" the answer, as in Part 6 of this test. They are inadvisable if the question lends itself readily to the coded choice form.

With respect to statistical data, the test is

not really ready for general use at the present time. The potential user is not furnished any data with the test on its reliability and validity, or on the procedures followed in its construction. However, a personal letter from the publisher gives the following information: reliability, .93; item difficulty, about 50 (range 25–65); discrimination index, about 23 for most of the items (range 20–45). A sheet of tentative norms accompanying the test gives a percentile table, but without information on the source or number of the scores used in preparing the table. It is indicated that new norms are being gathered, but they are not available at the present writing.

In summary, this test, yielding a single score of acceptable reliability, has possibilities of usefulness for the classroom teacher who scores his own tests, if he is willing to cope with scoring problems and to interpret the results without the help of adequate, and adequately defined, norms. The selection of content is, in general, good, and the questions, aside from reservations about the forms in which some of them are cast, are free from most of the common defects.

However, the printing and format, as well as the form of some of the questions, impose difficulties on both the examinee and the scorer. Because of these features, the test is not well adapted to large scale use with centralized scoring.

CLARENCE E. TURNER, *Professor of Romance Languages, Rutgers University, New Brunswick, New Jersey.*

This is a useful little test for its purposes. Its immediately striking characteristics are compactness and eclecticism.

Its 95 items cover four columns, two on each side of a single sheet. Some crowding inevitably results, and the print is quite fine. Good editing and printing have, however, protected clarity in the main. The authors have husbanded their testing time as carefully as their space, so that few items (scarcely over four) are so easy as to test nothing much, and the distractors are quite consistently of the sort which operate.

The authors have clearly tried to make the test reflect the variety which exists in teaching methods and emphases. There is something here for almost every taste. For example, vocabulary is tested in terms of English equiva-

lents (22 items) and French (3 items). Reading comprehension of three well chosen passages is tested in three different ways, by brief answers in French to questions in French (12 items), by brief answers in English to questions in English (8 items), and by marking statements in French true or false (5 items). There are questions on civilization to reflect that normal component of the second year curriculum. Grammar (30 items) is tested by completions in French of French sentences, one third of them multiple choice and the rest guided completion by the student. Even pronunciation (one is tempted to say the most fundamental and least tested of language skills) is dealt with in the form of matching vowel sounds (5 items). More could be done in this area, and should be done if relative importance is the criterion.

The authors may be said, then, to have sought a common center of second year curricula, and to have moved a hair's breadth to the left of it. A minimum of teachers should find this test objectionably unrelated to what they are doing.

A few details invite reproach. Item 8 has two correct answers, since *entendre* may mean "to intend" in certain contexts. Item 44 has an inoperative option, since *suis allé* can not follow *j'*, and might better be replaced by *irais,* the incorrect form most attractive to students in such a sentence. Item 76 has a pronoun with no clear antecedent. Item 81, "Est-ce que l'apprenti est intelligent?" seems to invite a value judgment and may militate against the more thoughtful student. To be sure, the text has described the apprentice as *leste et éveillé,* but it can be argued that he is not behaving very intelligently at the moment in question. Finally, why not in Part 6 simply call for the correct verb forms (which the key gives) instead of for the "subjunctive, if needed"? The student is left not knowing whether to write anything when the subjunctive is not needed, and perhaps feeling that verbs in the indicative are somehow not very important.

Can it be said that this trim and useful instrument promises to function equally well at school and college level? In the absence of statistical evidence we can only guess. The guess here recorded is that it fits the secondary somewhat better than the college situation. Its use at the end of the third college semester might be indicated.

Second Year French Test

GERMAN

[272]

*College Entrance Examination Board Achievement Test in German. Candidates for college entrance with 2–4 years high school; 1901–58; for more complete information, see 599; IBM; 60(80) minutes; program administered by Educational Testing Service for the College Entrance Examination Board. *

REFERENCES

1–3. See 4:244.
4. COLLEGE ENTRANCE EXAMINATION BOARD. *Foreign Languages: A Description of the College Board Tests in French, German, Latin, and Spanish.* Princeton, N.J.: the Board, April 1954. Pp. 31. * (PA 29:1444)
5. KING, RICHARD G. "The German Test—Good, Bad, or Indefinite?" *Col Board R* (23):444–8 My '54. *
6. HOLLMANN, WERNER. "The German Achievement Test of the College Board." *German Q* 31:128–32 Mr '58. *

HAROLD B. DUNKEL, *Professor of Education, The University of Chicago, Chicago, Illinois.* [Review of Form FAC.]

The German test of the CEEB series of achievement tests possesses all the usual virtues of that organization's examinations. The 110-item test achieves a reliability of .93 for students having two years of German and .94 for those having three years (as estimated by a modified form of the Kuder-Richardson formula 20). As is the practice of the CEEB, a considerable amount of detailed information concerning the number of students completing various portions of the material, the skewness of the distribution, the standard error of measurement, and the like is provided.

The test itself consists of five sections. In the first section of 20 items, the student is asked to select from among the offered responses that remark which a person in a situation already briefly sketched in German is most likely to make. The second section of 15 items consists of questions on three short reading passages. The third section of 30 items involves picking the proper German translation for parts of given English sentences. The fourth section of 25 items calls for supplying an omitted word or phrase in a given German sentence; and the fifth section of 20 items contains German passages with individual words or phrases underlined, for which English equivalents are to be selected. In this section there are also a few incomplete German statements about the passage which are to be completed by making a choice from four German possibilities offered for each.

The test was competently written and meticulously edited. Knowing from personal experience how difficult suitable passages are to find, this reviewer was particularly impressed by the felicity of the German passages used.

Within the range it covers, the examination is an extremely competent job. As it stands, it probably includes just about what teachers and students expect to appear on a "College Board." This very fact gives considerable food for reflection. The prestige of these examinations has always been great, and their content has undoubtedly influenced the thinking of students and teachers in regard to what is important in any academic field of study for the college oriented. The influence of these tests will undoubtedly increase still more as more and more schools come to rely on them as at least partial dams to stem the probable flood of students.

Under these circumstances, one may perhaps find fault, not with what the test includes, but rather with what it excludes. What is not measured by so influential a test will probably receive shorter and shorter shrift in the classroom. The varied and stupendous difficulties in measuring on a national scale such objectives as the aural-oral skills or that area commonly labeled "culture and civilization" are familiar. One readily understands why a national testing organization approaches them gradually and gingerly. But the neglect of these areas is something which both the College Entrance Examination Board and teachers who prepare students for these examinations should keep in their minds and on their consciences.

For a review by Herbert Schueler of earlier forms, see 4:244.

[273]

★College Entrance Examination Board Advanced Placement Examination: German. High school seniors desiring credit for college level courses; 1954–58; for more complete information, see 600; 2 tests; 180(200) minutes; program administered by Educational Testing Service for the College Entrance Examination Board. *
a) GERMAN 3. At least 3 years high school; IBM in part; 2 parts.
b) GERMAN 4. At least 4 years high school; 2 scores: aural comprehension and composition, literary composition.

HERBERT SCHUELER, *Professor of Education, and Director of Teacher Education, Hunter College, New York, New York.* [Review of Form FBP-DLC2.]

These two examinations, administered in 1957 as part of the CEEB Advanced Placement Program, are searching, difficult tests of understanding and use of the language. Unfortunately, the small number of candidates taking these examinations did not warrant the usual careful analysis of the results by the CEEB; this review, therefore, is based on one individual's opinion without the help of inferences to be drawn from such an analysis.

The tests were prepared to correspond to college courses at two different levels: German 3, to test primarily for the ability to understand and use the language; and German 4, to test knowledge of German literature as well. The difficulty level of each examination is at least up to the standard of competence expected in corresponding first-rate college courses. If the scores are reliably derived, there should be little hesitancy on the part of colleges in accepting the results for credit and advanced placement.

Both tests have an aural comprehension section in which the student responds to oral passages recorded on tape. In German 3 this section is a version of the CEEB *German Listening Comprehension Test,* featuring several voices, both male and female, in short repeated sentences to which the student responds in a series of multiple choice items, and in connected passages and dialogues requiring free response answers to oral questions. In the main, the material is presented clearly and in standard German, although one of the male voices is guilty of certain nonstandard regionalisms in pronunciation. Certain passages in the script are marred by a stilted, noncolloquial language. A transatlantic telephone dialogue, for example, between a man and his sweetheart making plans for their marriage is so unlikely in its polite formality of idiom and in its unemotional presentation as to sound utterly ridiculous. Most of the aural material is of acceptable quality, however.

The aural comprehension section of German 4 presents a single, 15-minute presentation by one voice of a comparative analysis of two works of literature. The student listens to the material, as if in a college lecture hall, and is asked to take "reasonably complete" notes, either in German or in English, during a single hearing of the material. These notes represent the student's total response to the aural section of the examination. (In view of wide variation in what constitutes acceptability in lecture note taking, and the wide range of acceptable individual differences in this activity, it is diffi-cult to conceive of commonly acceptable standards of rating for this question.)

The nonaural portion of the German 3 examination requires the answering in English of various reading comprehension items, the translation into English of a passage in German, and the writing of three compositions, one in English, and two in German. The stimuli used for the two German compositions are particularly noteworthy—a sequence of cartoon drawings and an English outline of suggested content. In German 4 the nonaural portion requires first the retelling in German of the story of an episode from a work of one of the six authors read in preparation for the examination, and then, based on selections from the authors read, the kind of literary analysis, in English, characteristic of this level of work in a college class in German literature. The nonaural portions of both the German 3 and German 4 tests present sound, testable material, and the student's controlled and free responses should furnish sufficient evidence of his command of the German language and of German literature. Whether the analysis of the student's response yields, in truth, accurate evidence of his competence depends, of course, on the quality of the rating. Each of these examinations is rated by a committee of readers who are expected to agree in advance on the criteria for rating. The instruction sheets to readers and the report of the chief reader on the procedures used for the examinations reveal a commendable regard for the necessity of establishing and following defensible and agreed criteria and standards. This reviewer is concerned, however, about the practice, evidently followed for all the advanced placement tests in 1957, of having each essay read by only one reader. While it is true that different readers read different essays in each booklet, with the result that at least two readers participated in the total rating of each booklet, the fact remains that each partial score was based on the unchecked judgment of a single reader. There is abundant evidence to indicate the fallibility of any given individual's ratings of free, written responses, no matter how thorough the prerating briefing. Since the bulk of each of these examinations is nonobjective, the necessity for achieving maximum objectivity in rating free responses should be obvious. It is this reviewer's opinion that the CEEB practice in this regard does not have sufficient

College Entrance Examination Board Advanced Placement Examination: German

checks and safeguards, however excellent the examinations themselves may be.

[274]

First Year German Test. High school and college; 1933; Form A; mimeographed directions sheet ['33]; tentative high school norms; $1.20 per 25 tests, postage extra; 25¢ per specimen set, postpaid; 40(45) minutes; J. R. Aiken and Cora Held; Bureau of Educational Measurements. *

HERBERT SCHUELER, *Professor of Education, and Director of Teacher Education, Hunter College, New York, New York.*

This short, 100-item, 40-minute test is intended to provide a measure of vocabulary recognition, reading comprehension, and command of elementary structure for students in first year college and first year high school classes. No distinction between the college and high school levels is suggested by the authors.

Part 1 consists of 35 vocabulary items in which the student is asked to choose one of three English translation alternatives of single German words. This section has several evident weaknesses: the words to be tested are not presented in context, and 15 of the items use an obvious, similar sounding misleader (like *Esel*-easel) as one of the three alternatives. This reviewer doubts whether this section provides a sufficiently searching measure of vocabulary recognition, and believes that an item analysis of a representative number of student responses will reveal serious shortcomings in many of the items.

Part 2 presents five German sentences, each of which is to be matched with a sentence of similar meaning to be chosen from among a group of 10 German alternatives. This section is unnecessarily cumbersome and time-consuming for the five items it covers. It actually represents, in an awkwardly camouflaged form, five 2-alternative items, in which the wrong answer in each case is a rather obvious misleader.

Part 3 requires the student to supply a missing word or expression in 40 short German sentences, with the English translation of the missing word supplied in each case. The majority of the items deal with verb forms; several require more than one word to be filled in. As is inevitable with such items, they vary greatly in difficulty and in the number of possibilities of error presented.

Part 4 consists of a single paragraph relating a German anecdote, followed by 20 true-false statements in German. The inclusion of but one short reading selection and the use of the outmoded true-false items, make this section both inadequate in scope and possibly insufficiently discriminating in the few short measures it offers.

A short manual accompanying the test offers percentile norms secured from 191 students in first year classes of 12 high schools. No norms are given for college students. Reliability coefficients were obtained on the basis of but 50 high school and 44 college cases. These are given as .84 and .94, respectively.

This is an unambitious and somewhat archaic test. It is neither long enough, comprehensive enough, nor discriminating enough to be useful in any but informal, casual applications.

[275]

*German I and II: Achievement Examinations for Secondary Schools. 1 or 2 years high school; 1951–53; Forms 1 ('51), 2 ('53); no specific manual; directions sheets [1, '51; 2, '53]; no data on reliability; norms: Forms 1 ['52], 2 ['53]; 10¢ per test, postage extra; (60–90) minutes; Emma Marie Birkmaier; Educational Test Bureau. *

[276]

★German I and II: Midwest High School Achievement Examinations. 2 years high school; 1953–55; Forms A ('55), B ('53, identical with Form 2 of *German I and II: Achievement Examinations for Secondary Schools*); no specific manual; directions sheet ['55]; no data on reliability; no norms; 10¢ per test, postage extra; (60) minutes; Gilbert C. Kettlekamp (A); Educational Test Bureau. *

HAROLD B. DUNKEL, *Professor of Education, The University of Chicago, Chicago, Illinois.*

According to the 4-page manual which accompanies this series of tests, they seemingly are intended to serve some special educational purpose. Since, however, the language in which this explanation is couched is something less than felicitous, the precise point is not clear. The first sentence, "The purpose of the American High School has had varying influences from time to time," is fairly illustrative of the difficulty which a reader has in figuring out just what is meant.

Be that as it may, the German test under review is of a familiar type, containing sections on reading, vocabulary, aural comprehension, and grammar, for a total of 87 items to be completed in an hour of testing time. It is too bad that the effort and expense which went into the manual were not devoted to matters more relevant to this test, especially since no useful information is given there. A sheet for tallying the distribution of class scores and a sheet of norms in terms of quartiles for several tests in the series are furnished with the manual. Unfortunately, German is not one of the tests covered by this list of quartiles, though this omission is a small loss since, even for those tests for which quartiles are supplied, no information is given concerning the number or type of student (or of institution) on which they are based. No estimate of reliability is provided. Thus, the teacher giving this test has only the equivalent of a homemade test since he has no data concerning its quality as a measuring device and no basis for comparing the performance of his own pupils with that of other groups. The question then is, apart from his having saved himself trouble by purchasing it rather than constructing it, whether he has as good a test as he would have built himself.

The sections on vocabulary and grammar (of 34 and 15 items, respectively) are perhaps no worse than what the average teacher would prepare, though they include some items with poor distractors and some with clumsy ones, and one item in which the wrong word is italicized and hence for which none of the offered responses is correct.

The reading section seems, however, poorer than the average teacher who was not in too much of a hurry might have come up with. In general, the section provides inefficient testing since often a whole paragraph must be read to answer one item which hangs on a single sentence. There are misprints, clumsy or dubious responses, and the other familiar shortcomings of the inexpertly prepared and insufficiently edited test. No attempt was made, even a priori, to arrange the items in order of ascending difficulty; hence the poorer students will never get to what seems probably the easiest item in this part, the last one. This entire section needs thoroughgoing revision before it should be used by anyone.

That a section endeavoring to measure aural comprehension is included is a welcome gesture in the direction of the aural-oral skills. In this instance, however, one doubts whether this section constitutes more than such a gesture. Without the reading's being standardized through being recorded on tape or disc, variations among the readers (especially with the additional visual and other clues which readers fall into unconsciously under these circumstances) certainly will not produce results which are comparable. The additional fact that each reader must work out his own timing within each aural part—with the probable result that readers will not work it out in advance and simply blunder through under the dubious inspiration of the moment—will raise further hob with the reliability of the results, as does one item with clumsy English and one item where English idiom permits two answers.

In sum, the reader has, at best, the equivalent of a test he could himself make the night before. If he is experienced and careful, he could probably make a better one. If he is spending money, he would do better to purchase, say, the *Cooperative German Test*.

GREEK

[277]
*College Entrance Examination Board Achievement Test in Greek.** Candidates for college entrance ; 1901–58 ; available only in the March testing program ; for more complete information, see 599 ; IBM ; 2 tests (candidate takes only one) : Attic Prose, Homer and Attic Prose ; 60(80) minutes ; program administered by Educational Testing Service for the College Entrance Examination Board. *

KONRAD GRIES, *Associate Professor of Classical Languages and Chairman of the Department, Queens College, Flushing, New York.* [Review of Form FAC.]

The comments of this reviewer on the CEEB Latin test (see 280) apply in principle also to the CEEB test in Greek, although here he has found no slips or errors, and only one doubtful item (Item 50 in the test on Homer, where too much is read into the Greek).

The test comes in two versions : one on Attic prose for those candidates who have followed the traditional Greek course, the other on Homer and Attic prose for candidates from those schools which introduce Homer at an early stage. Both versions have two parts : a short one, limited to 8 or 10 items, and a longer one with 57 or 58 assorted questions based on three passages. In the "old-style" test all of the passages are Xenophontic, whereas in the other test the first passage is identical with the first passage in the old-style test and the second and third passages are from *Odyssey* and *Iliad*. The two versions differ mainly in their first, and minor, part, where the eight items of the old-style test include four in which synonyms or synonymous expressions are to be chosen and four where the correct Greek translation of an

English phrase or clause is to be indicated, while the 10 items of the other test are simple vocabulary items. In either case, the sampling is much too small.

As only 32 and 36 students, respectively, took this test in March 1957, statistics are limited to a reporting of score distributions.

HEBREW

[278]

★**Uniform Achievement Tests.** Grades 1, 2, 3; 1951(?); 1 form; 3 tests; manual; teacher's mimeographed supplement; record blank; no data on reliability; no norms; 25¢ per test, postage extra; Jewish Education Committee of New York; the Committee. *
a) HEBREW LANGUAGE. (60–75) minutes.
b) JEWISH LIFE AND OBSERVANCES. (45–55) minutes.
c) THE JEWISH PEOPLE. (55–65) minutes.

ITALIAN

[279]

*College Entrance Examination Board Achievement Test in Italian.** Candidates for college entrance with 2–4 years high school; 1924–58; available only in the March testing program; for more complete information, see 599; IBM; 60(80) minutes; program administered by Educational Testing Service for the College Entrance Examination Board. *

LATIN

[280]

*College Entrance Examination Board Achievement Test in Latin.** Candidates for college entrance with 2–4 years high school; 1901–58; for more complete information, see 599; IBM; 60(80) minutes; program administered by Educational Testing Service for the College Entrance Examination Board.*

REFERENCES

1–2. See 4:250.
3. COLLEGE ENTRANCE EXAMINATION BOARD. *Foreign Languages: A Description of the College Board Tests in French, German, Latin, and Spanish.* Princeton, N.J.: the Board, April 1954. Pp. 31. * (PA 29:1444)

KONRAD GRIES, *Associate Professor of Classical Languages and Chairman of the Department, Queens College, Flushing, New York.* [Review of Form FAC.]

This test, like other CEEB tests, consists entirely of multiple choice items. There are 94 items, each with four choices, arranged in three parts.

The first part consists of 15 vocabulary items and two derivative items, each item being given in isolation. The words involved are not particularly abstruse; a second year student should know all but three or four. The suggested an-

swers are clever and sound, though one might quibble about Item 5: *curo;* the key designates "look out for" as the correct answer, but one could make out a good case for "want" (cf., e.g., Tibullus 1.1.58 *non ego laudari curo*). It is doubtful whether much is proved by so limited a sampling of the candidates' vocabulary, especially in view of the high frequency of most of the items. In any case, the practice of word matching here employed is reprehensible in itself.

The second part contains 22 items. In each an English phrase or sentence is translated in four different ways, only one of which is correct. Presumably meant to test recognitional knowledge of forms, syntax, and idiom, it is complicated by occasional vocabulary problems. Again, there would seem to be no functional value: college students of Latin will hardly be called upon to correct each other's written Latin, and under what other circumstances would they be likely to see the plethora of impossible Latinity contained in these two pages?

The last part, with 55 items, is based on three Latin passages, each a self-contained unit of about 20 lines, with occasional vocabulary aids. These three passages represent approximately the kind and the level of the Latin read respectively in the second, the third, and the fourth years of secondary school, the first being a straightforward prose narrative, the second (also in prose) involving ideas of a literary nature, and the third presenting a Vergilian episode from Valerius Flaccus in hexameters. The obvious difficulty of the second and third passages seems confirmed by the results achieved when the test was given in March 1957.

The aggregate of the items may aptly be described as a fruit salad, a vivid term used by Harold B. Dunkel in reviewing the *CEEB Achievement Test in Latin Reading* in *The Fourth Mental Measurements Yearbook.* There are items on syntax, on morphology, on derivation, on word and phrase translation, on content (both factual and interpretive), on poetry, and on scansion. It is not surprising that the candidates, given only one hour for the whole test and forced in this part to change their basis of operation almost from item to item, "found this test of greater than middle difficulty." Taken individually, on the other hand, these items are fair enough, provided the Latin itself

College Entrance Examination Board Achievement Test in Greek

has been understood, although several sore spots must be pointed out. In Item 44 the correct answer is B, not C, as indicated in the key. In Item 53 the correct answer, "Trajan.... did not want Hadrian to become emperor, but Plotina did," involves a straining of the Latin (*sine aliqua quidem voluntate Traiani*). Item 81, which calls upon the candidates to find a "symbolically....emotional counterpart" to a quoted phrase in one of four suggested lines, is completely beyond the reviewer. In Item 86, on *dapibus coeptis,* the answer given as correct, "only at this point do they really begin the banquet," is hardly right in view of the preceding *dum vincitur....prima fames....omnis aula silet.* In Item 93, where the correct answer is undoubtedly the one indicated by the key, the question itself speaks of a "dramatic effect" which is absent in all four suggested answers. And in Item 94, where the candidates are required to choose which of four lines "illustrates the quality of poetry defined by *duriora*" (with a good reference to the literary discussion contained in the second Latin passage), it is again difficult to identify the "hardness" of the line labeled correct by the key. The reviewer finds it euphonious.

Statistics on the 3,004 candidates who took the test in March 1957, are given in a test analysis bulletin. Whatever their interpretation, the test in itself is not one to inspire confidence in its ability to determine that rather nebulous conception "achievement in Latin," which is, by the way, not adequately defined in any literature connected with the test that the reviewer has seen.

For a review by Harold B. Dunkel of earlier forms, see 4:250.

[281]

★College Entrance Examination Board Advanced Placement Examination: Latin. High school seniors desiring credit for college level courses; 1954–58; for more complete information, see 600; 2 levels in 1 booklet: Latin 4 (candidates who present the advanced Vergil course), Latin 5 (candidates who have studied 2 of the following fields: prose, lyric poetry, comedy); 180(200) minutes; program administered by Educational Testing Service for the College Entrance Examination Board. *

[282]

*First Year Latin: Every Pupil Scholarship Test. 1 year high school; 1926–58; new form usually issued each January and April; norms available following testing program; no data on reliability; 4¢ per test; 4¢ per scoring key; postage extra; 40(45) minutes; Bureau of Educational Measurements. *

[283]

★Kansas First Year Latin Test. 1, 2 semesters high school; 1935–56; 2 levels; mimeographed manual ('56); $1.20 per 25 tests, postage extra; 25¢ per specimen set, postpaid; 40(45) minutes; Helen Pearson; Bureau of Educational Measurements. *
a) TEST 1, FORM A, FIRST SEMESTER. 1956.
b) TEST 1, FORM B, SECOND SEMESTER. 1956.

[284]

*Latin I and II: Achievement Examinations for Secondary Schools. 1 or 2 years high school; 1951–53; Form 1 ('51); no specific manual; no data on reliability; norms ['52]; 10¢ per test, postage extra; (60) minutes; Margaret M. Forbes; Educational Test Bureau. *

[285]

*Latin I and II: Every Pupil Test. 1 or 2 years high school; 1929–58; new form usually issued each December and April; norms available following testing program; no data on reliability; 3¢ per test; 1¢ per scoring key; cash orders postpaid; 40(45) minutes; Ohio Scholarship Tests. *

[286]

★Latin I and II: Midwest High School Achievement Examinations. 2 years high school; 1953–55; Forms A ('55), B ('53, identical with Form 2 of *Latin I and II: Achievement Examinations for Secondary Schools;* no specific manual; no data on reliability; no norms; 10¢ per test, postage extra; Form A: 60(65) minutes; Form B: 90(95) minutes; Margaret M. Forbes; Educational Test Bureau. *

SPANISH

[287]

*College Entrance Examination Board Achievement Test in Spanish. Candidates for college entrance with 2–4 years high school; 1902–58; for more complete information, see 599; IBM; 60(80) minutes; program administered by Educational Testing Service for the College Entrance Examination Board. *

REFERENCES
1–3. See 4:259.
4. COLLEGE ENTRANCE EXAMINATION BOARD. *Foreign Languages: A Description of the College Board Tests in French, German, Latin, and Spanish.* Princeton, N.J.: the Board, April 1954. Pp. 31. * (*PA* 29:1444)

[288]

★College Entrance Examination Board Advanced Placement Examination: Spanish. High school seniors desiring credit for college level courses; 1954–58; for more complete information, see 600; 180(200) minutes; program administered by Educational Testing Service for the College Entrance Examination Board. *

[289]

*The Graduate Record Examinations Advanced Tests: Spanish. College seniors and graduate students; 1946–58; for more complete information, see 601; IBM; 180(200) minutes; Educational Testing Service. *

For a review by Harold Seashore of the entire series, see 601.

[290]

★Kansas Second Year Spanish Test. High school and college; 1953; Form A; no college norms; $1.20

per 25 tests, postage extra; 30¢ per specimen set, post-paid; 40(45) minutes; Helen Johnson; Bureau of Educational Measurements. *

[291]

★Spanish and Latin American Life and Culture. 2 years high school or 1 year college; 1956; Form A; mimeographed directions sheet; tentative norms; $1.20 per 25 tests, postage extra; 25¢ per specimen set, postpaid; 40(45) minutes; Minnie M. Miller and Beulah Aiken; Bureau of Educational Measurements. *

KATHLEEN N. PERRET, *Interpreter, Department of Conference Services, Interpretation Division, United Nations, New York, New York.*

This test is designed to test students completing two years of high school or one year of college Spanish in the geography, history, government, art, literature, science, and customs of Spain and Latin America. It consists of 100 questions in English broken down into three sections. Part 1, consisting of 25 items, requires the student to write the answer in English (the student is told that one half point will be counted for spelling); Part 2, is made up of three groups of 10 questions each, the answers to which are to be selected from three lists of 15 possible replies; Part 3 gives 45 incomplete sentences, each followed by three choices of an English word or phrase to complete the text.

The authors display an obvious knowledge of the mechanics of testing, but the sum total of their efforts on this test is neither enlightened nor inspiring. What is more, Part 1 contains something which, to the reviewer's mind, is a totally unacceptable feature—the proviso that spelling count so heavily. This, after all, purports to be a test on a foreign civilization. How, in the circumstances, can the correct or incorrect spelling of the answer to Item 3 ("October 12") or to Item 13 ("green") be considered pertinent or valid?

Despite the all-embracing content coverage announced, geography and history account for approximately one third and one fifth, respectively, of the items, although much of this subject matter is certainly covered elsewhere in the normal high school or college curriculum. Cultural items, the catch-all category, constitute about two fifths of the test, leaving 5 per cent to be apportioned among the categories of art, literature, and science. There may be some question about the fine points of this breakdown, but the general distribution is unmistakable. It is depressing to feel that students in

Kansas Second Year Spanish Test

this field are confined to such an austere and trivial diet.

Examining the items in more detail, is it really useful to include 10 questions of the "What is the capital city" type? Surely a student knowing one or two capital cities is likely to know a fair proportion of the others as well; if teachers of Spanish are concentrating in so large measure on this type of material, it is a great pity. So many other items come to mind that might have been included on music, dance, and agriculture, to name only a few areas. Finer differentiation could certainly have been achieved by more items in neglected fields. There is another facet of the tests which seems questionable, namely the emphasis on Mexico (about 28 items, as compared with about 18 on Spain). Admittedly, it is difficult for teachers and testers to weigh the relative merits of the contributions of Spain and Latin America and to apportion time available fairly and sensibly. The mass of information is so overwhelming that it might be better to devote no time to this field at all if enough space cannot be allocated for the program to make it meaningful. But, if time is to be spent on this work, deeper and more lasting results might be achieved by using Spain as the starting point and developing understanding by later comparing and contrasting Spain with Latin America. To dismiss the all-pervading influence of Spain in so few items scattered over a wide field, while paying lip service to Latin America through a mass of items on its geography, serves no purpose, except perhaps to give the student an abiding dislike for "culture" and prevent him from pursuing these studies in later life.

In summary, the reviewer feels that the end product falls far short of the ambitious goal set by the authors. Much of the substance of the test has undoubtedly been conditioned by what is actually being taught. Even so, the range of content could have been considerably broader. The reliability and validity data reported in the manual are not sufficiently impressive to outweigh the many shortcomings of the test content. Before using the test, teachers would be well advised to consider carefully whether this is indeed a test suited to their needs.

[292]

✻Spanish I and II: Achievement Examinations for Secondary Schools. 1 or 2 years high school; 1951–53; Forms 1 ('51), 2 ('53); no specific manual; directions sheets [1, '51; 2, '53]; no data on reliability;

norms: Forms 1 ['52], 2 ('53) ; 10¢ per test, postage extra ; (60–90) minutes ; Emma Marie Birkmaier (2) ; Educational Test Bureau. *

[293]

★**Spanish I and II: Midwest High School Achievement Examinations.** 2 years high school ; 1951–55 ; Forms A ('51, title on test is *Spanish I and II: Achievement Examinations for Secondary Schools*), B ['52, identical with Form 2 of *Spanish I and II: Achievement Examinations for Secondary Schools*] ; no specific manual ; directions sheet ['55] ; no data on reliability ; Form A norms ['55] ; no norms

for Form B ; 10¢ per test, postage extra ; Form A : 35(60) minutes ; Form B : 45(90) minutes ; Educational Test Bureau. *

[294]

★**Spanish: Teacher Education Examination Program.** College seniors preparing to teach secondary school ; 1957 ; for more complete information, see 543 ; IBM ; no data on reliability ; no norms ; 80(95) minutes ; Educational Testing Service. *

For a review by Walter W. Cook of the entire series, see 543.

FOREIGN LANGUAGES — SIXTH MMY

REVIEWS BY *Nelson Brooks, John B. Carroll, Henry Chauncey, Harold B. Dunkel, Wayne D. Fisher, Walter V. Kaulfers, Gilbert C. Kettelkamp, Bertram B. Masia, Theodor F. Naumann, Paul Pimsleur, James H. Ricks, Jr., Herbert Schueler, Mariette Schwarz, Marion F. Shaycoft, Jack M. Stein, Mary E. Turnbull, and Clarence E. Turner.*

[355]

*Foreign Language Prognosis Test. Grades 8–9; 1930–59; 2 tests labeled Forms A ('59, c1930–59), B ('58, c1930–58), (8 pages, identical with tests copyrighted in 1930 except for cover page), either or both of which may be administered; manual ('59, c1930–59, 6 pages); $4 per 35 tests; 50¢ per specimen set of both tests (must be purchased to obtain manual); postpaid; 44(60) minutes; Percival M. Symonds; Bureau of Publications. *
a) FORM A. 5 scores: English inflection, word translation-English to Esperanto, sentence translation-Esperanto to English, related words, total.
b) FORM B. 5 scores: word translation-Esperanto to English, artificial language, sentence translation-English to Esperanto, formation of parts of speech in English, total.

REFERENCES

1–6. See 40:1340.
7. VEON, DOROTHY HELENE. *The Relationship of Learning Factors Found in Certain Modern Foreign-Language Aptitude Tests to the Prediction of Shorthand Achievement in College.* Stillwater, Okla.: Division of Commerce, Oklahoma Agricultural and Mechanical College, 1950. Pp. 74. *

WAYNE D. FISHER, *Assistant Professor of Education in Russian; and* BERTRAM B. MASIA, *Assistant Professor of Education; The University of Chicago, Chicago, Illinois.*

The *Foreign Language Prognosis Test,* which bears a first copyright date of 1930 and whose contents seem not to have been changed at the time of the 1959 copyright, has been outmoded by the application of principles of linguistics to the teaching of foreign languages. This relatively recent development conceives of language learning as based upon analytical contrastive studies of the signaling systems of the native and target languages. Instruction, therefore, focuses almost exclusively upon the problems indicated by the contrastive studies. The implications of this development for prognostic testing are clear. Such tests must be able to indicate the outcome of the encounter of the student with these linguistic problems. Whether the prognostic tests will have to vary with the particular native and target languages remains to be seen.

The usefulness of the *Foreign Language Prognosis Test* is therefore limited to those teachers whose instruction has little relation to the nature of language behavior. If the foreign language instruction emphasizes encoding and decoding, and looks upon language learning as essentially the acquisition of a large vocabulary, then success in such a course could be predicted fairly well with such a test. However, it is quite likely that this success can be predicted just as well with a shorter and more straightforward test of general verbal ability.

An inspection of test item types reveals both the author's conception of foreign language learning as being intellectual rather than behavioral, and the test's being at least a first cousin to tests of verbal fluency *in English*. Test 1 of Form A is a case in point. In this test the student is required to change a word in a sentence as indicated. For example, for the sentence, "Are you reading an interesting book?" he is directed to change the verb to the future perfect tense. This type of test item confuses (*a*) knowledge of terminology about language with (*b*) knowledge of language. It measures the first and presupposes that the first is necessary for the achievement of the second. Such an assumption is unwarranted. In the item cited a person might not be able to perform the task, yet could produce the future perfect structure whenever needed. In a deeper sense this type of task is no more than an intellectual exercise in manipulating rules of English grammar.

Test 2 of Form A reveals another fundamental weakness in the *Foreign Language Prognosis Test.* The student is presented with a story in Esperanto followed by its English translation. Then he is given a set of multiple choice items in which the task is to indicate one of five Esperanto words as being the equivalent of the English word presented. He makes his choice of the correct alternative by comparing the Esperanto and English renderings of the story. Here are two languages with similar signaling systems. At best this test could be useful in predicting performance in a language with an origin and an alphabet common to English. But it would not give any significant information concerning mastery of a language with different symbols such as Russian, Hebrew, and Chinese. What we have here essentially is a problem solving exercise which requires the use of mental processes whose relation to language as behavior is not clear.

A final example is from Test 4. Here the student is confronted with a series of sentences in Esperanto, each one containing an italicized word. His task is to translate the italicized word into English. Again we have a highly intellectualized exercise which possibly has face validity for knowledge about language but not for the acquisition of skills in the use of language. Performance on this type of test may be negatively correlated with success in a course which truly emphasizes the acquisition of language behavioral skills.

All eight subtests in the two noncomparable forms of the *Foreign Language Prognosis Test* are open to the same criticism. Since this appears to be nothing more than a test of verbal ability, nothing would be lost to evaluation of foreign language instruction if it were withdrawn from circulation.

For a review by William B. Michael, see 4:232; for a review by Walter V. Kaulfers, see 40:1340.

[356]

★**The Graduate School Foreign Language Testing Program.** Graduate level degree candidates required to demonstrate foreign language reading proficiency; 1963–64; tests administered 4 times annually (January, April, August, October) at participating graduate schools; departments must agree to test "all students deemed ready to meet reading proficiency requirements" in the languages; Forms K-LFG1, K-LFG2 ('63, 33–44 pages); 3 tests: French, German, Russian; for part of each test, examinees elect the 1 section out of 4 (biological sciences, humanities, physical sciences, social sciences) which contains materials related to their major field; handbook for deans and examiners ('63, 10 pages); bulletin of information for students ('63, 11 pages); guide for interpretation ('64, 21 pages); score interpretation leaflet for students ['64, 4 pages]; supervisor's handbook for administering the publisher's testing programs ('63, 24 pages); no data on reliability of section 2 of the Russian test; separate Scribe answer sheets must be used; examination fee: $6 per student tested, postage extra; fee includes scoring service and report of scores to the graduate school (extra copies of individual score reports are included for examinees); 80(100) minutes; Educational Testing Service. *

For a review of the French test, see 377; for a review of the German test, see 391.

[357]

★**Modern Language Aptitude Test.** Grades 9–16 and adults; 1959, c1955–58; earlier experimental form called *Psi-Lambda Foreign Language Aptitude Battery;* 4–6 scores: number learning (long form only), phonetic script (long form only), spelling clues, words in sentences, paired associates, total; IBM; Form A ('59, c1955–58) consists of 2 parts: test-answer sheet (2 pages) for parts 1 and 2, and test booklet (12 pages) for parts 3, 4, and 5; parts 3–5 may be administered as a short form; practice sheet ('59, c1955–58, 1 page); manual ('59, 27 pages); no norms for grades 12 and 14–16; separate answer sheets must be used; $3.50 per 25 tests; $3.60 per 50 IBM answer sheets and 50 practice sheets; 60¢ per set of stencils and manual; 75¢ per specimen set; $7.50 per 3¾ ips tape recording (essential for long form, optional for short form); postpaid; (30) minutes for short form, (60–70) minutes for long form; John B. Carroll and Stanley M. Sapon; Psychological Corporation. *

REFERENCES

1. CARROLL, JOHN B. "The Harvard Foreign Language Aptitude Tests." *Yearb Nat Council Meas Used Ed* 12:9–11 pt 2 '55. *
2. CARROLL, JOHN B. "A Factor Analysis of Two Foreign Language Aptitude Batteries." *J General Psychol* 59:3–19 Jl '58. * (*PA* 36:2KK03C)
3. CARROLL, JOHN B. "Use of the *Modern Language Aptitude Test* in Secondary Schools." *Yearb Nat Council Meas Used Ed* 16:155–9 '59. *
4. MARQUARDT, WILLIAM F. "Can Foreign Student Selection Be Based on Aptitude for Learning English?" *News B Inst Int Ed* 36:2–8 Ap '61. *
5. KJELDERGAARD, PAUL M. "Predicting Paired-Associate Learning Speed." *Psychol Rep* 11:353–4 O '62. * (*PA* 37:7587)
6. PIMSLEUR, PAUL; STOCKWELL, ROBERT P.; AND COMREY, ANDREW L. "Foreign Language Learning Ability." *J Ed Psychol* 53:15–26 F '62. * (*PA* 37:2003)
7. CIEUTAT, VICTOR J. "Predicting Speed of Serial and Paired-Associate Learning." *Psychol Rep* 13:786 D '63. *
8. KURLANDER, EDWIN D. "The Modern Language Aptitude Test as a Guidance Tool." *Sch Counselor* 10:129–31 Mr '63. *
9. MUELLER, KLAUS A., AND WIERSMA, WILLIAM, JR. "Correlation of Foreign Language Speaking Competency and Grades in Ten Midwestern Liberal Arts Colleges." *Mod Lang J* 47:353–5 D '63. *
10. WEAVER, WENDELL W., AND KINGSTON, ALBERT J. "A Factor Analysis of the Cloze Procedure and Other Measures of Reading and Language Ability." *J Commun* 13:252–61 D '63. * (*PA* 39:188)

WAYNE D. FISHER, *Assistant Professor of Education in Russian; and* BERTRAM B. MASIA, *Assistant Professor of Education; The University of Chicago, Chicago, Illinois.*

Tests designed to predict achievement in the study of a foreign language invariably reflect two rather serious weaknesses: (a) they are not rooted in psychological studies of language and language behavior, and (b) they do not indicate the specific language learning outcomes or instructional objectives the test is designed to predict.

The first weakness has given rise to validity coefficients between predictor and criterion variables which are not significantly higher than coefficients obtained when general scholastic ability tests are used as predictors. What appear as a result of cursory inspection to be measures of language abilities, turn out in statistical analysis to be nothing more than measures of general abilities.

The second weakness gives rise to a range of predictive validity coefficients when the prognostic instrument is used with foreign language classrooms of different teachers and in different schools. Since error and bias in the criterion variable, particularly when it is represented by teacher grades, is most likely random across teachers and schools, variability in predictive validity coefficients may in large measure be associated with variations in instructional objectives.

It is clear that the search for what might be termed "primary language abilities" which are operative for all goals of language instruction is as fruitless as the medieval search for the philosopher's stone. We do not mean to imply that there are no specific language learning abilities. But we do contend that such abilities are inextricably tied to purposes and goals of instruction, to the teacher's conception of the nature of foreign language behavior and how it is acquired. Thus aptitude must be viewed in terms of classroom implementation of foreign language instructional goals rather than in terms of language and language behavior *per se*. Often overlooked is the fact that a person has demonstrated his aptitude for learning a second language by having acquired skill in using his native language for his own purposes. An American student studying a foreign language has already gained practical, though perhaps not stylistic, proficiency in English. He is able to carry on a conversation, although he may not be able to do it with the skill of an Alexander Woollcott. He certainly can write, often not with any appreciable degree of precision, no less elegance. Yet in his proficiency in English, no matter what his level, he has demonstrated his linguistic aptitude. It is therefore unreasonable to expect the student of a second language to be more proficient in the basic language skills (e.g., speaking, listening, etc.) in the second language than he is in his native language. What is reasonable to expect is that the student of a foreign language should approximate the level of behavior of his counterpart in the cultural speech community of which the language is representative.

In terms of these two weaknesses of foreign language aptitude tests, to what extent does Carroll and Sapon's *Modern Language Aptitude Test* succeed in overcoming them? Predictive validities are generally .20 higher than those obtained for general ability and intelligence tests. But it is difficult to determine whether this overall increment in prediction is traceable to systematic psychological- and linguistic-oriented studies made by Carroll's Harvard Language Aptitude Project or to the more accidental effect of the test constructors' ingenuity in devising test models which are empirically more efficient for reasons which are not very clear. Since the MLAT manual does not provide a theoretical rationale for the instrument and does not claim that the parts of the test correspond with those cognitive ability factors reported elsewhere by the senior test author (3), we must accept the latter explanation for the reported overall increment in prediction.

Does the MLAT predict some types of instructional outcomes better than others? The manual states: "it was originally planned to study comparative validities of the MLAT in 'traditional' as opposed to 'new-type' courses, and efforts were made to collect data in both types of courses. It soon appeared, however, that there was no systematic fluctuation of validity dependent on teacher methodology. High validities were obtained for intensive courses, all of which laid much stress on oral work, but there were also some institutions stressing written work where reasonably high validities were obtained."

One problem is that the difference in methodology—the implementation of the teacher's views regarding the nature of language and how it is learned—between the so-called "traditional" course and the "new type" course is not as great in most cases as the literature would have us believe. More important than whether the course is labeled "traditional" or "new type" is whether the intention is to learn the new language in terms of its own linguistic elements or in terms of its restatement in the student's mother tongue. Our observations of both traditional and new type courses support the contention that courses of both types never relinquish the mother tongue. In Brooks' words, "language symbols are 'decoded' from one system to another, and comprehension,

Modern Language Aptitude Test

meaning, and value are all in terms of the student's first language." [1]

When a second language is learned as an alternate system of behavior, however, the ultimate goal must be the control of the linguistic elements (phonology, morphology, syntax, intonation, stress, graphic symbolization, and vocabulary) as the native speaker controls them. It is only further evidence in support of our criticism above that both teaching and testing in foreign languages place heavy emphasis on the acquisition of vocabulary. This one linguistic element not only is heavily stressed, it interferes with learning and testing of all the other linguistic elements. Language learning involves the acquisition of an alternate communication system which develops different signals, different sounds, different structures, and different structuring of reality from that of the native language.

In the MLAT the "target" language of the test is a restatement of American English. In every aspect of the test the similarities between English and a "target" language are emphasized, whereas in language learning it is precisely in these areas that transfer readily occurs and minimal difficulties are encountered by the student (unless language is taught as academic discipline, rather than as behavior). Language learning difficulties arise, to any significant degree, only at those points in the phonological system, the morphological system, the syntactical system, the rhythmical and intonational system which are *contrastive* to the native language.[2]

Our own consideration of the test content suggests that it measures the student's ability to recode English. The sound system used throughout the test is the English sound system. The structures used throughout the test are English structures. Even with vocabulary, nonsense words are here substituted for English words, thus giving the erroneous impression that language learning is in large measure a matter of the substitution of one set of words for another.

If the MLAT reveals, through "nonsense-substitute" vocabulary, the learner's knowledge of English sounds and structure, it is likely that the student's academic record in English classes would be as valid a predictor of success as the MLAT. Also, if our assertion of the pronounced English orientation of this test is a valid one, then the test should be a better predictor of English grades than of grades in a foreign language course.

In this connection our recommendation for improving the MLAT is the inclusion of non-English sounds in the taped portion, and the use of non-English linguistic characteristics in all other parts of the test. There should also be some non-Roman symbolization.

MARION F. SHAYCOFT, *Senior Research Scientist, American Institute for Research; and Director of Measurement Research, University of Pittsburgh Project Talent Office; Pittsburgh, Pennsylvania.*

The purpose of the *Modern Language Aptitude Test* is broader than its name implies, since the test is designed to measure aptitude for learning *any* foreign language—not just modern ones. It is suitable for high school and college students, and for adults.

The first two of the five parts involve oral presentation of the test material, via a prerecorded magnetic tape. The Short Form, which consists of the last three parts, is intended for use where available testing time is limited or where it is not feasible to use tape recorder playback equipment.

The test material itself is quite novel in character and represents an ingenious attack on the problem of getting a better measure of aptitude for learning a foreign language quickly and well than is yielded by IQ.

Part 1, Number Learning, is reported to have a fairly large specific variance, hypothesized to represent auditory alertness. Part 2, Phonetic Script, measures the ability to learn orthographic symbols corresponding to specific sounds. The authors suggest that it may also measure memory for speech sounds, and that it is correlated with ability to mimic these sounds. Part 3, Spelling Clues, the only highly speeded section of the test, also measures sound-symbol association to some extent but, unlike Part 2, is dependent in addition on size of the student's vocabulary. Part 4, Words in Sentences, is intended to measure sensitivity to grammatical structure. The item type, an ingenious one, yields scores that are not dependent on specific memory for grammatical

1 BROOKS, NELSON. *Language and Language Learning: Theory and Practice*, p. 104. New York: Harcourt, Brace & World, Inc., 1960. Pp. xv, 238. *
2 LADO, ROBERT. *Linguistics Across Cultures: Applied Linguistics for Language Teachers.* Ann Arbor, Mich.: University of Michigan Press, 1957. Pp. ix, 141. *

terminology. Part 5, Paired Associates, measures the rote memory aspect of learning a foreign language.

The test as a whole and the individual items that compose it are carefully constructed. The administrative procedures are well planned and easy to carry out, particularly if the tape is used. The directions might be improved slightly, however, by clarifying the instructions on guessing. Although the scores are not corrected for chance guessing, the students are neither explicitly instructed to attempt every item nor told that the score is number right. This lack could reduce the test's validity a little.

The manual is an exceptionally good one; it is clear and sound and contains suitable words of caution and explanation throughout, to keep the user from misinterpreting or misusing the results. It describes the test, contains instructions for administration and scoring, presents normative data, reliability coefficients, validity coefficients, expectancy tables, and auxiliary statistics, and discusses suggested uses of the test.

Percentile norms are presented for both the total test and the Short Form, for beginning language students (boys and girls separately) in grades 9, 10, and 11, and in the freshman year of college, and also for military and civilian personnel assigned to intensive foreign language training. Most of the norms groups are relatively small, however, consisting of only a few hundred cases each, and probably not comparable from grade to grade (if one may judge from the fact that the grade 10 boys' mean is somewhat lower than that for grade 9 boys, and from selection factors affecting the grade at which high school students embark on foreign language study). Thus the norms probably should be regarded as only suggestive, rather than definitive.

The validity coefficients (against course grades and proficiency test scores) are high enough, when criterion limitations are considered, to provide evidence that the test fulfills its basic purpose successfully.

Neither norms nor validity coefficients are presented for the part scores. Such data might be helpful in view of the fact that the intercorrelations among the parts are low enough to suggest that the part scores measure somewhat different aspects of foreign language aptitude. It appears to the reviewer that the

neglect of part scores may be partly responsible for the finding, reported in the manual, that the test does not have differential validity for different languages. Using the total score could easily wipe out any differential validity the parts have. The manual does suggest the use of part scores for predicting particular kinds of learning difficulties. Several of the parts are reliable enough to justify such use, although interpretations would have to be cautious.

Split-half reliability coefficients for scores on the total test and Short Form are excellent, most of them exceeding .90 and several exceeding .95.

One statistic that this reviewer hunted for in vain was the correlation between Short Form and total test scores. Potential users of the Short Form would probably be interested in this coefficient.

SUMMARY. The *Modern Language Aptitude Test* is ingeniously constructed, carefully developed, and a generally excellent instrument for measuring the ability to learn foreign languages. Its few weaknesses (such as the paucity of data presented on part scores) are very minor ones, vastly outweighed by its numerous and substantial merits.

French R 33:634–5 My '60. Harold B. Dunkel. At all educational levels both the cost and the mortality rate of language instruction are relatively high. Any device which enables us to counsel into language programs students able to profit from them and to keep out of these classes students likely to fail is more than merely useful. The long search for prognostic tests has, however, encountered a variety of fundamental problems. Because of the correlation between almost all educational tests, whether of academic achievement or intelligence (with most of the correlations being low positive ones of the order of .20–.50), nearly any test is to some degree a predictor of linguistic achievement. Of these general measures, the experience of most of us indicates that the tests of "verbal intelligence" (such as the L-score of the ACE Psychological Examination) usually give the best results, correlations in the neighborhood of .50 or a little better. Unfortunately, this degree of correlation between the predictor and the criterion of actual performance does not permit confident counseling in individual cases, precisely

Modern Language Aptitude Test

the situation in which prediction is most wanted. Earlier tests built specifically for language prognosis often do a little better, but usually not enough better to justify the additional testing time and money, since decisions in individual situations were still fairly precarious statistically. Finally, an inherent difficulty has been the diverse nature of foreign-language programs. It has seemed unlikely to many of us that a single instrument could predict later achievement in such varied courses as are suggested by the labels: "intensive aural-oral," "grammar-translation," "culture and civilization," "extensive reading," and the varied mixtures and compounds of all these and other emphases. It is against this background of past experience that we must consider the present effort. * The test has many good features, and in the manual the authors have presented users with a generous array of information about the test and its scores. Norms are based on about 1900 high-school students, 1200 college students and 1000 students in special language schools. The reliabilities of the parts and of the whole are good (usually in the .90's), and the parts show fairly low intercorrelations. The important question is, of course, how well it predicts later achievement. As might be expected, the answer here is complicated. The correlations between scores on the test and the various criteria (course grades, final exam grades, etc.) swing over a wide range, from .13 to .83, with the majority of them falling between .40 and .60. The kind of course involved, the validity and reliability of the criterion, and other familiar complications are all involved. In sum, this is a well planned and carefully developed test, but it is far from a magic bullet in slaying the problems of language prognosis. As the authors point out, teachers and programs will have to develop their own experience with it. For some it may prove a waste of time and money; for others, it may be a means of improving their present ability to predict student achievement in language courses.

J Consult Psychol 24:99–100 F '60. Edward S. Bordin. * Sufficient data bearing on reliability and validity are presented to warrant issuing the test and to establish confidence in its usefulness as a diagnostic device. The normative data, particularly for high school and adult norms, are weak.

J Counsel Psychol 6:319 w '59. Laurence Siegel. * appears to be a highly successful venture. It does what its authors claim it will do, and does it well. It is a more valid predictor of success in learning foreign languages than are various intelligence tests. There are undoubtedly many situations wherein this kind of predictor may be used advantageously.

Personnel & Guid J 38:582–4 Mr '60. Herschel T. Manuel. * The *Manual* of the MLAT has a wealth of information in addition to the detailed directions for administering and scoring the test. * Reported reliability coefficients are generally good * the *Manual,* which is excellent in many respects, could be improved by interpreting reliability in terms of its practical bearing upon the scores of individuals. Even the cautious language, such as "tend to mean," in the discussion of the use of the parts of the test in diagnosis does not seem to cover this need adequately. Validity coefficients.... are of the magnitude often found in correlating general scholastic aptitude with total college marks at the end of the first semester and are high enough to indicate that the test may be used effectively. * The authors have given education a new measuring instrument which promises to be useful in a field in which measurement is needed. Since it is so new, no complete evaluation can be made. It must be tried by others in various situations. The reviewer expresses the hope that the authors will continue their study of basic problems and especially the nature of aptitude for language. The MLAT is offered modestly as an instrument for predicting for a student "how rapidly he can acquire the basic knowledge of the foreign language which will enable him to speak, understand, read, or write, depending upon the training he is given in these aspects of performance." The authors have presented evidence that the test is related to achievement in these areas. Will they not now go forward with further analyses? Perhaps the reviewer may use this occasion to suggest the need for an integrated approach to the discovery of differences in ability to learn a foreign language. Instead of suggesting a test such as the MLAT as a *better* test than an intelligence test, for example, we should try to see how various tests fit together to give us the information which we need. Nor should we be satisfied by prediction coefficients, which express only the relation between a pretest and

Modern Language Aptitude Test

a measure of actual performance. We need also to explore what students *can* do, what abilities they have for language learning. This is not at all the same as predicting what they *will* accomplish. It might even be better in prediction to start with measures already in common use, such as tests of verbal ability, and ask what additional information special aptitude tests will provide. It would please the reviewer to have the emphasis shift from prediction to an analysis and measurement of the abilities which constitute aptitude for a foreign language—or perhaps better for any language. In such a shift of attention from prediction to abilities, from *will* to *can,* we must be prepared for longer measuring instruments and more time for using them. Measurement must not rob the student of time to learn, to be sure, but the analysis which we need will take more time than the 30 or even 70 minutes which "practical" considerations are forcing upon testing. There is a long history of attempts to discover the nature of aptitude for foreign language and to construct useful measures. The MLAT and the research out of which it grew are a significant contribution to the solution of this problem. The reviewer commends both to the careful attention of those who need a measuring instrument and of those who are interested in the general problem.

[Other Tests]
For tests not listed above, see the following entries in *Tests in Print:* 615 and 616.

ENGLISH

[358]
*English Usage Test for Non-Native Speakers of English. Non-native speakers of English; 1955-62; Forms A ['55, 8 pages], B ['57, 11 pages], C ['58, 11 pages], D ['60, 11 pages], E ['61, 7 pages], F ('62, 8 pages); directions sheets (2 pages): Forms A ['55], B–D ['60], E ['61], F ('62); reliability data for Form D only; distribution of Forms B–F restricted to the Agency for International Development or the Bureau of Educational and Cultural Affairs of the U.S. Department of State; distribution of Form A restricted to the Department of State; separate self-scoring answer sheets must be used; 60(65) minutes for Forms A, E, and F, 75(80) minutes for Forms B–D; A. L. Davis (A–C), Kenneth Croft (A–C), Harry Freeman (C), David P. Harris (D–F), Winifred E. Jones (D), and Leslie A. Palmer (F); American Language Institute. *

[359]
*Listening Test for Students of English as a Second Language. Non-native speakers of English; 1961-62; administered orally or by tape recording;

Forms A ('61), B ('62), (7 pages); examiner's booklets: Forms A ('61), B ('62), (10 pages); distribution restricted to the Agency for International Development or the Bureau of Educational and Cultural Affairs of the U.S. Department of State; separate self-scoring answer sheets must be used; [25] minutes; David P. Harris and Leslie A. Palmer; American Language Institute. *

[360]
*Michigan Test of English Language Proficiency. Applicants from non-English language countries for admission to American colleges; 1961-62; Form A ('61, 15 pages); manual ('62, 15 pages); separate answer sheets must be used; $9 per 20 tests, 100 answer sheets, key, and manual; $2 per specimen set; postpaid; 75(90) minutes; test by John Upshur, Leslie Palmer, John Harris, and Geraldine May; manual by Division of Testing and Certification, English Language Institute, University of Michigan; distributed for the Institute by Follett's Michigan Book Store, Inc. *

JOHN B. CARROLL, *Professor of Educational Psychology, Harvard University, Cambridge, Massachusetts.*

The test under review is only a part of a larger battery designed to estimate "whether a student whose native language is not English is able to pursue academic study in an English language college or university, and how much study he might be able to undertake at his present level of proficiency in English." The larger battery "includes an impromptu 30 minute written composition test" and either a test of aural comprehension or an oral interview rating. What validity data are given in the manual for this test pertain more to the larger battery than to this test specifically; it is thus difficult to appraise the *Michigan Test of English Language Proficiency* separately from the battery of which it is a part. Further, there is no indication in the manual as to how the results of this test are to be used in conjunction with the other tests of the battery.

The test contains 100 objective four-choice items in three sections: 40 items on grammar, 40 items on vocabulary, and 20 items for reading comprehension. The examinee is allowed 75 minutes to complete these 100 items; the sections are not separately timed, and the manual gives no clear statement on whether the test is intended as a power or a speed test, except that it is suggested that students who adopt a wrong approach (e.g., "parsing" in the grammar section) will generally not have sufficient time for the entire test. I judge, however, that highly proficient students should be able to complete the test easily within 75 minutes. On the other hand, it is unfortunate that what may be fairly time consuming for slower students, the reading comprehension test, is put at the end of the test; some slower students may never reach it and thus never be tested for reading comprehension as such. Separate timing of sections might have yielded more meaningful scores. The authors were probably wise in not providing for separate scores on the sections since these sections are too short to be sufficiently reliable.

The items seem to have been well selected and constructed to test difficulties that non-native speakers have with English. The items in the grammar and vocabulary sections were drawn from pools of items tried out in pretests so as to give "maximal valid discrimination"—of what, we are not told, though it was probably the total score on the pretest.

The leads in the grammar items present snatches of conversation to provide a suitable context for the filling in of a missing word or phrase from the four alternatives given: a well prepared student can in many cases immediately produce the desired response without even looking for it among the alternatives, thus saving time. One infers from the manual that the authors carefully decided upon an outline for the grammar section that would specify 16 items on verb forms, 11 on "function words" excluding verb auxiliaries, 8 on nominal structures, and 5 on modification structures. The function word items actually test what some would call vocabulary, e.g., the meaning of the word *otherwise,* and one suspects also a component of general reasoning ability in many of these items. For example, a kind of reasoning may be involved in deciding whether to fill in *otherwise* or *anyway* in the following context: "We have been waiting for you for over an hour." "The traffic was very heavy; ———— I would have been here 50 minutes sooner."

The vocabulary items are of two kinds: (*a*) a "selection" type where the examinee chooses one of four alternatives to fill in a blank in a sentence; and (*b*) a "substitution type" in which the examinee selects a synonym or substitute for an underlined word. The manual states that 30 of the 40 items test words in the range of the 4,000 to 6,000 most common words of the Thorndike-Lorge general word count. Some of the words appear to be rather literary, or specialized in application, e.g., *spouse, fettered, prune* (trees), but in view of the broad range of disciplines to which university students are exposed perhaps this catholicity is necessary. The fact is that it is difficult to test vocabulary at all adequately with a test of only 40 items.

The reading comprehension section contains four paragraphs of 139 to 217 words in length, each followed by five items. The items require rather close reading and careful interpretation of the passages, more or less on the style of the reading comprehension sections of the CEEB *Scholastic Aptitude Test* except that these passages are shorter. Here again, intellectual verbal ability is probably measured fully as much as proficiency in English; this is excusable only on the supposition that foreign students would be all of high intelligence if tested in their native language. A virtue of these items, however, is that they cannot be answered on the basis of general information or reasoning: answering them requires one to read the passages.

The test is well printed and contains no typographical errors. The special answer sheet seemed to me a bit crowded, however, and I could imagine some foreign students making merely clerical errors in indicating answers. On the other hand, provisions have been made to permit induction of the student into the process of test taking: the manual presents a sample test and answer sheet which the user may reproduce and give to students in advance. Template scoring of the answer sheets is about as easy and efficient as hand scoring can be.

The normative data are not as complete as one might expect. For example, even though the test is reported to have been administered to 284 foreign students at two midwest universities, the only data on this norming consist of a table for translating the test scores to scores on the *Test of Aural Comprehension* (see 5:261), Form A, also given to these students. Thus, no frequency distribution or table of percentiles is presented in the manual. In another section of the manual, under the heading of reliability, we are told that for a group of 300 students with 10 "unrelated" language backgrounds and constituting a random selection of applicants to 150 American universities, the mean raw score was 75.35 (maximum = 100, chance-level score = 25) with a standard deviation of 12.77. Split-half reliability for this group is reported as .965 (no indication is given as to whether it was "stepped up" in the usual way), with a resulting standard error of measurement of 3.35. A standard error of measurement of 3.54 was reported for another, somewhat more homogeneous group. Reliability of the test thus appears to be up to usual standards, although the standard error of measurement is actually a bit too large to inspire confidence in placements based on the test.

This latter statement is made in the light of the suggestions offered in the manual regarding the interpretations of the scores after they have been transformed into scores equated to the aural comprehension test. For example, depending upon which of the following score ranges the equated score lies in—96–100, 90–95, 85–89, 80–84, 70–79, or 69 and below—different recommendations are made with regard to the kind of academic load the student can bear and the further English language training the student should take. For example, if the student is to be an undergraduate in liberal arts or education and makes an equated score between 85 and 89, he "may take up to ¾ the normal academic load plus a special course (4 hrs. per week) in English as a foreign language." The fact that such a score band is not much greater than *one* standard error of measurement raises a question as to the appropriateness of such precise recommendations in individual cases, even if these recommendations were backed up by sound validity data. The authors report that at the University of Michigan, the recommendations of the English Language Institute, based presumably not only on the test under review, but also on other parts of the proficiency battery, have been regularly followed in selecting and placing students. They report further that "there have been too few cases in which recommendations have been waived to allow a meaningful determination of the efficiency of the test as a predictor of academic success." This is not an adequate excuse for failing to report some kind of follow-up data on the actual academic success of students placed in the various categories of recommendation. For example, how many students placed in the highest category ("Can compete with native speakers of English on equal or nearly equal terms—no restrictions need be placed on elections") did in fact appear to be able to compete with native speakers of English? Instead, the only predictive validity data reported in

the manual are a series of correlations between *battery* scores and academic success (average grades) in six different programs of the university, obtained at a time when student placement was not based upon English Language Institute recommendations. These correlations, ranging from .26 to .77, are uninterpretable because no means and standard deviations are given; i.e., one cannot judge the degree to which the various groups may have been selected. Also, there is no way of separating the validity of the test as a measure of *English proficiency* from its validity as a predictor of *academic success*. Of course, it can be argued that a battery whose purpose is described in such ambiguous terms as that of "estimating whether a student whose native language is not English is able to pursue academic study in an English language college or university" perhaps needs to contain both elements specifically valid for measuring English language proficiency and elements specifically valid for predicting academic success. If so, the test under review can be indicted both on the count that it fails to differentiate these two aspects of validity and on the count that it appears to emphasize the measurement of English proficiency over the prediction of academic success.

Despite the fact that the research underpinnings for recommendations based on the test are somewhat weak, this is a generally well constructed test and if the user acquires experience in interpreting scores it could help in selecting and placing non-English speaking foreign students. It must be recognized that the test under review is solely a written test; an assiduous student of English grammar books could easily get a high score on it even though he lacked the degree of facility in speaking and understanding English that would be prerequisite for succeeding in an English-speaking college or university. It would be dangerous to use this test as a sole predictor.

[361]

★Oral Rating Form for Rating Language Proficiency in Speaking and Understanding English. Non-native speakers of English; 1959–62; also called *AULC Interview Rating Form*; 6 ratings by interviewers: comprehension, pronunciation, grammar and word-order, vocabulary, general speed of speech and sentence length, total; individual; 1 form ('62, 2 pages, identical with form published in 1959 except for title and some wording changes); manual ('60, 11 pages); no data on reliability; distribution restricted to the Agency for International Development and the Bureau of Educational and Cultural Affairs of the U.S. Department of State; (15–30) minutes; [David P. Harris]; American Language Institute. *

[362]

★Test of Aural Perception in English for Japanese Students. Japanese students in American colleges; 1950; for research use only; orally administered; 1 form; manual (18 pages, including examiner's script); no data on reliability; no norms; separate answer sheets must be used; $4 per 100 answer sheets; $1.50 per set of manual and scoring stencil; postpaid; [30] minutes; Robert Lado and R. D. Andrade; distributed for English Language Institute, University of Michigan by Follett's Michigan Book Store, Inc. *

[363]

★A Vocabulary and Reading Test for Students of English as a Second Language, Revised Edition. Non-native speakers of English; 1960–62; Forms A ('61), VR-B ('62), (11 pages); directions sheets: Form A ['60, 2 pages], Form VR-B ('62, 2 pages); no data on reliability of revised edition; distribution restricted to the Agency for International Development and the Bureau of Educational and Cultural Affairs of the U.S. Department of State; separate answer sheets must be used; 60(65) minutes; David P. Harris and Leslie A. Palmer (VR-B); American Language Institute. *

[Other Tests]

For tests not listed above, see the following entries in *Tests in Print*: 619–22, 624, 626, and 628.

FRENCH

[364]

★Baltimore County French Test. 1 year high school; 1962; 2 scores: parts A, B; administered orally or by tape recording in part; IBM; 1 form (10 pages); manual (9 pages); no data on reliability; separate answer sheets must be used; $3.75 per 35 tests; $1.75 per 35 IBM answer sheets; 25¢ per scoring stencil; 50¢ per specimen set; $7.50 per 3¾ ips tape recording; postage extra; 80(90) minutes in 2 sessions; Baltimore County French Language Committee; Bobbs-Merrill Co., Inc. *

REFERENCES

1. JUNGEBLUT, ANN. "Experimentation With Baltimore County French Test in Independent Schools." *Ed Rec B* 84:67–71 Jl '63. *

NELSON BROOKS, *Associate Professor of French, Yale University, New Haven, Connecticut.*

This test is designed for use at the end of the first year's study of French in junior and senior high schools. It was planned, the authors say, to satisfy a new need resulting from a shift from a reading approach to a listening and speaking approach.

It is divided into two parts, Part A with 90 items and Part B with 50 items. Each part can be given in a single class period not less than 43 minutes long. In Part A, the first 60

items are done entirely with paper and pencil while the last 30 items involve a spoken stimulus only (these are true-false items, and no reading of response is necessary). In Part B a spoken stimulus is involved in every item, the response being printed and also read aloud. All the spoken parts have been recorded on one continuous tape prepared to accompany the test. A complete script is also provided in case the teacher wishes not to use tape but to give the spoken stimuli by live voice.

About a test with this new orientation we must ask certain key questions: What is the role of the different skills? What is the role of English? What is the role of translation? What is the relative emphasis placed upon structure and upon vocabulary? In this test only the receptive skills are brought into play; nothing is either said or written by the student. What we have, then, is a test of reading and listening. The reading of French is involved in 95 items. Listening comprehension is involved, more or less importantly, in 80 of them. English is an integral part of about a third of the items in Part A (15 items on culture are entirely in English). There is no English in the items of Part B. At no point is the candidate asked to translate, but there are 15 grammar items in which English sentences are translated into French except for a word or expression. In less than 20 per cent of the items is the focus upon problems of structure; in all the others it is a matter of vocabulary, idiom, and overall comprehension.

The items in which certain parts are spoken present a complicated pattern of listening alone and listening-plus-reading. In the 30 true-false items in Part A, there is merely the hearing of a statement, repeated once, on the basis of which it is deemed true or false. In Part B, in the first 42 items, the stimulus is heard but not seen, while the response is both heard and seen. For the final 8 items of Part B, the passage and the alternative answers to the questions are both heard and seen, while the questions are heard but not seen. Throughout the test, everything that is spoken is repeated, with the exception of the text of the brief story at the end of Part B, which is heard only once.

The tape that accompanies the test uses an American voice for English instructions and native speakers for the parts that are in French. The French voices are of good quality and are recorded clearly. The directing of the recording of these voices, however, was faulty. The speed of speech is not satisfactory, being almost uniformly too slow—so much so that at times the language is actually deformed Sometimes the French voices say English words, with quaint results. The word "number" is repeated over and over again, through dozens of items, to no purpose. With respect to speed, the American voice reading the instructions in English presents a good example of what should have been done in French.

Forty items in the test involve a true-false choice. This is regrettable because of the limited value of true-false items unless their number is considerably greater than it is here. One must admit that a candidate may know nothing whatever about a subject and still score 50 per cent when multiple-choice provides only two possible answers and, as in the case of this test, there is no correction for guessing. Though useful as a class exercise, the true-false technique has not proved satisfactory for the formal measurement of language learning.

In the overemphasis upon meaning and the lack of emphasis upon control of structure we find the most disappointing aspect of this test, an aspect which reveals the strong influence of the popular fallacy that a language is its vocabulary. The heart of a language is its sound system and its systems of order and form; these are what should receive major emphasis during the first levels of learning. In this test the student needs to know a few verb forms, a little about the forms of adjectives, and some uses of the partitive. But there is no reference at all to matters of pronoun substitution, to forms of negation and interrogation, or to comparison—to say nothing of face-to-face exchange between speaker and hearer as reflected in utterance and rejoinder. All these should be introduced very early in any basic course, and all lend themselves very readily to testing.

The authors have shown imagination and initiative in presenting an interesting variety of item types. It would be equally welcome if the content of the language referred more often than it does to something beyond the horizons of the classroom and the childlike preoccupations of the elementary school.

All will admit the extreme difficulty of preparing a standardized test for use at the end of the first year of work at the secondary level, for the patent reason that there is no widespread professional agreement on appropriate materials. The idea of the test attempted here is excellent; it is almost doomed to failure from the start because of the variety of curricular content appearing in various schools. If, as the authors imply on page 4 of the Teacher's Manual, the prospective user's students have been learning what the students in Baltimore County have been learning, the test will measure reasonably well.

MARY E. TURNBULL, *Formerly Head of Test Production, Educational Testing Service, Princeton, New Jersey.*

The *Baltimore County French Test* is a good achievement test which should be particularly useful at the end of a first-year French course or at the beginning of a second-year course, when its use could show the teacher the strengths and weaknesses of the class.

The test consists of Part A and Part B, each designed as a 40-minute test. Part A, the more varied, is divided into Part 1, Vocabulary (7 minutes), Part 2, Reading (6 minutes), Part 3, Culture (5 minutes), Part 4, Grammar (7 minutes), and Part 5, Aural Comprehension (15 minutes). This is not a speed test and, except for Part 5, students may go on to each part before time for the previous part has been called. Part B is an aural test, which students accustomed to a reading approach to French will probably find very difficult. Like Part 5 of Part A, it is recorded on a tape; alternatively, the examiner's voice may be substituted for the taped voices. Part B consists of three sections—30 French questions or incomplete sentences, 12 short French paragraphs, each describing an object that must be identified, and 8 French questions based on a short story that is read to the student and is also printed in the test book. Each of the 50 items of Part B has three given choices that are read to the student and are also printed in the test book.

The vocabulary section is made up of easy English-to-French items and French sentence completions. Mainly nouns and verbs are tested. Item 9, which includes "Sur *sa* tête," exposes the student to somewhat poor French. The reading section has 10 true-false French statements and two interesting short French paragraphs that are followed by questions based on them. One (item 26) of the questions could be answered without regard to the paragraph.

The culture section has 15 five-choice items in English; here the emphasis is mainly on points of interest in Paris and on French geography. To answer six of the questions the student must refer to a map of France in his test book. The map is well done except for a slight flaw—the letter C on the map could easily be mistaken for a G and C is the correct answer to item 42. If the order of the letter choices in this section had been alphabetical, selection of the desired answer might have been easier.

The grammar section tests mainly verb forms, although there are some questions on agreement of adjectives. In each item an incomplete French translation of a given English sentence is to be completed. Item 51 might be better placed in the vocabulary part and although choice 4 is given as the correct answer for item 52, a good argument could be made for choice 3.

The aural comprehension section is composed of 30 true-false French statements. On the tape these are read slowly and clearly; each statement is read twice, there are well timed pauses between each, and the item numbers are clearly indicated so that the student should have no difficulty recording his answers beside the correct item numbers.

Part B has good variety in the kinds of questions asked and should prove interesting to the student. The recording is excellent and shows much care in preparation and delivery. Again the student is exposed to rather awkward French in a couple of items (25 and 33), but, in general, this part is of high quality. For those who do not use the tape, the statements, questions and answers, and short story and its questions and answers are printed in the Teacher's Manual and are to be read by the examiner. Having more choice 2's as correct answers would give a better balance in correct answer-choice distribution in this part.

The printing and proofreading of the test book and of the Teacher's Manual have been very carefully done, except for the misplacement of two lines in column 2 of the first page of the manual.

One answer sheet can be used for both Parts A and B; however, it may be difficult to use only one for both parts if they are administered at different times. In the directions for scoring the test the scorer is told to record the score "in the box on the answer sheet after 'Total,'" but there is no "Total" box on the answer sheet.

The purpose of the test is clearly stated in the manual and a concise description of it is also given there. No attempt has been made at oral testing. The test's validity has not been measured nor are there any data on reliability. Phi coefficients have been computed for all the test items and a distribution of these is given in the manual. Separate percentile tables for Part A and Part B are given, based on 4,078 first-year French students in Baltimore County in 1960 and 1961.

One of the great assets of the *Baltimore County French Test* is the tape recording which is used for the last section of Part A and for the whole of Part B. This is particularly well done and should be very useful in schools where a listening and speaking approach to French is stressed.

[365]

★**Canadian Achievement Test in French (CATF).** Grade 10; 1961–63; this test and tests 5, 252, 565, and 566 make up the *Canadian Test Battery,* grade 10; 1 form ('61, 8 pages); 2 editions of manual (for use also with test 252): hand scoring ('63, 7 pages), machine scoring ('63, 8 pages); supplementary data ('63, 6 pages) for the battery; battery profile ('63, 1 page); separate answer sheets or cards must be used; $1.25 per 25 tests; $1 per set of 50 hand scoring answer sheets and hand scoring manual; 20¢ per hand scoring stencil; 20¢ per 15 battery profiles; 50¢ per set of 25 IBM answer cards (machine scoring through the Department of Educational Research only); 10¢ per machine scoring manual; 50¢ per specimen set; $2.15 per battery specimen set; postage extra; 60(70–75) minutes; Department of Educational Research, Ontario College of Education, University of Toronto; distributed by Guidance Centre (machine scoring manual and answer cards must be purchased from the Department of Educational Research). *

REFERENCES
1. D'OYLEY, VINCENT R. *Technical Manual for the Canadian Tests: Statistical Data on the Carnegie Study Tests of Academic Aptitude and Achievement in Grades 8, 9, and 10 in Ontario Schools and Grades 7 and 8 in Toronto Schools.* Carnegie Study of Identification and Utilization of Talent in High School and College, Bulletin No. 4. Toronto, Canada: Department of Educational Research, Ontario College of Education, University of Toronto, 1964. Pp. viii, 50. *
2. D'OYLEY, VINCENT R. *Testing: The First Two Years of the Carnegie Study 1959 to 1961: Analysis of Scores by Course, Sex, and Size of Municipality.* Carnegie Study of Identification and Utilization of Talent in High School and College, Bulletin No. 6. Toronto, Canada: Department of Educational Research, Ontario College of Education, University of Toronto, 1964. Pp. ix, 53. *

MARY E. TURNBULL, *Formerly Head of Test Production, Educational Testing Service, Princeton, New Jersey.*

The *Canadian Achievement Test in French* is a very good one-hour test for grade 10 students, consisting of four parts, not separately timed: 1, Vocabulary (35 items); 2, Grammar (45 items); 3, Comprehension (10 items); and 4, Pronunciation (12 items).

The test is accurately and attractively printed, the directions are clear, and it contains a good variety of questions. In almost all cases, the given choices are excellent, with many logical distractors included.

The first three parts are broken down into a number of short groups of questions—English to French, French to English, French sentence completion, French synonyms, French antonyms, etc.—a nice selection of slightly differing problems which should hold the students' interest and avoid monotony. Within the groups the questions seem usually to be in ascending order of difficulty.

Part 1, Vocabulary, concentrates mainly on nouns, verbs, and adjectives, whereas Part 2, Grammar, tests a good selection of verb forms, pronouns, adjectives, and prepositions. Part 3, Comprehension, contains three short and interesting paragraphs, each of which is followed by two good multiple choice questions. Part 4, Pronunciation, briefly tests words with the same pronunciation, underlined sounds, pronounced final consonants, silent consonants, and nasal vowels. No attempt has been made at aural testing.

In three groups of items where the sentences to be completed follow the given choices, having the sentences printed before the choices would probably assist the test taker. Two items (45 and 48) in the grammar part seem more appropriately classified as tests of vocabulary. The last group in the grammar part contains only two items, one of which (80) tests the same form of the same verb that has already been tested in item 43. The alert student will find the answer to item 54 given in item 33, and item 50 will tell him the answer to item 3, while item 81, in turn, will give him the answer to item 50.

The manuals tell of the development of the test, give clear and concise directions for administration, and include an answer key and percentile rank norms based on 42,264 grade 10 French students. A profile norm chart is available for the six tests in the *Canadian Test Battery* for grade 10, of which this test is one. An item analysis of this test and computation of validity coefficients between the grade 10 school French mark and the *Canadian Achievement Test in French* are in process of completion and reports on the findings will be available soon.[1]

This is an excellent French test covering a wide range of the different aspects of the mastery of the French language. It deserves widespread use and most students should almost enjoy taking it.

[366]

*College Entrance Examination Board Achievement Test: French.** Candidates for college entrance with 2–4 years high school French; 1901–64; for more complete information, see 760; 60(80) minutes; program administered for the College Entrance Examination Board by Educational Testing Service. *

REFERENCES

1–7. See 4:237.
8–9. See 5:263.
10. BLACK, D. B. "A Comparison of the Performance on Selected Standardized Tests to That on the Alberta Grade XII Departmental Examination of a Select Group of University of Alberta Freshmen." *Alberta J Ed Res* 5:180–90 S '59. * (*PA* 34:6559)
11. CABAT, LOUIS, AND GODIN, JACOB D. *How to Prepare for College Board Achievement Tests in French.* Great Neck, N.Y.: Barron's Educational Series, Inc., 1960. Pp. vi, 110. *
12. BRÉE, GERMAINE. "College Board French Tests." *French R* 36:119–24 D '62. *
13. SCHEIDER, ROSE M. "Evolution of the Listening Comprehension Tests." *Col Board R* 48:24–8 f '62. *

For a review by Walter V. Kaulfers of earlier forms, see 4:237. For reviews of the testing program, see 760.

[367]

★*College Entrance Examination Board Achievement Test: French Listening Comprehension.* Candidates for college entrance with 2–4 years high school French; 1960–63; tests administered at the local secondary school on a specified date in February; candidates must also be registered to take one or more achievement tests in one of the regular program administrations; for more complete information, see 760; (30–40) minutes; program administered for the College Entrance Examination Board by Educational Testing Service. *

For reviews of the testing program, see 760.

[368]

*College Entrance Examination Board Advanced Placement Examination: French.** High school students desiring credit for college level courses or admission to advanced courses; 1954–63; for more complete information, see 761; 180(200) minutes; program administered for the College Entrance Examination Board by Educational Testing Service. *

REFERENCES

1. VALLEY, JOHN R. "College Actions on CEEB Advanced Placement Language Examination Candidates." *Mod Lang J* 43:261–3 O '59. *

1 The supplementary data referred to in the entry above became available after this review was completed.—Editor.

2. NIESS, ROBERT J. "The Advanced Placement Program in French." *French R* 35:311–8 Ja '62. *
3. NELSON, ROBERT J. "The Relation of Language to Literature in the Advanced Placement Program." *French R* 36:617–28 My '63. *

[369]

★**College Entrance Examination Board Placement Tests: French Listening Comprehension Test.** Entering college freshmen; 1962–63, c1955–61; IBM; Forms DLC1, DLC2 in a single booklet ('55), KPL1, KPL2 in a single booklet (c1960–61, 11 pages, a reprint of inactive forms of *College Entrance Examination Board Achievement Test: French Listening Comprehension*); test administered by 7½ ips tape recording; for more complete information, see 759; 30(40) minutes; program administered for the College Entrance Examination Board by Educational Testing Service. *

[370]

★**College Entrance Examination Board Placement Tests: French Reading Test.** Entering college freshmen; 1962–63, c1955–63; IBM; Forms KPL1, KPL2 in a single booklet (c1955–57, 22 pages, a reprint of inactive forms of *College Entrance Examination Board Achievement Test: French*); for more complete information, see 759; 60(70) minutes; program administered for the College Entrance Examination Board by Educational Testing Service. *

For a review of the College Entrance Examination Board Achievement Test: French, *see 4:237.*

[371]

★**Common Concepts Foreign Language Test: French [Research Edition].** "Students [in any grade] who have had enough foreign language instruction to place them at the Level 1 stage in their achievement"; 1962–64; aural comprehension; may be administered using live voice but tape recording is recommended; IBM; Forms 1, 2; a single booklet ('62, 31 pages) presents response options for both forms of this test and the German and Spanish tests of the series; mimeographed preliminary manual ('64, 24 pages); interim norms (grades 7–12 only); separate answer sheets or cards must be used; 75¢ per test; $5.95 per 3¾ ips tape recording; 5¢ per IBM answer sheet; 20¢ per scoring stencil; 2¢ per Cal-Card; 20¢ per hand scoring stencil; 15¢ per manual; postage extra; $1 per specimen set without tape; $6.95 per specimen set with tape; postpaid; scoring service available; (40–45) minutes; Bela H. Banathy, Miles V. Zintz, W. James Popham, Joseph M. Sadnavitch, Rena Krichbaum, Fred B. Gannon, Valdemar Hempel, and Klaus A. Mueller; California Test Bureau. *

[372]

★**Ford-Hicks French Grammar Completion Tests.** High school; 1944; variously titled; Forms A, B, C, D, ['44, 4 pages]; manual ['44, 4 pages]; $1 per 12 tests; 10¢ per single copy; $1 per set of key and manual; postpaid; 35(40) minutes; H. E. Ford and R. K. Hicks; J. M. Dent & Sons (Canada) Ltd. *

[373]

*★French I and II: Minnesota High School Achievement Examinations.** 1 or 2 years high school; 1953–63; series formerly called *Midwest High School Achievement Examinations;* new norms issued each June; Form F ('60, 6 pages, originally called

Form C) used in 1963 testing; no specific manual; series manual ('63, 4 pages); series norms ['63, 4 pages]; series cumulative profile ('62, 2 pages); no data on reliability; no description of normative population; 12¢ per test; $2.50 per 100 profiles; postage extra; 20¢ per specimen set, postpaid; 60(65) minutes; American Guidance Service, Inc. *

For a review by Mary E. Turnbull of earlier forms, see 5:268.

[374]

French: Teacher Education Examination Program. College seniors preparing to teach secondary school; 1957; for more complete information, see 709; IBM; 80(95) minutes; Educational Testing Service. *

For a review of the testing program, see 5:543.

[375]

★**French Test (Two-Year Course): Affiliation Testing Program for Catholic Secondary Schools.** Grades 10–12 and students who are candidates for the high school diploma issued by the Catholic University of America; 1949–63; administered annually in May at individual schools; IBM; new form issued annually; Form Z ('63, 13 pages) used in 1963 program; separate answer sheets must be used; 50¢ per test and IBM answer sheet, postpaid; specimen set of the complete battery free; fee includes purchase of test booklets, scoring, and other services; for more complete information, see 758; 90(100) minutes; Program of Affiliation, Catholic University of America. *

HENRY CHAUNCEY, *President, Educational Testing Service, Princeton, New Jersey.* [Review of Forms Y and Z.]

The French test of the Affiliation Testing Program appears to be well suited for the two years of French it is designed to test.

Those areas of foreign language learning that can be tested by multiple choice questions (listening comprehension, reading comprehension, vocabulary, structure, and cultural background) are all covered by easy to difficult questions appropriate to two-year programs. However, the practice of having the proctor read the listening comprehension passages and questions hardly provides for standardized administration of this part of the test. In this age of widespread use of tape recorders, it would seem that a tape might well be used to provide more uniform testing conditions and thereby achieve greater reliability.

Instructions for taking the test are quite clear and understandable. The practice of using an English translation of the stem of sample items in describing the best answer for each sample question in Form Z is questionable.

This technique leads to statements such as: "The opposite of 'large' is *petit.*" Actually, of course, the opposite of large is small; petit is the opposite of grand. If it is felt necessary to indicate the English meaning of the stem, it might be preferable to say: "The opposite of 'grand' (large) is *petit.*"

Students should be able to finish the test in the allotted time, provided the proctor does not use more than the time specified for the listening comprehension part. The approximate time is indicated for the listening test, but no specific time is indicated for the remainder of the test; time allotments should be indicated for both these sections of the test, so that they will not vary from administration to administration. This, incidentally, is another reason why it might be wiser to tape the listening comprehension portion of the test.

The items are generally well written. Occasionally a nonexistent form is given as a distractor, for example, Form Y, item 53 (option 1); Form Z, items 22 (option 3), 23 (options 2, 3, 4), and 29 (option 2). This practice is questionable.

The test as a whole is well organized, well written, and well presented. A good balance of items in the various areas tested is provided. The avoidance of the use of English as a testing device is commendable.

For a review of the complete program, see 758.

[376]

The Graduate Record Examinations Advanced Tests: French. Grades 16–17; 1939–63; for more complete information, see 762; 180(200) minutes; Educational Testing Service. *

NELSON BROOKS, *Associate Professor of French, Yale University, New Haven, Connecticut.* [Review of Form K-GGR.]

The preparation of a multiple choice test to estimate a student's fitness for advanced work in cultural and literary studies in the field of French is no mean task. These are times in which successful candidates are likely to pursue their studies under the direction of faculty members, many of whom are made queasy at the very thought of measurement and selection by multiple choice tests, and one cannot deny that these test authors faced a serious challenge. Yet they have met this challenge with resourcefulness and aplomb, and have produced an instrument that does what it sets out

to do with thoroughness and distinction. Apart from a few flaws—only one of them serious—this test could well stand as an eloquent rebuttal to those who look upon this kind of measurement as intellectual heresy. From beginning to end, it requires just the kind of perception, knowledge, and range of acquaintance that the candidate had better be in possession of if he hopes to flourish in graduate school courses in this field.

The test is composed of 200 items, each with five proposed choices. There are in all nine separate (but continuously timed) sections of the test, each with its own set of directions. These directions are in English. There is no English in any of the items themselves. In three sections there are quoted passages of some length, each with a sequence of statements or questions based upon it. Five other sections ask for knowledge of general cultural and historical background, of literary vocabulary, of titles and characters famous in literature, of wide-ranging and detailed knowledge of literary history from medieval to modern. One section asks for the interpretation of a number of brief unidentified quotations. These nine sections are arranged in such a way as to vary the candidate's task from time to time, interspersing groups of self-contained items with other groups dealing with given texts. A few of the self-contained items deal with short quotations, but most of them refer only to knowledge the candidate is expected to possess. Some items deal with morphology, stylistics, and poetics, others with literary schools and salons. Still others present questions concerning the overall comprehension of quoted passages, the precise meaning of words and lines, and language change. The substance of the items differs widely, from acquaintance with the notions of important philosophies to the present day use of a written accent; all are germane to problems the student is sure to encounter in advanced studies.

The items themselves are of three varieties: (*a*) a question plus five answers, (*b*) a stem plus five completions, and (*c*) a word matched with one of five other words. In three sections of the test, only the last named variety appears. In the remaining sections the first two are intermixed at random.

In four of the nine sections the directions are adequate to describe the task that is set, in five sections they are not. The point at issue is the terminology "questions and answers" used to apply to items that are not question-and-answer but stem-and-completion. In one section this problem is handled with wording that is fully satisfactory; the same could easily have been true of the others. To mention this minor detail in the giving of directions may seem close to quibbling, yet a test of this kind sets up a situation in which the candidate must sensitize himself to preciseness and minute discrimination, and it is disturbing to him when laxness and inadequacy are apparent in the English that is telling him what to do. A test that is so well written, so important, and so widely used deserves better editing and printing. Not only should the directions be more accurately related to the nature of the items, but the page layout could be greatly improved, especially in the separation of one item from another. In some of the self-contained items that are preceded by a short quotation it looks at first, because of the way in which the item numbers are printed, as if this quotation belonged to the preceding item. Furthermore, the sections themselves are not clearly marked off. For psychological reasons, it would be better to make the candidate fully aware of the various phases and the change of pace in the questioning to which he is being subjected.

The wrongness of the wrong choice (in some cases the right one) is a basic problem in all tests of this kind. For the most part, the authors have handled this difficult matter in a fully commendable way, and it is regrettable that they did not do so all the way through. In most of the items the candidate is asked to *accept* one choice out of five, but in some cases he is to *reject* one out of five. It is in some of these last that the authors have left themselves open to criticism on this score. When wrongness is the result of a beginning and ending not fitting together, or of a statement, correct in itself, not being attributed to the appropriate author, we are within legitimate bounds. But when the wrongness of what is suggested appears only in the completion proper and results in the printing of statements that are incorrect or untrue, we have crossed a frontier that is of extreme importance in multiple choice testing. We are then in very deep water, and are involved with the philosophical distinction between term and proposition, with problems of learning psy-

chology, and above all with matters of professional principles. It is well known that the multiple choice technique has been shamefully cheapened in foreign language tests by offering in the printed choices examples of incorrect spelling, incorrect agreements, incorrect word order, and faulty meaning—the wrongness not being the result of appropriate terms wrongly fitted together into unsatisfactory propositions, but being an integral part of terms that are themselves spurious. In this test there are eight items in which the wrongness is exclusively in the completion. Seven of these present definitions or attributions rather loosely related, and, though suspect, they can be said to do little more than reflect the internal processes of fitting and matching that characterize this kind of test—though the inner processes of language behavior and the actuality of printing are of vastly different levels of reality. But one item contains in one of its completions a full-fledged sentence that is flatly inexact (it is, of course, the right answer). To have presented these eight items, and especially this last, is a regrettable lapse in what is otherwise an exemplary series of multiple choice items. The presence of these dubious items is not likely to affect the performance of the test as a discriminating instrument; statistical accuracy is not jeopardized. But *noblesse oblige.* Many of those who take this graduate school test will themselves be making tests for students, and before very long. And in their inexperienced and less capable hands, items containing the wrongness of the sort concerning us here can easily lead to poor measurement and to the further compromise of a test technique that is already in hazard. The introduction into such tests of completion elements that are *in themselves* wrong is tantamount to the intrusion into a jigsaw puzzle of pieces that do not fit into the puzzle in question, nor, for that matter, into any other. Professional scruples would appear to demand that problems of this degree of falsity be eschewed.

The student who takes this test is asked to deal with a total field of impressive proportions. He must be able to envisage vast areas in perspective, he must have a wide acquaintance with important persons and ideas, with literary history and with literary works in different forms, with significant cultural, historical, and geographical facts, and with memorable characters in fiction. He must time and again look closely at examples of literary art and report with accuracy on what he reads in the lines themselves and between the lines. And, happily, he is asked not only to display a knowledge acquired before presenting himself for the test, but also to call upon his command of language, his acquaintance with literature, and his own perceptive sensibilities to carry on constructive processes and arrive at conclusions that to him are new. This opportunity for synthesis during the test leads not only to fully satisfactory discrimination among competing candidates, but also provides a sense of intellectual accomplishment for the candidate himself. This is testing at its best.

For a review by Walter V. Kaulfers, see 5:270. For a review of the testing program, see 5:601.

[377]

★**Graduate School Foreign Language Test: French.** Graduate level degree candidates required to demonstrate reading proficiency in French; 1963–64; Forms K-LFG1, K-LFG2, ('63, 33 pages) ; for more complete information, see 356; 80(100) minutes; Educational Testing Service. *

CLARENCE E. TURNER, *Professor of Romance Languages, Rutgers, the State University, New Brunswick, New Jersey.* [Review of Form K-LFG2.]

The test at hand is in response to a long felt need. Graduate faculties, in order that their candidates may control research material published all over the world, are accustomed to require a reading knowledge usually of two foreign languages, one of which is nearly always French. A sound standardized test in this area would permit each year on a university campus the saving (depending on the testing methods now practiced) of up to 200 faculty man-hours. It would open up the prospect of reciprocity among faculties, today usually denied. The impersonality of the procedure would probably have a good effect on graduate student morale.

The operational realities must always be borne in mind. At least half of these graduate students, and among scientists the proportion is still higher, have had little or no French in school or college. To meet the requirement, they have learned French either on their own or through a special course adapted to their case. To this they can normally devote part of a year in addition to their full program in the courses and laboratories of their discipline. Typically, they attend one French session per week, whose oral-aural element is of necessity greatly reduced or omitted altogether. The accurate translation into English of specialized material is likely to be the one language skill in which they have been well trained, and at this they are often extremely good.

Section 1 of the present test seems not to be aimed at the persons just described. On the sound premise that knowledge of the structure of French is a relevant skill, Section 1 begins with 25 discrete items which would be wholly admirable to test students with two or more years of French in a modern secondary or college classroom. These items assume ear-training, experience in the construction of French sentences, the ability to think in French, and a sense of what "is French" and what is "not French." These things are all desirable and feasible in themselves, but all are denied to many, probably most, graduate students seeking to establish a research tool. Now there are frequently recurring aspects of structure which are vital to correct translation, and here was an opportunity to test them: for example, relative *qui* and *que,* telling noun from adjective by position, *ne....que,* the force of tenses, indefinite adjectives, or connectives like *il n'en est pas ainsi* and *quoi qu'il en soit.* In short, the structure items of Section 1 in their present form lack face validity for the population, and it is not surprising to read in the accompanying test analysis booklet that Section 1 proved "quite difficult." For graduate students as I have observed them, I should think Section 1 would be bewildering and demoralizing as well.

Section 2 offers each candidate four paragraphs of French with multiple choice questions in English. The material is generally well selected and ingeniously arranged in a system permitting each student to read in his own or a closely related field. Here, where vocabulary and concepts should be familiar, was the opportunity to construct a fairly rigorous test of accurate comprehension of details. Comparatively few items, however, pinpoint a specific problem of French. More typically, the problem lies in following the tentacles of the author's speculative thought and coming up with an opinion as to the author's purpose, or as to the main drift or general idea of a passage.

Graduate Record Examinations Advanced Tests: French

Not uncommonly the correct answer is obvious independently of the text. My suspicions aroused by student comment after administration of this test, I decided to pose as a graduate student in the social sciences and take *without reading a word of French text* those portions of Section 2 that such a candidate would answer, as well as those portions of Section 1 that are based on a text. I have assured myself in this fashion of a comfortable position at the 63rd percentile. A bright graduate student with advanced training in the subject matter could, of course, have done much better, still without reading a single word of any French text.

It should be mentioned that the test is speeded. On no section did 75 per cent of the students complete the test, and on some sections barely over half completed it. Since reasonable speed of reading is by definition part of the concept of a research tool, this is not out of line with the purpose of the test except when combined with the above-mentioned emphasis on skimming for the general idea.

It would be naïve to expect a test like this to yield a direct pass or fail score, yet of course this is just the kind of conversion that a graduate dean must ultimately make. To aid him in this, the accompanying Guide to Interpretation of Scores offers scaled scores and percentile norms based on administration of the test to 1,744 subjects in 37 institutions, 243 electing the biological sciences option, 560 the humanities, and the other groups falling between those extremes. Parallel testing by some other method is recommended, and demonstration is made with imaginary statistics of how this might be useful. Whatever circumstances may have prevented the inclusion of real data from cooperating institutions, the results of such experiments would have been most welcome here, and it is to be hoped that they will be forthcoming.

To conclude, I could recommend this test to a graduate dean for his purposes only after revision of Section 1 to bring it into line with graduate students' training and experience; revision of Section 2 to bring greater emphasis to accuracy of detail and less to the general idea; and study of experimental data from parallel testing in my own institution, but hopefully also in others.

[378]

★**MLA-Cooperative Foreign Language Tests: French.** 1 or 2 years high school or 2 semesters college, 3 or 4 years high school or 4 semesters college; 1963–64; 4 tests in a single booklet: listening, speaking, reading, writing; IBM in part; 2 levels; directions for administering and scoring ['64, 39 pages] for this and the German, Italian, Russian, and Spanish tests of the series; no data on reliability; no norms; $5 per 10 tests; separate answer sheets may be used for listening and reading tests; $1 per 20 IBM scorable answer sheets; $1 per 10 scoring stencils (answer pattern must be punched out locally); $7 per 3¾ ips tape for listening test; $7 per 3¾ ips tape for speaking test (blank tapes or discs for recording student responses must be obtained locally); postage extra; $2 per specimen set, cash orders postpaid; (25–35) minutes for listening, (10–20) minutes for speaking, 35(40) minutes for reading, 35(40) minutes for writing; prepared in cooperation with the Modern Language Association of America; Cooperative Test Division. *

a) [LOWER LEVEL.] 1 or 2 years high school or 2 semesters college; form LA ('63, 23 pages).

b) [HIGHER LEVEL.] 3 or 4 years high school or 4 semesters college; form MA ('63, 25 pages).

[379]

★**MLA Foreign Language Proficiency Tests for Teachers and Advanced Students: French.** Grades 15–17 and foreign language teachers; 1961–64; IBM in part; 7 tests; 2 forms ('61): Form JML1 (also called Form A, available for institutional programs), Form JML2 (also called Form B, restricted to state and local teacher certification programs); series supervisor's manual ['62, 34 pages]; series norms leaflet ('64, 4 pages); series interpretive leaflet ('64, 4 pages); examination fees: $15 per battery of 7 tests, $12.50 per battery of 4 skill tests (listening, speaking, reading, writing); fees include rental of test materials and scoring and reporting service; postage extra; fee for 30-day examination, $3.70 per battery; Modern Language Association of America and Educational Testing Service; program administered by Educational Testing Service. *

a) LISTENING COMPREHENSION TEST: FRENCH. IBM; 2 forms ('61, 6–7 pages, containing response options only); stimulus material presented on 3¾ or 7½ ips tape; $1.50 per examinee; (20–30) minutes.

b) SPEAKING TEST: FRENCH. 2 forms ('61, 9 pages, containing scripts for all languages in the series plus a section on 3¾ or 7½ ips tape); responses recorded on tapes or records supplied by the publisher; $6.75 per examinee; (15–30) minutes.

c) READING TEST: FRENCH. IBM; 2 forms ('61, 12 pages); $1.25 per examinee; 40(50) minutes.

d) WRITING TEST: FRENCH. IBM in part; 2 forms ('61, 8 pages); $3.50 per examinee; 45(55) minutes.

e) APPLIED LINGUISTICS TEST: FRENCH. IBM; 2 forms ('61, 10 pages); $1.25 per examinee; 40(50) minutes.

f) CIVILIZATION AND CULTURE TEST: FRENCH. IBM; 2 forms ('61, 10 pages); $1.25 per examinee; 30(40) minutes.

g) PROFESSIONAL PREPARATION TEST. IBM; 2 forms ('61, 10 pages) common to all languages in the series; $1.25 per examinee; 45(55) minutes.

REFERENCES

1. STARR, WILMARTH H. "Competency First: New Tests in Foreign Languages." *Proc Inv Conf Testing Probl* 1960: 97–110 '61. *
2. STARR, WILMARTH H. "Proficiency Tests in Modern Foreign Languages." *PMLA* 76:7–11 My '61. *
3. STARR, WILMARTH H. "MLA Foreign Language Proficiency Tests for Teachers and Advanced Students." *PMLA* 77:31–42 S '62. *

PAUL PIMSLEUR, *Director, The Listening Center, The Ohio State University, Columbus, Ohio.*

The publication of this series of tests is a major event for the foreign language teaching profession. This is the first time that this subject field—perhaps any subject field—has provided a reliable standard for evaluating prospective teachers on a nationwide scale. The tests are gradually being accepted by states as a basis for certification of teacher candidates, and by teacher training institutions as a means of assessing the preparation of their graduates. By holding up the present unevenness of teacher preparation to public scrutiny, they will no doubt have a beneficial effect on the quality of foreign language teacher preparation throughout the country.

The tests were prepared by committees of foreign language teachers and so represent, in a sense, an effort of the foreign language teaching profession to test itself. The French is correct, authentic, and representative of various social levels of discourse, from colloquial to literary. The item types are, on the whole, well chosen, and the items themselves are well constructed. Within the framework of this generally favorable evaluation, a certain number of criticisms, mostly minor, may be offered:

The Reading Test intends to measure both vocabulary (15 items) and reading comprehension (35 items). However, many of the comprehension items are really vocabulary items in another form, so that in all at least 25 of the 50 items are on vocabulary. Moreover, the item writers have succumbed occasionally to the easy way out of testing oddball vocabulary (e.g., "mettre le grappin dessus"). The test could be revised to weight comprehension more heavily and to eliminate a few comprehension items which can be answered without referring to the passage at all. This test, like several others in the series, is perhaps overly long in time; it takes 40 minutes for only 50 items.

The Writing Test is a compromise with feasibility. It confines itself to such technical matters as correct use of prepositions and subject-verb agreement, making no attempt to judge spelling and punctuation, much less choice of words, variety of expression, or originality of style. On the whole, the compromise is a reasonable one, and the testmakers are to be complimented on their willingness to forsake machine scorability for the sake of validity. The 45-minute time limit seems too generous for this 60-item test.

The Listening Comprehension Test, containing 36 items, is shorter than all the rest (except Speaking, which has to be short to limit scoring time). Part 3 is probably inefficient, taking three minutes to tell a story about which only eight true-false questions are asked, four of which may be right by chance. Either this test, which takes 20 minutes, is too short, or the others, which take twice that time, are too long. Probably the latter is the case, since the publisher indicates high reliability (.91–.92) for this test. It would be desirable to shorten the tests, since it now takes over five hours to administer the whole battery. As concerns the recording, the speech is too deliberate in speed and at times is unnatural (e.g., the liaison in "demander une").

The Speaking Test is an attempt to achieve objective measurement of the speaking skill—apparently a successful one, judging by the high interscorer reliability. However, all the scoring must be done by trained judges at the company's headquarters, which raises the cost as well as the reliability. In Part B, the examinee is instructed to read aloud in "natural colloquial style, treating liaison in accord with this style of speech"; this instruction is at variance with the speech style used in the Listening Comprehension Test. In Part C, the pictures which the examinee is to describe have been badly chosen. They depend too much on his knowing a single word, or on his "getting" a rather lame visual gag. This part of the test should be revised without delay.

The Professional Preparation Test is easily the most controversial of the battery, dealing, as it does, with methodology, about which teachers heartily disagree with each other. The test reflects a "new key" orientation toward language teaching. In the best sense, it will be an incentive to language teachers to learn (and to administrators to insist that they learn) of recent developments in methodology, including the contributions of structural linguistics and educational psychology. In the worst sense, this test shows what happens when creative attempts to develop effective teaching methods evolve into matters of dogma. It measures principally whether the examinee has attended

MLA Foreign Language Proficiency Tests: French

an NDEA Institute or otherwise been exposed to this set of doctrines about methodology. Users should be aware that, despite its title, this test does not measure a teacher's classroom effectiveness. Data on 1,007 participants in 1962 Spanish Institutes yielded a correlation of only .29 between scores on the Professional Preparation Test and instructor evaluations of the individuals' professional preparation. Corresponding validity figures for the other six tests were considerably higher.

The Civilization and Culture Test will be rough going for any teacher without graduate training and residence in France. It calls for considerable familiarity with the history of France, ancient and modern, its painters, its architecture, its political organization, and its literature. This reviewer finds it overloaded with literature, politics, and fine arts, and lacking in items about contemporary French life. School administrators may find it difficult to see how a knowledge of façades of buildings and backs of chairs makes a better French teacher.

The Applied Linguistics Test, like the Professional Preparation Test and the Civilization and Culture Test, has a didactic as well as a testing function; it is meant to upgrade the foreign language teaching field and hence represents what the foreign language teacher of the future *should* know, rather than what today's teacher *does* know. These three tests are visionary, and this is good, for they will lead to improved preparation of teachers. But the user has a right to know this fact so that, for example, a principal will not think his teachers are the only ones who did badly in the tests.

The publishers are gradually gathering and presenting information on the validity of the tests and the interpretation of scores. However, the user needs much more guidance than is yet available to help him interpret what a certain score—or set of scores—means, and what predictions he can make about a candidate's probable effectiveness as a teacher. More information of this kind will no doubt be forthcoming as experience accrues with this battery. In any event, and despite whatever shortcomings they may have, the publication of this set of tests is an important milestone in the efforts of the U.S. Office of Education to assist the foreign language teaching profession in upgrading the teaching of foreign

languages throughout the country and at all educational levels.

JAMES H. RICKS, JR., *Assistant Director, Test Division, The Psychological Corporation, New York, New York.*[1]

This ambitious and, on the whole, well realized testing program is at the time of this review (spring 1964) about to pass from experimental and special-situation use to the broader practical uses which were the goal of its construction. The preliminary and developmental research shows that the tests do what the battery title claims: provide useful and reliable information on the examinee's mastery of spoken and written French. The test constructors have done their work well; what remains to be seen is whether users of the test results will manifest equal skill.

For while "advanced students" appears in the title of the battery, the project will certainly have been a failure if these tests are not widely used as a basis for certifying teachers. In fact, at least one state already accepts scores on the tests as a basis for excusing teachers who are French natives from the usual academic requirements in the language itself, and James B. Conant, in *The Education of American Teachers,*[2] after certain reservations (pp. 181–2) says, "I am ready to recommend enthusiastically to all colleges and universities training foreign language teachers that they use this proficiency test to determine who is to be certified as a teacher." There can be little doubt that the battery constitutes a genuine advance over the kind of measurement represented by the Optional Examinations in various subjects that are part of the National Teacher Examinations.

The seven tests fall into three categories. There are four tests of proficiency in the language: Listening Comprehension Test, Speaking Test, Reading Test, and Writing Test. None of these involves translation from French to English or from English to French. Two tests, the Applied Linguistics Test and the Civilization and Culture Test, are peculiar to French but are made up of questions in English designed to sample mastery of the knowledge their titles indicate. One test, the Profes-

1 In reviewing test *content*, the writer gratefully acknowledges the assistance of Professor Daniel P. Girard of Teachers College, Columbia University.
2 CONANT, JAMES B. *The Education of American Teachers.* New York: McGraw-Hill Book Co., Inc., 1963. Pp. 275.

MLA Foreign Language Proficiency Tests: French

sional Preparation Test, is common to all of the languages included in the program (Spanish, Italian, German, Russian, and French). This review will consider the seven tests together as to technical and psychometric aspects, separately as to content.

MECHANICS. The first two tests, the Listening Comprehension Test and the Speaking Test, are administered by means of tape recordings, and for the Speaking Test the examinee's responses also must be recorded (on tape or disc). With these exceptions, the entire battery consists of paper and pencil procedures.

The Speaking Test is scored in Princeton by trained scorers. Interscorer reliability (language of the test studied is not specified) is reported as .89, and considerable care has been devoted to minimizing an observed tendency for scorers to raise their standards as they gain familiarity with the material. The Writing Test consists of completion items and an interlinear editing task; interscorer reliability (again, language unspecified) for these are reported as .99 and .95, respectively. (An essay section which appeared in experimental forms was finally discarded because of unsatisfactory interscorer reliability.) The remaining tests all are multiple choice, with entirely objective scoring. Scores are converted to an arbitrary scale based on the addition of 20 points to raw score on Form JML1.

Accompanying accessory materials and directions show appropriate care for high standards of examining, as evidenced by such details as provision for reporting of irregularities that may affect performance.

STATISTICS. An inconvenience to users and prospective users arises from the fact that data are spread through a number of separate leaflets and reports. A well organized manual bringing together the scattered data should have been prepared before the tests were offered for general use. Except for a pilot study of graduating foreign language majors in a Pennsylvania state program, all data are from NDEA Institutes.

Reliability. Kuder-Richardson formula 20 coefficients are .91 or higher for three of the skill tests: reading, writing, and listening. No such coefficient was computed for the Speaking Test because there was no way to estimate the degree of halo effect resulting from the rating of every item on a response tape by a single rater; as reported above, the

interscorer coefficient obtained was .89 (even when the three parts are rated by three different scorers). The K-R 20 values for the other three tests are in the upper .80's. For the Applied Linguistics Test, which definitely is speeded, test-retest coefficients are needed but were not computed; they would be of interest also for the Reading Test and the Civilization and Culture Test which are somewhat speeded. There may be some element of speed in scores on the paced or self-timed tests, listening and speaking, but it is not possible to estimate its magnitude and not reasonable to think that it is very important. It is stated that the Writing Test is "generously timed" and this is the reviewer's impression also, but the statistics on the per cent of examinees filling the last blanks in Part A and attempting corrections in the last sentence of Part B are not reported as they are for all the other tests except listening.

Intercorrelations. Among the four skill tests, intercorrelation coefficients range from .73 (reading with speaking) to .87 (reading with writing). The other three tests are less highly correlated with each other and with the skill tests, coefficients ranging from .20 to .67, mostly between .50 and .60. For each of the four skill tests, the multiple correlation was computed to determine how well the score on each could be estimated from the scores on the other three; the resulting coefficients were .83, .85, .89, and .89.

When an examinee scores high on the Speaking Test, might not at least a reasonable competence in listening comprehension be assumed without testing? If the Writing Test score is fairly high, is the level of reading comprehension for the same examinee ever really low? These questions, which may be important for situations where limited testing time is available, are not answered or even discussed in the test analysis reports. Simple expectancy (or experience) tables could present this information usefully.

In any event, all four of the skill tests should remain in the battery, whether or not their overlap is greater than the most efficient statistical design might dictate. The specification of these areas of competence by the MLA Steering Committee will lead to use of the battery in situations where obtaining high scores on these tests will become one of the goals of language study. This places upon the battery a demand for a kind of balance and

MLA Foreign Language Proficiency Tests: French

coverage that seems well met by the present design, whatever the intercorrelations. (For the three knowledge tests, this is less certain.)

Validity. Of criteria presently available for evaluating competence in a foreign language, probably none is superior to the four skill tests in this battery, even when allowance is made for continuing argument about the choice of specific items of content. As compared with the content validity of the skill tests, the content, construct, and predictive validities of the three other tests are much harder to estimate. In the end, nothing will serve as a satisfactory criterion but some yet to be developed means of measuring the performance of good and poor teachers. The teaming up of ETS and MLA for the present project offers some hope that we may be moving nearer to such an instrument or procedure. (The concurrent validation of the test scores against faculty ratings reported in one of the studies affords only the expected reassurance that the nature and goals of the tests are well accepted by the kind of people who helped make them up.)

Norms. Percentile norms for both the pretesting and the posttesting of graduate students enrolled in NDEA Foreign Language Institutes in 1961–1963—some 4,500–4,700 examinees—are the present basis of interpretation of the French test results. These are supplemented by norms based on about 160 French majors in a number of Pennsylvania colleges tested in the fall of their senior year. The seniors are more homogeneous than the institute enrollees and score about as high as the latter do at the beginning of the institutes. It may be surmised that both groups are somewhat superior to the general run of French teachers currently at work, but no data are available on this point.

States or institutions that may consider introducing the battery as a step in their certification procedures face a number of interesting questions: how high to set the requirements, whether to establish minima on all or several of the scores, whether to apply the tests in some sort of successive-hurdles fashion, and whether to use some single-number total, for example. Material accompanying the battery is silent on these problems, and their solution will presumably be empirical (and not necessarily the same in different states). With regard to the possible use of a single total score, simple summation would result in weighting the speaking

score more than twice as heavily and the reading and writing scores almost one and one half times as heavily as the listening comprehension, applied linguistics, civilization and culture, and professional preparation scores; to the reviewer, this seems a quite appropriate weighting for teacher selection purposes.

Other data. Data on skewness of presently available distributions and on frequency of below chance scores, and a summary of item analysis statistics are available to those to whom they may be of interest.

CONTENT. While the tests are not entirely free from flaws, the reviewer would like to say at once that participants in test construction selected by MLA and ETS clearly were both competent and conscientious and have done, on the whole, an excellent job.

Listening Comprehension Test. The examinee listens to a French question, or to a monologue or conversation followed by questions, and chooses the appropriate answer from among four printed (in French) in a booklet but not spoken (28 items); for the last 8 of the 36 items, a spoken response (not printed) is to be marked true or false on the answer sheet. The voices are good; both sexes and a variety of accents, tones, speeds, and contexts are represented. In only one of the 36 questions did it seem to the reviewer that the speaker perhaps contributed more difficulty to the item than the testmakers may have intended.

The composition and choice of distractors, perhaps more difficult here than for most multiple choice tests, reflect a nice blend of the testmaker's and the linguist's arts. Inevitably, however, the content at times becomes that which might be used to measure mental ability (as in a comprehension question on one of the Wechsler scales) or memory. In fact, at a lower level than college or graduate school, the test might function as an intelligence test for natives of France. One is required to assume that for its stated purposes, the test is freed from influence of this factor by the self-selection or circumstantial selection of those examined. If the test is used with French students or teachers currently at work in some situations, this assumption may not be justified. But it has to be accepted—at least the reviewer cannot imagine any way of surely getting around it.

Since the instructions are given entirely in French, one wonders why for the last eight questions an examinee who has been told to indicate whether the statement is *"Vraie ou fausse"* is then expected to mark T or F instead of V or F on the answer sheet (in the literature surrounding the tests, the statement is made frequently and with appropriate pride that the tests do not require translation at any point). The conversation or *"scène dramatique"* which, according to the instructions on the tape, is to be about three minutes long, actually runs for just two minutes.

Speaking Test. The examinee (after instructions given in English, unlike the preceding test) first repeats sentences spoken in French, then reads aloud a printed passage (involving dialogue), and lastly responds to pictured situations with a description, a story, and role playing. The first task is one of mimicry—exact reproduction of the sound as spoken is required—while in the second and third, the speech of an educated native regardless of regional accent is the standard of acceptability. As noted above, great care has been given to the scoring of these performances and a high degree of scorer reliability and interscorer equivalence has been achieved.

Unavoidably in such a test there is room for disagreement as to what should be credited and what counted wrong. At certain points (especially in the first part), the examinee may be counted wrong for speaking in a way that a great many native French *do* speak, but this cannot be helped and the necessary choices in such cases seem to have been made on the side of the angels. The scoring guide is not explicit in some instances—for example, as to whether in the case of an initial *r*, either the uvular Parisian or the trilled provincial *r* or both may be accepted. The usefulness of the test as a whole, however, is impaired very little by flaws of this kind.

Reading Comprehension Test. Fifteen French sentences each omit a word or two for which the examinee chooses among four French alternatives. Then vocabulary questions (French-French, not French-English) and questions of understanding or interpretation (in French) are asked about several prose passages. Finally there are five questions requiring the interpretation of poetry. The test seems to be moderately speeded but this may be partly a reflection of the change in item content for the later questions. Otherwise it

seems unexceptionable—a good, workmanlike instrument.

Writing Test. First, 30 blanks in two paragraphs are to be filled in, each by a single word or contraction. Both knowledge of what word is correct and knowledge of proper form, gender, tense, and spelling are measured by this part. Second, interlinear editing of two poorly written passages is required. Missing an error or a mistake in correcting it loses a point of score, but there is no penalty for "correcting" a word or expression that does not need correction—even if the "correction" contains an error. Vocabulary, grammar, and perhaps some rhetoric are involved. Alternative correct responses are indicated for some items in the scoring manual; the expert scorers (including some natives of France) are permitted, with the majority approval of the scoring group, to credit correct responses that do not appear in the manual. This test represents the best way the reviewer knows of approaching the goal of a measure of writing ability in the present state of the psychometric art; diehards who would insist on an essay or nothing ought to read the story of the essay test efforts in the address by Miriam M. Bryan, Director of the MLA Testing Programs at ETS, before the Conference on Teacher Education in Foreign Languages at the University of Minnesota in February 1963.[3]

Applied Linguistics Test. The five parts of this test include Pronunciation and Phonetics (12 items), The Writing System: Spelling and Pronunciation (10 items), Grammar: Morphology and Syntax (23 items), General Linguistics (7 items), and Historical Grammar (3 items). As the test analysis report duly notes, less than half the NDEA Institute examinees complete the test (even in the posttest use) and 10 per cent of examinees leave a quarter of the test unattempted, so either speed is a more important component of scores than it should be or (less likely) the last two sections of the test strike examinees as peculiarly difficult or threatening. With total working time for the battery already nearly four hours and practical administration time nearer to five, it might be profitable to allow 50 minutes instead of 40 for this test.

The almost impeccable editing and proofreading which characterize the four skill tests

[3] This address, available from ETS on request, is enlightening reading for all prospective users of the tests.

MLA Foreign Language Proficiency Tests: French

seem less evident in this and the two tests which follow. For example, in one item on this test either the key is wrong or the question stem must be rewritten, while in another a careless accent mark turns a verb into a preposition. In a third, choice of one wrong (according to the key) answer probably reflects lack of clarity in the definition contained in the stem more often than a mistake by the examinee in applying the definition. The apology contained in the overlengthy instructions preceding the last three items (historical grammar) will reinforce the convictions of those who think these questions have no necessary or useful place in the test anyway. On balance, however, the test is neither bad nor unfair and does seem to the reviewer worthy of inclusion in the battery. Like the Professional Preparation Test, the Applied Linguistics Test may or may not predict relative effectiveness of teaching among average and better teachers; it should help, though, to identify the pretender who knows French well but knows little about the teaching of it.

Civilization and Culture Test. The 60 multiple choice questions comprised in this test sample knowledge of French geography, history, economics, politics, art, literature, and ways. An adequate measure of no one of these, it seems to the reviewer to serve its general purpose well. It might easily have been made too hard or too easy, but on evidence of the data it seems pitched at about the right (rather stiff) level of difficulty, with plenty of room left under the ceiling.

It is marred by several specific flaws or errors. One question may have had a correct answer among the choices when it was written but no longer does because of changes in French election law. Several similar items could easily become out of date, as could some based on current information of other than legal nature. Still other items are questions of logic or explanation in no way dependent on acquaintance with the affairs of France. There is reflection of the profession's difficulty (remarked on by the program director in the address referred to above) in agreeing on the proper proportion of culture to Culture.

Professional Preparation Test. These 65 questions on teaching practices are not prepared especially for students or teachers of French; they are the same for all languages in the program. This test will certainly draw

the heaviest critical fire, especially while there continues to be honest disagreement between proponents of the traditional and the audiolingual methods. And of all seven tests, this is in fact the one about which there may be the greatest reasonable doubt that it contributes much in the settings in which the battery is to be used.

Some of the items are arguable (the instructions prudently ask for the "best" rather than the "correct" answer), and some are unarguably trivial. At least one item will be answered wrong if the examinee remembers the Writing Test he took earlier in the battery and assumes it to be an example of good foreign language test construction. The test as a whole is wordy, and some questions seem as appropriate to a reading comprehension (in English) measure as to one of professional knowledge and understanding.

Yet perhaps it cannot be otherwise. Professional preparation was specified as the seventh essential competence by the MLA Steering Committee; of the seven, it probably was the area that the testmakers felt least at peace with. Most likely, those who include this test and those who use only the first six will not hire or certify very different teachers.

SUMMARY. In the French version, the *MLA Foreign Language Proficiency Tests for Teachers and Advanced Students* are tests of good quality. Their flaws are not great and are, for the most part, correctible. The needed information that is not now available (e.g., better evidence of the all-around equivalence of alternate forms, norms on other than NDEA Institute samples) probably will become available in time. Very badly needed is a well organized manual to place in more coherent form and in better perspective the information already reported; it simply is not reasonable to expect prospective users to dig through the welter of current reports, and it is insulting to suggest the alternative that they take the tests on faith.

As noted in the test analysis report, "On the average, the tests are of greater than middle difficulty for these teachers." And teachers enrolling in NDEA Foreign Language Institutes may well be abler, on the average, than French teachers at large. With less able groups, there is a possibility that the tests' discriminating power may weaken as scores approach the chance level (especially on the three nonskill tests). Undoubtedly, however, it was wise to build the tests with room at the top for measurement of the superior teachers that new emphases, new techniques, and new money may develop.

The—*how* do people working regularly with the battery make an easy mouthful of that title? The *flipttas*, perhaps?—the tests almost certainly are better than most procedures previously available for deciding who should be certified and who should be hired. They may well provide a model for similar examinations in other teaching areas. They deserve wide use.

[380]

A Standardised French Grammar Test. Ages 11–17 with 1–5 years of French; 1951; Forms A, B, ['51, 4 pages]; manual ['51, 12 pages]; 3s. per 12 tests of Form A; 2s. 6d. per 12 tests of Form B; 4d. per single copy of Form A; 3d. per single copy of Form B; 2s. 6d. per manual; postage and purchase tax extra; 25(30) minutes; T. S. Percival; University of London Press Ltd. *

REFERENCES

1. PERCIVAL, THOMAS STURDY. *Achievement Tests in French Grammar and Vocabulary.* Master's thesis, University of Durham (Durham, England), 1950. (Abstract: *Brit J Ed Psychol* 21:156)

For reviews by Nelson Brooks and Donald G. Burns, see 4:242.

[381]

A Standardised French Vocabulary Test. Ages 11–17 with 1–5 years of French; 1951; Forms A, B, ['51, 4 pages]; manual ['51, 12 pages]; 3s. per 12 tests of Form A; 2s. 6d. per 12 tests of Form B; 4d. per single copy of Form A; 3d. per single copy of Form B; 2s. 6d. per manual; postage and purchase tax extra; 35(40) minutes; T. S. Percival; University of London Press Ltd. *

REFERENCES

1. PERCIVAL, THOMAS STURDY. *Achievement Tests in French Grammar and Vocabulary.* Master's thesis, University of Durham (Durham, England), 1950. (Abstract: *Brit J Ed Psychol* 21:156)

For reviews by Nelson Brooks and Donald G. Burns, see 4:243.

[Other Tests]

For tests not listed above, see the following entries in *Tests in Print:* 631, 635, 638–41, 643, 646, and 649–50; out of print: 630, 636, and 647.

GERMAN

[382]

★**AATG German Test.** 2 years high school or 1 year college, 4 years high school or 2 years college; 1960–63; IBM; 1 form ['60, 10–11 mimeographed pages]; 2 levels: lower level, higher level; mimeographed instructions for administration ['60, 1 page]; mimeographed interpretive data ['53, 4 pages]; separate answer sheets must be used; $1.25 per 5 tests with IBM scorable answer sheets; 10¢ per 5 IBM scorable answer sheets; 50¢ per scoring stencil; postpaid; 45(50) minutes; Harry Steinhauer and others; American Association of Teachers of German. *

GILBERT C. KETTELKAMP, *Professor of Education, University of Illinois, Urbana, Illinois.*

This test evaluates three aspects of German foreign language learning: reading comprehension, knowledge of correct language usage, and a combination of reading comprehension and correct language usage. It is set up to measure at two levels of student achievement. The Lower Level is constructed to evaluate achievement at the completion of two years of German study in high school or one year in college. The Higher Level is structured to evaluate four years of high school study or two years of work in college.

The lower level test is divided into three parts. Part 1 is in German and is structured to test vocabulary knowledge of the language. Part 2 employs a translation approach from English to evaluate the usage of correct German. Both parts are relatively free of ambiguous items. Part 3 evaluates reading comprehension by providing five selected passages in German. The student is then asked to select from multiple choice items in German the correct responses to statements or questions concerning these passages. The reading selections are varied enough in content to provide a reasonably broad sampling of vocabulary words.

The lower level test, as its name implies, has been constructed to evaluate student language achievement during the early period of study. The test contains only a limited number of samplings to evaluate correct language usage, but contains a much larger number of samplings to evaluate vocabulary knowledge. Possibly there is little need to evaluate in detail correct usage based on structural knowledge during this early period of study, but if there is, then more valid testing instruments will have to be utilized.

The time required to administer the lower level test is 45 minutes, hence it is well adapted for use during the average length class period. The instructions for administering the test are clear and concise. It can be scored by machine, hence is economical in time. The cost is generally well in line with the cost of test materials of this type.

In general, the higher level test is similar

in structure to the lower level test. Part 1 evaluates vocabulary knowledge. In a few instances as, for example, in items 7, 12, and 20, the multiple choice items are of such a nature as to make more than one answer acceptable. However, in general the items are free of this characteristic. In Part 2, English statements are used to test student ability to complete equivalent German statements. In this section there is a variety of content as well as an extended range of difficulty. Part 3, constructed to test reading comprehension, contains a wide range of material; the selection of multiple choice items is excellent. The cost and administrative characteristics of this test are the same as those for the lower level test.

The higher level test contains a broader sampling of correct language usage material than does the lower level test; this, of course, is to be expected of material of a more advanced nature. Both tests are relatively free of multiple choice answers which are not readily identifiable. The few such items that do occur in the higher level test are certainly not of such a critical nature as to affect the validity of the test.

In summary, the dual AATG test, constructed to evaluate at two levels of learning, is a valuable instrument for measuring achievement in correct usage of German and achievement in reading comprehension in German. However, it is not intended to evaluate audiolingual achievement in the language. Since this goal is at present a major objective in modern language learning, other instruments of measurement must be used for this aspect of learning. The test is concise in form, reasonable in cost, and easily administered. This instrument is a valuable addition to the standardized tests now being made available to evaluate instruction and learning in present day classrooms.

THEODOR F. NAUMANN, *Associate Professor of Psychology, Central Washington State College, Ellensburg, Washington.*

The Lower Level of this German test is for students who had German for two years in high school or for one year in college, while the Higher Level is for those who had four years of high school or two years of college German. Each level consists of three parts to assess German vocabulary, grammar, and reading comprehension. There are 78 multiple choice items in the Lower Level and 80 in the

Higher Level. Each form has 30 vocabulary items. The grammar parts have 25 items (Lower Level) and 20 items (Higher Level), and the comprehension parts have 23 and 30 items, respectively.

The content of both tests appears adequate. There are no unusual or outstanding characteristics. On the whole the tests are well written. (In the higher level form the surname of the physicist Hertz is consistently misspelled.)

Basic statistics are given for each form. The high school and college norm groups included 1,602 and 1,265 students, respectively, for the Lower Level, and 132 and 450 students, correspondingly, for the Higher Level. Percentile ranks are given for each of the four norm groups. Reliabilities are .88 and .84 for the Lower Level and .90 and .84 for the Higher Level (Kuder-Richardson 21), which may be considered fair for an achievement test.

It seems somewhat strange that a new test in this area fully follows traditional form and fails to reflect the language study approach based on modern linguistics. Oral-aural skills are not assessed by the tests, and no indication is given that any efforts to do so are being made in any supplementary tests. The absence of information about the representativeness of the norm groups reduces the value of the statistics provided. The reason for the time limit is not explained. These limitations indicate that the tests should in their present form be labeled "for research only" with the understanding that at best they may become good instruments for assessing the traditional type of German instruction.

[383]

College Entrance Examination Board Achievement Test: German. Candidates for college entrance with 2–4 years high school German; 1901–64; for more complete information, see 760; 60(80) minutes; program administered for the College Entrance Examination Board by Educational Testing Service. *

REFERENCES

1–3. See 4:244.
4–6. See 5:272.

GILBERT C. KETTELKAMP, *Professor of Education, University of Illinois, Urbana, Illinois.* [Review of Forms KAC and LAC1.]

The recent forms, KAC and LAC1 of this German test are constructed to evaluate language reading comprehension and knowledge of language structure and usage. The levels of achievement tested are broad enough in scope to include most of the possibilities that will arise in testing situations in the subject. The estimated reliability for Form KAC ranges from .90 for candidates with three semesters of German to .95 for candidates with three, five, and seven semesters of training combined. There are also data on the standard error of measurement. No statistical data are as yet available for Form LAC1.

Form KAC consists of five parts or sections. Part A, made up of 18 items, requires that the student select from among four multiple choice statements the one that is most likely to be made in the situation described in the key statement. All statements and choices are in German. The testing is at a reasonably low level of ability.

Part B contains three passages varying in length from 17 to 29 lines. For each item the student is to complete a statement by selecting the best completion from among four suggested possibilities. There are 15 items in the section. The testing here is not only at a somewhat higher level of ability but also provides a somewhat different approach to evaluating reading comprehension than is used in Part A.

In Part C there are 25 items in which the item stems are all in English. This section requires that the student select the German expression that correctly completes the translation of the English sentence. The testing here is again mainly for reading comprehension, but for the student to select the correct answer it is necessary for him to have some knowledge of correct language usage.

The 22 items of Part D consist of German sentences from which specific words or phrases have been omitted. The student is to select the expression which, when inserted in the sentence, best fits in with the meaning of the sentence as a whole. This section tests the student's knowledge of shades of meaning in words that have similarities in meaning or in spelling. The range of difficulty of the material is reasonably extensive.

Part E contains two 25- to 30-line passages in which certain words or expressions are underlined. From English expressions the student is to select the most appropriate translation of each underscored item. The section also contains a number of incomplete German statements which relate to the content of the passages. The student is to select the best completion for each item. This material is at a

fairly advanced level, hence is appropriate for testing student ability at a comparable level.

Form KAC is a well constructed test. It evaluates reading comprehension as well as correct language usage. The ability level range is broad. It is generally free from ambiguity in its multiple choice items. In this respect it is an improvement over earlier Form FAC in which it was not always possible to identify distinctly one correct answer from among the given multiple choice alternatives.

Form LAC1 is divided into five parts containing a total of 95 items. Part A is made up of 15 statements, each of which describes, in German, a situation or condition. From four multiple choices given, again in German, for each statement, the student is to select the remark most likely to be made in the situation described. It is obvious that this part of the test has been constructed to evaluate reading comprehension and association. All items are clear and concise with the possible exception of number 4 where either of the first two answers might be considered acceptable. The range of difficulty of the 15 selections is excellent.

Part B is structured to test ability to select the correct language form to complete the translation of a given English statement or question. Indirectly it evaluates the students' knowledge of grammar.

Part C contains three groups of four-choice items, each group based on a passage. The passage describes three dramatic situations in reasonable detail as a basis for the items. This part of the test is characterized by variety of content material, as well as appropriate range of difficulty.

Part D is a test of vocabulary knowledge. Each given statement is to be completed with the selection of an appropriate word. Here, as in Part C, there is variety along with reasonable range of difficulty.

Part E appears to be a valid measure of high level reading ability. The two descriptive passages which serve as sources for the questions are advanced in difficulty, yet the questions themselves are relatively simple in form.

Forms KAC and LAC1 have been constructed to evaluate achievement in German language usage and reading comprehension. For these purposes the forms appear to be valid instruments of measurement. Although they do not measure grammatical knowledge as such, a background knowledge of language structure

College Entrance Examination Board Achievement Test: German

is helpful to the student in selecting correct verb forms from among the listed choices. The test certainly measures ability to use the language correctly, regardless of the means by which the ability has been acquired.

It is encouraging to German teachers to find that the gap which has existed over the years in testing the listening phase of foreign language instruction is now being filled. The publication of the *College Entrance Examination Board Achievement Test: German Listening Comprehension* now makes available an instrument to cover that phase of instruction. As a result, the College Board's offerings in German now include tests to measure the three major objectives of listening, reading, and comprehension. Improvements on these tests will, of course, be made in the future, but for the present there are available instruments of measurement which were only dreamed of a few years ago.

For a review by Harold B. Dunkel of an earlier form, see 5:272; for a review by Herbert Schueler see 4:244. For reviews of the testing program, see 760.

[384]

★**College Entrance Examination Board Achievement Test: German Listening Comprehension.** Candidates for college entrance with 2–4 years high school German; 1960–63; tests administered at the local secondary school on a specified date in February; candidates must also be registered to take one or more achievement tests in one of the regular program administrations; for more complete information, see 760; (30–40) minutes; program administered for the College Entrance Examination Board by Educational Testing Service. *

REFERENCES
1. SCHEIDER, ROSE M. "Evolution of the Listening Comprehension Tests." *Col Board R* 48:24–8 f '62. *

HAROLD B. DUNKEL, *Professor of Education, The University of Chicago, Chicago, Illinois.* [Review of Forms IBA and KBA.]

Both of these forms follow the same general pattern in their four parts and have a total of 50 and 57 items, respectively. The first parts contain 15 or so two-sentence conversations, and the student is asked to judge whether or not the second sentence is coherent with the first. (The reviewer is not enthusiastic about this type of exercise since it seems particularly liable to the familiar difficulty of having the item actually hinge on a single word.) The second parts contain another set of 10 or so two-sentence conversations, with the student asked

to indicate the probable locale of the conversation. The third part again involves two-sentence conversations, but this time of a do-it-yourself sort, with the student required to select the proper second sentence from among four offered. In the fourth part, multiple choice questions test the student's comprehension of longer dialogues and readings.

In spite of the variety in the type of exercise, the test does not seem fragmented, but rather seems merely to reflect the different settings in which one does hear a foreign language (conversations, plays, lectures, and the rest). Moreover, dislike or distrust of any one sort of exercise does not ruin the entire test for any student, teacher, or critic since that part is merely one among several.

The reliabilities of both forms for groups with two years and with three years of training are .82 to .85 or better. In view of the variety of milieu and equipment used in administering aural tests, the smallness of the groups available for three-year norms, and other familiar factors, figures of this sort are not to be taken too seriously, but the present ones certainly suggest the adequate reliability of the two tests.

One can always think, of course, that reliability would be better if some of the weaker items had been removed. For example, in Form IBA a case can be made for the wrong answer to item 11 and the literal-minded student is likely to make it; in item 34 the keyed response is certainly the only possible one among those offered, but it doesn't seem quite the response which the student who has understood the item will be looking for as a right answer and this twist may cause confusion under pressure of time. But these and similar minor infelicities inevitably dog tests. Instead of worrying about them we should be happy that the CEEB has given us an examination which has all the earmarks of a valid and reliable test of the ability to understand spoken German.

HERBERT SCHUELER, *Director of Teacher Education, Hunter College of the City University of New York, New York, New York.* [Review of Forms IBA and LBA.]

These 30-minute listening comprehension tests are of extremely high quality in both conception and execution. They present tape recorded stimuli of ascending difficulty of four types: (*a*) 15 or 16 brief conversations between two people that are to be judged as either logical or illogical; (*b*) 10 additional conversations for each of which the student is to choose one of four locations as the most likely setting; (*c*) 10–13 questions for which one of four alternatives is to be chosen; and (*d*) three sustained passages (one an anecdote, the second a dialogue, and the third an excerpt from a speech) followed by 5–6 aural four-choice questions each.

Obviously, the quality of the aural stimulus material is crucial in a recorded listening comprehension test. The student has no recourse to repetition once the material is heard. For a listening comprehension test to be a true measure of the skill it purports to measure, it must provide recorded voices speaking the standard version of the language without distracting regionalisms, at a colloquial pace and manner, and with exemplary clarity. This is achieved to an admirable and consistent degree by both male and female voices on these tapes. Whatever faults these tests may have, therefore, are not due to the quality of the recordings. The language content itself is colloquial, appropriate, and generally free from the artificialities of some foreign language textbook material. Here and there, however, this reviewer feels that more careful editing, particularly in the sustained listening passages, might have removed some irrelevant bars to comprehension that may indeed detract from a valid measure of listening comprehension. The use in one passage, for example, of a highly unusual family name (when Schultz or Schmidt would have done as well) possibly introduces an unnecessary difficulty. Similarly, when a person is reported as saying something with a strong American accent and then says it instead in perfect native German, or when a piano selection, heard in the background and obviously played in a professional manner, is said to sound as if played by a child without notes, the material itself is in danger of introducing factors that may possibly skew the attention and the responses of the student. In addition, there is an occasional ambiguity in possible choices in earlier sections of each of the forms, but not enough to impair seriously the validity of the tests as a whole.

Analysis of the scores of 632 candidates on Form IBA and 2,213 on Form LBA reveals the two forms to be generally appropriate for students with three years of the language in secondary school, being pitched at the middle difficulty for the three-year sample, very difficult for the two-year sample, and quite easy for the four-year sample. In the main, these tests are quite satisfactory in appropriateness of content, and superior in recording quality and in test reliability. More careful editing of the linguistic material will make future forms even better.

For reviews of the testing program, see 760.

[385]

*College Entrance Examination Board Advanced Placement Examination: German. High school students desiring credit for college level courses or admission to advanced courses; 1954–63; 2 levels; for more complete information, see 761; 180(200) minutes; program administered for the College Entrance Examination Board by Educational Testing Service. *
a) INTERMEDIATE GERMAN. 3 years high school, including the equivalent of an intermediate college level course; discontinued during 1964.
b) ADVANCED GERMAN: INTRODUCTION TO GERMAN LITERATURE. 4 years high school, including the equivalent of a college level German literature course.

REFERENCES

1. PRESEL, ROSE. "German and the German Examination in the 'School and College Study for Admission With Advanced Standing.'" *German Q* 28:85–8 Ja '55. *
2. REICHARD, JOSEPH R. "The College Board and Advanced Placement in German." *German Q* 29:220–4 N '56. *
3. VALLEY, JOHN R. "College Actions on CEEB Advanced Placement Language Examination Candidates." *Mod Lang J* 43:261–3 O '59. *
4. REICHARD, JOSEPH R. "German Advanced Placement Under the College Board: Promising Signs." *German Q* 33:153–8 Mr '60. *
5. NEWMARK, MAXIM, AND SCHERER, PHILIP. *How to Prepare for College Board Achievement Tests: German.* Great Neck, N.Y.: Barron's Educational Series, Inc., 1962. Pp. viii, 134. *

For a review by Herbert Schueler of an earlier form, see 5:273.

[386]

★College Entrance Examination Board Placement Tests: German Listening Comprehension Test. Entering college freshmen; 1962–63, c1955–63; IBM; Forms DLC1, DLC2 in a single booklet ('55), KPL1, KPL2 in a single booklet (c1960–61, 12 pages, a reprint of inactive forms of *College Entrance Examination Board Achievement Test: German Listening Comprehension*); test administered by 7½ ips tape recording; for more complete information, see 759; 30(40) minutes; program administered for the College Entrance Examination Board by Educational Testing Service. *

For reviews of the College Entrance Examination Board Achievement Test: German Listening Comprehension, *see 384.*

[387]

★College Entrance Examination Board Placement Tests: German Reading Test. Entering college freshmen; 1962–63, c1957–63; test is a reprint, with 15 items omitted, of an inactive form of *College Entrance Examination Board Achievement Test: German;* IBM; Form KPL1 (c1957, 12 pages); for more complete information, see 759; program administered for the College Entrance Examination Board by Educational Testing Service. *

For reviews of the College Entrance Examination Board Achievement Test: German, *see 383, 5:272, and 4:244.*

[388]

★Common Concepts Foreign Language Test: German [Research Edition]. "Students [in any grade] who have had enough foreign language instruction to place them at the Level 1 stage in their achievement"; 1962–64; aural comprehension; may be administered using live voice but tape recording is recommended; IBM; Forms 1, 2; a single booklet ('62, 31 pages) presents response options for both forms of this test and the French and Spanish tests of the series; mimeographed preliminary manual ('64, 24 pages); interim norms (grades 7–12 only); separate answer sheets or cards must be used; 75¢ per test; $5.95 per 3¾ ips tape recording; 5¢ per IBM answer sheet; 20¢ per scoring stencil; 2¢ per Cal-Card; 20¢ per hand scoring stencil; 15¢ per manual; postage extra; $1 per specimen set without tape; $6.95 per specimen set with tape; postpaid; scoring service available; (40–45) minutes; Bela H. Banathy, Miles V. Zintz, W. James Popham, Joseph M. Sadnavitch, Rena Krichbaum, Fred B. Gannon, Valdemar Hempel, and Klaus A. Mueller; California Test Bureau. *

[389]

★German: Every Pupil Test. 1 or 2 years high school; 1962–64; test booklet titles vary; new form (4 pages) usually issued each April; forms from previous testing programs also available; general directions sheet ('63, 2 pages); no data on reliability; Ohio norms for new forms available following testing program; 5¢ per test; 3¢ per key; postpaid; 40(45) minutes; Ohio Scholarship Tests. *

[390]

*German I and II: Minnesota High School Achievement Examinations. 1 or 2 years high school; 1953–63; series formerly called *Midwest High School Achievement Examinations;* new norms issued each June; Form F ('51, 5 pages, formerly called Form I & D) used in 1963 testing; no specific manual; series manual ('63, 4 pages); series norms ['63, 4 pages]; series cumulative profile ('62, 2 pages); no data on reliability; no description of normative population; 12¢ per test; $2.50 per 100 profiles; postage extra; 20¢ per specimen set, postpaid; 60(65) minutes; American Guidance Service, Inc. *

For a review by Harold B. Dunkel, see 5:276.

[391]

★Graduate School Foreign Language Test: German. Graduate level degree candidates required to demonstrate reading proficiency in German; 1963–64; Forms K-LFG1, K-LFG2, ('63, 34 pages); for more complete information, see 356; 80(100) minutes; Educational Testing Service. *

JACK M. STEIN, *Professor of German, Harvard University, Cambridge, Massachusetts.* [Review of Form K-LFG2.]

The existence of this test is cause for hope that order, continuity, and reliability in testing the German competence of Ph.D. candidates in all fields will replace the inadequacy, unreliability, and general chaos of testing procedures used up to now for this purpose. Such procedures vary incredibly from department to department and from university to university, but there is general agreement that they share one chief characteristic: they are all unsatisfactory. The present test, though it is not without defects, to be discussed below, is unquestionably an enormous improvement over that which it is designed to replace. Developed by Educational Testing Service under a contract between the United States Office of Education and Cornell University after a preliminary study conference to determine acceptable specifications for standardized foreign language reading proficiency tests for graduate students, which was attended by representatives of 18 graduate schools, it has been extensively pretested at 37 cooperating institutions. A wide variety of explanatory material has wisely been prepared, since in the great majority of instances the persons in charge of testing at this level are not testing experts and are largely unfamiliar with the characteristics of machine scored multiple choice tests. This supplementary material gives clear and useful information, not only on the test itself, but on various methods of deriving local norms and determining local passing scores.

All examinees, from whatever department, take Section 1 (40 minutes, two parts). Part A consists of 25 items, brief sentences with words, phrases, or clauses underlined. The examinee is asked to choose that one of four alternative German expressions which is the equivalent of what is underlined. Both vocabulary and syntax are thus tested. Part 2 of Section 1 contains three passages, roughly 600 words in all, each passage followed by five items in German, with four alternatives each. The examinee is to choose the alternative which best matches the passage. The level of difficulty of this section is moderate and the passages are like those typically found in a magazine or newspaper. The vocabulary and subject matter is of a general nature, such as it is reasonable to assume could be readily grasped by anyone with a command of German sufficient to cope with the demands of a more specific and scholarly nature made in Section 2. Thus Section 1 serves admirably as a uniform base upon which the separate subdivisions of Section 2 are superimposed.

Section 2 is the really critical part of the examination. It is divided into four major subject matter areas (Biological Sciences, Humanities, Physical Sciences, Social Sciences), the examinee selecting that area in which his field of specialization lies. In this section (40 minutes) he is confronted with five or six passages totaling roughly 1,500 words, each passage followed by items to a total in the entire section of 30. These multiple choice statements, each with four alternatives, are in English, rather than in German as they were in Section 1. This change into English has presumably the effect of reducing the barrier of specialized vocabulary, since most, if not all, of the passages with which each examinee is dealing fall more or less outside his own area of specialization.

This, indeed, is the major dilemma of the examination. Of six faculty members (in as many large graduate departments) whom I consulted, only one was willing to go along with the necessarily broad coverage represented in the respective second sections. Thus a history man pointed out that only one of the social science passages was in history; and a social relations professor showed me that not one of the behavioral sciences (psychology, anthropology, sociology) was represented on the test at all. For better or worse, there was the feeling that an examination at this stage of the examinee's career which does not test in the immediate field of specialization, or at least very close to it, necessarily has a dilettantish flavor. Only one of the six men, I am pleased to report, objected to the absence of translation.

A more serious defect, indeed it would seem an inexcusable one, was pointed out in the physical sciences section. Here many of the distractors could be eliminated without reference to the passage because they consisted of scientific nonsense. Often two of the three distractors, and in some cases all three of them, in an item were thus nonfunctional, so that the correct answer could be selected entirely without reference to the German! Most of the items were carefully phrased "The author of this passage" etc., but obviously no selection would have been chosen which argues palpable error.

This does not seem to be the case with the other sections, though the reviewer cannot guarantee it except in the humanities, which is his own field.

Two bad misprints were found (*praussisch* for *preussisch* and *berufen, worden* for *berufen worden*), the latter being far more critical for the examinee than it may look. There was also inconsistency within the same passage in the use of the nineteenth century spelling *th* and its twentieth century equivalent *t,* and inconsistent use of the digraph ß.

Lest these deficiencies seem too grave, the reader should bear in mind three important points. First, the only alternatives to this test, with all its faults, are the grossly, sometimes grotesquely, inadequate present practices of graduate departments. Measured against these, rather than against some hypothetical ideal, the test is a major breakthrough. Second, this is a pioneer attempt in a testing area at once so diffuse and so highly compartmentalized that great vigilance (apparently more than was exercised) is necessary to avoid error. Third, and most important, the existence of this test establishes for the first time a professional framework to which improvements derived from cumulative experience can be annually adapted. It offers the happy prospect that nationwide respectability and uniformity can at last be achieved in what has been up to now the shoddiest testing area in our entire educational system.

[392]

★**MLA-Cooperative Foreign Language Tests: German.** 1 or 2 years high school or 2 semesters college, 3 or 4 years high school or 4 semesters college; 1963–64; 4 tests in a single booklet: listening, speaking, reading, writing; IBM in part; 2 levels; directions for administering and scoring ['64, 39 pages] for this and the French, Italian, Russian, and Spanish tests of the series; no data on reliability; no norms; $5 per 10 tests; separate answer sheets may be used for listening and reading tests; $1 per 20 IBM scorable answer sheets; $1 per 10 scoring stencils (answer pattern must be punched out locally); $7 per 3¾ ips tape for listening test; $7 per 3¾ ips tape for speaking test (blank tapes or discs for recording student responses must be obtained locally); postage extra; $2 per specimen set, cash orders postpaid; (25–35) minutes for listening, (10–20) minutes for speaking, 35(40) minutes for reading, 35(40) minutes for writing; prepared in cooperation with the Modern Language Association of America; Cooperative Test Division. *
a) [LOWER LEVEL.] 1 or 2 years high school or 2 semesters college; form LA ('63, 23 pages).
b) [HIGHER LEVEL.] 3 or 4 years high school or 4 semesters college; form MA ('63, 24 pages).

[393]

★MLA Foreign Language Proficiency Tests for Teachers and Advanced Students: German.
Grades 15–17 and foreign language teachers; 1961–64; IBM in part; 7 tests; 2 forms ('61): Form JML1 (also called Form A, available for institutional programs), Form JML2 (also called Form B, restricted to state and local teacher certification programs); series supervisor's manual ['62, 34 pages]; series norms leaflet ('64, 4 pages); series interpretive leaflet ('64, 4 pages); examination fees: $15 per battery of 7 tests, $12.50 per battery of 4 skill tests (listening, speaking, reading, writing); fees include rental of test materials and scoring and reporting service; postage extra; fee for 30-day examination, $3.70 per battery; Modern Language Association of America and Educational Testing Service; program administered by Educational Testing Service. *

a) LISTENING COMPREHENSION TEST: GERMAN. IBM; 2 forms ('61, 7 pages, containing response options only); stimulus material presented on 3¾ or 7½ ips tape; $1.50 per examinee; (20–30) minutes.

b) SPEAKING TEST: GERMAN. 2 forms ('61, 9 pages, containing scripts for all languages in the series plus a section on 3¾ or 7½ ips tape); responses recorded on tapes or records supplied by the publisher; $6.75 per examinee; (15–30) minutes.

c) READING TEST: GERMAN. IBM; 2 forms ('61, 12 pages); $1.25 per examinee; 40(50) minutes.

d) WRITING TEST: GERMAN. IBM in part; 2 forms ('61, 7–8 pages); $3.50 per examinee; 45(55) minutes.

e) APPLIED LINGUISTICS TEST: GERMAN. IBM; 2 forms ('61, 9 pages); $1.25 per examinee; 40(50) minutes.

f) CIVILIZATION AND CULTURE TEST: GERMAN. IBM; 2 forms ('61, 9–10 pages); $1.25 per examinee; 30(40) minutes.

g) PROFESSIONAL PREPARATION TEST. IBM; 2 forms ('61, 10 pages) common to all languages in the series; $1.25 per examinee; 45(55) minutes.

REFERENCES

1. STARR, WILMARTH H. "Competency First: New Tests in Foreign Languages." *Proc Inv Conf Testing Probl* 1960: 97–110 '61. *
2. STARR, WILMARTH H. "Proficiency Tests in Modern Foreign Languages." *PMLA* 76:7–11 My '61. *
3. STARR, WILMARTH H. "MLA Foreign Language Proficiency Tests for Teachers and Advanced Students." *PMLA* 77:31–42 S '62. *

HAROLD B. DUNKEL, *Professor of Education, The University of Chicago, Chicago, Illinois.*

Since three tests in this battery are efforts in areas relatively new to standardized testing (applied linguistics, civilization and culture, and professional preparation) while the four tests of the language skills (speaking, listening, reading, and writing) cover more familiar objectives, the limited space here will be devoted primarily to the three new varieties.

For obvious reasons of test security, reviewers are asked not to quote items. In some respects this limitation is unimportant; the Educational Testing Service usually does too competent a job to make quibbles about individual items profitable or even possible. The only unfortunate consequence is that comments on larger issues must appear somewhat vague

and *ex cathedra* since the supporting evidence cannot be cited.

The selection of "Professional Preparation" as the title for the one test is most interesting since the only aspect of professional preparation covered is knowledge of the theory of language teaching. If one wonders why the examination was not so named, one immediately realizes that this label would have highlighted the major inherent difficulty. Most of us think we know a good bit about language teaching and the right way of doing it, but whether our knowledge is of the sort that permits right and wrong answers is another matter. We should ask ourselves whether our theory has the comprehensiveness, coherence, and demonstrability possessed by those things called "theory" in other fields. In fact, a most stimulating seminar on language teaching could be conducted simply by having the group work through this test, item by item, and asking precisely what evidence there is, both in quality and quantity, for each correct response. Though most of us might agree with most of the items, our evidence for a good many points is tenuous. As a result, the test actually measures current received opinion. That most of us, or even all of us, receive these opinions makes little difference. Some danger exists, consequently, that this test may become a catechism on the doctrine of the language teaching establishment. The reviewer is old enough to belong to the generations which were worried by tests of orthodoxy.

As one who has grumbled for many years, both in previous *Mental Measurements Yearbooks* and elsewhere, that there is no point in talking about "Culture and Civilization" unless we test for knowledge of them and grade students on the results, the reviewer welcomes that part of the battery which is an objective and reliable test of these matters. But many of us will wonder as we read through these bits and pieces of geography, literature, history, and fine arts whether these snippets of knowledge are what we mean by culture and civilization. Probably to some extent they are. The person who knows a country, its culture, and its civilization does know its main rivers and mountains, its chief writers and what they wrote, important epochs in the country's history, and all the rest. The fact that the items are jumbled (probably in the order of empirical difficulty as observed in tryout forms) makes the test seem somewhat more of a hodgepodge than it probably is. Grouping the items by topics, as is done in the Applied Linguistics Test, would at least give this examination a more coherent appearance and might remind the testmaker as well as the test taker of the problem of some intelligible sampling of the major areas. The reviewer has no serious quarrel with the test as far as it goes; but most of us, including no doubt its constructors, probably hope that later versions will go further. A fruitful direction is indicated by the last item, which asks the student to explain why a joke is funny. What a culture sees as funny, honorific, disgraceful, unquestionable, and the like are important keys to that culture, and the person who understands the culture understands these viewpoints while the person strange to the culture finds them perplexing and absurd. Admittedly, items of this kind are extremely difficult to write, but is not this sort of insight the target at which we aim—particularly for advanced students and teachers? Possibly satire (from the standup comedian through the musical play to the satiric novel) would be a fruitful source of such items. To poke fun at the culture, the satirist must know where the chinks in a particular cultural armor are, and we might do well to follow the lead of these experts in detecting specific points of attack.

The Applied Linguistics Test is particularly interesting because of the long directions which inform the student why the questions are asked. Although the reviewer belongs to the school which believes that tests can and should constitute learning experiences and not just hurdles for the student, he is not certain that this learning should stem from the reading of test directions which are primarily justifications for the items rather than instructions for marking them. Considerations of testing aside, the test serves as an extensional definition of what is meant by the application of descriptive linguistics to foreign language teaching, with the directions giving the rationale and the items exemplifying the points. The items, covering pronunciation, phonetics, grammar, orthography, general linguistics, and historical and comparative philology, are familiar to takers and makers of advanced German tests.

Of the four tests of skills, the Reading Test seems weak in two of its parts. One group of items asks the students to supply a missing word in a sentence; a second set asks them to replace an underlined word by a synonym (which does not always seem easier or more familiar than the original word). Though exercises of this sort are related to reading, they are not reading; they patently demand a more active command of the language than mere reading requires. One can only hope that the prevailing doctrine of the priority of speech is not forcing us into reading tests thrown into the form of "what should I say next?" rather than "what is the author saying?"

The other three tests can briefly be noted as good. The Speaking Test, in its first part, measures the ability to read aloud, with the grade based on the correct pronunciation of certain phonemes appearing in the selection; the last part involves response to picture stimuli. The Listening Comprehension Test and the Writing Test involve familiar and well tested procedures. (In the first part of the listening test the continuous change of speakers for each brief isolated item is probably more troublesome for the student than valuable for measurement.) In general, all tests of the battery attain high reliabilities of .90 or better.

Though the reviewer is not a True Believer in all the current dogma, he applauds the appearance of a test which does take that doctrine seriously and which measures on a broad front the skills and knowledge stressed by the doctrine. As is usual with competent examinations, these tests make clearer than any number of more abstract statements the viewpoint on which they are based. Those who find the viewpoint acceptable will have here adequate and reliable tests.

HERBERT SCHUELER, *Director of Teacher Education, Hunter College of the City University of New York, New York, New York.*

The Modern Language Association proficiency tests for teachers and advanced students represent the culmination of a monumental effort on the part of the profession of foreign language teachers to establish national standards of linguistic and professional competence designed to help in the improvement of foreign language teaching in this country. Two major events provided the basis for these tests. The first was the promulgation in 1955 by a committee of the Modern Language Association of a statement of "Qualifications for Secondary School Teachers of Modern Foreign

Languages." This statement, subsequently endorsed by all the major regional and national professional organizations concerned with the teaching of modern foreign languages, established levels of proficiency for seven areas of language teaching competence: aural understanding, speaking, reading, writing, language analysis, culture, and professional preparation. The second was the establishment of Foreign Language Institutes, with the support of the National Defense Education Act, to provide the necessary upgrading in foreign language competence and in teaching methodology for the profession. The first event provided the necessary standards and the second the means, need, and initial population for the development of standardized tests in all aspects of foreign language competence for teachers. The tests resulting are therefore landmarks of wide professional involvement combining the resources of a representative cross section of foreign language scholars and teachers with test experts. The two forms of seven tests now available represent the end result of experimental tryouts with enrollees in the summer 1960, 1961, and 1962 Foreign Language Institutes. In addition, experimental forms were tested with graduating college seniors and applicants for study in foreign languages.

The Form JML1 versions of these tests are available for institutional programs; the Form JML2 equivalent versions are restricted to state and local teacher certification programs. While the seven tests are available separately, they divide themselves naturally into a battery of four skill tests (listening, speaking, reading, writing) and three tests particularly applicable to teachers (applied linguistics, civilization and culture, and professional preparation).

LISTENING COMPREHENSION TEST. This 20- to 30-minute test presents its stimulus material on 3¾ or 7½ ips tape, and requires candidates to react either to four response or true-false options. In the first part, the candidate hears a series of remarks or questions and must choose one response from four printed responses. In the second he hears a series of sustained dialogues or expositions to which he responds to a series of four-response descriptive options. In the third, he hears a protracted dialogue and must respond to a series of aural descriptive statements in the form of true or false options. The tapes are uniformly clear and the several voices, while speaking standard German, do exhibit regional differences in pronunciation, a feature deliberately built into the tapes and most appropriate for advanced measures of aural comprehension.

This test appears to be quite difficult, an opinion substantiated by results of available pre- and post-Institute test analysis made on the basis of testing during the summer of 1961. The extent to which the test is made more difficult by presenting single playings of each aural stimulus, particularly those of extended length, is undetermined. It might be interesting to ascertain changes in scores when the test provides repetitions of stimuli. In addition, the test provides further examples for speculation on the relationship between linguistic aural competence and general intelligence. It is this reviewer's contention that several of the items are more a measure of the respondent's intelligence than his aural command of the language. Perhaps the administration of this test to groups of native speakers of German of demonstrable variation on standard measures of intelligence might provide some interesting clues to the validity of this test as a measure of aural comprehension per se.

SPEAKING TEST. The MLA speaking tests represent the first widely available tests of speaking ability. While the United States Armed Forces Institute pioneered in experimenting with foreign language speaking tests during and immediately after World War II, unfortunately none of the many significant attempts of that time has been made available for subsequent civilian administration and study. The MLA tests must therefore be judged without reference to these earlier tests, nor have they had the benefit of these earlier experiments. The tests of 20–30 minutes duration are in three parts: (a) imitation exercises in which the candidate reproduces on his own tape or disc stimuli representing critical sounds and intonations usually difficult for the American student of a foreign language to master; (b) reading exercises in which the candidate reads orally, written material presented in the test booklet; (c) free oral responses stimulated by pictorial stimuli. It is obvious that in a speaking test the crucial problem is not so much the stimuli as the standards and uniformity of rating, particularly in the section testing the candidate's free speech. The achievement of a high degree of scorer consistency is a product of rigorous training of, and imposition of controls on, expert raters. The reported gains in interscorer reliability and in individual scorer consistency achieved by training sessions organized by the Educational Testing Service in 1961 and 1962 are impressive; interscorer reliabilities of .89 and better are almost too good to be true, and augur well for the usability of these tests.[1] The reliability (pre- and post-NDEA Institute testing) of the German Speaking Test is reported as .81 (3). The test requires painstaking attention to the details of administration; without proper facilities for recording students' responses on tape or disc, it should not be attempted. Without optimum conditions, candidates cannot fail to be handicapped.

READING TEST. This 40-minute test consists of three parts: (a) a completion test in which the candidates choose from among four alternatives to complete missing elements in a series of 15 sentences; (b) three extended reading passages followed by two types of items, (1) choices from four synonyms to substitute for underlined words in the passage, and (2) choices from four statements to complete a series of statements based on the passages; (c) short excerpts from poetry followed by four alternative interpretive statements. This is a challenging test, most suitable to advanced levels of reading competence. While conventional in form, it is nevertheless of demonstrated high reliability and presumed validity for testing advanced students and teachers of the language.

WRITING TEST. This test is in two parts: (a) a completion test requiring the student to insert missing words in two extended passages, and (b) a composition replete with errors which the candidate is required to correct as if he were the teacher. This test is interesting not so much for what it includes as for what is conspicuously missing. Unlike the speaking test, the written test provides no opportunity for free production of the language. The original specifications for the MLA testing program called for the inclusion of free writing stimuli, but frustrating experiences in seeking interscorer reliability resulted in their abandonment. While it was possible to achieve interscorer reliability of close to .90 in the

rating of the free speaking items, the best that could be achieved for the experimental free writing items was .62. It was wisely decided, therefore, to defer the inclusion of free writing items for the time being. As a result, this test gives an impression of incompleteness, however well conceived its two parts may be.

APPLIED LINGUISTICS TEST. This 40-minute test presents multiple choice items in six areas: English and German Pronunciation, Phonetics, Grammar, The Writing System, General Linguistics, and Historical and Comparative Philology. The test presents a fitting complement to the Professional Preparation Test (below) in providing a measure of the candidate's command of comparative linguistic analysis of his language with English and of both the basic terminology and applications to German of modern structural linguistics. While the candidate not versed in modern structural linguistics might do better in the historical and the writing system sections, he would be at a loss in the technical terminology of the others. This test, then, is, as is the Professional Preparation Test, firmly grounded in the so-called audio-lingual language teaching movement and its foundation in modern structural linguistics.

CIVILIZATION AND CULTURE TEST. This 60-item, multiple choice test presents a wide sampling of geographical, political, historical, literary, and artistic material, ranging from earliest times to the present. Fully half the questions present combinations of answers rather than calling for choice of single responses. Thus, in a four alternative item, the candidate is frequently expected to choose from among such combinations as I and II only; I and III only; I and IV only; and III and IV only. This device undoubtedly broadens the scope of any given item, makes possible the injection of subtleties of interpretation, and provides a greater range of difficulty. It may, however, introduce some mechanical difficulties unrelated to what is being tested, requiring as it does constant referral to numerical labels. The selection of but 60 items from among the broad sweep of German culture and civilization is a formidable task at best, and the test succeeds as well as any this reviewer has seen.

PROFESSIONAL PREPARATION TEST. This 65-item, 45-minute, multiple choice test is, as is the Applied Linguistics Test, thoroughly grounded in the so-called audio-lingual method of teaching foreign languages. This reviewer

---

[1] It is not indicated whether the studies which yielded these figures included the speaking tests in all languages and, if not, on which language test or tests the figures are based.

MLA Foreign Language Proficiency Tests: German

knows many foreign language teachers who would quarrel, sometimes even violently, with some of the items, and particularly with the scoring key. An analysis of particular items here would, however, violate the security of the tests and thus cannot be attempted in this review. It must be understood, particularly if certification authorities will make use of this test, that it is an expression of a particular foreign language teaching doctrine, and valid only if teachers are to be tested for their knowledge of, and commitment to, this movement. As a test of professional preparation within the scope, material, and method of the audio-lingual movement, it is admirable. Its use for teacher certification, therefore, will depend on the acceptance of this methodology and its precept as a requirement for the preparation and evaluation of foreign language teachers.

[Other Tests]

For tests not listed above, see the following entries in *Tests in Print*: 654–5; out of print: 657.

GREEK

[394]

*College Entrance Examination Board Achievement Test: Greek.** Candidates for college entrance with 2–3 years high school Greek; 1901–63; tests administered at the local secondary school on a specified date in February; candidates must also be registered to take one or more achievement tests in one of the regular program administrations; for more complete information, see 760; 3 parts (candidate takes only one): Attic prose, Homeric poetry, Attic prose and Homeric poetry; 90(100) minutes; program administered for the College Entrance Examination Board by Educational Testing Service. *

For a review by Konrad Gries of an earlier form, see 5:277. For reviews of the testing program, see 760.

[395]

★College Entrance Examination Board Placement Tests: Greek Test.** Entering college freshmen; 1962–63, c1957–63; test is a reprint of an inactive form of *College Entrance Examination Board Achievement Test: Greek;* IBM; Form KPL1 (c1957, 17 pages) in a single booklet with the Italian test of the series; 2 parts (student generally takes only one): Attic prose, Homer and Attic prose; for more complete information, see 759; 60(70) minutes per part; program administered for the College Entrance Examination Board by Educational Testing Service. *

For a review of the College Entrance Examination Board Achievement Test: Greek, *see 5:277.*

HEBREW

[396]

★College Entrance Examination Board Achievement Test: Hebrew.** Candidates for college entrance with 2–4 years high school Hebrew; 1961–64; available only in January testing program; for more complete information, see 760; 60(80) minutes; program administered for the College Entrance Examination Board by Educational Testing Service. *

For reviews of the testing program, see 760.

[397]

★Test on the Fundamentals of Hebrew.** Grades 2–5, 3–6, 4–7; 1955–59; 4–5 scores: sentences (grades 3–6 and 4–7 only), vocabulary, stories, grammar, total; 1 form; 3 levels: lower ('55, 5 pages), intermediate ('58, 7 pages), upper ('55, 7 pages); mimeographed manual ('59, 19 pages); no data on reliability; tentative norms; no norms for part scores; separate answer sheets must be used; 10¢ per test; $1 per 100 mimeographed answer sheets; $3 per 100 self-marking answer sheets; 35¢ per manual; 75¢ per specimen set; postpaid; (30–45) minutes; Committee on Tests of the American Association for Jewish Education; the Association. *

ITALIAN

[398]

★College Entrance Examination Board Achievement Test: Italian Listening Comprehension.** Candidates for college entrance with 2–4 years high school Italian; 1961–63; tests administered at the local secondary school on a specified date in February; candidates must also be registered to take one or more achievement tests in one of the regular program administrations; for more complete information, see 760; (30–40) minutes; program administered for the College Entrance Examination Board by Educational Testing Service. *

For reviews of the testing program, see 760.

[399]

*College Entrance Examination Board Achievement Test: Italian Reading and Essay.** Candidates for college entrance with 2–4 years high school Italian; 1924–63; tests administered at the local secondary school on a specified date in February; candidates must also be registered to take one or more achievement tests in one of the regular program administrations; for more complete information, see 760; 90(100) minutes; program administered for the College Entrance Examination Board by Educational Testing Service. *

For reviews of the testing program, see 760.

[400]

★College Entrance Examination Board Placement Tests: Italian Listening Comprehension.** Entering college freshmen; 1962–63; IBM; Form KBA ('62, 5 pages, an inactive form of *College Entrance Examination Board Achievement Test: Italian Listening Comprehension*); test administered by 7½ ips tape recording; for more complete information, see 759; 30(40) minutes; program administered for the College Entrance Examination Board by Educational Testing Service. *

[401]

★**College Entrance Examination Board Placement Tests: Italian Test.** Entering college freshmen; 1962–63, c1957–63; test is a reprint of an inactive form of *College Entrance Examination Board Achievement Test: Italian Reading and Essay;* IBM; Form KPL1 (c1957, 12 pages) in a single booklet with the Greek test of the series; for more complete information, see 759; 60(70) minutes; program administered for the College Entrance Examination Board by Educational Testing Service. *

[402]

★**MLA-Cooperative Foreign Language Tests: Italian.** 1 or 2 years high school or 2 semesters college, 3 or 4 years high school or 4 semesters college; 1963–64; 4 tests in a single booklet: listening, speaking, reading, writing; IBM in part; 2 levels; directions for administering and scoring ['64, 39 pages] for this and the German, French, Russian, and Spanish tests of the series; no data on reliability; no norms; $5 per 10 tests; separate answer sheets may be used for listening and reading tests; $1 per 20 IBM scorable answer sheets; $1 per 10 scoring stencils (answer pattern must be punched out locally); $7 per 3¾ ips tape for listening test; $7 per 3¾ ips tape for speaking test (blank tapes or discs for recording student responses must be obtained locally); postage extra; $2 per specimen set, cash orders postpaid; (25–35) minutes for listening, (10–20) minutes for speaking, 35(40) minutes for reading, 35(40) minutes for writing; prepared in cooperation with the Modern Language Association of America; Cooperative Test Division. *
a) [LOWER LEVEL.] 1 or 2 years high school or 2 semesters college; form LA ('63, 25 pages).
b) [HIGHER LEVEL.] 3 or 4 years high school or 4 semesters college; form MA ('63, 24 pages).

[403]

★**MLA Foreign Language Proficiency Tests for Teachers and Advanced Students: Italian.** Grades 15–17 and foreign language teachers; 1961–64; IBM in part; 7 tests; 2 forms ('61): Form JML1 (also called Form A, available for institutional programs), Form JML2 (also called Form B, restricted to state and local teacher certification programs); series supervisor's manual ['62, 34 pages]; series norms leaflet ('64, 4 pages); series interpretive leaflet ('64, 4 pages); tentative norms; examination fees: $15 per battery of 7 tests, $12.50 per battery of 4 skill tests (listening, speaking, reading, writing); fees include rental of test materials and scoring and reporting service; postage extra; fee for 30-day examination, $3.70 per battery; Modern Language Association of America and Educational Testing Service; program administered by Educational Testing Service. *
a) LISTENING COMPREHENSION TEST: ITALIAN. IBM; 2 forms ('61, 6–7 pages, containing response options only); stimulus material presented on 3¾ or 7½ ips tape; $1.50 per examinee; (20–30) minutes.
b) SPEAKING TEST: ITALIAN. 2 forms ('61, 9 pages, containing scripts for all languages in the series plus a section on 3¾ or 7½ ips tape); responses recorded on tapes or records supplied by the publisher; $6.75 per examinee; (15–30) minutes.
c) READING TEST: ITALIAN. IBM; 2 forms ('61, 12 pages); $1.25 per examinee; 40(50) minutes.

d) WRITING TEST: ITALIAN. IBM in part; 2 forms ('61, 8 pages); $3.50 per examinee; 45(55) minutes.
e) APPLIED LINGUISTICS TEST: ITALIAN. IBM; 2 forms ('61, 8–9 pages); $1.25 per examinee; 40(50) minutes.
f) CIVILIZATION AND CULTURE TEST: ITALIAN. IBM; 2 forms ('61, 9 pages); $1.25 per examinee; 30(40) minutes.
g) PROFESSIONAL PREPARATION TEST. IBM; 2 forms ('61, 10 pages) common to all languages in the series; $1.25 per examinee; 45(55) minutes.

REFERENCES

1. STARR, WILMARTH H. "Competency First: New Tests in Foreign Languages." *Proc Inv Conf Testing Probl* 1960: 97–110 '61. *
2. STARR, WILMARTH H. "Proficiency Tests in Modern Foreign Languages." *PMLA* 76:7–11 My '61. *
3. STARR, WILMARTH H. "MLA Foreign Language Proficiency Tests for Teachers and Advanced Students." *PMLA* 77:31–42 S '62. *

LATIN

[404]

*****College Entrance Examination Board Achievement Test: Latin.** Candidates for college entrance with 2–4 years high school Latin; 1901–64; for more complete information, see 760; 60(80) minutes; program administered for the College Entrance Examination Board by Educational Testing Service. *

REFERENCES

1–2. See 4:250.
3. See 5:280.

For a review by Konrad Gries of an earlier form, see 5:280; for a review by Harold B. Dunkel, see 4:250. For reviews of the testing program, see 760.

[405]

*****College Entrance Examination Board Advanced Placement Examination: Latin.** High School students desiring credit for college level courses or admission to advanced courses; 1954–63; for more complete information, see 761; 2 levels in 1 booklet: Latin 4 (candidates who present the advanced Vergil course), Latin 5 (candidates who have studied 2 of the following fields: prose, lyric poetry, comedy); 180(200) minutes; program administered for the College Entrance Examination Board by Educational Testing Service. *

[406]

★**College Entrance Examination Board Placement Tests: Latin Reading Test.** Candidates for college entrance; 1962–63, c1955–63; tests are reprints of inactive forms of *College Entrance Examination Board Achievement Test: Latin;* IBM; Forms KPL1, KPL2 in a single booklet (c1955–56, 22 pages); for more complete information, see 759; 60(70) minutes; program administered for the College Entrance Examination Board by Educational Testing Service. *

For reviews of the College Entrance Examination Board Achievement Test: Latin, *see 5:280 and 4:250.*

[407]

*****First- and Second-Year Latin: Every Pupil Test.** 1 or 2 years high school; 1929–64; new form

(4 pages) usually issued each December and April; forms from previous testing programs also available; general directions sheet ('63, 2 pages); no data on reliability; Ohio norms for new forms available following testing program; 5¢ per test; 3¢ per key; postpaid; 40(45) minutes; Ohio Scholarship Tests. *

[408]

*First Year Latin: Every Pupil Scholarship Test. 1 year high school; 1926–64; new form (2 pages) usually issued each January and April; forms from previous testing programs also available; general directions sheet ['63, 2 pages]; no data on reliability; norms for new forms available following testing program; 4¢ per test; 4¢ per key; postage extra; 40(45) minutes; Bureau of Educational Measurements. *

[409]

*Latin I and II: Minnesota High School Achievement Examinations. 1 or 2 years high school; 1953–63; series formerly called *Midwest High School Achievement Examinations;* new norms issued each June; Form F ('53, 3 pages, formerly called Form II, B, D and originally published as Form 2 of *Latin I and II: Achievement Examinations for Secondary Schools*) used in 1963 testing; no specific manual; series manual ('63, 4 pages); series norms ['63, 4 pages]; series cumulative profile ('62, 2 pages); no data on reliability; no description of normative population; 12¢ per test; $2.50 per 100 profiles; postage extra; 20¢ per specimen set, postpaid; 90(95) minutes; American Guidance Service, Inc. *

[410]

★Latin Test (Two-Year Course): Affiliation Testing Program for Catholic Secondary Schools. Grades 10–12 and students who are candidates for the high school diploma issued by the Catholic University of America; 1949–63; administered annually in May at individual schools; IBM; new form issued annually; Form Z ('63, 11 pages) used in 1963 program; separate answer sheets must be used; 50¢ per test and IBM answer sheet, postpaid; specimen set of the complete battery free; fee includes purchase of test booklets, scoring, and other services; for more complete information, see 758; 90(100) minutes; Program of Affiliation, Catholic University of America. *

HENRY CHAUNCEY, *President, Educational Testing Service, Princeton, New Jersey.* [Review of Forms Y and Z.]

These two forms are probably not too difficult for a candidate who has studied Latin for two years. Whether they are sufficiently demanding seems more questionable. Most of the objectives which the Program of Affiliation suggests the Latin course should cover, particularly those pertaining to a knowledge of the Latin language and to the ability to read it, are sampled. Gains in the understanding of the English language, which are also desired, are measured only indirectly.

The instructions for taking the test are clear, although the fact that four, not five, answer positions are used throughout could be pointed out in connection with the example on the cover, as well as each time a new item type is introduced.

The exercises in vocabulary in Part 1 probably have single answers for the two-year Latin student. There are, however, occasional questions (for example, Form Z, item 15, options 2 and 3) which have two possible answers. In others (for example, Form Z, item 16) the meaning given as correct is not the most common one. Thus the candidate who knows more than the average, or more than he has been taught in a particular class, may be at a disadvantage.

The questions testing knowledge of grammar are not of equal difficulty in the two forms. In Form Y, Part 2, the candidate is given Latin sentences containing English words or phrases for which he is to select the correct Latin replacement. This jumble of languages is not good, and the exercise is easier than the comparable one in Form Z, where the sentence contains a blank rather than an English word. In both exercises options can be eliminated because the forms offered are nonexistent in Latin (for example, Form Y, item 25, option 2, and item 45, option 4; Form Z, item 42, options 1 and 2). Thus these questions do not always fully test the kind of grammatical knowledge they purport to test.

In both forms the passages used to test the candidate's reading comprehension are extremely easy, and at least one question (Form Z, item 85) can be answered without reference to the passage. It is to be regretted that the passages are used only to test reading comprehension, and that knowledge of vocabulary, grammar, and syntax, and the ability to translate idiomatic Latin, are not tested by questions based on the passages, as well as by discrete items. A real understanding of Latin involves the ability to use it in the translation of the literature, not merely in fabricated exercises.

For a review of the complete program, see 758.

[411]

*Second Year Latin: Every Pupil Scholarship Test. 2 years high school; 1939–64; new form (2 pages) usually issued each January and April; forms from previous testing programs also available; general directions sheet ['63, 2 pages]; no data on reliability; norms for new forms available following testing program; 4¢ per test; 4¢ per key; postage extra; 40(45) minutes; Bureau of Educational Measurements. *

[Other Tests]

For tests not listed above, see the following entries in *Tests in Print:* 665, 668, 670-3, 675-6, 678-80, and 683-4; out of print: 681.

RUSSIAN

[412]

★**College Entrance Examination Board Achievement Test: Russian.** Candidates for college entrance with 2-4 years high school Russian; 1961-64; available only in January testing program; for more complete information, see 760; 60(80) minutes; program administered for the College Entrance Examination Board by Educational Testing Service. *

For reviews of the testing program, see 760.

[413]

★**College Entrance Examination Board Achievement Test: Russian Listening Comprehension.** Candidates for college entrance with 2-4 years high school Russian; 1963; tests administered at the local secondary school on a specified date in February; candidates must also be registered to take one or more achievement tests in one of the regular program administrations; for more complete information, see 760; (30-40) minutes; program administered for the College Entrance Examination Board by Educational Testing Service. *

For reviews of the testing program, see 760.

[414]

★**College Entrance Examination Board Placement Tests: Russian Listening Comprehension Test.** Entering college freshmen; 1962-63; IBM; Form LPL ('62, 8 pages, a reprint of an inactive form of *College Entrance Examination Board Achievement Test: Russian Listening Comprehension*); test administered by 7½ ips tape recording; for more complete information, see 759; 30(40) minutes; program administered for the College Entrance Examination Board by Educational Testing Service. *

[415]

★**Graduate School Foreign Language Test: Russian.** Graduate level degree candidates required to demonstrate reading proficiency in Russian; 1963-64; Forms K-LFG1, K-LFG2, ('63, 44 pages); for more complete information, see 356; 80(100) minutes; Educational Testing Service. *

[416]

★**MLA-Cooperative Foreign Language Tests: Russian.** 1 or 2 years high school or 2 semesters college, 3 or 4 years high school or 4 semesters college; 1963-64; 4 tests in a single booklet: listening, speaking, reading, writing; IBM in part; 2 levels; directions for administering and scoring ['64, 39 pages] for this and the German, Italian, French, and Spanish tests of the series; no data on reliability; no norms; $5 per 10 tests; separate answer sheets may be used for listening and reading tests; $1 per 20 IBM scorable answer sheets; $1 per 10 scoring stencils (answer pattern must be punched out locally); $7 per 3¾ ips tape for listening test; $7 per 3¾ ips tape for speaking test (blank tapes or discs for recording student responses must be obtained locally); postage extra; $2

per specimen set, cash orders postpaid; (25-35) minutes for listening, (10-20) minutes for speaking, 35(40) minutes for reading, 35(40) minutes for writing; prepared in cooperation with the Modern Language Association of America; Cooperative Test Division. *

a) [LOWER LEVEL.] 1 or 2 years high school or 2 semesters college; form LA ('63, 24 pages).

b) [HIGHER LEVEL.] 3 or 4 years high school or 4 semesters college; form MA ('63, 25 pages).

[417]

★**MLA Foreign Language Proficiency Tests for Teachers and Advanced Students: Russian.** Grades 15-17 and foreign language teachers; 1961-64; IBM in part; 7 tests; 2 forms ('61): Form JML1 (also called Form A, available for institutional programs), Form JML2 (also called Form B, restricted to state and local teacher certification programs); series supervisor's manual ['62, 34 pages]; series norms leaflet ('64, 4 pages); series interpretive leaflet ('64, 4 pages); examination fees: $15 per battery of 7 tests, $12.50 per battery of 4 skill tests (listening, speaking, reading, writing); fees include rental of test materials and scoring and reporting service; postage extra; fee for 30-day examination, $3.70 per battery; Modern Language Association of America and Educational Testing Service; program administered by Educational Testing Service. *

a) LISTENING COMPREHENSION TEST: RUSSIAN. IBM; 2 forms ('61, 6 pages, containing response options only); stimulus material presented on 3¾ or 7½ ips tape; $1.50 per examinee; (20-30) minutes.

b) SPEAKING TEST: RUSSIAN. 2 forms ('61, 9 pages, containing scripts for all languages in the series plus a section on 3¾ or 7½ ips tape); responses recorded on tapes or records supplied by the publisher; $6.75 per examinee; (15-30) minutes.

c) READING TEST: RUSSIAN. IBM; 2 forms ('61, 14-15 pages); $1.25 per examinee; 40(50) minutes.

d) WRITING TEST: RUSSIAN. IBM in part; 2 forms ('61, 7 pages); $3.50 per examinee; 45(55) minutes.

e) APPLIED LINGUISTICS TEST: RUSSIAN. IBM; 2 forms ('61, 8 pages); $1.25 per examinee; 40(50) minutes.

f) CIVILIZATION AND CULTURE TEST: RUSSIAN. IBM; 2 forms ('61, 9 pages); $1.25 per examinee; 30(40) minutes.

g) PROFESSIONAL PREPARATION TEST. IBM; 2 forms ('61, 10 pages) common to all languages in the series; $1.25 per examinee; 45(55) minutes.

REFERENCES

1. STARR, WILMARTH H. "Competency First: New Tests in Foreign Languages." *Proc Inv Conf Testing Probl* 1960: 97-110 '61. *
2. STARR, WILMARTH H. "Proficiency Tests in Modern Foreign Languages." *PMLA* 76:7-11 My '61. *
3. STARR, WILMARTH H. "MLA Foreign Language Proficiency Tests for Teachers and Advanced Students." *PMLA* 77:31-42 S '62. *

WAYNE D. FISHER, *Assistant Professor of Education in Russian, and Associate Coordinator of the Master of Arts in Teaching Program in Russian, The University of Chicago, Chicago, Illinois.*

The general impression I have of this battery is that it represents a most significant milestone along the path toward thoroughly reliable and valid tests which will yield specific information about language abilities. The battery does not represent the ideal, but not on that account should there be any hesitancy to make use of it. However, the limitations of the instruments should be kept in mind when making decisions about language abilities of examinees.

Developed by the Modern Language Association and the Educational Testing Service under contract with the United States Office of Education, the preparation of the tests in five languages has involved some 200 persons representing all teaching levels in many different institutions throughout the country. At least 25 teachers were directly involved in the Russian tests alone. The tests are designed to measure proficiency in seven areas: listening comprehension, speaking, reading, writing, applied linguistics, civilization and culture, and professional preparation. There are two parallel forms of each test, one available for institutional testing and the other for certification programs.

The Listening Comprehension Test is received from master tapes, and the examinee's responses are recorded on answer sheets. The Speaking Test is also received from master tapes, but the examinee's responses are recorded on tapes or discs. The Writing Test includes completion and interlinear exercises for which the examinee writes responses. The other four tests are of the written, multiple choice type. The Reading Test is presented in Russian; the Applied Linguistics Test, Civilization and Culture Test, and Professional Preparation Test are in English.

The reported K-R 20 reliability coefficients on all but the Speaking Test range from .82 to .96. That the Educational Testing Service was not able to overcome the difficulties associated with computing the statistical reliability of scores on the Speaking Test is a major shortcoming of the battery. The correlation between pre- and post-Institute scores (with training at summer 1961 NDEA Foreign Language Institutes intervening) is reported as .79.

As with most existing foreign language tests, the tests in this battery are so constructed that the single linguistic element of vocabulary has a controlling influence on the measurement of the examinee's grasp of all other elements. Thus the validity of the various tests as measures of proficiency in areas other than vocabulary remains open to serious doubt. It is unlikely that standardized tests in foreign languages will ever be valid as instruments for measuring general language proficiency until

vocabulary is controlled, for testing purposes. One simple way of accomplishing this would be for the testmakers to publish a list of the vocabulary used in their tests and to distribute it in advance to examinees. When we think we are measuring the examinee's "ability to reproduce critical sounds and intonations usually difficult for the American student" of the language, we should indeed be doing so, rather than measuring his control of vocabulary. When we think we are measuring the examinee's ability to comprehend spoken language, we should be certain that this is what we are doing, rather than measuring his control of vocabulary. When we think we are measuring the examinee's control of grammatical structure, we must be certain that we are not instead measuring his control of vocabulary. When we think we are measuring the examinee's ability to speak in response to picture stimuli, we should be certain that the stimuli are so broad and panoramic that any examinee would find something in them about which he might speak, in accordance with his own vocabulary experience and training. Testmakers must give this vocabulary problem closer attention, for language learning is much more than simply acquiring vocabulary.

Some questions concerning validity have to be raised in the parts of the Speaking Test where reading Russian print aloud is the testing situation; reading obviously enters as a factor affecting validity. Scoring of the Speaking Test is likely to be impressionistic rather than objective. Extraneous factors which are nonlanguage factors, such as the examinee's introversion-extroversion and creativity in story telling, are likely to influence the scorer's impression.

I suspect the Listening Comprehension Test is more of a clue-response measure of intellectual sleuthing ability than a measure of listening comprehension as normal language behavior. Examinees may be able to catch a word here and there, look at the printed Russian multiple choice answers, and draw upon their general knowledge of the Russian scene to fill in the gaps so that intelligence, memory, and general knowledge, as well as comprehension, are affecting performance on the test. The validity of this test must be further challenged because of the fact that the examinee is required to read the choice of answers in Russian, which, again, unnecessarily introduces the reading factor.

A very important use of the Applied Linguistics Test and the Professional Preparation Test would be for administration to native speakers who are being considered for teaching positions. A native speaker of Russian is not qualified, by virtue of that fact alone, to teach the language in American schools. On the college level, the effects of poor teaching may be overcome, occasionally, by the ingenuity of the students; but on the precollegiate levels the performance of a native speaker who is not also an effective teacher usually leads to disastrous results, or at best makes it possible for only the most talented students to succeed in the Russian classroom. American-educated teachers should also be given these two tests to determine if they are reasonably well informed on current linguistic and pedagogical practices.

Institutions engaged in teacher education might find it useful to administer the full battery of tests in pre- and post-training situations to ascertain the progress of their students and to help evaluate the effectiveness of their programs.

The four skill tests in this battery do represent the greatest advance in foreign language testing to date. They are infinitely better than teacher-made tests which, by their very nature, must interfere with learning. These professionally made tests hold out great promise that wholly valid and reliable tests can be constructed which do in fact measure what we want them to.

SPANISH

[418]

★**Baltimore County Spanish Test.** 1 year high school; 1962; 2 scores: parts A, B; administered orally or by tape recording in part; IBM; 1 form (10 pages); manual (9 pages); no data on reliability; separate answer sheets must be used; $3.75 per 35 tests; $1.75 per 35 IBM answer sheets; 25¢ per scoring stencil; 50¢ per specimen set; $7.50 per 3¾ ips tape recording; postage extra; 80(90) minutes in 2 sessions; Baltimore County Spanish Language Committee; Bobbs-Merrill Co., Inc. *

MARIETTE SCHWARZ, *Associate in Foreign Languages, Educational Testing Service, Princeton, New Jersey.*

This test was designed to satisfy a need resulting from the changing emphasis in for-

eign language teaching from a traditional reading approach to the aural-oral approach. The main purpose of the test is to measure achievement in the mastery of Spanish for students who have completed one year of high school study of the language. It also purports to serve three other purposes: to predict performance in a second-year course; to aid in appraising effectiveness of curriculum materials and methods of instruction; to aid in establishing objective standards for placement in second-year courses.

The test consists of two parts, each to be completed in 40 minutes of testing time. Part A contains 90 multiple choice and true-false items and measures the candidate's proficiency in vocabulary, reading, grammar, culture, and aural comprehension. Fifty of the questions have five choices and 40 are of the true-false type.

Part B contains 55 three-choice items and is intended to measure entirely aural comprehension. For all items in Part B all the choices are printed in the test booklet; for 10 of the items, not only the choices but even the short stories on which the items are based are printed in the booklet. For these items, selecting the correct answers does not necessarily prove listening skill; the candidate could arrive at them on the basis of reading skill.

Part 1 of Part A consists of 15 items testing vocabulary. In five items the student must choose the correct translation into Spanish from an English word or words. In light of present-day teaching methods, it would seem preferable to construct these similarly to the other 10 items which test vocabulary within the context of a Spanish sentence. A wide range of vocabulary with a considerable degree of interest is presented throughout the test, a feat which is often difficult when selection must be restricted to vocabulary within the competence of students with only one year of high school training in Spanish.

Part 2 consists of 15 items measuring reading comprehension. Individual statements which must be answered as true or false provide 10 scorable units which do not require much testing time. The others are multiple choice items based on a preceding paragraph. The questions, which are entirely in Spanish, are well chosen; they cannot be answered without the understanding of the passage.

Part 3 consists of 15 items testing both Spanish and Latin American culture. This part is written in English with some Spanish words interspersed and could be regarded as a contribution to the variety of approaches within the test.

Part 4, a grammar test, consists of 15 items. Each contains an English sentence followed by the Spanish translation with a word or phrase missing. The student must select the word or phrase which best completes the Spanish translation. Ten of the 15 items can be answered without referring to the English sentence, making the English sentences useless. The other five items could easily be revised so as not to necessitate the use of English in this part. Furthermore, two questions have more than one possible correct answer. One question presents a nonexistent word as a choice. It is likely that by the use of English, testing time is being wasted; in view of the trends of present-day language teaching the skill of translation might well be eliminated.

Part 5 tests aural comprehension. It can be administered either by tape or by the examiner reading the script, which is printed in the teacher's manual. This alternate choice of methods for administration, which also applies for all of Part B, suggests that the test cannot be considered completely standardized. Lack of standardization is further substantiated by the fact that there are approximately a dozen discrepancies between the tape and the script, although some of them are minor. In Part B, item number 23 as presented in the script is not the same item as presented on the tape, and the candidate will find no correct answer in his test booklet.

A rerecording of the tape would improve the test considerably. The English voice is pleasant and clear. However, the Spanish voice, which is not that of a native speaker of Spanish, commits serious errors in stress and pronunciation, as well as in basic grammar, by deviating from the script. This comment is made with the realization of the fact that regional differences do exist. For example, in question 35 of Part B, the stress is placed incorrectly on the word "país." No incorrect Spanish should be presented to students in a testing situation. Furthermore, the Spanish voice reads the question numbers in English with a strong German accent. It would be preferable to use an English voice for all of the English and a carefully chosen native speaker of Spanish for

the Spanish voice. Also, speed of the tape is unnatural to the extent of producing continuous open junctures and errors in pronunciation.

The fact that all the directions for the test are in English is to be commended especially at this level of language learning since it does not penalize students for their lack of comprehension of the directions. It might also have been helpful to the student to be presented, wherever possible, with an example for each different type of question. The directions for the second section of Part B need further editing. The student is told to identify objects which have been described. Some of the answers required are not names of objects. It would undoubtedly be of value in Part B to insert additional directions on the tape as an explanation and a warning to anticipate lengthy pauses.

The test is intended to be a power test and, although no data are given on speededness, it does not appear that the test is speeded.

In the section of the manual entitled "Validity and reliability," only data on item discrimination are given. Even these, however, are misleading because they consist of phi coefficients calculated on the basis of extreme groups. Furthermore, while no direct comparison can be made with data of other tests, it has been the reviewer's experience that more discriminating items can be constructed for tests of this type.

The only norms available are the Baltimore County norms ($n = 2,020$). There is no indication whether the norming administration was performed on a sample to which the aural comprehension parts were administered by means of the tape or by readings of the teacher or by a combination of both. No information is given regarding the correlation between Part A and Part B; neither are means and standard deviations given.

From the point of view of item construction, some improvements would be desirable mainly with regard to stems, but also to the choices, which lack consistency in the use or omission of articles.

This test is designed presumably for use with several types of foreign language curricula —those using a moderate oral-aural approach, those with a reading approach, and those with a strong oral-aural approach. This reviewer believes that it may be most satisfactory for the first type of curriculum. Part A cannot be compared to other tests due to the diversity of types of skills and knowledge measured. With regard to Part B, neither from the viewpoint of quality of Spanish nor of test construction does it compare favorably with the lower level listening test of the *MLA-Cooperative Foreign Language Tests: Spanish*. However, some capability is shown for testing the basic elements of elementary Spanish. Despite the shortcomings cited, there might be situations in which a teacher would find this test applicable.

[419]

*College Entrance Examination Board Achievement Test: Spanish.** Candidates for college entrance with 2–4 years high school Spanish; 1902–64; for more complete information, see 760; 60(80) minutes; program administered for the College Entrance Examination Board by Educational Testing Service. *

REFERENCES

1–3. See 4:259.
4. See 5:287.
5. CABAT, LOUIS, AND GODIN, JACOB D. *Spanish: How to Prepare for College Board Achievement Tests in Spanish.* Great Neck, N.Y.: Barron's Educational Series, Inc., 1960. Pp. vi, 107. *

For reviews of the testing program, see 760.

[420]

★**College Entrance Examination Board Achievement Test: Spanish Listening Comprehension.** Candidates for college entrance with 2–4 years high school Spanish; 1960–63; tests administered at the local secondary school on a specified date in February; candidates must also be registered to take one or more achievement tests in one of the regular program administrations; for more complete information, see 760; (30–40) minutes; program administered for the College Entrance Examination Board by Educational Testing Service. *

For reviews of the testing program, see 760.

[421]

*College Entrance Examination Board Advanced Placement Examination: Spanish.** High school students desiring credit for college level courses or admission to advanced courses; 1954–63; for more complete information, see 761; 180(200) minutes; program administered for the College Entrance Examination Board by Educational Testing Service. *

REFERENCES

1. VALLEY, JOHN R. "College Actions on CEEB Advanced Placement Language Examination Candidates." *Mod Lang J* 43:261–3 O '59. *

[422]

★**College Entrance Examination Board Placement Tests: Spanish Listening Comprehension Test.** Entering college freshmen; 1962–63, c1955–63; IBM; Forms DLC1, DLC2 in a single booklet (c1955), Forms JPL, KPL1 in a single booklet (c1960–61, 20 pages, a reprint of inactive forms of *College Entrance Examination Board Achievement Test: Spanish Listening Comprehension*); test administered by 7½ ips tape recording; for more complete information, see 759; 30(40) minutes; program ad-

ministered for the College Entrance Examination Board by Educational Testing Service. *

REFERENCES

1. SCHEIDER, ROSE M. "Evolution of the Listening Comprehension Tests." *Col Board R* 48:24–8 f '62. *

[423]

★**College Entrance Examination Board Placement Tests: Spanish Reading Test.** Entering college freshmen; 1962–63, c1955–63; tests are reprints of inactive forms of *College Entrance Examination Board Achievement Test: Spanish;* IBM; Forms KPL1, KPL2 in a single booklet (c1955–57, 22 pages); for more complete information, see 759; 60(70) minutes; program administered for the College Entrance Examination Board by Educational Testing Service. *

[424]

★**Common Concepts Foreign Language Test: Spanish [Research Edition].** "Students [in any grade] who have had enough foreign language instruction to place them at the Level 1 stage in their achievement"; 1962–64; aural comprehension; may be administered using live voice but tape recording is recommended; IBM; Forms 1, 2; a single booklet ('62, 31 pages) presents response options for both forms of this test and the French and German tests of the series; mimeographed preliminary manual ('64, 24 pages); interim norms (grades 7–12 only); separate answer sheets or cards must be used; 75¢ per test; $5.95 per 3¾ ips tape recording; 5¢ per IBM answer sheet; 20¢ per scoring stencil; 2¢ per Cal-Card; 20¢ per hand scoring stencil; 15¢ per manual; postage extra; $1 per specimen set without tape; $6.95 per specimen set with tape; postpaid; scoring service available; (40–45) minutes; Bela H. Banathy, Miles V. Zintz, W. James Popham, Joseph M. Sadnavitch, Rena Krichbaum, Fred B. Gannon, Valdemar Hempel, and Klaus A. Mueller; California Test Bureau. *

[425]

The Graduate Record Examinations Advanced Tests: Spanish. Grades 16–17; 1946–58; for more complete information, see 762; 180(200) minutes; Educational Testing Service. *

For a review of the testing program, see 5:601.

[426]

★**MLA-Cooperative Foreign Language Tests: Spanish.** 1 or 2 years high school or 2 semesters college, 3 or 4 years high school or 4 semesters college; 1963–64; 4 tests in a single booklet: listening, speaking, reading, writing; IBM in part; 2 levels; directions for administering and scoring ['64, 39 pages] for this and the German, Italian, Russian, and French tests of the series; no data on reliability; no norms; $5 per 10 tests; separate answer sheets may be used for listening and reading tests; $1 per 20 IBM scorable answer sheets; $1 per 10 scoring stencils (answer pattern must be punched out locally); $7 per 3¾ ips tape for listening test; $7 per 3¾ ips tape for speaking test (blank tapes or discs for recording student responses must be obtained locally); postage extra; $2 per specimen set, cash orders postpaid; (25–35) minutes for listening, (10–20) minutes for speaking, 35(40) minutes for reading, 35(40) minutes for writing; prepared in cooperation with the Modern Language Association of America; Cooperative Test Division. *

a) [LOWER LEVEL.] 1 or 2 years high school or 2 semesters college; form LA ('63, 24 pages).
b) [HIGHER LEVEL.] 3 or 4 years high school or 4 semesters college; form MA ('63, 24 pages).

[427]

★MLA Foreign Language Proficiency Tests for Teachers and Advanced Students: Spanish. Grades 15–17 and foreign language teachers; 1961–64; IBM in part; 7 tests; 2 forms ('61): Form JML1 (also called Form A, available for institutional programs), Form JML2 (also called Form B, restricted to state and local teacher certification programs); series supervisor's manual ['62, 34 pages]; series norms leaflet ('64, 4 pages); series interpretive leaflet ('64, 4 pages); examination fees: $15 per battery of 7 tests, $12.50 per battery of 4 skill tests (listening, speaking, reading, writing); fees include rental of test materials and scoring and reporting service; postage extra; fee for 30-day examination, $3.70 per battery; Modern Language Association of America and Educational Testing Service; program administered by Educational Testing Service. *
a) LISTENING COMPREHENSION TEST: SPANISH. IBM; 2 forms ('61, 6 pages, containing response options only); stimulus material presented on 3¾ or 7½ ips tape; $1.50 per examinee; (20–30) minutes.
b) SPEAKING TEST: SPANISH. 2 forms ('61, 9 pages, containing scripts for all languages in the series plus a section on 3¾ or 7½ ips tape); responses recorded on tapes or records supplied by the publisher; $6.75 per examinee; (15–30) minutes.
c) READING TEST: SPANISH. IBM; 2 forms ('61, 12 pages); $1.25 per examinee; 40(50) minutes.
d) WRITING TEST: SPANISH. IBM in part; 2 forms ('61, 8 pages); $3.50 per examinee; 45(55) minutes.
e) APPLIED LINGUISTICS TEST: SPANISH. IBM; 2 forms ('61, 9 pages); $1.25 per examinee; 40(50) minutes.
f) CIVILIZATION AND CULTURE TEST: SPANISH. IBM; 2 forms ('61, 9 pages); $1.25 per examinee; 30(40) minutes.
g) PROFESSIONAL PREPARATION TEST. IBM; 2 forms ('61, 10 pages) common to all languages in the series; $1.25 per examinee; 45(55) minutes.

REFERENCES

1. STARR, WILMARTH H. "Competency First: New Tests in Foreign Languages." *Proc Inv Conf Testing Probl* 1960:97–110 '61. *
2. STARR, WILMARTH H. "Proficiency Tests in Modern Foreign Languages." *PMLA* 76:7–11 My '61. *
3. STARR, WILMARTH H. "MLA Foreign Language Proficiency Tests for Teachers and Advanced Students." *PMLA* 77:31–42 S '62. *

WALTER V. KAULFERS, *Professor of Education, University of Illinois, Urbana, Illinois.*

This battery of seven tests represents a promising attempt to measure "three general levels of proficiency (Minimal, Good, and Superior) for seven areas of language teaching competencies: 1) aural understanding, 2) speaking, 3) reading, 4) writing, 5) language analysis, 6) culture, 7) professional preparation" (*3*). Administration of the battery in one sitting is impractical, not just because of its length (over four hours) but also because of the special equipment required for the Listening Comprehension Test and the Speaking Test. Fortunately, the examinations can be

given independently of each other, and in almost any order desired.

Percentile norms are available based on the converted scores of some 4,400 participants in the Spanish sections of the National Defense Education Act Foreign Language Institutes of 1961, 1962, and 1963. These, however, should be used only by evaluators competent to make allowances for the limitations governing the validity and reliability of the tests. The relationship between ratings given to the examinees by the faculties of the Institutes and the actual scores made by the participants on the tests is at times rather low—e.g., Professional Preparation Test scores versus ratings in all test areas including professional preparation. Percentile norms for a limited sampling (33–138 cases) of Pennsylvania college seniors are also available. The number of cases involved, however, is at present too limited for the norms to be useful as criteria of evaluation.

Inasmuch as a "Superior" level of competence in reading, writing, aural comprehension, and speaking was defined by the Steering Committee of the Foreign Language Program of the Modern Language Association of America as proficiency approximating that of an educated native, it is regrettable that the tests of the aforementioned abilities could not have been administered to a representative sampling of educated natives of Spanish-speaking countries. This would have provided scores with some point of reference or anchorage in reality. It might then be possible to tell, at least within reasonable limits, whether an examinee's performance approximates that of a native, whether it is about half as good, or nearly two thirds as good, etc. In the absence of such validation the reviewer would prefer some of the tests prepared for the College Entrance Examination Board as measures of proficiency in Spanish proper.

The unique features of the battery are the Applied Linguistics Test, the Speaking Test, and the Professional Preparation Test. These are probably the first tests in these fields published for widespread professional use. Unfortunately each falls somewhat short of the reliability commonly expected of examinations designed to differentiate between individuals. Although the battery has already been revised to reduce its original length by nearly two hours, some of the standard errors of measurement are still a little high for tests consisting of only 36 to 65 items. The reviewer has been assured that further revisions are already under way.

The Listening Comprehension Test attempts to measure ability to understand spoken Spanish by means of 36 tape recorded multiple choice questions divided into three parts. As throughout most of the battery, the Spanish of the test, whether printed or recorded on tape, is idiomatic, well edited, and generally above criticism. The use of both male and female voices is well advised. So, too, is the use of acceptable regional variations in the speech of educated natives of Spain and the Spanish-speaking Americas. Only Part 3, however, is strictly an aural comprehension test. The preceding two sections require the examinee to read and choose among four possible answers involving a total of from 8 to 37 words. In fact, some of the items in Parts 1 and 2 of the Listening Comprehension Test actually involve more "reading" than is required in Part 1 of the Reading Test proper. For this reason the validity of the test—namely, the exact meaning of the scores obtained from it—is open to question. In Part 2 the length of some of the comprehension items also suggests that they may measure memory as much as understanding. The examinee is constantly distracted by the necessity of choosing the correct response from among four possible answers printed in Spanish.

The reliability of .91 as measured by Kuder-Richardson formula 20 is satisfactory. That this is an unnecessarily difficult test for many people, however, is confirmed by the fact that while "the mean number of unanswered items is less than one * the score distributions show substantial numbers of scores not only below the dashed lines [99th percentile of the theoretical chance score distribution] but also below the expected mean chance score of 11.00." It is the reviewer's opinion that not a small part of the trouble lies not in the difficulty of the spoken Spanish which the examinees are expected to comprehend, but in the involved printed statements from among which they are so often expected to make a choice. While selecting an answer the examinee can easily forget some of what he heard on tape.

The Speaking Test is administered entirely on tape from directions given in English. The examinee records his responses for evaluation by scorers trained by the Educational Testing Service. Part 1 has him repeat verbatim short spoken sentences and questions. Part 2 requires him to read aloud a printed passage of Spanish dialogue. Part 3 requests him to describe in Spanish what he sees in a series of situation drawings. Since Parts 1 and 2 are essentially tests of pronunciation, intonation, and ability in oral reading, only Part 3 is actually a "speaking" test in the everyday sense of the word. To score the latter the evaluator is obliged to keep in mind simultaneously a rating scale embracing 20 different levels of performance—5 each for vocabulary, pronunciation, structure, and fluency!

The fact that even with scoring done by specially trained evaluators interscorer reliabilities in the .80's are difficult to obtain shows that this is not an examination to be scored or interpreted by amateurs. As one of the first tests of speaking ability in Spanish to be produced for widespread professional use since the days of the Army Student Training Program, however, it is an additional milestone in foreign language achievement testing.

The three parts of the 40-minute Reading Test are designed to afford a measure of comprehension in silent reading. Since an educated native of Spain or Spanish America would be able to complete the examination in much less time than the 40 minutes allowed, it is essentially a power test. It will not always discriminate between fast and slow readers—between those who can actually "read" Spanish and those who can do little more than "decode" it. Although Part A is well constructed and apparently scaled in ascending order of difficulty, some of the items actually require less "reading" than is involved in the Listening Comprehension Test.

Part B consists of four passages of from approximately 130 to 250 words each. The reviewer found it possible to choose the correct answers to several questions here without reading the selection itself. Items 16 through 21 of Form JML1 are more tests of vocabulary than of reading comprehension. Part C consists of five passages of poetry. The abstract symbolism of some of the verses will present a challenge even to able readers.

Although the Kuder-Richardson reliability coefficients of .91 and .90 for the two forms appear satisfactory, the validity of the examination is limited by the fact that it provides no measure of ability to comprehend material presented in a conversational or dialogue context, as is often the case in plays, novels, and short stories.

The Writing Test consists of two parts. In the two printed passages of Part A each numbered line replaces a word that has been omitted. Since some of the 30 blanks permit more than one acceptable answer, scoring the test objectively is not an easy matter. The scorer is permitted to use personal judgment in the case of dubious or far-fetched responses —a seeming throwback to the infancy of foreign language achievement testing a generation ago. Space 28 (in Form JML1), for example, suggested five acceptable alternatives to the reviewer who made no attempt to exhaust the possibilities. Applied to Part A the title, "Writing Test," is a misnomer since this part involves far more reading than writing. Little more writing is involved here than was frequently required in tests of "active vocabulary" a generation ago.

Part B confronts the examinee with two poorly written passages. He is to treat them as though they were student compositions and to revise them so that they conform to standard Spanish. This part is highly functional in that it affords an indication of the examinee's ability to correct student compositions, written exercises, board work, etc. However, by its very nature it is more a measure of "proof-reading" ability than of proficiency in original composition.

The reliability coefficients of .94 and .95 for the two forms show that satisfactory reliability can be achieved even for tests which are not entirely objective, provided the scorers are agreed from previous orientation sessions regarding just how they will evaluate such things as minor slips in the omission of accent marks, minor misspellings, or cases of borderline legibility.

The Applied Linguistics Test is divided into four parts. Part A covers phonetics, pronunciation, and orthography. Part B covers morphology and syntax with a view to testing the examinee's "knowledge of some of the differences and similarities among Spanish grammatical patterns on the one hand, and between Spanish and English on the other." Part C tests the examinee's understanding of some of the terms of phonetics and descriptive linguistics, and more importantly his "ability to identify Spanish illustrations of the concepts represented by these terms." The last part consists of only three items dealing with historical linguistics.

Inasmuch as the Applied Linguistics Test is probably the first objective examination in this field to be published for widespread professional use it is unfortunate that neither form has a reliability of more than .85—a little short of the reliability of .90 commonly considered desirable if a test is to differentiate between individuals. Scaling the items in ascending order of difficulty (of which there is little evidence in the examination) should help here, as would recasting the multiple choice items to reduce the word length of the four responses. In general, the greater the word length of the multiple choice answers the more time consuming and "difficult" taking the test becomes regardless of the examinee's knowledge of the subject. Moreover, there are other types of machine scorable test items that could have been employed to advantage here as in other parts of the battery.

The Civilization and Culture Test covers mainly the geography, history, and literature of Spain and Spanish America, with passing attention to art, music, and politico-economic conditions. Items 1, 2, 15, 17, 22, and 45 in Form JML1, as well as all items of this type in Form JML2, should be cast in another form. Selecting the correct response here is exasperatingly time consuming because of the amount of "decoding" involved. The sequence of items without any apparent attempt either to scale them in ascending order of difficulty or to group them according to topic (as in the linguistics test) is unfortunate. The omnibus scores provided by the test prevent it from affording ready suggestions concerning the specific aspects of Spanish or Spanish-American civilization and culture in which an examinee may be strong or weak. A reconstruction of the test to meet these objections should enhance its utility and also increase its present reliability of .89 so as to make it even more dependable in differentiating between individuals.

The 45-minute, 65-item multiple choice Professional Preparation Test is primarily an attempt to measure an examinee's acquaintance with objectives, methods, and resource materials approved by exponents of the audio-lingual ("linguistic") approach in foreign language teaching. Several items relate to the teaching of foreign languages in the elementary grades. Knowledge of the ways and means for accommodating students of different abilities, however—viz., gifted as compared with very slow learners, stammerers, etc.—is apparently beyond the purview of this examination. Moreover, even a perfect score will provide no assurance that the teacher can give intelligent counsel to parents asking, for example, if their five-year-old son is too immature to begin learning a second language.

The reliability coefficients of .86 and .87 for Forms JML1 and JML2 barely approximate the reliability generally expected of tests designed to differentiate between individuals. A grouping of items by topic into three or more parts should help raise the test's reliability by reducing the number of shifts in mindset which the present unscaled, unorganized sequence requires. Recasting items 34 and 35 in Form JML1 should also help. As presently framed they are unnecessarily time consuming because of the "decoding" involved and hence probably more difficult to answer than the subject justifies. Grouping the items by topics into three or more parts might also increase both the validity and the utility of the examinations by affording a diagnosis of the respects in which an examinee's professional preparation is adequate or deficient. As probably the first test of this kind to be published for widespread professional use it is an important first step in the right direction. In its present form, however, it should be regarded as tentative and experimental. Fortunately, this test has been under almost continuous revision since its first printing.

In summary, the *MLA Foreign Language Proficiency Tests for Teachers and Advanced Students: Spanish* are designed to serve an important need which to date they barely succeed in meeting satisfactorily. The excellent statistical analyses of the tests, however, indicate that they have enough promise to warrant further revision. In their present state they should be used only by examiners thoroughly acquainted with the nature of the subject matter tested, aware of the limitations of the individual tests, and willing to give borderline examinees either a supplementary test or the benefit of any doubt.

[428]

★**National Spanish Examination.** 2, 3, 4 year's high school; 1957–63; new form issued annually for admin-

istration in April at local secondary schools or centers established by local chapters of the AATSP; 4 scores: aural, usage, reading, total; 3 levels; Forms G2S, G3S, G4S, ['63, 4 pages] used in 1963 program; no manual; no directions for administration; no data on reliability; summary of results (based on locally scored papers returned to the test development committee) is published in *Hispania* in September following the testing program; 10¢ per test; $5.50 per 7½ ips tape recording for aural subtest; postpaid; copies of previous year's tests and tapes available at the same prices; (105–115) minutes; [Test Development Committee, American Association of Teachers of Spanish and Portuguese]; the Association (distributed by local chapter treasurers and the national chairman). *

REFERENCES

1. SAPORTA, SOL, AND CHARLY, H. T. "Report on the 1957 National Spanish Examinations." *Hispania* 40:333–5 S '57. *
2. POWELL, JAMES D. "Second Report on the 1958 National Spanish Examinations." *Hispania* 41:499–501 D '58. *
3. POWELL, JAMES D., AND CHARLY, HARRY T. "Preliminary Report on the 1958 National Spanish Examinations." *Hispania* 41:336–7 S '58. *
4. POWELL, JAMES D.; HARTSOOK, JOHN H.; AND CHARLY, HARRY T. "Report on the 1959 National Spanish Examinations." *Hispania* 42:356–7 S '59. *
5. HARTSOOK, JOHN H., AND CHARLY, HARRY T. "Report on the 1960 National Spanish Examinations." *Hispania* 43: 422–4 S '60. *
6. CHARLY, HARRY T., AND HARTSOOK, JOHN H. "Report on the 1961 National Spanish Examinations." *Hispania* 44: 499–500 S '61. *
7. CHARLY, HARRY T. "Report on the 1962 National Spanish Examinations." *Hispania* 45:498–500 S '62. *
8. BOYER, MILDRED V., AND CHARLY, HARRY T. "Report on the 1963 National Spanish Examinations." *Hispania* 46: 587–90 S '63. *

[429]

★**Spanish I and II: Minnesota High School Achievement Examinations.** 1 or 2 years high school; 1951–63; series formerly called *Midwest High School Achievement Examinations*; new norms issued each June; Form F ('53, 5 pages, formerly called Form II, B, D and originally published as Form 2 of *Spanish I and II: Achievement Examinations for Secondary Schools*) used in 1963 testing; no specific manual; series manual ('63, 4 pages); series norms ['63, 4 pages]; series cumulative profile ('62, 2 pages); no data on reliability; no description of normative population; 12¢ per test; $2.50 per 100 profiles; postage extra; 20¢ per specimen set, postpaid; 90(95) minutes; American Guidance Service, Inc. *

[430]

Spanish: Teacher Education Examination Program. College seniors preparing to teach secondary school; 1957; for more complete information, see 709; IBM; 80(95) minutes; Educational Testing Service. *

For a review of the testing program, see 5:543.

[431]

★**Spanish Test (Two-Year Course): Affiliation Testing Program for Catholic Secondary Schools.** Grades 10–12 and students who are candidates for the high school diploma issued by the Catholic University of America; 1949–63; administered annually in May at individual schools; IBM; Form Y ['62, 12 pages] used in 1963 program; tests loaned only; separate answer sheets must be used; 50¢ per test and IBM answer sheet, postpaid; specimen set of the complete battery free; fee includes scoring and other services; for more complete information, see

758; 90(100) minutes; Program of Affiliation, Catholic University of America. *

HENRY CHAUNCEY, *President, Educational Testing Service, Princeton, New Jersey.* [Review of Form Y.]

According to the data for interpretation, as well as personal judgment, the test in its entirety is of average difficulty for students having had a two-year sequence of Spanish study in high school. Although Part 2, which purports to measure reading comprehension, borders on the easy side with a mean per cent of right answers of 60, and Part 5, measuring cultural background, is a difficult part with 32 per cent of right answers, the test appears to be well suited for its educational level, and it is not speeded.

It is questionable, however, that the test really measures all four language skills—listening, speaking, reading, and writing—as implied on page 51 of the booklet Program of Affiliation. This booklet states, "Oral and written expression can be tested only indirectly by an objective test, especially by questions on grammar and syntax." However, questions on grammar and syntax can hardly be said, even indirectly, to provide a measure of speaking and writing, at least not now with the absence of any correlation studies to prove the contrary. Furthermore, Part 2 of the test does not represent a true measure of reading comprehension. Although a paragraph is presented, it appears to be there mainly for face validity. Following the first paragraph, for example, 18 out of the 20 questions can be answered with-

out ever having read the passage. The candidate merely chooses the English translation of a word or group of words. At best, this could be called the testing of vocabulary in context, providing that the candidate is helped by referring to the paragraph. Each of the two remaining questions has only one attractive distractor. In other words, it is necessary to read the passage only in order to choose between two of the options.

In terms of the syllabus, the area of the content tested is broad and still realistic, although the vocabulary of the test is based upon a designated word list. In certain respects, both the Spanish course outline and the test seem to retain features of the traditional grammar-translation approach, while also incorporating some characteristics of audio-lingual language teaching and testing. It appears that, in light of the syllabus, translation of vocabulary and testing of grammar partially through translation are justified. It is commendable that nowhere are incorrect structures presented to the candidate. However, in light of the changing emphasis of present-day foreign language curricula, perhaps some of the course objectives, as well as the resulting test specifications, might be reexamined and item types modified or new ones employed.

For a review of the complete program, see 758.

[Other Tests]
For tests not listed above, see the following entries in *Tests in Print:* 691–2, 694–6, 699–701, and 703; out of print: 690, 697, and 704.

REPRINTED FROM *The Seventh Mental Measurements Yearbook*

FOREIGN LANGUAGES — SEVENTH MMY

REVIEWS BY *John B. Carroll, Clinton I. Chase, John L. D. Clark, George Domino, Michio Peter Hagiwara, A. Ralph Hakstian, Walter V. Kaulfers, Robert Lado, Walter F. W. Lohnes, Joseph A. Murphy, T. F. Naumann, Josephine Bruno Pane, Gino Parisi, Glen W. Probst, Jean-Guy Savard, Jack M. Stein, and Paolo Valesio.*

[253]

*Common Concepts Foreign Language Test. Students in any grade who are at the Level 1 stage of achievement; 1962–66; CCFLT; 3 aural comprehension tests: French, German, Spanish; may be administered using live voice but tape recording (3¾ ips) is recommended; Forms 1, 2, ('62, 31 pages, the same booklet is used for both forms and all 3 languages); manual ('66, 41 pages); separate answer sheets (IBM 1230) must be used; $1.10 per test; $2.50 per 50 answer sheets; $5.95 per tape recording; 75¢ per scoring stencil for a given form and language; $1 per manual; postage extra; $2.25 per specimen set (without tape), postpaid; scoring service, 22¢ and over per test; (40–45) minutes; Bela H. Banathy, Miles V. Zintz, W. James Popham, Joseph M. Sadnavitch, Rena Krichbaum, Fred B. Gannon, Valdemar Hempel, and Klaus A. Mueller; CTB/McGraw-Hill. *

WALTER V. KAULFERS, *Professor of Foreign Language Education, University of Illinois, Urbana, Illinois.*

Although the title page of the manual suggests that the battery includes English as a foreign language, the current edition is incomplete in this respect. "An English version had been contemplated at one time, but was subsequently dropped. Users in situations demanding an English edition are urged to utilize the appropriate language and simply reverse the process; that is, the preliminary instructions should be given in the native tongue (French, for example) and the stimulus sentences spoken in English." Since no supporting data are available to substantiate the validity and reliability of this procedure, it is doubtful if users of the test should place much confidence in scores for English obtained in this manner.

In fact, the title of this test does not indicate that it is exclusively a test of aural comprehension. The test requires no ability whatsoever to read, write, or speak the foreign language. With changes in the directions, it could be administered to illiterates in almost any language. It is therefore difficult to accept the authors' claim that a student's "basic language competence can be estimated more readily by testing aural comprehension or oral production than by using measurement techniques based on the secondary skills of reading and writing." This would seem true only if "basic language competence" is narrowly defined in esoteric terms to describe the most primitive of language skills. The claim that the examination "is designed primarily to measure and evaluate overall level of proficiency in another language" is therefore not warranted in this reviewer's judgment.

In structure the examination is exclusively a multiple choice test "presenting a stimulus sentence which is heard in the foreign language while the student looks at a panel of four small pictures. The student's task is to identify from the four frames [i.e., choices] the one picture which matches the spoken sentence. * Twenty-three clearly delineated, multi-colored pictures are used for the eighty test sentences that are incorporated in each form of the test. These are common scenes that are easily interpretable." The pictures, while small, are generally attractive, interesting, and readily intelligible.

Tapes in Spanish, French, and German (one for each of the two forms for each language, but none for English) are available for administering the test entirely by tape recorder. The directions (given in impeccable English by a separate administrator) are clear and so detailed as to occupy over a third of each recording. The test sentences are spoken by a male native. The same male voice is heard exclusively throughout both forms of the test for each language. The recordings are of high fidelity, the voices pleasing, and the diction that of educated natives. However, the use of only one native voice throughout (using only the Latin American pronunciation in the case of Span-

ish) seems an unfortunate limitation in a test measuring nothing but aural comprehension.

Use of the tapes should simplify administration of the test and is recommended to assure uniformity of administration when data are to be obtained for comparative purposes from students taught by different methods. Their use is also desirable if the scores are to provide a measure of how well the students can understand German, French, or Spanish when the language is spoken by someone other than their teacher.

Statistically, the *Common Concepts Foreign Language Test* compares favorably with the better foreign language achievement tests now on the market. The reliability of the two forms for French, German, and Spanish extends from .73 for elementary school pupils in French to .96 for junior high school students in Spanish. Most reliability coefficients in the three languages fall within the .88–.92 range. As measured by the correlation of raw scores with teachers' course marks, the validity of the test ranges from .40 in junior high school Spanish (71 cases only) to .72 in elementary school Spanish (172 cases).

Tables giving percentiles, standard scores, and stanine reference distributions for the elementary school, junior high school, and senior high school levels are included for each language and form in the manual. However, since the publishers do not indicate whether the data are based on tape recorded administrations of the test, derived from administration by the students' own teachers, or from scores obtained by a mixture of methods, these "reference distributions" have very limited application. Comparison of a particular student's score with scores other than the average for his own classmates is unwarranted because of (a) the lack of data concerning the norming population, (b) the impracticability of providing separate norms for highly selected vs. unselected groups, and (c) the impracticability of providing norms for specific grades—because of the wide variations in the number ·of contact hours in different schools.

The chief limitations of the *Common Concepts Foreign Language Test,* however, are qualitative rather than statistical. Five deserve attention:

a) The 80 items of each form of the test consist almost exclusively of simple declarative sentences. In all of Form 1 of the German test, for example, nine items are simple questions, but only two items are exclamatory. No items whatever are compound, complex, or complex-compound in structure and only one (one of the exclamations) is imperative. The French and Spanish forms have comparable shortcomings. A picture identification test apparently does not lend itself readily to other than simple declarative statements.

b) The tests are phrased almost exclusively in the present indicative. For example, Form 1 of the French examination contains not a single sentence in a past or present perfect tense and only one future tense. In the German and Spanish tests, the number of other than simple present indicative statements is much too limited for evaluative purposes.

c) Apparently none of the tests are scaled in difficulty from easiest item first to hardest item last. Translated into English, item 43 in Form 2 of the French test reads, "They walk, ride, and drive to school," while item 80 at the end of the test simply says, "The walls are green." A relatively hard item early in a test often disheartens an examinee unnecessarily.

d) No evidence is available showing to what extent the two forms for each language are statistically of equal difficulty. Thus, if a pupil scores 10 points higher on Form 2 at the end of the third semester than he scores on Form 1 at the end of the second, no one can be sure whether the gain is a measure of the student's progress, or a measure of the degree to which Form 2 is easier.

e) Correct answers can at times be selected without necessarily comprehending the statement as a whole. In translation, item 59 in Form 2 of the French test reads, "I see the number 50." Since only one picture in the booklet contains this number, a pupil would not necessarily have to understand the entire sentence to choose the right answer. Just recognizing the French word for "fifty" would suffice.

In summary, the *Common Concepts Foreign Language Test* can provide a rough measure of the extent to which a pupil understands spoken French, German, or Spanish when the speaker talks almost exclusively in the present tense and rarely in other than short, simple declarative sentences. In no circumstances should it be used as the sole means for measuring and evaluating "overall level of proficiency in another language."

[254]

*MLA Cooperative Foreign Language Tests. 1–2 years high school or 2 semesters college, 3–4 years high school or 4 semesters college; 1963–65; 2 levels; 5 tests; for additional information and reviews, see the separate test entries; Cooperative Tests and Services. *
a) FRENCH. See 277.
b) GERMAN. See 290.
c) ITALIAN. See 302.
d) RUSSIAN. See 312.
e) SPANISH. See 322.

J Ed Meas 2:234–44 D '65. John L. D. Clark. * Although a number of specific criticisms of these tests may be advanced, it should be borne in mind that the emphasis and scope of these tests is such as to secure for them a very important place in present day language teaching and evaluation endeavors. * Listening and Speaking norms for level L are given only for "audio-lingual" classes at the first and second year high school levels, since tests of these two skills were not considered appropriate for the "traditional" courses at these levels. Although it is certainly true that the development of listening and speaking skills usually receives greater stress in "audio-lingual" courses, even the more traditional courses do provide at least some opportunity for listening and speaking practice, if only through the occasional repetition of memorized material or the reading of blackboard sentences. Thus, it would appear suitable (and particularly helpful for comparative and other research purposes) to provide listening and speaking norms for "traditional" groups as well. * At the college level, general norms are provided for all four skills at each of two levels: first year (level L) and second year (level M). A worthwhile future undertaking might be to provide separate "audio-lingual" and "traditional" norms at the elementary *college* level; a candid view of beginning undergraduate courses will suggest considerable variations in course content and emphasis which would make the definition of different norming groups appropriate. For the most part, the normative data described above are uniformly available across languages; in a few instances, however, and particularly for certain Italian and Russian groups, the total number of cases tested was too small to permit even tentative norming; test users in these two languages particularly should make sure that norms are listed for the forms and levels to be used. * For the most part, considerable care seems to have been taken to assist the user in his interpretation of the norms tables and other statistical information presented. * Although claims made for the measurement applications of the tests are in general carefully delineated, a few rather serious overstatements seem to have been made concerning their potential usefulness for *diagnostic* purposes for pinpointing specific language areas in which individual students or test groups are experiencing difficulty. The Handbook states in this respect that the tests will be found useful for "discovering the kinds of errors that foreign language students make," and for "identifying idioms and structures in a foreign language that are troublesome for a class or for individual students." The reviewer seriously doubts that either the test developers or potential users would be able to identify in most of the items the unitary linguistic features which are both necessary and sufficient for success or failure on that item. The linguistic redundancies always present in meaningful continuous discourse, both spoken and written, make it extremely difficult to specify particular lexical or syntactical elements which the student must "know" to answer the item correctly. Put somewhat differently, there are usually a number of "linguistic roads" (or detours) that the student may follow in passing or failing an item; and from the item response alone, it is generally impossible to determine which particular route the student has taken. * A clear warning against the attempted use of the tests for diagnostic purposes is particularly in order in view of the recent establishment by ETS of a scoring-reporting service for the "A" forms of the Listening and Reading tests. This service provides the teacher with such item analysis data as the percentage of students passing each item, the group frequency of answer alternatives, and individual student response patterns including the designation of correctly and incorrectly answered items and indication of the particular answer options chosen. A leaflet describing the scoring service states among other things that the data provided will "facilitate the use of test results in improving instruction" and will permit the identification of "common difficulties revealed by the individual response patterns." It is somewhat ironic that this type of scoring is not available for the Speaking and Writing tests—the two tests which do in certain limited instances permit the identification of particular linguistic problems (the pronunciation of certain sounds and the knowledge of tense, gender,

and number markers, respectively). But to expect that similarly close identifications will be afforded by commercial or private analysis of responses to Listening and Reading test items (or by private analysis of most Speaking and Writing test items) is to court disillusionment. In keeping with the above discussion, it is suggested that the Cooperative tests will *not* be found appropriate in such content-oriented applications as the following: 1) determining student grades, insofar as such grades are expected to reflect the extent to which particular linguistic patterns, vocabularies, etc. have been learned; 2) evaluating the success of training programs in meeting goals cast in specific linguistic terms (for example, as given in course syllabi); 3) identifying particular linguistic problems for diagnostic and correctional purposes, either on an individual or group basis. On the other hand, as more general-purpose tests of the level of students' competence in different skill areas, the Cooperative tests could be expected to serve effectively in such measurement tasks as: 1) determining the standing of certain schools or school districts with respect to the overall outcomes of the language programs; 2) establishing the general level of competence of individual students for such purposes as initial class placement, assignment to teaching sections, and so forth; 3) determining, for counseling or other purposes, the relative standings of particular students with respect to "developed proficiency" in any or all of the four skill areas, by reference either to the performance of other students in a locally defined group or to the performance of a nationwide sample of students engaged in "similar" language programs. In these and comparable undertakings, the fact that the Cooperative tests are not bound to materials presented in a specific textbook or training sequence gives appreciable assurance that the tests will be "fair" to large numbers of students regardless of the particular classrooms or school systems in which they have studied. * the Cooperative series is made up of four entirely different tests, each with unique characteristics and logic of measurement corresponding to the particular skill involved * The order in which the tests are discussed below is established for convenience only; the suggested order of administration is not made clear in the test literature, although it may be an important variable in the light of possible "warm-up" or practice effects among the different tests. * *Reading.* In the Reading tests....the reading passages, questions, and answer alternatives are all in the foreign language. Although it would appear generally desirable to reduce the use of English as much as possible in foreign language tests, measurement validity may be adversely affected. Thus, in the Reading test, the student's inability to understand a particular printed question may prevent a proper response to that item, regardless of his overall comprehension of the passage itself. * In the absence of distracting factors of the type described above, it may fairly be said that the Cooperative Reading tests measure the student's ability to comprehend various written passages to the extent that he is able to answer certain questions based on the factual content and, for some of the upper level items, the "tone" of the material involved. * *Listening.* * When played on a high quality and properly adjusted reproducing system, the sound quality of both the Listening and Speaking tapes is unquestionably excellent. * the speech heard on these tapes may be considered somewhat "too good" in that it often exceeds in clarity and carefulness the speech which would usually be employed in the various real-life situations being modeled * It is not suggested that test constructors are ill-advised to seek high electronic and vocal quality in test tapes (on the contrary, there are cogent pedagogical and evaluative justifications for such an approach), but rather that students who respond successfully in the various situations presented on the Listening test tapes might not by this token be expected to perform with comparable facility in analogous real-life situations encountered, for example, during a trip abroad. A more serious problem with the Listening tests lies in the fact that these tests are to a certain extent tests of *reading* ability: the student must read and understand the answer alternatives in order to indicate his responses to the spoken stimuli. Here, as with the Reading tests, it is always possible that the student may understand the test passages themselves but experience confounding difficulties with the "answer" portions. In the Listening tests, however, the problem is compounded, since an entirely different linguistic modality is involved, a modality in which the student may well not be expected to have the requisite degree of facility. Indeed, for those language classes that postpone the introduction of printed material in favor of intensive preliminary work on listening comprehension and speaking, the necessity for the student to *read* a number of printed answer alternatives may in some instances proscribe use of these tests as valid measures of aural comprehension. Teachers who wish to make use of the Listening tests in their own classes should determine through careful prior examination of the test booklets that their students would probably not have difficulty in understanding the printed alternatives. Another potential problem with the Listening tests is the occasional inclusion of spoken passages based on factual or historical material. In Spanish Listening MA, for example, a passage is read describing the history of bullfighting; in Spanish Listening MB, there is a description of the history and geography of Bolpebra, a rather well-known city near the borders of Bolivia, Peru, and Brazil. In these and similar cases, students who have had previous exposure to the factual material presented (not necessarily in a language learning situation) are in a more favorable position to answer the questions correctly than persons for whom the material is entirely novel. For that matter, students who are well acquainted with the probable content of a given passage may need to catch only a few random words to "understand" quite clearly what the passage is about. Fortunately, such factual passages are in the minority, and most of the conversations, dialogues, and other passages used appear to have been created expressly for the tests, a procedure that insures against prior familiarity with the content of the passages. *Writing.* * Although the Writing test is subjectively scored in the sense that trained human judgment is required, the inter-rater scoring reliability (independent scoring by two judges) seems to be quite high. * In general terms, the producers of the Writing tests appear to have struck a happy balance between, on the one hand, a structuring of student responses sufficient to allow for well-defined grading procedures, and on the other, provision for a certain amount of freedom in the actual writing process including the "creation" of an entire paragraph. Like the Listening tests, the Writing tests do not measure exclusively the language skill for which they are named. On the contrary, the student is required to read and understand a number of foreign words and sentences to fill in the required words or alter the sentences as requested. Not all tests of writing skill necessarily require some element of reading proficiency in the foreign language: for example, the simple direction "Write a story about...." would successfully bypass questions of reading ability altogether. However, in view of the fact that the Cooperative test constructors for a number of practical reasons have elected to construct the Writing test in a way which includes a reading ability factor, the test user should satisfy himself that his students are experiencing little difficulty with the reading of the sentences as such if he intends to consider the obtained results to be reflections of writing ability *per se*. Certain possibly minor problems in the mechanics of the Writing test may be suggested. For example, is the test so arranged as to place a premium on handwriting speed? In this connection, it is interesting to note that the scoring directions ask the rater to overlook "minor errors that might be due to hurried copying of words in the model sentence." Another question is raised by a sentence in the scoring directions which asks the rater to "overlook a student's failure to observe" an instruction printed in the test booklets (for some languages) that only a certain number of words (e.g. from 3 to 10) are to be used in composing certain responses. There seems to be in these instances no legitimate reason to misinform the student as to the nature of the task requested. Aside from such minor considerations, which are probably easily correctable, the Writing tests appear to provide a convenient and straightforward means for presenting the student an opportunity to produce words, phrases, and longer passages in the foreign language with attention to spelling, agreement of persons and gender, proper sequence of tenses, and so forth, all of which are certainly valid elements in the totality of performance known as "writing in the foreign language." *Speaking.* Among the tests in the four skill areas, the development of a valid and reliable test of speaking ability is at once of the most immediate importance to the teaching profession and of the greatest technical difficulty in terms of the measurement problems encountered. * the undertaking on the part of the MLA-ETS group to provide alternate forms of a speaking test for five different languages at each of two ability levels is of major significance. Although the tests so produced may be considered in many respects the least successful of the four Cooperative skill tests, the importance of the undertaking cannot be overemphasized: rather than curse the darkness which has surrounded the evaluation of foreign language speaking ability, the Cooperative test constructors have lit several candles for which the entire language profession may be grateful. Administration of the Speaking test requires the use of the test booklet, a test tape, and in addition, blank tapes (locally obtained) for recording the student responses. Administration is almost necessarily confined to the language laboratory, where the number of student recording positions available sets an upper limit on the number of students who may be tested at one time. * In the first part of the Speaking test, the student listens to short utterances that he repeats aloud, attempting to imitate the model voice as closely as possible. * The second section of the test asks the student to read a short printed passage aloud * In the third section, the student looks at simple line drawings (for example, a book lying on a table) and answers a spoken question about each drawing ("Where is the book?"). * In the fourth and final part of the test, the student looks at and "tells a story about" both a single picture (for example, a wife bringing her husband a cake from the kitchen) and a series of four pictures (for example, a family visiting the zoo). * A number of questions may immediately be raised concerning the first section of the test (sound imitation). First, there is some indication that trained judges may not be able to rate consistently the right-wrong quality of the imitated sounds. * In the same connection, it may be wondered whether sounds produced by native speakers themselves would be uniformly judged as "right," or whether certain features of the speakers' idiolects might be considered "wrong" by the judges. In the latter case, the validity of the right-wrong scoring method might be called into question. For the picture description sections, one could ask whether rather laconic native speakers might be assigned lower scores than more verbose speakers; presumably, such individual personality factors would be out of place in a test of basic speaking skill. In the absence of validity information obtained through the administration of the Speaking (and other skills) tests to representative groups of native speakers, these and similar questions which might be raised about test performance must go unanswered. It should be noted briefly that the reading section of the Speaking test again involves two different linguistic modalities, and that student scores on this part of the test might be expected to vary to some extent on the basis of their prior exposure to printed materials. A serious practical shortcoming in the use of the published Speaking test norms is that these norms have been based on the scoring performance of "largely native or very fluent" speakers of the test language who had also participated in a number of preliminary training sessions at ETS. Since an in-field test usage would involve a rather different group of scorers (presumably, high school and college teachers with varying degrees of linguistic proficiency and no preliminary practice in the judging procedure) the scores assigned by these raters might not be comparable to those which would have been assigned in the same cases by the norming judges. The in-field scoring problem is addressed, at least in a nominal way, by the provision at the end of each Speaking test tape of a special section containing responses of one student "judged by his teacher to have a high degree of competence for a student at this level." Suggested ratings for this model student on the various sections of the test are not provided, nor is there any discussion of the linguistic merits or shortcomings of the responses made. Further, in the absence of other recordings made by "poor" or "average" students, little idea of the range of possible responses can be obtained through listening to the single voice provided on the practice tape. It would not be technically difficult to produce and make available a detailed "scorer training tape" for each language that would contain a number of representative student performances together with a detailed discussion of the scores to be assigned in each case. The scoring directions for the Writing test do in fact present samples of student responses, giving both the particular scores assigned in each case and the rationale underlying their assignment; in the case of the Speaking test, an aural analog for this type of scoring aid would seem clearly in order. *Summary.* The MLA Cooperative Foreign Language Tests are considered to represent, for the most part, well based and carefully developed measures of overall linguistic achievement at the beginning and intermediate levels of proficiency. Their wide scope and general orientation make them especially suitable for use in larger-scale testing programs which cut across lines of particular course content. On the individual student level, the tests allow for broadly

defined statements of competence which should be of value in such areas as initial course placement and academic counseling. The MLA tests are not recommended for use in measuring the attainment of particular linguistic goals, such as the knowledge of specific lexicon, control of certain syntactical patterns, and so forth. Although individual linguistic elements may be isolated for some of the items, the tests as a whole do not lend themselves to such analysis. In certain tests or test sections, the confounding of linguistic modalities as a consequence of the format employed makes it advisable for the user to determine that students who are to take the tests would not reasonably experience difficulty as a result. Additional research on various other aspects of test performance may be suggested, including a detailed examination of the responses of native speakers to the linguistic tasks presented. The MLA Cooperative tests are to be praised for their extensiveness and for the emphasis which they bring to the testing of all four language skills. It can be hoped that the precedent so established will be followed by both the MLA-ETS group and others in continuing the work that has been so auspiciously begun.

For reviews of individual tests, see 277, 290, 302, 312, and 322.

[255]
★**Modern Language Aptitude Test—Elementary.** Grades 3-6; 1960-67; EMLAT; downward extension of the *Modern Language Aptitude Test;* 5 scores: hidden words, matching words, finding rhymes, number learning, total; Form EA ('65, 15 pages) ; manual ('67, 12 pages) ; 3¾ ips test tape, 5 inch reel; $4.50 per 25 tests; 60¢ per set of keys; $7.50 per test tape; 40¢ per manual; $1.20 per specimen set; postage extra; 61(75) minutes; John B. Carroll and Stanley M. Sapon; Psychological Corporation. *

A. RALPH HAKSTIAN, *Associate Professor of Educational Psychology, University of Alberta, Edmonton, Alberta, Canada.*

The EMLAT contains many of the features found in the older, well-conceived MLAT (for grades 9 and over). In Part 1, Hidden Words, the examinee must find a synonym or definition for a stimulus consisting of a group of letters which, when uttered, approximates an English word (e.g., "silns," for which the correct answer is "quiet"). Both vocabulary and sound-symbol association—verbal and auditory skills, respectively—are presumably measured. In Part 2, Matching Words, two sentences are presented together, the task being to find the word in the second sentence having the same syntactic function as a particular word in the first. "Sensitivity to grammatical structure" is said to be measured. In Part 3, Finding Rhymes, the examinee must identify, from a list, the word that rhymes with the stimulus word, so that, although both stimulus and response are written, something akin to sound discrimination—an auditory skill—is measured. In Part 4, Number Learning, the examinee learns the names of numbers in an artificial language and then must write them down when he hears them presented. Thus, memorizing ability is measured along with, perhaps, "auditory alertness." Parts 1, 2, and 4 are found in the MLAT; Part 3 is totally new.

ADMINISTRATION AND SCORING. Instructions are given almost entirely on a tape. The test stimuli for Parts 1, 2, and 3 are in an expendable test booklet; for Part 4, on the tape. All responses are recorded in the test booklet. Thus, test booklets and a single tape recording are needed for administration. The test booklets are hand scored using stencils which are provided. Overall, administration and scoring are clearly explained in the manual and require no special training other than in the operation of a tape recorder.

INTERPRETATION AND NORMS. Norms are based on a fairly small but adequately representative sample (18 elementary schools), and are given for both sexes in each of grades 3 to 6. Since normative data are provided only for total scores, the diagnostic purposes for which this test can be used are rather limited. The part scores and the constructs which they represent are not discussed or interpreted in the manual. Although in the higher-level MLAT norms are available only for total scores, some information is given in the manual on using part scores to diagnose learning difficulties (it might prove difficult, of course, to know what is really a "low" score without norms). It seems reasonable that if language aptitude can be conceived of as multi-factorial, the uses to which a test such as the EMLAT could be put might well have been extended beyond prediction to include diagnosis.

The very sensible feature, present also in the MLAT, of norms reported in terms of percentile bands is found in the manual. Unfortunately, however, and unlike the MLAT, no mention is made of developing local normative data. Some directions are given on using scores for placement and guidance. Overall, however, some important interpretive uses of the test have been overlooked.

RELIABILITY AND VALIDITY. The statistical data gathered on the EMLAT are particularly well presented. The inappropriateness for speeded tests of the usual split-half method of estimating reliability is acknowledged (three of the four parts may be considered speeded), and instead an alternative estimate is presented, based upon independently administered and timed half-tests, with the resulting correlations corrected with the Spearman-Brown formula. The obtained reliabilities, data on which were gathered from four schools, and which were estimated at each of the four grade levels for each sex, are extremely high, ranging from .93 to .96. Also included are standard errors of measurement and an excellent explanation of their uses.

Reliabilities (based on the same groups) of the part scores range between .70 and .95. Also presented are the intercorrelations among the parts for samples comprising each of the eight sex-by-grade-level combinations. Part 1, Hidden Words, and Part 3, Finding Rhymes, tend to correlate highly—from .55 to .81 over the samples. The other interpart correlations tend to be lower, but still substantial enough (approximately half of the 48 interpart correlations—six each for the eight samples—are above .50), when one considers the shortness and hence deflated reliabilities of the parts, to call into question the authors' contention that the interpart correlations are "only moderate" and represent evidence that the parts measure "distinct aspects of aptitude." It would appear that the separate component skills are quite substantially interrelated.

Evidence for criterion-related validity is presented in the form of correlations between total scores and course grades given two to three months later. The authors correctly acknowledge that such correlations can be more properly considered concurrent than predictive validity estimates. Forty samples were used in the validation study, with N's ranging between 26 and 89. Although each sample was homogeneous with regard to sex, grade, language (French or Spanish), and school (seven were used), the obtained validity estimates are impressively high, ranging between .23 and .84 over the 40 coefficients presented, with 37 at or above .40

and 10 above .60. The validities could perhaps have been even higher had the authors combined the students examined into larger subsets with consequently less restriction in the range of ability, but such estimates would not have been nearly as meaningful. Some demographic information on the schools in the study, however, might have helped the prospective user better estimate the test's validity for his school. In any case, the criterion-related validity appears more than adequate to make this test a useful predictor of success in foreign language learning. In short, reliability and validity are not only excellent, but also well documented.

SUMMARY. The EMLAT appears to be a carefully constructed and useful instrument for assessing language aptitude in grades 3–6. In spite of certain interpretative failings of the manual—such as no emphasis on establishing local norms and no way to interpret part scores —this test can be used to make reliable and valid assessment of language aptitude among young students. It is hoped that subsequent manuals will offer more direction on possible interpretive uses of the test.

[256]

★Pimsleur Language Aptitude Battery. Grades 6–10; 1966–67; 5 scores: grade-point average, interest, verbal, auditory, total; Form S ('66, 4 pages); manual ('66, 19 pages); student performance chart and report to parents ('67, 2 pages); separate answer sheets (Digitek, IBM 805, IBM 1230) must be used; $7 per 35 tests; $9.50 per 7½ ips test tape, 7 inch reel; $2.30 per 35 IBM 805 answer sheets; $2.80 per 35 Digitek or IBM 1230 answer sheets; $1.40 per set of scoring stencils; $2.70 per 35 student performance charts; $2.25 per specimen set; postage extra; IBM scoring service, 33¢ and over per test; (50–60) minutes; Paul Pimsleur; Harcourt Brace Jovanovich, Inc. *

REFERENCES
1. PIMSLEUR, PAUL; STOCKWELL, ROBERT P.; AND COMREY, ANDREW L. "Foreign Language Learning Ability." *J Ed Psychol* 53:15–26 F '62. * (*PA* 37:2003)
2. PIMSLEUR, PAUL. "Predicting Success in High School Foreign Language Course." *Ed & Psychol Meas* 23:349–57 su '63. * (*PA* 38:1387)
3. FAY, BETTE LANNERT. *A Study of the Validity of the Pimsleur Language Aptitude Battery With Beginning French Students.* Master's thesis, Ohio State University (Columbus, Ohio), 1965.
4. PIMSLEUR, PAUL, AND STRUTH, JOHANN F. "Knowing Your Students in Advance." *Mod Lang J* 53(2):85–7 F '69. *
5. THOMAS, JESSE C. *A Study of the Correlation Between the Pimsleur Language Aptitude Battery and Foreign Language Grade Point Average Among Seventh Grade Students in the Anaheim Union High School District.* Master's thesis, Chapman College (Orange, Calif.), 1969.

A. RALPH HAKSTIAN, *Associate Professor of Educational Psychology, University of Alberta, Edmonton, Alberta, Canada.*

The *Pimsleur Language Aptitude Battery* is composed of six parts: (1) Grade Point Average, (2) Interest, (3) Vocabulary, (4) Language Analysis (from a list of foreign expressions and their English equivalents, deducing how sentences may be formed in the foreign language), (5) Sound Discrimination (differentiating between pitch, orality, and nasality in spoken words), and (6) Sound-Symbol Association (associating sounds with their written symbols). The four factors seen by the author as underlying language aptitude, and on which part scores are used, are GPA, Interest, Verbal (Parts 3 and 4), and Auditory (Parts 5 and 6).

ADMINISTRATION AND SCORING. In Part 1, GPA, the examinee records from memory his last letter grade in English, social studies, mathematics, and science. From a predictive viewpoint, such an assessment appears weak, not only because considerable inaccuracy is probable, but also because the precise meaning of letter grades can vary over local settings; longer-term GPA's with greater predictive efficacy could be obtained from school records. Perhaps, however, the advantage of not having to search out these grades outweighs any small loss in predictive power. One wonders whether the equal weighting of grades in the four subjects, when summing to get the GPA score, could not effectively be replaced by some optimal unequal weighting system, since it is unlikely that grades in the four subjects predict foreign language aptitude equally well.

Part 2, Interest, is assessed via a *single item* with a 5-point scale running from "Rather uninterested" (in studying a modern foreign language) through "Strongly interested." Such an assessment seems very unreliable, since the measurement of such fluctuating, noncognitive constructs is somewhat unreliable *at best*. It seems strange that a longer interest test used experimentally by the author and referred to in the manual was abandoned.

Parts 3 through 6 are administered by using directions on tape; Parts 3 and 4 have the test stimuli in a booklet, whereas Parts 5 and 6 have the stimuli also on tape. Responses to *all* parts are recorded on machine scorable answer sheets. Thus, test booklets, answer sheets, and a single tape recording are needed. Overall, no special training is required of the teacher giving the test, and directions for administration and scoring are clear and complete.

INTERPRETATION AND NORMS. Norms, based on an admirably large and representative standardization sample, are provided in terms of both percentile ranks and stanines at four levels—the beginning of grades 7, 8, and 9, and the end of a first-level course—for total raw scores, verbal scores, and auditory scores. The manual unfortunately stresses the use of the stanine, the disadvantages of which seem to far outweigh the merits. Comparative judgments among students can more accurately be made with such other standard scores as the T score. Further, the size of stanines 1 and 9 is *not* equal to that of the others (although in the manual one is informed that all nine intervals are of equal size), and the reflection of truly exceptional scores—both low and high—is somewhat precluded. Percentile bands (used, for example, in the *Modern Language Aptitude Test*) would have constituted a preferable acknowledgment of the errors of measurement in mental testing.

Thorough interpretive information is presented. The user is advised to interpret scores cautiously and always with an eye to the most relevant norms group. Highly commendable are the rationale and directions provided for establishing local normative information using expectancy tables. Further, multiple regression analysis is suggested, and the publisher offers such a service. Advice is included on using the test for selection, classification, and diagnosis.

RELIABILITY AND VALIDITY. Corrected split-half reliability estimates, based on scores in the normative samples, are presented for Parts 3 through 6 separately and for the total of these parts, for four levels. Reliabilities appear adequate—running from .57 to .82 for the part scores and .85 to .89 for the composite scores— for tests of such length (Part 4, for example, has only 15 items), although it is not clear just how much elevating effect speededness may have had on these estimates. One can only guess, of course, at the reliability of the one-item interest test. Test-retest reliability estimates are promised in a future publication. It is most unfortunate that standard errors of measurement are not presented, as (*a*) they tend to be considerably more stable, over samples differing in homogeneity, than do the associated reliability coefficients, and (*b*) they can be used to set limits about obtained scores for more judicious interpretation. Their absence, then, must be considered a shortcoming.

The construct validation procedures are described, and tables of intercorrelations among the six part scores are presented at four levels. These correlations, varying between .14 and .50, are presented as evidence that the abilities

measured are relatively distinct. Actually, however, the .14 and most of the correlations below .20 involve the interest test, which undoubtedly has low correlations with the other parts because of low reliability. In fact, of the remaining correlations presented, the majority are above .35, and many above .40. Given the short tests used to measure the six components, it would seem that the constructs represented are quite highly interrelated.

Concurrent validity data are the results of two studies. In one, correlations between total raw scores and (*a*) final grades in first-level courses in French and Spanish and (*b*) scores on experimental forms of the Pimsleur tests of Reading and Listening Comprehension ranged (over samples) between .44 and .79 for final grades, .25 and .72 for the Reading Comprehension Test, and .39 and .78 for the Listening Comprehension Test. Unfortunately, a different set of weights than that recommended in the manual was used with Parts 1 and 2 of the aptitude battery. In the other study, part scores, but not total scores, were correlated with the same criteria. Some predictive validity data are presented with the criterion being the *MLA— Cooperative Foreign Language Tests: French,* but again regression weights different from those recommended were used. Thus, no substantial predictive or concurrent validity data for the present test are presented. Had the test been published a year later, perhaps adequate validity data could have been included, rather than merely promised in a future publication.

SUMMARY. It may be true that data on the first two components of language aptitude— GPA and Interest—could be more effectively obtained by means other than the same test used to assess verbal and auditory ability. Overall, however, the *Pimsleur Language Aptitude Battery* appears to offer easy administration and scoring, adequate interpretive guidelines, but, as yet, incomplete reliability and validity data (although the reliability and validity may well be quite adequate). It is hoped that as these data are obtained they will be made available to users of the test.

J Counsel Psychol 15:299–300 My '68. Donald C. Ryberg. * The norms....summarize data for nearly 4,000 students beginning Grades 7, 8, and 9 in the fall of 1965–1966. Means and standard deviations are reported for each level by sex and with sexes combined for each of the parts and for the total scores. Intercorrelations are given. However, data are cross-sectional, and the population sample is not specified. * Correlations of Aptitude scores with final course grades and with raw scores for the Pimsleur Listening and Reading Comprehension Tests in French and Spanish are reported. Aptitude scores (total raw scores) yield coefficients ranging from .44 to .79, with final course grades ranging from .39 to .78 with Listening Test raw scores and from .31 to .72 with Reading Comprehension Test raw scores. While these data provide information on performance, the measures were obtained concurrently and cannot be considered evidence of predictive validity. * The LAB appears to be appropriate to the age levels for which it was intended and appears to measure relevant characteristics for foreign language learning. The battery is easily administered and scored. Given the scores, prediction and guidance, however, should proceed cautiously. The part scores seem particularly useful. For example, scores on Part 1 indicating general academic achievement could tell a great deal about perseverance and application in general, and scores on Part 2 indicating interest in studying a modern foreign language could be crucial when there is an unusually low score in either verbal or auditory ability. The interest score depends largely on a student's background of information and interests rather than on interest which may be developed through contact, study, and maturity. Total score on this type of test is of questionable value when one considers the various abilities or skills that make up the spectrum of language learning. Scores on the various parts of the battery will tell more about the facets of language learning that might pose problems for the student. The manual suggests that local norms collected over a period of years may be most helpful. The norms presented in the manual are useful references, but are not necessarily relevant to local groups of students and programs of instruction. On the other hand, once local norms are established, it may be valuable to compare them with those quoted in the manual as a basis for judgments about the program itself. Validity and reliability data in the manual are incomplete. The publisher is reporting results of investigations in progress as they are available. *

[257]
★Pimsleur Modern Foreign Language Proficiency Tests. First, second level courses in grades 7–12 or first, second semesters college; 1967; 3 tests; for additional information and reviews, see the separate test entries; Harcourt Brace Jovanovich, Inc. *
a) PIMSLEUR FRENCH PROFICIENCY TESTS. See 279.
b) PIMSLEUR GERMAN PROFICIENCY TESTS. See 292.
c) PIMSLEUR SPANISH PROFICIENCY TESTS. See 325.

J Ed Meas 6(1):44–6 sp '69. A. Ralph Hakstian. * Administration and Scoring. Clear and detailed instructions for administration and scoring are provided in the manual. The fifteen minute listening comprehension test is administered via tape and answers are recorded on machine-scorable answer sheets. The thirty-five minute reading comprehension test utilizes test booklets and machine-scorable answer sheets. The speaking and writing proficiency tests, requiring sixteen and thirty-five minutes, respectively, represent necessarily more subjective scoring (spoken answers to the former are recorded on tape; written answers to the latter, in a booklet), but commendable attempts have been made to make the scoring as objective as possible. * Interpretation and Norms. Substantial interpretive materials are provided in the manual. Relevant information is given on the standardization sample. The sample seems admirably representative, geographically, and certainly large enough—8595 students in all, from 90 schools and 21 states. There is no information given on the degree of selectivity introduced as a function of the degree to which schools showed a willingness to participate. It is interesting to note that when teachers were asked to send back only every fifth *writing* test booklet in order to facilitate scoring in the standardization program, the listening and reading test scores of this "random" sample were slightly higher than those for the total normative group. * It is somewhat unfortunate that considerable stress is given to the stanine scale, since this scale does little more than add additional crudeness to already crude measures. The manual points out that a difference of two stanines or more between a person's scores on two of the subtests can be considered a reliable difference. Actually, however, the standard error of a difference for a difference between listening and reading comprehension scores on Form A of the French test, for example, is 1.28 stanines. Thus, the probability by chance alone, of a difference of two stanines on these two tests for an individual whose scores are at the top of the lower stanine and the bottom of the upper stanine could be as high as .28, clearly too high to consider such a difference reliable. A weakness in the interpretive tables lies in the fact that percentiles and stanines are based upon the total first- and second-level standardization groups. The first-level norming group contains students from grades 8 to 12; the second-level group, from grades 9 to 12. It might be more informative for teachers to be able to make comparisons with more finely delineated reference groups or at least have data showing the degree of similarity of performance between the various grades included in each level. With these few exceptions, however, the interpretive materials are informative and well presented. *Validity and Reliability.* Data on validity are well presented in the manual. A breakdown of items into well defined categories constitutes the content validity data, and the author wisely suggests that prospective users of the tests use this analysis in judging the appropriateness of the tests for their own language program. * Concurrent validity is presented in terms of correlations of the various tests (except for speaking proficiency) with final grades and teachers' ratings in a sample of students other than the standardization sample. Unfortunately, it is not clear from the manual whether or not teachers had knowledge of their students' scores on the tests prior to assignment of final grades and ratings. It is interesting to note that Form A of the French writing test, for example, correlates more highly with teachers' ratings of listening (.63) than does the listening test (.52). Similarly, the writing test correlates as highly with teachers' ratings of reading (.60) as does the reading test (.58). Also, the reading test appears to correlate more highly with the teachers' ratings of listening (.59) than does the listening test (.52). It is the reviewer's belief that these seeming incongruities are attributable to halo effect, in that teachers are more familiar with a student's reading and writing capabilities, perhaps, than his listening ability and knowledge of these more familiar skills transfers to assessment of listening ability. These results also bring up the issue of the relative purity of the four tests in all three languages, and the discriminant validity inherent in the tests. The listening test, and, to a lesser degree, the speaking test, are somewhat contaminated with a reading component. In the former, the student hears a sentence and chooses among four *written* alternatives the one he thinks he has heard. As Scherer and Wert-

heimer (1964) have suggested,[1] a better measure of listening as a separate skill would have been to have the alternatives also presented on tape. Moreover, the relatively high correlations among the listening, reading, and writing tests (.56 to .78) and between these three tests and teachers' ratings of speaking (.48 to .72) suggest, as Scherer and Wertheimer found, that, even had the tests been as free as possible of the overlapping of hypothesized skills, the existence of four language communication skills as meaningfully discriminable entities may be an unwarranted conception among teachers of foreign languages. * It is a mystery, though, why the Kuder-Richardson formula 21 was used in estimating reliabilities for the writing proficiency test, when it was freely admitted in the manual that assumptions implied in formula 21 were not met (the possible scores on some of the items of this test range from 0 to 3). * In general, however, validity and reliability data are clearly presented and complete. *Summary.* With the few exceptions noted, the Pimsleur Tests are well designed technically, and clearly and completely documented in the manual. The tests for each language will be discussed at greater length in the following sections.

For reviews of individual tests, see 279, 292, and 325.

ARABIC

[258]
★**First-Year Arabic Qualifying Examination.** 1 year college; 1964; 1 form (25 pages); manual (4 pages); no data on reliability; no norms, publisher recommends use of local norms; separate answer sheets (IBM 805) must be used; $3 per test and manual, postage extra; answer sheets free; (110–130) minutes; Sami A. Hanna; Middle East Center, University of Utah. *

CHINESE

[259]
★**Harvard-MLA Tests of Chinese Language Proficiency.** College and adults; 1959–65; 2 tests; manual ('65, 12 pages); no data on reliability; 35¢ per test; 5¢ per answer sheet; 35¢ per manual; cash orders postpaid; Modern Language Association of America and Educational Testing Service; program administered by Educational Testing Service. *
a) PICTORIAL AUDITORY COMPREHENSION TEST. 2 semesters; 1959–65; PACT; 1 form ('59, 21 pages);

1 SCHERER, G. A. C. AND WERTHEIMER, M. *A Psycholinguistic Experiment in Foreign-Language Teaching.* New York: McGraw-Hill Book Co., 1964. Pp. 256.

Harvard-MLA Tests of Chinese Language Proficiency

7½ ips tape, 7 inch reel; separate answer sheets may be used; $5 per tape; (30–40) minutes; John B. Carroll and Wai-Ching Ho.

b) INTERMEDIATE READING COMPREHENSION TEST IN MODERN CHINESE. 4 semesters; 1964–65; 4 scores: vocabulary, structure, reading comprehension, total; 1 form ('64, 31 pages); separate answer sheets must be used; (120–130) minutes; K. P. Chou, John de Francis, Y. K. Kao, H. C. Mills, R. C. Pian, and J. Wrenn.

ENGLISH

[260]

★A Comprehensive English Language Test for Speakers of English as a Second Language. Nonnative speakers of English; 1970; CELT; 3 tests; preliminary manual (16 pages); tentative norms; publisher recommends use of local norms; separate answer sheets must be used; $4 per 100 answer sheets, postage extra; David P. Harris and Leslie A. Palmer; McGraw-Hill Book Co. *

a) LISTENING. Administered orally or by a recording; Form L-A (7 pages); examiner's book (13 pages); $8 per 20 tests; $20 per 20 tests, 100 answer sheets, examiner's book, and 3¾ ips tape recording ($15 with 33⅓ rpm record instead of tape); $3 per specimen set; (35–45) minutes.

b) STRUCTURE. Form S-A (10 pages); directions (1 page); $8 per 20 tests; $10.50 per 20 tests and 100 answer sheets; $2.50 per specimen set; 45(55) minutes.

c) VOCABULARY. Form V-A (10 pages); directions (1 page); $8 per 20 tests; $10.50 per 20 tests and 100 answer sheets; $2.50 per specimen set; 35(45) minutes.

JOHN B. CARROLL, *Senior Research Psychologist, Educational Testing Service, Princeton, New Jersey.*

To judge from the data arrayed in the preliminary manual, this battery would appear to be a promising instrument for gauging the English proficiency of persons (high school age and above) who are learning English as a second language. It is "comprehensive" in the sense that it provides information in three critical areas: listening comprehension, knowledge of "structure," and reading vocabulary. The intertest correlations are not so high as to suggest that the subscores are all measuring the same thing, yet they are not so low as to give the impression that they are measuring totally different domains. The materials evidently went through a considerable amount of pretesting, item analysis, and refinement. Sufficient normative data, although of a provisional character, are offered to enable the user to interpret scores with some confidence. The authors are to be commended for presenting data on the performance of native English speakers on the tests—data that show that American high school students of only moderate ability achieved "extremely high scores" on

them. Thus, one may infer that the tests measure fundamental rather than high-level skills in English.

It is unlikely that there will ever be a perfect all-purpose test of English as a second language; any battery of reasonable length must be designed with particular purposes in mind. This test is intended for persons who have had some formal instruction in English, usually abroad, and who come to the U.S. for further training or education. All parts of the test assume reading knowledge of English. Thus, the listening test is a test not only of aural comprehension but also of reading skill, even though the authors claim to have taken care "to keep the printed alternatives brief and lexically and grammatically simple so as to minimize the reading factor." Nevertheless, one can find items in which the total word count for the four alternatives (which must be inspected within the 15 seconds allowed for selecting the answer) is as high as 40. A learner of English with a native language background in a non-Roman alphabet or syllabary, or with just poor reading ability, might do poorly on the test despite good aural comprehension. Occasionally the items demand more than comprehension, that is to say, they demand the making of inferences about fairly complex situations. On the other hand, a few items seem too simple, depending almost exclusively on the recognition of introductory question words (*what, how,* etc.). But on the whole, given the assumptions on which it was based, this is a good test of global auditory comprehension of idiomatic American English spoken at a relatively rapid rate. Unless they object to the particular American dialect used in the recordings, users are strongly encouraged to employ the tape or phonograph recording that is available rather than to try to have the script read aloud locally —requiring the use of three speakers, two males and one female.

The structure test is introduced as a test of how well the learner knows the "grammar" of English. This is a correct claim only if one assumes that "knowing the grammar of English" corresponds to the ability to read and select constructions that are acceptable and idiomatic in choice of words or word order. These are constructions that tend to cause difficulty for foreign learners. Teachers of English as a second language justifiably place much emphasis on such constructions, hoping that the student who masters them will be more likely to speak and write acceptably. One could imagine, however, a student with a rather good technical knowledge of the theory of English grammar who might nevertheless fail to recognize, say, that "lunch room" is more idiomatic than "room for lunches," or to find a better word order than "hardly ever he leaves his house now." But this structure test will please most teachers of English as a second language, for the constructions tested are well selected and the items well written.

If any of the subtests can be rather seriously faulted, it would be the vocabulary test. According to the authors, the 280 words included in the test (counting words in both stems and alternatives) "were selected to represent the vocabulary which students might encounter in mature reading materials of the kinds assigned in general college courses." This reviewer was struck, however, with the rather high frequency of what he would call "everyday household words" like *shrink, rake, dyed,* and *strap* that would be more likely to occur in *Woman's Day* magazine than in mature college reading material; conversely, core concept words like *excel* and *reject* were poorly represented in the test. By selecting only words from the 4th to the 7th thousand in frequency-rank in the Thorndike-Lorge *Teacher's Word Book of 30,000 Words,* the authors missed the opportunity to test some of the less usual meanings of words occurring in the 1st to 3rd thousand of the frequency list. Incidentally, item 25 of the vocabulary test Form V-A is miskeyed in the scoring key that was supplied to the reviewer (the answer should be D, not B).

Since CELT comes in three separate modules, it will be convenient and economical to use only those parts that are appropriate for one's purpose. It is to be hoped that more forms will become available so that it may be used for varied purposes in placement and in the measurement of course achievement. As a practical and flexible test that can be easily procured by a teacher (in contrast to "secure" tests like the ETS *Test of English as a Foreign Language*), it will fill a need. The CELT total score is reported as having a correlation of .91 with the TOEFL scores in one group of 29 students.

[261]

★**English Knowledge and Comprehension Test.** High school; 1965; EKCT; Form 165 ['65, 13 pages]; mimeographed manual ['65, 14 pages]; authors recom-

mend use of local norms; separate answer sheets must be used; Rs. 1.60 per test; Rs. 75 per 50 tests; Rs. 6 per 100 answer sheets; Rs. 3.50 per scoring stencil; Rs. 4 per manual; postage extra; 90(100) minutes; S. Chatterji and M. Mukerjee; S. Chatterji. *

[262]

***English Usage Test for Non-Native Speakers of English.** Non-native speakers of English; 1955–70; Forms U-A ('62, 8 pages), G, H, I, ('63, 8 pages), J ('67, 8 pages), K ('70, 8 pages); directions sheets: Form U-A ('62, 2 pages), Forms G-K ('67, 2 pages); combined manual ('67, 15 pages) for this and tests 263, 265, and 267; distribution of Forms G-K restricted to the Agency for International Development and the Bureau of Educational and Cultural Affairs of the U.S. Department of State; distribution of Form U-A restricted to the Department of State; separate answer sheets must be used; manual free on request; 60(65) minutes; David P. Harris and Leslie A. Palmer; American Language Institute. *

[263]

***Listening Test for Students of English as a Second Language.** Non-native speakers of English; 1961–67; administered orally or by tape recording; Forms A ('61, 7 pages), B ('62, 7 pages), C ('64, 7 pages); examiner's booklets: Forms A ('61, 10 pages), B ('62, 10 pages), C ('64, 10 pages); combined manual ('67, 15 pages) for this and tests 262, 265, and 267; distribution restricted to the Agency for International Development and the Bureau of Educational and Cultural Affairs of the U.S. Department of State; separate answer sheets must be used; manual free on request; (25) minutes; David P. Harris and Leslie A. Palmer; American Language Institute. *

[264]

***Michigan Test of English Language Proficiency.** Applicants from non-English language countries for admission to American colleges; 1961–65; MTELP; Forms A ('61, 15 pages), B, revised ('65, 16 pages); manual ('62, 15 pages); separate answer sheets must be used; $8 per 20 tests, 100 answer sheets, scoring stencil, and manual; $3 per 100 answer sheets; $2 per specimen set; postpaid; 75(90) minutes; test by John Upshur, Geraldine May, Leslie Palmer (A), John Harris (A), Miho Tanaka (B), and Rudolph Thrasher (B); manual by Division of Testing and Certification, English Language Institute, University of Michigan; distributed for the Institute by Follett's Michigan Book Store, Inc. *

REFERENCES

1. DIZNEY, HENRY. "Concurrent Validity of the Test of English as a Foreign Language for a Group of Foreign Students at an American University." *Ed & Psychol Meas* 25: 1129–31 w '65. * (PA 40:3566)
2. URSUA, AURORA RICARDO. *The Relationship Between Adeptness in the English Language and Social Adjustment of Foreign Graduate Students.* Doctor's thesis, Catholic University of America (Washington, D.C.), 1969. (DAI 30:2390A)

For a review by John B. Carroll of Form A, see 6:360.

[265]

***Oral Rating Form for Rating Language Proficiency in Speaking and Understanding English.** Non-native speakers of English; 1959–67; also called *AULC Interview Rating Form;* 6 ratings by interviewers: comprehension, pronunciation, grammar and word-order, vocabulary, general speed of speech and sentence length, total; individual; 1 form ('62, 2 pages, identical with form published in 1959 except for title); manual ('60, 11 pages); combined manual ('67, 15 pages) for this and tests 262–3 and 267; distribution restricted to the Agency for International Development and the Bureau of Educational and Cultural Affairs of the U.S. Department of State; manual free on request; (15–30) minutes; [David P. Harris]; American Language Institute. *

[266]

★**Test of English as a Foreign Language.** Applicants from non-English language countries for admission to American colleges; 1964–70; TOEFL; test administered 4 times annually (January, March, June, October) in approximately 100 countries; 6 scores: listening comprehension, English structure, vocabulary, reading comprehension, writing ability, total; 4 forms published annually; last 3 forms: Forms SEF2 ('70, 26 pages), SEF3 ('70, 25 pages), SEF4 ('70, 25 pages); bulletin of information ('70, 16 pages); handbook for candidates ('70, 19 pages); supervisor's manual ('70, 24 pages); revised interpretive manual ('70, 31 pages); listening comprehension subtest administered by record or tape; supervisor's script ['70, 7 pages]; separate answer sheets (SCRIBE) must be used; examination fee, $10 per student; fee includes reporting of scores to the examinee and to 3 colleges designated at time of application; 140(160) minutes; program sponsored jointly by the College Entrance Examination Board and Educational Testing Service; Educational Testing Service. *

REFERENCES

1. HARRIS, DAVID. "English as a Second Language: Testing." *Overseas* 3:22–5 Ja '64. *
2. LADO, ROBERT. "English and the Foreign Student." *Nat Cath Ed Assn B* 61:210–2 Ag '64. *
3. DIZNEY, HENRY. "Concurrent Validity of the Test of English as a Foreign Language for a Group of Foreign Students at an American University." *Ed & Psychol Meas* 25: 1129–31 w '65. * (PA 40:3566)
4. PALMER, LESLIE A. "TOEFL: Testing of English as a Foreign Language." *Nat Cath Ed Assn B* 62:235–8 Ag '65. *
5. CHASE, CLINTON I., AND STALLINGS, WILLIAM M. *Tests of English Language as Predictors of Success for Foreign Students.* Indiana University, Monograph of the Bureau of Educational Studies and Testing, Indiana Studies in Prediction, No. 8. Bloomington, Ind.: the Bureau, 1966. Pp. 24. *
6. MAXWELL, ALICE. *A Comparison of TOEFL and the UCB/EFL Test.* Master's thesis, Sacramento State College (Sacramento, Calif.), 1966.
7. HWANG, KWO-YANN. *A Study of TOEFL Test Scores and Academic Success for Chinese Graduate Students at an American University.* Master's thesis, University of Oregon (Eugene, Ore.), 1969.
8. DARNELL, DONALD K. "Clozentropy: A Procedure for Testing English Language Proficiency of Foreign Students." *Speech Monogr* 37(1):36–46 Mr '70. *
9. HWANG, KWO-YANN, AND DIZNEY, HENRY F. "Predictive Validity of the Test of English as a Foreign Language for Chinese Graduate Students at an American University." *Ed & Psychol Meas* 30(2):475–7 su '70. *
10. VROMAN, CLYDE, AND WILCOX, LEE. "Research on A.I.D. Sponsored Foreign Students." *Col & Univ* 45(4):717–23 su '70. *

CLINTON I. CHASE, *Professor of Educational Psychology and Chairman of the Department; and Director, Bureau of Educational Studies and Testing; Indiana University, Bloomington, Indiana.*

This test is designed to assess the English language skills of persons whose native language is not English and who are applicants for admission to American colleges and universities. There are five subtests: Listening Comprehension, English Structure, Vocabulary, Reading Comprehension, and Writing. A total score is also reported.

The Listening Comprehension test has three parts: direct questions, conversation followed by questions, and a lecture followed by questions on its content. Tape recordings provide the stimuli in all parts of this subtest. The first two parts are general in content and only casually exploit the verbal skills that reflect one's ability for movement within the American culture. Also, the first part deals heavily with personal responses, using 16 American given names, such as Bob and Eloise, in 20 items. While the lecture provided in the third part of Listening Comprehension appears to simulate activity in which students will participate in college, one wonders what is being measured. Is it understanding of English, ability to take permitted notes, recall of details, general intelligence, or prior knowledge of the topic of the lecture? Certainly more than listening skill goes into this subscale.

The second section of TOEFL is English Structure. Each item provides a segment of a dialogue with a blank and four options from which the examinee selects the correct response with which to fill the blank. This subtest deals with tense, sequence of nouns and adjectives, etc., but no rationale is given for the selection of structure included. Although rules of grammar are important to communication, it is clear that much communication goes on amid obvious violations of these rules. The responses demanded by this subtest simulate little behavior that will be required of a foreign student in an American college.

Vocabulary, Part A, is basically like English Structure in that it uses a "fill in the blank" procedure with four options. Part B provides definitions or synonyms with four options, one of which corresponds to the stimulus. There are 15 items in Part A and 25 in Part B, a meager sample of total vocabulary. Another format, possibly selecting synonyms, would have allowed a much wider sampling of vocabulary in essentially the same amount of time, divorced from any burden of sentence reading. With an obvious overlap in format between the Vocabulary and the English Structure subtests, it is not surprising to see that the intercorrelation between them is substantial, .72. Further, there is no rationale presented for selecting the vocabulary in the test. With the number of word counts available, it seems reasonable to believe that a test based on graded difficulty and abstractness could be developed.

The fourth subtest is Reading Comprehension. A short text is provided and several questions asked about the content. Text and questions are on the same page and students may refer to the reading passage to look up the answers to the questions. A test-wise student would first scan the questions and skim the passage for the answers. This is an important skill for research work in college but is not what is typically defined as reading comprehension.

The last subtest is Writing Ability. Part A contains sentences with four words or phrases underlined in each sentence. The underlinings are labelled A, B, C, D. In each sentence one underlined word or phrase is incorrect. The letter of that word is to be marked on the answer sheet. Part B contains incomplete sentences with four options presented for completing each statement. This subtest, like English Structure, is essentially tied to basic grammar. The format of the test is so similar to other subtests that it is not surprising that it correlates in the .70's with several other subtests. Again, this test asks the student to do nothing that he will be asked to do later in his college career. Recognition of an inconsistency in grammatical form tells us very little about how the student would manage the form in his own writing. A writing sample like that used in the *Sequential Tests of Educational Progress,* although difficult to manage, would clearly be more intimately associated with writing tasks the student will be asked to perform in college than is the TOEFL writing ability exercise.

The TOEFL manual is clearly written and provides a considerable amount of useful data. The test results are reported in percentile ranks based on nearly 114,000 persons tested between 1964 and 1969.

Reliabilities, based on K-R 20, are relatively substantial, ranging from .84 for Reading Comprehension to .91 for Vocabulary. For the total test the reliability was .97. However, these reliabilities are none too high for tests designed for making decisions about individuals. The tests are timed, but the degree of their speededness is probably not a major factor in their reliability, since for the most part at least 90 percent of the examinees finish within the time limits.

The manual states that "the part scores are particularly relevant for diagnostic....interpretation." This statement is highly questionable. The intercorrelation between the subtest scores is substantial, ranging from .54 to .79 with a median of .68. The reliability of the difference score between the most reliable and least reliable subtests would be .60. A considerable score difference would have to appear between these two subtests before it could be considered more than a chance variation. The test reliabilities and intercorrelations suggest that this generalization would be true for all tests in the battery. Therefore, diagnostic application of the test is clearly limited.

The validity of the TOEFL is reflected in three types of studies: concurrent validity studies, predictive studies, and construct validity studies.

Studies of concurrent validity typically correlate TOEFL with either ratings of proficiency in English or with other test scores. Although ratings are typically less than satisfactory assessments, the TOEFL total score has been shown to correlate with them in the .70 and .80 range. TOEFL also has correlated with other tests of English well into the .80 range (.89 with the *Michigan Test of English Language Proficiency*). It should, however, be pointed out that test-taking behavior common to these tests may be increasing their intercorrelation. In any case, TOEFL is measuring about the same things as other tests of English, although it should be noted that most of the studies are based on rather small groups of students with little information on their mode of selection.

Studies showing the validity of TOEFL as a predictor of later criterion performance, typically grade point average, produce much lower correlations than do the concurrent validity studies. The correlations are, in fact, so low (e.g., .17 at the University of California, .26 at the University of Washington) as to suggest that the test may be of almost no value as a predictor of grade achievement.

Although all of the above data are relevant to construct validation of the test, the use of construct validity as described in the manual is scarcely permissible. There is little evidence of a nomological network out of which hypotheses may be constructed and tested. Hence, the nature of the construct is obscure.

In summary, the TOEFL subscales appear by title to be assessing important subskills in language behavior; however, there is obvious overlap in format from test to test, and many common behaviors are required by the various subtests in the battery. This contention is sup-

Test of English as a Foreign Language

ported by the substantial intercorrelations between the subtests. Reliabilities are satisfactory, but the reliability of differences between two subtest scores is so low that making diagnostic decisions about individuals becomes perilous. The test has evidence of acceptable concurrent validity where other measures of English language ability are used as criteria. However, TOEFL is not a useful predictor of grade achievement. The manual suggests that TOEFL is best used for admission only in conjunction with corroborating data on the candidate. This appears to be excellent advice for the test user.

GEORGE DOMINO, *Associate Professor of Psychology and Director, Counseling Center, Fordham University, New York, New York.*

The TOEFL is designed to test competence in English of foreign students applying for admission to American colleges and universities. It is an objective test divided into five timed sections: Listening Comprehension, English Structure, Vocabulary, Reading Comprehension, and Writing Ability. Part scores, based on a mean of 50 and a standard deviation of 10, as well as a total score, are reported for each candidate, with the interpretive manual indicating that "the part scores are particularly relevant for diagnostic, as well as admissions, interpretation."

Normative data are given so that part scores can be translated into percentile ranks; these ranks were, however, computed on the basis of all candidates taking the TOEFL within a five year period, rather than a breakdown by sex, undergraduate versus graduate status, and intended field major. These breakdowns are available for total scores. Mean total scores for candidates classified by native language and by native country are also given, with an explicit cautionary note that mean differences may be the result of myriad factors rather than a reflection of native differences.

Kuder-Richardson reliability coefficients for the individual subparts range from .84 to .91 and appear satisfactory. Intercorrelations of the five subparts range from .54 to .79; although these values are high, the interpretive manual argues that each of the parts contributes something unique to the total since these values are all lower than the K-R reliability coefficients. Statistically, this may be a cogent argument; practically, one wonders whether for admission purposes, there is much redundancy. The sub-

parts may be differentially relevant to both diagnostic interpretations and admissions decisions, but there is little if any empirical evidence either to support or to dispute this.

Thirteen validation studies are reported in the interpretive manual, seven focusing on concurrent validity, five concerned with predictive validity, and one with construct validity. The seven concurrent validity studies report substantial correlations of TOEFL total scores with performance on other English proficiency tests, and in several instances, with faculty ratings. Most of the five studies focusing on predictive validity report low correlations between TOEFL scores and grade point average. As the manual points out, however, grades may not be a reasonable criterion of the validity of the TOEFL, since proficiency in English is a necessary but not sufficient prerequisite for academic achievement.

Finally, the manual contains a useful example for setting up institutional norms and expectancies tables, while repeatedly underscoring the fact that academic decisions should not be based solely on TOEFL scores and that there are no cut off scores of general applicability.

As with most ETS tests, the TOEFL appears to be a carefully constructed test. The manual and other interpretive aids are well written, and skillfully present a proper balance of technical details and interpretive comments. Although there are other English proficiency tests available of comparative validity, none approach the TOEFL in general availability both to the foreign applicant and to American institutions.

From the consumer's viewpoint, however, it has been this reviewer's experience that a number of foreign student advisors and admissions committees use (misuse?) the TOEFL either to assess in a global manner a candidate's English proficiency or to predict his potential for academic achievement. If, indeed, institutions are merely interested in knowing whether a candidate possesses a minimal knowledge of English, then a standard vocabulary test might be as satisfactory. If prediction of academic achievement is the major goal, then the effort is doomed at the beginning.

[267]

*A Vocabulary and Reading Test for Students of English as a Second Language, Revised Edition.** Non-native speakers of English; 1960-67; Forms A ('61, 11 pages), VR-B ('62, 11 pages); directions sheets: Form A ['60, 2 pages], Form VR-B ('62, 2 pages); combined manual ('67, 15 pages) for this and tests 262-3 and 265; distribution restricted to the Agency for International Development and the Bureau of Educational and Cultural Affairs of the U.S. Department of State; separate answer sheets must be used; manual free on request; 60(65) minutes; David P. Harris and Leslie A. Palmer (VR-B); American Language Institute. *

FRENCH

[268]
Advanced Placement Examination in French. High school students desiring credit for college level courses or admission to advanced courses; 1954-70; Forms RBP ('69, 15 pages), SBP ('70, 17 pages) in 2 booklets (objective, essay); listening comprehension tapes: 7½ ips for Form RBP, 3¾ ips for Form SBP; tape script ['69-70, 5 pages] for each form; for more complete information, see 662; 180(200) minutes; program administered for the College Entrance Examination Board by Educational Testing Service. *

REFERENCES
1-3. See 6:368.
4. "CEEB Advanced Placement Examination in French." *French R* 39:439-49 D '65. *

For a review of the testing program, see 662.

[269]
College Board Achievement Test in French. Candidates for college entrance with 2-4 years high school French; 1901-71; test administered each January at centers established by the publisher; for more complete information, see 663; 60(80) minutes; program administered for the College Entrance Examination Board by Educational Testing Service. *

REFERENCES
1-7. See 4:237.
8-9. See 5:263.
10-13. See 6:366.

For a review by Walter V. Kaulfers of earlier forms, see 4:237. For reviews of the testing program, see 6:760 (2 reviews).

[270]
College Placement Test in French Listening Comprehension. Entering college freshmen; 1962-70, c1955-70; CPTFLC; irregularly scheduled reprintings of inactive forms of *College Board Achievement Test in French Listening Comprehension;* Forms NPL ['65, reprint of 1963 test], QPL ['68, reprint of 1967 test] in a single booklet (13 pages); test administered by 7½ ips tape recording; for more complete information, see 665; 30(40) minutes; program administered for the College Entrance Examination Board by Educational Testing Service. *

REFERENCE
1. ALEAMONI, LAWRENCE M., AND MATSUNAGA, ALLEN. *A Study of Foreign Language at the University of Illinois Using the CEEB Foreign Language Placement Tests and End-of-Course Grades.* Research Report No. 317. Champaign, Ill.: Measurement and Research Division, Office of Instructional Resources, University of Illinois, 1970. Pp. i, 42. *

For a review of the testing program, see 665.

[271]
College Placement Test in French Reading. Entering college freshmen; 1962-70, c1955-70; CPTFR; irregularly scheduled reprintings of inactive forms of *College Board Achievement Test in French;* Forms SPL1 ('70, reprint of 1963 test), SPL2 ('70, reprint of 1964 test) in a single booklet (19 pages); for more complete information, see 665; 60(70) minutes; program administered for the College Entrance Examination Board by Educational Testing Service. *

REFERENCE
1. ALEAMONI, LAWRENCE M., AND MATSUNAGA, ALLEN. *A Study of Foreign Language at the University of Illinois Using the CEEB Foreign Language Placement Tests and End-of-Course Grades.* Research Report No. 317. Champaign, Ill.: Measurement and Research Division, Office of Instructional Resources, University of Illinois, 1970. Pp. i, 42. *

For a review by Walter V. Kaulfers of earlier forms, see 4:237. For a review of the testing program, see 665.

[272]
Common Concepts Foreign Language Test: French. Students in any grade who are at the Level 1 stage of achievement; 1962-66; aural comprehension; same booklet also used to test German and Spanish; may be administered using live voice but tape recording (3¾ ips) is recommended; Forms 1, 2, ('62, 31 pages) in a single booklet; manual ('66, 41 pages); separate answer sheets (IBM 1230) must be used; $1.10 per test; $5.95 per tape recording; $2.50 per 50 answer sheets; 75¢ per scoring stencil for either form; $1 per manual; postage extra; $2.25 per specimen set (without tape), postpaid; scoring service, 22¢ and over per test; (40-45) minutes; Bela H. Banathy, Miles V. Zintz, W. James Popham, Joseph M. Sadnavitch, Rena Krichbaum, Fred B. Gannon, Valdemar Hempel, and Klaus A. Mueller; CTB/McGraw-Hill. *

For a review covering the three languages, see 253.

[273]
First Year French Test, [Revised Edition]. High school and college; 1956-68; FYFT; Form A ('68, 2 pages); manual ('68, 2 pages); no data on reliability; $1.75 per 25 tests, postage extra; 75¢ per specimen set, postpaid; 50(55) minutes; Jean Leblon and Minnie M. Miller; Data Processing and Educational Measurement Center. *

For reviews by Nelson Brooks and Mary E. Turnbull of an earlier edition, see 5:266.

[274]
The Graduate Record Examinations Advanced French Test. Graduate school candidates; 1939-70; 3 current forms ('64-69, 32-36 pages); descriptive booklet ('70, 8 pages); for more complete information, see 667; 180(200) minutes; Educational Testing Service. *

For a review by Nelson Brooks of an earlier form, see 6:376; for a review by Walter V. Kaulfers, see 5:270. For reviews of the testing program, see 667 (1 review) and 5:601 (1 review).

[275]
Graduate School Foreign Language Test: French. Graduate level degree candidates required to

demonstrate reading proficiency in French; 1963-71; GSFLTF; 3 current forms ('70-71, 31-32 pages); for more complete information, see 668; 100(120) minutes; Educational Testing Service. *

REFERENCES

1. BARTLETT, ALBERT ALLEN. "The Foreign Language Requirement for the Ph.D.: A New Approach." *Foreign Lang Ann* 2:174-84 D '68. *
2. CLARK, JOHN L. D. "The Graduate School Foreign Language Requirement: A Survey of Testing Practices and Related Topics." *Foreign Lang Ann* 2:150-64 D '68. *
3. HARVEY, PHILIP R. "Minimal Passing Scores on the Graduate School Foreign Language Tests." *Foreign Lang Ann* 2:165-73 D '68. *

For a review by Clarence E. Turner of an earlier edition, see 6:377.

[276]

*MLA Cooperative Foreign Language Proficiency Tests: French. French majors and advanced students in college; 1960-68; formerly called *MLA Foreign Language Proficiency Tests for Teachers and Advanced Students: French;* 7 tests in 3 booklets (formerly in 7 booklets); Forms HA ('61, identical except for format and directions with earlier tests variously designated Forms A, JML1, and K-JML1), HB ('66, identical except for format and directions with tests copyrighted in 1961 and variously designated Forms B, JML2, K-JML2, and OML1); temporary series directions for administering ('68, 12 pages); series norms ('66, 2 pages); mimeographed series score conversion directions ['68, 8 pages]; separate answer sheets (Digitek, SCRIBE) must be used except for speaking and writing tests; $4 per 100 answer sheets, cash orders postpaid; Digitek scoring stencils not available; SCRIBE scoring and statistical analysis service, 35¢ per student for all tests except speaking and writing; scoring by special arrangement with language specialists: $3 per speaking test tape, $1.50 per writing test; Modern Language Association of America and Educational Testing Service; Cooperative Tests and Services. *

a) BOOK 1: READING, LISTENING COMPREHENSION, SPEAKING. Forms HA (24 pages), HB (21 pages); $9 per 10 tests; 90¢ per single copy; $12 per 7½ ips listening/speaking test tape; blank tapes for student responses must be obtained locally; 40(50) minutes for reading, (20-30) minutes for listening comprehension, (15-30) minutes for speaking.

b) BOOK 2: WRITING. Forms HA (8 pages), HB (7 pages); $6 per 20 tests; 30¢ per single copy; 45(55) minutes.

c) BOOK 3: APPLIED LINGUISTICS, CIVILIZATION AND CULTURE, PROFESSIONAL PREPARATION. Forms HA, HB, (29 pages); professional preparation test is common to all languages in series; $9 per 10 tests; 90¢ per single copy; 40(50) minutes for linguistics, 30(40) minutes for civilization and culture, 45(55) minutes for professional preparation.

REFERENCES

1-3. See 6:379.
4. PAQUETTE, F. ANDRÉ; WALLMARK, MADELINE; SPENCER, RICHARD E.; AND CHURCHILL, FREDERICK J. *A Comparison of the MLA Foreign Language Proficiency Tests for Teachers and Advanced Students With the MLA Foreign Language Cooperative Tests.* An unpublished report to the U.S. Office of Education, Project No. BR-6-2619. Modern Language Association of America, 1966. Pp. 58. * (ERIC ED 019 017)
5. TOLLINGER, SUZANNE, AND PAQUETTE, F. ANDRÉ, Editors. *The MLA Foreign Language Proficiency Tests for Teachers and Advanced Students: A Professional Evaluation and Recommendations for Test Development,* pp. 1-23, 118-24, 144-7, 161-5, passim. Sections on this test by Dora S. Bashour, Michel Beaujour, Jacques Ehrmann, Alexander Hull, Tora T. Ladu, James C. McKinney, Douglas C. Sheppard, and Rebecca M. Valette. An unpublished report to the U.S. Office of Edu-

cation, Project No. BR-6-2619, Modern Language Association of America, June 1966. Pp. viii, 366. * (ERIC ED 019 016)

6. CARROLL, JOHN B. "Foreign Language Proficiency Levels Attained by Language Majors Near Graduation From College." *Foreign Lang Ann* 1:131-51 O '67. *
7. DIZNEY, HENRY F., AND GROMEN, LAUREN. "Predictive Validity and Differential Achievement on Three MLA-Cooperative Foreign Language Tests." *Ed & Psychol Meas* 27:1127-30 w '67. * (*PA* 42:9417)
8. PAQUETTE, F. ANDRÉ; WITH THE COOPERATION OF MADELINE WALLMARK. *The MLA Foreign Language Proficiency Tests for Teachers and Advanced Students: Analysis of the Performance of Native Speakers and Comparison With That of NDEA Summer Institute Participants.* An unpublished report to the U.S. Office of Education, Project No. BR-6-2619, Modern Language Association of America, June 1968. Pp. ii, 42. * (ERIC ED 019 017)
9. PERKINS, JEAN A. "State Certification and Proficiency Tests: The Experience in Pennsylvania." *Foreign Lang Ann* 2:195-9 D '68. *
10. CARROLL, JOHN B. "What Does the Pennsylvania Foreign Language Project Tell Us?" *Foreign Lang Ann* 3(2):214-36 D '69. *
11. OTTO, FRANK. "The Teacher in the Pennsylvania Project." *Mod Lang J* 53(6):411-20 O '69. * (*PA* 44:21642)
12. SMITH, PHILIP D., JR. "The Pennsylvania Foreign Language Research Project: Teacher Proficiency and Class Achievement in Two Modern Languages." *Foreign Lang Ann* 3(2):194-207 D '69. *

JOSEPH A. MURPHY, *Professor of French, Lycoming College, Williamsport, Pennsylvania.*

In evaluating the MLA Proficiency tests, one cannot avoid reference to the central issue in evaluating any teacher-education program: Are the in-put experiences on which the program (or test) rests predictive of the competencies required of the practitioner? In this age of deep educational malaise, the reviewer should look beyond a mere correlation between these variables to the values on which current educational practice stands. More specifically, is the discipline involved in a program or test battery attuned to the perceived needs of those served by it? Only after this nagging question has been confronted, however unsatisfactorily, can we meaningfully consider the problem of test efficiency.

Proficiency in something called the four skills has long been the central objective of foreign language programs. This logical categorization has led to very real kinds of separation in preparing curriculum objectives, activities, and tests. The MLA Proficiency tests represent the ultimate in compartmentalization of skills. Given the lack of demonstrated correlation between teacher proficiency and student achievement,[1] doubts must be raised about this separatist form of teaching and testing. This thought will reappear in the analysis of particular tests.

THE WRITING TEST. In the first of the two sections, the student completes sentences with structure words. In the second he corrects a

[1] SMITH, PHILIP D., AND BARANY, HELMUT A. *A Comparison Study of the Effectiveness of the Traditional and Audiolingual Approaches to Foreign Language Instruction Utilizing Laboratory Equipment.* Unpublished report to the U.S. Office of Education, Project No. 7-0133, Pennsylvania State Department of Public Instruction, October 1968. (ERIC ED 030 013)

poorly written passage. The former stands as an effective procedure for testing key grammatical concepts. The items themselves span elementary to low-level advanced French grammar. However, there is something unnatural about a test in which a student revises incorrect French that is not his own. A more authentic question type would encourage students to produce synonyms or paraphrased equivalents for underlined words. This does not qualify as an authentic writing test if by writing one means the production of original language patterns. French grammar will continue to be treated as a static body of knowledge until national examinations provide model evaluations of comprehensive writing samples. Despite serious administrative and scoring difficulties, ways should be found to test writing as a total skill. Knowledge of structure cannot be *realistically* tested except in a situation where the student is given some freedom to decide content as well as form. Objectivity must be re-defined within a nonstatistical framework.

THE READING TEST. The first section of the reading test contains 15 multiple choice items about idioms. Other sections contain many vocabulary recognition and implication type questions. The last part presents five questions on analysis of poetry. In general, the questions appear carefully designed. There is a balance between the word-study inventory and the comprehension questions themselves. It is notable that there are no questions which stimulate analogous, logical (in the sense of cause-effect recognitions), or evaluative thinking. In this area too the test provides teacher education programs with powerful motivation for sustaining the inertia of present low thought levels. For example, five efficient questions requiring higher mental operations would be more revealing of reading aptitude than all the questions assigned to word study. As a reading test it succeeds only partially as a measure of the process of reading.

THE SPEAKING TEST. The first thing notable about this test is the angry voice of the announcer. Despite such a frightening beginning, the test does offer the means of evaluating oral production. It consists of a taped sampling of oral French cued in three ways. First one repeats 15 sentences, each of which contains two phonetic elements for scoring. In the next part the subject reads a passage "in a natural colloquial style, treating liaison in accord with

this style." The final section requires one to comment on pictures—in isolation, in a series, and with general directions in English.

These three question types afford the test a commendable pedagogical balance. The first and last parts especially seem to have been prepared with a keen critical sense. In Part A most of the phonetic units are quite appropriately vowel sounds. The few consonants chosen for testing are dentals and liquids. A minor recommendation might be to substitute initial plosives for the relatively simple and insignificant dentals. Degrees of acceptability might be more easily detected for plosives. In fact, none of the consonant mistakes are likely to interfere with comprehension of a message. Moreover, specific intonation features were not tested in this part but were relegated to the more subjective sections in which rating scales were used. Intonation should be tested more rigorously.

In Part C the pictures are simple and clear, but rich enough in detail to stimulate a series of coherent utterances. They command speech involving narration, description, and "formules de politesse," while allowing the imaginative student to go beyond the physical stimulus.

Part B might be questioned on the reasoning that few if any undergraduate courses stress the precise characteristics of colloquial versus formal French, especially as applied to optional liaisons. Basing an entire section on this precarious foundation undoubtedly introduces an emotional shock with a concomitant error factor, the extent of which would be difficult to ascertain. Clearer directions would require the subject to make obligatory liaisons and to refrain from forbidden ones.

THE LISTENING TEST. In the listening test 36 questions are cued in three ways. First, short snatches of conversation are followed by four possible written responses. Next a radio broadcast is followed by oral questions and four written answers. Finally a three-minute "dramatic" scene is followed by eight oral true-false questions. The style of the utterances progresses from carefully enunciated to rapid colloquial in the last section. The items in both forms have been meticulously constructed. Most are difficult for beginners but attainable by a person with average sound discrimination ability and moderate exposure to the foreign tongue. It is improbable that a subject without foreign experience could perform successfully in the last part. Moreover, there are some disturbing facts that warrant further study. Because the answers are read, the purity of the listening factor becomes tainted. In Form HA especially, there seem to be some items in which an unreasonably brief pause is given to peruse the printed answers and make a selection. This is not to argue against combining skills in a testing situation for that would only lead to further compartmentalization. What is needed is synchronization based on an average reading speed of representative test subjects. Without this kind of knowledge, a speed reading factor is introduced into a test where listening skill should dominate. Also, because the test is administered in a language laboratory, one can only wonder about the effect of moving the booklet around so that printed answers are always within normal seeing distance. There is definite distraction in manipulating the answer booklet in a crowded space. Despite these doubts, the listening test remains a fair and significant measure within realistic limits.

THE APPLIED LINGUISTICS TEST. The applied linguistics test includes 55 items covering pronunciation and phonetics, the writing system, morphology and syntax, general linguistics, and historical linguistics. The questions are pertinent, treating the kind of knowledge taught in the better applied linguistics courses. Moreover, it contains many application questions in which knowledge of principles must be accompanied by a more practical penetrating kind of intelligence. Such a test presents a problem for the many institutions lacking trained personnel to teach modern applied linguistics. However, this gives no legitimate basis for abandoning evaluation of this vital related discipline.

THE CIVILIZATION AND CULTURE TEST. To test culture and civilization, there are 60 objective questions about French history, politics, literature, geography, economics, religion, education, and sports. The range of questions is commendable. The underlying assumption can be identified with the validity of a "culture" in the broad French meaning. Regardless of the inherent value of such a "culture," problems arise in the course of achieving and evaluating it. Specific aspects of this assumption will have to receive honest investigation. Is the information embodied in the questions of greatest worth to the student of French life? Is the scope of the test realistic for a novice teacher? Does any part of the test reflect a compromise with the scientific view of culture as a social science?

Does the test provide an excuse for continuing the boring un-intellectual approaches to the teaching of culture and civilization? If the test contained the germs of positive response to these questions, it would be analyzed further at this point.

THE PROFESSIONAL PREPARATION TEST. The professional preparation test contains 65 multiple choice questions of pedagogical interest. As stated in the preceding section, the most crucial question about an "objective" question is "What information is most worth examining?" The 65 questions can be categorized as pertaining to either fact or theory. There is little justification in an "objective" test of "right" answers for the latter. In the absence of convincing research, it is intellectually dishonest to parade theories as facts. For example, there is no "right" answer as to whether choral or individual drills are more effective, whether dictation is inappropriate for the language laboratory, whether the mental discipline argument for learning a language is less defensible than the pragmatic one, whether literature is a better tool for learning culture than history, geography, or economics, or whether one method of dialogue presentation is superior to another. On the other hand, professional questions like that dealing with the values of linguistics for a language teacher, should be kept and increased. The test could be made considerably more objective by including application questions on topics like the use of the media, psychological foundations on which a consensus has been reached, unit planning, and evaluation procedures. The absence of such professional topics and the inclusion of so much partisan bias tarnish a potentially important test.

CONCLUSION. Results of external validation of the MLA Proficiency tests have not yet appeared in the professional literature, but such studies are not necessary to raise doubts about the importance to be granted this battery. Given the inherent limitations of the separate tests, no educator can securely interpret scores on this test as a predictor of teaching effectiveness. This is true mostly because the static parts separately united do not create a dynamic whole. The test does offer an uneven gauge of mastery of a few skills and a mass of factual information.

JEAN-GUY SAVARD, *Research Officer, International Center for Research on Bilingualism;*

MLA Cooperative Foreign Language Proficiency Tests: French and Assistant Professor of Linguistics, Université Laval, Quebec, Canada.

The *MLA Foreign Language Proficiency Tests: French* are worthy of top-rank listing among present-day foreign language testing materials for advanced students and foreign language teachers. This reviewer made it a point personally to answer each item contained in this test, so that an analysis of each of the subtests might bring forth a more accurate evaluation of the test as a whole.

READING. The 40 minutes allotted for the 50 items of the reading test seem more than adequate. I wonder, however, about the use of certain difficult and rarely used words and expressions, such as: "mettre le grappin dessus," "primesautier," and "lamente la faiblesse" in a test of reading comprehension. On the other hand, in one item the correct word, "cafard," might be selected by a greater number of testees simply because the other choices are so outstandingly irrelevant to the meaning of the sentence. To be fair with the examinees it would also seem advisable to mention the author of a literary quotation, and perhaps the year in which it was written. The interpretation of the meaning may depend on whether the passage was taken from works signed Corneille, Rousseau, Sartre, etc. This test definitely measures what it was meant to measure, the meanings of words and sentences, knowledge of grammatical categories (nouns, pronouns, adverbs, prepositions, verbs, etc.) and structures. In a sense, it could be said that the test measures more than what it is intended to measure. Some questions appear to measure a degree of intelligence as well as a degree of proficiency in literary analysis. Unfortunately, it does not seem possible to specify the equivalence of the two forms owing to the lack of statistical data.

LISTENING COMPREHENSION. In this test it would seem quite admissible to allow for an occasional and perhaps intentional flaw in articulation. In fact, such is the case in several items where the first three words are literally dropped. This minor detail is a bit more obvious with the hissing sounds in the first four spoken words of one item. The testmakers are to be complimented for the commendable feature of alternating masculine and feminine voices on the test tape. The only drawback here is that the feminine voice, in certain instances, tends to exaggerate the natural flow of enunciation. In general, the masculine and feminine voices in

Form HB have a twangy tone on the tape and slurring seems unnecessarily overdone. At this advanced level, however, this procedure could very well be admissible. Assuming that this procedure is part of the intentional difficulties included in the test, it would be advisable to present them in both forms. At present the difficulties differ from one form to the other. In Form HA, item 7, the intonation is a little misleading; it seems to lack the upward movement of the pitch needed to make it sound like a question. In item 11 the rolling of *rrr* as in "aller et retour" seems somewhat excessive at a normal speed of conversation. Item 13 is given rather rapidly on tape, and thereby seems to skip syllables. These are reasons for doubting the equivalence of the forms.

The spacing of questions given on tape deserves some attention. The following is the result of our trial in timing the tape. In the first part, a statement is given, and 10 seconds are allotted to choose the correct answer. It takes approximately 5 seconds to read the four choices and then another 3 to 4 seconds to select the answer. More time could be given: 2 additional seconds would suffice. In the third part, the description of a scene seems to be a bit long and drawn out. The dialogue must be retained and recalled. The student may easily forget what he has heard. In this case we tend to measure memorizing ability rather than listening comprehension.

SPEAKING. Both forms of the test are well balanced, well constructed, adequate, and comprehensive. Part A, Form HA, tends to measure the 16 phonemes most apt to create certain difficulties for English-speaking students learning French. Time allotment for reading of the text in Part B is quite sufficient. The reading calls for a natural colloquial style of speech. In Part C the examinee is asked to give an oral description of pictures and he may also give his version of what they suggest. This pictorial feature is well chosen and should give rise to favorable comments. Objective evaluation of this type of test would, however, bring about certain problems in scoring. The testmakers are to be commended on their effort to give clear and concise instructions in order to avoid a completely subjective scoring system. Nevertheless, Parts B and C most likely present certain scoring difficulties. I should imagine that even trained judges could interpret differently the meaning of "Performance like a native who reads well," "Easily intelligible," or "Frequent approximation of native features," etc. In all fairness we must admit that this particular problem of scoring method is not peculiar to the MLA tests. The authors of the MLA battery have devised a worthy measuring instrument. The five-point scale which they have devised will no doubt help to reduce the error factor.

WRITING. Part A (HA) of this test mostly measures the use of function words: relative pronouns, demonstrative pronouns, prepositions, articles, adverbs, and auxiliary verbs. The relative importance of each of these grammatical categories has been fairly well determined. Among 30 measured elements there are 11 prepositions. It is a well-known fact that prepositions do bring about numerous problems to students learning a foreign language. In Part B-1 (HA), the choice of words and structures to be measured is entirely relevant. However, in Part B-2 (HA), the word "matineux," which is so archaic that few native speakers could be expected to understand the subtleties of its usage, is a good example of French language subtleties which should be avoided in this type of test. It may be noted that poorly written passages which "present some incorrect forms for students to correct" are, according to item 58 of the Professional Preparation Test (HA), the LEAST desirable practice in constructing a foreign language test.

APPLIED LINGUISTICS. In this subtest, a good knowledge of French phonetics, morphology, and syntax is a requisite. If a diploma is to be of importance then it is high time to demand that foreign language teachers be proficient in the language they intend to teach. The authors have wisely de-emphasized the importance of a knowledge of historical linguistics. Items 23, 24, 27, and 50 in Form HA are long and complicated. They present such comprehension difficulties that I wonder if they truly measure the knowledge of the grammar rule involved. In Form HB the range and order of item difficulties are questionable. For a native speaker items 9 and 12 seem much easier to answer than item 1. Statistical data only could prove the validity of such an observation.

CIVILIZATION AND CULTURE. It is undoubtedly an excellent idea to include a sound knowledge of French culture and civilization among the requirements for advanced students and future teachers of French. Indeed, true bilingualism supposes a certain degree of biculturalism. The construction of this type of test, however, involves many difficulties. It should be pointed out to users of the test that the answers given in the Table of Correct Answers should be checked for possible modifications due to the passage of time. I would also be inclined to put considerably less emphasis on the history and economy of France. It would then be possible to include a few questions concerning ways and customs and institutions of contemporary French-speaking communities (la Francophonie) throughout the world with particular reference to North America. It would be a means of giving better balance to this subtest, thereby rendering it a bit more comprehensive.

PROFESSIONAL PREPARATION. This subtest is of utmost importance to those who have chosen language teaching as a profession. The purpose of this test is to measure knowledge of principles and techniques of language teaching at the primary and secondary levels. Granted that there is a world of difference between theory and practice, we must still take available means to ascertain the degree of professional competency of teachers of a foreign language. The content of the subtest seems to correspond to a curriculum based on the audio-lingual approach to foreign language teaching. The theories and practices which this test emphasizes are hardly questionable, and it takes much careful probing to single out questions which could be considered irrelevant. In this perspective, even the less satisfactory questions are still acceptable. In order to answer items 25 and 63 (HA) the testee would have to be familiar with the specific documents mentioned. This point in itself deprives the test of its universal character. The same remark applies to items 25 and 62, where reference is made to the abbreviation FLES. Current fashions should be banned by testmakers. The importance given to the audio-lingual approach in language teaching may lead one to wonder whether the pedagogical value of this test is not as important as its measuring value. As a means for measuring knowledge of audio-lingual methodology this test is undoubtedly adequate.

CONCLUSIONS. The one problem to which a definite answer had yet to be found when this test was designed was that of content: linguistic, cultural, or professional. This observation can be applied, in a very general manner, to all known language tests and professional preparation tests. *We do not know exactly what to test because we do not know exactly what to teach.* In practice, we do make a choice, but is it always the best one? In the light of what is currently known on the subject, the authors were wise in giving priority to their own most pressing needs. This, however, does not eliminate the need for a new approach to research in the field. It should be possible to establish a more or less precise operational definition of the subject matter to be taught at the different stages of language teaching. Only such an operational definition could constitute an adequate criterion for the validity of a test.

It appears that constructors of this MLA test have achieved the proposed objectives at a high level. The techniques and procedures are in conformity with the specifications supplied by responsible authorities. The committees designated to make up the test have without doubt succeeded in devising a measuring instrument which permits an evaluation of the candidates' (future teachers) degree of proficiency. Classification is then established as minimal, good, or superior.

Those who might find the testing time excessive should be reminded that the professional objectives pursued by this test fully justify the required four to five hours. Independently of correlations between subtests, it is quite evident that the seven lengthy subtests will enable administrators to establish a more reliable diagnosis of specific weaknesses and skills.

A complete and well organized manual giving the coefficients of reliability and validity, as well as a detailed item analysis for HA and HB forms, would be of great value. Data from the NDEA experimental testing of native speakers (*8*) and other programs and surveys should be available in one exhaustive report. The figures compiled up to now are encouraging; for example, the following reliability coefficients were reported: Listening (.91), Reading (.93), Writing (.94), Applied Linguistics (.87), Civilization and Culture (.86), and Professional Preparation (.87).

This MLA French test is, to my knowledge, the most adequate, comprehensive, and objective test of its kind. Notwithstanding all the aforementioned observations, I do not hesitate in recommending the *MLA Cooperative Foreign Language Proficiency Tests: French* to those who have the responsibility of selecting and appointing teachers of French as a foreign language.

For reviews by Paul Pimsleur and James H. Ricks, Jr., see 6:379.

[277]

*MLA-Cooperative Foreign Language Tests: French. 1–2 years high school or 2 semesters college, 3–4 years high school or 4 semesters college; 1963–65; 4 tests in a single booklet: listening, speaking, reading, writing; writing test available as separate; 2 forms; 2 levels; no specific manual; series directions for administering and scoring ('64, 40 pages); series handbook ('65, 24 pages); series booklet of norms ('65, 82 pages); student bulletin ('65, 2 pages) for each level; $7 per 10 tests; $5 per 20 writing tests only; separate answer sheets (Digitek, Digitek-IBM 805, IBM 1230, SCRIBE) may be used for listening and reading tests; $4 per 100 answer sheets; $1.25 per 10 IBM 805 or IBM 1230 scoring stencils (answer pattern must be punched out locally); Digitek scoring stencils not available; $8.50 per 3¾ ips tape, 5 inch reel, for listening test; $8.50 per 3¾ ips tape, 5 inch reel, for speaking test (blank tapes or discs for recording student responses must be obtained locally); $2 per series directions for administering and scoring; $2 per series handbook; $2 per series norms booklet; $3 per 100 student bulletins; $3 per specimen set; cash orders postpaid; SCRIBE scoring and statistical analysis service (listening and reading tests), 35¢ per student; no scoring service for speaking and writing tests, but arrangements for professional scoring can be made; 25(35) minutes for listening, 10(20) minutes for speaking, 35(40) minutes for reading, 35(40) minutes for writing; prepared in cooperation with the Modern Language Association of America; Cooperative Tests and Services. *
a) [LOWER LEVEL.] 1–2 years high school or 2 semesters college; Forms LA ('63, 23 pages), LB ('63, 24 pages); writing test: Forms LA, LB, ('63, 8 pages).
b) [HIGHER LEVEL.] 3–4 years high school or 4 semesters college; Forms MA, MB, ('63, 25 pages); writing test: Forms LA, LB, ('63, 9 pages).

REFERENCES
1. PAQUETTE, F. ANDRÉ; WALLMARK, MADELINE; SPENCER, RICHARD E.; AND CHURCHILL, FREDERICK J. *A Comparison of the MLA Foreign Language Proficiency Tests for Teachers and Advanced Students With the MLA Foreign Language Cooperative Tests.* An unpublished report to the U.S. Office of Education, Project No. BR-6-2619, Modern Language Association of America, 1966. Pp. 58. * (ERIC ED 019 017)
2. SPENCER, RICHARD E. "The Influence of Disc or Tape Language Laboratory Equipment on Foreign Language Speaking Test Scores." *Mod Lang J* 50:207–8 Ap '66. *
3. VOCOLO, JOSEPH M. "The Effect of Foreign Language Study in the Elementary School Upon Achievement in the Same Foreign Language in High School." *Mod Lang J* 51: 463–9 D '67. *
4. MUELLER, THEODORE H. "Programmed Language Instruction—Help for the Linguistically 'Underprivileged.'" *Mod Lang J* 52:79–84 F '68. * (PA 44:20888)
5. ALEAMONI, LAWRENCE M., AND SPENCER, RICHARD E. "A Comparison of Biserial Discrimination, Point Biserial Discrimination, and Difficulty Indices in Item Analysis Data." *Ed & Psychol Meas* 29(2):353–8 su '69. * (PA 44:17314)

MICHIO PETER HAGIWARA, *Associate Professor of French, University of Michigan, Ann Arbor, Michigan.*

Foreign language methodology that has been dominant in the past two decades is the "audiolingual" approach. It aims to develop the four fundamental language skills of listening comprehension, speaking, reading, and writing in a systematic manner, with a stress on the first two, often called "primary communication skills," in the early stages of instruction. The advent of this teaching method made traditional reading-oriented proficiency tests all too inadequate. The *MLA-Cooperative Foreign Language Tests* were issued in 1963 in the light of the "new key" method. They measure the linguistic competence of a student in the four basic language skills at two different levels.

LISTENING COMPREHENSION. Forms LA and LB have 45 items (45 maximum points), and MA and MB, 40 items (40 maximum points), to be completed in 25 minutes. Pure auditory test items are found only in LA and LB, where the first four items require the student to choose the one of four simple line drawings that matches the statement he has heard. The remainder of the items are a conventional "hybrid" type combining listening and reading. They are also grouped according to general topics, so that the context of the sentences does not jump abruptly from one item to another. Forms LA and LB contain 13 and 12 items, respectively, after the pictorial-cue items, and each item is a single utterance for which the student chooses one out of four possible answers that are printed in the booklet. The next 13 or 14 items are "conversations" between two speakers, usually a male and a female. The student is to select a printed statement that best describes each conversation. In the next 10 items, the auditory stimuli are lengthened, up to four utterances per item; in each item, however, there are normally two cues embedded, so that missing one out of several sentences may not adversely affect the selection of the correct response. The pauses are also longer in order to accommodate the increased amount of reading. Items 41 through 43 concern a brief telephone conversation, and the student is to play the role of the second speaker in answering statements made by the first speaker which are heard on the tape. Finally, the last two items are preceded by a dialogue of 12 lines or more and two questions concerning its content. Forms MA and MB follow the same patterns as LA and LB, except that there are no picture-based items and the auditory stimuli are much longer and somewhat more complicated.

The heavy reliance on hybrid test items to evaluate listening comprehension is rather unfortunate. Although the 10–15 second pauses may enable most students to glance over the printed multiple choice answers quickly, the slow reader will more likely be penalized as the answers become progressively longer. Furthermore, there is a possibility that a wrong response may be due to a faulty reading of the answers or an unfamiliarity with their vocabulary, rather than to a misunderstanding of the auditory cues. As a result, the score on this test may reflect reading ability as much as listening comprehension. A more extensive use of pictorial multiple choice items would be preferable for both levels. As an additional means of increasing the difficulty level, the phonation rate of the aural stimuli might have been gradually increased, or some background noise or "white noise" might have been introduced in the last few items. The telephone conversation that occurs in all the tests could have utilized the actual pitch and timbre of voices on the telephone.

SPEAKING. This is probably the most original of the four tests. It aims to evaluate the student's oral production on the basis of pronunciation, grammar, vocabulary, and fluency, through 32 items with a maximum possible score of 82 points. The test, which lasts 10 minutes, requires the student to record his oral responses on a tape. The first 15 items measure his pronunciation in terms of mimicry. The student repeats 10 short utterances given by the master tape, each sentence within 3 or 4 seconds. The responses are checked according to specific sounds or successions of sounds and basic intonation patterns, each item to be scored as right or wrong. The next 10 items are embedded in a short passage containing a dialogue which the student reads aloud from his test booklet. Each item is scored right or wrong even though it contains several sounds. There is also a global rating scale (item 26) on which the student's general ability to pronounce accurately is judged on a five-point scale. The first part can be scored relatively objectively by a trained ear, but in the second part scorer subjectivity increases. Obviously, in speech production the correct pronunciation of a sequence of phonemes is more important than that of single phonemes. But since each item is made up of several sounds, an error in any one sound segment will mark the entire item wrong even if the remainder are pronounced acceptably. No intonation patterns are checked in the second part. In both parts, certain sound segments that

MLA-Cooperative Foreign Language Tests: French

are often mispronounced by students, such as /i/ and /a/, are not tested alone, but each is combined with at least one other sound. The rising intonation is not sufficiently covered in any of the four test forms. Perhaps the reading passage should be a dialogue without extraneous descriptive elements and should test intonation, linking of syllables, liaison, and a limited number of morphologically important segments, such as the /d/ of *vendent* as against *vend,* /n/ of *italienne* as against *italien,* /l/ of *journal* as against *journaux,* and so forth.

Part 3 consists of four questions concerning simple line drawings, thus combining auditory comprehension and speaking. Each response is globally rated on a 0–3 point scale, so that the total possible score is 12 points. Subjectivity increases in this part, since the definition of "major" versus "minor" errors is lacking, and relative weights of vocabulary, grammar, and pronunciation in scoring are not clearly established in the instructions. The last part consists of a single picture and a series of four sequential pictures telling a story, to be described in 60 and 120 seconds, respectively. The student responses are scored in terms of vocabulary, pronunciation, structure, and fluency, each factor on a 0–5 point scale. There is a brief description of these scoring categories to aid the teacher.

The testing method, patterned after similar items in the *MLA Cooperative Foreign Language Proficiency Tests,* is ingenious but it also has several drawbacks. Since the tests consist of a few pictures, the transmission of items from one student to another is almost inevitable unless it can be insured that all students take the test simultaneously. Secondly, speaking activity is seldom a monologue, and the one-sidedness of the responses may not accurately reflect the student's ability to communicate in the target language. True speaking fluency may be better measured by a panel of judges in interviews or role playing, even though such procedures are more time-consuming and have less scorer reliability. In any case, the evaluative criteria of these tests do not take into account the total length of the responses. The recorded sample student responses for the single-picture item were 53, 40, 25, and 20 seconds, respectively, for the four forms, and for the sequential picture item, 27, 67, 40, and 27 seconds. Obviously, as any experienced teacher can testify, the longer the response, the more errors it is likely to contain. Therefore, length should be considered in scoring speech production, perhaps along with a simple measure of the ability to phonate a certain number of syllables within so many seconds. Moreover, in view of the short sample responses, the maximum recording time for the last two items could be reduced by at least one-third, which would also facilitate scoring. The evaluation could be based on the first ten utterances, in terms of grammar and vocabulary, on a more simplified scoring scale, with a global rating of pronunciation and fluency for each picture description. It should be noted, in fact, that pronunciation seems to receive an inordinate emphasis in the speaking test, to the disadvantage of those students who have acquired a reasonable control of structure and vocabulary but who speak with an obvious "foreign" accent.

In order to guide the teacher in applying the rating scales, sample student responses are recorded on the test tape, without extraneous pauses, and separated from the test itself by a white leader tape. Each of the four male and female students is judged to have a "high degree of competence for a student" at the given level. Contrary to our expectation, there is no discussion whatsoever of the scoring procedures to be applied to these sample responses, and the excellent answers given by the students offer little clue as to how their responses were actually graded. It should also be mentioned that the student answering the single-picture item in Form LA tended to enumerate the objects in the picture despite the instructions to "describe what seems to be going on" rather than simply list all the objects. The directions to the student could be more specific; for example, the master tape could tell him to make up an imaginary dialogue or tell a story in the first person from the viewpoint of one of the persons depicted in the picture.

READING. This test is composed of two parts with a total of 50 items (50 maximum points), to be administered in 35 minutes. Part 1, consisting of 25 items in LA and LB and 20 in MA and MB, contains statements which must be completed with appropriate words or expressions supplied in multiple choice. There appears to be a rather heavy emphasis on vocabulary. In order to answer as many as two-thirds of LA or LB, the student needs to know especially the single key word in each statement as well as the fill-in items. According to the handbook these forms are "specifically aimed at the middle of the second year"; they will prove excessively difficult for students who have completed only one year of language instruction, particularly through the audio-lingual method, which intentionally limits the number of lexical items in the early stages in favor of a more firm mastery of structures. False cognates are not utilized to any appreciable extent.

As many as 8 out of 20 items in MA and MB are idiom-oriented. One might question on what basis certain idioms have been selected; for instance, *se faire prier* and *en savoir gré* instead of *s'agir de, au lieu de,* or *avoir beau.* Since there are numerous reading materials available today, the criteria used for the choice of lexical items and idiomatic expressions for the construction of the reading tests should be listed as a guide to the teacher who needs to determine the suitability of the test as a measuring instrument for his particular purpose. If the test writers do not wish to publish such lists, they should at least state whether or not the vocabulary is based on any known frequency list.

The second part consists of 8 to 10 journalistic and literary prose readings, including dramatic scenes, with multiple choice questions that must be answered. The reading passages are longer and more difficult in MA and MB, as they should be. There is again the question of the criteria for selecting the lexical items, idiomatic expressions, and structural points employed in this part. In order to respond correctly, the student must either find *corroborating* information in the passage or judge what is *implied* in it. The first type demands a good knowledge of vocabulary and structure, while the second requires a somewhat more sophisticated analysis of the text in order to draw the necessary inferences. Forms LA and LB appear to contain about an equal number of both types of items. On the other hand, in MA and MB, less than one-third of the items seem to be inference-oriented. This is somewhat surprising since at more advanced levels of language instruction there is an increased amount of reading, and the discussions of stories in terms of plot, characterization, apparent themes, underlying ideas, and the author's intentions are more frequent. Furthermore, students who have reached the fourth-year level are often introduced to the fundamental concepts of the *explication de texte,* an important part of French literary studies. There are, however, no items

requiring elementary stylistic analysis, even though the majority of the passages are literary rather than journalistic prose.

WRITING. The writing test, to be completed in 35 minutes, consists of four parts which combine reading and writing. Part 1 is made up of 25 fill-in items in LA and LB, and 30 items in MA and MB. The student inserts one word in each of the sentences, none of which are related to the other. The context in these sentences requires a relative pronoun, question word, object pronoun, preposition, verb in the appropriate tense and form, and so on. Forms LA and LB concentrate on somewhat more elementary aspects of grammar, such as the use of articles, noun-markers, relative pronouns, and object pronouns. Forms MA and MB, in addition to the type of structural points found in the lower forms, contain items such as demonstrative pronouns, adjectives, and verbs requiring a preposition before a dependent infinitive, and verb tenses used in "contrary-to-fact" statements. One may question the validity of the selection criteria for certain items. While the coverage of the grammatical points in the four forms combined seems fairly comprehensive, some common constructions are missing: the passive voice, the comparison of adjectives and adverbs, and simple idioms with *avoir,* to name a few. On the other hand, somewhat idiomatic expressions such as *en vouloir à* and *s'en aller* are included in MA. Grading is simple and rapid, for each item receives one point or zero.

Part 2 of LA and LB consists of five sentences. The student must rewrite the verb in the embedded clause of each sentence to match its tense with the verb in the main clause which has been already rewritten so as to provide a cue. The verb tenses involved are the future and the *passé composé,* and there is no attempt made to check the correct use and form of the imperfect tense. Grading here is also one point or zero per item. Part 3 of LA and LB comprises 15 items requiring the student to rewrite sentences according to the changes indicated, usually a switch in the gender or number of the key nouns or pronouns. Most items do not check syntax but rather the adjective and verb morphology. Scoring is based on a 0–3 point scale, and there is a short description of each category to assist the scorer. The distinction of these categories depends mostly on the number of errors found in each sentence as well as on the nature of the errors (major or minor).

MLA-Cooperative Foreign Language Tests: French

Scoring can thus be quite subjective, particularly because the number of changes to be effected by the student in each sentence is not kept uniform.

Part 2 of MA and MB consists of seven questions to be answered with the appropriate object pronouns, and Part 3 has eight pairs of sentences to be combined by embedding one sentence into the other. The grading procedure is the same as in the corresponding parts of LA and LB. We may question whether or not it is desirable to have seven or eight items on a single grammatical point, such as the object pronouns and the subjunctive, with a high maximum score for the part. Furthermore, the verb tenses in the pronoun substitution items are exclusively in the past tense, thus penalizing some students as many times as they have failed to make the agreement of the past participle with the preceding direct object pronoun. The change in the subject occurs twice, from *vous* to *je,* with a concomitant change in the auxiliary verb, adding still another operation to perform in these sentences. One of them even requires the addition of a negative element. Perhaps the majority of the sentences should have been in the present tense, with a mandatory change of subject from *je* to *vous* or vice versa. At least one item should have dealt with the affirmative imperative, in which the sequence of object pronouns differs from the normal pattern. The scoring could have been greatly simplified by using a uniform 0–1 point scale for the object pronouns, for the verb form (preferably a common irregular verb), and for the rest of the sentence.

In Part 4 of Forms LA and LB, the student must write a short dialogue based on a given topic, including in his sentences the words or expressions listed in the booklet. Scoring is in terms of the number of specified words covered in the response, their appropriate use, the accuracy of each sentence, the continuity of meaning, and a global rating, to each of which are assigned 0, 1, 3, or 5 points. In order to assist the scorer, sample responses are given, with an indication of the scores on each of the five factors. The scoring fails to distinguish between major and minor errors which affect differently the general intelligibility of the dialogue. In fact, a single minor error can result in a loss of two points rather than one, since the scoring system does not permit assigning four points. The total scores of students on this part of the examination may thus show considerable variation without reflecting accurately the intelligibility or the originality of their compositions.

Part 4 of MA and MB consists of a very long connected passage, approximately half of which is "dehydrated." Students are to use all the given elements in completing sentences, while supplying grammar to them in view of the given context. It is an excellent way of testing writing, inasmuch as the passage as a whole has a good continuity of meaning and the responses are controlled just enough to facilitate evaluation. The scoring method, however, is similar to that for the lower forms and is subject to the same type of criticism. It is extremely time-consuming to have to count the words used by the student to determine how many of the specified elements (63 in MA, 78 in MB) have been included in the response. It would have been much simpler and far more efficient to divide the expected answers into segments, such as *le monde/attendait/avec impatience,* or *faire/une longue promenade/à bicyclette.* One point or zero can be assigned to each segment, with a global rating using a 0–5 point scale at the end.

CONCLUSION. The MLA-Cooperative tests were produced after rigorous item analyses and correlation studies. They should prove to be of use to many language teachers who are acquainted with statistical methods of interpreting test results. However, as has been mentioned earlier, they are not really designed to measure the four basic language skills separately. Listening, speaking, reading, and writing are interdependent activities in the language classroom. The extensive use of hybrid test items may be justifiable but it will give only broad indications of the relative strength or weakness of a student or group of students in regard to the different linguistic skills involved in language learning. According to the handbook, one of the purposes of the tests is the identification of the "idioms and structures in a foreign language that are troublesome for a class or for individual students." Yet the implied "sensitivity" of the test batteries may be questioned, particularly in view of the biases present in some of the tests, such as the vocabulary emphasis in reading and pronunciation emphasis in speaking, and the rarity of pure test items. There are, moreover, no lists indicating the sources of the vocabulary, idioms, and structures that are utilized in the tests. As pointed out earlier, such lists are essential to the users, especially because of the myriad of instructional materials available today and of the numerous psycholinguistic research projects that require the use of reliable standardized tests. The avoidance of English as test items is also regrettable. Translation is an important activity in our culture and is utilized by many language teachers, even though the early audiolingual methodology proscribed it in language instruction. The avoidance of English has resulted in an outright exclusion from these tests of many problems of pattern conflicts and vocabulary distinctions which are found commonly in classroom quizzes and examinations. Finally, the reliability and the norms of the tests need to be re-examined in view of the developments in language methodology and instructional materials since 1963. The findings of contrastive linguistic analysis, along with the experience of many teachers with their locally-produced tests, should be considered in the revision of the tests.

It should be pointed out that the criticisms of the MLA-Cooperative tests by no means detract from their excellent overall quality and usefulness. They reflect both the traditional and "new key" teaching methods and constitute an admirable attempt to introduce innovation as well as renovation in the field of foreign language testing. The need for nationally standardized tests has been felt for a long time, and these tests have made significant contributions, particularly in the areas of evaluating speaking and writing skills.

For an excerpted review of the series, see 254.

[278]

★**National Teacher Examinations: French.** College seniors and teachers; 1970–71; modified version of secure form of *MLA Foreign Language Proficiency Tests for Teachers and Advanced Students: French;* Form TNT1 ('71, 22 pages); descriptive booklet ('70, 8 pages); listening comprehension section administered by 3¾ ips tape recording; for more complete information, see 582; 120(165) minutes; Educational Testing Service. *

For reviews of the testing program, see 582 (2 reviews), 6:700 (1 review), 5:538 (3 reviews), and 4:802 (1 review).

[279]

★**Pimsleur French Proficiency Tests.** First, second level courses in grades 7–12 or first, second semesters college; 1967; 4 scores: listening, speaking, reading, writing; 1 form; 2 levels labeled Forms A, C; manual (23 pages); no college norms; $1.75 per manual;

$1.75 per specimen set (without tapes or manual); postage extra; Paul Pimsleur; Harcourt Brace Jovanovich, Inc. *
a) TEST 1, LISTENING COMPREHENSION. Digitek, IBM 805, and IBM 1230 test-answer sheets (2 pages); 7½ ips test tape, 5 inch reel; $7.50 per test tape; $3.80 per 35 test-answer sheets; $1.40 per set of scoring stencils; IBM scoring service, 33¢ and over per test; 15(25) minutes.
b) TEST 2, SPEAKING PROFICIENCY. Test (4 pages); scoring sheet (2 pages); 7½ ips test tape, 5 inch reel; $7.50 per test tape; $4.50 per 35 tests; $2.70 per 35 scoring sheets; 16(26) minutes.
c) TEST 3, READING COMPREHENSION. Test (4 pages); separate answer sheets (Digitek-IBM 805, IBM 1230) must be used; $4.50 per 35 tests; $2.30 per 35 Digitek-IBM 805 answer sheets; $2.80 per 35 IBM 1230 answer sheets; 70¢ per scoring stencil; IBM scoring service, 19¢ and over per test; 35(45) minutes.
d) TEST 4, WRITING PROFICIENCY. Test (6 pages); answer key and scoring directions (4 pages); $7.40 per 35 tests; 35(45) minutes.

REFERENCE
1. PIMSLEUR, PAUL. "A French Speaking Proficiency Test." *French R* 34:470–9 Ap '61. *

JOHN L. D. CLARK, *Examiner in Foreign Languages, Test Development Division, Educational Testing Service, Princeton, New Jersey.*

The *Pimsleur French Proficiency Tests* consist of two batteries, each containing four separate skills tests: Listening Comprehension, Speaking Proficiency, Reading Comprehension, and Writing Proficiency. The two levels are labeled Form A and Form C. These are somewhat misleading designations, because the two batteries are not alternate forms but rather two different sets of instruments designed for students completing either a "first-level" course (Form A) or a "second-level" course (Form C). The absence of true alternate forms at each level renders problematical the use of the Pimsleur tests for pre- and post-testing of a single group of students or for other applications requiring the use of equivalent instruments. The test manual, advisedly, does not recommend such use but suggests that tests at either level be used on a year-to-year basis to compare the achievement of different class groups using a stable curriculum or to evaluate the results of modifications in the language teaching program (under the apparent assumption that inherent student ability remains constant over the time period in question).

Normative information consisting of raw score percentile ranks and stanine score equivalents is presented for the listening, reading, and writing tests at each level, but similar data are regrettably not available for the Speaking Proficiency test. According to the manual, the speaking test did not undergo a complete norming analysis but was subjected to a "smaller, separate study." Results of this study are shown only in the form of a simple table of suggested proficiency ratings of "good," "fair," and "poor" for each of three raw-score ranges; in addition, the user is cautioned that "because of the nature of this test and the limitations of the study on which the classifications are based," even these limited ratings should be considered only as estimated cutting points. Reliability coefficients, means, standard deviations, analysis group size, and related statistical data are completely lacking. The upshot is quite simply that the Pimsleur battery contains only three standardized tests: listening, reading, and writing. Evaluation of student competence in speaking must for all practical purposes be limited to comparisons based on local norms, and in view of the apparently unsatisfactory results of the test developers' own analysis of the speaking test data, it is difficult to be sanguine about the reliability and usefulness of similar analyses carried out at the local level.

Normative data for the listening, reading, and writing tests are based on the results of a standardization study involving 4,543 "first-level" students and 3,052 "second-level" students from junior and senior high schools in the U.S. "First" and "second" levels are not explicitly defined in either the test catalog or manual. Although most language teachers would be expected to have a general notion of the curricula and student attainment levels implied by these two designations, a closer definition in terms of various combinations of course length and grade level (e.g., two years of junior high school study, one year of high school study, one semester of college study, etc.) or the number of units covered in widely used language programs would allow the potential test user to determine more accurately the appropriateness of the tests for a particular group of students.

The composition of the two norming groups is not clearly indicated in the test literature. The manual mentions the use of 90 participating schools that are described as having been selected on the basis of responses to a school questionnaire covering such factors as amount of material covered in the French classes, the type of language program, and the size and geographical location of the school system. Unfortunately, only the geographical distribution of the schools is shown in the manual. More crucial breakdowns such as the type of schools

represented (public, private, parochial) and, especially, their instructional orientation (e.g., "audio-lingual," "traditional," "eclectic") are not given. In the absence of specific information in these areas, the prospective user can only guess as to the particular "mix" of schools and instructional emphases represented by the standardization groups and the degree of correspondence of these groups to the local group whose performance he intends to evaluate. In this regard, one may wonder why only one general norms group was identified at each level rather than two or more separate groups, such as "audio-lingual" and "traditional." The information needed to make such categorizations would presumably have been available from the school questionnaires, and the total number of students tested would easily have permitted the establishment of two or more norming groups at each level.

Norming considerations notwithstanding, the Pimsleur test manual presents a considerable amount of useful information in other areas of test usage and interpretation. Administration instructions for each test are set forth clearly and completely, and the test user should have little difficulty in following them correctly. The very detailed instructions for administering the Speaking Proficiency test—including the procedures to be followed in labeling the student response tapes, setting the tape recorder controls, and even threading the tape ("thread to the take-up reels, and make a few turns")—should help to reassure the nontechnically oriented user and increase the chances of a smooth and valid administration.

It should be pointed out that the order of administration of the four skills tests is not specified but is left to the judgment of the test user. As discussed elsewhere (see 254) in my review of the *MLA Cooperative Foreign Language Tests,* different administration sequences may produce varying warm-up or practice effects for one or more tests in a skills battery. Thus, in the absence of a single prescribed administration sequence, the user would be well advised to adopt a specific administration order of his own and to follow this order in testing any and all groups whose performance he will later wish to compare.

The authors of the test manual are candid and helpful in their discussion of the proper interpretation of test results. A basic caveat not often emphasized in test literature is succinctly stated in the Pimsleur manual: "standardized tests can measure only a representative sample of those aspects of learning commonly accepted as being important and measurable"; for this reason, "the extent to which the content and objectives actually correspond to those of a local program must be determined by the prospective test user." To aid in this determination, test items from those sections of the speaking and writing tests that lend themselves to close content analysis are classified in the manual according to the pronunciation feature or grammatical element represented. Although these classifications should not be used as a substitute for careful examination of the tests themselves, they do provide a succinct content overview of the test sections involved and should also be of value in any post-test analysis of individual item results.

Separate descriptions and discussions of each test in the Pimsleur battery are given below. Unless otherwise indicated, all comments apply to both first-level and second-level tests.

READING COMPREHENSION. The content of this test is typical of several other published reading tests: the student reads French passages of varying lengths and degrees of difficulty and answers multiple choice questions, also in French, dealing with the literal meaning of the passage or with easily drawn inferences about it. At both levels, the passages chosen are well varied in style and content and include brief selections on general topics as well as the usual literary narratives and dramatic scenes. Several passages have been drawn, with considerable adaptation, from well-known authors, including Maupassant, Jean-Jacques Rousseau, Théophile Gautier, and Saint-Exupéry (*Le Petit Prince*). With the exception of *Le Petit Prince*—which may have been encountered by some students— prior acquaintance with the reading passages would not be expected; nonetheless, the careful test user may wish to verify this fact through prior examination.

Although each of the reading tests has only 36 items, odd-even split-half reliabilities are satisfactorily high (.85 and .88 for first and second levels, respectively). Mean raw scores of 15.5 and 19.5 for the first and second level norming samples indicate that the tests are reasonably well pitched in difficulty, at least for the "general" standardization group. However, in view of the wide difference in emphasis accorded the reading skill under "traditional"

and "audio-lingual" methods (especially at the first level), the presentation of separate "traditional" and "audio-lingual" norming data would have been quite welcome.

LISTENING COMPREHENSION. The format of the listening test differs in that there is no student test booklet. Instead, a special answer sheet is used on which the answer options for each question are printed immediately beside the corresponding answer spaces. This technique deserves some praise as it substantially reduces the amount of paper handling which the student must do in the course of the test.

The test has two parts. In the first part, the student listens to short tape-recorded sentences such as "Charles ne la voit guère" and chooses from among four printed sentences the one that was spoken: "Charles ne la voit guère/Charles la voit à la guerre/Charles a la voix gaie/ Charles voit la gare." The testing intent of this section, as stated in the manual, is to "measure the student's ability to listen attentively, to distinguish individual French sounds in the context of a complete sentence, and to associate these sounds with their written symbols." Although the first two goals would probably have the general approval of language teachers regardless of their instructional philosophy, there may well be some question about using at the elementary or intermediate level—and particularly with audio-lingually trained students—a testing procedure that requires the student to deal with a wide variety of sound-grapheme relationships. Although most students, even those in audio-lingual courses, would have had some exposure to elementary reading tasks by the time they were tested, it is questionable whether they would have mastered the sound-spelling correspondences involved in discriminating among such sentences as: "J'ai su sauter/Je sais sauter /J'ai sursauté/Je sais souder" or "Vous dites qu'il était déçu?/Vous dites qu'il était dessus?/ Vous dites qu'il était dessous?/Vous dites qu'il était dissous?" One should also note the uncommon vocabulary required in some cases to make meaningful parallel sentences.

The sound-grapheme discrimination problem is compounded by the short (8 seconds) pauses allowed for student responses. If it is assumed that two of the 8 seconds are used for mechanically marking the response and the remaining 6 seconds for reading the options, it may be calculated that an average reading speed of 187 words per minute would be required to answer each of the second-level questions in the time allotted and 195 words per minute to answer the first-level questions. Reading speed for individual questions ranges from a low of 110 words per minute (item 18, first level) to a high of 300 words per minute (item 12, first level).

The manual states candidly that "the four tests in the Pimsleur series do not measure the individual skills in isolation" and suggests that "the teacher must therefore be alert to the possibility of interactions among the skills in evaluating performance." This advice is especially applicable to the first part of Listening Comprehension, in which the reading load and the speed with which the student is required to respond may for some student groups largely invalidate this section of the test as a measure of aural comprehension.

The second part of the test makes use of "rejoinder" questions, in which the student hears a conversational statement or question in French and chooses from among four printed French choices the most appropriate reply. Although student reading ability is also at issue in this part of the test, the printed choices are generally shorter than in the first part and embody a much more common vocabulary.

In both parts of the test, the spoken material for each question consists of a short utterance by a single voice. The student hears no spoken dialogues, radio broadcasts, *récits,* or other longer passages typical of other published listening tests. Since the Pimsleur test tapes run only about 15 minutes and since the manual suggests that a full class period be set aside for each test, it may be wondered why a somewhat longer test was not specified, both to increase total test reliability beyond the rather low figure of .74 reported for both levels and to permit the inclusion of various other types of spoken material.

An interesting feature of the listening test tapes is that the speakers read their scripts throughout at a normal to slightly rapid speed and elide mute E's wherever phonetically possible. The prospective test user would be advised to listen in advance to the test tapes to determine whether the speed of delivery is generally in keeping with the type of listening practice that his students have had in the classroom. If classroom speech has for the most part been at a slower pace, it may be helpful for the teacher to devote one or more preliminary class periods to practice in listening at a somewhat faster speed.

WRITING PROFICIENCY. This test uses a free response format in which the student writes all of his answers in the test booklet; the tests must therefore be scored individually by the classroom teacher or some other person competent in French. In the first part of the test, the student reads a French paragraph in which certain words have been omitted and writes in the appropriate completions. The missing words include pronouns, demonstrative adjectives, prepositions, and other grammatical elements. For the most part, the sentence context is such that only one specific word can be considered correct. The scoring instructions state, however, that the teacher should give credit for the occasional use of some other correct word that is not shown on the scoring key. No partial credit is allowed, and the word must be spelled correctly, including any necessary accents.

The second part, which is also a fill-in exercise, tests the student's ability to write verb forms in various persons and tenses. The first-level test includes present, imperfect, past indefinite, and future tenses of regular and common irregular verbs; the second-level test adds the conditional and present subjunctive.

In the third part, the student writes complete sentences based on model sentences but requiring certain modifications, such as changing the number or gender of adjectives, converting nouns to direct and indirect object pronouns, and so forth. For example, "J'ai un beau manteau blanc (robe)" would be rewritten: "J'ai une belle robe blanche." Scoring is on a right-wrong basis for each critical element (in this example, the correct formation of the three feminine adjectives).

The fourth and final part consists of somewhat freer writing tasks based on pictorial stimuli. In the first-level test, the student writes descriptive sentences for each of several pictures; the time cue "maintenant" or "hier" written above each picture indicates whether present or past tense is to be used. In the second-level test, the student writes a single paragraph describing a series of chronologically related pictures. For both levels, scoring of the fourth part is carried out subjectively on the basis of guidelines provided in the scoring instructions leaflet.

The Writing Proficiency test appears to be a quite straightforward measure of such basic components of writing skill as verb formation, grammatical agreement, and pronoun selection and placement. Inter-scorer reliabilities for the entire test are .988 (first level) and .979 (second level), reported for the independent rating of a sample of 50 tests by two scorers. Within-scorer reliability is not indicated, except for the results of a limited study in which one rater rescored the fourth part of 82 second-level tests with a reliability of .961.

It should be noted in evaluating these statistics that scoring was carried out by raters who had undergone special preliminary training and had discussed the rating procedure in detail in group meetings. Although one would not expect in-field users to have difficulty in scoring the essentially right-wrong items in the first three parts of the test, there might be some question as to whether persons scoring the test locally and having recourse only to the printed scoring guides could reach reported reliability levels for the less structured exercises in the fourth part. A somewhat stronger case for the reliability of the writing test in general and of the fourth part in particular could have been made by asking teachers to administer and score the tests just as they would in the school situation. Reliabilities based on these more realistic conditions would be of both practical and research interest.

SPEAKING PROFICIENCY. The Pimsleur speaking test may be administered on a group basis in language laboratories equipped to record the responses of each student on an individual tape. Although not so indicated in the manual, the test may also be administered on an individual student basis through the use of two regular tape recorders, one to play the test tape and the other to record student responses. This technique would of course be feasible only for rather small groups of students.

Test instructions to the student are recorded on the master tape, and the tape also automatically times the approximately 16 minutes required for administration. A useful feature of the Pimsleur test is that the student is instructed to start and stop his own tape recorder so as to record only those portions of the test in which he is actually speaking. In this way, the overall length of each student-response tape is reduced to about six and one-half minutes, and the listening time of the person scoring the test is substantially reduced. By contrast, the student-response tapes for the MLA Cooperative speaking test run approximately 11 minutes, and

the person scoring these tapes must either listen to long periods of re-recorded instructions or laboriously shuttle the tape back and forth to locate the spots at which the student is speaking. In either case, the time and effort involved is substantially greater than for the Pimsleur tests.

In the first part of the speaking test (Vocabulary), the student looks at line drawings depicting common objects and is given four seconds per drawing to name the object aloud in French. Use of the definite article is not required. This use of pictures to test spoken vocabulary is a potentially rewarding technique in that a great number of scorable items can be introduced within a short time span. By the same token, it is possible to sample a number of different vocabulary domains (such as *vêtements, parties du corps, articles de cuisine,* etc.) within a relatively brief period. The technique is limited to those vocabulary items that can be easily and unambiguously pictured, but for beginning and intermediate language courses, which typically involve common noun vocabulary to a large extent, this restriction should not be critical. Scoring reliability of a pictured vocabulary section should be very high, since only one specific response would be considered correct in most cases. Novel correct responses might occasionally be made, but these could be easily resolved by the teacher-scorer.

In the second part of the test (Pronunciation), the student reads aloud a number of printed French sentences. For each sentence, the scorer judges as right or wrong the student's pronunciation of two "critical sounds." For example, the phrase "Buvez du café" is evaluated for the proper pronunciation of the two /e/ sounds. In "C'est une question de temps," the /k/ of *question* and the nasal vowel of *temps* are scored as right or wrong. It is the reviewer's opinion, based on close acquaintance with similar sound judging exercises in other testing situations, that satisfactory scoring reliability is difficult to attain even through the use of scorers who are both highly sophisticated in the phonetic considerations at issue and thoroughly practiced in the judging standards to be applied to a particular test form. Neither the Pimsleur nor the MLA test manual provides information on the scoring reliability that could be expected in regular in-field use of the test, and it may be seriously doubted that many teachers or other local persons would be able to

Pimsleur French Proficiency Tests

score accurately the sound-judging section of either the Pimsleur or the MLA Cooperative test simply on the basis of their own phonetic backgrounds and the printed scoring instructions.

In the third and final part of the test (Fluency), the test booklet is not used. Instead, the student listens to simple questions such as "Quelle est la date d'aujourd'hui?" or "Où allez-vous après l'école?" and answers the questions using complete French sentences. Scoring is done on a four-point scale in accordance with reasonably specific verbal criteria. There is considerable face validity to this part of the test in that question-answer sequences are an important aspect of everyday conversation. It is also worth noting that no printed materials are required and that the procedure is thus entirely audio-lingual in nature. However, the question of scoring reliability may again be raised, and it is unfortunate that specific information on this matter is not available in the manual.

As previously discussed, the major shortcoming of the Speaking Proficiency test is the unavailability of normative and other statistical data that would allow it to be classified and used as a standardized test. This second-class status of the Speaking Proficiency test in comparison to the other three tests in the battery is unfortunate in that the absence of suitable interpretive information will in all probability reinforce the already apparent trend on the part of school systems and research groups to forego direct testing of student speaking ability as a regular part of their evaluation programs. When lack of standardization of the Pimsleur speaking test is added to the list of drawbacks already identified for speaking tests in general (complexity of administration, time and expense of scoring, problems of reliability), those in the language teaching and testing professions who continue to see important advantages to the formal evaluation of speaking skill will have an even more difficult battle.

MICHIO PETER HAGIWARA, *Associate Professor of French, University of Michigan, Ann Arbor, Michigan.*

Though it appears that the preliminary version of these tests had at least two equated sets, the present tests are available only in one form for each level, thereby lessening somewhat their usefulness in educational research where inde-

pendent measures of language competence for groups of students are needed.

LISTENING COMPREHENSION. The listening test, consisting of two parts with 20 items each, has a maximum total score of 40 points and is administered in approximately 15 minutes. All aural stimuli are read at normal conversational speed by alternating male and female voices on the test tape. Part 1 presents basically sound-symbol association items. The student matches within an eight-second pause the sentence he has heard with one of the four similar-looking sentences printed on the answer sheet. Generally, the aural stimulus is a single utterance composed of four to seven words. Form C has a comparatively larger number of items based on verb morphology, since students completing two years of French will have learned many verb tenses and forms which often sound alike. The sound-symbol association takes up exactly 50 percent of the entire test, and we may question whether or not such inordinate emphasis is warranted. Furthermore, there is no attempt to graduate the difficulty level of the test items. As a result, the sentences at the beginning are just as long as those occurring toward the middle or the end of this part. Thus, the student who is a slow reader or who has a short auditory retention will undoubtedly be handicapped from the outset. It would have been more desirable to begin the test with single words or short phrases and gradually increase the length of utterances.

In Part 2, the student matches the aural cue, usually a question or a statement, with one of the four printed sentences that constitutes the most appropriate answer or rejoinder. As in the other Pimsleur tests, some of the test items in Form A are repeated in Form C, in order to elicit responses from underachievers and also to discriminate among the varying abilities of students. The aural cues are repeated twice in succession, unlike the practice of many other standardized listening comprehension tests, to insure that many students will attempt to answer most of the items. The test items do not appear to be graded according to their difficulty levels. From the beginning, there are fairly long spoken cues and equally long multiple choice answers, to the disadvantage of slow readers. The aural cues are almost invariably single utterances and do not become longer throughout the twenty items. Some items are based on auditory discrimination of two or three sound segments—rather than on vocabulary, structure, or context—and should have been incorporated in Part 1. Since there is no attempt to group the test items on the basis of common general topics, the context jumps from one item to another. In Form C, several items have a distinct vocabulary bias: the student cannot select the correct response unless he knows the key words or expressions—such as *avocat, veuve,* and *s'en aller*—used in the aural stimuli. Although the hybrid types are more economical to produce, it would have been preferable to include a few items in which simple line drawings replace printed sentences, as used, though insufficiently, in the MLA Cooperative tests. It also would have been desirable either to increase the length of the aural cues progressively or to include one or two short connected passages. Background noise or an increased rate of phonation might also have been used. Except for the addition of the sound-symbol association items—which are rather excessive in number—the Pimsleur listening comprehension test is less systematic and sophisticated than its counterparts in the MLA and the College Board tests.

SPEAKING. Speaking skill is measured by a three-part test of approximately 16 minutes with a maximum possible score of 91. Part 1, scored one point or zero per item, consists of 27 drawings designed to elicit vocabulary. Spontaneity, one of the aspects of speech fluency, is also tested inasmuch as the recording time for each item hardly exceeds three seconds. Pronunciation is not an important factor since the scoring instructions state that it "need not be perfect, but the word must be readily understandable," implying that all kinds of substitution of English phonemes are permissible as long as the substitution does not distort a given French word to the point of making it unintelligible. Although the use of pictorial cues is an excellent idea, one may wonder if a set of 27 lexical items is really sufficient to evaluate the student's active vocabulary. The vaguely stated criterion for the evaluation of pronunciation does not seem to qualify this part as a true speaking test. We note, in addition, that several illustrations are culturally unauthentic, such as the pictures of an American church, kitchen, breakfast, and bread. They may give an erroneous impression that the semantic range—connotational, denotational, and circumstantial

—of the 27 words is identical in English and French.

Part 2 is a combination of mimicry and reading pronunciation test in that first the 20 short utterances are heard first on the master tape and the student is allowed to follow them with the test booklet open. The pause allowed for the recording of each sentence is approximately three to four seconds. The model on the master tape may encourage some students to mark the difficult words as they follow the text while listening. The embedding of two test items in each short utterance, recorded in rapid succession, will make scoring extremely difficult without stopping the answer tapes frequently. Moreover, as many as 14 phonemes in Form A and 8 in Form C occur twice in the same sentence, potentially adding to the confusion of the inexperienced scorer and penalizing students twice for the same kind of error. At least 7 items in Form A and 11 in Form C border on sound-symbol association in that the sounds to be produced are represented by the *c* of *lac,* and *ch, s,* and *x,* while the absence of sounds as indicated by the verb ending -*ent* and the plural marker of nouns occur also as pronunciation items. The sound /œ̃/, virtually nonexistent in the standard Parisian French, is included although the more important /œ/ is not. Finally, there are no items designed to check the intonation patterns and syllabification. As a result, Part 2 measures pronunciation only imperfectly, despite the fact that it is assigned a maximum of 40 points in the entire speaking test.

Part 3 is made up of eight questions, all of which begin with question words. They center around a vaguely common topic so that the context does not jump abruptly from one question to another. In order to insure correct listening comprehension and to elicit appropriate responses, each question is repeated. Five items in Form A and seven in Form C require personalized answers, such as, "What time did you get up this morning?" and "Where do you go after school?" Students are told to respond in complete sentences, and each response is scored globally in terms of pronunciation, meaning, and grammar on a 0–3 point scale. Scorer subjectivity is inherent in this type of evaluation. There is no sample recording, but a brief description of the scoring categories is given. Unlike the MLA Cooperative tests, this test provides no items to check the continuous speech production of the student.

Pimsleur French Proficiency Tests

READING. Reading comprehension (35 minutes) is tested by 12 short paragraphs representing authentic as well as adapted journalistic and literary prose. Each passage is followed by three multiple choice completion items, with a maximum score of 36 points. The lexical items used in both the paragraphs and statements are quite simple, so that there is little vocabulary bias in the two tests, as contrasted with the MLA Cooperative and the College Board tests. Six items from Form A are repeated in Form C. The manual mentions that the "ability to locate and understand information set forth" in the passage and the ability to make inferences are more or less evenly tested, 18 to 18 items in Form A, and 17 to 19 in Form C. However, such a distinction is so subtle that another person analyzing the contents can easily come up with different results. This reviewer's classification shows that the ratio of the two types of test items is 21 to 9 in Form A, with 6 items bordering on both categories, and 19 to 12 in Form C, with 5 items having both characteristics. The only general agreement thus seems to be that Form C has a comparatively larger number of items requiring the ability to draw inferences from a given passage. These tests are adequate for Levels 1 and 2 of secondary-school French or the first and second semester of college French, even though the difficulty levels of the test items and the length of paragraphs are not graduated.

WRITING PROFICIENCY. Writing competence is evaluated in four parts, to be completed in 35 minutes. Part 1, scored one point or zero per item, consists of 19 fill-in items in Form A and 22 in Form C. The sentences, which require a preposition, noun marker, object pronoun, and so forth, constitute a connected passage.

On Part 2, scored the same as the preceding part and containing 9 items in Form A, the student is to supply the correct forms of the verbs whose infinitives are given in parentheses. The verb tenses involved are the present, future, imperfect, and the passé composé of regular and common irregular verbs. Each of the 10 items in Form C consists of a pair of sentences, a complete model and an incomplete transformation for which the correct verb form must be supplied. In addition to the tenses already mentioned, the conditional and the present subjunctive are included. As is the case with the MLA Cooperative tests, the number of verbs is extremely limited and the choice seems almost arbitrary.

Part 3 contains 10 sentences to be rewritten to incorporate the transformation required by a change in the noun, object pronoun, adjective, or verb in the original. The scoring shows an improvement over the similar test items in the MLA Cooperative tests in that *each* change receives one point or zero, thereby insuring a higher degree of scorer objectivity. The number of changes to be made varies from one sentence to another, so that the maximum score for each item ranges between one and four points. Form C duplicates three sentences (nine points) of Form A. Students who make mistakes in copying the unchanged portion of the sentences will be penalized, the degree of penalty depending on the type of errors involved.

Part 4 is the most original section of the writing test. In Form A, the student describes each of four unrelated pictures in a sentence and then writes three sentences concerning a scene that contains a good number of details. The scoring is global for each of the five sentences, based on a 0–3 point scale, and there is a description of each numerical category with sample responses. Although the scoring is simpler than for the comparable part of the MLA Cooperative tests, scorer subjectivity cannot be avoided. Furthermore, those students who have chosen more "original" expressions and sentence patterns have more chances of being penalized for the possible number of errors they may make, as compared to those who stay with the conventional subject-verb-object type of sentence structure. If the subject of each sentence were indicated in the test booklet, perhaps more varied constructions might be elicited.

Form C contains eight sequential drawings representing a simple story. There is no limit to the number of sentences the student can write to tell the story, again with the possibility that the longer the composition, the more errors it may contain. No credit is given for originality of expressions, and the student who writes a series of simple sentences will be better off than the one who attempts to produce complex and compound sentences. Scoring is global: the composition is evaluated from the viewpoint of grammar, verb formation and usage, and content (completeness, continuity, vocabulary, appropriate use of idioms, and the absence of extraneous sentences). Each of these factors is to be rated on a 0–4 point scale and the

Pimsleur French Proficiency Tests

resultant score to be multiplied by two. The doubling of the score is necessary in order to weight this part of the test and give a sufficient range of scores. Nevertheless, it also increases the likelihood of magnifying scorer errors. In addition, the "content" factor could be divided into at least two separate categories, vocabulary and idioms on one hand, and completeness and continuity on the other.

A rather high interscorer agreement is claimed in the manual, the tables indicating the results of scoring Parts 1–3 and of Part 4 by two similarly trained scorers and that of one scorer evaluating the same compositions of Part 4 twice. The crucial point of the degree of unanimity among three or more scorers remains to be established. As with the MLA Cooperative tests, the Pimsleur tests preclude the use of English as test cues. As a result, many pattern conflicts and vocabulary distinction problems are not included, even though they constitute very common errors made by students in their writing assignments. Moreover, there are no items dealing with relative pronouns, interrogative pronouns and adverbs, and the various equivalents of the English *how* plus adjectives. The writing test is somewhat fragmentary in Parts 1–3, and the nature of Part 4, particularly in Form A, is such that it may not be comprehensive enough to yield a sufficient sampling of the student's writing ability.

CONCLUSION. The *Pimsleur French Proficiency Tests* serve basically the same objectives as the MLA Cooperative tests. They can assess the linguistic competence of a student or a group of students in terms of national or local norms. They are useful to some extent in evaluating the effectiveness of a local language curriculum and may also be used for guidance and counseling purposes. Both batteries of tests will reveal to a degree the relative strengths and weaknesses of students in the four fundamental language skills. The choice between the Pimsleur tests and the MLA Cooperative tests will depend on the purchasing and scoring cost factors. Generally speaking, the Pimsleur tests are shorter and much less complicated to administer and score, an important point to consider if a fairly large-scale local scoring is contemplated. The usefulness of the Pimsleur tests as a diagnostic instrument is somewhat superior, since they provide some information concerning the content and objectives of each test. Simplicity and economy seem to have been a key factor

in the production of the Pimsleur tests. They are not necessarily an improvement over the MLA Cooperative tests, and in certain areas they tend to magnify the latter's defects. Form A of the Pimsleur tests provides a more appropriate instrument to evaluate the language proficiency of the first-year French students at the high school level, for whom the Forms LA and LB of the MLA Cooperative tests will prove to be rather difficult. On the other hand, for Level 2 and above, the MLA tests, despite their shortcomings, may be more effective because of their amplitude and systematic treatment of testing methods. Furthermore, the usefulness of the Pimsleur tests is severely limited because they lack alternate forms, college norms, and more advanced tests for third-year and fourth-year high school French students.

J Ed Meas 6(1):46–7 sp '69. C. Richards Pusey. The most serious weaknesses....are in the listening and speaking tests. Noticeable positive features of these tests include clear, authentic, French recordings, ample time to record responses, adequate increase in question difficulty from Form A to Form C, and answer choices all expressed in correct language. Negative features observed in the listening and speaking tests include questions requiring only vocabulary knowledge for a correct answer and some ambiguity in the choice of answers. These two tests appear to be strongly influenced by two common misconceptions held by teachers of foreign languages; first that French (or any other "foreign" language) has its real meaning in English, and second, that language and writing are the same thing. Evidence of these negative features is found in the translation used in the directions of the listening proficiency test and in the highly objectionable use of reading skills to measure listening comprehension. The listening comprehension test should be revised so as to measure aural and not visual discriminations. In the listening test directions, Part 2, contrary to what Mr. Pimsleur says on the tape, the French speaker did not say "I'm sick today"; she said "Je suis malade aujourd'hui." The author is wrongfully assuming that French has its real meaning in English. This, of course, is not so, nor should the author assume that it is so for students taking his test. In the speaking test the author might just as well cause direct translation by using written English words to evoke the pronunciation of French vocabulary items as to cause indirect translation by using American drawings of objects. It would, however, be much more appropriate to have the student use the picture-suggested noun in a complete sentence than to simply record the noun with neither a context nor an article indicating its gender. The second part of the test called pronunciation measures oral reading ability rather than speaking proficiency. It is unfortunate that the speaking test, along with its questions and answers, makes no use of the statement-comment, or rejoinder exercise, an extremely appropriate means of measuring student ability to interact in a language, for speaking proficiency is "interaction in the language" rather than vocabulary recall, pronunciation, or oral reading. The reading test presents varied and interesting passages and thought-provoking questions. For some reason, not immediately apparent to this reviewer, this test is much more advanced than either the listening test or the speaking test. This discrepancy in difficulty levels contradicts commonly accepted modern foreign language pedagogy which demands more listening and speaking than reading and writing experience in the first two years of language study. The reason for identical passages in Forms A and C is not apparent. There is an objectionable ambiguity of answer choice in at least four of the questions causing the student's point of view to determine his response rather than the information given him in the reading passage. It is commendable that in the writing test any right answer is to be considered correct even though not found on the correction sheet, and that no answer using English is to be accepted. This reviewer finds it difficult to see why the student is never required to write the future tense in the more advanced form of the test and only once in the first level form. The directions telling the student not to write everything he can about the rather detailed picture in his test booklet do not seem to be necessary. Why not simply give a less detailed picture? Suggestions for improvement would include the use of "action" pictures as opposed to "thing" pictures in both the listening and speaking tests. In conclusion, the Pimsleur French Proficiency Tests show a noble aim if not noteworthy marksmanship. The listening and speaking tests need serious revision; the reading and writing tests are well designed and for the most part valid.

[280]

*Second Year French Test, [Revised Edition]. High school and college; 1956–68; SYFT; Form A ('68, 2 pages); manual ('68, 2 pages); no data on reliability; $1.75 per 25 tests, postage extra; 75¢ per specimen set, postpaid; 50(55) minutes; Jean Leblon and Minnie M. Miller; Data Processing and Educational Measurement Center. *

JOHN L. D. CLARK, *Examiner in Foreign Languages, Test Development Division, Educational Testing Service, Princeton, New Jersey.*

The *Second Year French Test* is a paper-and-pencil test containing 100 items. The entire test is printed on the front and back of a single sheet of paper, on which the student makes all of his responses. Seven of the ten parts use a multiple choice format in which the student writes in the number (not letter) corresponding to the intended answer. (There are five true-false items in one part.) The remaining three parts use questions of the "completion" type, in which the student must fill in a word or words to complete a sentence.

Extremely sketchy information on test use and interpretation is given in a one-page Manual of Directions. Administration instructions are presented in only two sentences: "After the students have filled in the blanks on the first page, direct them to read the directions and answer the items of each part. Allow exactly 50 minutes of working time." The students are not told, for example, how they should indicate a changed answer or, for the multiple choice items, how they should handle questions about which they are not certain (since there is no correction for guessing, the appropriate instruction would be for the student to attempt to answer every question).

Normative information is restricted to a single percentile table based on the scores of 240 "students of second-year French classes." The number of classes represented, the type and location of the participating schools, and the course history of the students tested are not described. In the absence of more specific information about the norming group, the potential user is at a loss to evaluate the appropriateness of the norms for a local test group. Basic statistical data, such as whole-test reliability and standard deviation of the norming group scores, are also lacking.

The test places heavy weight on reading-related tasks and on grammatical exercises. Of the ten parts, three involve recognitional vocabulary and textual reading, and five are concerned with verb formation and usage, pronoun selection, contraction of articles, use of prepositions, and other basic grammatical features.

In the reading area, there are two multiple choice parts in which the student finds synonyms and antonyms for various nouns, verbs, and idiomatic expressions. A third part presents a reading passage of about 240 words on which are based four 3-option multiple choice questions and five true-false questions. Rather than base the entire reading part on a single passage representing only one writing style and topical area, it would be preferable to use two or three shorter passages by different authors and on different topics. One may also wonder why 3-choice questions were used rather than the more reliable 4- or 5-choice questions.

The largest proportion of the test—five parts and 51 items—is devoted to questions testing grammatical points. The student is asked to identify appropriate verb forms, select correct pronouns or other forms for a given context, supply the correct person and tense of verbs given in the infinitive, convert a short paragraph written in the present tense into a past-tense narration by changing the verbs into the past indefinite or imperfect, and write in pronouns or prepositions drawn from a short list of designated forms.

In working through the test, the student may be hindered by the extremely cramped format used to print the entire test on a single sheet of paper; this is particularly likely for the fill-in questions.

A single part containing five multiple choice items is addressed to questions of pronunciation. The student sees a word (such as mais**on**) and is asked to choose from among three other words (monsieur, pompe, donner) the one which has "the same sound" as the boldface letters in the stimulus word. Under the perhaps questionable assumption that there is a high correspondence between the ability to recognize similar-sounding elements in printed words and the ability accurately to produce the same sounds, this part of the test could be considered to deal with one aspect of pronunciation. However, since the part consists of only five items, the overall contribution of the "pronunciation" section to total test score is minimal.

The last part of the test consists of ten multiple choice questions on French civilization and culture. Teachers who attempt to give their students a broader picture of French history,

customs, and daily life than that represented by a simple collection of facts about dates, places, and famous personages will find this part of the test insufficient.

No provision is made to test listening comprehension, either directly or indirectly. For this reason, many teachers would probably wish to supplement the *Second Year French Test* with a tape-recorded listening test produced locally or obtained from some other source. Any intention to evaluate student speaking ability would also call for the administration of a supplementary test specifically aimed at this skill.

In summary, the *Second Year French Test* may be of general informational use to the teacher who has by the time of testing given his students suitable exposure to the various vocabulary-reading and grammatical tasks represented. In the absence of sufficient normative information, student performance on the test should not be evaluated in other than local terms; and for classes in which all four language skills receive emphasis, the use of additional tests of listening comprehension and speaking ability would be indicated.

For reviews by Geraldine Spaulding and Clarence E. Turner of an earlier edition, see 5:271.

[281]

★**The Undergraduate Record Examinations: French Test.** College; 1969–70; Form K-RUR ('69, 21 pages); descriptive booklet ('70, 8 pages); for more complete information, see 671; 120(140) minutes; Educational Testing Service. *

JOSEPH A. MURPHY, *Professor of French, Lycoming College, Williamsport, Pennsylvania.*

This new standardized test of achievement in French has the following stated purposes:

To measure the level of certain kinds of competence achieved by the college senior who has majored in French.
To provide information useful in assessing a student's achievement in undergraduate work and his competence for further study.
To serve as one useful source of information for student counseling.
To provide information that will prove useful in institutional self-evaluation, both curricular and departmental.

It is a two-hour test of reading comprehension, literature (including literary history, criticism and interpretation), and culture and civilization.

The test is reported to have a reliability coefficient of .93, one of the highest reported for a UP test. However, the content validity of the test is more difficult to ascertain. Following ETS guidelines for determining validity, one must decide (a) to what extent the test questions are representative of particular courses of study, and (b) the extent to which the questions are representative of the content to which the person has been exposed.

With the limited data published at this time, one can only make inferences about validity from an item analysis of the reference-group sample. In that analysis only 64 of the 110 items fell within the difficulty range of 40 to 75 percent. A significant number of questions (32) were missed by more than 60 percent of students while only 14 items were answered correctly by 60 percent or more of the student population. Although a good test should contain a wide range of item difficulty, such a sustained high level of difficulty creates doubt as to whether the test is a representative sampling of subject matter actually taught by the institutions serviced. A more detailed analysis will clarify the strengths and weaknesses of this test.

An analysis of the 49 items testing reading comprehension has revealed them to be fair and discriminating. The questions span many cognitive areas from vocabulary recognition, paraphrasing, implications, comparative thinking, and evaluation. This large subsection would certainly be useful to individuals and institutions wishing to evaluate reading competence.

Although there is no section numbering, it is possible to place the questions into ten sets. Five sets test exclusively reading comprehension, vocabulary and literary analysis. Two sets treat culture and civilization, with one set apiece for literary terms, literary characters, and literary criticism. In terms of item-weight per area of achievement, 61 items measure reading comprehension and literary analysis, while 18 items are assigned to literary criticism, 16 to culture and civilization, 8 to literary terms, and 7 to literary characters. It is thus clear that the instrument is above all a test of reading comprehension and literature. There are no questions pertaining to customs and values of everyday French life. Moreover, the small sampling of questions in the culture-civilization sets does not permit reliable generalizations about individual competence in those areas. This is perhaps the most serious deficiency in a test that purports to provide comprehensive individual and institutional self-evaluation. With rare exceptions the

questions are well written and challenging. There are perhaps two questionable items, items 48 and 83.

In testing factual information about culture and civilization, one should select material having the utmost significance and applicability. Most of the questions meet this criterion, but with only 13 questions asked about geography, history, and music, it does not seem balanced to select names like Jean Monnet and Leon Blum as bases for questions. In this section also, the questions are technically effective and demanding. It is the size of the sampling and the absence of culture with a small "c" that render this part useless for generalizations.

Only one of the eight questions on literary terminology was answered correctly by a majority of students in the reference group. While a few of the difficult items would seem appropriate for undergraduate testing ("pasticher," "hiatus," "romanesque," "le vers régulier"), others lend themselves to more sophisticated literary study at the graduate level (Voltaire's "pamphlets," "chevilles," "le drame selon Victor Hugo," "ouvrages inédits"). These kinds of questions would be more appropriate in a graduate examination. In general the literary questions should be reviewed item by item by a number of experienced undergraduate teachers. These are precisely the questions that seem to function the least efficiently.

As stated above, the test performs most adequately as a measure of the level of reading competence. It performs less effectively as a measure of literary knowledge and ability, and is of little use as a test of culture and civilization. If institutions are to evaluate comprehensively their undergraduate programs, they will need supplementary modular tests in culture and civilization, listening, speaking, and writing skills. In the interim, this test will provide useful feedback on reading skills.

For reviews of the testing program, see 671 (2 reviews).

GERMAN

[282]

*Advanced Placement Examination in German. High school students desiring credit for college level courses or admission to advanced courses; 1954–70; Forms RBP ('69, 17 pages), SBP ('70, 15 pages) in 2 booklets (objective, essay); listening comprehension tapes: 7½ ips for Form RBP, 3¾ ips for Form SBP;

tape script ['69–70, 6 pages] for each form; for more complete information, see 662; 180 (200) minutes; program administered for the College Entrance Examination Board by Educational Testing Service. *

REFERENCES

1–5. See 6:385.
6. "The Advanced Placement German Examination of 1965." *German Q* 38:480–505 S '65. *
7. LEDERER, HERBERT. "Evaluating Advanced Placement Candidates: Notes From the Chief Reader's Desk." *German Q* 38:506–13 S '65. *
8. REICHARD, JOSEPH R. "The First Ten Years of German Advanced Placement: Theory and Practice." *German Q* 38: 440–9 S '65. *
9. SCHEIDER, ROSE M. "The Role of Educational Testing Service in the German Advanced Placement Program." *German Q* 38:514–21 S '65. *

For a review by Herbert Schueler of an earlier form, see 5:273. For a review of the testing program, see 662.

[283]

*College Board Achievement Test in German. Candidates for college entrance with 2–4 years high school German; 1901–71; test administered each January at centers established by the publisher; for more complete information, see 663; 60(80) minutes; program administered for the College Entrance Examination Board by Educational Testing Service. *

REFERENCES

1–3. See 4:244.
4–6. See 5:272.

For a review by Gilbert C. Kettelkamp of earlier forms, see 6:383; for a review by Harold B. Dunkel, see 5:272; for a review by Herbert Schueler, see 4:244. For reviews of the testing program, see 6:760 (2 reviews).

[284]

*College Placement Test in German Listening Comprehension. Entering college freshmen; 1962–70, c1955–70; irregularly scheduled reprintings of inactive forms of *College Board Achievement Test in German Listening Comprehension;* Forms PPL1 ('67, reprint of 1966 test), PPL2 ('67) in a single booklet (12 pages); test administered by 7½ ips tape recording; for more complete information, see 665; 30(40) minutes; program administered for the College Entrance Examination Board by Educational Testing Service. *

REFERENCES

1. SPENCER, RICHARD E., AND SEGUIN, EDMOND L. "The Relative Effectiveness of Earphones and Loudspeakers as a Means of Presenting a Listening Test in a Foreign Language." *Mod Lang J* 48:346–9 O '64. *
2. ALEAMONI, LAWRENCE M., AND MATSUNAGA, ALLEN. *A Study of Foreign Language at the University of Illinois Using the CEEB Foreign Language Placement Tests and End-of-Course Grades.* Research Report No. 317. Champaign, Ill.: Measurement and Research Division, Office of Instructional Resources, University of Illinois, 1970. Pp. i, 42. *

For reviews by Harold B. Dunkel and Herbert Schueler of earlier forms, see 6:384. For a review of the testing program, see 665.

[285]

*College Placement Test in German Reading. Entering college freshmen; 1962–70, c1957–70; CPTGR; irregularly scheduled reprintings of inactive forms of *College Board Achievement Test in German;* Forms QPL1 ['68, reprint of 1965 test], QPL2 ['68, reprint

of 1966 test] in a single booklet (24 pages); for more complete information, see 665; 60(70) minutes; program administered for the College Entrance Examination Board by Educational Testing Service. *

REFERENCES

1. SPENCER, RICHARD E., AND SEGUIN, EDMOND L. "The Relative Effectiveness of Earphones and Loudspeakers as a Means of Presenting a Listening Test in a Foreign Language." *Mod Lang J* 48:346–9 O '64. *
2. ALEAMONI, LAWRENCE M., AND MATSUNAGA, ALLEN. *A Study of Foreign Language at the University of Illinois Using the CEEB Foreign Language Placement Tests and End-of-Course Grades.* Research Report No. 317. Champaign, Ill.: Measurement and Research Division, Office of Instructional Resources, University of Illinois, 1970. Pp. i, 42. *

For a review by Gilbert C. Kettelkamp of earlier forms, see 6:383; for a review by Harold B. Dunkel, see 5:272; for a review by Herbert Schueler, see 4:244. For a review of the testing program, see 665.

[286]

*Common Concepts Foreign Language Test: German. Students in any grade who are at the Level 1 stage of achievement; 1962–66; aural comprehension; same booklet also used to test French and Spanish; may be administered using live voice but tape recording (3¾ ips) is recommended; Forms 1, 2, ('62, 31 pages) in a single booklet; manual ('66, 41 pages); separate answer sheets (IBM 1230) must be used; $1.10 per test; $5.95 per tape recording; $2.50 per 50 answer sheets; 75¢ per scoring stencil for either form; $1 per manual; postage extra; $2.25 per specimen set (without tape), postpaid; scoring service, 22¢ and over per test; (40–45) minutes; Bela H. Banathy, Miles V. Zintz, W. James Popham, Joseph M. Sadnavitch, Rena Krichbaum, Fred B. Gannon, Valdemar Hempel, and Klaus A. Mueller; CTB/McGraw-Hill. *

WALTER F. W. LOHNES, *Professor of German, Stanford University, Stanford, California.*

This test, designed to measure proficiency in German after the first level of instruction, is an aural comprehension test based on visual cues. It was developed in the early 1960's, following the widespread introduction of the audio-lingual method. The assumption upon which the test is based is that listening and speaking are primary skills and more basic than the secondary skills of reading and writing. Hence, these primary skills should be tested without recourse to the printed or written word. To date, no satisfactory way has been found to test speaking on a large scale, but the authors claim that "aural comprehension is a better index of oral production than the ability to read or write the language." Thus, though measuring only listening comprehension, this test should also give an indication of the student's manifest or latent speaking ability.

The test is ingeniously devised. There are 80 items in all, each requiring the student to identify one of four pictures in a set. There are, however, only 23 multicolored pictures of familiar scenes. On the tape, each of these scenes is described in a few sentences, prior to the actual test, thus familiarizing the student with the content of the pictures. From picture 24 on, the first 23 reappear in various arrangements; subsequent questions deal with different aspects of the pictures, and as the aural stimuli increase in difficulty, the student becomes increasingly familiar with the pictures. The stimuli are all complete utterances rather than isolated words, so that each item creates a mini-situation connecting the spoken word with its visual representation. There are various types of sentences; some are descriptive, some narrative, others are statements that could be made by one of the people in the pictures.

The nature of the test also circumscribes its limitations. It cannot be used to test proficiency in all skills; however, if given in a strictly audio-lingual situation, where the mode of instruction is exclusively aural-oral, it is very well suited indeed. The content of both pictures and aural stimuli is such that use of the test beyond a certain age limit, say the second year in high school, would seem precarious.

There are two parallel forms of the test, both based on the same set of pictures, but with different stimuli. Aside from the fact that there are more statistical data available for Form 1 than for Form 2, the two are interchangeable.

The test can be administered by the teacher, but, in order to achieve uniform results, use of the tape is mandatory. The quality of the taped instructions, including the description of the pictures, is very good, but the German stimulus sentences are not as clearly spoken as they could be. The voice of the (male) speaker is somewhat distorted and muffled. (In one instance, it took three replays to determine whether the word spoken was *badet* or *wartet*.)

By and large, the German sentences are idiomatic and well suited for the age level and achievement level of the presumed test population. There are, however, a number of words one would not expect in the vocabulary of beginning German students, e.g., *Fächer* or *Karton*. In item 76 of Form 1, there is a sudden shift of gears that is apt to throw the student off. Some of the stimuli are somewhat far-fetched (Hier schläft wahrscheinlich ein Mann), a few others have lost their idiomatic genuineness in favor of simplification.

The manual contains a description of the test,

statistical data, directions for administration and scoring, and the stimulus sentences as well as their translations. The manual is not as logically and clearly arranged as it might be; it takes several readings before its scope is completely understood. For instance, the reader is informed that pauses will be indicated throughout the test script, but this is true only of the introductory section of the script where the pauses are not needed; in the test proper, these indications are missing, although it is here that the length of pauses is most crucial if the test is not administered by tape.

The tables of percentile, standard score, and stanine distributions are based on rather small populations: 55 cases for Form 2, Junior High, 1–3 semesters, to 866 cases for Form 1, Senior High, 1–3 semesters; the highest number of cases for over three semesters is 230 for Senior High. For this reason, and also "because of vast differences in foreign language instructional programs, especially at the elementary and junior high levels, the norms have been presented as illustrative 'reference distributions.' "

As an instrument for testing listening comprehension in the early stages of audio-lingual instruction, this test is excellent. It is hoped that the flaws pointed out above will be corrected in an early revision.

For a review covering the three languages, see 253.

[287]

*The Graduate Record Examinations Advanced German Test. Graduate school candidates; 1939–70; 2 current forms ('70, 32 pages); descriptive booklet ('70, 8 pages); for more complete information, see 667; 180(200) minutes; Educational Testing Service. *

For reviews of the testing program, see 667 (1 review) and 5:601 (1 review).

[288]

*Graduate School Foreign Language Test: German. Graduate level degree candidates required to demonstrate reading proficiency in German; 1963–71; GSFLTG; 3 current forms ('70–71, 31–33 pages); for more complete information, see 668; 100(120) minutes; Educational Testing Service. *

REFERENCES

1. BARTLETT, ALBERT ALLEN. "The Foreign Language Requirement for the Ph.D.: A New Approach." *Foreign Lang Ann* 2:174–84 D '68. *
2. CLARK, JOHN L. D. "The Graduate School Foreign Language Requirement: A Survey of Testing Practices and Related Topics." *Foreign Lang Ann* 2:150–64 D '68. *
3. HARVEY, PHILIP R. "Minimal Passing Scores on the Graduate School Foreign Language Tests." *Foreign Lang Ann* 2:165–73 D '68. *

For a review by Jack M. Stein of an earlier edition, see 6:391.

[289]

*MLA Cooperative Foreign Language Proficiency Tests: German. German majors and advanced students in college; 1960–68; formerly called *MLA Foreign Language Proficiency Tests for Teachers and Advanced Students: German;* 7 tests in 3 booklets (formerly in 7 booklets); Forms HA ('61, identical except for format and directions with earlier tests variously designated Forms A, JML1, and K-JML1), HB ('66, identical except for format and directions with tests copyrighted in 1961 and variously designated Forms B, JML2, K-JML2, and OML1); temporary series directions for administering ('68, 12 pages); series norms ('66, 2 pages); mimeographed series score conversion directions ['68, 8 pages]; separate answer sheets (Digitek, SCRIBE) must be used except for speaking and writing tests; $4 per 100 answer sheets, cash orders postpaid; Digitek scoring stencils not available; SCRIBE scoring and statistical analysis service, 35¢ per student for all tests except speaking and writing; scoring by special arrangement with language specialists: $3 per speaking test tape, $1.50 per writing test; Modern Language Association of America and Educational Testing Service; Cooperative Tests and Services. *

a) BOOK 1: READING, LISTENING COMPREHENSION, SPEAKING. Forms HA (24 pages), HB (21 pages); $9 per 10 tests; 90¢ per single copy; $12 per 7½ ips listening/speaking test tape; blank tapes for student responses must be obtained locally; 40(50) minutes for reading, (20–30) minutes for listening comprehension, (15–30) minutes for speaking.

b) BOOK 2: WRITING. Forms HA (8 pages), HB (7 pages); $6 per 20 tests; 30¢ per single copy; 45(55) minutes.

c) BOOK 3: APPLIED LINGUISTICS, CIVILIZATION AND CULTURE, PROFESSIONAL PREPARATION. Forms HA, HB, (29 pages); professional preparation test is common to all languages in series; $9 per 10 tests; 90¢ per single copy: 40(50) minutes for linguistics, 30(40) minutes for civilization and culture, 45(55) minutes for professional preparation.

REFERENCES

1–3. See 6:393.
4. PAQUETTE, F. ANDRÉ; WALLMARK, MADELINE; SPENCER, RICHARD E.; AND CHURCHILL, FREDERICK J. *A Comparison of the MLA Foreign Language Proficiency Tests for Teachers and Advanced Students With the MLA Foreign Language Cooperative Tests.* An unpublished report to the U.S. Office of Education, Project No. BR-6-2619, Modern Language Association of America, 1966. Pp. 58. * (ERIC ED 019 017)
5. TOLLINGER, SUZANNE, AND PAQUETTE, F. ANDRÉ, EDITORS. *The MLA Foreign Language Proficiency Tests for Teachers and Advanced Students: A Professional Evaluation and Recommendations for Test Development,* pp. 24–41, 137–5, 148–50, 161–75, passim. Sections on this test by Frederick J. Churchill, Tora T. Ladu, James C. McKinney, James W. Marchand, Klaus A. Mueller, Helmut Rehder, Frank G. Ryder, and Douglas C. Sheppard. An unpublished report to the U.S. Office of Education, Project No. BR-6-2619, Modern Language Association of America, June 1966. Pp. viii, 366. * (ERIC ED 019 016)
6. CARROLL, JOHN B. "Foreign Language Proficiency Levels Attained by Language Majors Near Graduation From College." *Foreign Lang Ann* 1:131–51 O '67. *
7. DIZNEY, HENRY F., AND GROMEN, LAUREN. "Predictive Validity and Differential Achievement on Three MLA-Cooperative Foreign Language Tests." *Ed & Psychol Meas* 27: 1127–30 w '67. * (PA 42:9417)
8. PAQUETTE, F. ANDRÉ; WITH THE COOPERATION OF MADELINE WALLMARK. *The MLA Foreign Language Proficiency Tests for Teachers and Advanced Students: Analysis of the Performance of Native Speakers and Comparison With That of NDEA Summer Institute Participants.* An unpublished report to the U.S. Office of Education, Project No. BR-6-2619, Modern Language Association of America, June 1968. Pp. ii, 42. * (ERIC ED 019 017)
9. PERKINS, JEAN A. "State Certification and Proficiency Tests: The Experience in Pennsylvania." *Foreign Lang Ann* 2:195–9 D '68. *
10. CARROLL, JOHN B. "What Does the Pennsylvania For-

eign Language Project Tell Us?" *Foreign Lang Ann* 3(2): 214–36 D '69. *
11. SMITH, PHILIP D., JR. "The Pennsylvania Foreign Language Research Project: Teacher Proficiency and Class Achievement in Two Modern Languages." *Foreign Lang Ann* 3(2):194–207 D '69. *

For reviews by Harold B. Dunkel and Herbert Schueler, see 6:393.

[290]

*MLA-Cooperative Foreign Language Tests: German. 1–2 years high school or 2 semesters college, 3–4 years high school or 4 semesters college; 1963–65; 4 tests in a single booklet: listening, speaking, reading, writing; writing test ('63, 8 pages) available as separate; 2 forms; 2 levels; no specific manual; series directions for administering and scoring ('64, 40 pages); series handbook ('65, 24 pages); series booklet of norms ('65, 82 pages); student bulletin ('65, 2 pages) for each level; $7 per 10 tests; $5 per 20 writing tests only; separate answer sheets (Digitek, Digitek-IBM 805, IBM 1230, SCRIBE) may be used for listening and reading tests; $4 per 100 answer sheets; $1.25 per 10 IBM 805 or IBM 1230 scoring stencils (answer pattern must be punched out locally); Digitek scoring stencils not available; $8.50 per 3¾ ips tape, 5 inch reel, for listening test; $8.50 per 3¾ ips tape, 5 inch reel, for speaking test (blank tapes or discs for recording student responses must be obtained locally); $2 per series directions for administering and scoring; $2 per series handbook; $2 per series norms booklet; $3 per 100 student bulletins; $3 per specimen set; cash orders postpaid; SCRIBE scoring and statistical analysis service (listening and reading tests), 35¢ per student; no scoring service for speaking and writing tests, but arrangements for professional scoring can be made; 25(35) minutes for listening, 10(20) minutes for speaking, 35(40) minutes for reading, 35(40) minutes for writing; prepared in cooperation with the Modern Language Association of America; Cooperative Tests and Services. *

a) [LOWER LEVEL.] 1–2 years high school or 2 semesters college; Forms LA ('63, 23 pages), LB ('63, 24 pages).

b) [HIGHER LEVEL.] 3–4 years high school or 4 semesters college; Forms MA, MB, ('63, 24 pages).

REFERENCES

1. PAQUETTE, F. ANDRÉ; WALLMARK, MADELINE; SPENCER, RICHARD E.; AND CHURCHILL, FREDERICK J. *A Comparison of the MLA Foreign Language Proficiency Tests for Teachers and Advanced Students With the MLA Foreign Language Cooperative Tests.* An unpublished report to the U.S. Office of Education, Project No. BR-6-2619, Modern Language Association of America, 1966. Pp. 58. * (ERIC ED 019 017)
2. ALEAMONI, LAWRENCE M., AND SPENCER, RICHARD E. "A Comparison of Biserial Discrimination, Point Biserial Discrimination, and Difficulty Indices in Item Analysis Data." *Ed & Psychol Meas* 29(2):353–8 su '69. * (PA 44:17314)

T. F. NAUMANN, *Professor of Psychology, Central Washington State College, Ellensburg, Washington.*

The stated purpose of the MLA-Cooperative tests is to measure the learner's knowledge of structures which are common in speech and writing, and to assess his knowledge of vocabulary and idiom in their receptive and productive aspects. By design the tests measure language skills in a functional context of the language for which skills are tested.

No specific study or discussion of validity

was found. It can be assumed fairly safely that adequate content validity has been obtained due to the outstanding technical know-how of ETS and the specialists selected by MLA.

The content of the Listening Test seems adequate, but some minor improvements are indicated. For example on Form LA item 39 should begin the response stems C and D with "Über's" or "Über das." Also, in the same test item 43 should have an idiomatically more adequate introduction on the tape containing "erzahlte mir meine Schwester" instead of "meine Schwester had mir erzahlt." Item 7, Form MB, should use the term "Butterbrote" (sandwiches) instead of "Brote" (breads) in the taped conversation. When listening to items 35 to 37 of the same form the question arises to what extent memory is tested rather than listening comprehension skill. It is suggested that the taped directives give more often the number of the page to be turned to. Scoring of the listening skill test is objective and simple.

In the Speaking Test, the learner interacts with a test tape, recording his own statements on a separate tape. Scoring is subjective with specific directions provided for the tester. The learner's responses are scored for proper reproduction of German sounds ("mimicry"), adequacy of expression within word groups, rhythm, intonation patterns, correctness, naturalness and meaningfulness of responses. For a number of responses a point system is applied. This is obviously the weakest section of the tests since it is open to rater bias and the scorer's own competency in German.

The Reading Test consists of 50 multiple choice items which range from selecting small parts of speech in a given sentence to completing a dialogue or a paragraph from multiple choices. Scoring is objective. This is the most comprehensive of the four subtests. With the native German speaker sample referred to above, reading had the highest correlation with other subtests, viz., .41 with listening and .42 with writing, the first a receptive communication skill, the other an expressive skill.

The types of responses in the 50-item Writing Test range from filling in small parts of speech to rewriting sentences and, finally, writing a dialogue or paragraph based on a specified situation or topic. Part of the scoring is subjective with items scored on a point system. Item 39 of Forms MA and MB should be changed to

avoid unnecessary ambiguity with respect to gender in the third person singular.

The MLA-Cooperative German tests are undoubtedly the best of this type available. Improvements of small details here and there could readily be made in a new edition. The potential user should realize that the tests are for students beyond beginner's level. Reports of validity studies should be made available as soon as possible, particularly with data on predictive validity. On the whole, these tests set standards which deserve emulation.

For an excerpted review of the series, see 254.

[291]

★**National Teacher Examinations: German.** College seniors and teachers; 1970–71; modified version of secure form of *MLA Foreign Language Proficiency Tests for Teachers and Advanced Students: German;* Form TNT1 ('71, 21 pages); descriptive booklet ('70, 11 pages); listening comprehension section administered by 3¾ ips tape recording; for more complete information, see 582; 120(165) minutes; Educational Testing Service. *

For reviews of the testing program, see 582 (2 reviews), 6:700 (1 review), 5:538 (3 reviews), and 4:802 (1 review).

[292]

★**Pimsleur German Proficiency Tests.** First, second level courses in grades 7–12 or first, second semesters college; 1967; 4 scores: listening, speaking, reading, writing; 1 form; 2 levels labeled Forms A, C; manual (23 pages); no college norms; $1.75 per manual; $1.75 per specimen set (without tapes or manual); postage extra; Paul Pimsleur; Harcourt Brace Jovanovich, Inc. *
a) TEST 1, LISTENING COMPREHENSION. Digitek, IBM 805, and IBM 1230 test-answer sheets (2 pages); 7½ ips test tape, 5 inch reel; $7.50 per test tape; $3.80 per 35 test-answer sheets; $1.40 per set of scoring stencils; IBM scoring service, 33¢ and over per test; 15(25) minutes.
b) TEST 2, SPEAKING PROFICIENCY. Test (4 pages); scoring sheet (2 pages); 7½ ips test tape, 5 inch reel; $7.50 per test tape; $4.50 per 35 tests; $2.70 per 35 scoring sheets; 16(26) minutes.
c) TEST 3, READING COMPREHENSION. Test (4 pages); separate answer sheets (Digitek-IBM 805, IBM 1230) must be used; $4.50 per 35 tests; $2.30 per 35 Digitek-IBM 805 answer sheets; $2.80 per 35 IBM 1230 answer sheets; 70¢ per scoring stencil; IBM scoring service, 19¢ and over per test; 35(45) minutes.
d) TEST 4, WRITING PROFICIENCY. Test (6 pages); answer key and scoring directions (4 pages); $7.40 per 35 tests; 35(45) minutes.

WALTER F. W. LOHNES, *Professor of German, Stanford University, Stanford, California.*

These tests examine proficiency in the four skills: listening, speaking, reading, and writing. Both forms, A and C, follow the same pattern, the sole difference being the degree of difficulty of the material tested. The primary usefulness of the tests is for high school testing and as an instrument for placing incoming freshmen into early college courses. The content of parts of the tests, notably the reading and writing tests, does not seem to be suitable for today's college students and may, in fact, soon outlive its appeal to high school students as well. The tests can be used for other purposes: evaluating individual and class achievement as well as evaluating local German programs.

The Pimsleur tests were developed during several years of thorough research and experimentation, starting in 1960. They follow the pattern set by the *MLA Foreign Language Proficiency Tests for Teachers and Advanced Students* and closely resemble the *MLA Co-operative Foreign Language Tests*. The manual reflects the thoroughness with which the tests were produced. It contains not only easy-to-follow directions for administering and scoring the tests, but also detailed statistical information on the interpretation of test results and on validity and reliability.

The tapes for the Listening and the Speaking Tests are excellent. The English instructions are clear and precise; the German voices, one male and one female, are very good; all texts are spoken at normal speed.

The Listening Test has two parts. Part 1 tests sound discrimination. For each of the 20 spoken sentences, the student has to identify the correct written equivalent from among four printed choices. Each item concentrates on one problem, such as *s* versus *z*. Each sentence is spoken only once. In Part 2, the student hears 20 statements or questions, each spoken twice, and has to select the most logical rejoinder from among four printed choices. There are a few unhappy choices of words; for example, the German equivalent of *athlete* is not *Athlet,* but *Sportler.* By and large, however, the items are very good, some with excellent distractors that play on possible misunderstandings of the stem. In Part 1 of Form C, a few items are quite artificial, doubtless due to the fact that it is very difficult in German to find minimal pairs (let alone minimal quadruplets) of phonemic distinction. There is some duplication of items in the two forms, presumably for equating purposes.

Part 1 of the Speaking Test tests vocabulary. The student has to identify 27 nouns (article

not required) from simple line drawings in the test booklet. This part appears to test speaking proficiency only secondarily. Speed is of the essence here, and if the student cannot think of the correct word immediately, he will miss out, no matter how good his speaking ability. It can be argued, of course, that the ability to transfer instantaneously a visual image into sound is a major part of speaking proficiency. Part 2 tests pronunciation. Each item contains two critical sounds: vowels, consonants, diphthongs, or glottal stops. (A classification of these items is given in the manual.) All 20 phrases and sentences are read by the speaker; the student records them from his printed text only after he has heard all of them, thus being forced to rely on what he has learned and knows rather than on immediate imitation of the taped voice. In Part 3, the student hears eight questions, to which he must respond freely, though in complete sentences. This is apt to create artificial statements, since the normal way of responding to questions such as these is in incomplete sentences. In a revision of the test, it might be advisable to increase the number of questions and to encourage the student to reply as he would in a normal conversation.

Both forms of the Reading Test contain ten very short passages and a total of 36 multiple choice questions; thus, the same answer sheet can be used for both. Again, there is an overlap between the two forms: two passages appear in both, though the choices are scrambled differently. As far as language is concerned, this is the poorest of the four tests. The wording of some of the passages, especially in Form A, simply does not ring true. There are a number of ungrammatical forms in the choices as well. In a revision of the test, some of the texts should be improved or replaced by passages of more immediate concern to the student.

The format of the Writing Test is again the same for both forms. Strictly speaking, only Parts 1 and 4 test the student's writing ability. In Part 1, the student is given a passage with a number of function words left out; this type of exercise has proved to be an excellent indicator of writing ability. In Part 4, the student is asked to write freely, using pictures as cues. Parts 2 and 3 simply require the student to rewrite a number of sentences, either by changing tenses or by substituting other indicated elements, which necessitates some additional

Pimsleur German Proficiency Tests

changes. These two parts demand nothing more than the kind of manipulation required in pattern drills. A classification of the items in Parts 1, 2, and 3 is provided in the manual. Like the Reading Test, the Writing Test could profit from some updating.

The interpretation of test results in the manual gives percentiles and stanines based on standardization samples of 2,390 students for Level 1 and 2,025 students for Level 2 in 21 states across the United States.

Two final points: In the next printing of the test booklets, the digraph ß should be used instead of *ss,* and on the cover of the test package, the picture of Hohenschwanstein, which is about as representative of Germany as Disneyland is of the United States, should be replaced by a more appropriate picture.

Despite my criticisms and suggestions for revision, I consider the Pimsleur Tests one of the best available test batteries. Its shortcomings are primarily of a linguistic nature and can be easily remedied in a future revision.

JACK M. STEIN, *Professor of German, Harvard University, Cambridge, Massachusetts.*

The *Pimsleur German Proficiency Tests* are an excellent medium for evaluating achievement in the first and second levels of German study in grades 7–12. They are less useful for college placement purposes (more below). Separate tests in each of the four skills combine to make a larger unit, while each can be administered independently. The tests make use of established techniques; there are no innovations. A splendid 25-page printed manual gives accurate descriptions of the separate units, including excellent classification tables, item by item. The manual provides careful guidance in administering and scoring the tests, with copious tables. There are also lucid sections on interpreting and using the test results, including some cautious but sound advice on evaluating individual and class achievement, as well as on evaluating the local language program as a whole. The manual also contains six pages describing the validity and reliability of the tests. Reliability coefficients, item analysis summaries (difficulty, discrimination), and other detailed information are given in statistical tables.

The overwhelming majority of the items in all the tests are sound, natural, and functional. There are occasional slips, however, which, it seems, could easily have been eliminated. I noticed the following: in each listening comprehension test there was at least one sentence which was spoken on tape with an unnatural intonation. On the second level test, the sentences "Verzieh es nicht" and "Er wäscht nicht" are spoken. Both are artificial. In the vocabulary part of the speaking tests, where pictures are given to elicit nouns from the student, the pictures are occasionally ambiguous. Since the responses must be given with very little deliberation, this is all the more objectionable. For instance, a theater ticket looks a lot like a safety razor blade; a store front could be any number of things; etc. One picture in Form C shows an unmistakably American farmer (der Farmer? der Bauer?). Part 2 of the Form A speaking test, which tests pronunciation, contains a silly sentence: "Sie ist dünn und müde." In Part 3 of each speaking proficiency test occurs the most serious fault. This part tests fluency by requiring responses to basic questions. The directions insist that the student respond in "simple but complete German sentences." The reason for the directions is clear, but the technique is nonetheless artificial. The natural response would in most cases be an incomplete sentence. Occasionally a complete sentence would be downright unnatural, e.g., the response to "Wohin werden Sie heute nach der Schule gehen?" In the writing test there are a couple of bad sentences, e.g., "Die Jungen essen immer viele Brötchen und werden später krank," which is to be rewritten as "Robert isst immer viel Brot und wird später krank." One would think he (or they) would eventually learn not to.

These and a few additional examples notwithstanding, the Pimsleur tests are in general excellent and are certain to give reliable achievement scores when administered as advised in the excellent printed manual (the test packet includes in addition a 3-page brochure giving the information from the 25-page manual in summary form; if this offers any temptation not to read the full manual carefully, it should be eliminated). The tests can be administered at any time after a certain minimum amount of material has been covered, defined in the manual as "at least two-thirds of a first-level German course" for Form A and "at least two-thirds of a second-level German course" for Form C. Form A is too elementary for college placement; Form C could be used for college placement only if none of the entering students had had more than two years of secondary school German. It is simply not advanced enough to be reliable otherwise. For this reason it is not an acceptable alternative for college placement purposes to the Higher Level of the *MLA-Cooperative Foreign Language Tests: German.*

J Ed Meas 6(1):47–8 sp '69. Garold N. Davis. Although a nominal effort is made to test the four language skills independent of one another, this effort is never entirely successful. The listening test, for example, could not be taken by even a native speaker of German if he had not yet learned to read. The speaking test is also dependent in part on the ability to read. Since it is assumed that the students taking the tests will have been trained in the four skills, this relationship between the spoken and the written language is not necessarily a disadvantage as long as the tests are taken as a unit. Any attempt to use the individual parts to test one of the skills independently will be unsuccessful. The vocabulary and structure used for the Form A tests seem to be of adequate difficulty for students with one year of high school training in German. The language proficiency level tested with the Form C tests, however, does not seem to be much higher than that of the Form A tests. Of the 20 sentences presented in the Form C listening test, for example, 5 sentences are repetitions from Form A. Such repetitions are found throughout the Form C tests. There are a few unfortunate test items. On the Form C listening test students are asked to distinguish from a single hearing the difference between "machst du" and "magst du." Although a phonetic distinction does exist, I found that a Professor of German Linguistics whose native language is English, and a native speaker of German were both unable to identify the distinction as it was presented on the test tape without several hearings and a lengthy discussion. Also, the Form C reading test includes the strange construction: "Diese Reise wäre ein Grund, damit ich zeitlebens barfuss ginge," instead of the more normal: "Diese Reise wäre ein Grund für mich, dass ich...." Such items which will tend to confuse even the better students should be eliminated from the tests. Fortunately these confusing items are few in number. Perhaps there is no simple, efficient way to test reading comprehension. The "reading" test in both Form A and Form C

is actually an exercise in identifying the synonymous relationship between words or phrases used in a prose passage with the words or phrases used in the "questions." For example, a reading passage contains the sentence : Konrad hat ein Auto, aber er ist kaputt." In the "question" section the student sees the partial sentence : "Sie fahren mit dem Bus, denn Konrads Auto....," followed by four possible "completions." The correct completion in this case is "fährt nicht." Thus if the student knows that "kaputt" and "fährt nicht" are used synonymously he will mark the correct completion. It is possible that a student could read and understand the prose passage, however, and still not be able to identify the correct completion. Perhaps as long as it is understood that the "answers" as well as the reading passages constitute a part of the "reading" test, there is no problem. There will be no way to identify the source of the error, however, without further testing. The most outstanding part of the test in my estimation is the writing test, which makes use of drawings to stimulate written responses. This attenuates the possibility of interference from a written English model, and seems to be the most natural way to conduct a controlled writing test. The problem of this part of the test is in the scoring, but even here the author has done an admirable job of preparing an objective and uniform method of grading the written responses. Since testing is still one of the most neglected phases of language teaching, these tests will be a welcome addition to the materials available, and, taking into consideration the problems suggested in this review, they will be a useful tool to the teacher who wants to evaluate the relative progress of a group of students.

[293]
★**The Undergraduate Record Examinations: German Test.** College ; 1969–70 ; Forms K-RUR ('69, 23 pages), SUR ('70, 23 pages) ; descriptive booklet ('70, 11 pages) ; for more complete information, see 671 ; 120(140) minutes ; Educational Testing Service. *

For reviews of the testing program, see 671 (2 reviews).

GREEK

[294]
*****College Board Achievement Test in Greek.** Candidates for college entrance with 2–3 years high school Greek ; 1901–71 ; test administered at local sec-

ondary schools in February; candidates must also be registered to take Achievement Tests (see 663b) during a regular program administration; 3 parts (candidate takes only one): Attic prose, Homeric poetry, Attic prose and Homeric poetry; descriptive booklet ('70, 7 pages); supervisor's manual ('71, 14 pages); no data on reliability; no additional fee; 90(100) minutes; program administered for the College Entrance Examination Board by Educational Testing Service. *

For a review by Konrad Gries of an earlier form, see 5:277. For reviews of the testing program, see 6:760 (2 reviews).

[295]
*College Placement Test in Greek. Entering college freshmen; 1962–70, c1957–70; CPTG; irregularly scheduled reprintings of inactive forms of *College Board Achievement Test in Greek;* Form K-KPLi ['62, reprint of 1957 test]; 2 tests (student takes only one): Attic prose (10 pages), Homer and Attic prose (11 pages); for more complete information, see 665; 60(70) minutes per test; program administered for the College Entrance Examination Board by Educational Testing Service. *

For a review by Konrad Gries (then Form FAC), see 5:277. For a review of the testing program, see 665.

HEBREW

[296]
*College Board Achievement Test in Hebrew. Candidates for college entrance with 2–4 years high school Hebrew; 1961–71; test administered each January at centers established by the publisher; for more complete information, see 663; 60(80) minutes; program administered for the College Entrance Examination Board by Educational Testing Service. *

For reviews of the testing program, see 6:760 (2 reviews).

[297]
★College Placement Test in Hebrew Reading. Entering college freshmen; 1962–70, c1961–70; CPTHR; irregularly scheduled reprintings of inactive forms of *College Board Achievement Test in Hebrew;* Form SPL ('70, reprint of 1964 test, 19 pages); for more complete information, see 665; 60(70) minutes; program administered for the College Entrance Examination Board by Educational Testing Service. *

For a review of the testing program, see 665.

[298]
★[NCRI Achievement Tests in Hebrew.] Grades 5–7, 7–9; 1965–67; 2 levels; 2 forms; directions ['65, 1 page]; combined interpretation guide ('67, 14 pages) for this test and 6:397; no data on reliability; separate answer sheets (IBM 1230) must be used; 15¢ per test; 2¢ per answer sheet; scoring stencil not available; 5¢ per directions sheet; 75¢ per interpretation guide; 10% extra for postage, cash orders only; scoring service, 9¢ per test; [40–50] minutes; Simon Bugatch and

Judah Pilch (test); National Curriculum Research Institute, American Association for Jewish Education. *
a) ACHIEVEMENT TEST IN HEBREW. Grades 5–7; Forms 1, 2, ['65, 8 pages].
b) ACHIEVEMENT TESTS IN HEBREW. Grades 7–9; 2 forms labeled Tests 3, 4, ('65, 8 pages).

ITALIAN

[299]
*College Placement Test in Italian Listening Comprehension. Entering college freshmen; 1962–70; irregularly scheduled reprintings of inactive forms of *College Board Achievement Test in Italian Listening Comprehension;* Form PPL ['67, reprint of 1966 test, 9 pages]; test administered by 7½ ips tape recording; for more complete information, see 665; 30(40) minutes; program administered for the College Entrance Examination Board by Educational Testing Service. *

PAOLO VALESIO, *Associate Professor of Romance Languages and Literatures, Harvard University, Cambridge, Massachusetts.*

In dialogue 9, the expression *Stasera danno l'Aida a Caracalla* is perhaps too concise and allusive. A version like *Stasera danno l'Aida al Teatro Comunale* (where the presence of the common noun *teatro* clarifies the context) would spare the listener some difficulty.

In the dialogue "La signorina Rossi e il direttore d'ufficio," there are some points which do not seem to me to be fully idiomatic: (*a*) *Capoufficio* (or *capo ufficio,* or *capufficio*) is more appropriate than *direttore d'ufficio.* (*b*) The phrase *scuola media,* with no further qualification, usually designates in Italian the period of schooling between 10 and 13 years; a 20-year-old Italian typist would probably name a *scuola commerciale* or *scuola professionale* as her recent scholastic background. (*c*) In Italy one speaks of *chilometri* (at least in a technical, nonliterary context such as this one) rather than *miglia.* (*d*) Unlike the English phrase *letters of recommendation,* the superficially equivalent Italian phrase *lettere di raccomandazione* implies a very informal kind of communication; a more appropriate equivalent here would be *lettere di presentazione.*

Perhaps an effort could be made to make these short dialogues slightly broader in scope and more lively. For instance, one or two of the shorter exchanges could have a polemical, or a humorous tone, and the longer dialogue could concern some historical or cultural problems relevant to Italy.

In general, this test seems to be adequate to

the task of evaluating the familiarity of the candidate with the everyday use of the language.

For a review of the testing program, see 665.

[300]

*College Placement Test in Italian Reading. Entering college freshmen; 1962–70, c1957–70; CPTIR; irregularly scheduled reprintings of inactive forms of *College Board Achievement Test in Italian Reading and Essay;* Form PPL ('67, reprint of 1966 test, 12 pages); for more complete information, see 664; 60(70) minutes; program administered for the College Entrance Examination Board by Educational Testing Service. *

PAOLO VALESIO, *Associate Professor of Romance Languages and Literatures, Harvard University, Cambridge, Massachusetts.*

The criteria implicit in the lists of lexical items in sections 1, 2, and 3 seem to be different for each section: in 1 there are three items (A, B, D) which are clearly out of place in the proposed context, and two (C, E) of which only one is the normal answer but which are semantically and phonologically very close, although morphologically unrelated; in 2 there are no special relationships (phonological, morphological, or semantic) among the five items; in 3, three of the items (A, D, E) are morphologically related, insofar as they are all formed on the basis of the same suffix, and to that extent they are also semantically related (the relation between A and D is particularly close). It is not clear to me whether this different treatment was planned or not, i.e., whether or not there is a plan to put lexical choices within a specific phonological and/or morphological framework. Concerning section 3, the form *scarpellino* is less usual in Italian than *scalpellino*.

In 5, it seems confusing to present D and E as mutually exclusive choices, since the distinction between them is essentially graphemic; the form in E is the most usual, but the form in D, although less common in modern Italian writing, is not incorrect.

In section 11, there is a sort of semantic hierarchy: although A is the normal solution, E is still possible as an answer here, while the other three items are clearly "out." It seems to me that such a hierarchy is missing in sections 9 and 10; in each of them there is only one likely answer, while the other answers are clearly not normal in the context. (Answer C in 10 could be an exception, if one considers *cucinare* as a metaphor for the making of the movie; but if so, this should have been made clearer.) This situation (hierarchy of acceptability in one section versus absence of such a hierarchy in the other two sections) could puzzle the reader.

In section 14, since the verb *sentire* in Italian may refer to either acoustic or tactile perceptions, it is not clear whether answer B is meant as an unacceptable answer or as a less acceptable but still possible answer with respect to the normal one, E.

The most interesting and delicate problem arises in connection with sentence 4, *Domani mattina voi....questo o niente!* This sentence is syntactically ambiguous, in the context of the available choices, because it can have two different interpretations, for both of which the sentence is grammatical: in one interpretation, it can be paraphrased in English as "Tomorrow you will eat this, otherwise you will not get anything," (from the answer presented as correct, A, it is obvious that the writers had this interpretation in mind); in the other interpretation, the sentence can be paraphrased in English as "Tomorrow you would be capable of refusing to eat, if you were not offered this," implying an (admirative or ironical) "this-is-the-kind-of-person-you-are" attitude. In other words, this sentence can be interpreted *either* as a descriptive statement (although, as things now stand, this is not completely true, as will be shown later) in which, given the choices available and the reference to the future expressed by the adverbial phrase (*Domani mattina*), the appropriate choice is the future tense form (A), *or* as an emphatic statement, for which the Italian "conditional mood" form, *mangereste* (C), would be the appropriate choice. The ambiguity could be solved (but not fully, even for a native speaker of Italian, because of intonation problems in reading an incomplete sentence) if the sentence were uttered, because the intonation symbolized by the exclamation point in connection with the first interpretation, although it could be generically described as "emphatic," is different from the intonation symbolized by the exclamation point in connection with the second interpretation. But since this is a printed sentence presented to a reader, the ambiguity remains. This ambiguity is all the more damaging because the two interpretations presuppose two opposite attitudes of the subject of the sentence toward the action described: in the first interpretation, the presupposition is that the subject (the group of persons designated by the pronoun *voi*) does not want to eat the thing referred to, while in the second interpretation, the presupposition is that the subject strongly wants to eat it.

Since it is almost impossible to find a sentence, in any language, whose surface syntactic structure does not possess some measure of ambiguity, inconveniences like these are probably unavoidable. But if this is true, it shows that clearcut evaluations of grammaticality such as the ones required in these tests have relatively little to do with the actual linguistic knowledge of the speaker. However, it is perhaps possible to clarify this sentence. In the first interpretation (the one desired by the test writers) the sentence remains grammatical even if a different, less emphatic intonation is adopted. In fact, in the framework of the first interpretation, the emphatic intonation symbolized by the exclamation point adds an imperative meaning to the sentence; a less emphatic intonation, symbolized by a period, would make of the sentence a descriptive statement (the indication of a choice), without a specific imperative implication. On the other hand, the second interpretation implies a structure which requires the kind of emphatic intonation represented by the exclamation point, in order for the sentence to be grammatical; the only other kind of intonation normally possible would be the "suspensive," usually one represented by a comma. Then, the conditional form would make of this structure merely a clause in a complex sentence, and thus the sentence as presented in the text would be ungrammatical (as required). One could, therefore, simply substitute a period for the exclamation point here; in this way, the solution desired for the test would really become the only one which is normally acceptable in the language.

In conclusion, provided that some adjustments are made, this test should prove useful.

For a review of the testing program, see 665.

[301]

*MLA Cooperative Foreign Language Proficiency Tests: Italian.** Italian majors and advanced students in college; 1961–68; formerly called *MLA Foreign Language Proficiency Tests for Teachers and Advanced Students: Italian;* 7 tests in 3 booklets (formerly in 7 booklets); Form HA ('61, identical except for format and directions with earlier tests variously designated Forms A, JML1, and K-JML1); temporary series directions for administering ('68, 12 pages); series norms ('66, 2 pages, Italian norms tentative);

mimeographed series score conversion directions ['68, 8 pages]; separate answer sheets (Digitek, SCRIBE) must be used except for speaking and writing tests; $4 per 100 answer sheets, cash orders postpaid; Digitek scoring stencils not available; SCRIBE scoring and statistical analysis service, 35¢ per student for all tests except speaking and writing; scoring by special arrangement with language specialists: $3 per speaking test tape, $1.50 per writing test; Modern Language Association of America and Educational Testing Service; Cooperative Tests and Services. *

a) BOOK 1: READING, LISTENING COMPREHENSION, SPEAKING. Form HA (24 pages); $9 per 10 tests; 90¢ per single copy; $12 per 7½ ips listening/speaking test tape; blank tapes for student responses must be obtained locally; 40(50) minutes for reading, (20–30) minutes for listening comprehension, (15–30) minutes for speaking.

b) BOOK 2: WRITING. Form HA (8 pages); $6 per 20 tests; 30¢ per single copy; 45(55) minutes.

c) BOOK 3: APPLIED LINGUISTICS, CIVILIZATION AND CULTURE, PROFESSIONAL PREPARATION. Form HA (29 pages); professional preparation test is common to all languages in series; $9 per 10 tests; 90¢ per single copy; 40(50) minutes for linguistics, 30(40) minutes for civilization and culture, 45(55) minutes for professional preparation.

REFERENCES

1–3. See 6:403.
4. TOLLINGER, SUZANNE, AND PAQUETTE, F. ANDRÉ, EDITORS. *The MLA Foreign Language Proficiency Tests for Teachers and Advanced Students: A Professional Evaluation and Recommendations for Test Development,* pp. 42–61, 128–9, 151–4, 161–75, passim. Sections on this test by Pierina B. Castiglione, Robert J. Di Pietro, Tora T. Ladu, Graziana Lazzarino, Archibald T. MacAllister, James C. McKinney, Paul R. Olson, and Douglas C. Sheppard. An unpublished report to the U.S. Office of Education, Project No. BR-6-2619, Modern Language Association of America, June 1966. Pp. viii, 366. * (ERIC ED 019 016)
5. PAQUETTE, F. ANDRÉ; WITH THE COOPERATION OF MADELINE WALLMARK. *The MLA Foreign Language Proficiency Tests for Teachers and Advanced Students: Analysis of the Performance of Native Speakers and Comparison With That of NDEA Summer Institute Participants.* An unpublished report to the U.S. Office of Education, Project No. BR-6-2619, Modern Language Association of America, June 1968. Pp. ii, 42. * (ERIC ED 019 017)

JOSEPHINE BRUNO PANE, *Associate Professor of Foreign Language Education, Rutgers, The State University, New Brunswick, New Jersey.*

These tests are based on the 1955 MLA "Qualifications for Secondary School Teachers of Modern Foreign Languages." The MLA statement establishes three levels of proficiency: Minimal, Good, Superior, for seven areas of competency: Listening Comprehension, Speaking, Reading, Writing, Applied Linguistics, Culture and Civilization, and Professional Preparation.

To review in 1970 tests which appeared in 1961 is difficult. At the time the MLA Proficiency Tests were written, the foreign language profession was in the midst of re-evaluating itself. In all of the areas, but especially in applied linguistics, culture and civilization, and professional preparation, it was treading on unfamiliar ground. Since there was uncertainty regarding content, it follows naturally that there had to be uncertainty in the matter of testing it. The MLA Proficiency Tests are a reflection of their time.

Since then, however, the foreign language profession has moved forward both in definition of content and in the science of testing. In view of these facts, this reviewer suggests that the MLA Proficiency Tests be revised to reflect these advances. In most urgent need of revision is Book 3 (Applied Linguistics, Culture and Civilization, and Professional Preparation) because these areas are constantly changing and must be kept contemporary, and also because their relationship to modern foreign language teaching is now better defined.

The science of linguistics, for example, is growing and changing rapidly. The Applied Linguistics Test reflects neither the growth nor the changes, the most obvious omission being any mention of transformational grammar. In addition, it is the application of linguistics to foreign language teaching that is being stressed today. Yet, this aspect is not emphasized in the test. Interestingly, whatever items there are on applied linguistics actually appear in the Professional Preparation Test. Perhaps the most important result of this test is that it has forced foreign language teachers to investigate the science of linguistics.

The Culture and Civilization Test is another which needs constant up-dating, because it must include items of contemporary culture along with those of basic, unchanging character. In addition, the foreign language teaching profession now has a clearer understanding of culture in the anthropological sense and of its relation to foreign language teaching. In the Italian Culture and Civilization Test little mention is made of language as culture or of contrasts in culture. Instead, the test stresses fine arts, history, music, architecture, and literary appreciation. The last of these, incidentally, might better be included in the Reading Test. As for the identification questions, luck might play a very important part in answering some of them. In the items connected with pictures, for example, the unlucky examinee might know all of the cathedrals in Italy except the one pictured in the test item whereas the lucky examinee might know no other cathedral but that one!

The Professional Preparation Test also needs constant up-dating. The original criticism of this test, that it is biased toward the audio-lingual approach, still holds true. In 1970, it

shows, in addition, serious omissions in areas reflecting recent developments in research, media, curriculum, and the "New Key" itself.

In the Listening Comprehension Test the examinee hears spoken passages (questions, monologues, conversations) and chooses appropriate responses from those printed in his booklet. In general, the spoken passages are too long. This is unfortunate, because it limits the kinds of situations and themes that can be presented and therefore also the variety and levels of language usage. Also, if the examinee does not know the key words, he is at a loss on too large a number of items. In addition to being too long, the spoken passages are also overinvolved and contain too many people, with the result that it is difficult to remember who is who and who did what. All of this raises the important question of whether the test really measures comprehension, or, rather if it measures retention. As for the answers themselves, they often require knowledge of unimportant details rather than ideas. Much of the vocabulary is either uncommon or archaic and the structural forms are often so involved as to sound unnatural and contrived. The voices are native and represent several regions of Italy.

The Speaking Test includes mimicry, reading from a script, and describing a picture or a series of pictures. This reviewer seriously questions the mimicry section. Is it not more important to judge the examinee's own performance instead of his ability to mimic a model? Especially since in some cases the model's speech is open to question. Furthermore, even a native speaker of Italian from one region of Italy would have difficulty reproducing the pronunciation and intonation of a native from another region. In any case, the ability to imitate is not the same as the ability to speak. As for scoring, it is difficult to achieve reliability on speaking tests, because it cannot be done objectively, and so much depends upon the expectations and linguistic prejudices of the judges.

The Reading Test sets out to measure vocabulary and reading comprehension. The format is similar to previous reading tests. The questions emphasize vocabulary more than reading, however; in many cases the correct answer depends not on understanding an idea but rather on a specific word. To make matters worse, many of the words and idioms are unusual, and the passages are long and abstruse.

The Writing Test shares the format of the

MLA Cooperative Foreign Language Proficiency Tests: Italian writing tests in the other four languages. According to the MLA Statement of Qualifications, even the minimal level of proficiency in writing includes "the ability to write" in the foreign language. Yet, nowhere in the proficiency tests is the examinee asked to write. Instead, he fills blanks and corrects passages. Filling in the blanks limits the morphological items that can be tested. As for the correction of passages, one such exercise might be sufficient instead of three. The remainder of the test might be devoted to writing a passage, in the manner of the Speaking Test. This reviewer would recommend such a change, even with the attendant problems that it would create for scoring.

In 1966 the MLA conducted an evaluative study (4) of the existing forms of the MLA tests with teams of foreign language teachers as reviewers. This study points out many weaknesses in the tests. It also points out the strengths, the chief ones being that they evaluate teacher proficiency objectively, and perform well statistically. (In regard to the latter, data on the Italian tests should be considered as tentative because of the small numbers involved.)

To help in validating the tests the MLA sponsored another study (5) which analyzes the performance of native speakers and compares it with that of NDEA Institute participants. Listening Comprehension, Speaking, Reading, and Writing were given to native speakers in the corresponding country in the summer of 1964. Results show that the native speaker groups performed at a level considerably higher than that achieved by the NDEA Institute participants in the posttest, and suggest that because of some overlap in performance "the best among the NDEA participants approach the 'educated native speaker' in competence." The fact that native speakers sometimes received mediocre or even low scores in speaking points to the difficulty of scoring the speaking test. The fact that some native speakers scored lower in reading than non-native speakers suggests that they might have had difficulty with those parts of the test which require literary analysis.

The *MLA Cooperative Foreign Language Proficiency Tests* represent an important achievement in the foreign language profession. They still remain the only such tests available, serve an important need, and are being used extensively in research projects of all kinds. A number of states use the scores on these tests as a basis for certification of foreign language teachers. Both of the studies sponsored by the MLA point out the strengths and weaknesses of the tests and can be very helpful in the interpretation of test results. This reviewer recommends that users of the MLA tests read these studies.

[302]

MLA-Cooperative Foreign Language Tests: Italian. 1–2 years high school or 2 semesters college, 3–4 years high school or 4 semesters college; 1963–65; 4 tests in a single booklet: listening, speaking, reading, writing; writing test ('63, 8 pages) available as separate; 2 forms; 2 levels; no specific manual; series directions for administering and scoring ('64, 40 pages); series handbook ('65, 24 pages); series booklet of norms ('65, 82 pages); student bulletin ('65, 2 pages) for each level; $7 per 10 tests; $5 per 20 writing tests only; separate answer sheets (Digitek, Digitek-IBM 805, IBM 1230, SCRIBE) may be used for listening and reading tests; $4 per 100 answer sheets; $1.25 per 10 IBM 805 or IBM 1230 scoring stencils (answer pattern must be punched out locally); Digitek scoring stencils not available; $8.50 per 3¾ ips tape, 5 inch reel, for listening test; $8.50 per 3¾ ips tape, 5 inch reel, for speaking test (blank tapes or discs for recording student responses must be obtained locally); $2 per series directions for administering and scoring; $2 per series handbook; $2 per series norms booklet; $3 per 100 student bulletins; $3 per specimen set; cash orders postpaid; SCRIBE scoring and statistical analysis service (listening and reading tests), 35¢ per student; no scoring service for speaking and writing tests, but arrangements for professional scoring can be made; 25(35) minutes for listening, 10(20) minutes for speaking, 35(40) minutes for reading, 35(40) minutes for writing; prepared in cooperation with the Modern Language Association of America; Cooperative Tests and Services. *
a) [LOWER LEVEL.] 1–2 years high school or 2 semesters college; Forms LA, LB, ('63, 25 pages).
b) [HIGHER LEVEL.] 3–4 years high school or 4 semesters college; Forms MA, MB, ('63, 24 pages).

JOSEPHINE BRUNO PANE, *Associate Professor of Foreign Language Education, Rutgers, The State University, New Brunswick, New Jersey.*

The lower level Listening test has 45 items and the higher level, 40. Instructions, narrative passages, and questions are presented on tape and the student selects the appropriate answer from the multiple choices printed in the test booklet. The spoken passages are usually single utterances, conversations, or prose selections. To be sure, the listening tests are also partially reading tests, since they require a reading knowledge of Italian in order to answer the questions. To the credit of these examinations, the reading load is usually no greater than the difficulty presented in the spoken material. And further, the answers do give the student the opportunity to demonstrate understanding of ideas as well as words. The situations are varied, thereby giving opportunity for different levels of language, vocabulary and structure. The voices are native, the Italian is authentic, the speed of delivery is normal.

The Speaking test for both levels contains 38 items. Instructions and questions are spoken and students' responses are recorded on their own individual tapes. The test includes mimicry, reading from a script, answering questions about line drawings, and describing a picture or a series of pictures that tell a story (the drawings and pictures are in the test booklet). Speaking stimuli, both spoken and pictured, are very good. The drawings are clear, and present a variety of situations. The weakest part of this test is the mimicry section. Certainly the ability to imitate is not the same as the ability to speak; good imitators may not be able to speak the language while good speakers may not be able to imitate. Perhaps the greatest problem with any test of speaking is the scoring, since it is open to subjectivity on the part of the scorer.

The Reading test for both levels has 50 items. The format is not unlike some reading tests which preceded it, consisting, as it does, of reading selections followed by multiple choice items. Where it does differ from them is in the questions, which really test ideas rather than just vocabulary. The Italian is largely contemporary, and always appropriate contextually.

The Writing test for both levels has 50 items. It is intended as a test of structure, but like all writing tests necessarily implies reading comprehension and vocabulary. The first part calls for filling in blanks and includes such items as articles, prepositions, pronouns, and subjunctive. Another section calls for rewriting sentences requiring such changes as tense, person, number, mood. The last part requires writing a composition on a given subject. Too many test-makers shy away from actual writing items because of the difficulty of scoring them. The MLA is to be congratulated first for including the item and then for giving helpful suggestions for scoring.

One aspect of these tests which ought to be studied is the matter of lexicon in the first level. It is difficult to know what formula was used for determining the vocabulary found in all four skill tests. One even wonders if such a formula could be devised and herein lies the greatest difficulty in all first-level tests. In the first year of foreign language instruction, vo-cabulary acquisition is based on the textbook used. Vocabulary selection in textbooks is anarchic, with the result that there is very little common vocabulary across the lower level materials. This is not so much a problem in upper level tests because students at this stage of the language sequence should be able to handle vocabulary across a wide range of frequency. This is not intended as a criticism of the tests, but rather as a comment on the vocabulary situation in the lower level in general.

The MLA-Cooperative test in Italian is not only the first and only one available for measuring the four skills, but it is also an excellent one. This reviewer recommends it highly to teachers of Italian at both the high school and college level.

For an excerpted review of the series, see 254.

LATIN

[303]

*Advanced Placement Examination in Latin. High school students desiring credit for college level courses or admission to advanced courses; 1954–70; 4 tests (candidate elects 1 or 2): Comedy, Lyric, Prose, Vergil; Forms RBP ('69, 10–11 pages), SBP ('70, 10–11 pages) in 2 booklets (objective, essay); for more complete information, see 662; 90(100) minutes; program administered for the College Entrance Examination Board by Educational Testing Service. *

For a review of the testing program, see 662.

[304]

*College Board Achievement Test in Latin. Candidates for college entrance with 2–4 years high school Latin; 1901–71; test administered each January and May at centers established by the publisher; for more complete information, see 663; 60(80) minutes; program administered for the College Entrance Examination Board by Educational Testing Service. *

REFERENCES

1–2. See 4:250.
3. See 5:280.

For a review by Konrad Gries of an earlier form, see 5:280; for a review by Harold B. Dunkel, see 4:250. For reviews of the testing program, see 6:760 (2 reviews).

[305]

*College Placement Test in Latin Reading. Entering college freshmen; 1962–70, c1955–70; CPTLR; irregularly scheduled reprintings of inactive forms of *College Board Achievement Test in Latin;* Forms PPL1 ['67, reprint of 1963 test], PPL2 ['67, reprint of 1964 test] in a single booklet (15 pages); for more complete information, see 665; 60(70) minutes; program administered for the College Entrance Examination Board by Educational Testing Service. *

For a review by Konrad Gries of an earlier form, see 5:280; for a review by Harold B. Dunkel, see 4:250. For a review of the testing program, see 665.

[306]

*Emporia First Year Latin Test. 1 year high school; 1962–64; first published 1962–63 in the Every Pupil Scholarship Test series; Forms A, B, ('64, 2 pages); 2 levels labeled Tests 1, 2; manual ('64, 3 pages); $1.75 per 25 tests, postage extra; 75¢ per specimen set, postpaid; 40(45) minutes; Bernadine Sitts, Minnie M. Miller, Lillian A. Wall, and M. W. Sanders; Data Processing and Educational Measurement Center. *

[307]

*Emporia Second Year Latin Test. 2 years high school; 1962–64; first published 1962–63 in the Every Pupil Scholarship Test series; Forms A, B, ('64, 2 pages); 2 levels labeled Tests 1, 2; manual ('64, 3 pages); $1.75 per 25 tests, postage extra; 75¢ per specimen set, postpaid; 40(45) minutes; Bernadine Sitts, Minnie M. Miller, Lillian A. Wall, and M. W. Sanders; Data Processing and Educational Measurement Center. *

RUSSIAN

[308]

*College Placement Test in Russian Listening Comprehension. Entering college freshmen; 1962–70; irregularly scheduled reprintings of inactive forms of *College Board Achievement Test in Russian Listening Comprehension;* Form SPL ['70, reprint of 1968 test, 13 pages]; test administered by 7½ ips tape recording; for more complete information, see 665; 30(40) minutes; program administered for the College Entrance Examination Board by Educational Testing Service. *

REFERENCE

1. ALEAMONI, LAWRENCE M., AND MATSUNAGA, ALLEN. *A Study of Foreign Language at the University of Illinois Using the CEEB Foreign Language Placement Tests and End-of-Course Grades.* Research Report No. 317. Champaign, Ill.: Measurement and Research Division, Office of Instructional Resources, University of Illinois, 1970. Pp. i, 42. *

For a review of the testing program, see 665.

[309]

★College Placement Test in Russian Reading. Entering college freshmen; 1962–70; CPTRR; irregularly scheduled reprintings of inactive forms of *College Board Achievement Test in Russian;* Forms PPL1 ['67, reprint of 1964 test], PPL2 ['67, reprint of 1965 test] in a single booklet (28 pages); for more complete information, see 665; 60(70) minutes; program administered for the College Entrance Examination Board by Educational Testing Service. *

For a review of the testing program, see 665.

[310]

*Graduate School Foreign Language Test: Russian. Graduate level degree candidates required to demonstrate reading proficiency in Russian; 1963–70; GSFLTR; 2 current forms ('68–69, 47–49 pages); for more complete information, see 668; 100(120) minutes; Educational Testing Service. *

REFERENCES

1. BARTLETT, ALBERT ALLEN. "The Foreign Language Requirement for the Ph.D.: A New Approach." *Foreign Lang Ann* 2:174–84 D '68. *
2. CLARK, JOHN L. D. "The Graduate School Foreign Language Requirement: A Survey of Testing Practices and Related Topics." *Foreign Lang Ann* 2:150–64 D '68. *
3. HARVEY, PHILIP R. "Minimal Passing Scores on the Graduate School Foreign Language Tests." *Foreign Lang Ann* 2:165–73 D '68. *
4. ALEAMONI, LAWRENCE M., AND MATSUNAGA, ALLEN. *A Study of Foreign Language at the University of Illinois Using the CEEB Foreign Language Placement Tests and End-of-Course Grades.* Research Report No. 317. Champaign, Ill.: Measurement and Research Division, Office of Instructional Resources, University of Illinois, 1970. Pp. i, 42. *

[311]

*MLA Cooperative Foreign Language Proficiency Tests: Russian. Russian majors and advanced students in college; 1960–68; formerly called *MLA Foreign Language Proficiency Tests for Teachers and Advanced Students: Russian;* 7 tests in 3 booklets (formerly in 7 booklets); Forms HA ('61, identical except for format and directions with earlier tests variously designated Forms A, JML1, and K-JML1), HB ('66, identical except for format and directions with tests copyrighted in 1961 and variously designated Forms B, JML2, K-JML2, and OML1); temporary series directions for administering ('68, 12 pages); series norms ('66, 2 pages); mimeographed series score conversion directions ['68, 8 pages]; separate answer sheets (Digitek, SCRIBE) must be used except for speaking and writing tests; $4 per 100 answer sheets, cash orders postpaid; Digitek scoring stencils not available; SCRIBE scoring and statistical analysis service, 35¢ per student for all tests except speaking and writing; scoring by special arrangement with language specialists: $3 per speaking test tape, $1.50 per writing test; Modern Language Association of America and Educational Testing Service; Co-operative Tests and Services. *

a) BOOK 1: READING, LISTENING COMPREHENSION, SPEAKING. Forms HA (24 pages), HB (21 pages); $9 per 10 tests; 90¢ per single copy; $12 per 7½ ips listening/speaking test tape; blank tapes for student responses must be obtained locally; 40(50) minutes for reading, (20–30) minutes for listening comprehension, (15–30) minutes for speaking.

b) BOOK 2: WRITING. Forms HA (8 pages), HB (7 pages); $6 per 20 tests; 30¢ per single copy; 45(55) minutes.

c) BOOK 3: APPLIED LINGUISTICS, CIVILIZATION AND CULTURE, PROFESSIONAL PREPARATION. Forms HA, HB, (29 pages); professional preparation test is common to all languages in series; $9 per 10 tests; 90¢ per single copy; 40(50) minutes for linguistics, 30(40) minutes for civilization and culture, 45(55) minutes for professional preparation.

REFERENCES

1–3. See 6:417.
4. TOLLINGER, SUZANNE, AND PAQUETTE, F. ANDRÉ, EDITORS. *The MLA Foreign Language Proficiency Tests for Teachers and Advanced Students: A Professional Evaluation and Recommendations for Test Development,* pp. 62–89, 131–5, 155–6, 161–75, passim. Sections on this test by Robert L. Baker, David Chandler, Edith Ignatieff, Tora T. Ladu, James C. McKinney, Charles A. Moser, Douglas C. Sheppard, and Leon I. Twarog. An unpublished report to the U.S. Office of Education, Project No. BR-6-2619, Modern Language Association of America, June 1966. Pp. viii, 366. * (ERIC ED 019 016)
5. CARROLL, JOHN B. "Foreign Language Proficiency Levels Attained by Language Majors Near Graduation From College." *Foreign Lang Ann* 1:131–51 O '67. *
6. PERKINS, JEAN A. "State Certification and Proficiency Tests: The Experience in Pennsylvania." *Foreign Lang Ann* 2:195–9 D '68. *

For a review by Wayne D. Fisher, see 6:417.

[312]

*MLA-Cooperative Foreign Language Tests: Russian. 1–2 years high school or 2 semesters college, 3–4 years high school or 4 semesters college; 1963–65; 4 tests in a single booklet: listening, speaking, reading, writing; writing test ('63, 8 pages) available as separate; 2 forms; 2 levels; no specific manual; series directions for administering and scoring ('64, 40 pages); series handbook ('65, 24 pages); series booklet of norms ('65, 82 pages); student bulletin ('65, 2 pages) for each level; $7 per 10 tests; $5 per 20 writing tests only; separate answer sheets (Digitek, Digitek-IBM 805, IBM 1230, SCRIBE) may be used for listening and reading tests; $4 per 100 answer sheets; $1.25 per 10 IBM 805 or IBM 1230 scoring stencils (answer pattern must be punched out locally); Digitek scoring stencils not available; $8.50 per 3¾ ips tape, 5 inch reel, for listening test; $8.50 per 3¾ ips tape, 5 inch reel, for speaking test (blank tapes or discs for recording student responses must be obtained locally); $2 per series directions for administering and scoring; $2 per series handbook; $2 per series norms booklet; $3 per 100 student bulletins; $3 per specimen set; cash orders postpaid; SCRIBE scoring and statistical analysis service (listening and reading tests), 35¢ per student; no scoring service for speaking and writing tests, but arrangements for professional scoring can be made; 25(35) minutes for listening, 10(20) minutes for speaking, 35(40) minutes for reading, 35(40) minutes for writing; prepared in cooperation with the Modern Language Association of America; Cooperative Tests and Services. *
a) [LOWER LEVEL.] 1–2 years high school or 2 semesters college; Forms LA, LB, ('63, 24 pages).
b) [HIGHER LEVEL.] 3–4 years high school or 4 semesters college; Forms MA, MB, ('63, 25 pages).

REFERENCES

1. BAIR, RAYMOND L. "The MLA Cooperative Foreign Language Tests in Russian." *Slavic & East Europ J* 9:308–14 f '65. *
2. ALFAMONI, LAWRENCE M., AND SPENCER, RICHARD E. "A Comparison of Biserial Discrimination, Point Biserial Discrimination, and Difficulty Indices in Item Analysis Data." *Ed & Psychol Meas* 29(2):353–8 su '69. * (PA 44:17314)

Slavic & East Europ J 9:308–14 f '65. Raymond L. Bair. * The first test in form LA, the Listening Test, is....to be given to the students on tape * these questions are excellent and the range of difficulty extremely wide * However, language, unlike Gaul, does not lend itself so neatly to division into four parts (listening, speaking, reading, and writing). Although this first test is labeled "Listening," it is not just that. This portion of the entire test requires the student not only to comprehend spoken Russian, but also to read Russian. In the test booklet, four answers are given for each question, and the student must read all four in order to select the correct one. This test might be more accurately labeled "Listening and Reading." This may sound like a picayune criticism, but having taken the MLA *Proficiency Tests for Teachers* at NDEA Institutes four times, I vividly recall having had much more difficulty with reading the phrases jammed with poly-

syllabic words that I had never seen, than with comprehending what was being said by the voice on the tape. If listening is actually being tested, why not have the voice on the tape read the answer choices? * If two skills are to be combined in order to provide a testing situation, why not combine listening and writing? A short passage might be read in Russian, then a question asked in Russian to be answered by the examinee in Russian in his test booklet. This answer need be graded only for content, not for form. The present number of questions, forty or forty-five, could be reduced to thirty while retaining the same accuracy. The present questions, with four choices in each answer, mean that every fourth question might be guessed right. If the examinee wrote his answer in Russian, this possibility would be less likely. Listening and writing might make a more reliable appraisal of the student's progress in Russian than listening and reading. The second section of the MLA *Cooperative Russian Tests,* "Speaking," contains thirty-eight questions with a total of eighty-two points. This test is comprehensive and cleverly devised. Mimicry; reading aloud; questions about pictures, to be answered in Russian; descriptions, the first of a single picture and the second of a four-picture sequence, are the techniques employed to test speaking ability. * The method used for rating speaking performance is excellent and deserves the highest praise. * the vocabulary is carefully and fairly chosen * The "Reading" test has fifty questions of the multiple-choice type, each with four answers. * "Passages drawn from periodicals and appropriate literary sources are used to test word and phrase discrimination and ability to understand the main idea, find details, and draw conclusions." Once again the range of difficulty is wide, and the questions, for the most part, well chosen. My weakest student answered five correctly, the strongest—forty-five. Some of the first twenty-five questions are what would have been called a few years ago vocabulary questions, but here they are dressed up to suit the label "Reading." * The reading passages that follow are well chosen as to vocabulary and topics. * These passages are appropriate and seem to increase gradually in degree of difficulty. It is unfortunate that five of them can be answered without reference to the selection from which the information for the answer is supposed to come. This is true of questions 26, 29, 34, 37, and 42 * The final test in form

LA, the "Writing" test, sems to me the weakest of the four. This test contains one hundred units of credit. The range of questions is limited and several grammatical categories neglected. The consequence of this is to make it pedagogically unsound. It is obvious that teachers will use these tests as syllabi for their teaching of Russian. In the lower level form LA and in the higher level form MA there is no question to test aspect. These MLA *Cooperative Foreign Language Tests* are of such scope that in the future they will determine the mode of instruction of Russian. It is, therefore, vital that they contain a fair sampling of questions covering the entire grammar of Russian. Here is my count of the parts of speech covered in form LA: pronouns—3, adjectives—8, correlatives—2, numbers—1, nouns—29, adverbs—3, prepositions—5, verbs—19, demonstrative adjectives—3, possessive adjectives—7. Not questioned at all were: aspect, inflection of cardinal and ordinal numbers, reflexive verbs, future tense of perfective or imperfective verbs, verb prefixes, actual and potential verbs, imperatives, and the declension of *sebja, sam,* and *čej,* to mention a few. Although verbs are requested nineteen times, six of these are to be written in the past tense, for regular verbs a rather easy task in Russian. The features that make Russian verbs difficult—consonant mutation, changing stress, and aspect—go untested. Evidence that some of the question forms were written with a language other than Russian in mind can be found in the contradiction in the directions. For questions 31 to 36 they read: "Rewrite each of the following sentences so that the word or words printed on the line below it fit correctly into the new sentence. Make all changes necessary to produce a correct Russian sentence, but do not add any words and do not leave any out." Immediately below, a Russian sentence must be changed from the positive to the negative and a double negative used—ergo a word added. * Sentence 34 is to be rewritten in the past tense and the model is in the present. The verb is "to be," which is expressed in the past and not in the present and therefore must be added here to make a correct sentence, contrary to the directions! * In order to rewrite the next sentence correctly two words must be deleted and two added. * A tabulation of the parts of speech of the "Writing" test of the higher level form MA shows an increase in the percentage of nouns asked for. The declension of nouns is tested thirty-one times; 38 percent of the words asked for are nouns. Fifteen verbs must be altered or supplied, and this number represents 19 percent of the words tested. In descending order then are adjectives, prepositions, pronouns, and adverbs. For the most part there is only *one* word each for the remaining speech categories. After four years of secondary school Russian, aspect, declension of cardinals, actual and potential verbs, and a few more categories go untested. For us secondary school teachers, it is comforting to know exactly what is to be taught during the first, second, third, and fourth years of Russian language study. These tests will serve as outlines for teachers, to guide them as to how to teach and what to teach. In the past we have often noticed a reluctance on the part of publishers and experienced teachers to state dogmatically just exactly what to teach, at what speed, and how. * The importance of the MLA *Cooperative Foreign Language Tests* hinges on the fact that these tests include listening and speaking sections. Students are reluctant to recognize the worth of listening and speaking, if these skills are not tested and credit given for them in a formal manner. This, then, is the real contribution of the MLA *Cooperative Foreign Language Tests.* Who can fool a student? He knows full well that when listening and speaking are not tested as part of the final examination they are not as important as reading and writing. *

For an excerpted review of the series, see 254.

SPANISH

[313]

*Advanced Placement Examination in Spanish. High school students desiring credit for college level courses or admission to advanced courses; 1954–70; Forms RBP ('69, 16 pages), SBP ('70, 17 pages) in 2 booklets (objective, essay); listening comprehension tapes: 7½ ips for Form RBP, 3¾ ips for Form SBP; tape script ['69–70, 5–6 pages] for each form; for more complete information, see 662; 180(200) minutes; program administered for the College Entrance Examination Board by Educational Testing Service. *

REFERENCES

1. See 6:421.
2. ENGLEKIRK, JOHN E. "The Evolution of the College Board Advanced Placement Program in Spanish: What Will the 1968 Program Be Like?" *Hispania* 50:558–68 S '67. *
3. TURNER, ALBERT R. "New Developments in the Spanish Advanced Placement Program of the College Entrance Examination Board." *Hispania* 50:348–53 My '67. *

For a review of the testing program, see 662.

[314]

*College Board Achievement Test in Spanish.
Candidates for college entrance with 2–4 years high
school Spanish; 1902–71; test administered each January at centers established by the publisher; for more
complete information, see 663; 60(80) minutes; program administered for the College Entrance Examination Board by Educational Testing Service. *

REFERENCES

1–3. See 4:259.
4. See 5:287.
5. See 6:419.

*For reviews of the testing program, see 6:760
(2 reviews).*

[315]

***College Placement Test in Spanish Listening
Comprehension.** Entering college freshmen; 1962–
70, c1955–70; irregularly scheduled reprintings of inactive forms of *College Board Achievement Test in
Spanish Listening Comprehension;* Forms NPL ('65,
reprint of 1963 test), OPL ('66, reprint of 1964 test)
in a single booklet (18 pages); test administered by
7½ ips tape recording; for more complete information,
see 665; 30(40) minutes; program administered for
the College Entrance Examination Board by Educational Testing Service. *

REFERENCES

1. See 6:422.
2. ALEAMONI, LAWRENCE M., AND MATSUNAGA, ALLEN. *A
Study of Foreign Language at the University of Illinois Using
the CEEB Foreign Language Placement Tests and End-of-
Course Grades.* Research Report No. 317. Champaign, Ill.:
Measurement and Research Division, Office of Instructional
Resources, University of Illinois, 1970. Pp. i, 42. *

For a review of the testing program, see 665.

[316]

*College Placement Test in Spanish Reading.
Entering college freshmen; 1962–70, c1955–70;
CPTSR; irregularly scheduled reprintings of inactive
forms of *College Board Achievement Test in Spanish;*
Forms PPL1, PPL2, ['67, reprint of 1963 tests] in a
single booklet (20 pages); for more complete information, see 665; 60(70) minutes; program administered for the College Entrance Examination Board
by Educational Testing Service. *

REFERENCE

1. ALEAMONI, LAWRENCE M., AND MATSUNAGA, ALLEN. *A
Study of Foreign Language at the University of Illinois Using
the CEEB Foreign Language Placement Tests and End-of-
Course Grades.* Research Report No. 317. Champaign, Ill.:
Measurement and Research Division, Office of Instructional
Resources, University of Illinois, 1970. Pp. i, 42. *

For a review of the testing program, see 665.

[317]

***Common Concepts Foreign Language Test:
Spanish.** Students in any grade who are at the Level
1 stage of achievement; 1962–66; aural comprehension; same booklet also used to test French and German; may be administered using live voice but tape
recording (3¾ ips) is recommended; Forms 1, 2, ('62,
31 pages) in a single booklet; manual ('66, 41 pages);
separate answer sheets (IBM 1230) must be used;
$1.10 per test; $5.95 per tape recording; $2.50 per 50
answer sheets; 75¢ per scoring stencil for either form;
$1 per manual; postage extra; $2.25 per specimen set
(without tape), postpaid; scoring service, 22¢ and
over per test; (40–45) minutes; Bela H. Banathy,
Miles V. Zintz, W. James Popham, Joseph M. Sadna-

vitch, Rena Krichbaum, Fred B. Gannon, Valdemar
Hempel, and Klaus A. Mueller; CTB/McGraw-Hill. *

*For a review covering the three languages,
see 253.*

[318]

*First Year Spanish Test. High school and college;
1947–68; FYST; revision of *Kansas First Year Spanish Test;* Form A ('68, 2 pages); manual ('68, 2
pages); no data on reliability; $1.75 per 25 tests,
postage extra; 75¢ per specimen set, postpaid; 50(55)
minutes; Oscar F. Hernández and Minnie M. Miller;
Data Processing and Educational Measurement Center. *

[319]

***The Graduate Record Examinations Advanced
Spanish Test.** Graduate school candidates; 1946–70;
3 current forms ('64–69, 24–28 pages); descriptive
booklet ('70, 9 pages); for more complete information,
see 667; 180(200) minutes; Educational Testing Service. *

GINO PARISI, *Assistant Professor of Spanish,
Georgetown University, Washington, D.C.*
[Review of Form RGR.]

There are different ways of grouping the 200
items that make up this test. Exact analysis is
difficult because some items test several factors
simultaneously. The breakdown used by the
publisher follows: (*a*) Literature, 50 items (33
Spanish, 17 Spanish-American); (*b*) Culture
and Civilization, 60 items (40 Spanish, 20
Spanish-American); (*c*) Structure and Linguistics, 40 items; (*d*) Reading Comprehension, 49 items.

The analysis shows the Literature section to
be the most difficult and the language sections
(*c* and *d*) the easiest. Reliability for the total
test is highest of all the GRE tests: within a
range of .83 to .96, the Spanish has a coefficient
of .96, shared only by the Music test. However,
the prime consideration in this case is not the
reliability, which may be expected in a test of
predominantly factual material, but the predictive validity of the scores, which must be determined by each graduate department as it
collects data over the years.

A three-way classification along different
lines shows the following proportions: (*a*)
Factual information, 4 parts; (*b*) Literary
appreciation, 2 parts; (*c*) Language proficiency, 1 part. The desirability of such a preponderance of factual material must be judged
by each graduate school according to its program. For those requiring a high level of proficiency, the important question is whether there
is a sufficient degree of language ability implicit
in the literature and culture sections of this test.

In view of the fact that acquisition of the language is often a goal in itself, there could be a better balance between what may be called simple language proficiency on the one hand and knowledge of literature, culture, and linguistics on the other. Furthermore, the scores in each area could be explicitly stated. Although the subscores are used in the publisher's analysis, apparently the usual practice is to report only the total score to the graduate school.

The items in different categories are grouped in short sections alternating throughout the test. A majority of the answers are five-choice; some are four-choice; and one section uses a format in which four questions are matched with five answers. This last device would seem to complicate the guessing factor as a student eliminates the possible answers.

Usage is tested in items that cover the fundamental areas of verbs, syntax, and vocabulary. Except for one item, apparently based on prescriptive rules, the knowledge required is appropriate for college level.

The section on linguistics contains only 10 items, mostly in the field of dialectology. For a school offering a program in linguistics this number is too small to be significant, and for a literature program the section is irrelevant. It is not clear why it has been included, except for the contemporary sound of the label "linguistics."

The prose and poetry selections require the student to understand both the literal and the implied meaning. He must be aware of the tone of the writer, the literary devices employed, and the period represented. There is one section in Old Spanish with the attendant problems of orthography and vocabulary.

In conclusion, this is a highly reliable test of the student's achievement in Spanish and Spanish-American literature and culture; language proficiency, primarily passive skills, is tested for the most part indirectly. Users should first satisfy themselves that the content is appropriate for their programs, then decide how much weight to give to the scores. For the future, a test with clearly labeled subtests and subscores in different areas—language, literature, culture, linguistics—might facilitate this task. It would also be advantageous for the student or school to be able to use only parts of the test. Finally, predictive validity studies must be carried out by the schools themselves. Judgment concerning the value of GRE scores must

therefore be deferred until more data are accumulated.

For reviews of the testing program, see 667 (1 review) and 5:601 (1 review).

[320]

★**Graduate School Foreign Language Test: Spanish.** Graduate level degree candidates required to demonstrate reading proficiency in Spanish; 1963-70; GSFLTS; 2 current forms ('69-70, 29-31 pages); for more complete information, see 668; 100(120) minutes; Educational Testing Service. *

REFERENCES

1. BARTLETT, ALBERT ALLEN. "The Foreign Language Requirement for the Ph.D.: A New Approach." *Foreign Lang Ann* 2:174-84 D '68. *
2. CLARK, JOHN L. D. "The Graduate School Foreign Language Requirement: A Survey of Testing Practices and Related Topics." *Foreign Lang Ann* 2:150-64 D '68. *
3. HARVEY, PHILIP R. "Minimal Passing Scores on the Graduate School Foreign Language Tests." *Foreign Lang Ann* 2:165-73 D '68. *

ROBERT LADO, *Dean, School of Languages and Linguistics, Georgetown University, Washington, D.C.*

The *Graduate School Foreign Language Test: Spanish* is designed to measure the ability to read and understand professional literature in Spanish. It was developed to test reading proficiency in fulfilling the foreign language requirement for advanced degrees. It may also be used to measure reading at the end of an undergraduate program of study or a graduate reading course, or to assess the reading proficiency of those who judge their preparation to be adequate without formal course work.

An initial version of the test was developed in 1967. The present version, Form RFG, is the result of a 1969 revision, which incorporated a specialized reading section with a choice of three fields: humanities, natural sciences, and social sciences, making the Spanish test parallel to the French, German, and Russian forms of the same program. The test is administered nationally by the Educational Testing Service, which provides scaled and percentile scores. The scaled scores range from 200 to 800, with a mean of 500. Since this is a new version, score interpretation charts are based on the scores of approximately 625 students who took the test in November 1969. The total test reliability estimates are .94 for humanities, .92 for natural sciences, and .93 for social sciences. These are in the same range as those for the French, German, and Russian tests.

Administration of the test, which consists of two sections, requires 100 minutes: 40 minutes for Section 1 and 60 minutes for Section 2.

Section 1 consists of 60 multiple choice items. Section 2 consists of passages in the humanities, the natural sciences, and the social sciences, drawn from professional literature in Spanish. All candidates take Section 1 and choose one of the options of Section 2 according to their field of professional interest. The passages vary in length from about 75 to 300 words, each passage being followed by a series of multiple choice questions in English that are to be answered through comprehension of the Spanish text.

This is a test developed in the pattern of the Educational Testing Service in which the ETS cooperates with qualified members of the profession in the preparation of items and the refinement and standardization of the test on the basis of statistical analysis of field performance. The present revision in format followed a survey of the language requirements and testing practices of 1,604 graduate school departments in the spring of 1967. The availability of this test service in Spanish represents a welcome advance in the assessment of the reading proficiency of graduate students in fulfilling their foreign language requirement. We now have the option of a professionally prepared objective instrument to substitute for the great variety of practices with subjective and often arbitrary procedures and standards which contribute to the fear and frustration on the part of graduate students and the waste of valuable hours of faculty time. Any reservations one might have about the validity of the test for a particular student or program or about the various parts and items of the test do not begin to compare with the weaknesses of the various practices which were the only fare before the appearance of this test.

The ability to read connected texts at an advanced level in a foreign language is in itself a complex skill. The reader must be able to extract the meanings of lexical items that are brought up by the context; to understand stylistic variations; and to handle longer sequences of material. Section 1 of the test is intended to measure the candidate's knowledge of specific structure elements, while Section 2 concentrates on the more complex task of overall comprehension and abstraction of meaning.

Section 1 consists of two parts, A and B, with 30 items each. The 30 items of Part A present Spanish sentences with a blank for certain words or phrases, followed by four suggested

choices of possible fillers. The functional structure elements, such as verbs, sequence signals, and adverbs are emphasized. Vocabulary is not tested directly, although a good command of the lexical meanings of the sentences is required in order to establish the context. The validity of this section can be justified in terms of the specific elements being tested. However, the skill that is being measured seems to be productive knowledge of Spanish structure rather than interpretation of structural elements as an aid to comprehension. A candidate who has followed a reading course, or who intends to use his second language only for reading purposes, will probably have been trained in the recognition and interpretation of Spanish texts that are already stylistically and grammatically well formed. The task of choosing items to be used in active production is more demanding and may lead to some frustration, particularly at the beginning of the test, since many of the choices present stylistic or grammatical distractors rather than matters of interpretation of meaning. Thus, some of the choices offer answers with no semantic difference, although one of the two may be chosen as stylistically more appropriate or more 'correct' according to grammar norms. It is true that the students who are able to choose a stylistically or grammatically more appropriate form are likely to understand the meaning better, but the two abilities are not the same and therefore the substitution of one for the other introduces an unnecessary problem of validity.

The 30 items of Part B, Section 1, are more directly related to the task of determining whether the candidate understands specific Spanish items. Here the student is presented with complete Spanish sentences where certain words or phrases have been underlined. Following each sentence are four English words or phrases among which the candidate is to select the one that is the best translation of the underlined items in the stimulus sentence. A wider sample of language elements is evaluated in this section, including idioms, vocabulary, and the main grammatical categories. Most of the items offer good distractors, although a few include choices that may be decided on the basis of English criteria: that is, the student may decide on the correct item by judging which one of the choices will fit into the English version of the Spanish sentence. In some cases there may be a doubt as to whether to choose an item because

Graduate School Foreign Language Test: Spanish

it is the best translation of the Spanish—as specified in the directions—or because it represents better English.

The three specialized options of Section 2 measure the candidate's ability to extract meaning from longer texts in a broad area within which his own field of specialization falls. A frequent objection to this necessarily broad field in the selection of the reading passages is the fact that the student's research interests may be highly specialized by the time he reaches this advanced stage of his graduate studies. There is no question that the ability to read with understanding the professional literature in Spanish depends in part upon the student's knowledge of the concepts, methods, and terminology in his own special field. But these are most likely to be similar across languages and therefore most will be readily understandable to the student if he is able to read the foreign language in the general context of the humanities, natural sciences, or social sciences. Therefore, a well-developed objective test of reading in the broader field is likely to be more valid and reliable than an ad hoc translation or a reading chosen from material which is specifically within the student's field.

In the present test the natural sciences option seems to contain the largest number of questions that might be answered merely from knowledge of subject matter without reading the Spanish text, since the questions are based on natural facts and phenomena with which the student may be familiar. This may be inherent in any test of reading in the natural sciences that discusses realistic material.

In all sections most of the questions and choices seem to focus on the student's general reasoning ability and on his skill at making inferences from the authors' statements. Relatively few questions test his grasp of the specific language clues to a given meaning. Some of the selections, particularly in the humanities and social sciences, include paragraphs of unusual complexity. The English questions and choices themselves are also quite complex and will test the candidate's general reading ability and power of abstraction in his own language. Efficient readers of English may have more than the usual advantage in decoding the subtleties involved in the various choices.

The test is not intended as a speeded instrument and the standardization procedures report that enough students finished both parts to eliminate the factor of speed. This is presumably a desideratum in a reading test for students who will be doing untimed reading of some critical source material in their research. Actually, the ability to read at an efficient speed is also important. Future revisions might consider a speed section as well.

The need for a second language at the advanced level of graduate study, where the scholar needs to have access to professional literature written abroad, has always been great and will continue to be so in spite of the availability of translations of most major works. The increasing volume of periodical literature and professional journals will continue to require a knowledge of foreign languages in order to have up-to-date information on new developments reported in such publications. The task of measuring a graduate's proficiency in a second language can be greatly simplified by using tests such as GSFLT. Maximum simplification would have been achieved by adopting national norms and standards for passing scores with a range for superior to minimum performance. In the absence of such national norms, each school or department may establish its own standards. Suggestions for relating the scaled and percentile scores on the test to other scores and criteria for passing are presented in the Guide to the Interpretation of Scores.

This, then, is a professionally developed test of reading prepared according to correct professional standards and administered within the practices of the ETS. It can be used with confidence for its intended purpose.

[321]

*MLA Cooperative Foreign Language Proficiency Tests: Spanish. Spanish majors and advanced students in college; 1960–68; formerly called *MLA Foreign Language Proficiency Tests for Teachers and Advanced Students: Spanish;* 7 tests in 3 booklets (formerly in 7 booklets); Forms HA ('61, identical except for format and directions with earlier tests variously designated Forms A, JML1, and K-JML1), HB ('66, identical except for format and directions with tests copyrighted in 1961 and variously designated Forms B, JML2, K-JML2, and OML1); temporary series directions for administering ('68, 12 pages); series norms ('66, 2 pages); mimeographed series score conversion directions ['68, 8 pages]; separate answer sheets (Digitek, SCRIBE) must be used except for speaking and writing tests; $4 per 100 answer sheets, cash orders postpaid; Digitek scoring stencils not available; SCRIBE scoring and statistical analysis service, 35¢ per student for all tests except speaking and writing; scoring by special arrangement with language specialists; $3 per speaking test tape, $1.50 per writing test; Modern Language Association of America and Educational Testing Service; Cooperative Tests and Services. *

a) BOOK 1: READING, LISTENING COMPREHENSION, SPEAKING. Forms HA (24 pages), HB (21 pages); $9 per 10 tests; 90¢ per single copy; $12 per 7½ ips listening/speaking test tape; blank tapes for student responses must be obtained locally; 40(50) minutes for reading, (20–30) minutes for listening comprehension, (15–30) minutes for speaking.

b) BOOK 2: WRITING. Forms HA (8 pages), HB (7 pages); $6 per 20 tests; 30¢ per single copy; 45(55) minutes.

c) BOOK 3: APPLIED LINGUISTICS, CIVILIZATION AND CULTURE, PROFESSIONAL PREPARATION. Forms HA, HB, (29 pages); professional preparation test is common to all languages in series; $9 per 10 tests; 90¢ per single copy; 40(50) minutes for linguistics, 30(40) minutes for civilization and culture, 45(55) minutes for professional preparation.

REFERENCES

1–3. See 6:427.

4. PAQUETTE, F. ANDRÉ; WALLMARK, MADELINE; SPENCER, RICHARD E.; AND CHURCHILL, FREDERICK J. *A Comparison of the MLA Foreign Language Proficiency Tests for Teachers and Advanced Students With the MLA Foreign Language Cooperative Tests.* An unpublished report to the U.S. Office of Education, Project No. BR-6-2619, Modern Language Association of America, 1966. Pp. 58. * (ERIC ED 019 017)

5. TOLLINGER, SUZANNE, AND PAQUETTE, F. ANDRÉ, EDITORS. *The MLA Foreign Language Proficiency Tests for Teachers and Advanced Students: A Professional Evaluation and Recommendations for Test Development,* pp. 90–112, 136–9, 157–60, 161–75, passim. Sections on this test by Joan E. Ciruti, David Griffin, Tora T. Ladu, James C. McKinney, Robert G. Meade, Jr., Lucrecia Ruisanchez-Lopez, Douglas C. Sheppard, and George W. Wilkins, Jr. An unpublished report to the U.S. Office of Education, Project No. BR-6-2619, Modern Language Association of America, June 1966. Pp. viii, 366. * (ERIC ED 019 016)

6. CARROLL, JOHN B. "Foreign Language Proficiency Levels Attained by Language Majors Near Graduation From College." *Foreign Lang Ann* 1:131–51 O '67. *

7. DIZNEY, HENRY F., AND GROMEN, LAUREN. "Predictive Validity and Differential Achievement on Three MLA—Cooperative Foreign Language Tests." *Ed & Psychol Meas* 27:1127–30 w '67. * (PA 42:9417)

8. PAQUETTE, F. ANDRÉ; WITH THE COOPERATION OF MADELINE WALLMARK. *The MLA Foreign Language Proficiency Tests for Teachers and Advanced Students: Analysis of the Performance of Native Speakers and Comparison With That of NDEA Summer Language Institute Participants.* An unpublished report to the U.S. Office of Education, Project No. BR-6-2619, Modern Language Association of America, June 1968. Pp. ii, 42. * (ERIC ED 019 017)

9. PERKINS, JEAN A. "State Certification and Proficiency Tests: The Experience in Pennsylvania." *Foreign Lang Ann* 2:195–9 D '68. *

GLEN W. PROBST, *Professor of Spanish, Michigan State University, East Lansing, Michigan.*

Several years have passed since the publication of this test. And although much has been said and done in conjunction with it, there are still some questions which need to be answered, as well as some updating and revision that need to be accomplished.

The listening, reading, and writing parts of this test have acceptable reliability coefficients, but those for the other parts are questionable. An attempt at securing a validity index was carried out by administering the test to samples of native speakers in Latin America and Spain. The results were not conclusive enough to establish the test's validity for determining language proficiency in non-native speakers of Spanish. Therefore, its role in testing for certification purposes and institutional testing programs may be limited.

Listening comprehension skill is tested in combination with the testing of reading skill. The examinee must choose his response from the printed options. This hybrid-type test may deliver inaccurate results because the score achieved is dependent upon the examinee's ability to recognize the correct response from the written word. It does not test one's ability to listen to and understand spoken Spanish without reference to the written word. Although reality cannot be duplicated as long as the examinee knows he is being tested, an attempt must be made to represent it as closely as possible by not testing one skill based on ability in another skill.

Part A of the Speaking test aims at an evaluation of ability to pronounce with correct intonation while repeating model sentences spoken by a native speaker on the tape. Part B tests the ability to read aloud from the printed page. Both of these parts are weak in their attempt to deliver valid results concerning the examinee's ability to speak. Part C does a much better job by asking the examinee to respond extemporaneously to certain situations which are cued through the use of visuals. This part has three subparts, each one setting up a different situation. A negative aspect of the two latter parts is that the situations illustrated are too contrived and restrict the examinee to a narrow line of theme development. A lack of knowledge or lapse in recall of key words could inhibit the examinee's performance in general. Wider contextual situations are needed which will allow the examinee flexibility in topic choice and development.

The Reading test appears to be the least valid part of the examination. The primary disadvantage of the Reading test is that the vocabulary treats more the rare, exceptional, and obscure than the common, real life situations. Since extensive vocabulary acquisition is not a primary goal in audio-lingual teaching, it seems to be a paradox that many items are based upon a knowledge of very low frequency vocabulary, and not of structure and syntax. The structure and syntax need to be given more attention while a common, high frequency vocabulary inventory is used. The Reading test takes for granted a good basic proficiency in reading skill and aims at testing a proficiency based too much on a knowledge of obscure vocabulary in a literary context. This is a narrow dimension when compared with all the different kinds of content available in Spanish reading material. Perhaps the test is an accurate measure of one's ability to handle literary readings at the upper college level. If this is the case, it will serve to define the competence of a narrow segment of individuals in the profession. A check on the difficulty of the Reading test was made by this reviewer by applying the Spaulding Spanish Readability Formula[1] to seven passages in both test forms. Three of the passages were rated "exceptionally difficult," two were rated "difficult," and two were rated "moderately difficult."

The Writing test does not measure the examinee's ability to write. It measures his ability to understand grammar or appropriate word choice controlled by a contrived word environment. The test reveals no indication of the examinee's proficiency at writing out his thoughts in Spanish or at accurately recording on paper Spanish sounds which he has heard; nor does it give any indication as to the examinee's ability to extemporize in writing on a given subject. The Writing test requires more reading comprehension skill than writing skill. It reveals that the examinee has either not understood what he has read, if he is unable to fill in the blank correctly, or that he does not know a specific word or the grammar concept involved. Instead of measuring ability in writing skill, this examination tests the production of grammar.

In the Applied Linguistics test the questions posed in the negative would be clearer and more easily understood if stated in the affirmative. Question 24, Part B of Form HB is more of a pedagogical question than a linguistic question and should be deleted.

The Civilization and Culture test contains too much information concerning formal culture. About 20 percent of this section of the test on both forms deals with anthropological culture. In order to establish a more valid basis for testing, at least a balance, if not an overbalance in favor of anthropological culture, needs to be included in the questions of this part of the test. Some questions on formal culture have no apparent validity or relevance. For example, one question asks what country leads the Hispanic world in motion-picture production. Until more information concerning the social be-

havior patterns of the people is included in this test, it will remain a weak indicator of the examinee's knowledge of the target cultural patterns.

The Professional Preparation test impresses this reviewer as the most valid for its purpose of the seven tests in the battery. Several changes and modifications could be made in order to update and improve it. Question 8, Form HB is cloudy because the wording is misleading. Question 22 of the same form should be updated to include ACTFL as a possible answer. Question 36, Form HB should be placed in the Applied Linguistics section or deleted. Questions 43 and 52, Form HB are based too much on subjectivity which could result in more than one correct answer among the four possibilities. Question 5, Form HA also has as its correct answer a statement which has not yet been established as being more pedagogically sound than some of the alternate possibilities. Five of the questions on the two forms are asked in the negative. These would be better put in the affirmative.

This MLA battery may reveal some relative differences between those examinees who take it, but it could be missing the target completely in testing the four basic skills and knowledge of culture and civilization because of an apparent lack of content validity in these areas. An examinee's results in the four basic skills tests may not be a realistic representation of his true ability since the Spanish used is of a low frequency vocabulary, the skills are mixed in testing, and there is too much emphasis on the production of grammar. The Culture and Civilization test results might not be representative of the examinee's knowledge because it relies too heavily on formal culture content instead of anthropological culture content.

It is quite possible that many prospective teachers could fail this test battery and still become adequate teachers in the classroom at the beginning levels of instruction. Perhaps too many have already been screened out in such a manner. In light of the weaknesses discussed here, it is suggested that administrators judiciously use a candidate's results on this test, keeping in mind that the degree of proficiency should be commensurate with the requirements of the position—not way beyond them, nor in a semi-related content area.

In summary, these MLA tests in Spanish were designed to serve a definite need and give impetus to a field which was almost nonexistent

---

1 SPAULDING, SETH. "A Spanish Readability Formula." *Mod Lang J* 40:433–41 D '56. *

until their publication. However, no one should consider the tests valid enough to use them as the only criterion in selecting students for graduate study, for certification, or for hiring Spanish teachers. The administrator who is selecting students for graduate study may rely on the candidate's results in certain sections of the test, while the administrator who is seeking prospective teachers may rely more on the candidate's proficiency in other sections of the test, depending on the requirements for the position involved. In all cases it is strongly suggested that the results of this test be used in conjunction with other methods of measuring achievement, such as a personal interview in Spanish or recommendations from previous advisors to the candidate in question.

For a review by Walter V. Kaulfers, see 6:427.

[322]

*MLA-Cooperative Foreign Language Tests: Spanish.** 1–2 years high school or 2 semesters college, 3–4 years high school or 4 semesters college; 1963–65; 4 tests in a single booklet: listening, speaking, reading, writing; writing test ('63, 8 pages) available as separate; 2 forms; 2 levels; no specific manual; series directions for administering and scoring ('64, 40 pages); series handbook ('65, 24 pages); series booklet of norms ('65, 82 pages); student bulletin ('65, 2 pages) for each level; $7 per 10 tests; $5 per 20 writing tests only; separate answer sheets (Digitek, Digitek-IBM 805, IBM 1230, SCRIBE) may be used for listening and reading tests; $4 per 100 answer sheets; $1.25 per 10 IBM 805 or IBM 1230 scoring stencils (answer pattern must be punched out locally); Digitek scoring stencils not available; $8.50 per 3¾ ips tape, 5 inch reel, for listening test; $8.50 per 3¾ ips tape, 5 inch reel, for speaking test (blank tapes or discs for recording student responses must be obtained locally); $2 per series directions for administering and scoring; $2 per series handbook; $2 per series norms booklet; $3 per 100 student bulletins; $3 per specimen set; cash orders postpaid; SCRIBE scoring and statistical analysis service (listening and reading tests), 35¢ per student; no scoring service for speaking and writing tests, but arrangements for professional scoring can be made; 25(35) minutes for listening, 10(20) minutes for speaking, 35(40) minutes for reading, 35(40) minutes for writing; prepared in cooperation with the Modern Language Association of America; Cooperative Tests and Services. *

a) [LOWER LEVEL.] 1–2 years high school or 2 semesters college; Forms LA, LB, ('63, 24 pages).
b) [HIGHER LEVEL.] 3–4 years high school or 4 semesters college; Forms MA, MB, ('63, 24 pages).

REFERENCES

1. PAQUETTE, F. ANDRÉ; WALLMARK, MADELINE; SPENCER, RICHARD E.; AND CHURCHILL, FREDERICK J. *A Comparison of the MLA Foreign Language Proficiency Tests for Teachers and Advanced Students With the MLA Foreign Language Cooperative Tests.* An unpublished report to the U.S. Office of Education, Project No. BR-6-2619, Modern Language Association of America, 1966. Pp. 58. * (ERIC ED 019 017)
2. ALEAMONI, LAWRENCE M., AND SPENCER, RICHARD E. "A Comparison of Biserial Discrimination, Point Biserial Dis-

crimination, and Difficulty Indices in Item Analysis Data." *Ed & Psychol Meas* 29(2):353–8 su '69. * (PA 44:17314)

ROBERT LADO, *Dean, School of Languages and Linguistics, Georgetown University, Washington, D.C.*

The MLA tests were developed specifically to measure language learning by the audio-lingual approach. With major emphasis being given to audio-lingual skills in the teaching of languages after World War II and especially after the enactment of the National Defense Education Act in 1958, the need for tests that would measure these skills became imperative.

The tests are aimed at two levels: the L or low level for the second year of high school and second semester in college, and the M or middle level for the fourth year of high school and fourth semester in college.

These tests are designed to measure Spanish language skills functionally and are completely in Spanish except for directions on taking the test, which are given in English. Since they test the four skills separately and functionally, they can be used for traditional as well as progressive classes by simply omitting or including the audio-lingual tests.

Approximately 40,000 tests were administered to 10,000 students in the pretesting phase of the work. These tests plus the development of the *MLA Cooperative Foreign Language Proficiency Tests* constitute the largest undertaking in the history of the profession with regard to testing.

The preparation of the test followed the general procedures of the ETS, first bringing together the various tests committees to draw up test specifications and outlines, then writing test items for three experimental forms at each level, submitting them to extensive pretesting and detailed item analyses, and finally selecting items from every three pretested forms for the two final forms of each test. The pretesting phase was more elaborate than usual because of the new ways of testing language achievement being attempted.

The listening test gives the instructions and the utterances to be comprehended on a tape-recording. The utterances are single sentences, short conversations, paragraphs read by a speaker, telephone conversations, and dramatic scenes played by several speakers. The student responds by selecting one of four choices in his test booklet.

The speaking test gives instructions and questions on a tape and the student records his spoken responses on another tape. "He repeats ....short statements that he hears; he reads from a printed script; he answers spoken questions that refer to simple line drawings; and he describes, at some length, a picture or series of pictures that convey a message or story."

The reading test consists of 50 multiple choice items of two types. Approximately one-half of the items are incomplete sentences. These items seem to require only reading comprehension since the selection of the correct choice depends on the meaning of the context and the choices, and the distractors must be rejected on the basis of their meaning rather than grammatical incorrectness. The remaining items test comprehension of paragraphs selected from periodicals and appropriate literary sources. The paragraphs of the L forms are simple, straightforward factual prose free from archaisms. Those of the M forms are slightly longer and more literary but still clearly within the style limits that a student can be expected to understand if he has succeeded in learning.

The writing test breaks up the skill into five partial tasks that are involved in writing. They are (1) filling a blank with a word that fits the context lexically and grammatically. There are 24 items of these, requiring such words as *a, la, del, que, es, le,* etc. Only one of these seems dubious in each L form (LA item 3, LB item 3) because it requires a lexical item representing a cultural choice rather than a grammatical one. Forms MA and MB have twenty items each in this section. They all require grammatically and lexically determined words or in some cases words required as part of an idiom. (2) The second task is to supply the appropriate verb form in a sentence. The items cleverly obviate the need for using the technical names of the tenses by giving a base sentence with two verbs and providing a transformed sentence with the test verb left blank. The student knows what tense is required by analogy with the one supplied. The example makes this clear:

> Primero como y luego trabajo
> Primero comí y luego *trabajé*

In this fashion the test requires that the student use tenses that are difficult, e.g., the subjunctive, the imperfect indicative, etc. (3) In the third type of task the student has to rewrite a sentence changing the number, gender and/or person to agree with one word that has been changed. Again no grammatical terminology is necessary: if the word is the 3rd person singular pronoun *él,* and the base sentence is in 1st person plural *nosotros* the response must change the sentence accordingly. Each form has eight items of this type.

The first three parts can be scored objectively since only one response per item is fully acceptable. The fourth and fifth tasks are obviously intended to approximate actual writing more closely, and they allow more than one acceptable answer. This is commendable in the crucial problem of developing a valid test, but it represents the loss of fully objective scoring. In task (4) several content words are given and the student has to write a complete sentence in Spanish using all of the words in the order given, changing their form if necessary and adding other necessary words. For example,

> Libro/mesa/sala
> Tus libros están en una mesa en la sala

This sample item could be answered correctly in many different ways, e.g., *Los libros de mi hermano habían quedado sobre la mesa monumental detrás de la Sala.* This response is within the 7 to 15 word limit of the instructions. It uses more complicated tenses and phrase structure. The problem is how do we score this if a mistake is made in an element that the simpler answer did not attempt? It may well be that if this student had attempted the simpler sentence he might have been successful.

The last task (5) is to write a six- or seven-line dialogue using a given expression in each line. The scoring on this part is done on a four-slot scale (5, 3, 1, 0) applied separately on five variables: coverage of elements, correct word, sentences and phrases meaningful in themselves, sentences and phrases contributing to paragraph meaning, and general quality. As the scale and variables clearly show, there is room for considerable subjectivity in scoring this part in spite of the controls imposed by the expressions and the particular speakers and situation given.

The test norms are given for first through fourth year high school and first through second year of college. The first and second year high school norms for reading and writing are given separately for traditional and audio-lingual classes. Audio-lingual norms for first and second year high school are given only for audio-lingual classes. Third and fourth year high school norms and those for first and second year college are for undifferentiated groups as to teaching method and are called "general." The number of cases in the norming samples seems small in several cases. It would seem that establishing national percentile norms on samples of less than 100 cases must be taken as very preliminary. Such is the case with the listening and speaking, L level, high school audio-lingual norms, first year (91 students), second year (95 students) ; listening and speaking, level M, high school general norms, third year (58 students), fourth year (79 students).

The norms show a steady progression from first through fourth year high school Spanish and from first through second year college. This progression must be assumed to include a factor of selection of students as they advance to the later years.

Reliability is high for all the tests. This is particularly noticeable for the speaking and the writing tests, which one would expect to have lower reliabilities due to the subjective scoring. The reliability of both these tests was computed on samples with greater spread of language study (college and high school samples were included), but even so, the highest reliability is that reported for LB Writing (.96) which did not include college grades.

SUMMARY. It is obvious that the MLA tests represent a major effort and accomplishment of the profession. They give fully equal status to the audio-lingual skills (listening and speaking) ; they do away with translation altogether ; they introduce items that approximate actual functional use of the language ; they are objective for the most part ; and they are professionally developed and standardized.

With these credentials the tests can be recommended and used confidently. Naturally, they are not everything we might need, and their limitations must be pointed out. They are diagnostic as to the four skills—i.e., they show separate scores for them, but they are not diagnostic in detail (nor were they designed to be) within each skill. They are general level tests and may be used as achievement tests in general but not as the single achievement measure for a particular course. They are not speed tests, and they are not exhaustive power tests ; they are based on samples on which typical performance may be measured.

The norms are internal and relative for the population of students intended. They do not tell us if a student will know enough to perform well in typical real life use of the language with native speakers. The cost of scoring the speaking and writing tests limits their use on a mass scale. Finally, the absence of new forms will eventually diminish their usefulness through possible compromise of the present forms.

For an excerpted review of the series, see 254.

[323]

*National Spanish Examination. 1, 2, 3, 4, 5 years junior high school and high school ; 1957–70 ; NSE ; new form issued annually for administration in April at local secondary schools or centers established by local chapters of the AATSP ; 4 scores : aural, usage, reading comprehension, total ; 5 levels ; Forms O1S, O2S, O3S, O4S, O5S, ('70, 4 pages) used in 1970 program ; tape recording (7½ ips, 7 inch reel) for each level of aural subtest ; directions for administering ['70, 3 pages, mimeographed] ; no data on reliability ; summary of results (based on locally scored papers returned to the test development committee) is published in *Hispania* in September following the testing program ; 15¢ per test ; separate answer sheets may be used ; $5.50 per tape recording ; postpaid ; answer sheets must be obtained locally ; copies of previous year's tests and tapes available at the same prices ; 70(90) minutes ; [Test Development Committee, American Association of Teachers of Spanish and Portuguese] ; the Association (distributed by local chapter treasurers and the national chairman). *

REFERENCES
1–8. See 6:428.
9. CHARLY, HARRY T. "History of the AATSP National Spanish Examination Program." *Hispania* 50:857–9 D '67. *

WALTER V. KAULFERS, *Professor of Foreign Language Education, University of Illinois, Urbana, Illinois.* [Review of 1969 and 1970 forms.]

Since March 1957, some 25,000 *National Spanish Examinations* have been administered yearly as a basis for allocating the 300 awards sanctioned by the American Association of Teachers of Spanish and Portuguese. Because of the AATSP Test Development Committee's 14-year experience in the preparation of objective achievement tests, the examinations reveal a high level of expertise in test construction. The directions are clear, the Spanish is idiomatic, and the high-fidelity tape recordings are impeccable in diction and intonation.

Since new examinations have to be prepared each year, time limitations prevent standardization of the tests in such a way as to make them comparable in reliability, validity, and difficulty to those of previous years. That the examinations are not statistically comparable is revealed in the variations in medians and means since

1957. In 1957, for example, the mean for the 100-item Level 3 Examination (first or second semester of the third year) was 73.4 while in 1965 it was 57.57—a difference of nearly 16 points.

Inspection of the medians, means, and percentile distributions of scores for the 1969 tests (structured along lines similar to those of 1970) leads the reviewer to believe that the reliability of the examinations as a whole should be .85 or better. It is unfortunate that coefficients of reliability have not actually been reported for previous years, since the tests for the preceding term are commonly available for use either as achievement tests or as means for acquainting prospective contestants with the general nature and scope of the *National Spanish Examinations* for the current academic year. Where the previous year's examination is used as an achievement test, the median, mean, and percentile distribution of scores can serve as norms in evaluating individual achievement.

In any case, tryout of prospective contestants on one or more earlier examinations is strongly recommended for the following reasons:

a) The oral directions for some of the subtests of auditory discrimination and aural comprehension are given only once on tape and hence promote a feeling of insecurity because of their complexity. Note, for example, the following exclusively oral directions for Part 1 of the 1970 Auditory Discrimination Test:

For each item you will hear a series of three words. If all three words are identical in sound, mark *A* on your answer sheet or in your test booklet. If two of the words are identical and a third is different, indicate your choice of answer as *B*. If all three are different, mark answer *C*. Each set of words will be read once.

Note also the insecurity that the following directions for the true-false section are likely to produce when given only once orally, exclusively on tape, without printed confirmation of the directions on the students' answer sheets:

You will now hear a series of simple statements in Spanish. Select the letter *A* on your answer sheet or in your test booklet if the statement is generally true. Select the letter *B* if the statement is logically false. Select the letter *C* if the statement could be considered either true or false, or is only partially true.

The reviewer feels strongly that student response on these parts of the test may in many cases be as much a measure of ability to comprehend and remember the directions as of actual performance in Spanish. In fact, some of the items require a level of philosophical

discrimination comparable to that needed to make a value judgment between tweedledee and tweedledum.

b) The voices on the tapes are those of adult males. Students who have been taught exclusively by women teachers, with little opportunity to hear other than feminine voices in Spanish, may find themselves disadvantaged without advance practice using the tests for a previous year.

c) The pronunciation on the tapes is exclusively Highland Latin American. Students who have been taught the pronunciation of Castile or have grown up in families of Castilian descent may find themselves somewhat disadvantaged if they have not had frequent exposure to pronunciation different from that of Old or New Castile. The difference in pronunciation and intonation is in some respects as great as the difference between Oxford English and Midwest American.

If the reviewer has any specific suggestion for the improvement of the examinations (beyond those implied in the preceding paragraphs), it is that the Auditory Discrimination subtest be eliminated. It is essentially a *diagnostic* test of aural acuity. As such it does not belong in a functional test of actual ability to use Spanish in connected discourse in everyday life. Diagnostic tests have their place in locating the *reasons* for inferior or superior performance, not in evaluating achievement or performance itself.

[324]

★**National Teacher Examinations: Spanish.** College seniors and teachers; 1970-71; modified version of secure form of *MLA Foreign Language Proficiency Tests for Teachers and Advanced Students: Spanish;* Form TNT1 ('71, 19 pages); descriptive booklet ('70, 8 pages); listening comprehension section administered by 3¾ ips tape recording; for more complete information, see 582; 120(165) minutes; Educational Testing Service. *

For reviews of the testing program, see 582 (2 reviews), 6:700 (1 review), 5:538 (3 reviews), and 4:802 (1 review).

[325]

★**Pimsleur Spanish Proficiency Tests.** First, second level courses in grades 7-12 or first, second semesters college; 1967; 4 scores: listening, speaking, reading, writing; 1 form; 2 levels labeled Forms A, C; manual (23 pages); no college norms; $1.75 per manual; $1.75 per specimen set (without tapes or manual); postage extra; Paul Pimsleur; Harcourt Brace Jovanovich, Inc. *
a) TEST I, LISTENING COMPREHENSION. Digitek, IBM 805, and IBM 1230 test-answer sheets (2 pages);

7½ ips test tape, 5 inch reel; $7.50 per test tape; $3.80 per 35 test-answer sheets; $1.40 per set of scoring stencils; IBM scoring service, 33¢ and over per test; 15(25) minutes.
b) TEST 2, SPEAKING PROFICIENCY. Test (4 pages); scoring sheet (2 pages); 7½ ips test tape, 5 inch reel; $7.50 per test tape; $4.50 per 35 tests; $2.70 per 35 scoring sheets; 16(26) minutes.
c) TEST 3, READING COMPREHENSION. Test (4 pages); separate answer sheets (Digitek-IBM 805, IBM 1230) must be used; $4.50 per 35 tests; $2.30 per 35 Digitek-IBM 805 answer sheets; $2.80 per 35 IBM 1230 answer sheets; 70¢ per scoring stencil; IBM scoring service, 19¢ and over per test; 35(45) minutes.
d) TEST 4, WRITING PROFICIENCY. Test (6 pages); answer key and scoring directions (4 pages); $7.40 per 35 tests; 35(45) minutes.

GINO PARISI, *Assistant Professor of Spanish, Georgetown University, Washington, D.C.*

The emphasis during the sixties on teaching the four skills, which brought about fundamental changes in textbooks and methodology, has obviously influenced the writers of these tests. It has become acceptable to discuss the four skills as independent areas. Yet the feasibility of such a separation is open to question. As pointed out in the manual, "The four tests.... do not measure the individual skills in isolation * The teacher must therefore be alert to the possibilities of interaction among the skills in evaluating performance."

Prospective users of these tests should become thoroughly acquainted with the manual beforehand. Its description of the tests and various tables give a clear idea of the abilities measured in the four tests, each of which will be taken up in turn below.

PASSIVE SKILLS: LISTENING COMPREHENSION. In the 20 items of the first part, or Side 1, the student hears a short sentence once and must match it with the correct written form by choosing among four possibilities. The tapes are clear, with male and female voices alternating; pronunciation is Spanish-American. The four choices are often subtle, differing only by a phoneme, a syllable, or an intonation pattern indicated by the punctuation. A considerable amount of rapid reading is required. Recognizing individual differences in mental processes, one might assume that some students would continue repeating silently what they heard as they scan the four options. In such a case, the written sentences might cause a student to forget or confuse what he heard. Furthermore, the slow or careless reader might be handicapped even if he understood the Spanish perfectly, especially when the correct choice was the fourth one listed.

Another factor relative to the validity of items of this type is the difficulty of perceiving minimal differences unaided by context. The formal test situation provides none of the code redundancy that characterizes natural conversation and facilitates comprehension.

The 20 items of Side 2 are based less on fine distinctions. They consist of oral sentences to be matched by suitable rejoinders, chosen from four printed possibilities. As in Side 1, the reading factor is important, but here the procedure seems more reasonable because the correct rejoinder is completely different from the incorrect ones and therefore easily distinguishable.

It is unfortunate that listening and reading are combined in this test. Understandably, the burden on one's memory would be excessive if the four choices were presented orally. On the other hand, if this test were presented entirely in written form, it would be false to attribute a student's mistakes to either a listening deficiency or a reading deficiency. He simply would not know the items, regardless of the skill involved.

An idea of the difficulty of the levels can be formed from a comparison of the verb tenses used in each test. The first level (Form A) uses mostly present tense in both parts, with an occasional preterite or imperfect form. In the second level (Form C), the first part consists of slightly more than half present tense and the remainder preterite, imperfect, and present perfect; in the second part, about three-fourths of the verbs are in the present and one-fourth are in the preterite. This information is not included in the manual for the Listening test.

PASSIVE SKILLS: READING COMPREHENSION. In this test the student reads short passages of one to nine sentences followed by three questions with four-choice answers. Form A uses simple narratives, dialogues, and letters. Vocabulary and verb forms seem appropriate. Form C also includes literary, historical, and cultural examples; the prose is more sophisticated.

Ability to draw inferences as well as to understand literal meaning is tested. The manual provides a table which classifies the questions according to these two factors. A reasonable knowledge of synonyms is required, but meanings are straightforward and the authors have avoided the type of item in which all interpretation hinges on an unusual idiom or a punch line.

This is a fairly traditional type of test and easily controlled. Based on samples of from 500 to 2,340 students per grade from grades 8 to 12, split-half reliability coefficients range from .83 to .88, a natural consequence of the complete objectivity of scoring. The lower figures of .72 to .83 for the Listening test, also objectively scored, may be attributable to the many skills tested simultaneously.

Table 10 of the manual gives the results of a comparison of the Listening and Reading tests. For Form A, based on over 5,000 subjects, the mean score for Listening is 19.8 (50% of possible score) and for Reading, 13.6 (38%); and the correlation between the two is .60. These figures should be interpreted carefully for many reasons. They imply that students perform better in listening than in reading, but such a conclusion would be a result of the assumption that the two tests are testing the same material in different form, an assumption not borne out by close examination. In length, variety, and complexity, the Reading test is more advanced than the Listening test. No significant conclusions can be drawn unless the two tests deal with the same level of material. Nor is it valid to argue that the reading skill requires a more developed vocabulary than the listening skill. Because of the elementary level of these tests, all its vocabulary could be called conversational. The major difference between these two tests is one of quantity. The student clearly has to know more Spanish for the Reading test.

ACTIVE SKILLS: WRITING PROFICIENCY. Part 1 consists of a dialogue, with missing items to be supplied from the context. Form A contains 19 items; Form C contains 26, with longer sentences and more advanced syntax. The words required are mostly prepositions, articles, and pronouns, plus a few verbs.

Here again the overlapping of the separate tests is apparent. The missing words are no more peculiar to writing than to speaking. Their inclusion in this section is obviously due to the practical consideration of control. A student might be able to produce these forms in writing without having the necessary fluency to speak them; on the other hand, if a student did not know these forms in writing it is safe to assume that he would not be able to use them in speaking either. Thus the relation between writing and speaking, if only measurable negatively through mistakes, is real and could be made explicit if the techniques were available.

This observation is equally applicable to Parts 2 and 3. Part 2 tests recognition (reading) and production (writing) of verb forms in 10 items. In Form A the student is expected to recognize the tense used in one part of the sentence and match it by conjugating the infinitive given in the other part. In Form C the student changes a verb from one tense to another on cue. One item which calls for a choice between preterite or imperfect seems ambiguous.

These devices to test control and usage of verb forms are an improvement over the once common practice of asking for a specific tense of a verb given in parentheses. Yet they require recognition before production and thus serve to underline the difficulty of separating active and passive skills.

Part 3 of both forms consists of nine items of the pattern drill type, involving cued changes in number and gender. The directions for correction specify that copying errors are not to be considered. Since such items could easily be tested orally, there seems to be no reason for calling this a test of writing rather than speaking proficiency.

At issue is not the relevance of a given ability to the skill being tested, but rather the implication that such an ability is more relevant to one skill than to another. Indeed, pattern drills are usually associated with oral practice and involve both active and passive skills.

Part 4, Form A, asks the student to write one sentence about each of four pictures and a three-sentence description of a larger picture. Form C is similar to Form A, except that eight pictures tell a story which must be written in the past tense. For scoring there is a factor guide which gives credit for content, verb formation and usage, and structure. Instructions for scoring are detailed, mentioning completeness of story, vocabulary, phrasing, smoothness, word order, spelling, tense usage, and many other aspects.

Obviously, the most important consideration in Part 4 is scorer reliability. The manual gives data based on two studies, one involving the same scorer and a set of 82 tests corrected at two different times, and another involving two scorers and a set of 50 tests. Correlations are high: .96 for the first study and .94 for the second. The conclusion arrived at in the manual is the following: "Although the extremely high correlation coefficients and the marked agreements in means and standard deviations may reflect to a certain extent the training and backgrounds of the scorers, classroom teachers should also be able to achieve high reliability in scoring *if they follow carefully and conscientiously the prescribed scoring system* [italics added]." This is far from convincing. First, as is frankly stated in the manual, the coefficients are based on figures treated as though the total of points arrived at by applying scoring standards (Part 4) is comparable to a number of separate items answered correctly (Parts 1, 2 and 3). Second, the classroom teacher may not be highly trained. And third, objectivity is difficult when a teacher knows the students whose work he is evaluating. The only valid conclusion is that there is a *possibility* of high scoring reliability, subject to the important variables of care, conscience, training, and background. These are precisely the qualities one expects in a standardized test. It does not seem fair to shift the responsibility to the teacher. It would be safer to use the scoring service provided by the publishers and trust that all the trained scorers are equally competent. For writing proficiency (and speaking proficiency) there continues to be a need for reliability studies involving significant numbers of scorers. Indeed, elimination of scorer subjectivity should be the goal. As long as the teacher is required to use his own judgment he might operate more effectively within the framework of classroom tests which he could control according to his particular needs.

ACTIVE SKILLS: SPEAKING PROFICIENCY. In Part 1 of both forms the student is asked to record without the article the names of 27 pictured items. Directions for correcting instruct the scorer that "pronunciation need not be perfect, but the word must be readily understandable." The format dictates that all the items be concrete nouns.

A voice on the master tape paces the student by reading numbers, so that a reasonable speed of response is maintained. Aside from this, what is tested is vocabulary, and the omission of the article does not seem well advised. A sure control of gender is certainly essential for speaking.

Part 2 tests pronunciation by having the student first listen to all of 20 sentences of two to seven words as he reads them in the test booklet. Then he records all the sentences as a voice reads the numbers, again controlling the speed. What is being tested, rather than simple pronunciation, is ability to read orally.

The scoring focuses on two sounds in each sentence, disregarding all other elements. Test results would be affected if a student trained to read had had any oral practice, since some of the mistakes anticipated involve pronouncing Spanish letters ("silent h") as in English. A suggested improvement would be to lengthen the test so that the student would have more than one sentence devoted to each sound. This repetition would allow discrimination between those who never mispronounce, those who sometimes mispronounce, and those who habitually mispronounce.

Part 3, Form A, includes eight taped questions to be answered orally by the student, preferably in complete sentences, and in the present tense. In Form C five answers are in the present and three in the past tense. Some of the questions are personal and would require answers of varying length from different individuals. Listening ability is a factor in this section.

The answer tape runs 6 to 7 minutes, including only the student's responses for Parts 1 and 2, and both questions and answers for Part 3.

As noted above, very little can be said about scorer reliability for this test. No norms are given, and no scoring service is available. When one considers that to correct 100 test tapes—a reasonable number for high school—the teacher would have to spend about 13 hours, there is little advantage in using this test. A good teacher could probably evaluate his students' pronunciation informally with as much accuracy. There is no need to consider the poor teacher; he would have difficulty correcting the tapes objectively in any event.

For the teacher the promise of a standardized test is uniformity and ease of correction. A test which shifts the burden of reliability back on the teacher does not answer any purpose. It has only the appearance of objectivity. The teacher's evaluation is at least frankly subjective and therefore more honest. The teacher should be aware of the problems connected with standardization of speaking (and writing) proficiency tests and not assume that they have been solved yet.

CONCLUSION. The eight tests of this series cover about one-half of a complete language course, judging by the fact that virtually no subjunctives have been included. They have been carefully developed, the Spanish is consistently appropriate, and many pertinent statistical tables are published in the manual. They can be said to represent the best of the past decade; but if we are to take seriously the publisher's promise—"A new decade, a new challenge. Old concepts must go and new ones take their place"—these tests must be judged unsatisfactory. Face validity is still the guiding factor in many cases: the student speaks for a speaking test; he writes for a writing test.

The chief shortcoming is the overlapping of the abilities in the separate tests. This stems from the framework which dictates that the four skills can or should be tested independently, creating a problem of validity for all tests and of reliability for Speaking and Writing. Perhaps a new approach will focus on the elements or abilities rather than the skills. In the search for new techniques, the following questions may be kept in mind: (*a*) What is the approximate range of the student's vocabulary? (*b*) Is there any difference between his oral and written command of this vocabulary? (*c*) How does his active vocabulary compare to his passive vocabulary? (*d*) At what speed of delivery is he competent in listening? (*e*) How much code noise can he tolerate? (*f*) Is he able to distinguish between Spanish and non-Spanish—e.g., how many of the following are not Spanish nouns: *masa, maso, casa, caso?* (*g*) Does he know the patterns of derivation as well as all the words to which they apply—e.g., is it *conocimento* or *conocimiento?* (*h*) How secure is his command of verbs, oral or written? (*i*) How correct is his pronunciation? (*j*) Does he command both formal and informal styles? The new tests may try to tell us first *what* the student knows, then *how* he is able to manifest that knowledge.

J Ed Meas 6(*1*):48–50 sp '69. E. E. Bilyeu. * basically well constructed and contain many excellent testing techniques. However, they do not completely avoid some of the pitfalls common to standardized testing. There is a lack of procedure from the simple to the complex in each part of the tests as well as from Form A to Form C. With few exceptions, the testing techniques of the two forms are identical, and

Level C is not always sufficiently more difficult than Level A. Indeed, many of the test items appear without change in both forms. For example, items 31 through 36 of the Reading Comprehension Test of Form A are repeated as items 1 through 6 of Form C. In the Listening and the Reading Comprehension Tests the questions are multiple choice. In enough test items to be of some concern, two of the four alternatives could be considered logical responses. To illustrate: in an item the student hears "¿Qué hay allí?" (What's over there?). Two of the four alternatives are easily eliminated, leaving "No tiene nada" and "No veo nada." A student might legitimately argue that "He has nothing" is as logical an answer as "I see nothing." Once an oral statement or a reading passage has been understood, it is desirable that the correct response be readily apparent and that the matter of student conjecture be eliminated. One minor problem pertains only to Part I of the Listening Comprehension Test. The student hears a statement and from four similar sentences printed on the answer sheet he must choose the one he heard. For example, he hears: "Caminó hacia la universidad." He reads: Caminó hasta la universidad, Caminó hacia la universidad, Camino hasta la universidad, Camino hacia la universidad. If it occurs to the student to read ahead in order to identify the areas of contrast and to listen attentively to *only* those areas, he will have a distinct advantage over the student who fails to make the analogy in time and who continues to treat all of the sounds of all four sentences as problems demanding his attention as he attempts to remember what he has heard. Thus, the possibility exists that the student's success may relate directly to his ability to discover a test-taking technique. The above item reveals another problem of greater concern—the interdependence of skills. Although, in the above example, the student must correctly perceive the oral stimulus, his success, nevertheless, depends upon his ability to relate what he has heard to the graphic representation. The emphasis upon visual perception is so great that the student who has been taught by an intensive audio-lingual approach, with little emphasis on reading and writing, will find himself at a distinct disadvantage. Of greater significance is the over emphasis throughout the tests on the student's knowledge of vocabulary. Reference is not made here to those areas of the test which are constructed to test vocabulary knowledge, but rather to certain parts of the tests which are designed to measure a comprehensive skill, but in which the student's success is dependent upon his knowledge of a particular vocabulary item. The problem is particularly prevalent in the Listening and in the Reading Comprehension Tests. In many cases it is possible that the student may have understood the oral statement or the reading passage, yet may answer the test item incorrectly because a particular word among the alternatives is unfamiliar to him. One example, chosen at random from many, will illustrate the point. One reading passage discusses the return of a student from Peru. To successfully complete one of the following test items the student must know the idioms *acabar de* (to have just) and *hacer un viaje* (to take a trip), neither of which appears in the reading passage. Thus, the item does not actually measure the student's ability to read and understand the passage, but rather assesses his knowledge of vocabulary equivalency. In spite of the above problems, the Pimsleur tests are a good measure of the basic skills of listen-ing, speaking, reading and writing. Representative samples of most of the major structures of the language are included, and matters of sound, order, form, and choice are adequately tested. Particularly excellent are the Writing Proficiency Tests and the Fluency portions of the Speaking Tests. Much thought and considerable effort clearly have been employed in constructing all the tests. Certainly, they must be recognized as a worthwhile contribution to the profession.

[326]

*Second Year Spanish Test. High school and college; 1953–68; SYST; revision of *Kansas Second Year Spanish Test;* Form A ('68, 4 pages); manual ('68, 2 pages); no data on reliability; $1.75 per 25 tests, postage extra; 75¢ per specimen set, postpaid; 50(55) minutes; Oscar F. Hernández and Minnie M. Miller; Data Processing and Educational Measurement Center. *

[327]

★The Undergraduate Record Examinations: Spanish Test. College; 1969–70; Form K-RUR ('69, 17 pages); descriptive booklet ('70, 8 pages); for more complete information, see 671; 120(140) minutes; Educational Testing Service. *

For reviews of the testing program, see 671 (2 reviews).

TIP II SCANNING INDEX

This classified index of all tests in *Tests in Print II* can be used to determine what tests are available in areas besides foreign language. Citations are to test entry numbers in TIP II. The population for which a test is intended is included. Stars indicate tests not previously listed in an MMY; asterisks indicate tests revised or supplemented since last listed. The foreign language portion of this index, the only part relevant to this monograph, is repeated at the end of this volume.

ACHIEVEMENT BATTERIES

Academic Proficiency Battery [South Africa], college entrants, see 1

Adult Basic Education Student Survey, poorly educated adults in basic education classes, see 2

Adult Basic Learning Examination, adults with achievement levels grades 1–12, see 3

American School Achievement Tests, grades 1–9, see 4

Bristol Achievement Tests [England], ages 8–13, see 5

*CLEP General Examinations: Humanities, 1–2 years of college or equivalent, see 6

*California Achievement Tests, grades 1–14, see 7

Canadian Tests of Basic Skills [Canada], grades 3–8, see 8

Classification and Placement Examination, grade 8 and high school entrants, see 9

*College-Level Examination Program General Examinations, 1–2 years of college or equivalent, see 10

*Comprehensive Tests of Basic Skills, grades kgn–12, see 11

Cooperative Primary Tests, grades 1.5–3, see 12

★Educational Skills Tests: College Edition, open-door college entrants, see 13

General Tests of Language and Arithmetic [South Africa], standards 5–7, see 14

Gray-Votaw-Rogers General Achievement Tests, grades 1–9, see 15

★Guidance Test for Junior Secondary Bantu Pupils in Form 3 [South Africa], see 16

High School Fundamentals Evaluation Test, grades 9–12, see 17

Iowa High School Content Examination, grades 11–13, see 18

*Iowa Tests of Basic Skills, grades 1.7–9, see 19

*Iowa Tests of Educational Development, grades 9–12, see 20

Ligondé Equivalence Test [Canada], adults who left elementary or secondary school 15–20 years ago, see 21

*Metropolitan Achievement Tests, grades kgn–9, see 22

National Achievement Tests, grades 4–9, see 23

*National Educational Development Tests, grades 7–10, see 24

*National Teacher Examinations: Common Examinations, college seniors and teachers, see 25

Peabody Individual Achievement Test, grades kgn–12, see 26

★Primary Survey Tests, grades 2–3, see 27

Public School Achievement Tests, grades 3–8, see 28

*SRA Achievement Series, grades 1–9, see 29

*SRA Assessment Survey, grades 1–12, see 30

*SRA High School Placement Test, grade 9 entrants, see 31

*STS Closed High School Placement Test, grade 9 entrants, see 32

*STS Educational Development Series, grades 2–12, see 33

*Scholastic Proficiency Battery [South Africa], standards 8–10, see 34

*Sequential Tests of Educational Progress, grades 4–14, see 35

*Stanford Achievement Test, grades 1.5–9, see 36

Stanford Achievement Test: High School Basic Battery, grades 9–12, see 37

*Stanford Early School Achievement Test, grades kgn–1.5, see 38

★Stanford Test of Academic Skills, grades 8–12 and first year junior/community college, see 39

Survey of College Achievement, grades 13–14, see 40

*Teacher Education Examination Program: General Professional Examinations, college seniors preparing to teach, see 41

*Test for High School Entrants, high school entrants, see 42

Test of Reading and Number: Inter-American Series, grade 4 entrants, see 43

*Tests of Academic Progress, grades 9–12, see 44

ENGLISH

Test of English Usage [India], English-speaking high school and college students and adults, see 118
Tests of Academic Progress: Composition, grades 9–12, see 119
Tests of Basic Experiences: Language, prekgn–grade 1, see 120
Tressler English Minimum Essentials Test, grades 8–12, see 121
Walton-Sanders English Test, 1–2 semesters in grades 9–13, see 122
Watson English Usage and Appreciation Test [Canada], grades 4–8, see 123
Writing Skills Test, grades 9–12, see 124
Writing Test: McGraw-Hill Basic Skills System, grades 11–14, see 125

LITERATURE

American Literature Anthology Tests, high school, see 126
★*CLEP Subject Examination in American Literature,* 1 year or equivalent, see 127
CLEP Subject Examination in Analysis and Interpretation of Literature, 1 year or equivalent, see 128
CLEP Subject Examination in English Literature, 1 year or equivalent, see 129
College Board Achievement Test in Literature, candidates for college entrance, see 130
College Placement Test in Literature, entering college freshmen, see 131
★*Cooperative Literature Tests,* grades 9–12, see 132
English Literature Anthology Tests, high school, see 133
English Tests for Outside Reading, grades 9–12, see 134
Graduate Record Examinations Advanced Literature in English Test, graduate school candidates, see 135
Hollingsworth-Sanders Junior High School Literature Test, grades 7–8, see 136
Hoskins-Sanders Literature Test, 1–2 semesters in grades 9–13, see 137
Iowa Tests of Educational Development: Ability to Interpret Literary Materials, grades 9–12, see 138
Literature Test: National Achievement Tests, grades 7–12, see 139
Literature Tests/Objective, high school, see 140
Look at Literature: NCTE Cooperative Test of Critical Reading and Appreciation, grades 4–6, see 141
★*Poetry Test/Objective,* grades 7–12, see 142
Tests of Academic Progress: Literature, grades 9–12, see 143
Undergraduate Program Field Tests: Literature Tests, college, see 144
★*World Literature Anthology Tests,* high school, see 145

SPELLING

Buckingham Extension of the Ayres Spelling Scale, grades 2–9, see 146

★*Correct Spelling,* grades 10–13, see 147
Group Diagnostic Spelling Test, grades 9–13, see 148
Iowa Spelling Scales, grades 2–8, see 149
Kansas Spelling Tests, grades 3–8, see 150
Kelvin Measurement of Spelling Ability [Scotland], ages 7–12, see 151
Lincoln Diagnostic Spelling Tests, grades 2–12, see 152
N.B. Spelling Tests [South Africa], standards 1–10 for English pupils and 3–10 for Afrikaans pupils, see 153
Nationwide Spelling Examination, grades 4–12, see 154
New Iowa Spelling Scale, grades 2–8, see 155
Sanders-Fletcher Spelling Test, 1–2 semesters in grades 9–13, see 156
Spelling: Differential Aptitude Tests, grades 8–12 and adults, see 157
Spelling Errors Test, grades 2–8, see 158
Spelling Test for Clerical Workers, stenographic applicants and high school, see 159
Spelling Test: McGraw-Hill Basic Skills System, grades 11–14, see 160
Spelling Test: National Achievement Tests, grades 3–12, see 161
Traxler High School Spelling Test, grades 9–12, see 162

VOCABULARY

A.C.E.R. Word Knowledge Test [Australia], ages 18 and over, see 163
American Literacy Test, adults, see 164
Bruce Vocabulary Inventory, business and industry, see 165
Iowa Tests of Educational Development: General Vocabulary, grades 9–12, see 166
Johnson O'Connor English Vocabulary Worksamples, ages 9 and over, see 167
Johnson O'Connor Vocabulary Tests, professionals, see 168
Nationwide English Vocabulary Examination, grades 4–12, see 169
Purdue Industrial Supervisors Word-Meaning Test, supervisors, see 170
RBH Vocabulary Test, applicants for clerical and stenographic positions, see 171
Sanders-Fletcher Vocabulary Test, 1–2 semesters in grades 9–13, see 172
Survey Test of Vocabulary, grades 3–12, see 173
Test of Active Vocabulary, grades 9–12, see 174
★*Vocabulary Survey Test,* grades kgn–1, see 175
Vocabulary Test for High School Students and College Freshmen, grades 9–13, see 176
Vocabulary Test: McGraw-Hill Basic Skills System, grades 11–14, see 177
Vocabulary Test: National Achievement Tests, grades 3–12, see 178
Wide Range Vocabulary Test, ages 8 and over, see 179
Word Clue Tests, grades 7–13 and adults, see 180
Word Dexterity Test, grades 7–16, see 181
Word Understanding, grades 6–12, see 182

FINE ARTS

ART

★*Advanced Placement Examination in Art,* high school students desiring credit for college level courses or admission to advanced courses, see 183

Art Vocabulary, grades 6–12, see 184
Graves Design Judgment Test, grades 7–16 and adults, see 185
Horn Art Aptitude Inventory, grades 12–16 and adults, see 186

MUSIC

FOREIGN LANGUAGES

ARABIC

CHINESE

ENGLISH

FRENCH

GERMAN

GREEK

HEBREW

ITALIAN

LATIN

RUSSIAN

SPANISH

INTELLIGENCE

GROUP

INDIVIDUAL

Passalong Test: A Performance Test of Intelligence, ages 8 and over, see 515
Peabody Picture Vocabulary Test, ages 2.5–18, see 516
Pictorial Test of Intelligence, ages 3–8, see 517
Porteus Maze Test, ages 3 and over, see 518
Preschool Attainment Record, ages 6 months to 7 years, see 519
Queensland Test [Australia], ages 7 and over, see 520
Quick Screening Scale of Mental Development, ages 6 months to 10 years, see 521
Quick Test, ages 2 and over, see 522
Ring and Peg Tests of Behavior Development, birth to age 6, see 523
Slosson Intelligence Test, ages 2 weeks and over, see 524
*Stanford-Binet Intelligence Scale, ages 2 and over, see 525; *Clinical Profile for the Stanford Binet Intelligence Scale (L–M),* ages 5 and over, see 526
Stanford-Ohwaki-Kohs Block Design Intelligence Test for the Blind, blind and partially sighted ages 16 and over, see 527
Vane Kindergarten Test, ages 4–6, see 528
Wechsler Adult Intelligence Scale, ages 16 and over, see 529; *Rhodes WAIS Scatter Profile,* see 530; ★*WAIS Test Profile,* see 531
Wechsler-Bellevue Intelligence Scale, ages 10 and over, see 532
Wechsler Intelligence Scale for Children, ages 5–15, see 533; *California Abbreviated WISC,* educable mentally retarded ages 8–13.5 and intellectually gifted elementary school children, see 534; *Rhodes WISC Scatter Profile,* see 535; ★*WISC Mental Description Sheet,* see 536; ★*WISC Test Profile,* see 537
Wechsler Preschool and Primary Scale of Intelligence, ages 4–6.5, see 538; ★*WPPSI Test Profile,* see 539
Williams Intelligence Test for Children With Defective Vision [England], blind and partially sighted ages 5–15, see 540

SPECIFIC

★*Abstract Spatial Relations Test* [South Africa], Bantu industrial workers with 0–12 years of education, see 541
Alternate Uses, grades 6–16 and adults, see 542
Benton Visual Retention Test, ages 8 and over, see 543
★*Biographical Inventory—Creativity,* "adolescents and young adults," see 544
Block-Design Test, mental ages 5–20, see 545
*Christensen-Guilford Fluency Tests, grades 7–16 and adults, see 546
Closure Flexibility (Concealed Figures), industrial employees, see 547
Closure Speed (Gestalt Completion), industrial employees, see 548
Concept Assessment Kit—Conservation, ages 4–7, see 549
★*Concept Attainment Test* [South Africa], college and adults, see 550

Consequences, grades 9–16 and adults, see 551
★*Consequences* [South Africa], ages 15 and over, see 552
★*Creativity Attitude Survey,* grades 4–6, see 553
★*Creativity Tests for Children,* grades 4–6, see 554
Decorations, grades 9–16 and adults, see 555
Feature Profile Test: Pintner-Paterson Modification, ages 4 and over, see 556
★*Gottschaldt Figures* [South Africa], job applicants with at least 10 years of education, see 557
Healy Pictorial Completion Tests, ages 5 and over, see 558
Hidden Figures Test, grades 6–16, see 559
Higgins-Wertman Test: Threshold of Visual Closure, ages 5–15, see 560
Jensen Alternation Board, ages 5 and over, see 560A
Kit of Reference Tests for Cognitive Factors, grades 6–16, see 561
Making Objects, grades 9–16 and adults, see 562
Manikin Test, ages 2 and over, see 563
Match Problems, grades 9–16 and adults, see 564
*Match Problems 5, grades 9–16, see 565
★*Memory for Events,* grades 9–13, see 566
★*Memory for Meanings,* grades 7–16, see 567
*New Uses, grades 10–16, see 568
★*Pattern Relations Test* [South Africa], college graduates, see 569
Perceptual Speed (Identical Forms), grades 9–16 and industrial employees, see 570
Pertinent Questions, grades 9–16 and adults, see 571
*Plot Titles, grades 9–16, see 572
Possible Jobs, grades 6–16 and adults, see 573
*Remote Associates Test, grades 9–16 and adults, see 574
Rutgers Drawing Test, ages 4–9, see 575
★*Seeing Faults* [South Africa], ages 15 and over, see 576
*Seeing Problems, grades 9–16, see 577
Seguin-Goddard Formboard, ages 5–14, see 578
*Simile Interpretations, grades 10–16, see 579
★*Similes Test,* grades 4–16 and adults, see 580
★*Sketches,* grades 9 and over, see 581
Subsumed Abilities Test, ages 9 and over, see 582
★*Symbol Identities,* grades 10 and over, see 583
Symbol Series Test [South Africa], illiterate and semiliterate adults, see 584
★*Test of Concept Utilization,* ages 4.5–18.5, see 585
★*Test of Creative Potential,* grades 2–12 and adults, see 586
★*Thinking Creatively With Sounds and Words,* grades 3–12 and adults, see 587
Time Appreciation Test, ages 10 and over, see 588
Torrance Tests of Creative Thinking, kgn through graduate school, see 589
Two-Figure Formboard, ages 4 and over, see 590
*Utility Test, grades 9–12, see 591
Wechsler Memory Scale, adults, see 592
★*Willner Instance Similarities Test,* adults, see 593
Word Fluency, industrial employees, see 594

MATHEMATICS

★*ACER Mathematics Tests* [Australia], grades 4–6, see 595
ACT Mathematics Placement Examination, college entrants, see 596
*Advanced Mathematics (Including Trigonometry): Minnesota High School Achievement Examinations, high school, see 597

★*Annual High School Mathematics Examination,* high school students competing for individual and school awards, see 598
*Basic Mathematics Tests [England], ages 7–14.5, see 599
Bristol Achievement Tests: Mathematics [England], ages 8–13, see 600

ALGEBRA

ARITHMETIC

CALCULUS

GEOMETRY

SPECIAL FIELDS

TRIGONOMETRY

MISCELLANEOUS

AGRICULTURE

BLIND

BUSINESS EDUCATION

COMPUTATIONAL & TESTING DEVICES

★*Bowman Chronological Age Calculator,* see 802
Bowman M.A. and I.Q. Kalculator, see 803
**Chronological Age Computer,* ages 3–7 to 19-5, see 804
Dominion Table for Converting Mental Age to I.Q. [Canada], see 805
Grade Averaging Charts, see 806
I.Q. Calculator, see 807
★*Mental Age Calculator,* see 808
**Multiple Purpose Self Trainer,* high school and adults, see 809
Psychometric Research and Service Chart Showing the Davis Difficulty and Discrimination Indices for Item Analysis [India], see 810
Rapid-Rater, see 811
★*Ratio I.Q. Computer,* see 812

COURTSHIP & MARRIAGE

★*Albert Mate Selection Check List,* premarital counselees, see 813
California Marriage Readiness Evaluation, premarital counselees, see 814
Caring Relationship Inventory, marital counselees, see 815
Courtship Analysis, adults, see 816
Dating Problems Checklist, high school and college, see 817
El Senoussi Multiphasic Marital Inventory, premarital and marital counselees, see 818
★*I-Am Sentence Completion Test,* marital counselees, see 819
Individual and Family Developmental Review, counselees and therapy patients, see 820
★*Love Attitudes Inventory,* grades 12–16, see 821
Male Impotence Test, adult males, see 822
Marital Communication Inventory, adults, see 823
★*Marital Diagnostic Inventory,* marital counselees, see 824
Marital Roles Inventory, marital counselees, see 825
Marriage Adjustment Form, adults, see 826
Marriage Adjustment Inventory, marital counselees, see 827
Marriage Adjustment Sentence Completion Survey, marital counselees, see 828
Marriage Analysis, married couples in counseling, see 829
★*Marriage Expectation Inventories,* engaged and married couples, see 830
Marriage-Personality Inventory, individuals and couples, see 831
Marriage Prediction Schedule, adults, see 832
Marriage Role Expectation Inventory, adolescents and adults, see 833
**Marriage Scale (For Measuring Compatibility of Interests),* premarital or married counselees, see 834
★*Marriage Skills Analysis,* marital counselees, see 835
Otto Pre-Marital Counseling Schedules, adult couples, see 836
★*Pair Attraction Inventory,* college and adults, see 837
Sex Knowledge Inventory, sex education classes in high school and college and adults, see 838
Sexual Development Scale for Females, adult females, see 839
**Taylor-Johnson Temperament Analysis,* grades 7–16 and adults, see 840
Thorman Family Relations Conference Situation Questionnaire, families receiving therapy, see 841

DRIVING & SAFETY EDUCATION

**American Automobile Association Driver Testing Apparatus,* drivers, see 842
**Bicycle Safety—Performance and Skill Tests,* ages 10–16, see 843
Driver Attitude Survey, drivers, see 844
★*Driving Skill Exercises,* automobile drivers, see 845
General Test on Traffic and Driving Knowledge, drivers, see 846
Hannaford Industrial Safety Attitude Scales, industry, see 847
McGlade Road Test for Use in Driver Licensing, Education and Employment, prospective drivers, see 848
Road Test Check List for Passenger Car Drivers, passenger car drivers, see 849
Siebrecht Attitude Scale, grades 9–16 and adults, see 850
★*Simplified Road Test,* drivers, see 851

EDUCATION

Academic Freedom Survey, college students and faculty, see 852
**CLEP Subject Examination in History of American Education,* 1 semester or equivalent, see 853
**CLEP Subject Examination in Tests and Measurements,* 1 semester or equivalent, see 854
★*Classroom Atmosphere Questionnaire,* grades 4–9, see 855
★*Comprehensive Teaching and Training Evaluation,* college and training programs, see 856
★*Counseling Services Assessment Blank,* college and adult counseling clients, see 857
★*Course Evaluation Questionnaire,* high school and college, see 858
Diagnostic Teacher-Rating Scale, grades 4–12, see 859
★*Educational Values Assessment Questionnaire,* adults, see 860
Faculty Morale Scale for Institutional Improvement, college faculty, see 861
★*General Tests of Language and Arithmetic for Students* [South Africa], first and second year Bantu candidates for primary teacher's certificate, see 862
**Graduate Record Examinations Advanced Education Test,* graduate school candidates, see 863
**Illinois Course Evaluation Questionnaire,* college, see 864
Illinois Ratings of Teacher Effectiveness, grades 9–12, see 865
Illinois Teacher Evaluation Questionnaire, grades 7–12, see 866
**Junior Index of Motivation,* grades 7–12, see 867
Minnesota Teacher Attitude Inventory, elementary and secondary school teachers and students in grades 12–17, see 868
**National Teacher Examinations,* college seniors and teachers, see 869
**National Teacher Examinations: Early Childhood Education,* college seniors and teachers, see 870
**National Teacher Examinations: Education in an Urban Setting,* college seniors and teachers, see 871
**National Teacher Examinations: Education in the Elementary School,* college seniors and teachers, see 872
**National Teacher Examinations: Education of Mentally Retarded,* college seniors and teachers, see 873
★*National Teacher Examinations: Educational Administration and Supervision,* prospective principals, see 874
★*National Teacher Examinations: Guidance Counselor,* prospective guidance counselors, see 875

HANDWRITING

HEALTH & PHYSICAL EDUCATION

HOME ECONOMICS

Minnesota Check List for Food Preparation and Serving, grades 7–16 and adults, see 951
★National Teacher Examinations: Home Economics Education, college seniors and teachers, see 952
★Nutrition Information Test, grades 9–16 and adults, see 953
Scales for Appraising High School Homemaking Programs, pupils, teachers, community members, and administrators, see 954
★Teacher Education Examination Program: Home Economics Education, college seniors preparing to teach secondary school, see 955
★Test of Family Life Knowledge and Attitudes, grade 12 boys and girls seeking Betty Crocker college scholarships and awards, see 956–66

INDUSTRIAL ARTS

Drawing: Cooperative Industrial Arts Tests, 1 semester grades 7–9, see 967
Electricity/Electronics: Cooperative Industrial Arts Tests, 1 semester grades 7–9, see 968
Emporia Industrial Arts Test, high school, see 969
General Industrial Arts: Cooperative Industrial Arts Tests, 1 year grades 7–9, see 970
Metals: Cooperative Industrial Arts Tests, 1 semester grades 7–9, see 971
★National Teacher Examinations: Industrial Arts Education, college seniors and teachers, see 972
★Teacher Education Examination Program: Industrial Arts, college seniors preparing to teach secondary school, see 973
Technical and Scholastic Test: Dailey Vocational Tests, grades 8–12 and adults, see 974
Woods: Cooperative Industrial Arts Tests, 1 semester grades 7–9, see 975

LEARNING DISABILITIES

★Automated Graphogestalt Technique, grades 1–4, see 976
★Basic Screening and Referral Form for Children With Suspected Learning and Behavioral Disabilities, grades 1–12, see 977
★Cutrona Child Study Profile of Psycho-Educational Abilities, grades kgn–3, see 978
First Grade Screening Test, first grade entrants, see 979
★Grassi Basic Cognitive Evaluation, ages 3–9, see 980
Illinois Test of Psycholinguistic Abilities, ages 2–10, see 981; *Filmed Demonstration of the ITPA*, see 982
★Individual Learning Disabilities Classroom Screening Instrument, grades 1–3, see 983
Meeting Street School Screening Test, grades kgn–1, see 984
★Psychoeducational Inventory of Basic Learning Abilities, ages 5–12 with suspected learning disabilities, see 985
Psychoeducational Profile of Basic Learning Abilities, ages 2–14 with learning disabilities, see 986
★Pupil Rating Scale: Screening for Learning Disabilities, grades 3–4, see 987
Screening Test for the Assignment of Remedial Treatments, ages 4-6 to 6-5, see 988
Screening Tests for Identifying Children With Specific Language Disability, grades 1–4, see 989
Specific Language Disability Test, "average to high IQ" children in grades 6–8, see 990
Valett Developmental Survey of Basic Learning Abilities, ages 2–7, see 991

LISTENING COMPREHENSION

★Assessment of Children's Language Comprehension, ages 2–6, see 992
Brown-Carlsen Listening Comprehension Test, grades 9–16 and adults, see 993
Cooperative Primary Tests: Listening, grades 1.5–3, see 994
Orr-Graham Listening Test, junior high school boys, see 995
★Progressive Achievement Tests of Listening Comprehension [New Zealand], standards 1–4 and Forms I–IV (ages 7–14), see 996
Sequential Tests of Educational Progress: Listening, grades 4–14, see 997
★Tests for Auditory Comprehension of Language, ages 3–7, see 997A

PHILOSOPHY

★Graduate Record Examinations Advanced Philosophy Test, graduate school candidates, see 998
★Undergraduate Program Field Tests: Philosophy Test, college, see 999
★Undergraduate Program Field Tests: Scholastic Philosophy Test, college, see 1000

PSYCHOLOGY

Aden-Crosthwait Adolescent Psychology Achievement Test, college, see 1001
★CLEP Subject Examination in Educational Psychology, 1 semester or equivalent, see 1002
★CLEP Subject Examination in General Psychology, 1 semester or equivalent, see 1003
Cass-Sanders Psychology Test, high school and college, see 1004
★Graduate Record Examinations Advanced Psychology Test, graduate school candidates, see 1005
★Undergraduate Program Field Tests: Psychology Test, college, see 1006

RECORD & REPORT FORMS

★A/9 Cumulative Record Folder, grades kgn–12, see 1007
American Council on Education Cumulative Record Folders, grades 1–16, see 1008
California Cumulative Record and Health Insert, grades 1–12, see 1009
★Cassel Developmental Record, birth to death, see 1010
Florida Cumulative Guidance Record, grades 1–12, see 1011
G.C. Anecdotal Record Form [Canada], teachers' recordings of student actions, see 1012
★Guidance Cumulative Folder and Record Forms, grades kgn–12, see 1013
★Height Weight Interpretation Folders, ages 4–17, see 1014
Junior High School Record, grades 7–10, see 1015
★Ontario School Record System [Canada], grades kgn–13, see 1016
★Permanent Record Folder, exceptional children, see 1017
★Psychodiagnostic Test Report Blank, psychologists' test data on clients, see 1018
★Secondary-School Record, grades 9–12, see 1019

RELIGIOUS EDUCATION

Achievement Test in Jewish History, junior high school, see 1020

★*Achievement Test—Jewish Life and Observances,* grades 5–7, see 1021

★*Achievement Test—The State of Israel,* "pupils who have completed an organized course of study on the State of Israel," see 1022

★*Bible and You,* ages 13 and over, see 1023

★*Biblical Survey Test,* college, see 1024

Concordia Bible Information Inventory, grades 4–8, see 1025

Inventory of Religious Activities and Interests, high school and college students considering church-related occupations and theological school students, see 1025A

Religious Attitudes Inventory, religious counselees, see 1026

Standardized Bible Content Tests, Bible college, see 1027

Theological School Inventory, incoming seminary students, see 1028

Youth Research Survey, ages 13–19, see 1029

SCORING MACHINES & SERVICES

Automata EDT 1200 Educational Data Terminal, see 1030

Hankes Scoring Service, see 1031

IBM 1230 Optical Mark Scoring Reader, see 1032

★*IBM 3881 Optical Mark Reader,* see 1033

MRC Scoring and Reporting Services, see 1034

NCS Scoring and Reporting Services, see 1035

NCS Sentry 70, see 1036

OpScan Test Scoring and Document Scanning System, see 1037

Psychological Resources, see 1038

SOCIOECONOMIC STATUS

American Home Scale, grades 8–16, see 1039

Environmental Participation Index, culturally disadvantaged ages 12 and over, see 1040

Home Index, grades 4–12, see 1040A

Socio-Economic Status Scales [India], urban students, adults, and rural families, see 1041

STATISTICS

CLEP Subject Examination in Statistics, 1 semester or equivalent, see 1042

★*Objective Tests in Mathematics: Statistics* [England], ages 15 and over, see 1043

TEST PROGRAMS

ACT Assessment, candidates for college entrance, see 1044

Advanced Placement Examinations, high school students desiring credit for college level courses or admission to advanced courses, see 1045

Canadian Test Battery, Grade 10 [Canada], see 1046

Canadian Test Battery, Grades 8–9 [Canada], grades 8.5–9.0, see 1047

College Board Admissions Testing Program, candidates for college entrance, see 1048

★*College Guidance Program,* grade 11, see 1049

College-Level Examination Program, 1–2 years of college or equivalent, see 1050

College Placement Tests, entering college freshmen, see 1051

Comparative Guidance and Placement Program, entrants to two-year colleges and vocational-technical institutes, see 1052

Graduate Record Examinations: National Program for Graduate School Selection, graduate school candidates, see 1053

Junior College Placement Program, junior college entrants, see 1054

National Guidance Testing Program, grades 1.5–14, see 1055

National Science Foundation Graduate Fellowship Testing Program, applicants for N.S.F. fellowships for graduate study in the sciences, see 1056

★*Ohio Survey Tests,* grades 4, 6, 8, and 10, see 1057

Project Talent Test Battery, grades 9–12, see 1058

Secondary School Admission Test, grades 5–10, see 1059

★*Service for Admission to College and University Testing Program* [Canada], candidates for college entrance, see 1060

★*Testing Academic Achievement,* high school students desiring credit for college level courses or advanced placement, entering college freshmen, and 1–2 years of college or equivalent, see 1061

Undergraduate Program for Counseling and Evaluation, college, see 1062

MULTI-APTITUDE BATTERIES

Academic Promise Tests, grades 6–9, see 1063

★*Academic-Technical Aptitude Tests* [South Africa], "coloured pupils" in standards 6–8, see 1064

★*Aptitude Test for Junior Secondary Pupils* [South Africa], Bantus in Form I, see 1065

Aptitude Tests for Occupations, grades 9–13 and adults, see 1066

★*Armed Services Vocational Aptitude Battery,* high school, see 1067

Detroit General Aptitudes Examination, grades 6–12, see 1068

Differential Aptitude Tests, grades 8–12 and adults, see 1069

Differential Test Battery [England], ages 7 to "top university level," see 1070

Employee Aptitude Survey, ages 16 and over, see 1071

Flanagan Aptitude Classification Tests, grades 9–12 and adults, see 1072

General Aptitude Test Battery, grades 9–12 and adults, see 1073

Guilford-Zimmerman Aptitude Survey, grades 9–16 and adults, see 1074

High Level Battery: Test A/75 [South Africa], adults with at least 12 years of education, see 1075

★*International Primary Factors Test Battery,* grades 5 and over, see 1076

Jastak Test of Potential Ability and Behavior Stability, ages 11.5–14.5, see 1077

Job-Tests Program, adults, see 1078

★*Junior Aptitude Tests for Indian South Africans* [South Africa], standards 6–8, see 1079

Measurement of Skill, adults, see 1080

Multi-Aptitude Test, college courses in testing, see 1081

Multiple Aptitude Tests, grades 7–13, see 1082

N.B. Aptitude Tests (Junior) [South Africa], standards 4–8, see 1083

National Institute for Personnel Research Intermediate Battery [South Africa], standards 7–10 and job applicants with 9–12 years of education, see 1084

*National Institute for Personnel Research Normal Battery [South Africa], standards 6–10 and job applicants with 8–11 years of education, see 1085

*Nonreading Aptitude Test Battery, disadvantaged grades 9–12 and adults, see 1086

SRA Primary Mental Abilities, grades kgn–12 and adults, see 1087

*Senior Aptitude Tests [South Africa], standards 8–10 and college and adults, see 1088

PERSONALITY

NONPROJECTIVE

★Ai3Q: A Measure of the Obsessional Personality or Anal Character [England], sixth form and intelligent adults, see 1089

A-S Reaction Study, college and adults, see 1090

*Activity Vector Analysis, ages 16 and over, see 1091

*Adaptive Behavior Scales, mentally retarded and emotionally maladjusted ages 3 and over, see 1092

Addiction Research Center Inventory, drug addicts, see 1093

Adjective Check List, grades 9–16 and adults, see 1094

Adjustment Inventory, grades 9–16 and adults, see 1095

★Adolescent Alienation Index, ages 12–19, see 1096

★Affect Scale, college, see 1097

Alcadd Test, adults, see 1098

★Animal Crackers: A Test of Motivation to Achieve, grades kgn–1, see 1099

Anxiety Scale for the Blind, blind and partially sighted ages 13 and over, see 1100

Attitude-Interest Analysis Test, early adolescents and adults, see 1101

Attitudes Toward Industrialization, adults, see 1102

Attitudes Toward Parental Control of Children, adults, see 1103

Ayres Space Test, ages 3 and over, see 1104

Babcock Test of Mental Efficiency, ages 7 and over, see 1105

Baker-Schulberg Community Mental Health Ideology Scale, mental health professionals, see 1106

★Balthazar Scales of Adaptive Behavior, "profoundly and severely mentally retarded adults and the younger less retarded," see 1107

★Barclay Classroom Climate Inventory, grades 3–6, see 1108

Barron-Welsh Art Scale, ages 6 and over, see 1109

Behavior Cards, delinquents having a reading grade score 4.5 or higher, see 1110

Behavior Status Inventory, psychiatric inpatients, see 1111

Bristol Social Adjustment Guides [England], ages 5–15, see 1112

Brook Reaction Test [England], ages 13 and over, see 1113

Burks' Behavior Rating Scale for Organic Brain Dysfunction, grades kgn–6, see 1114

Burks' Behavior Rating Scales, preschool and grades kgn–8, see 1115

C-R Opinionaire, grades 11–16 and adults, see 1116

Cain-Levine Social Competency Scale, mentally retarded children ages 5–13, see 1117

California Life Goals Evaluation Schedules, ages 15 and over, see 1118

California Medical Survey, medical patients ages 10–18 and adults, see 1119

California Preschool Social Competency Scale, ages 2.5–5.5, see 1120

California Psychological Inventory, ages 13 and over, see 1121; *Behaviordyne Psychodiagnostic Lab Service, see 1122

California Test of Personality, grades kgn–14 and adults, see 1123

Cassel Group Level of Aspiration Test, grades 5–16 and adults, see 1124

Chapin Social Insight Test, ages 13 and over, see 1125

Child Behavior Rating Scale, grades kgn–3, see 1126

*Children's Embedded Figures Test, ages 5–12, see 1127

Children's Hypnotic Susceptibility Scale, ages 5–16, see 1128

*Children's Personality Questionnaire [South Africa], ages 8–12, see 1129

Client-Centered Counseling Progress Record, adults and children undergoing psychotherapeutic counseling, see 1130

Clinical Analysis Questionnaire, ages 18 and over, see 1131

Clinical Behavior Check List and Rating Scale, clinical clients, see 1132

College and University Environment Scales, college, see 1133

College Inventory of Academic Adjustment, college, see 1134

*College Student Questionnaires, college entrants and students, see 1135

★College Student Satisfaction Questionnaire, college, see 1136

Community Adaptation Schedule, normals and psychiatric patients, see 1137

Community Improvement Scale, adults, see 1138

Comrey Personality Scales, ages 16 and over, see 1139

Concept Formation Test, normal and schizophrenic adults, see 1140

★Concept-Specific Anxiety Scale, college and adults, see 1141

★Conceptual Systems Test, grades 7 and over, see 1142

Conservatism Scale [England], ages 12 and over, see 1143

Cornell Index, ages 18 and over, see 1144

Cornell Medical Index, ages 14 and over, see 1145

Cornell Word Form 2, adults, see 1146

Cotswold Personality Assessment P.A.1 [Scotland], ages 11–16, see 1147

★Crawford Psychological Adjustment Scale, psychiatric patients, see 1148

Cree Questionnaire, industrial employees, see 1149

Current and Past Psychopathology Scales, psychiatric patients and nonpatients, see 1150

DF Opinion Survey, grades 12–16 and adults, see 1151

Defense Mechanism Inventory, ages 16 and over, see 1152

Demos D Scale: An Attitude Scale for the Identification of Dropouts, grades 7–12, see 1153

Depression Adjective Check Lists, grades 9–16 and adults, see 1154

Detroit Adjustment Inventory, grades kgn–12, see 1155

PROJECTIVE

Social Relations Test [South Africa], adult males, see 1509

Sound-Apperception Test, ages 16 and over, see 1510

South African Picture Analysis Test [The Netherlands], ages 5–13, see 1511

Structured Doll Play Test, ages 2–6, see 1512

Structured-Objective Rorschach Test, adults, see 1513

Symbol Elaboration Test, ages 6 and over, see 1514

Symonds Picture-Story Test, grades 7–12, see 1515

Szondi Test [Switzerland], ages 5 and over, see 1516

*Tasks of Emotional Development Test, ages 6–11 and adolescents, see 1517

Test of Family Attitudes [Belgium], ages 6–12, see 1518

Thematic Apperception Test, ages 4 and over, see 1519

Thematic Apperception Test for African Subjects [South Africa], ages 10 and over, see 1520

★*This I Believe Test*, grades 9 and over, see 1521

Tomkins-Horn Picture Arrangement Test, ages 10 and over, see 1522

Toy World Test [France], ages 2 and over, see 1523

Tree Test [Switzerland], ages 9 and over, see 1524

Twitchell-Allen Three-Dimensional Personality Test, ages 3 and over (sighted and sightless), see 1525

Visual Apperception Test '60, ages 6 and over, see 1526

Washington University Sentence Completion Test, ages 12 and over, see 1527

Zulliger Individual and Group Test [Switzerland], ages 3 and over, see 1528

READING

A.C.E.R. Lower Grades Reading Test: Level 1 [Australia], grade 1, see 1529

★*ACER Primary Reading Survey Tests* [Australia], grades 3–6, see 1530

A.C.E.R. Silent Reading Tests: Standardized for Use in New Zealand [New Zealand], ages 9–12, see 1531

American School Achievement Tests: Reading, grades 2–9, see 1532

American School Reading Tests, grades 10–13, see 1533

Buffalo Reading Test for Speed and Comprehension, grades 9–16, see 1534

Burnett Reading Series: Survey Test, grades 1.5–12, see 1535

*California Achievement Tests: Reading, grades 1–14, see 1536

*Carver-Darby Chunked Reading Test, grades 9–16 and adults, see 1537

Commerce Reading Comprehension Test, grades 12–16 and adults, see 1538

Comprehension Test for Training College Students [England], training college students and applicants for admission, see 1539

Comprehensive Primary Reading Scales, grade 1, see 1540

Comprehensive Reading Scales, grades 4–12, see 1541

*Comprehensive Tests of Basic Skills: Reading, grades kgn–12, see 1542

Cooperative Primary Tests: Reading, grades 1.5–3, see 1543

Cooperative Reading Comprehension Test, Form Y [Australia], secondary forms 5–6 and university, see 1544

Cooperative Reading Comprehension Test, Forms L and M [Australia], secondary forms 2–4, see 1545

Davis Reading Test, grades 8–13, see 1546

Delaware County Silent Reading Test, grades 1.5–8, see 1547

★*Edinburgh Reading Tests* [England], ages 8.5–12.5, see 1548

Emporia Reading Tests, grades 1–8, see 1549

GAP Reading Comprehension Test [Australia], grades 2–7, see 1550

★*GAPADOL* [Australia], ages 10 and over, see 1551

*Gates-MacGinitie Reading Tests, grades 1–9, see 1552

Gates-MacGinitie Reading Tests: Survey F, grades 10–12, see 1553

Group Reading Assessment [England], end of first year junior school, see 1554

Group Reading Test [England], ages 6–10, see 1555

High School Reading Test: National Achievement Tests, grades 7–12, see 1556

Individual Reading Test [Australia], ages 6-0 to 9-9, see 1557

★*Informal Reading Assessment Tests* [Canada], grades 1–3, see 1558

★*Inventory-Survey Tests*, grades 4–8, see 1559

*Iowa Silent Reading Tests, grades 4–16, see 1560

Kelvin Measurement of Reading Ability [Scotland], ages 8–12, see 1561

Kingston Test of Silent Reading [England], ages 7–11, see 1562

Lee-Clark Reading Test, grades 1–2, see 1563

McGrath Test of Reading Skills, grades 1–13, see 1564

McMenemy Measure of Reading Ability, grades 3 and 5–8, see 1565

Maintaining Reading Efficiency Tests, grades 7–16 and adults, see 1566

*Metropolitan Achievement Tests: Reading Tests, grades 2–9, see 1567

Minnesota Reading Examination for College Students, grades 9–16, see 1568

Monroe's Standardized Silent Reading Test, grades 3–12, see 1569

N.B. Silent Reading Tests (Beginners): Reading Comprehension Test [South Africa], substandard B, see 1570

*National Teacher Examinations: Reading Specialist, college seniors and teachers, see 1571

Nelson-Denny Reading Test, grades 9–16 and adults, see 1572

Nelson Reading Test, grades 3–9, see 1573

New Developmental Reading Tests, grades 1–6, see 1574

OISE Achievement Tests in Silent Reading: Advanced Primary Battery [Canada], grade 2, see 1575

Pressey Diagnostic Reading Tests, grades 3–9, see 1576

★*Primary Reading Survey Tests*, grades 2–3, see 1577

Primary Reading Test: Acorn Achievement Tests, grades 2–3, see 1578

Progressive Achievement Tests of Reading [New Zealand], standards 2–4 and Forms I–IV (ages 8–14), see 1579

RBH Basic Reading and Word Test, disadvantaged adults, see 1580

RBH Test of Reading Comprehension, business and industry, see 1581

*Reading Comprehension: Canadian English Achievement Test [Canada], grades 8.5–9.0, see 1582

Reading Comprehension: Cooperative English Tests, grades 9–14, see 1583

Reading Comprehension Test, college entrants, see 1584

*Reading Comprehension Test DE [England], ages 10–12.5, see 1585

Reading Comprehension Test: National Achievement

DIAGNOSTIC

MISCELLANEOUS

OC Diagnostic Syllabizing Test, grades 4–6, see 1668
Phonics Test for Teachers, reading methods courses, see 1669
Reader Rater With Self-Scoring Profile, ages 15 and over, see 1670
Reader's Inventory, entrants to a reading improvement course for secondary and college students and adults, see 1671
Reading Eye II, grades 1–16 and adults, see 1672
Reading Versatility Test, grades 5–16, see 1673
Roswell-Chall Auditory Blending Test, grades 1–4, see 1674
Word Discrimination Test, grades 1–8, see 1675
★*Word Recognition Test* [England], preschool to age 8.5, see 1676

ORAL

★*Concise Word Reading Tests* [Australia], ages 7–12, see 1677
Flash-X Sight Vocabulary Test, grades 1–2, see 1678
Gilmore Oral Reading Test, grades 1–8, see 1679
Graded Word Reading Test [England], ages 5 and over, see 1680
Gray Oral Reading Test, grades 1–16 and adults, see 1681
Holborn Reading Scale [England], ages 5.5–10, see 1682
Neale Analysis of Reading Ability [England], ages 6–13, see 1683
★*Oral Reading Criterion Test,* reading level grades 1–7, see 1684
Oral Word Reading Test [New Zealand], ages 7–11, see 1685
★*Reading Miscue Inventory,* grades 1–7, see 1686
★*St. Lucia Graded Word Reading Test* [Australia], grades 2–7, see 1687
Slosson Oral Reading Test, grades 1–8 and high school, see 1688
Standardized Oral Reading Check Tests, grades 1–8, see 1689
Standardized Oral Reading Paragraphs, grades 1–8, see 1690

READINESS

ABC Inventory to Determine Kindergarten and School Readiness, entrants to kgn and grade 1, see 1691
APELL Test, Assessment Program of Early Learning Levels, ages 4.5–7, see 1692
Academic Readiness and End of First Grade Progress Scales, grade 1, see 1693
American School Reading Readiness Test, first grade entrants, see 1694
★*Analysis of Readiness Skills: Reading and Mathematics,* grades kgn–1, see 1695
Anton Brenner Developmental Gestalt Test of School Readiness, ages 5–6, see 1696
Basic Concept Inventory, preschool and kgn, see 1697
Binion-Beck Reading Readiness Test for Kindergarten and First Grade, grades kgn–1, see 1698
Clymer-Barrett Prereading Battery, first grade entrants, see 1699
Contemporary School Readiness Test, first grade entrants, see 1700
★*Delco Readiness Test,* first grade entrants, see 1701
Gates-MacGinitie Reading Tests: Readiness Skills, grades kgn–1, see 1702
Gesell Developmental Tests, ages 5–10, see 1703
Group Test of Reading Readiness, grades kgn–1, see 1704
Harrison-Stroud Reading Readiness Profiles, grades kgn–1, see 1705

★*Initial Survey Test,* first grade entrants, see 1706
★*Inventory of Primary Skills,* grades kgn–1, see 1707
★*Kindergarten Behavioural Index* [Australia], grades kgn–1, see 1708
Kindergarten Evaluation of Learning Potential, kgn, see 1709
★*LRS Seriation Test,* ages 4–6, see 1710
Lee-Clark Reading Readiness Test, grades kgn–1, see 1711
Lippincott Reading Readiness Test, grades kgn–1, see 1712
McHugh-McParland Reading Readiness Test, grades kgn–1, see 1713
Macmillan Reading Readiness Test, first grade entrants, see 1714
Maturity Level for School Entrance and Reading Readiness, grades kgn–1, see 1715
Metropolitan Readiness Tests, grades kgn–1, see 1716
Murphy-Durrell Reading Readiness Analysis, first grade entrants, see 1717
Parent Readiness Evaluation of Preschoolers, ages 3–9 to 5–8, see 1718
★*Pre-Reading Assessment Kit* [Canada], grades kgn–1, see 1719
★*Prereading Expectancy Screening Scales,* first grade entrants, see 1720
Pre-Reading Screening Procedures, first grade entrants of average or superior intelligence, see 1721
★*Preschool and Kindergarten Performance Profile,* preschool and kgn, see 1722
Primary Academic Sentiment Scale, ages 4–4 to 7–3, see 1723
Reading Aptitude Tests, grades kgn–1, see 1724
★*Reading Inventory Probe 1,* grades 1–2, see 1725
Reversal Test [Sweden], grade 1 entrants, see 1726
Riley Preschool Developmental Screening Inventory, ages 3–5, see 1727
School Readiness Checklist, ages 5–6, see 1728
School Readiness Survey, ages 4–6, see 1729
Screening Test of Academic Readiness, ages 4–0 to 6–5, see 1730
Sprigle School Readiness Screening Test, ages 4–6 to 6–9, see 1731
Steinbach Test of Reading Readiness, grades kgn–1, see 1732
Van Wagenen Reading Readiness Scales, first grade entrants, see 1733
Watson Reading-Readiness Test [Canada], grades kgn–1, see 1734

SPECIAL FIELDS

ANPA Foundation Newspaper Test, grades 7–12, see 1735
Adult Basic Reading Inventory, functionally illiterate adolescents and adults, see 1736
Iowa Tests of Educational Development: Ability to Interpret Reading Materials in the Social Studies, grades 9–12, see 1737
Iowa Tests of Educational Development: Ability to Interpret Reading Materials in the Natural Sciences, grades 9–12, see 1738
Purdue Reading Test for Industrial Supervisors, supervisors, see 1739
RBH Scientific Reading Test, employees in technical companies, see 1740
Reading Adequacy "READ" Test: Individual Placement Series, adults in industry, see 1741
Reading: Adult Basic Education Student Survey, poorly educated adults, see 1742
Reading Comprehension Test for Personnel Selection [England], applicants for technical training programs with high verbal content, see 1743

★*Reading/Everyday Activities in Life*, high school and "adults at basic education levels," see 1744
Robinson-Hall Reading Tests, college, see 1745
SRA Reading Index, job applicants with poor educational backgrounds, see 1746
Understanding Communication (Verbal Comprehension), industrial employees at the skilled level or below, see 1747

SPEED

*Basic Reading Rate Scale, grades 3–12, see 1748
Minnesota Speed of Reading Test for College Students, grades 12–16, see 1749

STUDY SKILLS

Bristol Achievement Tests: Study Skills [England], ages 8–13, see 1750
College Adjustment and Study Skills Inventory, college, see 1751
*Comprehensive Tests of Basic Skills: Study Skills, grades 2.5–12, see 1752
★*Cornell Class-Reasoning Test*, grades 4–12, see 1753
★*Cornell Conditional-Reasoning Test*, grades 4–12, see 1754
Cornell Critical Thinking Test, grades 7–16, see 1755
★*Cornell Learning and Study Skills Inventory*, grades 7–16, see 1756
Evaluation Aptitude Test, candidates for college and graduate school entrance, see 1757

**Iowa Tests of Educational Development: Use of Sources of Information*, grades 9–12, see 1758
Library Orientation Test for College Freshmen, grade 13, see 1759
★*Library Tests*, college, see 1760
Logical Reasoning, grades 9–16 and adults, see 1761
★*National Test of Library Skills*, grades 2–12, see 1762
Nationwide Library Skills Examination, grades 4–12, see 1763
OC Diagnostic Dictionary Test, grades 5–8, see 1764
SRA Achievement Series: Work-Study Skills, grades 4–9, see 1765
★*Study Attitudes and Methods Survey*, high school and college, see 1766
Study Habits Checklist, grades 9–14, see 1767
Study Habits Inventory, grades 12–16, see 1768
Study Performance Test, high school and college, see 1769
Study Skills Counseling Evaluation, high school and college, see 1770
Study Skills Test: McGraw-Hill Basic Skills System, grades 11–14, see 1771
Survey of Study Habits and Attitudes, grades 7–14, see 1772
Test on Use of the Dictionary, high school and college, see 1773
★*Uncritical Inference Test*, college, see 1774
Watson-Glaser Critical Thinking Appraisal, grades 9–16 and adults, see 1775
★*Wisconsin Tests of Reading Skill Development: Study Skills*, grades kgn–7, see 1776

SCIENCE

Adkins-McBride General Science Test, high school, see 1777
Borman-Sanders Elementary Science Test, grades 5–8, see 1778
*CLEP General Examinations: Natural Sciences, 1–2 years of college or equivalent, see 1779
Cooperative Science Tests: Advanced General Science, grades 8–9, see 1780
Cooperative Science Tests: General Science, grades 7–9, see 1781
Elementary Science Test: National Achievement Tests, grades 4–6, see 1782
Emporia General Science Test, 1–2 semesters high school, see 1783
★*General Science Test* [South Africa], matriculants and higher, see 1784
General Science Test: National Achievement Tests, grades 7–9, see 1785
General Science III: Achievement Examinations for Secondary Schools, high school, see 1786
*Iowa Tests of Educational Development: General Background in the Natural Sciences, grades 9–12, see 1787
*National Teacher Examinations: Biology and General Science, college seniors and teachers, see 1788
*National Teacher Examinations: Chemistry, Physics and General Science, college seniors and teachers, see 1789
SRA Achievement Series: Science, grades 4–9, see 1790
*Science: Minnesota High School Achievement Examinations, grades 7–9, see 1791
Science Tests: Content Evaluation Series, grades 8–9, see 1792

Scientific Knowledge and Aptitude Test [India], high school, see 1793
*Sequential Tests of Educational Progress: Science, grades 4–14, see 1794
Stanford Achievement Test: High School Science Test, grades 9–12, see 1795
Stanford Achievement Test: Science, grades 5.5–9.9, see 1796
*Teacher Education Examination Program: Biology and General Science, college seniors preparing to teach secondary school, see 1797
*Teacher Education Examination Program: Chemistry, Physics and General Science, college seniors preparing to teach secondary school, see 1798
Tests of Academic Progress: Science, grades 9–12, see 1799

BIOLOGY

*Advanced Placement Examination in Biology, high school students desiring credit for college level courses or admission to advanced courses, see 1800
*BSCS Achievement Tests, grade 10, see 1801
*Biological Science: Interaction of Experiments and Ideas, grades 10–12, see 1802
*Biology: Minnesota High School Achievement Examinations, high school, see 1803
*CLEP Subject Examination in Biology, 1 year or equivalent, see 1804
*College Board Achievement Test in Biology, candidates for college entrance, see 1805
*College Placement Test in Biology, entering college freshmen, see 1806

CHEMISTRY

GEOLOGY

MISCELLANEOUS

PHYSICS

SENSORY-MOTOR

D-K Scale of Lateral Dominance, grades 2–6, see 1874
Developmental Test of Visual-Motor Integration, ages 2–15, see 1875
★*Frostig Movement Skills Test Battery,* ages 6–12, see 1876
Harris Tests of Lateral Dominance, ages 7 and over, see 1877
Leavell Hand-Eye Coordinator Tests, ages 8–14, see 1878
MKM Picture Arrangement Test, grades kgn–6, see 1879
Moore Eye-Hand Coordination and Color-Matching Test, ages 2 and over, see 1880
Perceptual Forms Test, ages 5–8, see 1881
Primary Visual Motor Test, ages 4–8, see 1882
Purdue Perceptual-Motor Survey, ages 6–10, see 1883
★*Rosner Perceptual Survey,* ages 5–12, see 1884
Southern California Kinesthesia and Tactile Perception Tests, ages 4–8, see 1885
Southern California Perceptual-Motor Tests, ages 4–8, see 1886
Southern California Sensory Integration Tests, ages 4–10 with learning problems, see 1887
★*Spatial Orientation Memory Test,* ages 5–8, see 1888
★*Symbol Digit Modalities Test,* ages 8 and over, see 1889
Trankell's Laterality Tests [Sweden], left-handed children in grades 1–2, see 1890
★*Wold Digit-Symbol Test,* ages 6–16, see 1891
★*Wold Sentence Copying Test,* grades 2–8, see 1892
★*Wold Visuo-Motor Test,* ages 6–16, see 1893

MOTOR

★*Devereux Test of Extremity Coordination,* emotionally handicapped and neurologically impaired ages 4–10, see 1894
Lincoln-Oseretsky Motor Development Scale, ages 6–14, see 1895
★*Manual Accuracy and Speed Test,* ages 4 and over, see 1896
★*Motor Problems Inventory,* preschool–grade 5, see 1897
Oseretsky Tests of Motor Proficiency: A Translation From the Portuguese Adaptation, ages 4–16, see 1898
Perrin Motor Coordination Test, adults, see 1899
Rail-Walking Test, ages 5 and over, see 1900
Smedley Hand Dynamometer, ages 6–18, see 1901
Southern California Motor Accuracy Test, ages 4–7 with nervous system dysfunction, see 1902
★*Teaching Research Motor-Development Scale,* moderately and severely retarded (preschool–grade 12), see 1903
★*Test of Motor Impairment* [Canada], ages 5–14, see 1904

VISION

A-B-C Vision Test for Ocular Dominance, ages 5 and over, see 1905
AO Sight Screener, adults, see 1906
Atlantic City Eye Test, grades 1 and over, see 1907
Basic Screen Test—Vision: Measurement of Skill Test 12, job applicants, see 1908
Burnham-Clark-Munsell Color Memory Test, adults, see 1909
Dennis Visual Perception Scale, grades 1–6, see 1910
Dvorine Pseudo-Isochromatic Plates, ages 3 and over, see 1911
Farnsworth Dichotomous Test for Color Blindness: Panel D–15, ages 12 and over, see 1912
Farnsworth-Munsell 100-Hue Test for the Examination of Color Discrimination, mental ages 12 and over, see 1913
★*Guy's Colour Vision Test for Young Children* [England], ages 3–5 and handicapped, see 1914
Inter-Society Color Council Color Aptitude Test, adults, see 1915
Keystone Ready-to-Read Tests, school entrants, see 1916
Keystone Tests of Binocular Skill, grades 1 and over, see 1917
Keystone Visual Screening Tests, preschool and over, see 1918
MKM Binocular Preschool Test, preschool, see 1919
MKM Monocular and Binocular Reading Test, grades 1 and over, see 1920
Marianne Frostig Developmental Test of Visual Perception, ages 3–8, see 1921
★*Motor-Free Visual Perception Test,* ages 4–8, see 1922
Ortho-Rater, adults, see 1923
Pseudo-Isochromatic Plates for Testing Color Perception, ages 7 and over, see 1924
School Vision Tester, grades kgn and over, see 1925
★*Sheridan Gardiner Test of Visual Acuity* [England], ages 5 and over, see 1926
★*Sloan Achromatopsia Test,* individuals suspected of total color blindness, see 1927
Southern California Figure-Ground Visual Perception Test, ages 4–10, see 1928
Spache Binocular Reading Test, nonreaders and grades 1 and over, see 1929
★*Speed of Color Discrimination Test,* college, see 1930
Stycar Vision Tests [England], ages 6 months to 7 years, see 1931
Test for Colour-Blindness [Japan], ages 4 and over, see 1932
★*3-D Test of Visualization Skill,* ages 3–8, see 1933
Titmus Vision Tester, ages 3 and over, see 1934
★*Visualization Test of Three Dimensional Orthographic Shape,* high school and college, see 1935

SOCIAL STUDIES

American History—Government—Problems of Democracy: Acorn Achievement Tests, grades 9–16, see 1936
American School Achievement Tests: Social Studies and Science, grades 4–9, see 1937
CLEP General Examinations: Social Sciences and History, 1–2 years of college or equivalent, see 1938
College Board Achievement Test in American History and Social Studies, candidates for college entrance, see 1939
College Board Achievement Test in European History

and World Cultures, candidates for college entrance, see 1940

College Placement Test in American History and Social Studies, entering college freshmen, see 1941

College Placement Test in European History and World Cultures, entering college freshmen, see 1942

History and Civics Test: Municipal Tests, grades 3–8, see 1943

Iowa Tests of Educational Development: Understanding of Basic Social Concepts, grades 9–12, see 1944

National Teacher Examinations: Social Studies, college seniors and teachers, see 1945

Primary Social Studies Test, grades 1–3, see 1946

SRA Achievement Series: Social Studies, grades 4–9, see 1947

Sequential Tests of Educational Progress: Social Studies, grades 4–14, see 1948

Social Studies: Minnesota High School Achievement Examinations, grades 7–9, see 1949

Social Studies Test: Acorn National Achievement Tests, grades 7–9, see 1950

Social Studies Test: National Achievement Tests, grades 4–9, see 1951

Stanford Achievement Test: High School Social Studies Test, grades 9–12, see 1952

Stanford Achievement Test: Social Studies Tests, grades 5.5–9, see 1953

Teacher Education Examination Program: Social Studies, college seniors preparing to teach secondary school, see 1954

Tests of Academic Progress: Social Studies, grades 9–12, see 1955

Tests of Basic Experiences: Social Studies, prekgn– grade 1, see 1956

Zimmerman-Sanders Social Studies Test, grades 7–8, see 1957

CONTEMPORARY AFFAIRS

Current News Test, grades 9–12, see 1958

Newsweek NewsQuiz, grades 9–12, see 1959

School Weekly News Quiz, high school, see 1960

Time Current Affairs Test, grades 9–12 and adults, see 1961

★*Time Monthly News Quiz,* grades 9–12 and adults, see 1962

ECONOMICS

CLEP Subject Examination in Introductory Economics, 1 year or equivalent, see 1963

★*Economics/Objective Tests,* 1 semester high school, see 1964

Graduate Record Examinations Advanced Economics Test, graduate school candidates, see 1965

★*Modern Economics Test: Content Evaluation Series,* grades 10–12, see 1966

★*Primary Test of Economic Understanding,* grades 2–3, see 1967

Test of Economic Understanding, high school and college, see 1968

★*Test of Elementary Economics,* grades 4–6, see 1969

Test of Understanding in College Economics, 1–2 semesters college, see 1970

★*Test of Understanding in Personal Economics,* high school, see 1971

Undergraduate Program Field Tests: Economics Test, college, see 1972

GEOGRAPHY

Brandywine Achievement Test in Geography for Secondary Schools, grades 7–12, see 1973

Economic Geography: Achievement Examinations for Secondary Schools, high school, see 1974

Geography Test: Municipal Tests, grades 3–8, see 1975

Geography Test: National Achievement Tests, grades 6–8, see 1976

Graduate Record Examinations Advanced Geography Test, graduate school candidates, see 1977

Hollingsworth-Sanders Geography Test, grades 5–7, see 1978

Undergraduate Program Field Tests: Geography Test, college, see 1979

HISTORY

Advanced Placement Examination in American History, high school students desiring credit for college level courses or admission to advanced courses, see 1980

Advanced Placement Examination in European History, high school students desiring credit for college level courses or admission to advanced courses, see 1981

★*American History: Junior High—Objective,* grades 7–9, see 1982

American History: Senior High—Objective, 1–2 semesters high school, see 1983

American History Test: National Achievement Tests, grades 7–8, see 1984

★*CLEP Subject Examination in Afro-American History,* 1 semester or equivalent, see 1985

CLEP Subject Examination in American History, 1 year or equivalent, see 1986

CLEP Subject Examination in Western Civilization, 1 year or equivalent, see 1987

Cooperative Social Studies Tests: American History, grades 7–8, 10–12, see 1988

Cooperative Social Studies Tests: Modern European History, grades 10–12, see 1989

Cooperative Social Studies Tests: World History, grades 10–12, see 1990

Cooperative Topical Tests in American History, high school, see 1991

Crary American History Test, grades 10–13, see 1992

Emporia American History Test, 1–2 semesters high school, see 1993

Graduate Record Examinations Advanced History Test, graduate school candidates, see 1994

Hollingsworth-Sanders Intermediate History Test, grades 5–6, see 1995

Meares-Sanders Junior High School History Test, grades 7–8, see 1996

Modern World History: Achievement Examinations for Secondary Schools, high school, see 1997

Sanders-Buller World History Test, 1–2 semesters high school, see 1998

Social Studies Grade 10 (American History): Minnesota High School Achievement Examinations, grade 10, see 1999

Social Studies Grade 11 (World History): Minnesota High School Achievement Examinations, grade 11, see 2000

Undergraduate Program Field Tests: History Test, college, see 2001

World History/Objective Tests, 1–2 semesters high school, see 2002

World History Test: Acorn National Achievement Tests, high school and college, see 2003

POLITICAL SCIENCE

CLEP Subject Examination in American Government, 1 semester or equivalent, see 2004

Cooperative Social Studies Tests: American Government, grades 10–12, see 2005

Cooperative Social Studies Tests: Civics, grades 8–9, see 2006

Cooperative Social Studies Tests: Problems of Democracy, grades 10–12, see 2007

★*Government/Objective Tests*, 1 semester grades 11–12, see 2008

Graduate Record Examinations Advanced Political Science Test, graduate school candidates, see 2009

★*National Teacher Examinations: Texas Government*, college seniors and teachers, see 2010

Patterson Test or Study Exercises on the Constitution of the United States, grades 9–16 and adults, see 2011

Principles of Democracy Test, grades 9–12, see 2012

Sare-Sanders American Government Test, high school and college, see 2013

Sare-Sanders Constitution Test, high school and college, see 2014

Social Studies Grade 12 (American Problems): Minnesota High School Achievement Examinations, grade 12, see 2015

Undergraduate Program Field Tests: Political Science Test, college, see 2016

SOCIOLOGY

CLEP Subject Examination in Introductory Sociology, 1 year or equivalent, see 2017

Graduate Record Examinations Advanced Sociology Test, graduate school candidates, see 2018

Sare-Sanders Sociology Test, high school and college, see 2019

Undergraduate Program Field Tests: Sociology Test, college, see 2020

SPEECH AND HEARING

★*Diagnostic Test of Speechreading*, deaf children ages 4–9, see 2021

★*Multiple-Choice Intelligibility Test*, college, see 2022

★*Ohio Tests of Articulation and Perception of Sounds*, ages 5–8, see 2023

Preschool Language Scale, ages 2–6, see 2024

Reynell Developmental Language Scales [England], children ages 1–5 with delayed or deviant language development, see 2025

Undergraduate Program Field Tests: Speech Pathology and Audiology Test, college, see 2026

HEARING

Ambco Audiometers, ages 10 and over, see 2027

Ambco Speech Test Record, ages 3 and over, see 2027A

Auditory Discrimination Test, ages 5–8, see 2028

★*Auditory Memory Span Test*, ages 5–8, see 2029

★*Auditory Sequential Memory Test*, grades 5–8, see 2030

Auditory Tests, grades 2 and over, see 2031

Beltone Audiometers, grades kgn and over, see 2032

Comprehension of Oral Language: Inter-American Series, grade 1, see 2033

Eckstein Audiometers, grades kgn and over, see 2034

★*Flowers-Costello Tests of Central Auditory Abilities*, grades kgn–6, see 2035

★*Four Tone Screening for Older Children and Adults*, ages 8 and over, see 2036

Goldman-Fristoe-Woodcock Test of Auditory Discrimination, ages 4 and over, see 2037

Grason-Stadler Audiometers, ages 6 and over, see 2038

Hearing of Speech Tests, ages 3–12, see 2039

Hollien-Thompson Group Hearing Test, grades 1 and over, see 2040

★*Kindergarten Auditory Screening Test*, grades kgn–1, see 2041

★*Lindamood Auditory Conceptualization Test*, grades kgn–12, see 2042

Maico Audiometers, grades kgn and over, see 2043

Maico Hearing Impairment Calculator, see 2044

Massachusetts Hearing Test, grades 1–16 and adults, see 2045

Modified Rhyme Hearing Test, grades 4 and over, see 2046

National Teacher Examinations: Audiology, college seniors and teachers, see 2047

New Group Pure Tone Hearing Test, grades 1 and over, see 2048

★*Oliphant Auditory Discrimination Memory Test*, grades 2–6, see 2049

★*Oliphant Auditory Synthesizing Test*, grade 1, see 2050

Pritchard-Fox Phoneme Auditory Discrimination Tests: Test Four, kgn and over, see 2051

Robbins Speech Sound Discrimination and Verbal Imagery Type Tests, ages 4 and over, see 2052

Rush Hughes (PB 50): Phonetically Balanced Lists 5–12, grades 2 and over, see 2053

Screening Test for Auditory Perception, grades 2–6, see 2054

Stycar Hearing Tests [England], ages 6 months to 7 years, see 2055

Test of Listening Accuracy in Children, ages 5–9, see 2056

★*Test of Non-Verbal Auditory Discrimination*, ages 6–8, see 2057

★*Tracor Audiometers*, infants and older, see 2058

Verbal Auditory Screening for Children, ages 3–8, see 2059

★*Washington Speech Sound Discrimination Test*, ages 3–5, see 2060

★*Word Intelligibility by Picture Identification*, hearing impaired children ages 5–13, see 2061

★*ZECO Pure Tone Screening for Children*, ages 3–8, see 2062

Zenith Audiometers, preschool and over, see 2063–4

SPEECH

Arizona Articulation Proficiency Scale, mental ages 2–14 and over, see 2065

★*Boston Diagnostic Aphasia Examination*, aphasic patients, see 2066

★*Bzoch-League Receptive-Expressive Emergent Language Scale: For the Measurement of Language Skills in Infancy*, birth to age 3, see 2067

Communicative Evaluation Chart From Infancy to Five Years, see 2068

Deep Test of Articulation, all reading levels, see 2069

★*Edinburgh Articulation Test* [Scotland], ages 3–5, see 2070
Examining for Aphasia, adolescents and adults, see 2071
★*Fairview Language Evaluation Scale,* mentally retarded, see 2072
★*Fisher-Logemann Test of Articulation Competence,* preschool and over, see 2073
Forms From Diagnostic Methods in Speech Pathology, children and adults with speech problems, see 2074
*Goldman-Fristoe Test of Articulation, ages 2 and over, see 2075
Halstead Aphasia Test, adults, see 2076
Houston Test for Language Development, ages 6 months to 6 years, see 2077
Language Facility Test, ages 3 and over, see 2078
Language Modalities Test for Aphasia, adults, see 2079
*Minnesota Test for Differential Diagnosis of Aphasia, adults, see 2080
*National Teacher Examinations: Speech-Communication and Theatre, college seniors and teachers, see 2081
*National Teacher Examinations: Speech Pathology, college seniors and teachers, see 2082
Nationwide Speech Examination, grades 4–12, see 2083
★*Northwestern Syntax Screening Test,* ages 3–7, see 2084

Orzeck Aphasia Evaluation, mental and brain damaged patients, see 2085
Photo Articulation Test, ages 3–12, see 2086
*Porch Index of Communicative Ability, adults, see 2087
Predictive Screening Test of Articulation, grade 1, see 2088
*Riley Articulation and Language Test, grades kgn–2, see 2089
Screening Deep Test of Articulation, grades kgn and over, see 2090
*Screening Speech Articulation Test, ages 3.5–8.5, see 2091
*Sklar Aphasia Scale, brain damaged adults, see 2092
Speech Defect Questionnaire, ages 6 and over, see 2093
Speech Diagnostic Chart, grades 1–8, see 2094
Templin-Darley Tests of Articulation, ages 3 and over, see 2095
★*Undergraduate Program Field Tests: Drama and Theatre Test,* college, see 2096
Utah Test of Language Development, ages 1.5 to 14.5, see 2097
*Verbal Language Development Scale, birth to age 15, see 2098
Weidner-Fensch Speech Screening Test, grades 1–3, see 2099

VOCATIONS

★*ACT Assessment of Career Development,* grades 8–11, see 2100
★*ACT Career Planning Program,* entrants to postsecondary educational institutions, see 2101
*Aptitude Inventory, employee applicants, see 2102
★*Career Maturity Inventory,* grades 6–12, see 2103
★*Classification Test Battery* [South Africa], illiterate and semiliterate applicants for unskilled and semi-skilled mining jobs, see 2104
Dailey Vocational Tests, grades 8–12 and adults, see 2105
*ETSA Tests, job applicants, see 2106
*Flanagan Industrial Tests, business and industry, see 2107
Individual Placement Series, high school and adults, see 2108
★*New Mexico Career Education Test Series,* grades 9–12, see 2109
Personal History Index, job applicants, see 2110
Steward Basic Factors Inventory, applicants for sales and office positions, see 2111
Steward Personnel Tests, applicants for sales and office positions, see 2112
TAV Selection System, adults, see 2113
Vocational Planning Inventory, vocational students in grades 8–12 and grade 13 entrants, see 2114
WLW Employment Inventory, adults, see 2115
★*Wide Range Employment Sample Test,* ages 16–35 (normal and handicapped), see 2116

CLERICAL

ACER Short Clerical Test—Form C [Australia], ages 13 and over, see 2117
A.C.E.R. Speed and Accuracy Tests [Australia], ages 13.5 and over, see 2118
APT Dictation Test, stenographers, see 2119
★*Appraisal of Occupational Aptitudes,* high school and adults, see 2120
Clerical Skills Series, clerical workers and applicants, see 2121

Clerical Tests, applicants for clerical positions, see 2122
Clerical Tests, Series N, applicants for clerical positions not involving frequent use of typewriter or verbal skill, see 2123
Clerical Tests, Series V, applicants for typing and stenographic positions, see 2124
Clerical Worker Examination, clerical workers, see 2125
Cross Reference Test, clerical job applicants, see 2126
Curtis Verbal-Clerical Skills Tests, applicants for clerical positions, see 2127
*General Clerical Ability Test, job applicants, see 2128
*General Clerical Test, grades 9–16 and clerical job applicants, see 2129
*Group Test 20 [England], ages 15 and over, see 2130
*Group Tests 61A, 64, and 66A [England], clerical applicants, see 2131
*Hay Clerical Test Battery, applicants for clerical positions, see 2132
L & L Clerical Tests, applicants for office positions, see 2133
McCann Typing Tests, applicants for typing positions, see 2134
Minnesota Clerical Test, grades 8–12 and adults, see 2135
Office Skills Achievement Test, employees, see 2136
*Office Worker Test, office workers, see 2137
O'Rourke Clerical Aptitude Test, Junior Grade, applicants for clerical positions, see 2138
Personnel Institute Clerical Tests, clerical personnel and typists-stenographers-secretaries, see 2139
Personnel Research Institute Clerical Battery, applicants for clerical positions, see 2140
Personnel Research Institute Test of Shorthand Skills, stenographers, see 2141
Purdue Clerical Adaptability Test, applicants for clerical positions, see 2142
RBH Checking Test, applicants for clerical and stenographic positions, see 2143
RBH Classifying Test, business and industry, see 2144
RBH Number Checking Test, business and industry, see 2145

INTERESTS

MANUAL DEXTERITY

APT Manual Dexterity Test, automobile and truck mechanics and mechanics' helpers, see 2222

Crawford Small Parts Dexterity Test, high school and adults, see 2223

Crissey Dexterity Test, job applicants, see 2224

Hand-Tool Dexterity Test, adolescents and adults, see 2225

Manipulative Aptitude Test, grades 9–16 and adults, see 2226

Minnesota Rate of Manipulation Test, grade 7 to adults, see 2227

O'Connor Finger Dexterity Test, ages 14 and over, see 2228

O'Connor Tweezer Dexterity Test, ages 14 and over, see 2229

★*One Hole Test,* job applicants, see 2230

Pennsylvania Bi-Manual Worksample, ages 16 and over, see 2231

Practical Dexterity Board, ages 8 and over, see 2232

Purdue Hand Precision Test, ages 17 and over, see 2233

Purdue Pegboard, grades 9–16 and adults, see 2234

Stromberg Dexterity Test, trade school and adults, see 2235

Yarn Dexterity Test, textile workers and applicants, see 2236

MECHANICAL ABILITY

A.C.E.R. Mechanical Comprehension Test [Australia], ages 13.5 and over, see 2237

A.C.E.R. Mechanical Reasoning Test [Australia], ages 13–9 and over, see 2238

Bennett Mechanical Comprehension Test, grades 9–12 and adults, see 2239

Chriswell Structural Dexterity Test, grades 7–9, see 2240

College Placement Test in Spatial Relations, entering college freshmen, see 2241

Cox Mechanical and Manual Tests [England], boys ages 10 and over, see 2242

Curtis Object Completion and Space Form Tests, applicants for mechanical and technical jobs, see 2243

Detroit Mechanical Aptitudes Examination, grades 7–16, see 2244

Flags: A Test of Space Thinking, industrial employees, see 2245

Form Perception Test [South Africa], illiterate and semiliterate adults, see 2246

Form Relations Group Test [England], ages 14 and over, see 2247

Group Test 80A [England], ages 15 and over, see 2248

Group Test 81 [England], ages 14 and over, see 2249

Group Test 82 [England], ages 14.5 and over, see 2250

MacQuarrie Test for Mechanical Ability, grades 7 and over, see 2251

Mechanical Aptitude Test: Acorn National Aptitude Tests, grades 7–16 and adults, see 2252

Mechanical Comprehension Test [South Africa], male technical apprentices and trainee engineer applicants, see 2253

Mechanical Information Test [England], ages 15 and over, see 2254

Mechanical Movements: A Test of Mechanical Comprehension, industrial employees, see 2255

Mechanical Reasoning: Differential Aptitude Tests, grades 8–12 and adults, see 2256

Mellenbruch Mechanical Motivation Test, grades 6–16 and adults, see 2257

Minnesota Spatial Relations Test, ages 11 and over, see 2258

O'Connor Wiggly Block, ages 16 and over, see 2259

O'Rourke Mechanical Aptitude Test, grades 7–12 and adults, see 2260

Perceptual Battery [South Africa], job applicants with at least 10 years of education, see 2261

Primary Mechanical Ability Tests, applicants for positions requiring mechanical ability, see 2262

Purdue Mechanical Adaptability Test, males ages 15 and over, see 2263

RBH Three-Dimensional Space Test, industrial workers in mechanical fields, see 2264

RBH Two-Dimensional Space Test, business and industry, see 2265

Revised Minnesota Paper Form Board Test, grades 9–16 and adults, see 2266

SRA Mechanical Aptitudes, grades 9–12 and adults, see 2267

Space Relations: Differential Aptitude Tests, grades 8–12 and adults, see 2268

Spatial Tests EG, 2, and 3 [England], ages 10–13 and 15–17, see 2269

Spatial Visualization Test: Dailey Vocational Tests, grades 8–12 and adults, see 2270

Vincent Mechanical Diagrams Test [England], ages 15 and over, see 2271

Weights and Pulleys: A Test of Intuitive Mechanics, engineering students and industrial employees, see 2272

MISCELLANEOUS

Alpha Biographical Inventory, grades 9–12, see 2273

Biographical Index, college and industry, see 2274

Business Judgment Test, adults, see 2275

Conference Evaluation, conference participants, see 2276

Conference Meeting Rating Scale, conference leaders and participants, see 2277

★*Continuous Letter Checking and Continuous Symbol Checking* [South Africa], ages 12 and over, see 2278–9

Gullo Workshop and Seminar Evaluation, workshop and seminar participants, see 2280

Job Attitude Analysis, production and clerical workers, see 2281

Mathematical and Technical Test [England], ages 11 and over, see 2282

Minnesota Importance Questionnaire, vocational counselees, see 2283

★*Minnesota Job Description Questionnaire,* employees and supervisors, see 2284

Minnesota Satisfaction Questionnaire, business and industry, see 2285

Per-Flu-Dex Tests, college and industry, see 2286

RBH Breadth of Information, business and industry, see 2287

Self-Rating Scale for Leadership Qualifications, adults, see 2288

Tear Ballot for Industry, employees in industry, see 2289

Test Orientation Procedure, job applicants and trainees, see 2290

Tests A/9 and A/10 [South Africa], applicants for technical and apprentice jobs, see 2291

Whisler Strategy Test, business and industry, see 2292

Work Information Inventory, employee groups in industry, see 2293

SELECTION & RATING FORMS

SPECIFIC VOCATIONS

ACCOUNTING

BUSINESS

COMPUTER PROGRAMMING

DENTISTRY

ENGINEERING

LAW

MEDICINE

Colleges of Podiatry Admission Test, grades 14 and
over, see 2354
Medical College Admission Test, applicants for admission to member colleges of the Association of
American Medical Colleges, see 2355
Medical School Instructor Attitude Inventory, medical school faculty members, see 2356
★*Optometry College Admission Test,* optometry college applicants, see 2357
Veterinary Aptitude Test, veterinary school applicants, see 2358

MISCELLANEOUS

Architectural School Aptitude Test, architectural
school applicants, see 2359
Chemical Operators Selection Test, chemical operators
and applicants, see 2360
Fire Promotion Tests, prospective firemen promotees,
see 2361
Firefighter Test, prospective firemen, see 2362
Fireman Examination, prospective firemen, see 2363
*General Municipal Employees Performance (Effi-
ciency) Rating System,* municipal employees, see
2364
Journalism Test, high school, see 2365
★*Law Enforcement Perception Questionnaire,* law
enforcement personnel, see 2366
Memory and Observation Tests for Policeman, pros-
pective policemen, see 2367
Police Performance Rating System, policemen, see
2368
Police Promotion Tests, prospective policemen promotees, see 2369
Policeman Examination, prospective policemen, see
2370
Policeman Test, policemen and prospective policemen,
see 2371
*Potter-Nash Aptitude Test for Lumber Inspectors
and Other General Personnel Who Handle Lumber,* employees in woodworking industries, see 2372
★*Test for Firefighter B-1,* firemen and prospective
firemen, see 2373
★*Test for Police Officer A-1,* policemen and prospective policemen, see 2374
Visual Comprehension Test for Detective, prospective
police detectives, see 2375

NURSING

Achievement Tests in Nursing, students in schools of
registered nursing, see 2376
Achievement Tests in Practical Nursing, practical
nursing students, see 2377
Empathy Inventory, nursing instructors, see 2378
Entrance Examination for Schools of Nursing, nursing
school applicants, see 2379
*Entrance Examination for Schools of Practical Nurs-
ing,* practical nursing school applicants, see 2380
George Washington University Series Nursing Tests,
prospective nurses, see 2381
Luther Hospital Sentence Completions, prospective
nursing students, see 2382
*NLN Achievement Tests for Schools Preparing
Registered Nurses,* students in state-approved
schools preparing registered nurses, see 2383
NLN Aide Selection Test, applicants for aide positions in hospitals and home health agencies, see 2384
NLN Practical Nursing Achievement Tests, students
in state-approved schools of practical nursing, see
2385
NLN Pre-Admission and Classification Examination,
practical nursing school entrants, see 2386
NLN Pre-Nursing and Guidance Examination, ap-

plicants for admission to state-approved schools
preparing registered nurses, see 2387
Netherne Study Difficulties Battery for Student Nurses
[England], student nurses, see 2388
Nurse Attitudes Inventory, prospective nursing students, see 2389
PSB-Aptitude for Practical Nursing Examination,
applicants for admission to practical nursing schools,
see 2390

RESEARCH

Research Personnel Review Form, research and engineering and scientific firms, see 2391
Supervisor's Evaluation of Research Personnel, research personnel, see 2392
*Surveys of Research Administration and Environ-
ment,* research and engineering and scientific firms,
see 2393
Technical Personnel Recruiting Inventory, research
and engineering and scientific firms, see 2394

SELLING

Aptitudes Associates Test of Sales Aptitude, appli-
cants for sales positions, see 2395
Combination Inventory, Form 2, prospective debit life
insurance salesmen, see 2396
Detroit Retail Selling Inventory, candidates for train-
ing in retail selling, see 2397
Evaluation Record, prospective life insurance agency
managers, see 2398
Hall Salespower Inventory, salesmen, see 2399
Hanes Sales Selection Inventory, insurance and print-
ing salesmen, see 2400
Information Index, life and health insurance agents,
see 2401
LIAMA Inventory of Job Attitudes, life insurance
field personnel, see 2402
Personnel Institute Hiring Kit, applicants for sales
positions, see 2403
SRA Sales Attitudes Check List, applicants for sales
positions, see 2404
Sales Aptitude Test, job applicants, see 2405
Sales Comprehension Test, applicants for sales posi-
tions, see 2406
Sales Method Index, life insurance agents, see 2407
Sales Motivation Inventory, applicants for sales posi-
tions, see 2408
Sales Sentence Completion Blank, applicants for sales
positions, see 2409
Steward Life Insurance Knowledge Test, applicants
for life insurance agent or supervisory positions,
see 2410
Steward Occupational Objectives Inventory, appli-
cants for supervisory positions in life insurance
companies or agencies, see 2411
Steward Personal Background Inventory, applicants
for sales positions, see 2412
*Test for Ability to Sell: George Washington University
Series,* grades 7–16 and adults, see 2413
★*Test of Retail Sales Insight,* retail clerks and students, see 2414

SKILLED TRADES

Electrical Sophistication Test, job applicants, see 2415
Fiesenheiser Test of Ability to Read Drawings, trade
school and adults, see 2416
Mechanical Familiarity Test, job applicants, see 2417
Mechanical Handyman Test, maintenance workers,
see 2418
Mechanical Knowledge Test, job applicants, see 2419

SUPERVISION

TRANSPORTATION

PUBLISHERS DIRECTORY
AND INDEX

This directory and index gives the addresses and tests of all publishers represented in this volume. References are to entry numbers, not to page numbers. Stars indicate test publishers with test catalogs listing 10 or more tests.

American Association for Jewish Education, 114 Fifth Ave., New York, N.Y. 10011:
Achievement Test—Hebrew Language, 278
NCRI Achievement Tests in Hebrew, 281
Test on the Fundamentals of Hebrew, 282

American Association of Teachers of German, Inc., 339 Walnut St., Philadelphia, Pa. 19106:
National German Examination for High School Students, 273

American Association of Teachers of Spanish and Portuguese, 1810 Chadbourne Ave., Madison, Wis. 53705:
National Spanish Examination, 316

American Language Institute (The), Georgetown University, 3605 O St. N.W., Washington, D.C. 20007:
English Usage Test for Non-Native Speakers of English, 230
Oral Rating Form for Rating Language Proficiency in Speaking and Understanding English, 234
Vocabulary and Reading Test for Students of English as a Second Language, 239

★Bobbs-Merrill Co., Inc. (The), 4300 West 62nd St., Indianapolis, Ind. 46268:
Achievement Examinations for Secondary Schools
  French I and II, 251
  German I and II, 268
  Latin I and II, 294
  Spanish I and II, 320
Baltimore County French Test, 241
Baltimore County Spanish Test, 303

★Bureau of Educational Measurements, Kansas State Teachers College, 1200 Commercial, Emporia, Kan. 66802:
Emporia First Year Latin Test, 292
Emporia Second Year Latin Test, 293
First Year French Test, 249
First Year Spanish Test, 309
Second Year French Test, 259
Second Year Spanish Test, 319

★Bureau of Educational Research and Service, University of Iowa, Iowa City, Iowa 52240:
Iowa Placement Examinations
  Foreign Language Aptitude, 220
  French Training, 254
  Spanish Training, 313

Chatterji (S.), Indian Statistical Institute, 203 Barrackpore Trunk Road, Calcutta-35, India:
English Knowledge and Comprehension Test, 228

College Entrance Examination Board, 888 Seventh Ave., New York, N.Y. 10019:
Advanced Placement Examinations

Classics, 288
French, 240
German, 262
Spanish, 302
College Board Achievement Tests
  French Listening-Reading, 243
  French Reading, 244
  German Listening-Reading, 263
  German Reading, 264
  Hebrew, 279
  Latin, 289
  Russian Listening-Reading, 295
  Spanish Listening-Reading, 304
  Spanish Reading, 305
College Placement Tests
  French Listening Comprehension, 245
  French Listening-Reading, 246
  French Reading, 247
  German Listening Comprehension, 265
  German Listening-Reading, 266
  German Reading, 267
  Greek Reading, 277
  Hebrew Reading, 280
  Italian Listening Comprehension, 283
  Italian Listening-Reading, 284
  Italian Reading, 285
  Latin Reading, 290
  Russian Listening Comprehension, 296
  Russian Listening-Reading, 297
  Russian Reading, 298
  Spanish Listening Comprehension, 306
  Spanish Listening-Reading, 307
  Spanish Reading, 308
Test of English as a Foreign Language, 238

★Cooperative Tests and Services, Educational Testing Service, Princeton, N.J. 08540:
Cooperative French Listening Comprehension Test, 248
Cooperative Latin Test: Elementary and Advanced Levels, 291
MLA Cooperative Foreign Language Proficiency Tests
  French, 255
  German, 271
  Italian, 286
  Russian, 300
  Spanish, 314
MLA Cooperative Foreign Language Tests
  French, 256
  German, 272
  Italian, 287
  Russian, 301
  Spanish, 315

Dent (J. M.) & Sons (Canada) Ltd., 100 Scarsdale Road, Don Mills, Ont. M3B 2R8, Canada:
Ford-Hicks French Grammar Completion Tests, 250

★Educational Testing Service, Princeton, N.J. 08540
(*See also* College Entrance Examination Board,
Cooperative Tests and Services, and Educational
Testing Service [Atlanta Office]) :
Graduate Record Examinations
  Advanced French Test, 252
  Advanced German Test, 269
  Advanced Spanish Test, 311
Graduate School Foreign Language Tests, 219
  French, 253
  German, 270
  Russian, 299
  Spanish, 312
National Teacher Examinations
  French, 257
  German, 274
  Spanish, 317
Teacher Education Examination Program
  French, 260
  Spanish, 321
Test of English as a Foreign Language, 238
Undergraduate Program Field Tests
  French Test, 261
  German Test, 276
  Spanish Test, 322
Educational Testing Service (Atlanta Office), Suite
100, 17 Executive Park Drive, Atlanta, Ga. 30329:
Harvard-MLA Tests of Chinese Language Proficiency, 225
Follett's Michigan Book Store, Inc., 322 South State
St., Ann Arbor, Mich. 48108:
English Placement Test, 229
Examination in Structure (English as a Foreign Language),
  231
Michigan Test of Aural Comprehension, 232
Michigan Test of English Language Proficiency, 233
Test of Aural Perception in English for Japanese Students,
  236
Test of Aural Perception in English for Latin-American Stu-
  dents, 237
★Guidance Centre, University of Toronto, 1000 Yonge
St., Toronto, Ont. M4W 2K8, Canada :
Canadian Achievement Test in French, 242

★Harcourt Brace Jovanovich, Inc., 757 Third Ave.,
New York, N.Y. 10017:
Pimsleur French Proficiency Tests, 258
Pimsleur German Proficiency Tests, 275
Pimsleur Language Aptitude Battery, 223
Pimsleur Spanish Proficiency Tests, 318
Kansas State Teachers College. *See* Bureau of Educa-
tional Measurements.
McGraw-Hill Book Co., Inc., 1221 Avenue of the
Americas, New York, N.Y. 10020:
Comprehensive English Language Test for Speakers of Eng-
  lish as a Second Language, 226
Diagnostic Test for Students of English as a Second Language,
  227
Middle East Center, University of Utah, Salt Lake
City, Utah 84112:
First Year Arabic Final Examination, 224
National Curriculum Research Institute. *See* American
Association for Jewish Education.
★National Institute for Personnel Research, P.O. Box
10319, Johannesburg, Republic of South Africa :
Test A/65, 235
National Textbook Co., 8259 Niles Center Road,
Skokie, Ill. 60076:
Furness Test of Aural Comprehension in Spanish, 310
★Psychological Corporation (The), 304 East 45th St.,
New York, N.Y. 10017:
Modern Language Aptitude Test, 221
Modern Language Aptitude Test—Elementary, 222
Teachers College Press, 1234 Amsterdam Ave., New
York, N.Y. 10027:
Foreign Language Prognosis Test, 218
University of Iowa. *See* Bureau of Educational Re-
search and Service.
University of Toronto. *See* Guidance Centre.
University of Utah. *See* Middle East Center.

INDEX OF TITLES

This index lists (*a*) foreign language tests in print as of February 1, 1974, and (*b*) foreign language tests out of print or status unknown since last listed in a *Mental Measurements Yearbook* (MMY). Citations are to test entries, not to pages. Numbers without colons refer to in print tests; numbers with colons refer to tests out of print or status unknown. All tests cited are in this volume. The guide numbers next to the outside margins in the running heads of the reprint sections should be used to locate a particular test. The first reprint section, from *Tests in Print II*, has guide numbers in the range 218 to 322; the second reprint section, from the 1st MMY, 1:984 to 1:1157; the third reprint section, from the 2nd MMY, 2:1340 to 2:1375; etc. Superseded titles are listed with cross references to the current title. Tests which are part of a series are listed under their individual titles and also their series titles.

INDEX OF NAMES

This analytical index indicates whether a citation refers to authorship of a test, test review, excerpted review, or a reference for a specific test. Citations are to test numbers, not to page numbers. In the reprint sections, the numbers of the first and last tests on facing pages are given in the running heads next to the outside margins. Numbers without colons refer to in print tests presented in the section reprinted from TIP II. Interpret abbreviations and numbers for in print tests as follows: "*test,* 248" indicates authorship of test 248; "*rev,* 254," authorship of a review of test 254; "*exc,* 258," authorship of an excerpted review of test 258; and "*ref,* 310," authorship of one or more references for test 310. (The Cumulative Name Index for that test must be consulted to locate the references.) Numbers with colons (e.g., 4:236, test 236 in the 4th MMY) refer to out of print tests included in the material reprinted from the MMY's, unless otherwise indicated. In the reprint sections, the yearbook digit preceding the colon is given in the running head only.

ACKERMAN, T. J.: *ref,* 221
Agard, F. B.: *rev,* 310, 3:208, 3:211
Aiken, B.: *test,* 5:291
Aiken, J. R.: *test,* 5:274
Aleamoni, L. M.: *ref,* 245, 247, 256, 265, 267, 272, 296, 299, 301, 306, 308, 315
Alexander, R. L.: *test,* 1:1067
Allen, B. M.: *test,* 1:1064
American Association for Jewish Education: *test,* 282
American Association of Teachers of German: *test,* 273
American Association of Teachers of Spanish and Portuguese: *test,* 316
Andrade, R. D.: *test,* 236
Andrus, L.: *rev,* 2:1371, 2:1373
Angoff, W. H.: *ref,* 238, 269
Appelt, E. P.: *test,* 2:1358
Arendt, J. D.: *ref,* 221
Arndt, C. O.: *rev,* 2:1371, 2:1374
Atkins, S. D.: *rev,* 291, 2:1363, 2:1367

BABCOCK, J. C.: *rev,* 2:1372, 2:1375
Bair, R. L.: *exc,* 301; *ref,* 301
Baker, R. L.: *ref,* 300
Baltimore County French Language Committee: *test,* 241
Baltimore County Spanish Language Committee: *test,* 303

Banathy, B. H.: *test,* 7:253, 7:272, 7:286, 7:317
Bartlett, A. A.: *ref,* 219, 253, 270, 299, 312
Bartley, D. E.: *ref,* 221
Bashour, D. S.: *ref,* 255
Beatley, B.: *ref,* 2:1342(3)
Beaujour, M.: *ref,* 255
Bebeau, D. E.: *ref,* 233
Bedell, R.: *rev,* 5:256, 5:258
Bellinger, L.: *test,* 3:206
Bickley, A. C.: *ref,* 221
Bilyeu, E. E.: *exc,* 318
Birkmaier, E. M.: *test,* 268, 320
Black, D. B.: *ref,* 244
Blatchford, C. H.: *ref,* 227
Bordin, E. S.: *exc,* 221
Bovee, A. G.: *ref,* 4:238(2)
Boyer, M. V.: *ref,* 316
Brée, G.: *ref,* 244
Breed, F. S.: *ref,* 2:1342(6)
Brogden, H. E.: *rev,* 220, 3:179
Brooks, N.: *rev,* 227, 241, 249, 252, 1:984–5, 2:1343, 2:1354, 3:183, 3:185, 4:242–3; *test,* 248; *ref,* 244
Brueckner, L. J.: *ref,* 4:253(2)
Buchanan, M. A.: *test,* 2:1371
Buck, E. S.: *test,* 1:1066
Bugatch, S.: *test,* 281
Bureau of Educational Measurements: *test,* 6:408, 6:411
Burns, D. G.: *rev,* 4:242–3
Buynitzky, K. C.: *test,* 3:179

CABAT, L.: *ref,* 244, 305
Callcott, F.: *test,* 2:1372
Campbell, H. S.: *ref,* 3:181(6)
Campbell, R. N.: *test,* 5:258
Carr, W. L.: *rev,* 2:1366, 2:1369; *test,* 1:1065
Carroll, J. B.: *rev,* 226, 233; *test,* 221–2, 225; *ref,* 221, 255, 271, 300, 314
Cartwright, C. W.: *ref,* 2:1372(2)
Castiglione, P. B.: *ref,* 286
Chandler, D.: *ref,* 300
Charly, H. T.: *ref,* 316
Chase, C. I.: *rev,* 238; *ref,* 238
Chastain, K.: *ref,* 221
Chatterji, S.: *test,* 228
Chauncey, H.: *rev,* 6:375, 6:410, 6:431
Cheydleur, F. D.: *test,* 2:1345–6; *ref,* 2:1345(1–3, 5), 2:1348(3)
Chou, K. P.: *test,* 225
Churchill, F. J.: *ref,* 255–6, 271–2, 314–5
Cieutat, V. J.: *ref,* 221
Ciruti, J. E.: *ref,* 314
Clapp, H. L.: *ref,* 4:260(2)
Clark, J. L. D.: *rev,* 258–9; *exc,* 256, 272, 287, 301, 315; *ref,* 219, 253, 270, 299, 312
Clark, M. G.: *ref,* 221
Clarke, F. M.: *test,* 2:1343; *ref,* 2:1343(2–3)
Cloos, R. I.: *ref,* 221, 223
Cochran, G.: *test,* 220

306

FOREIGN LANGUAGE SCANNING INDEX

This scanning index is an expanded table of contents listing all tests in this volume. Foreign tests are identified by listing the country of origin in brackets immediately after the title. The population for which a test is intended is presented to facilitate the search for tests for use with a particular group. Stars indicate tests not previously listed in a *Mental Measurements Yearbook;* asterisks indicate tests revised or supplemented since last listed. Numbers refer to test entries, not to pages.

FOREIGN LANGUAGES

Baltimore County French Test, 1 year high school, see 241

*Canadian Achievement Test in French [Canada], grade 10, see 242

★College Board Achievement Test in French Listening-Reading, candidates for college entrance with 2–4 years high school French, see 243

*College Board Achievement Test in French Reading, candidates for college entrance with 2–4 years high school French, see 244

*College Placement Test in French Listening Comprehension, entering college freshmen, see 245

★College Placement Test in French Listening-Reading, entering college freshmen, see 246

*College Placement Test in French Reading, entering college freshmen, see 247

Cooperative French Listening Comprehension Test, 2–5 semesters high school or college, see 248

First Year French Test, high school and college, see 249

Ford-Hicks French Grammar Completion Tests [Canada], high school, see 250

French I and II: Achievement Examinations for Secondary Schools, 1–2 years high school, see 251

*Graduate Record Examinations Advanced French Test, graduate school candidates, see 252

*Graduate School Foreign Language Test: French, graduate level degree candidates required to demonstrate reading proficiency in French, see 253

Iowa Placement Examinations: French Training, grades 12–13, see 254

MLA Cooperative Foreign Language Proficiency Tests: French, French majors and advanced students in college, see 255

MLA-Cooperative Foreign Language Tests: French, 1–4 years high school or 1–2 years college, see 256

*National Teacher Examinations: French, college seniors and teachers, see 257

Pimsleur French Proficiency Tests, grades 7–16, see 258

Second Year French Test, high school and college, see 259

*Teacher Education Examination Program: French, college seniors preparing to teach secondary school, see 260

*Undergraduate Program Field Tests: French Test, college, see 261

GERMAN

*Advanced Placement Examination in German, high school students desiring credit for college level courses or admission to advanced courses, see 262

★College Board Achievement Test in German Listening-Reading, candidates for college entrance with 2–4 years high school German, see 263

*College Board Achievement Test in German Reading, candidates for college entrance with 2–4 years high school German, see 264

*College Placement Test in German Listening Comprehension, entering college freshmen, see 265

★College Placement Test in German Listening-Reading, entering college freshmen, see 266

*College Placement Test in German Reading, entering college freshmen, see 267

German I and II: Achievement Examinations for Secondary Schools, 1–2 years high school, see 268

*Graduate Record Examinations Advanced German Test, graduate school candidates, see 269

*Graduate School Foreign Language Test: German, graduate level degree candidates required to demonstrate reading proficiency in German, see 270

MLA Cooperative Foreign Language Proficiency Tests: German, German majors and advanced students in college, see 271

MLA-Cooperative Foreign Language Tests: German, 1–4 years high school or 1–2 years college, see 272

*National German Examination for High School Students, 2–4 years high school, see 273

*National Teacher Examinations: German, college seniors and teachers, see 274

Pimsleur German Proficiency Tests, grades 7–16, see 275

*Undergraduate Program Field Tests: German Test, college, see 276

GREEK

*College Placement Test in Greek Reading, entering college freshmen, see 277

HEBREW

★Achievement Test—Hebrew Language, grades 5–7, see 278

*College Board Achievement Test in Hebrew, candidates for college entrance with 2–4 years high school Hebrew, see 279

*College Placement Test in Hebrew Reading, entering college freshmen, see 280

NCRI Achievement Tests in Hebrew, grades 5–9, see 281

Test on the Fundamentals of Hebrew, grades 2–7, see 282

ITALIAN

*College Placement Test in Italian Listening Comprehension, entering college freshmen, see 283

★College Placement Test in Italian Listening-Reading, entering college freshmen, see 284

*College Placement Test in Italian Reading, entering college freshmen, see 285

MLA Cooperative Foreign Language Proficiency Tests: Italian, Italian majors and advanced students in college, see 286

MLA-Cooperative Foreign Language Tests: Italian, 1–4 years high school or 1–2 years college, see 287

LATIN

*Advanced Placement Examination in Classics, high school students desiring credit for college level courses or admission to advanced courses, see 288

*College Board Achievement Test in Latin, candidates for college entrance with 2–4 years high school Latin, see 289

*College Placement Test in Latin Reading, entering college freshmen, see 290

Cooperative Latin Test: Elementary and Advanced Levels, grades 9–16, see 291

Emporia First Year Latin Test, 1 year high school, see 292

Emporia Second Year Latin Test, 2 years high school, see 293

Latin I and II: Achievement Examinations for Secondary Schools, 1–2 years high school, see 294

RUSSIAN

★College Board Achievement Test in Russian Listening-Reading, candidates for college entrance with 2–4 years high school Russian, see 295

SPANISH